Not For Tourists™ Guide to **SEATTLE**

2009

Not For Tourists Inc

published and designed by
Not For Tourists Inc
NFT~TM~—Not For Tourists~TM~ Guide to SEATTLE 2009
www.notfortourists.com

Publisher
Jane Pirone

Information Design
Jane Pirone
Rob Tallia
Scot Covey
Ben Bray

Managing Editors
Craig Nelson

Database Manager
Ben Bray

City Editor
Jessica Baxter

Writing and Editing
Jessica Baxter
Meiwa Chen
Shirley Hendrickson
Rebecca Katherine Hirsch
Craig Nelson
Karen Watson

Contributors
Robin Barker
Chika Eustace
Lara Johannsen
Gary McGuire
Robin Martin
Jared Randall
Patrick Romero

Research
Melissa Burgos
Michael Dale
Bryce Evans

Graphic Design/Production
Bethany Covey
Yumi Endo
Aaron Schielke
Emily Steinfeld

Cartographer
Jonathan Levy

Proofing
Sho Spaeth

Sales & Marketing
Lea Garrett
Sarah Hocevar
Annie Holt

Web Guru
Juan Molinari

Printed in China
ISBN# 978-0-9815591-1-7 $19.95
Copyright © 2008 by Not For Tourists, Inc.

Every effort has been made to ensure that the information in this book is as up-to-date as possible at press time. However, many details are liable to change—as we have learned. The publishers cannot accept responsibility for any consequences arising from the use of this book.

Not For Tourists does not solicit individuals, organizations, or businesses for listings inclusion in our guides, nor do we accept payment for inclusion into the editorial portion of our book; the advertising sections, however, are exempt from this policy. We always welcome communications from anyone regarding ANYTHING having to do with our books; please visit us on our website at www.notfortourists.com for appropriate contact information.

Dear NFT User:

So what brought you to Seattle? Computers? Airplanes? Coffee? Please, don't tell us it was Kurt…seriously, are there still deluded youngsters hopping Greyhounds and freight trains for the Emerald City in hopes of reflected glory that they'll never find? Try Haight Street or the Sunset Strip, Bra.

Anywho, ever since the city's humble beginnings we've been a transient's town, full of sailors on leave, gold rush/dot-com/grunge rock hopefuls, and gentlemen loafers sleeping beneath the stars. Microsoft, Starbucks, Amazon, and Sub Pop changed all that, and suddenly the city's reputation changed in the eyes of the world and itself, becoming an international hub of commerce, technology, and youth culture. The dot-com bust punctured the economy but not Seattle's upwardly mobile self-image, so we steadfastly cling to the notion that we can once again rule the earth (even if many of us are working in cafés instead of writing code or selling books).

You might need to be a millionaire to buy a house here, but you only need a couple of bucks to buy this book. So while you wait for whatever big break you seek, there is a vibrant music scene, great food, amazing art, incredible libraries, quirky landmarks, and thousands of friendly panhandlers willing to accept any spare change that's weighing you down. And this second edition of NFT is here to help you navigate it all!

So whether you were born in Wallingford or just moved from Wichita, beginning a start-up venture or hastily spending your venture capital, you need this book. You'll find each and every one of Seattle's neighborhoods represented within, mapped out in full detail and carefully evaluated for both leisurely pursuits and essential services. Nightlife, restaurants, shopping spots, banks, schools, gas stations, coffee shops—it's all inside, meticulously researched by a crack staff of folks who actually live here. Hell, we've even included a whole section on—gulp—the Eastside.

The '09 book is full of hundreds of new listings and updates thanks, in part, to the submissions of our dear readers. But if there's still something amiss or missing (since a new Hipster Hot Spot seems to open here monthly) by all means let us know. Your feedback is essential in helping us make this the ultimate guide to Seattle. Dig www. notfortourists.com to give us feedback, pro or con. While you're there, check out our fabulous Seattle website where you can read longer reviews of stuff around town, sign up for the NFT newsletter, and see what's going on in your neighborhood.

Come as you are,
Jessica, Craig, Rob, and Jane

Table of Contents

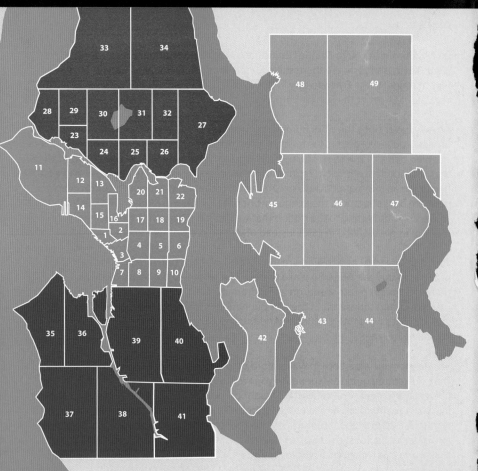

Map 1 · **Belltown**

The formerly seedy Belltown now bursts with pricey condos, boutique eateries, and metrosexual (or is it metronatural?) nightlife destinations. But don't fret, heroin can still be scored on the proper street corners. Homeless shelters and public health centers neighbor the rock clubs, art galleries, and sushi joints, making for an occasionally jarring mix of people. To escape the craziness, take a stroll through SAM's fabulous sculpture park.

Banks

- **Bank of America** • 566 Denny Wy [Vine St]
- **Bank of America (ATM)** • 2035 4th Ave [Virginia St]
- **Bank of America (ATM)** • 2711 Alaskan Wy [Cedar St]
- **Wells Fargo** • 2800 3rd Ave [Clay St]

Car Rental

- **Avis** • 1919 5th Ave [Stewart St]

Coffee

- **Caffe Bella** • 2621 5th Ave [Vine St]
- **Cherry St Coffee Belltown** • 2121 1st Ave [Lenora St]
- **Cherry Street Coffee House** • 2719 1st Ave [Cedar St]
- **Midtown Espresso** • 2133 5th Ave [Lenora St]
- **Starbucks** • 2101 4th Ave, Ste 150 [Lenora St]
- **Starbucks** • 211 Lenora St [2nd Ave]
- **Starbucks** • 2200 Alaskan Wy [Blanchard St]
- **Starbucks** • 2326 1st Ave [Bell St]
- **Starbucks** • 620 Denny Wy [6th Ave]
- **Top Pot Donuts** • 2124 5th Ave [Lenora St]
- **Tully's** • 2929 1st Ave [Broad St]
- **Uptown Espresso** • 2504 4th Ave [Wall St]
- **Uptown Espresso** • Pier 70 • Alaskan Wy & Broad St
- **World Cup Coffee Inc** • 2819 2nd Ave [Clay St]

Community Gardens

Gas Stations

- **76** • 351 Broad St [Denny Wy]
- **Shell** • 10 Denny Wy [Queen Anne Ave N]
- **Shell** • 2461 4th Ave [Wall St]

Landmarks

- **Cinerama** • 2100 4th Ave [Lenora St]
- **Edgewater Hotel** • 2411 Alaskan Wy [Battery St]
- **Olympic Sculpture Park** • Western Ave & Broad St
- **Seattle P.I. Globe** • 101 Elliott Ave W [Denny Wy]

Parking

Pharmacies

- **Cornerstone Pharmacy** • 2502 5th Ave [Wall St]
- **Rite Aid** • 2603 3rd Ave [Vine St]

Post Offices

- **Cpu Harbor Heights 111** • 2512 5th Ave [Wall St]

Schools

- **Art Institute Of Seattle** • 2323 Elliott Ave [Bell St]
- **Special Education Service** • 2445 3rd Ave [Battery St]

Map 1 · **Belltown**

Sundries / Entertainment

Shorty's is the closest thing to heaven in Seattle with pinball, booze, and hot dogs. Cinerama is a close second, offering one of the best movie-going experiences in the world. Other highlights: Macrina's pastries, Marco's Supperclub, 24-7 grub at The Five Point, and a drink at the Rendevous. (But we still miss the Croc big time.) Swing with the cool art crowd, daddy-o, at the McLoed Residence, part gallery, part bar, and recently opened to the public.

Map 1

Copy Shops

- **Digicopy N Print** • 164 Denny Wy [2nd Ave N]
- **FedEx Kinko's** • 2500 2nd Ave [Wall St]
- **Minuteman Press** • 307 Battery St [3rd Ave]
- **Seattle Photocopy** • 111 Battery St [1st Ave]
- **Swifty Printing & Digital Imaging** • 2001 3rd Ave [Virginia St]

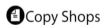Gyms

- **Rain Fitness** • 159 Western Ave W [2nd Ave W]
- **X Gym** • 11 Vine St [Wall St]
- **Zum** • 2235 5th Ave [Bell St]

Liquor Stores

- **Champion Wine Cellars-Since 1969** • 108 Denny Wy [1st Ave N]
- **Seattle Cellars** • 2505 2nd Ave [Wall St]

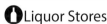Movie Theaters

- **AMC Cinerama 1** • 2100 4th Ave [Lenora St]
- **Big Picture** • 2505 1st Ave [Wall St]
- **Jewel Box Theatre** • 2322 2nd Ave [Bell St]

Nightlife

- **Amber** • 2214 1st Ave [Blanchard St]
- **Belltown Billiards** • 90 Blanchard St [1st Ave]
- **The Black Bottle** • 2600 1st Ave [Vine St]
- **Buddha** • 2222 2nd Ave [Blanchard St]
- **Cyclops Café and Lounge** • 2421 1st Ave [Battery St]
- **Del Rey** • 2332 1st Ave [Bell St]
- **Five Point Café** • 415 Cedar St [4th Ave]
- **Frontier Room** • 2203 1st Ave [Blanchard St]
- **Hula Hula** • 106 1st Ave N [Denny Wy]
- **Lava Lounge** • 2226 2nd Ave [Blanchard St]
- **Marjorie** • 2331 2nd Ave [Bell St]
- **McLoed Residence Lounge** • 2209 2nd Ave [Blanchard St]
- **Palace Kitchen** • 2030 5th Ave [Virginia St]
- **Queen City Grill** • 2201 1st Ave [Blanchard St]
- **Rendezvous** • 2322 2nd Ave [Bell St]
- **Shorty's** • 2222 2nd Ave [Blanchard St]
- **Spitfire Grill** • 2219 4th Ave [Blanchard St]
- **Tia Lou's** • 2218 1st Ave [Blanchard St]
- **Tini Bigs Lounge** • 100 Denny Wy [1st Ave N]
- **Twist Restaurant and Lounge** • 2313 1st Ave [Bell St]
- **Umi Sake House** • 2230 1st Ave [Blanchard St]
- **Viceroy** • 2332 2nd Ave [Bell St]
- **Wasabi Bistro** • 2311 2nd Ave [Bell St]
- **The Waterfront Seafood Grill** • 2801 Alaskan Wy [Clay St]
- **Whisky Bar** • 2000 2nd Ave [Virginia St]

Pet Shops

- **Belltown Feed & Seed** • 2218 2nd Ave [Blanchard St]
- **Wags 2 Whiskers** • 113A Bell St [1st Ave]

Restaurants

- **Anthony's Bell Street Diner** • 2201 Alaskan Wy [Blanchard St]
- **Anthony's Pier 66** • 2201 Alaskan Wy [Blanchard St]
- **Assaggio Ristorante** • 2010 4th Ave [Virginia St]
- **Black Bottle** • 2600 1st Ave [Vine St]
- **Boat Street Café** • 3131 Western Ave [Queen Anne Ave N]
- **Brasa** • 2107 3rd Ave [Lenora St]
- **Buenos Aires Grill** • 2000 2nd Ave [Virginia St]
- **Buffalo Deli** • 2123 1st Ave [Lenora St]
- **Cascadia** • 2328 1st Ave [Bell St]
- **Dahlia Lounge** • 2001 4th Ave [Virginia St]
- **El Gaucho** • 2505 1st Ave [Wall St]
- **Five Point Café** • 415 Cedar St [4th Ave] ⌚
- **Flying Fish** • 2234 1st Ave [Blanchard St]
- **The Frontier Room** • 2203 1st Ave [Blanchard St]
- **icon Grill** • 1933 5th Ave [Stewart St]
- **La Fontana Siciliana** • 120 Blanchard St [1st Ave]
- **La Vita E Bella** • 2407 2nd Ave [Battery St]
- **Lampreia** • 2400 1st Ave [Battery St]
- **Lola** • 2000 4th Ave [Virginia St]
- **Macrina Bakery & Café** • 2408 1st Ave [Battery St]
- **Mama's Mexican Kitchen** • 2334 2nd Ave [Bell St]
- **Marco's Supperclub** • 2510 1st Ave [Wall St]
- **Marjorie** • 2331 2nd Ave [Bell St]
- **Marrakesh Moroccan Restaurant** • 2334 2nd Ave [Bell St]
- **Mistral** • 113 Blanchard St [1st Ave]
- **Nara Grill** • 2027 5th Ave [Virginia St]
- **Noodle Ranch** • 2228 2nd Ave [Blanchard St]
- **Ohana** • 2207 1st Ave [Blanchard St]
- **Palace Kitchen** • 2030 5th Ave [Virginia St]
- **Queen City Grill** • 2201 1st Ave [Blanchard St]
- **Saito's Japanese Café & Bar** • 2122 2nd Ave [Lenora St]
- **Shallots** • 2525 4th Ave [Wall St]
- **Shiro's Sushi** • 2401 2nd Ave [Battery St]
- **Six Seven** • Pier 67, 2411 Alaskan Wy [Battery St]
- **Two Bells Tavern** • 2313 4th Ave [Bell St]
- **Txori Bar** • 2207 2nd Ave [Bell St]
- **Wasabi Bistro** • 2311 2nd Ave [Blanchard St]
- **Waterfront Seafood Grill** • 2801 Alaskan Wy [Clay St]
- **Zeek's Pizza** • 419 Denny Wy [4th Ave]
- **Zoë** • 2137 2nd Ave [Lenora St]

Shopping

- **Rudy's Barbershop** • 89 Wall St [Western Ave]
- **Singles Going Steady** • 2219 2nd Ave [Blanchard St]

Video Rental

- **Belltown Video** • 2500 3rd Ave [Wall St]

Map 2 • **Downtown / Denny Triangle**

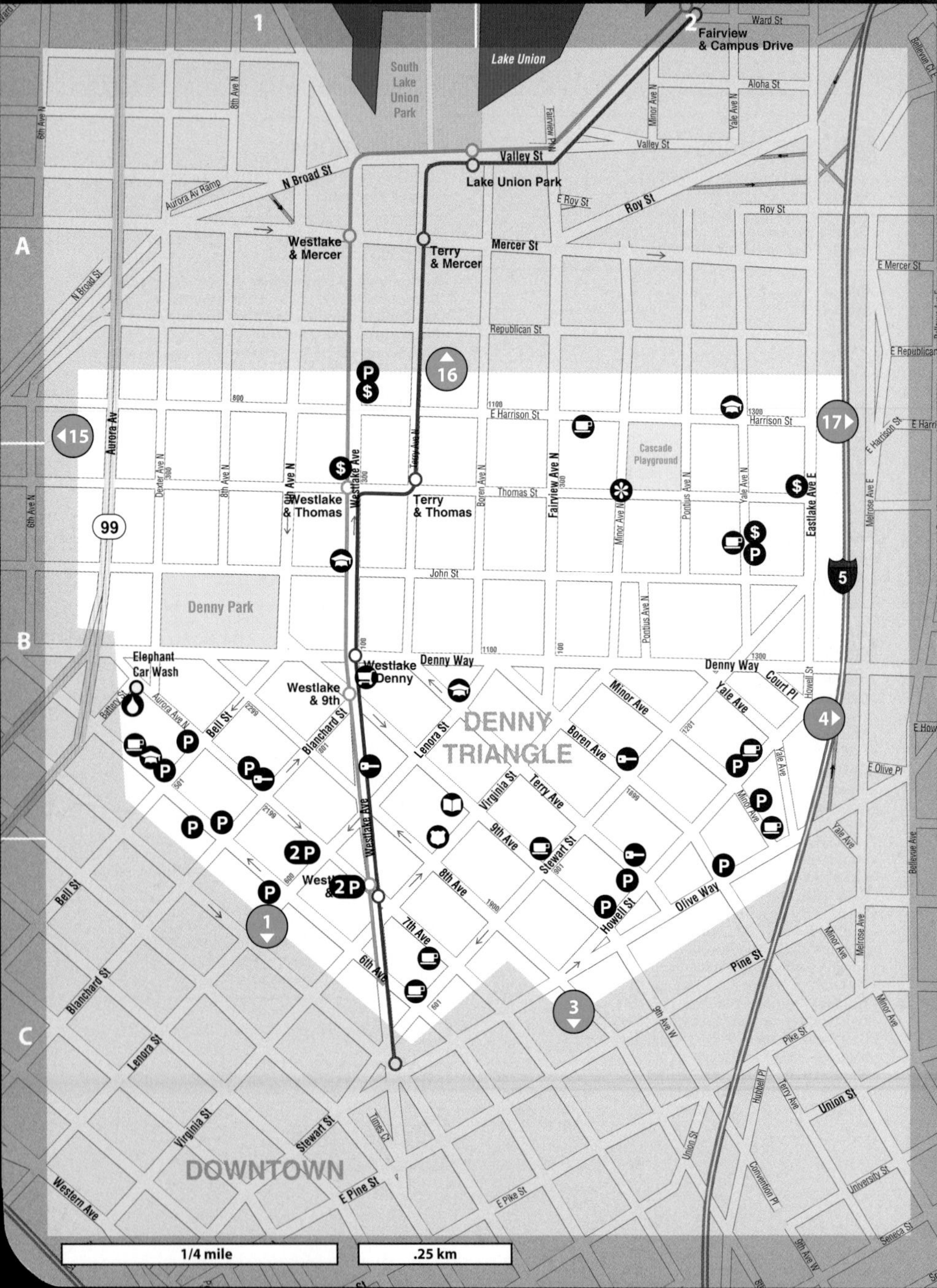

N

1

Ward St

2 Fairview
& Campus Drive

Lake Union

Aloha St

South
Lake
Union
Park

Minor Ave N

Yale Ave N

Valley St

Valley St

Aurora Ave Ramp

N Broad St

E Roy St

Roy St

Roy St

Lake Union Park

A

Westlake
& Mercer

Terry
& Mercer

Mercer St

E Mercer St

N Broad St

Republican St

E Republican

E Harrison St

Harrison St

17

E Harri

15

P
$

16

Cascade
Playground

Aurora Ave

Denny Ave N

8th Ave N

Ave N

Westlake Ave

Boren Ave N

Fairview Ave N

Minor Ave N

$

Westlake
& Thomas

Terry
& Thomas

Thomas St

$
P

Eastlake Ave E

99

$

Westlake
& Thomas

John St

Portus Ave N

Yale Ave N

$

5

Denny Park

B

Elephant
Car Wash

Westlake
Denny

Denny Way

1100

Denny Way

1300

Denny Way

Court Pl

4

E Olive Pl

Westlake
& 9th

Lenora St

Minor Ave

Boren Ave

Yale Ave

Howell St

E Ho

**DENNY
TRIANGLE**

Bell St

Aurora Ave N

Blanchard St

Blanchard St

Virginia St

9th Ave

Terry Ave

Stewart St

Minor Ave

Yale Ave

E Olive Pl

Bellevue Ave

2 P

1

West

2 P

8th Ave

7th Ave

Howell St

Olive Way

Pine St

Minor Ave

Melrose Ave

3

6th Ave

Pike St

Pike St

Boren Ave

Terry Ave

Minor Ave

C

Bell St

Lenora St

Stewart St

7th Ave

Union St

Hubbell Pl

Terry Ave

Boren Ave

Melrose Ave

Seneca

Blanchard St

Virginia St

Time Ct

E Pike St

Union St

Convention Pl

University St

DOWNTOWN

Western Ave

Stewart St

E Pike St

┌─────────────┬─────────────┐
│ 1/4 mile   │   .25 km   │
└─────────────┴─────────────┘

It's not the prettiest part of town, especially with the always horribly congested stretch of Denny Way running through the middle. But if you get out of the car and wander around, you can certainly uncover a few gems. And it's impossible not to feel a little warm and fuzzy when you're under the soft neon glow of the famous pink Elephant Car Wash sign.

Banks

- **Bank of America (ATM)** · 222 Yale Ave N [John St]
- **Evergreen Bank** · 301 Eastlake Ave E [Thomas St]
- **Evergreen Bank** · 315 Westlake Ave N [Thomas St]
- **Key Bank** · 428 Westlake Ave N [Harrison St]

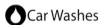 Car Rental

- **Advantage** · 1820 Terry Ave [Howell St]
- **Budget** · 2200 7th Ave [Blanchard St]
- **Dollar** · 1900 Boren Ave [Stewart St]
- **Enterprise** · 2116 Westlake Ave [8th Ave]

Car Washes

- **Elephant Car Wash** · 616 Battery St [6th Ave]

 Coffee

- **Espresso Vivace Roasteria** ·
  227 Yale Ave N [John Street]
- **Kapow Coffee** · 1165 Harrison St [Fairview Ave N]
- **Motore** · 1904 9th Ave [Stewart St]
- **Starbucks** · 1220 Howell St [Minor Ave]
- **Starbucks** · 1730 Minor Ave [Olive Wy]
- **Starbucks** · 600 Stewart St [6th Ave]
- **Tully's** · 2326 6th Ave [Bell St]
- **Uptown Espresso** · 1933 7th Ave [Stewart St]

✳ Community Gardens

○ Landmarks

- **Elephant Car Wash** · 616 Battery St [6th Ave]

📖 Libraries

- **Washington Talking Book & Braille Library** ·
  2021 9th Ave [Virginia St]

Ⓟ Parking

🅞 Police

- **West Precinct** · 810 Virginia St [8th Ave]

🏫 Schools

- **Antioch University** · 2326 6th Ave [Bell St]
- **Cornish College Of The Arts** · 1000 Lenora St [Terry Ave]
- **Morningside Academy** · 201 Westlake Ave N [John St]
- **Spruce St** · 411 Yale Ave N [Harrison St]

🛒 Supermarkets

- **Whole Foods** · 2210 Westlake Ave [Denny Wy]

Map 2 • Downtown / Denny Triangle

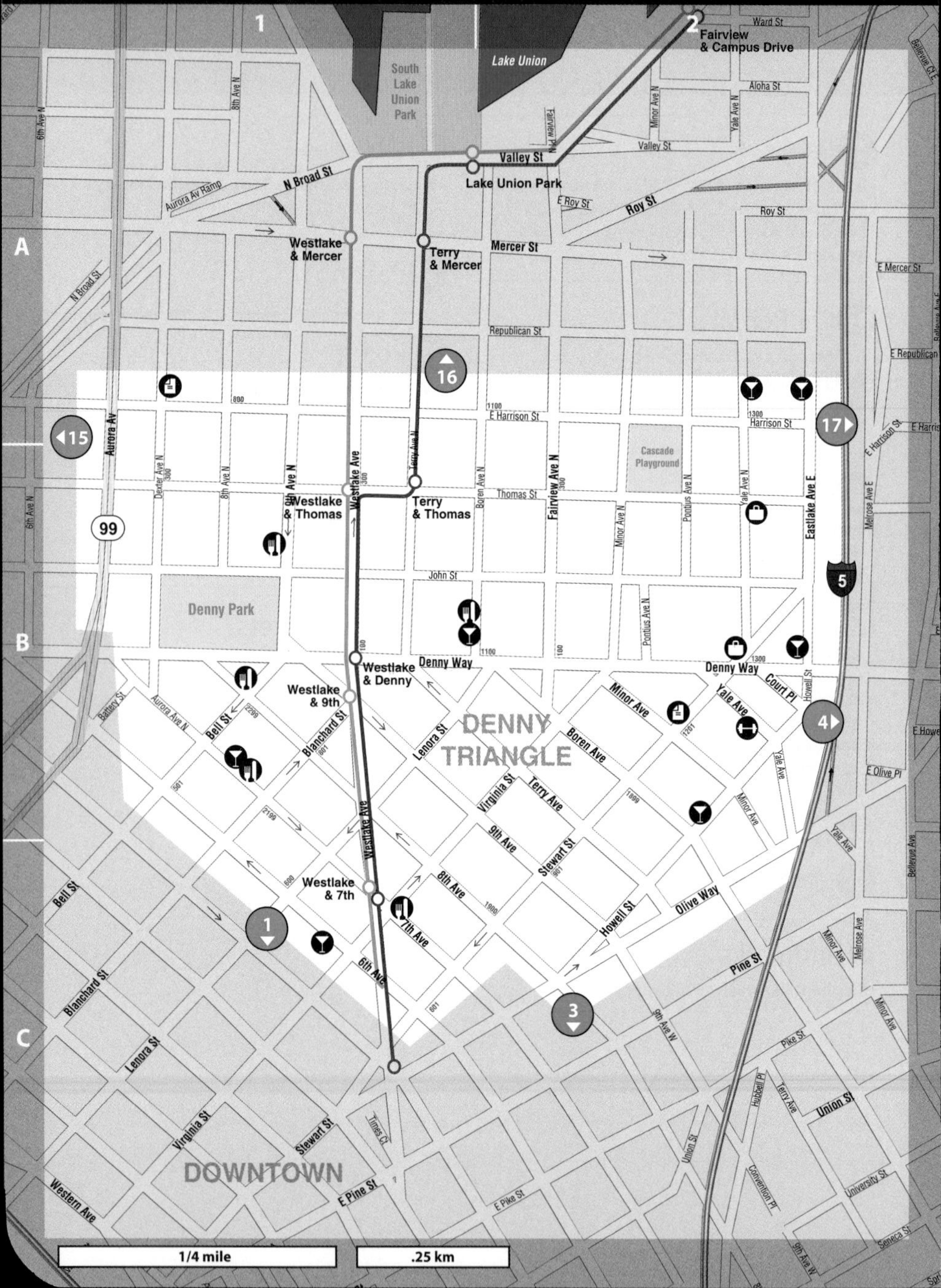
N
1
2
Fairview
& Campus Drive
Ward St
Lake Union
South
Lake
Union
Park
Aloha St
8th Ave N
6th Ave N
Fairview Pl N
Minor Ave N
Yale Ave N
Valley St
Valley St
Lake Union Park
N Broad St
Aurora Av Ramp
E Roy St
Roy St
Roy St
A
Westlake
& Mercer
Terry
& Mercer
Mercer St
E Mercer St
N Broad St
Republican St
E Republican
16
890
1100
E Harrison St
1300
Harrison St
17
E Harrison St
15
Aurora Av
Dexter Ave N
300
8th Ave N
9th Ave N
Westlake Ave
300
Terry Ave N
Cascade
Playground
Westlake
& Thomas
Terry
& Thomas
Boren Ave N
Thomas St
Fairview Ave N
300
Minor Ave N
Pontius Ave N
Yale Ave N
Eastlake Ave E
Melrose Ave E
6th Ave N
99
John St
5
Denny Park
Pontius Ave N
B
100
1100
100
1300
Westlake
& Denny
Denny Way
Denny Way
Court Pl
Howell St
Westlake
& 9th
Battery St
Aurora Ave N
Bell St
2299
Blanchard St
801
Lenora St
DENNY
TRIANGLE
Minor Ave
Yale Ave
1201
4
Boren Ave
Yale Ave
E Howe
501
Virginia St
Terry Ave
1899
Minor Ave
E Olive Pl
2199
Westlake Ave
9th Ave
Stewart St
901
Yale Ave
Bellevue Ave
600
Westlake
& 7th
8th Ave
1900
Howell St
Olive Way
Bell St
1
7th Ave
6th Ave
Pine St
Minor Ave
Melrose Ave
Blanchard St
3
601
9th Ave W
Minor Ave
C
Lenora St
Pike St
Hubbell Pl
Terry Ave
Union St
Virginia St
Stewart St
Times Ct
Union St
DOWNTOWN
Convention Pl
University St
Western Ave
E Pine St
E Pike St
9th Ave W
Seneca St
1/4 mile
.25 km

After you've ridden the SLUT (a.k.a. streetcar), line your stomach with grease on the cheap at the 24-hour Hurricane Café. Learn what the kids are listening to at El Corazon. Make merry on the dance floor or see some amazing fringe theater at ReBar. Feierabend has awesome large pretzels and German beer. Stab or be stabbed in Denny Park.

Copy Shops
- **Lazerquick Printing** • 1204 Stewart St [Minor Ave]
- **United Reprographics** • 420 Dexter Ave N [Harrison St]

Gyms
- **24 Hour Fitness** • 1827 Yale Ave [Howell St] ☼

Nightlife
- **13 Coins** • 125 Boren Ave N [Denny Wy] ☼
- **Dimitriou's Jazz Alley** • 2033 6th Ave [Virginia St]
- **El Corazon** • 109 Eastlake Ave E [Denny Wy]
- **Feierabend** • 422 Yale Ave N [Harrison St]
- **Hurricane Café** • 2230 7th Ave [Blanchard St] ☼
- **Lo Fi** • 429B Eastlake Ave E [Harrison St]
- **Rebar** • 1114 Howell St [Boren St]

Restaurants
- **13 Coins** • 125 Boren Ave N [Denny Wy] ☼
- **FareStart** • 700 Virginia St [7th Ave]
- **The Hurricane Café** • 2230 7th Ave [Blanchard St] ☼
- **Shilla Restaurant** • 2300 8th Ave [Bell St]
- **Venik Lounge** • 227 9th Ave N [John St]

Shopping
- **Play it Again Sports** • 1304 Stewart St [Yale Ave N]
- **REI** • 222 Yale Ave N [John St]

Map 3 · **Downtown**

N

Denny Park

Denny Way

Aurora

Clay St
Vine St
Wall St
Battery St
Bell St
Battery St
Blanchard St
Bell St
Lenora St
5th Ave
4th Ave
3rd Ave
2nd Ave
1st Ave
1st Ave
Lenora St
Blanchard St

Minor Ave
Yale Ave
Court Pl
Howell
E Olive
Denny Way
Boren Ave
Terry Ave
Minor Ave
9th Ave
8th Ave
Stewart St
Virginia St
7th Ave
6th Ave
Howell St
Olive Way

Pine St
E Olive
Minor Ave
Melrose Ave
Pike St
Yale Ave
Union St
Terry Ave
9th Ave W

A

Giant Rotating
Shuttlecock

Westlake Ave

Paramount
Theatre

PAGE 302

Regrade
Park

Western Ave
Virginia St
Stewart St

Moore Theater

PAGE 301

Pine St

Pike St

"Seattle Police Are
Communists" Guy

E Pine St

E Pike St

Washington State
Convention and
Trade Center

Union St

Victor
Steinbrueck
Park

PAGE 216

Pike Place
Market

Rachel the Pig

Gum Wall

The Blade

Union St

PAGE 299

Benaroya
Hall

University St

5th Avenue
Theatre

Rainier Tower

PAGE 205

Freeway
Park

B

Waterfront
Park

Seattle
Art Museum

Lusty
Lady

The Hammering
Man

Seneca St

Spring St

Seattle
Central
Library

PAGE 223

Alaskan Way

99

1st Ave

Post Ave

Western Ave

Madison St

Marion St

Columbia St

Cherry St

James St

Columbia Center

Seattle
Central
Library

Elliott Bay

Western Ave

Pioneer
Square Park

Yesler Way

City Hall
Park

Dilling Way

Terrace St

C

S Washington St

S Main St

S Jackson St

S King St

2nd Avenue Ext S

3rd Ave S

Jefferson St

1/4 mile   .25 km

Like most downtowns, Seattle's mainly caters to tourists, consumers, and the work-a-day crowd. Therefore department stores, happy hours, and Starbucks are plentiful. But fancy condos are starting to spring up on every block, and more people are calling this 'hood home. You can get your culture on at Benaroya Hall or the Seattle Art Museum. Westlake Center is flavor country in terms of colorful characters, religious zealots, LaRouche bags, and the occasional "Personality Test" booth.

$ Banks

- **Bank of America** • 1001 4th Ave [Madison St]
- **Bank of America** • 1309 4th Ave [University St]
- **Bank of America** • 408 Pike St [4th Ave]
- **Bank of America** • 500 Olive Wy [Westlake Ave]
- **Bank of America** • 701 2nd Ave [Cherry St]
- **Bank of America** • 701 5th Ave [Cherry St]
- **Bank of America** (ATM) •
  1100 2nd Ave [Spring St]
- **Bank of America** (ATM) •
  1401 1st Ave [Union St]
- **Evergreen Bank** • 1111 3rd Ave [Spring St]
- **Frontier Bank** • 1200 5th Ave [Seneca St]
- **Key Bank** • 1329 4th Ave [University St]
- **Key Bank** • 700 5th Ave [Cherry St]
- **Key Bank** • 815 2nd Ave [Columbia St]
- **Key Bank** (ATM) • 601 Union St [6th Ave]
- **Sterling Savings Bank** •
  1191 2nd Ave, Ste 1900 [Seneca St]
- **Sterling Savings Bank** •
  1406 4th Ave [Union St]
- **Sterling Savings Bank** •
  601 Union St, Ste 1717 [6th Ave]
- **US Bank** • 1301 5th Ave [University St]
- **US Bank** • 1420 5th Ave [Union St]
- **US Bank** • 1525 1st Ave Ste 4 [Pike St]
- **US Bank** • 723 1st Ave [Columbia St]
- **US Bank** (ATM) • 1221 1st Ave [Seneca St]
- **US Bank** (ATM) • 1916 Pike St [Stewart St]
- **US Bank** (ATM) • 800 Convention Pl [Union St]
- **US Bank** (ATM) • 85 Pike St [1st Ave]
- **Washington Federal Savings** •
  215 Columbia St, Ste 723 [2nd Ave]
- **Washington Federal Savings** •
  425 Pike St [4th Ave]
- **Washington Mutual** •
  1201 3rd Ave [Seneca St]
- **Washington Mutual** •
  1301 2nd Ave [University St]
- **Washington Mutual** •
  1401 5th Ave [Union St]
- **Washington Mutual** • 1501 4th Ave [Pike St]
- **Washington Mutual** • 600 Pine St [6th Ave]
- **Washington Mutual** •
  1191 2nd Ave [Seneca St]
- **Wells Fargo** • 1215 4th Ave [Seneca St]
- **Wells Fargo** • 1620 4th Ave [Pine St]
- **Wells Fargo** • 720 Olive Wy, Ste 107 [7th Ave]
- **Wells Fargo** • 999 3rd Ave [Madison St]
- **Wells Fargo** (ATM) • 102 Pike St [1st Ave]
- **Wells Fargo** (ATM) • 1301 5th Ave [University St]
- **Wells Fargo** (ATM) • 999 3rd Ave [Madison St]

🚗 Car Rental

- **Airways Rent A Car** • 801 4th Ave [Columbia St]
- **Alamo** • 1301 6th Ave [University St]
- **Budget** • 801 4th Ave [Columbia St]
- **Hertz** • 1501 8th Ave [Pike St]
- **National** • 1301 6th Ave [University St]

☕ Coffee

- **Ancient Grounds** • 1220 1st Ave [Seneca St]
- **Bottega Italiana** • 1425 1st Ave [Union St]
- **Caffe Appassionato** •
  801 Alaskan Wy [Marion St]
- **Caffe D'Arte** • 1625 Second Ave [Pine St]
- **Caffe Ladro** • 108 Union St [1st Ave]
- **Caffe Ladro** • 801 Pine St [8th Ave]
- **Cherry Street Coffee House** •
  103 Cherry St [1st Ave]
- **Cherry Street Coffee House** •
  808 3rd Ave [Columbia St]
- **Espresso Caffe DIOR** •
  725 Pike St, Ste 3 [7th Ave]
- **Fergy's Café** • 1303 6th Ave [University St]
- **Local Color** • 1606 Pike Pl [Pine Street]
- **M Coy Books & Espresso** • 117 Pine St [1st Ave]
- **Online Coffee Company** •
  1111 1st Ave [Spring St]
- **Pegasus Coffee Bar** • 1218 3rd Ave [Seneca St]
- **Pegasus Coffee Bar** • 711 3rd Ave [Cherry St]
- **Seattle's Best Coffee** • 102 Pike St [1st Ave]
- **Seattle's Best Coffee** •
  1100 4th Ave [Spring St]
- **Seattle's Best Coffee** • 1530 Post Aly [Pine St]
- **Seattle's Best Coffee** • 400 Pike St [4th Ave]
- **Seattle's Best Coffee** •
  621 2nd Ave [James St]
- **Starbucks** • 1000 2nd Ave [Madison St]
- **Starbucks** • 1101 Alaskan Wy [Spring St]
- **Starbucks** • 1111 3rd Ave [Spring St]
- **Starbucks** • 1125 4th Ave [Spring St]
- **Starbucks** • 1191 2nd Ave [Seneca St]
- **Starbucks** • Washington Mutual Center •
  1301 2nd Ave [University St]
- **Starbucks** • 1325 4th Ave [University St]
- **Starbucks** • 1420 5th Ave [Union St]
- **Starbucks** • 1420 5th Ave [Union St]
- **Starbucks** • 1501 4th Ave [Pike St]
- **Starbucks** • Elliot Hotel • 1524 7th Ave [Pike St]
- **Starbucks** • 1700 7th Ave [Olive Wy]
- **Starbucks** • 1912 Pike Pl [Stewart St]
- **Starbucks** • Benaroya Symphony Hall •
  200 University St [2nd Ave]
- **Starbucks** • 221 Pike St [2nd Ave]
- **Starbucks** • 400 Pine St [4th Ave]
- **Starbucks** • 515 Pine St [5th Ave]
- **Starbucks** • 600 Pine St [6th Ave]
- **Starbucks** • 600 Union St [6th Ave]
- **Starbucks** • 700 5th Ave [Cherry St]
- **Starbucks** • 701 5th Ave [Cherry St]
- **Starbucks** • 721 Pine St [7th Ave]
- **Starbucks** • 800 Convention Pl [Union St]
- **Starbucks** • 823 1st Ave [Columbia St]
- **Starbucks** • 999 3rd Ave [Madison St]
- **Tully's** • 1000 2nd Ave [Madison St]
- **Tully's** • 1015 3rd Ave [Madison St]
- **Tully's** • 1015 3rd Ave [Madison St]
- **Tully's** • 1222 Post Aly [Pine St]
- **Tully's** • 1401 4th Ave [Union St]
- **Tully's** • 1601 5th Ave [Pine St]
- **Tully's** • 2000 1st Ave [Virginia St]
- **Tully's** • 2001 Western Ave [Virginia St]
- **Tully's** • 601 Union St [6th Ave]
- **Tully's** • 701 5th Ave [Cherry St]
- **Tully's** • 821 2nd Ave [Columbia St]
- **Tully's** • 824 Pike St [8th Ave]
- **Valdez Juan** • 1427 5th Ave [Union St]

⊙ Landmarks

- **5th Avenue Theatre** •
  1308 5th Ave [University St]
- **The Blade** • Pike St & 2nd Ave
- **Columbia Center** • 701 5th Ave [Cherry St]
- **Freeway Park** • 700 Seneca St [6th Ave]
- **Giant Rotating Shuttlecock** •
  Western Ave & Lenora St
- **Gum Wall** • Lower Post Aly [Pike St]
- **The Hammering Man** •
  100 University St [1st Ave]
- **Lusty Lady** • 1315 1st Ave [University St]
- **Paramount Theatre** • 911 Pine St [9th Ave]
- **Pike Place Market** • 1501 Pike Pl # 510 [Pike St]
- **Rachel the Pig** • Pike Pl & Pike St
- **Rainier Tower** • 1301 5th Ave [University St]
- **Seattle Art Museum** • 100 University St [1st Ave]
- **Seattle Central Library** •
  1000 4th Ave [Madison St]
- **"Seattle Police Are Communists" Guy** •
  6th Ave & Pine St

📖 Libraries

- **Central Library** • 1000 4th Ave [Madison St]

P Parking

℞ Pharmacies

- **Bartell Drug Store** • 1404 3rd Ave [Union St]
- **Bartell Drug Store** • 1628 5th Ave [Pine St]
- **Bartell Drug Store** • 910 4th Ave [Marion St]
- **Kelley-Ross Pharmacy** • 616 Olive Wy [6th Ave]
- **Pacific Drugs** • 822 1st Ave [Columbia St]
- **Rite Aid Pharmacies** • 319 Pike St [3rd Ave]
- **Rite Aid Pharmacies** •
  802 3rd Ave [Columbia St]
- **Walgreens** • 222 Pike St [2nd Ave]

🚓 Police

- **Seattle Police Headquarters** •
  610 5th Ave [James St]

✉ Post Offices

- **Columbia Center** •
  701 5th Ave, Ste 306 [Cherry St]
- **Federal Station** • 909 1st Ave, Ste 100 [Marion St]
- **Midtown** • 301 Union St [3rd Ave]
- **Seafirst** • 1001 4th Ave [Madison St]

Map 3 · **Downtown**

1

2

Denny Park

Denny Way

Clay St

Vine St

Wall St

Battery St

Aurora Ave

Battery St

Bell St

8th Ave

Blanchard St

Lenora St

Minor Ave

Yale Ave

Court Pl

E Olive Pl

Boren Ave

Terry Ave

Yale Ave

A

1st Ave

5th Ave

4th Ave

3rd Ave

2nd Ave

Lenora St

Virginia St

9th Ave

8th Ave

Stewart St

7th Ave

6th Ave

Howell St

Olive Way

Pine St

Minor Ave

Melrose Ave

Pike St

9th Ave W

Bell St

Regrade Park

Blanchard St

1st Ave

Lenora St

Virginia St

Westlake Ave

Times Ct

E Pine St

E Pine St

Pike St

Convention and Trade Center

Union St

University St

2

PAGE 301

Moore Theater

6th Ave

5th Ave

Terry Ave

Convention Pl

Hubbell Pl

9th Ave W

Western Ave

Victor Steinbrueck Park

Stewart St

Virginia St

1

2

4

5

3

3

3

Pine St

Pike St

Pine St

5th Ave

6th Ave

PAGE 205

Freeway Park

PAGE 216

Pike Place Market

8

4

6

4

3

1

Union St

PAGE 299

Benaroya Hall

University St

Pike St

Post Al

3rd Ave

4th Ave

2

Seneca St

Spring St

5th Ave

6th Ave

99

Alaskan Way

Waterfront Park

Madison St

2nd Ave

1st Ave

Western Ave

Post Al

Marion St

Columbia St

Cherry St

4th Ave

5th Ave

3rd Ave

James St

4

B

5

Elliott Bay

2

1

Western Ave

7

Pioneer Square Park

City Hall Park

Dilling Way

Terrace St

C

Yesler Way

2nd Avenue Ext S

S Washington St

S Main St

S Jackson St

S King St

Jefferson St

Prefontaine Pl S

1/4 mile	.25 km

Sundries / Entertainment

Map 3

Get up early, brave the tourists, and shop like a local at Pike Place Market. The fresh food and flowers are all worth sticking out the crowds. For seafood go highbrow at Etta's or Matt's or lowbrow at Emmett's or Jack's. Grab a bar stool at the Zig Zag for a stiff cocktail. The Showbox and the Moore have top-notch music calendars. Sneak away from the family for a peep show at the conveniently located Lusty Lady.

Copy Shops

- **FedEx Kinko's** • 1200 6th Ave [Seneca St]
- **FedEx Kinko's** • 735 Pike St [7th Ave]
- **FedEx Kinko's** • 816 3rd Ave [Columbia St]
- **Golem Copy Center Llc** • 720 Olive Wy [7th Ave]
- **Mail Boxes Etc** • 800 5th Ave [Columbia St]
- **Minuteman Press** • 515 Union St [5th Ave]
- **Minuteman Press** • 920 Alaskan Wy [Marion St]
- **Office Depot** • 1423 4th Ave [Union St]
- **One Step Copy Center** •
  600 University St [6th Ave]
- **UPS Store** • 1700 7th Ave [Olive Wy]
- **UPS Store** • 815 1st Ave [Columbia St]

Gyms

- **All Star Fitness** • 509 Olive Wy [5th Ave]
- **All Star Fitness** • 700 5th Ave [Cherry St]
- **Epicenter** • 1419 3rd Ave [Union St]
- **Gold's Gym** • 825 Pike St [8th Ave]
- **Headquarters Health & Fitness** •
  217 Pine St [2nd Ave]
- **Pure Fitness** • 808 2nd Ave [Columbia St]
- **Seattle Athletic Club** •
  2020 Western Ave [Lenora St]
- **Washington Athletic Club** •
  1325 6th Ave [University St]

Liquor Stores

- **Pike & Western Wine Shop** •
  1934 Pike Pl [Stewart St]
- **Sixth Avenue Wine Seller** •
  600 Pine St [6th Ave]
- **Washington State Liquor Store** •
  1201 2nd Ave [Seneca St]

Movie Theaters

- **Regal Meridian 16** • 1501 7th Ave [Pike St]
- **AMC Pacific Place 11** • 600 Pine St [6th Ave]

Nightlife

- **Alibi Room** • 85 Pike St, Ste 410 [Post Aly]
- **Athenian Inn** • 1517 Pike Pl [Post Aly]
- **Can Can** • 94 Pike St [1st Ave]
- **Contour** • 807 1st Ave [Columbia St]
- **Déjà Vu** • 1510 1st Ave [Pike St]
- **Fado Irish Pub** • 801 1st Ave [Columbia St]
- **Gameworks** • 1511 7th Ave [Pike St]
- **Kells Irish Restaurant and Pub** •
  1916 Post Aly [Stewart St]
- **Le Pichet** • 1933 1st Ave [Stewart St]
- **The Lusty Lady** • 1315 1st Ave [University St]
- **Moore Theatre** • 1932 2nd Ave [Stewart St]
- **Nite Lite Restaurant & Bar** •
  1926 2nd Ave [Stewart St]
- **Noc Noc** • 1516 2nd Ave [Pike St]
- **Oliver's Lounge** • 405 Olive Wy [4th Ave]
- **The Owl & Thistle** • 808 Post Ave [Columbia St]
- **Paramount Theatre** • 911 Pine St [9th Ave]
- **The Pink Door** • 1919 Post Aly [Stewart St]
- **Purple Café & Wine Bar** •
  1225 4th Ave [Seneca St]
- **Shea's Lounge** • 94 Pike St #34 [1st Ave]
- **The Showbox** • 1426 1st Ave [Union St]

- **The Triple Door** • 216 Union St [2nd Ave]
- **Vino Vino Room** • 102 Cherry St [1st Ave]
- **The Virginia Inn** • 1937 1st Ave [Stewart St]
- **W Bar** • 1112 4th Ave [Spring St]
- **White Horse Trading Company** •
  1908 Post Aly [Stewart St]
- **Zig Zag Café** • 1501 Western Ave [Pike St]

Pet Shops

- **Fetch Pet Grocery** • 1411 34th Ave [6th Ave]
- **Three Dog Bakery** • 1408 1st Ave [Union St]

Restaurants

- **94 Stewart** • 94 Stewart St [1st Ave]
- **Andaluca** • 407 Olive Wy [4th Ave]
- **Bakeman's** • 122 Cherry St [1st Ave]
- **The Brooklyn** • 1212 2nd Ave [Seneca St]
- **Café Campagne** • 1600 Post Aly [Pine St]
- **Campagne** • 86 Pine St [Post Aly]
- **Chez Shea** • 94 Pike St [1st Ave]
- **Crêpe de Paris** • 1333 5th Ave [University St]
- **Crumpet Shop** • 1503 1st Ave [Pike St]
- **DeNunzio** • 102 Cherry St [1st Ave]
- **Dilettante Chocolates** • 400 Pine St [4th Ave]
- **Dragonfish Asian Café** • 722 Pine St [7th Ave]
- **Earth and Ocean** • 1112 4th Ave [Spring St]
- **El Puerco Lloron** • 1501 Western Ave [Pike St]
- **Elliot's Oyster House** •
  1201 Alaskan Wy [Seneca St]
- **Emmett Watson's Oyster Bar** •
  1916 Pike Pl [Stewart St]
- **Etta's Seafood** • 2020 Western Ave [Lenora St]
- **Fish Club** • 2100 Alaskan Wy [Lenora St]
- **Fox Sports Grill** • 1522 6th Ave [Pike St]
- **Gelatiamo** • 1400 3rd Ave [Union St]
- **The Georgian** • 411 University St [4th Ave]
- **Il Bistro** • 93A Pike St [1st Ave]
- **Il Fornaio** • 600 Pine St [6th Ave]
- **Jack's Fish Spot** • 1514 Pike Pl [Pike St]
- **Kells Irish Pub** • 1916 Post Aly [Stewart St]
- **Le Pichet** • 1933 1st Ave [Stewart St]
- **Library Bistro** • 92 Madison St [1st Ave]
- **Mae Phim Thai Restaurant** •
  94 Columbia St [Post Ave]
- **Market Grill** • 1509 Pike Pl #3 [Pike St]
- **Matt's Famous Chili Dogs** •
  801 Alaskan Wy [Marion St]
- **Matt's in the Market** • 94 Pike St [1st Ave]
- **Maximilien in the Market** •
  81A Pike St [1st ave]
- **McCormick & Schmick's** •
  1103 1st Ave [Spring St]
- **McCormick's Fish House & Bar** •
  722 4th Ave [Columbia St]
- **Metropolitan Grill** • 820 2nd Ave [Columbia St]
- **Morton's, The Steakhouse** •
  1511 6th Ave [Pike St]
- **New Orleans Creole** • 114 1st Ave S [Yesler Wy St]
- **Oceanaire Seafood Room** •
  1700 7th Ave [Olive Wy]
- **Osaka Grill** • 128 Pike St [1st Ave]
- **Palomino** • 1420 5th Ave [Union St]
- **Pan Africa** • 1521 1st Ave [Pike St]
- **Pellini** • 515 Madison St [5th Ave]
- **PF Chang's China Bistro** • 400 Pine St [4th Ave]
- **The Pink Door** • 1919 Post Aly [Stewart St]

- **Place Pigalle** • 81 Pike St [1st ave]
- **Porta by the Market** • 113 Virginia St [1st Ave]
- **Purple Café & Wine Bar** •
  1225 4th Ave [Seneca St]
- **Ruth's Chris Steak House** • 727 Pine St [7th Ave]
- **Sazerac** • 1101 4th Ave [Spring St]
- **Shuckers** • 411 University St [4th Ave]
- **Three Girls Bakery** • 1514 Pike Pl [Pike St]
- **Tulio Ristorante** • 1100 5th Ave [Spring St]
- **Turkish Delight** • 1930 Pike Pl [Stewart St]
- **Union** • 1400 1st Ave [Union St]
- **Union Square Grill** • 621 Union St [6th Ave]
- **Von's Grand City Café** • 619 Pine St [6th Ave]
- **Wild Ginger** • 1401 3rd Ave [Union St]
- **World Class Chili Inc** •
  93 Pike St [1st Ave]
- **Zaina Food, Drink & Friends** •
  108 Cherry St [1st Ave]
- **Zaina Food, Drink & Friends** •
  1619 3rd Ave [Pine St]

Shopping

- **Baby and Company** • 1936 1st Ave [Stewart St]
- **Beecher's Cheese** • 1600 Pike Pl [Pine St]
- **Bottega Italiana** • 1425 1st Ave [Union St]
- **Decaro Sartoria Custom Tailors** •
  2025 1st Ave [Virginia St]
- **Don & Joe's Meats** • 85 Pike St [1st Ave]
- **First and Pike News** • 93 Pike St [1st Ave]
- **Golden Age Collectibles** •
  1501 Pike Pl [Pike St]
- **Hair Fair Wig Shop** • 124 Pike St [1st Ave]
- **Isadoras** • 1915 1st Ave [Stewart St]
- **Left Bank Books Collective** •
  92 Pike St [1st Ave]
- **Leroy's Menswear** • 204 Pike St [2nd Ave]
- **Market Magic** • 1501 Pike Pl [Pike St]
- **Market Optical** • 1906 Pike Pl [Stewart St]
- **Metsker Maps** • 1511 1st Ave [Pike St]
- **Nordstrom** • 500 Pine St [5th Ave]
- **The Nordstrom Rack** • 1601 2nd Ave [Pine St]
- **Opus 204** • 2004 1st Ave [Virginia St]
- **Peter Miller Books** •
  1930 1st Ave [Stewart St]
- **Pike Place Creamery** • 1514 Pike Pl [Pike St]
- **Pike Place Market** • Pike St @ First Ave
- **Pure Food Fish** • 1515 Pike Pl [Pike St]
- **Riveted** • 1113 1st Ave [Spring St]
- **Schmancy** • 1932 2nd Ave [Stewart St]
- **Seattle Art Museum Gallery** •
  1220 3rd Ave [Seneca St]
- **Seattle Mystery Bookshop** •
  117 Cherry St [1st Ave]
- **Sephora** • 415 Pine St [4th Ave]
- **Sneaker City** • 110 Pike St [1st Ave]
- **Spanish Table** • 1427 Western Ave [Union St]
- **Sway & Cake** • 1631 6th Ave [Pine St]
- **Tenzing Momo** • 93 Pike St [1st Ave]
- **Twist** • 600 Pine St [6th Ave]
- **Uli's Famous Sausage** • 1511 Pike Pl [Pike St]
- **Vain** • 2018 1st Ave [Virginia St]
- **Watson Kennedy Fine Living** •
  1022 1st Ave [Madison St]
- **Westlake Center** • 1601 5th Ave [Pine St]
- **Zanadu Comics** •
  1923 3rd Ave [Stewart St]

Map 4 · **First Hill / Pike / Pine**

If you absolutely have to get sick, try to do it on "Pill Hill," where numerous hospitals, medical centers, and private practices make having a heart attack or getting injured downright convenient. Meanwhile, the nearby Pike/Pine corridor is the epicenter of Seattle hipster culture, where twenty-something bohemians waste their youth in assorted tattoo parlors, carefully-designed dive bars, and vintage clothing stores. Stop by Stumptown or Bauhaus for your caffeine fix.

Banks

- **Bank of America** • 1201 Madison St [Minor Ave]
- **Bank of America** • 801 Madison St [M Street Grocery]
- **Bank of America** • 1300 E Madison St [13th Ave]
- **Bank of America (ATM)** • 1401 Broadway [E Union St]
- **Bank of America (ATM)** • 1701 Broadway [E Pine St]
- **Bank of America (ATM)** • 925 Seneca St [9th Ave]
- **Key Bank** • 1224 Madison St [Minor Ave]
- **US Bank** • 1830 Broadway Ste A [E Howell St]
- **US Bank (ATM)** • 1145 Broadway [Harvard Ave]
- **US Bank (ATM)** • 900 E Madison St [Harvard Ave]
- **Washington Mutual** • 1429 Broadway [E Union St]
- **Wells Fargo** • 1317 Madison St [Summit Ave]

Car Rental

- **Enterprise** • 1605 Boylston Ave [Boylston Ave]

Coffee

- **Bauhaus Books & Coffee** • 301 E Pine St [Melrose Ave]
- **Buzz Stop** • 1122 E Madison St [E Union St]
- **Café Stellina** • 1429 12th Ave [E Union St]
- **Caffe Vita** • 1005 E Pike St [10th Ave E]
- **Chatterbox Café** • 1100 12th Ave [E Spring St]
- **Coffee Animals** • 550 12th Ave [E James Court]
- **Online Coffee Company** • 1404 E Pine St [14th Ave]
- **Pettirosso** • 1101 E Pike St [11th Ave]
- **Starbucks** • 1101 Madison St [Boren Ave N]
- **Starbucks** • 1301 Madison St [Summit Ave]
- **Starbucks** • QFC • 1401 Broadway [E Union St]
- **Starbucks** • 800 12th Ave [E Columbia St]
- **Stumptown** • 1115 12th Ave [E Spring St]
- **Stumptown** • 616 E Pine St [Belmont Ave]
- **Tully's** • 925 Seneca St [9th Ave]
- **Uncle Elizabeth's Internet Café** • 1123 Pike St [Boren Ave]
- **Victrola Coffee** • 310 E Pike St [Melrose Ave]

 Gas Stations

- **76** • 914 James St [9th Ave]
- **Arco** • 427 12th Ave [E Remington Ct]
- **Shell** • 1500 Broadway [E Pike St]
- **Shell** • 700 12th Ave [E Cherry St]

Emergency Rooms

- **Swedish Medical Center - First Hill** • 747 Broadway [E Columbia St]
- **Virginia Mason Medical Center** • 1100 9th Ave [Spring St]

Landmarks

- **Egyptian Theatre** • 805 E Pine St [Harvard Ave]
- **Jimi Hendrix Statue** • Broadway & E Pine St

Parking

Pharmacies

- **Bartell Drug Store** • 1101 Madison St [Boren Ave N]
- **Bartell Drug Store** • 1407 Broadway [E Union St]
- **Eastern's** • 515 Minor Ave [Broadway]
- **Kelley-Ross Pharmacy** • 1120 Harvard Ave [Broadway]
- **Moms Pharmacy** • 1120 Cherry St [Boren Ave]
- **Rite Aid Pharmacies** • 1300 Madison St [Summit Ave]

Police

- **East Precinct** • 1519 12th Ave [E Pike St]

Schools

- **The Northwest School** • 1415 Summit Ave [Summit Ave]
- **O Dea High** • 802 Terry Ave [Columbia St]
- **Seattle Academy** • 1201 E Union St [E Madison St]
- **Seattle Central Community College** • 1701 Broadway [E Pine St]
- **Seattle University** • 901 12th Ave [E Marion St]

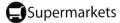 Supermarkets

- **Quality Food Center** • 1401 Broadway [E Union St]

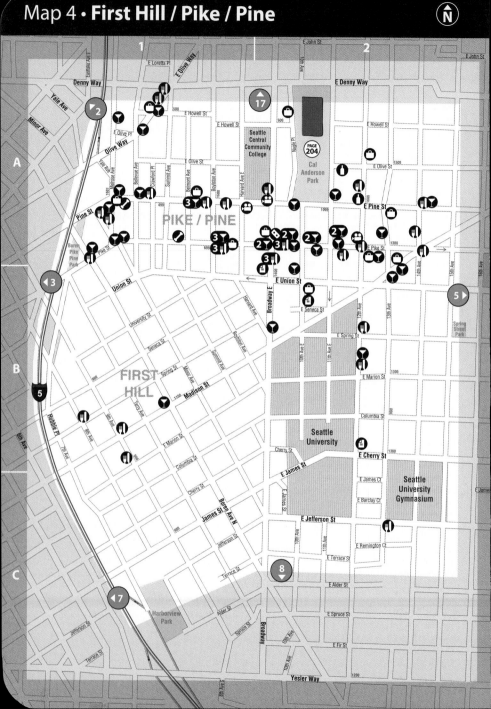

Map 4 • First Hill / Pike / Pine

Sundries / Entertainment

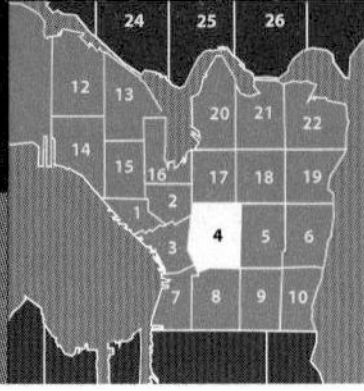

If you're under thirty (or over and still like to party down), you'll find the bars along Pike and Pine to be absolutely fabulous. Linda's is a comfortable, friendly tavern with a great jukebox, while its evil stepsister, the Cha Cha, is a dimly-lit, claustrophobic lounge with cooler-than-thou bartenders. Meet some ladies at the Wild Rose, take a date to Machiavelli, score some late-night tasty tacos at Taco Gringos, or hit the Hideout to escape it all.

Map 4

Copy Shops

- **Copy Mart** • 1018 E Seneca St [10th Ave]
- **UPS Store** • 1425 Broadway [E Union St]

Liquor Stores

- **Tarragona Wine & Food** •
  1125 E Olive St [11th Ave]
- **Washington State Liquor Store** •
  1605 12th Ave [E Pine St]

Movie Theaters

- **Broadway Performance Hall** •
  1625 Broadway [E Pine St]
- **Landmark Egyptian Theatre** •
  805 E Pine St [Harvard Ave]
- **Northwest Film Forum** •
  1515 12th Ave [E Pike St]

Nightlife

- **611 Supreme** •
  611 E Pine St [Belmont Ave]
- **Bad JuJu Lounge** •
  1425 10th Ave [E Union St]
- **Baltic Room** • 1207 Pine St [Minor Ave]
- **Barca** • 1510 11th Ave [E Pike St]
- **Capitol Club** •
  414 E Pine St [Bellevue Ave]
- **Century Ballroom** •
  915 E Pine St [Naple Pl]
- **Cha Cha Lounge** •
  1013 E Pike St [Summit Ave]
- **Chapel** • 1600 Melrose Ave [Pine St]
- **Chez Gaudy** •
  1802 Bellevue Ave [E Olive Pl]
- **Chop Suey** •
  1325 E Madison St [13th Ave]
- **Clever Dunne's Irish House** •
  1501 E Olive Wy [E Howell St]
- **The Comet Tavern** •
  922 E Pike St [Broadway]
- **Crescent Lounge** •
  1413 E Olive Wy [E Olive Pl]
- **The Cuff** • 1533 13th Ave [E Pike St]
- **The Eagle** • 314 E Pike St [Melrose Ave]
- **Elysian Brewing Company** •
  1221 E Pike St [12th Ave]
- **The Garage** •
  1130 Broadway [E Madison St]
- **HaLo** • 500 E Pike St [Summit Ave]
- **Havana** • 1010 E Pike St [10th Ave]
- **The Hideout** • 1005 Boren Ave [Madison St]
- **Honey Hole** • 703 E Pike St [Boylston Ave]
- **King Cobra** • 916 E Pike St [Broadway]
- **Licorous** • 928 12th Ave [E Marion St]

- **Linda's Tavern** •
  707 E Pine St [Belmont Ave]
- **Madison Pub** •
  1315 E Madison St [13th Ave]
- **Manray Video Bar** •
  514 E Pine St [Summit Ave]
- **Neighbours Disco** •
  1509 Broadway [E Pike St]
- **Neumos** • 925 E Pike St [Broadway]
- **Poco Wine Room** •
  1408 E Pine St [14th Ave]
- **Purr** • 1518 11th Ave [E Pike St]
- **R Place** • 619 E Pine St [Belmont Ave]
- **The Redwood** •
  514 E Howell St [Summit Ave]
- **Richard Hugo House** •
  1634 11th Ave [E Pine St]
- **Rosebud Restaurant** •
  719 E Pike St [Boylston Ave]
- **The Saint** •
  1416 E Olive Way [Bellevue Ave E]
- **Satellite Lounge** •
  1118 E Pike St [11th Ave]
- **Six Arms** • 300 E Pike St [Melrose Ave]
- **Sugar** • 916 E Pike St [Broadway]
- **Tango** • 1100 Pike St [Boren Ave]
- **Vito's Madison Grill** •
  929 9th Ave [Marion St]
- **The War Room** •
  722 E Pike St [Boylston Ave]
- **The Wild Rose** • 1021 E Pike St [10th Ave]

Pet Shops

- **Feed Bag** • 516 E Pike St [Summit Ave]
- **Mud Bay Granary** •
  321 E Pine St [Melrose Ave]

Restaurants

- **611 Supreme** •
  611 E Pine St [Belmont Ave]
- **Annapurna Café** •
  1833 Broadway [E Pine St]
- **Ayutthaya Thai Cuisine** •
  727 E Pike St [Boylston Ave]
- **Baguette Box** • 1203 Pine St [Minor Ave]
- **Ballet Restaurant** •
  914 E Pike St [Broadway]
- **Bill's Off Broadway** •
  725 E Pine St [Boylston Ave]
- **Bimbo's Bitchin' Burrito Kitchen** •
  506 E Pine St [Summit Ave]
- **Capitol Club** •
  414 E Pine St [Bellevue Ave]
- **Crave** • 1621 12th Ave [E Pine St]
- **Dinette** • 1514 E Olive Wy [E Howell St]
- **Frites Belgian Frites** •
  925 E Pike St [Broadway]

- **Geneva** • 1106 8th Ave [Spring St]
- **The Globe Café and Bakery** •
  1531 14th Ave [E Pike St]
- **The Green Papaya** •
  600 E Pine St [Summit Ave]
- **Honeyhole Sandwiches** •
  703 E Pike St [Boylston Ave]
- **Hunt Club** • 900 Madison St [9th Ave]
- **Lark** • 926 12th Ave [E Marion St]
- **Machiavelli** • 1215 Pine St [Minor Ave]
- **Mediterranean Kitchen** •
  1417 Broadway [E Union St]
- **Mesob** • 1325 E Jefferson St [13th Ave]
- **Osteria la Spiga** •
  1401 Broadway [E Union St]
- **Piecora's** • 1401 E Madison St [14th Ave]
- **Pike Street Fish Fry** •
  925 E Pike St [Broadway]
- **Poco Wine Room** •
  1408 E Pine St [14th Ave]
- **Rosebud** • 719 E Pike St [Boylston Ave]
- **Tacos Gringos** •
  1510 E Olive Wy [E Howell St]
- **Tango** • 1100 Pike St [Boren Ave]
- **Taqueria Guaymas** •
  1415 Broadway [E Union St]
- **Via Tribunali** • 913 E Pike St [Broadway]

Shopping

- **Atlas Clothing Co** •
  1515 Broadway [E Pike St]
- **Babeland** • 707 E Pike St [Boylston Ave]
- **Backstage Thrift** •
  1512 11th Ave [E Pike St]
- **Bootyland** • 1317 E Pine St [13th Ave]
- **Jive Time Records** •
  411 E Pine St [Bellevue Ave]
- **Le Frock** • 317 E Pine St [Melrose Ave]
- **Life Long Thrift** •
  1017 E Union St [10th Ave]
- **Lucky Devil Tattoo** •
  1720 12th Ave [E Olive St]
- **RE Load Baggage/Tandem** •
  1205 E Pike St, Ste 1D [12th Ave]
- **Revolution Books** •
  1833 Nagle Pl [E Howell St]
- **Rudy's Barbershop** •
  614 E Pine St [Belmont Ave]
- **That's Atomic** •
  1502 E Olive Wy [E Howell St]

Video Rental

- **Blockbuster** • 1514 Broadway [E Pike St]

21

Map 5 · **Central District (North)**

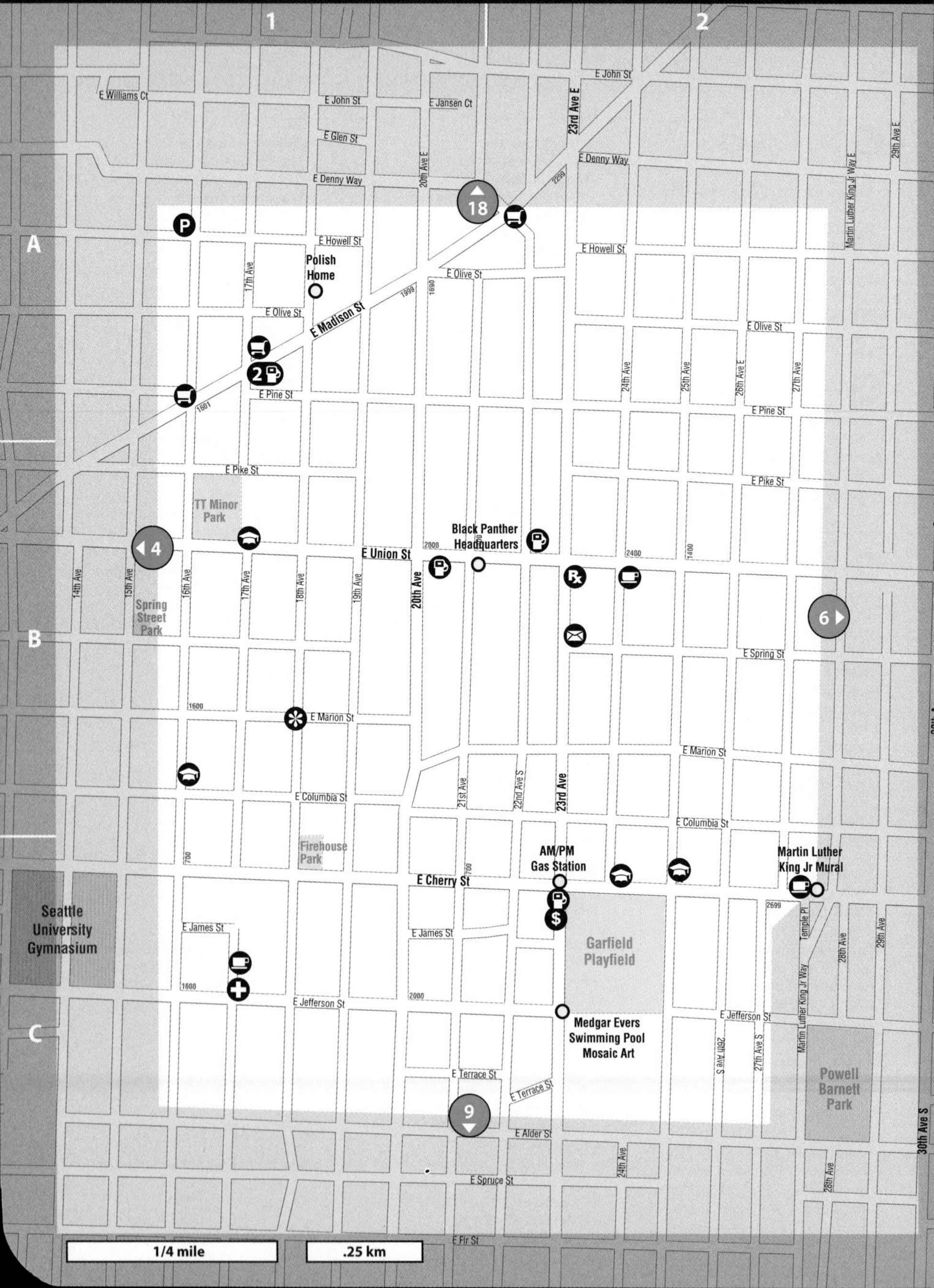

1

2

N

E Williams Ct

E John St

E Jansen Ct

E John St

E Glen St

23rd Ave E

E Denny Way

E Denny Way

18

A

P

E Howell St

E Howell St

17th Ave

20th Ave E

E Madison St

Polish
Home

E Olive St

E Olive St

E Olive St

E Pine St

2

22nd Ave

24th Ave

25th Ave

26th Ave E

27th Ave

28th Ave E

E Pine St

E Pike St

E Pike St

TT Minor
Park

4

14th Ave

15th Ave

16th Ave

17th Ave

18th Ave

19th Ave

20th Ave

E Union St

Black Panther
Headquarters

P

2400

6

B

Spring
Street
Park

E Spring St

E Marion St

E Marion St

E Marion St

E Columbia St

21st Ave

22nd Ave S

23rd Ave

E Columbia St

Firehouse
Park

E Cherry St

AM/PM
Gas Station

Martin Luther
King Jr Mural

Seattle
University
Gymnasium

E James St

E James St

Garfield
Playfield

$

2699

27th Ave S

28th Ave

29th Ave

Temple Pl

Martin Luther King Jr Way

1600

E Jefferson St

2000

Medgar Evers
Swimming Pool
Mosaic Art

E Jefferson St

C

Powell
Barnett
Park

E Terrace St

E Terrace St

9

E Alder St

30th Ave S

E Spruce St

24th Ave S

26th Ave

| 1/4 mile | | .25 km |

E Fir St

The north side of the Central District is an Ethiopian and African-American community being swallowed by new developments. Family-owned groceries and restaurants sit quietly between the busy streets of Adler, 23rd Avenue, MLK, and Union where Garfield community center and a mural of Martin Luther King, Jr. are located.

Banks

- **Key Bank** • 2320 E Union St [23rd Ave]

Coffee

- **Fatima Café** • 2401 E Union St [24th Ave]
- **Seattle Central Grind** • 2724 E Cherry St [Temple Pl]
- **Starbucks** • 550 17th Ave [E Jefferson St]

Community Gardens

Gas Stations

- **76** • 2220 E Union St [22nd Ave S]
- **Arco** • 5620 Martin Luther King Jr Wy S [S Findlay St]
- **Arco** • 665 23rd Ave [E Cherry St]
- **Shell** • 1701 E Madison St [17th Ave]
- **Shell** • 2015 E Union St [20th Ave]
- **Shell** • 1701 E Madison St [17th Ave]

Emergency Rooms

- **Swedish Medical Center - Providence** • 500 17th Ave [E Jefferson St]

Landmarks

- **AM/PM Gas Station** • 23rd Ave & E Cherry St
- **Black Panther Headquarters** • 2111 E Union St [21st Ave]
- **Martin Luther King, Jr Mural** • 2726 E Cherry St [Temple Pl]
- **Medgar Evers Swimming Pool Mosaic Art** • 500 23rd Ave [E Jefferson St]
- **Polish Home** • 1714 18th Ave [E Olive St]

Parking

 Pharmacies

- **Chesterfield Pharmacy** • 2301 E Union St [23rd Ave]

Post Offices

- **East Union** • 1110 23rd Ave [E Spring St]

Schools

- **The Islamic School of Seattle** • 720 25th Ave [E Cherry St]
- **Nova High** • 2410 E Cherry St [24th Ave]
- **Seahawks Academy** • 810 18 Av [E Columbia St]
- **TT Minor Elementary** • 1700 E Union St [17th Ave]

Supermarkets

- **Madison Market** • 1600 E Madison St [16th Ave]
- **Safeway** • 2201 E Madison St [22nd Ave S]
- **Trader Joe's** • 1700 E Madison St [17th Ave]

Map 5 · **Central District (North)**

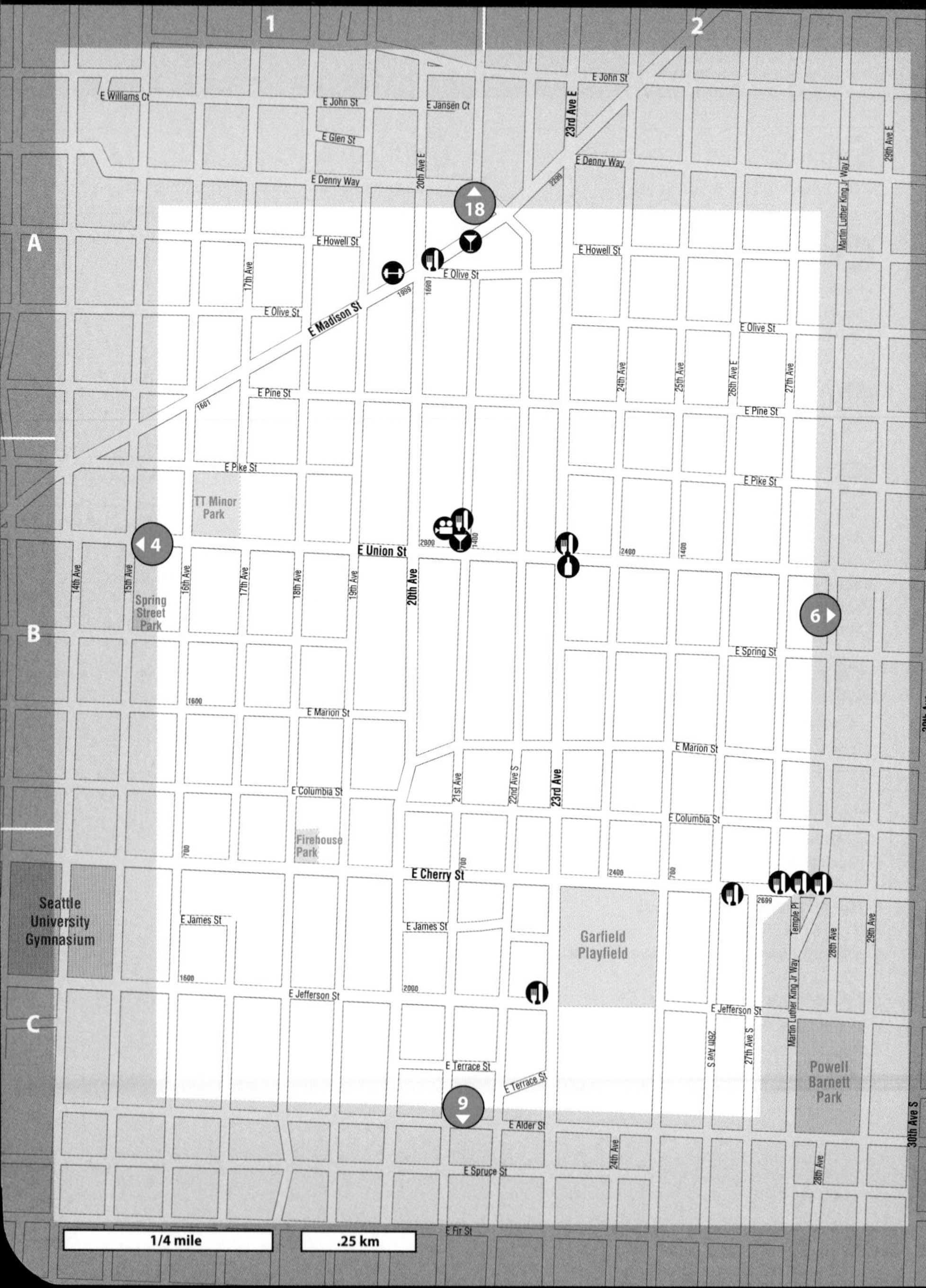

N

1 **2**

E Williams Ct

E John St

E John St

E Jansen Ct

E Glen St

23rd Ave E

E Denny Way

E Denny Way

A

E Howell St

17th Ave

20th Ave

E Olive St

E Howell St

24th Ave E

25th Ave

26th Ave E

27th Ave

28th Ave E

29th Ave E

Martin Luther King Jr Way E

18

E Olive St

E Madison St

1695

1696

E Olive St

E Olive St

1661

E Pine St

E Pine St

E Pike St

E Pike St

TT Minor Park

◄ 4

14th Ave

15th Ave

16th Ave

17th Ave

18th Ave

19th Ave

20th Ave

2900

2800

E Union St

2500

2400

6 ►

Spring Street Park

B

E Spring St

1600

E Marion St

E Marion St

700

E Columbia St

21st Ave

22nd Ave S

23rd Ave

E Columbia St

Firehouse Park

700

E Cherry St

2400

700

2600

Garfield Playfield

Temple Pl

Martin Luther King Jr Way

28th Ave

29th Ave

Seattle University Gymnasium

E James St

E James St

1600

2000

S 26th Ave S

27th Ave S

E Jefferson St

E Jefferson St

E Jefferson St

Powell Barnett Park

C

E Terrace St

E Terrace St

9 ▼

E Alder St

30th Ave S

24th Ave

28th Ave

E Spruce St

| 1/4 mile | .25 km |

E Fir St

Take your pick among the many Ethiopian restaurants that line the streets of Cherry and Union. Assimba and Meskel are standouts. And then there's chicken, creole, and catfish. Ezell's fries up tasty cluckers, Thompson's Point of View is all about southern soul, and fish swim in batter at Catfish Corner. Wash it all down with a drink at Twilight Exit.

Gyms

- **Curves** • 1920 E Madison St [20th Ave]

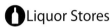Liquor Stores

- **Washington State Liquor Store** •
  2307 E Union St [23rd St]

Movie Theaters

- **Central Cinema** • 1411 21st Ave [E Union St]

Nightlife

- **Central Cinema** • 1411 21st Ave [E Union St]
- **The Twilight Exit** • 2051 E Madison St [20th Ave]

Restaurants

- **Assimba Ethiopian Cuisine** •
  2722 E Cherry St [Temple Pl]
- **Café Selam** • 2715 E Cherry St [27th Ave]
- **Catfish Corner** • 2726 E Cherry St [Temple Pl]
- **Central Cinema** • 1411 21st Ave [E Union St]
- **El Gallito** • 1700 20th Ave [E Madison St]
- **Ezell's Famous Chicken** • 501 23rd Ave [E Jefferson St]
- **Meskel Ethiopian Restaurant** •
  2605 E Cherry St [26th Ave]
- **Thompson's Point of View** •
  2308 E Union St [23rd Ave]

Map 6 • Madrona

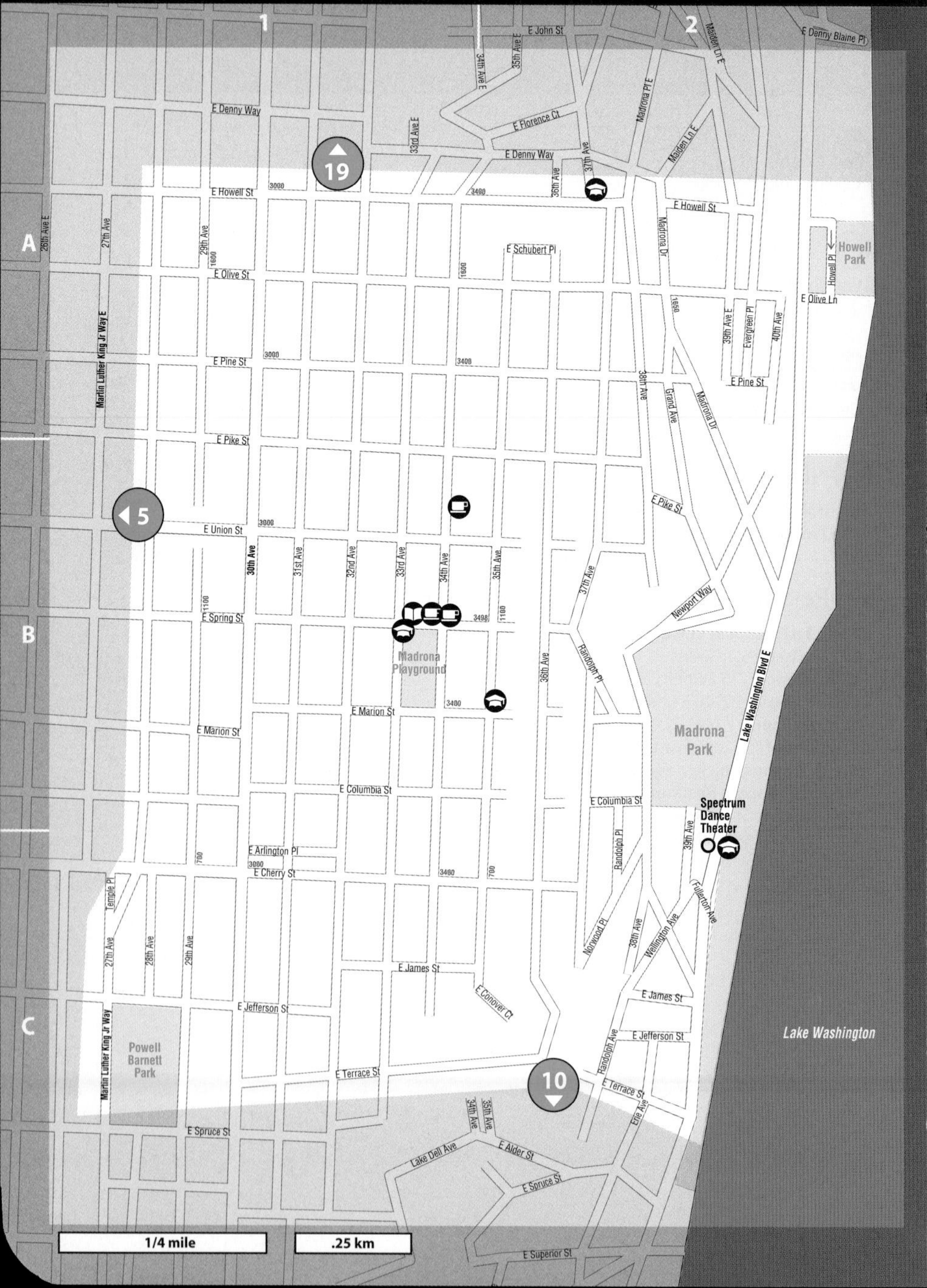

N
1
2
A
B
C
E John St
E Denny Blaine Pl
Maiden Ln E
34th Ave E
35th Ave E
E Denny Way
Madrona Pl E
E Florence Ct
33rd Ave E
Maiden Ln E
19
E Denny Way
37th Ave
36th Ave
E Howell St
3000
3400
E Howell St
Madrona Dr
26th Ave E
27th Ave
29th Ave
1600
E Schubert Pl
Howell Park
Howell Pl
E Olive St
1600
E Olive Ln
1650
39th Ave E
Evergreen Pl
40th Ave
Martin Luther King Jr Way E
E Pine St
3000
3400
38th Ave
Grand Ave
Madrona Dr
E Pine St
E Pike St
E Pike St
5
3000
E Union St
30th Ave
31st Ave
32nd Ave
33rd Ave
34th Ave
35th Ave
37th Ave
Newport Way
1100
E Spring St
3498
1100
Randolph Pl
38th Ave
Madrona Playground
Lake Washington Blvd E
3400
E Marion St
E Marion St
Madrona Park
E Columbia St
E Columbia St
Spectrum Dance Theater
39th Ave
Randolph Pl
E Arlington Pl
700
3000
E Cherry St
3400
700
Fullerton Ave
Temple Pl
27th Ave
28th Ave
29th Ave
Norwood Pl
38th Ave
Wellington Ave
E James St
E Conover Ct
E James St
Martin Luther King Jr Way
E Jefferson St
E Jefferson St
Lake Washington
Powell Barnett Park
Randolph Ave
E Terrace St
10
E Terrace St
Erie Ave
34th Ave
35th Ave
E Spruce St
Lake Dell Ave
E Alder St
E Spruce St
1/4 mile
.25 km
E Superior St

Map 6

What's steeper? Madrona's rising home values or the walk from the lake? A short bus ride from downtown Seattle, this lovely area on Lake Washington is home to staid matriarchs, gay couples, artists, and multi-generational families residing in everything from Seattle big-money mansions to shabby cottages. Locals covet life on the beach with astounding views of Mount Rainier, but it's the variety of food and drink on 34th Avenue that's the real draw.

Coffee
- **Cupcake Royale/Verite Coffee ·**
  1101 34th Ave [E Spring St]
- **The Hi-Spot Café ·** 1410 34th Ave [E Union St]
- **Verite Coffee ·** 1101 34th Ave [E Spring St]

Libraries
- **Madrona-Sally Goldmark Branch ·**
  1134 33rd Ave [E Spring St]

Schools
- **Epiphany ·** 3710 E Howell St [37th Ave]
- **Madrona Dance Studio ·**
  800 Lake Washington Blvd [Fullerton Ave]
- **Madrona K-8 ·** 1121 33rd Ave [E Spring St]
- **St Therese Elementary ·** 900 35th Ave [E Marion St]

o Landmarks
- **Spectrum Dance Theater ·**
  800 Lake Washington Blvd [Fullerton Ave]

Map 6 · **Madrona**

Lake Washington

The stretch on 34th between Pike and Union features wonderful dining amid artsy shops. Start with Dulce's Latin Bistro for aperitifs, Cremant for cassoulet, and St Clouds for tasty late night vittles. Get burgers at the kid friendly Madrona Alehouse. Cozy into the Hi-Spot for brunch or relax at Soleil. See Spot's tail wag while chomping biscuits from Fetch and romping at King's Palace doggie daycare.

Nightlife

• **Madrona Ale House** • 1138 34th Ave [E Spring St]

Pet Shops

• **Fetch Pet Grocery** • 1411 34th Ave [6th Ave]

Restaurants

• **Café Soleil** • 1400 34th Ave [E Union St]
• **Coupage** • 1404 34th Ave [E Union St]
• **Cremant** • 1423 34th Ave [E Union St]
• **Dulce's Latin Bistro** • 1430 34th Ave [E Union St]
• **Hi-Spot Cafe** • 1410 34th Ave [E Union St]
• **Lalibela** • 2800 E Cherry St [Martin Luther King Jr Blvd]
• **Madrona Ale House** • 1138 34th Ave [E Spring St]
• **St Clouds** • 1131 34th Ave [E Spring St]

Shopping

• **Decor on 34th**• 1421 34th Ave [E Union St]
• **Jaywalk** • 1105 34th Ave [Spring St]
• **King's Palace** • 1411 34th Ave [E Pike St]
• **Madrona Moose** • 1421 34th Ave [E Union St]

Map 7 · **Pioneer Square / SoDo**

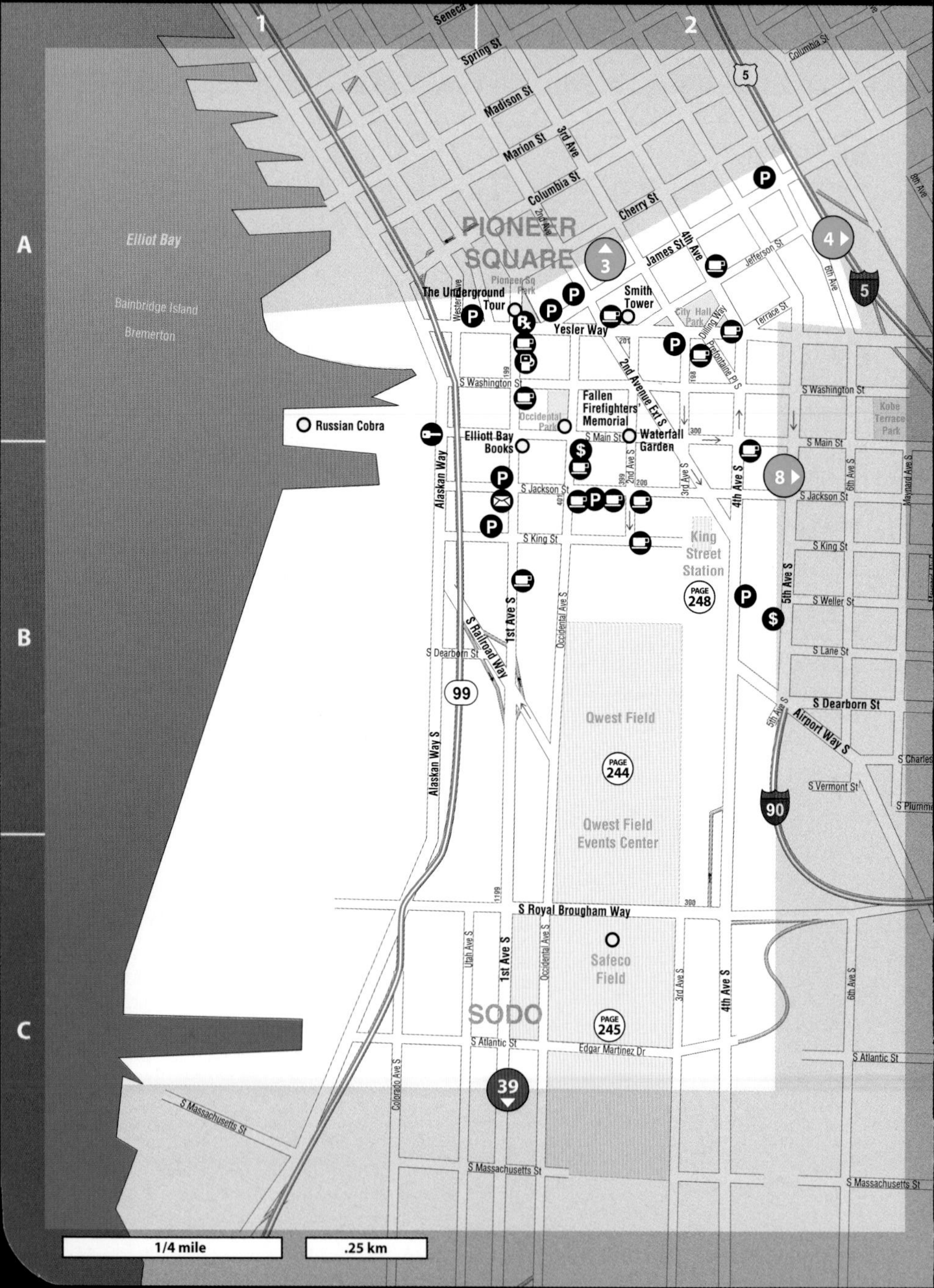

N

1   **2**

Seneca

Spring St

Columbia St

Madison St

5

Marion St

3rd Ave

Columbia St

A

Elliot Bay

Cherry St

P

PIONEER
SQUARE

James St

4th Ave

4

Pioneer Sq
Park

Jefferson St

5

Bainbridge Island

The Underground
Tour

P

P

Smith
Tower

Bremerton

Yesler Way

City Hall
Parking Way

Terrace St

P

Prefontaine Pl S

S Washington St

S Washington St

Kobe
Terrace
Park

Occidental
Park

Fallen
Firefighters'
Memorial

2nd Avenue Ext S

Russian Cobra

S Main St

Waterfall
Garden

S Main St

5th Ave S

Elliott Bay
Books

$

3rd Ave S

P

S Jackson St

2nd Ave S

4th Ave S

S Jackson St

Alaskan Way

P

S Jackson St

P

King
Street
Station

P

S King St

S King St

S Weller St

PAGE
248

P

S Lane St

1st Ave S

Occidental Ave S

S Dearborn St

$

S Railroad Way

B

S Dearborn St

99

Qwest Field

Airport Way S

PAGE
244

S Charles

5th Ave S

90

S Vermont St

S Plumme

Qwest Field
Events Center

Alaskan Way S

S Royal Brougham Way

Utah Ave S

1st Ave S

Occidental Ave S

3rd Ave S

4th Ave S

6th Ave S

Safeco
Field

SODO

PAGE
245

C

S Atlantic St

S Atlantic St

Colorado Ave S

Edgar Martinez Dr

39

S Massachusetts St

S Massachusetts St

S Massachusetts St

1/4 mile	.25 km

Essentials

Map 7

As the city's oldest neighborhood, there's a mystique about Pioneer Square, the nation's original "Skid Road" where the early settlers toiled through harsh conditions. Today, Pioneer Square entertains a tenuous mix of tourists, art galleries, and frat bars around its community living room, Occidental Square. Start your day at All City Coffee or swing by Grand Central Bakery for homemade pastries.

$ Banks

- **Bank of America** · 300 Occidental Ave S [S Main St]
- **Key Bank** · 666 S Dearborn St [Maynard Ave S]
- **Wells Fargo** · 625 5th Ave S [S Weller St]

Car Rental

- **Thrifty** · 101 Alaskan Wy S [S Main St]

Coffee

- **4th Avenue Caffe** · 500 4th Ave [Jefferson St]
- **All City Coffee** · 125 Prefontaine Pl S [Yesler Wy]
- **Caffe Umbria Retail** · 320 Occidental Ave S [S Main St]
- **Grand Central Bakery** · 214 1st Ave S [S Washington St]
- **Joelle's Espresso Café** · 101 4th Ave S [Yesler Wy]
- **Starbucks** · 102 1st Ave S [Yesler Wy]
- **Starbucks** · 400 Occidental Ave S [S Jackson St]
- **Starbucks** · 502 2nd Ave [Yesler Wy]
- **Starbucks** · Safeway · 516 1st Ave S [S King St]
- **TID Coffee House** · 304 4th Ave S [S Main St]
- **Trabant Coffee & Chai** · 602 2nd Ave [James St]
- **Tully's** · 201 S Jackson St [2nd Ave S]
- **Tully's** · 408 2nd Ave S [S Jackson St]
- **Zeitgeist Kunst And Kaffee** · 171 S Jackson St [2nd Ave S]

Gas Stations

- **Shell** · 156 1st Ave S [Yesler Wy]

Landmarks

- **Elliott Bay Books** · 101 S Main St [1st Ave S]
- **Fallen Firefighters' Memorial** · Occidental Park, Occidental Ave S & S Main St
- **Russian Cobra** · 101 Alaskan Wy S, Pier 48 [S Main St]
- **Safeco Field** · Occidental Ave S & S Royal Brougham Wy
- **Smith Tower** · 506 Second Ave [Yesler Wy]
- **The Underground Tour** · 610 1st Ave [Yesler Way]
- **Waterfall Garden** · Second Ave S & S Main St

P Parking

Rx Pharmacies

- **Bartell Drugs** · 600 1st Ave [Yesler Wy]

Post Offices

- **Pioneer Square** · 91 S Jackson St [1st Ave S]

Map 7 · **Pioneer Square / SoDo**

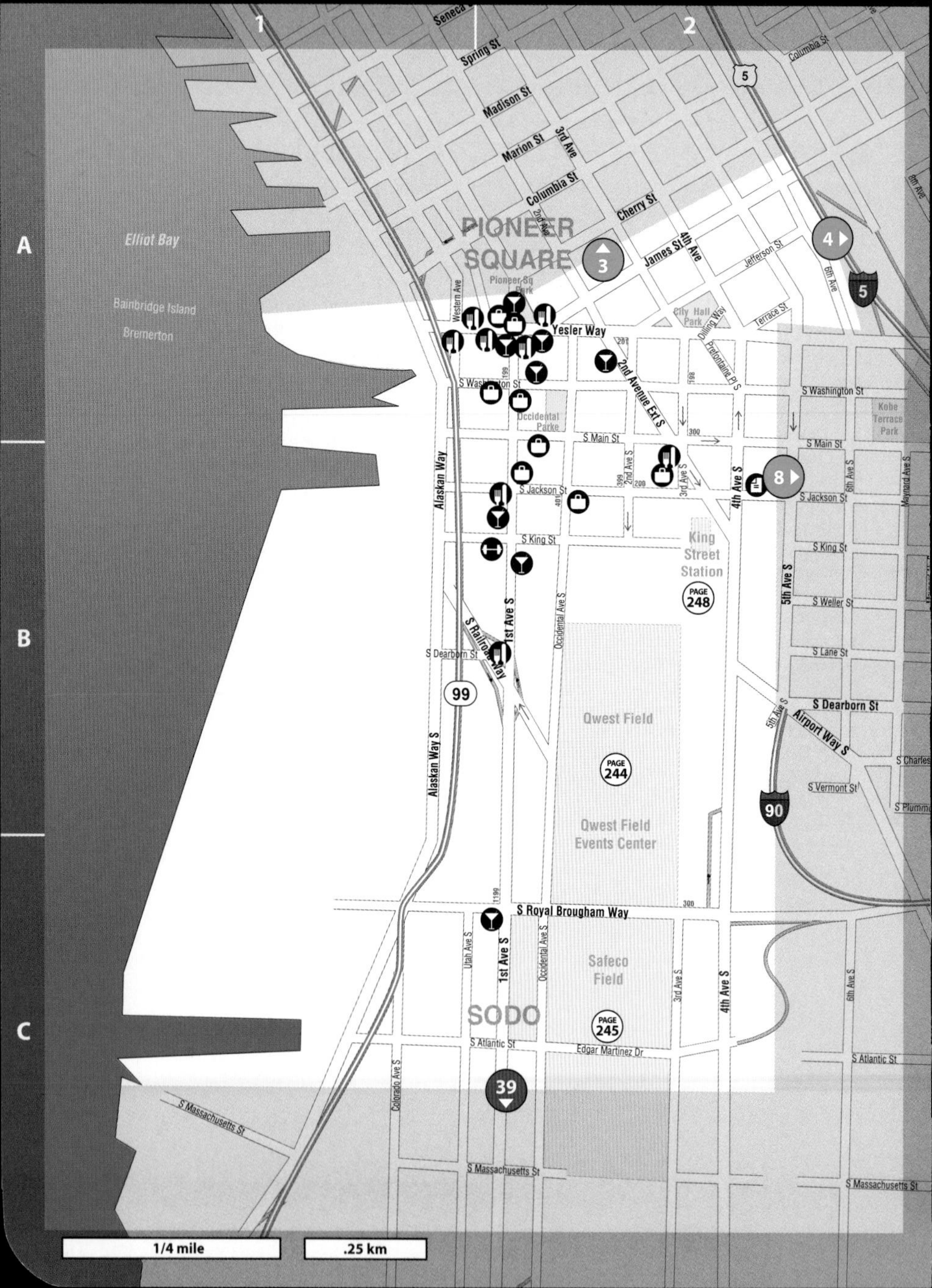

Ⓝ

1

2

Seneca St

Spring St

Madison St

Marion St

3rd Ave

Columbia St

Columbia St

5

A

Elliot Bay

Cherry St

**PIONEER
SQUARE**

James St

4th Ave

Jefferson St

4

6th Ave

5

Bainbridge Island

Bremerton

Pioneer Sq
Park

Western Ave

Yesler Way

2nd Ave

City Hall
Park

Terrace St

3

Terrace St

S Washington St

Kobe
Terrace
Park

S Washington St

Occidental
Parke

S Main St

Prefontaine Pl S

200

S Main St

Alaskan Way

2nd Ave Ext S

S Main St

2nd Ave S

3rd Ave S

4th Ave S

8

S Jackson St

S Jackson St

S King St

King
Street
Station

5th Ave S

S King St

S Weller St

PAGE
248

B

1st Ave S

S Railroad Way

Occidental Ave S

S Lane St

S Dearborn St

S Dearborn St

99

5th Ave S

Airport Way S

S Charles

Qwest Field

PAGE
244

S Vermont St

S Plummer

90

Qwest Field
Events Center

S Royal Brougham Way

Utah Ave S

1st Ave S

Occidental Ave S

Safeco
Field

3rd Ave S

4th Ave S

6th Ave S

C

SODO

PAGE
245

Colorado Ave S

S Atlantic St

Edgar Martinez Dr

S Atlantic St

39

S Massachusetts St

S Massachusetts St

S Massachusetts St

| 1/4 mile | | .25 km |

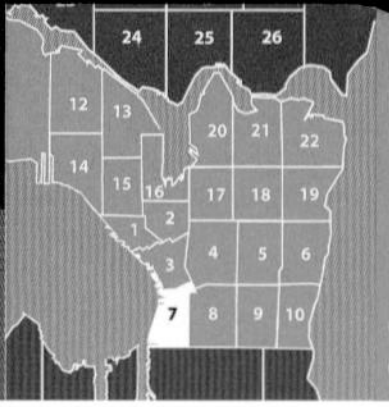

its old-fashioned charm, even if it's hidden under the grimy veil of homelessness, petty crime, and drunken revelers. It's also a refuge for men's men seeking cheap booze and thrills at bars like Cowgirls Inc, while the literary set hunkers down at Elliot Bay Books for the afternoon. Foodies flock to Salumi to taste the heavenly pork products.

Map 7

Copy Shops

- **FedEx Kinko's** · 418 S Jackson St [4th Ave S]

Gyms

- **Seattle Fitness Inc** · 83 S King St [1st Ave S]

Nightlife

- **Central Saloon** · 207 1st Ave S [S Washington St]
- **Cowgirls Inc** · 421 1st Ave S [S Jackson St]
- **Doc Maynard's** · 610 First Ave [Yesler Wy]
- **Double Header** · 407 Second Ave [S Washington St]
- **Elysian Fields** · 542 1st Ave S [S King St]
- **The Last Supper Club** · 124 S Washington St [1st Ave S]
- **New Orleans Creole Restaurant** · 114 1st Ave S [Yesler Wy]
- **Pyramid Alehouse** · 1201 1st Ave S [S Royal Brougham Wy]
- **Triangle Pub** · 553 1st Ave S [S King St]
- **Trinity Night Club** · 111 Yesler Wy [James St]

Restaurants

- **Al Boccalino** · 1 Yesler Wy [Alaskan Wy S]
- **Café Paloma** · 93 Yesler Wy [1st Ave S]
- **Grand Central Bakery** · 214 1st Ave S [S Washington St]
- **Green Leaf Vietnamese Restaurant** · 418 8th Ave S [S Jackson St]
- **Il Terrazzo Carmine** · 411 1st Ave S [S Jackson St]
- **Marcela's Cookery** · 106 James St [Yesler Wy]
- **Salumi** · 309 3rd Ave S [2nd Ave Ext S]
- **Slim's Last Chance Chili Shack & Watering Hole** · 663 1st Ave S [S Railroad Wy]
- **Trattoria Mitchelli** · 84 Yesler Wy [Western Ave]

Shopping

- **Bud's Jazz Records** · 102 S Jackson St [1st Ave S]
- **Ebbets Field Flannels** · 408 Occidental Ave S [S Jackson St]
- **Elliot Bay Book Company** · 101 S Main St [1st Ave S]
- **Magic Mouse Toys** · 603 1st Ave [Yesler Wy]
- **Pioneer Square Antique Mall** · 602 1st Ave [1st Ave]
- **Rialto Movie Art** · 81 1/2 S Washington St [1st Ave S]
- **Salumi** · 309 3rd Ave S [2nd Ave Ext S]
- **Synapse 206** · 206 1st Ave S [S Washington St]

Map 8 • International District

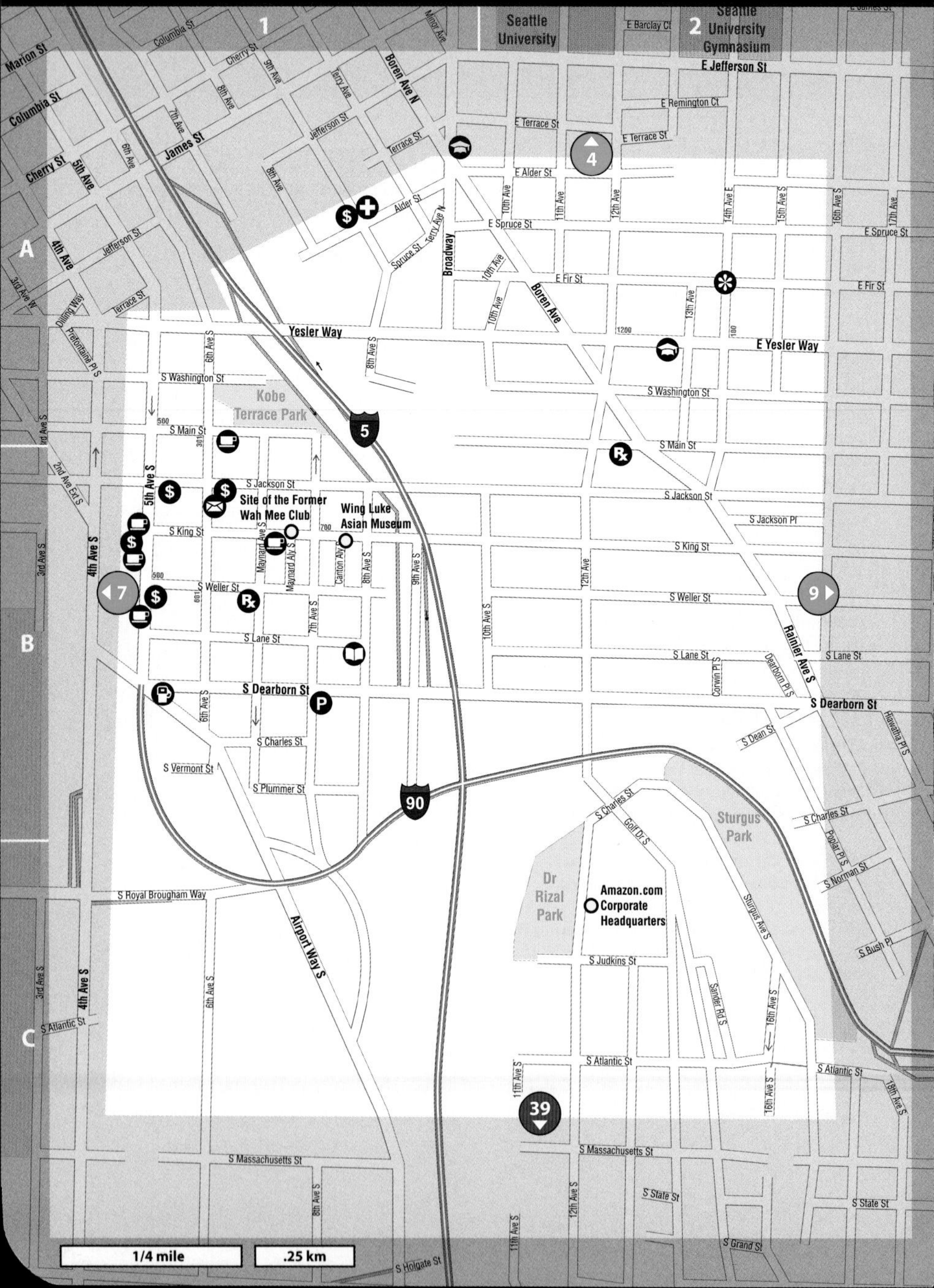
N
1
2
A
B
C
Seattle University
Seattle University Gymnasium
E Barclay Ct
E Jefferson St
E Remington Ct
E Terrace St
E Alder St
E Spruce St
E Fir St
E Yesler Way
Marion St
Columbia St
Cherry St
James St
Jefferson St
Terrace St
Alder St
Spruce St
Terry Ave N
Terry Ave
Boren Ave N
Boren Ave
Minor Ave
Broadway
4th Ave
5th Ave
6th Ave
7th Ave
8th Ave
9th Ave
10th Ave
11th Ave
12th Ave
13th Ave
14th Ave E
15th Ave S
16th Ave S
17th Ave
E Spruce St
E Fir St
3rd Ave W
Dilling Way
Prefontaine Pl S
Yesler Way
S Washington St
S Main St
S Jackson St
S Jackson Pl
S King St
S Weller St
S Lane St
S Dearborn St
S Charles St
S Vermont St
S Plummer St
S Dean St
Hiawatha Pl S
Kobe Terrace Park
Site of the Former Wah Mee Club
Wing Luke Asian Museum
Maynard Ave S
Maynard Aly S
Canton Aly S
2nd Ave Ext S
3rd Ave S
4th Ave S
5th Ave S
6th Ave S
7th Ave S
8th Ave S
9th Ave S
10th Ave S
12th Ave
Corwin Pl S
Dearborn Pl S
Rainier Ave S
500
301
700
601
1200
180
5
90
4
7
9
39
Sturgus Park
S Charles St
Poplar Pl S
S Norman St
S Bush Pl
Golf Dr S
Dr Rizal Park
Amazon.com Corporate Headquarters
S Judkins St
Sander Rd S
Sturgus Ave S
16th Ave S
S Royal Brougham Way
Airport Way S
S Atlantic St
11th Ave S
18th Ave S
S Massachusetts St
12th Ave S
S State St
S Grand St
S Holgate St
1/4 mile
.25 km

This historic neighborhood has provided a cultural hub for Seattle's sizable Asian-American population since the 19th century. Home to Filipino, Vietnamese, Cambodian, Japanese, and Chinese businesses of every stripe, the International District truly feels, well, international. It's hardly the most glamorous area of the city, but strolling through the ID is highly recommended.

Banks

- **Bank of America** · 525 S Jackson St [5th Ave S]
- **Bank of America (ATM)** · 325 9th Ave S [Alder St]
- **Bank of America (ATM)** · 505 5th Ave S [S King St]
- **Washington Federal Savings** ·
  601 S Jackson St [6th Ave S]
- **Washington Mutual** · 600 5th Ave S [S Weller St]

Coffee

- **The Gossip Espresso & Tea** ·
  651 S King St [Maynard Ave S]
- **Oasis Tea Zone** · 519 5th Ave S [S King St]
- **Panama Hotel Tea & Coffee House** ·
  607 S Main St [6th Ave S]
- **Starbucks** · 505 5th Ave S [S King St]
- **Tully's** · 625 5th Ave S [S Weller St]

Community Gardens

Gas Stations

- **Shell** · 511 S Dearborn St [5th Ave S]

Emergency Rooms

- **Harborview Medical Center** · 325 9th Ave [Alder St]

oLandmarks

- **Amazon.com Headquarters** ·
  1200 12th Ave S [S Judkins St]
- **Site of the Former Wah Mee Club** ·
  Maynard Aly & S King St
- **Wing Luke Asian Museum** ·
  719 S King St [S Jackson St]

Libraries

- **International District / Chinatown Branch** ·
  713 8th Ave S [S Lane St]

Parking

Pharmacies

- **Luke's Pharmacy** · 611 Maynard Ave S [S Weller St]
- **Nguyen's Pharmacy** · 1221 S Main St [Boren Ave S]

Post Offices

- **International** · 414 6th Ave S [S Jackson St]

Schools

- **Childhaven** · 316 Broadway [Boren Ave]
- **Gatzert Elementary** · 1301 E Yesler Wy [13th Ave]

Map 8 · **International District**

N

1

2

Seattle
University

Seattle
University
Gymnasium

E Barclay Ct

E Jefferson St

Marion St

Columbia St

Columbia St

Cherry St

Cherry St

James St

E Terrace St

E Terrace St

4

E Alder St

E Remington Ct

Jefferson St

Alder St

Spruce St

E Spruce St

Broadway

E Fir St

E Spruce St

A

4th Ave

3rd Ave

Terrace St

E Fir St

Quilango Way
Prefontaine Pl S

Yesler Way

E Yesler Way

S Washington St

Kobe
Terrace Park

5

S Washington St

S Main St

S Main St

2

S Jackson St

S Jackson St

2

5th Ave S

S King St

S Jackson Pl

2

3

S King St

S Weller St

7

Maynard Ave S

Carlton Aly S

8th Ave S

9th Ave S

S Weller St

9

B

4th Ave S

3rd Ave S

2nd Ave Ext S

S Lane St

S Lane St

S Lane St

Rainier Ave S

Dearborn Pl S

S Dearborn St

S Dearborn St

S Dean St

S Charles St

Corwin Pl S

T

S Charles St

S Plummer St

90

S Charles St

S Charles St

Goal Dr S

Sturgus
Park

S Norman St

S Vermont St

Dr
Rizal
Park

S Royal Brougham Way

Sturgus Ave S

S Bush Pl

Airport Way S

8th Ave S

S Judkins St

Seiler Rd S

16th Ave S

C

3rd Ave S

4th Ave S

S Atlantic St

S Atlantic St

S Atlantic St

11th Ave S

12th Ave S

39

S Massachusetts St

S Massachusetts St

S State St

S State St

15th Ave S

S Grand St

S Holgate St

| 1/4 mile | .25 km |

Uwajimaya Village features an awesome food court, a bookstore, apartments, and even a bank—you could move in and never leave. But hit the streets of the ID for the real eats. The China Gate restaurant has been serving the community since the 1920s. Maneki, a Seattle gem, has been dishing up sushi and traditional Japanese for over 100 years. Take some of the mystery out of dim sum by dining at the meat-free Vegetarian Bistro. Or grab a super cheap bahn mi at Saigon Deli.

Copy Shops
- **Copy Company** • 616 6th Ave S [S Weller St]

Hardware Stores
- **KDL Hardware Supply Inc** • 850 Poplar Pl S [S Dean St]

Nightlife
- **Bush Gardens** • 614 Maynard Ave S [S Weller St]
- **Fort St George** • 601 S King St [6th Ave S]
- **Joe's** • 500 S King St [5th Ave S]

Pet Shops
- **Liem's Aquarium & Bird Shop** • 511 Maynard Aly S [S King St]

Restaurants
- **663 Bistro** • 663 S Weller St [Maynard Alley S]
- **Blue & Pink** • 502 S King St [5th Ave S]
- **The China Gate Restaurant** • 516 7th Ave S [S King St]
- **Hing Loon** • 628 S Weller St
- **House of Hong** • 409 8th Ave S [S Jackson St]
- **Jade Garden** • 704 S King St [7th Ave S]
- **Made In Kitchen** • 725 S Lane St [7th Ave S]
- **Malay Satay Hut** • 212 12th Ave S [S Main St]
- **Maneki** • 304 6th Ave S [S Main St]
- **Phnom Penh** • 660 S King St [Maynard Ave S]
- **Pho Bac** • 415 7th Ave S [S Jackson St]
- **The Rocket** • 110 Boren Ave S [12th Ave S]
- **Saigon Deli** • 1032 S Jackson St [10th Ave S]
- **Samurai Noodle** • 606 5th Ave S [S Weller St]
- **Sea Garden** • 509 7th Ave S [S King St]
- **Shanghai Garden** • 524 6th Ave S [S King St]
- **Szechuan Noodle Bowl** • 420 8th Ave S [S Jackson St]
- **Tai Tung** • 655 S King St [Maynard Ave S]
- **Tamarind Tree** • 1036 S Jackson St [12th Ave S]
- **Tea Garden** • 708 Rainier Ave S [S Lane St]
- **Tsukushinbo Japanese Restaurant** • 515 S Main St [5th Ave S]
- **Uwajimaya Food Court** • 600 5th Ave S [S Weller St]
- **Vegetarian Bistro** • 668 S King St [Maynard Ave S]

Shopping
- **Kinokuniya Bookstore** • 525 S Weller St [5th Ave S]
- **Re-Pc Recycled Computers** • 1565 6th Ave S [S Atlantic St]
- **Tsue Chung Co Inc** • 800 S Weller St [8th Ave S]
- **Uwajimaya** • 600 5th Ave S [S Weller St]

Video Rental
- **Hop Video (Japanese)** • 601 S King St [6th Ave S]
- **Van Loc Video** • 1221 S Main St [Boren Ave S]

Map 9 · **Central District (South)**

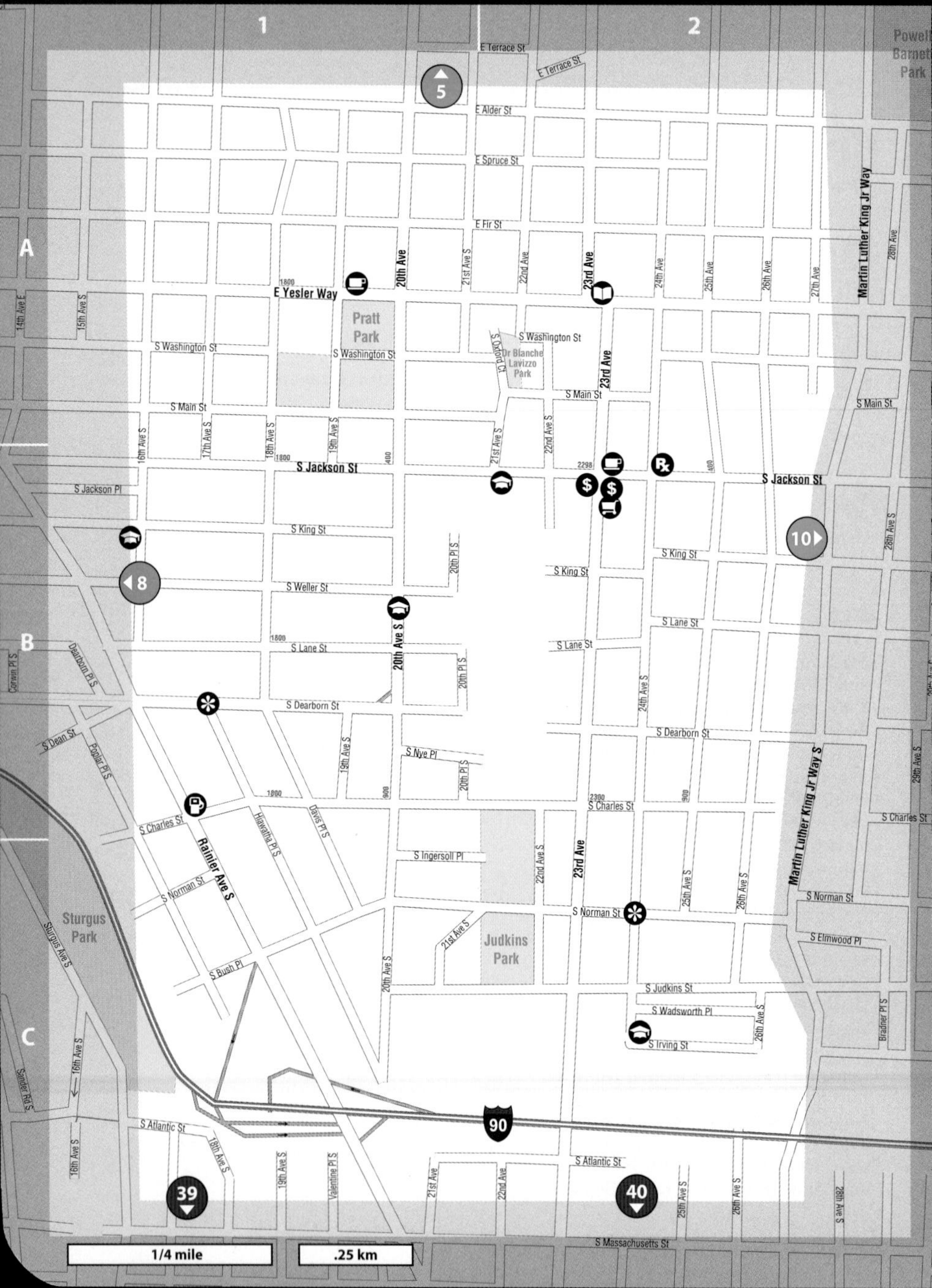

N

1   2

Powell
Barnett
Park

5

E Terrace St
E Terrace St
E Alder St
E Spruce St
E Fir St

A

20th Ave
21st Ave S
22nd Ave
23rd Ave
24th Ave
25th Ave
26th Ave
27th Ave

Martin Luther King Jr Way

28th Ave

1800
E Yesler Way

Pratt
Park

S Washington St

Blanche
Lavizzo
Park

S Washington St
S Washington St
S Main St.

23rd Ave

14th Ave E
15th Ave S

S Washington St

S Main St

16th S
17th Ave S
18th Ave S
19th Ave S

1800
4400

S Jackson St

21st Ave S

22nd Ave S

2200

S Jackson St

S Jackson St

8

S King St

S King St

S King St

20th Pl S

Rx

4600

26th Ave S

B

S Weller St

S Lane St

S Lane St

10

1800
20th Ave S

20th Pl S

S Lane St

Corwin Pl S

S Dearborn St

S Dearborn St

S Dearborn St

Davis Pl S

S Dean St

S Nye Pl

S Charles St

2300
S Charles St

S Charles St

19th Ave S

20th Pl S

25th Ave S

26th Ave S

Rainier Ave S

S Charles St

S Ingersoll Pl

22nd Ave S

23rd Ave

28th Ave S

Hiawatha Pl S

S Norman St

S Norman St

S Norman St

Martin Luther King Jr Way S

S Elmwood Pl

Sturgus
Park

21st Ave S

S Bush Pl

Judkins
Park

S Judkins St

S Wadsworth St

24th Ave S

26th Ave S

Bradner Pl S

C

16th Ave S

20th Ave S

S Irving St

Sturgus Ave S

Snoqualmie Pl S

90

S Atlantic St

18th Ave S

Valentine Pl S

S Atlantic St

S Atlantic St

25th Ave S

26th Ave S

28th Ave S

39

21st Ave
22nd Ave

40

S Massachusetts St

| 1/4 mile | .25 km |

Can you say gentrification? Well, promenade along the main streets of CD's south side and experience the word itself. The high traffic streets of Martin Luther King, 23rd Avenue, Massachusetts, and Yesler contain a regurgitated version of Pleasantville. But at least parks are pretty green respites from the irreality.

$ Banks

• **Bank of America** • 2301 S Jackson St [23rd Ave]
• **Washington Mutual** • 401 23rd Ave S [S Jackson St]

Coffee

• **Café Vega** • 1918 E Yesler Wy [19th Ave]
• **Starbucks** • 2300 S Jackson St [23rd Ave]

✳ Community Gardens

Gas Stations

• **Shell** • 852 Rainier Ave S [S Charles St]

Libraries

• **Douglass-Truth Branch** • 2300 E Yesler Wy [23rd St]

℞ Pharmacies

• **Walgreens** • 2400 S Jackson St [24th Ave]

Schools

• **Happy Medium** • 620 20th Ave S [S Weller St]
• **Lake Washington Girls Middle** •
  511 16th Ave S [S King St]
• **Thurgood Marshall Elementary** •
  2401 S Irving St [24th Ave S]
• **Washington Middle** • 2101 S Jackson St [21st Ave S]

Supermarkets

• **Red Apple** • 2301 S Jackson St [23rd Ave]

Map 9 · **Central District (South)**

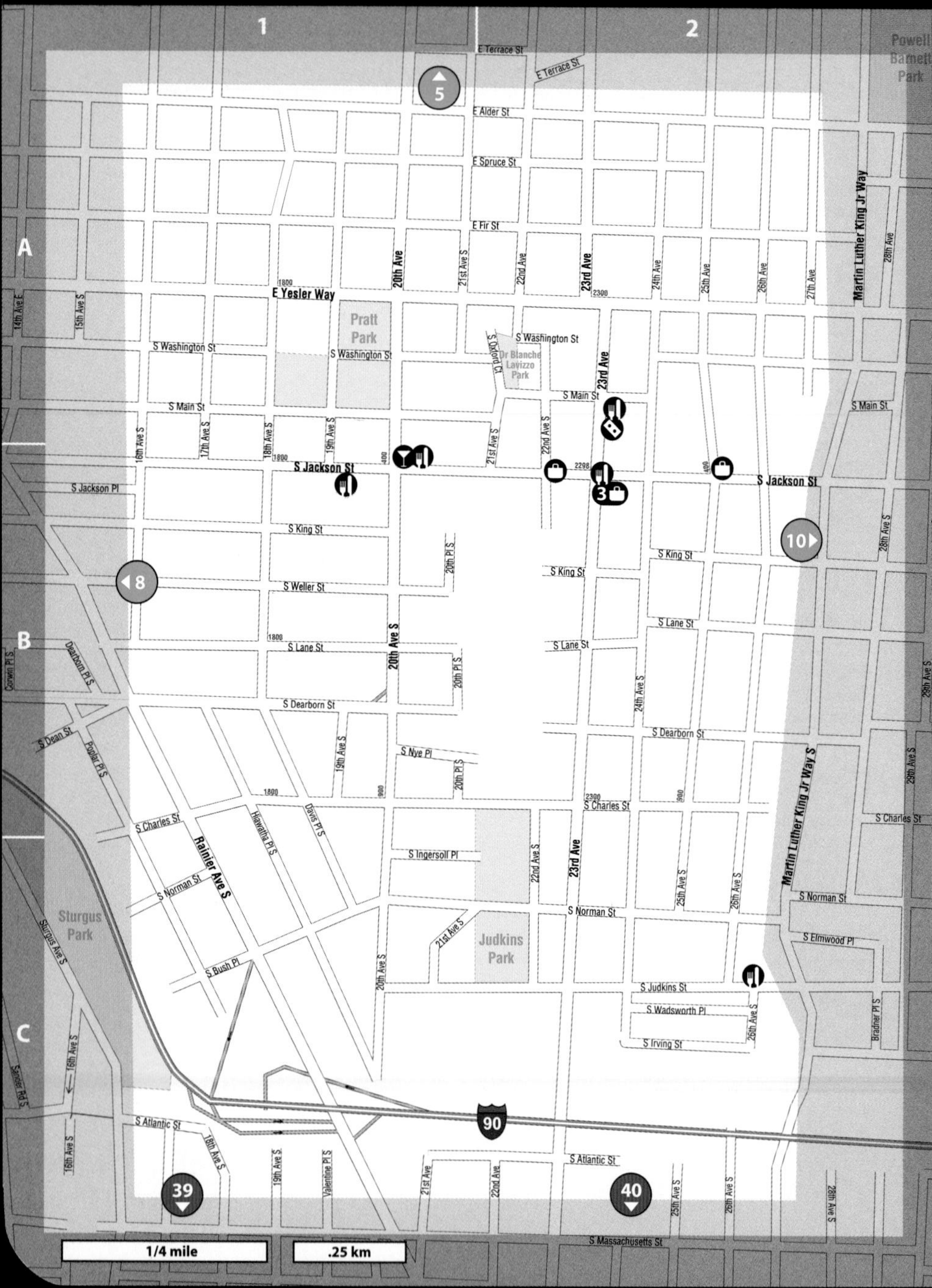

N

1

2

Powell
Barnett
Park

E Terrace St
E Terrace St
E Alder St
E Spruce St
E Fir St

5

A

E Yesler Way

1800

20th Ave
21st Ave S
22nd Ave
23rd Ave
24th Ave
25th Ave
26th Ave
27th Ave

Martin Luther King Jr Way

28th Ave

16th Ave E

15th Ave S

Pratt
Park

S Washington St
S Washington St
S Washington St

Dr Blanche
Lavizzo
Park

S Main St
S Main St
S Main St

23rd Ave
2300

19th Ave S
18th Ave S
17th Ave S
16th Ave S

21st Ave S
22nd Ave S

S Jackson St
S Jackson St
S Jackson St

2200

400

400

8

S Jackson Pl

3

10

S King St
S King St
S King St

20th Pl S

20th Ave S

24th Ave S

B

S Weller St

S Lane St
S Lane St
S Lane St

1800

Cornell Pl S

S Dearborn St
S Dearborn St

19th Ave S
20th Pl S

S Nye Pl

Dearborn Pl S

S Dean St
Poplar Pl S

1800

S Charles St
S Charles St
S Charles St

1900

2300

1900

23rd Ave

Martin Luther King Jr Way S

S Norman St
S Norman St

S Norman St

S Ingersoll Pl

Rainier Ave S

Hiawatha Pl S

Davis Pl S

21st Ave S

22nd Ave S

25th Ave S
26th Ave S

S Elmwood Pl

Sturgus
Park

S Charles St

Judkins
Park

S Bush Pl

S Judkins St
S Wadsworth Pl
S Irving St

26th Ave S

Bradner Pl S

C

Sturgus Pl S

16th Ave S

18th Ave S

S Atlantic St

90

S Atlantic St

39

40

S Pl S
17th Ave S

16th Ave S
17th Ave S
18th Ave S
19th Ave S

Valentine Pl S

21st Ave
22nd Ave

24th Ave S
25th Ave S
26th Ave S

28th Ave S

1/4 mile

.25 km

S Massachusetts St

Want to impress your date without traveling too far? Do up yourself in a phat get-up from Two Big Blondes Plus Consignment, grab something exotic at Africa Braids and Jewelry, splurge at Flowers Just For You, and dine at Hidmo East African Cuisine. Feel like being a well-versed romantic? Read poetic words from Jackson Street Books while watching the sun set from Sam Smith Park. Don't want a second date? Visit Taco Del Mar, Starbucks, and Hollywood Video.

 ## Nightlife

- **Hidmo East African Cuisine** ·
  2000 S Jackson St [20th Ave S]

 ## Restaurants

- **Hidmo East African Cuisine** ·
  2000 S Jackson St [20th Ave S]
- **Island Soul** · 2608 S Judkins St [26th Ave S]
- **Magic Dragon Chinese Eatery** ·
  306 23rd Ave S [S Main St]
- **Moonlight Cafe** · 1919 S Jackson St [19th Ave S]
- **Taco Del Mar** · 2309 S Jackson St [23rd Ave S]

 ## Shopping

- **Africa Braids and Jewelry** ·
  2506 S Jackson St [25th Ave S]
- **Flowers Just For You** · 2216 S Jackson St [22nd Ave S]
- **Jackson Street Books** · 2301 S Jackson St [23rd Ave S]
- **Two Big Blondes Plus Consignment Shop** ·
  2501 S Jackson St [23rd Ave S]
- **Western Beauty** · 2301 S Jackson St [23rd Ave S]

 ## Video Rental

- **Hollywood Video** · 306 23rd Ave S [S Main St]

Map 10 · Leschi

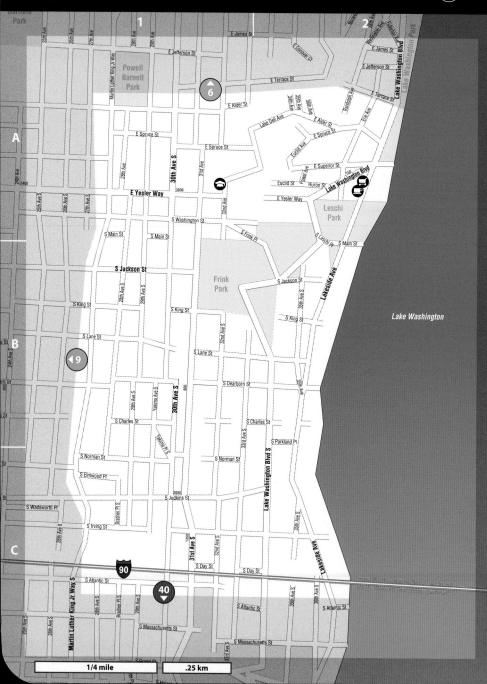

Gee, Toto, there's no place like Leschi. The neighborhood rises quietly above the shores of Lake Washington, boasting spectacular views of Mt. Rainier, the Cascade Range, Mt. Baker, the screaming Blue Angels in August, and decorated Christmas ships during December. The packed retail core is home to throngs of weekend cyclists, kayakers, and boaters, but there's plenty of room to toss Frisbees and chase kids in the spacious parks.

Coffee

• **Starbucks** • 121 Lakeside Ave [Erie Ave]

Schools

• **Leschi Elementary** • 135 32nd Ave [E Yesler Wy]

Supermarkets

• **Leschi Food Mart** • 103 Lakeside Ave [Lake Washington Blvd]

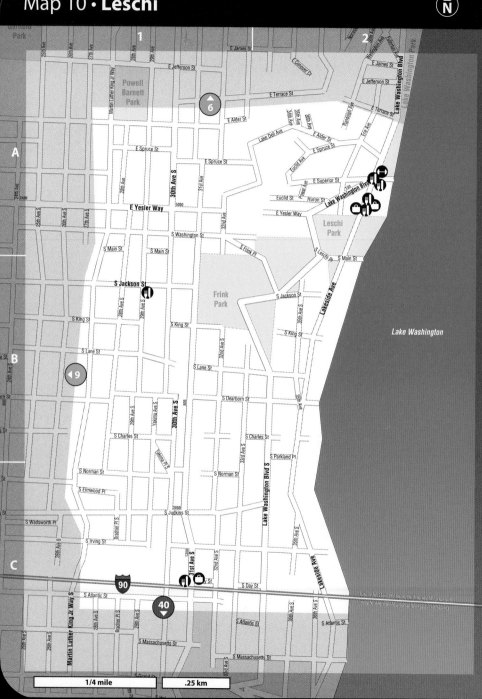

Map 10 · **Leschi**
N

Garfield Park

E James St

E Jefferson St

E Conover Ct

E James St

E Jefferson St

E Terrace St

Powell Barnett Park

E Alder St

Lake Dell Ave

E Alder St

Lake Washington Park

A

E Spruce St

E Spruce St

E Spruce St

30th Ave S

31st Ave

Euclid St

E Superior St

Lake Washington Blvd

E Yesler Way

Euclid St

Huron St

E Yesler Way

Leschi Park

32nd Ave

S Washington St

S Main St

S Main St

S Frink Pl

S Lesch Pl

S Main St

S Jackson St

Frink Park

S Jackson St

S King St

S King St

S King St

Lakeside Ave

Lake Washington

S Lane St

S Lane St

B

S Dearborn St

28th Ave S

29th Ave S

Yakima Ave S

30th Ave S

33rd Ave S

35th Ave

S Charles St

S Charles St

S Parkland Pl

Yakima Pl S

S Norman St

S Norman St

S Elmwood Pl

Lake Washington Blvd S

S Judkins St

35th Ave S

S Wadsworth Pl

Brandon Pl S

Lakeside Ave

S Irving St

26th Ave S

C

90

31st Ave S

32nd Ave S

S Day St

Martin Luther King Jr Way S

S Atlantic St

28th Ave S

Brandon Pl S

29th Ave S

36th Ave S

S Atlantic St

40

30th Ave S

S Atlantic St

25th Ave S

S Massachusetts St

33rd Ave S

S Massachusetts St

Hudson M. Hardy Jr Memorial Bridge (Westbound)
Lacey V. Morrow Memorial Bridge (Eastbound)

1/4 mile

.25 km

Along the waterfront, Daniel's Broiler attracts the steak and martini crowd, Ruby Asian Dining and Pert's Deli offer casual fare. Sidewalk service and fireside ale drinkers pack the Bluwater Bistro. Just try to go a week without wine, homemade sausage, or roast chicken from friendly Leschi Food Mart or a pain au chocolat from Sweet and Savory's Parisian Bakery. Cross 31st to enjoy spectacular city views, sunsets, and Italian fare at That's Amore.

Gyms

- **Curves** • 200 Lake Washington Blvd [Lakeside Ave]

Restaurants

- **All Purpose Pizza** • 2901 S Jackson St [29th Ave S]
- **Bluwater Bistro** •
  102 Lakeside Ave [Lake Washington Blvd]
- **Daniel's Broiler** •
  200 Lake Washington Blvd [Lakeside Ave]
- **Pert's Deli on Leschi** •
  120 Lakeside Ave [Lake Washington Blvd]
- **Ruby Asian Dining** •
  200 Lake Washington Blvd [Lakeside Ave]
- **That's Amore** • 1425 31st Ave [S Day St]

Shopping

- **Il Vecchio Bicycles** •
  140 Lakeside Ave [Lake Washington Blvd]
- **Leschi Food Mart** •
  103 Lakeside Ave [Lake Washington Blvd]
- **Sweet and Savory's Parisian Bakery** •
  1418 31st Ave S [S Day St]

Map 11 · **Magnolia / Interbay**

1

2

Shilshole
Bay

NW 70th St

NW 69th St

NW 67th St

NW 67th St

NW 65th St

Seaview Ave NW

NW 64th St

NW 63rd St

NW 62nd St

32nd Ave NW

30th Ave NW

28th Ave NW

26th Ave NW

24th Ave NW

22nd Ave NW

20th Ave NW

NW 60th St

NW 61st St

NW 59th St

NW 58th St

NW 57th St

15th Ave NW

14th Ave NW

A

W Sheridan St

W Hooker St

W Parry Way

43rd Ave W

42nd Ave W

40th Ave W

W Cramer St

W Sheridan St

47th Ave W

W Cramer St

34th Ave NW

32nd Ave NW

30th Ave NW

NW Market St

Barnes Ave NW

Leary Ave NW

Russell Ave NW

NW Ypsit Pl

NW 53rd St

NW 49th St

28

W Commodore Way

40th Ave W

Lawton Ln W

W Lawton St

Salmon Bay

Shilshole Ave NW

NW Leary Way

PAGE
208

○ Discovery Park

Lawton Ln W

W Lawton St

W Lawton St

Kiwanis
Memorial
Preserve
Park

W Mccord Pl

W Fort St

Ohman Dr

W Fort St

Brygger Dr

33rd Ave W

Gay Ave W

W Fort St

W Government St

W Harley St

Jameson St

Gilman Ave W

21st Ave W

23

Fort
Lawton
Cemetery

Fort Lawton Military Reservation

W Jameson St

36th Ave W

W Mansell St

34th Ave W

33rd Pl W

W Jameson St

W Elmore St

Gilman Ave W

Gilman Ave W

W Elmore St

21st Ave W

W Elmore St

W Harley St

21st Ave W

W Thurman St

47th Pl W

W Elmore Pl

W View Pl

28th Ave W

27th Ave W

W Thurman St

18th Ave W

15th Ave W

W Thurman St

Lawton
Park

W Emerson Pl

$

W Emerson St

W Emerson St

W Emerson St

Williams Ave W

W Emerson St

B

Puget
Sound

W Ruffner St

W Raye's Way

45th Ave W

W Mclaren Way

Magnolia Blvd W

44th Ave W

42nd Ave W

41st Ave W

39th Ave W

W Ruffner St

38th Ave W

37th Ave W

Arapahoe Pl W

33rd Ave W

31st Ave W

W Tilden St

W Ruffner St

29th Ave W

27th Ave W

25th Ave W

24th Ave W

23rd Ave W

22nd Ave W

21st Ave W

Thorndyke Ave W

W Tilden St

W Grover St

W Ruffner St

W Bertona St

Viewmont Way W

W Bertona St

W Bertona St

Manor Pl

20th Ave W

15th Ave W

W Ruffner St

W Prosper St

W Dravus St

35th Ave W

34th Ave W

33rd Ave W

31st Ave W

30th Ave W

Valley W

W Dravus St

□
$

R

12

W Ruffner St

13th Ave W

W Barrett St

Sound View Dr W

W Bertona St

W Fulton St

W Barrett St

W Barrett St

24th Ave W

20th Ave W

15th Ave W

W Barrett St

W Barrett St

Perkins Ln W

Montfort Pl

W Armour St

W Fulton Pl

⊙

W Armour St

W Fulton St

W Armour St

Palm Ave W

W Halladay St

Thorndyke Ave W

Interbay
Athletic
Field

W Raye St

38th Ave W

37th Ave W

35th Ave W

West
Magnolia
Playfield

W Raye St

30th Ave W

29th Ave W

28th Ave W

27th Ave W

26th Ave W

Bayview
Playground

W Halladay St

W Smith St

W Wheeler St

Interbay
Family
Golf
Center

W Raye St

W Smith St

Condon Way W

36th Ave W

R

$

E Magnolia Blvd

W Mcgraw St

W Lynn St

24th Ave W

23rd Ave W

Gilman Ave W

W Bothwell St

$

W Mcgraw St

W Boston St

Magnolia Way W

W Mcgraw St

2 $ 2 $

✉
$

W Lynn St

W Crockett St

W Newton St

W Lynn St

W Boston St

22nd Ave W

National
Guard
Armory

10th Ave W

Clise Pl W

R

W Blaine St

28th Ave W

W Plymouth St

W Howe St

Kinnear
Park

Magnolia
Park

34th Ct W

W Hayes St

W Garfield St

W Eaton St

Magnolia Way W

W Howe St

14

14th Ave W

13th Ave W

12th Ave W

11th Ave W

W Galer St

W Galer St

Smith Cove
Park

W Garfield St

W Galer St

W Lee St

C

W Marina Pl

Elliott Ave W

W Prospect St

Elliott Bay

1/2 mile

.5 km

Essentials

Map 11

Since it's on a peninsula, Magnolia residents rely on a trio of bridges to connect them to the rest of the city (unless landslides or earthquakes interfere). However, the relative isolation suits this quiet, family-friendly community. Dominated by the 500-acre Discovery Park and surrounded by Shilshole Bay and Puget Sound, Magnolia is prime real estate, boasting some of Seattle's most expensive homes. Interbay is an industrial strip useful mostly for getting to and from other neighborhoods.

$ Banks

- **Bank of America** • 1810 W Emerson Pl [18th Ave W]
- **Bank of America** • 3425 W Mcgraw St [34th Ave W]
- **Key Bank** • 2401 34th Ave W [W McGraw St]
- **Key Bank (ATM)** • 3201 20th Ave W [W Dravus St]
- **US Bank** • 3124 W McGraw St [31st Ave W]
- **US Bank (ATM)** • 2550 32nd Ave W [W Raye St]
- **Washington Federal Savings** •
  3219 W McGraw St [32nd Ave W]
- **Washington Mutual** • 2424 34th Ave W [W Smith St]
- **Wells Fargo (ATM)** • 3310 W Mcgraw St [33rd Ave W]

 Coffee

- **Discovery Espresso & Juice** •
  3103 W Jameson St [31st Ave W]
- **Starbucks** • 1607 W Dravus St [16th Ave W]
- **Starbucks** • 3300 W McGraw St [33rd Ave W]
- **Tully's** • 3223 W McGraw St [32nd Ave W]

Gas Stations

- **Arco** • 3201 20th Ave W [W Dravus St]
- **Shell** • 3317 W Government Wy [33rd Ave W]

o Landmarks

- **Discovery Park** • 3801 W Government Wy [36th Ave W]

Libraries

- **Magnolia Branch** • 2801 34th Ave W [W Armour St]

 Pharmacies

- **Albertson's** • 2550 32nd Ave W [W Raye St]
- **Bartell Drugs** • 2222 32nd Ave W [W Lynn St]
- **Quality Food Center** • 1600 W Dravus St [16th Ave W]

Post Offices

- **Magnolia** • 3211 W Mcgraw St [32nd Ave W]

Schools

- **Catharine Blaine K-8** • 2550 34th Ave W [W Raye St]
- **Discovery Montessori** • 2836 34th Ave W [W Armour St]
- **Lawton Elementary** • 4000 27th Ave W [Lawton Park]
- **Our Lady of Fatima** • 3301 W Dravus St [33rd Ave W]

 Supermarkets

- **Quality Food Center** • 1600 W Dravus St [16th Ave W]
- **Thriftway** • 3830 34th Ave W [W Emerson St]

Map 11 · **Magnolia / Interbay**

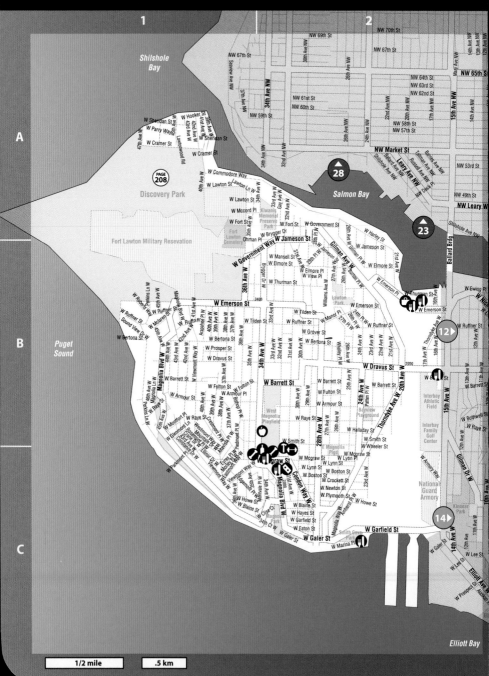

Shilshole Bay

Salmon Bay

Puget Sound

Discovery Park

Fort Lawton Military Reservation

PAGE
208

Elliott Bay

1/2 mile   .5 km

Though there's not much in the way of wild nightlife, Magnolia is known for several excellent restaurants. Palisade offers elegant waterfront seating and fine dining with Hawaiian flair, Szmania's is the place for European cuisine, and the Bay Café is as good a low-brow breakfast joint as you're likely to find. Interbay features golf, a National Guard Armory, and not a whole lot else.

Farmers Markets

- **Magnolia (Sat, 10 am–2 pm, June–Sept)** ·
  Magnolia Community Center ·
  2550 34th Ave W [W Raye St]

Gyms

- **Mieko's Fitness** · 2438 32nd Ave W [W Smith St]

Hardware Stores

- **Magnolia Ace Hardware** ·
  2420 32nd Ave W [W Smith St]

Liquor Stores

- **Washington State Liquor Store** ·
  3310 W McGraw St [33rd Ave W]

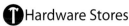Pet Shops

- **Pet Pros** · 3411 W McGraw St [34th Ave W]
- **Pj's Paws And Claws** ·
  3320 W McGraw St, Ste 3 [33rd Ave W]

Restaurants

- **Bay Café** · 1900 W Nickerson St [18th Ave W]
- **Chinook's at Salmon Bay** ·
  1900 W Nickerson St [18th Ave W]
- **Mondello Ristorante** · 2435 33rd Ave W [W Wheeler St]
- **Palisade** · 2601 W Marina Pl [23rd Ave W]
- **Red Mill Burgers** · 1613 W Dravus St [16th Ave]
- **Szmania's** · 3321 W McGraw St [33rd Ave W]

Shopping

- **Wild Salmon Seafood Market** ·
  1900 W Nickerson St [18th Ave W]

Video Rental

- **Hollywood Video** · 2236 32nd Ave W [W Lynn St]

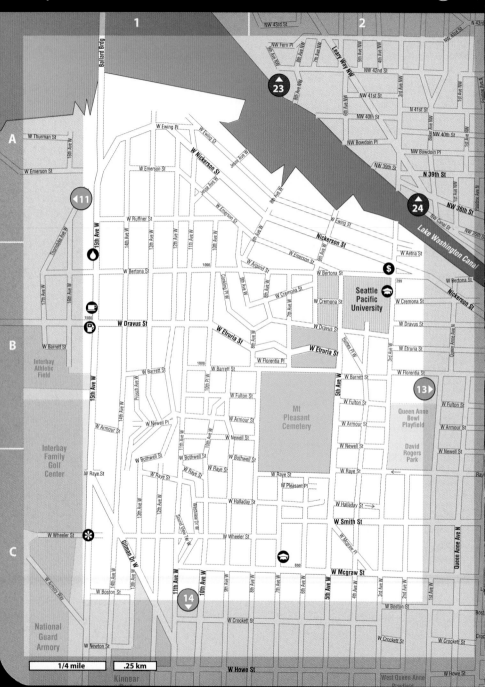

Map 12 · Queen Anne (North)

1 | 2

NW 43rd St
NW Fern Pl
8th Ave NW
6th Ave NW
5th Ave NW
3rd Ave NW
1st Ave NW
Palatine Ave N

Leary Way NW
NW 42nd St
NW 41st St
N 41st St
NW 40th St
Baker Ave NW
2nd Ave NW
NW Bowdoin Pl
NW Bowdoin Pl
NW 39th St
N 39th St

23

A
W Thurman St
15th Ave W
W Ewing Pl
W Ewing St
W Nickerson St
Jesse Ave W

W Emerson St
W Emerson St
Thorndike Ave W
W Emerson St
Jesse Ave W
8th Ave W
W Emerson St
NW 35th St
Lake Washington Canal

11
15th Ave W
W Ruffner St
14th Ave W
13th Ave W
12th Ave W
11th Ave W
10th Ave W
W Ewing St
Nickerson St
Nickerson St
W Aetna St
299

17th Ave W
16th Ave W
W Bertona St
W Argand St
8th Ave W
W Emerson St
8th Ave W
W Bertona St
W Bertona St
W Cremona St
6th Ave W
W Cremona St
Colorado Pl W
W Cremona St
7th Ave W
Seattle Pacific University
W Cremona St
W Dravus St
W Dravus St
W Dravus St
5th Ave W
W Etruria St
3rd Ave W
W Etruria St
Queen Anne Ave N

B
W Barrett St
Interbay Athletic Field
W Dravus St
W Etruria St
8th Ave W
W Etruria St
Nickerson St
1500
1000
W Florentia Pl
W Florentia St
1000
W Barrett St
W Barrett St
10th Pl W
W Barrett St
5th Ave W
W Barrett St
13
W Fulton St
W Fulton St
W Fulton St
Prosch Ave W
W Armour St
W Armour St
W Armour St
Queen Anne Bowl Playfield
Mt Pleasant Cemetery
W Newell Pl
W Newell St
W Newell St
W Newell St
David Rogers Park
11th Ave W
W Bothwell St
W Bothwell St
W Bothwell St
Interbay Family Golf Center
W Raye St
13th Ave W
12th Ave W
W Raye St
W Raye St
W Raye St
W Raye St
W Pleasant Pl
W Halladay St
W Halladay St
W Halladay St
W Smith St
Sound View Pl W
W Wheeler St
W Wheeler St
W Wheeler St

C
W Armory Way
Gilman Dr W
11th Ave W
10th Ave W
9th Ave W
8th Ave W
7th Ave W
6th Ave W
5th Ave W
4th Ave W
3rd Ave W
2nd Ave N
1st Ave W
Queen Anne Ave N
W Mcgraw St
W Mcgraw St
600
14
W Boston St
13th Ave W
W Boston St
W Crockett St
W Crockett St
W Crockett St
National Guard Armory
W Newton St
W Howe St
W Howe St
West Queen Anne

1/4 mile **.25 km**

Kinnear

This neighborhood perches atop Queen Anne Hill, the highest point in Seattle and thus a magnet for those with wealth. Along with yuppie families, millionaires, and thrifty octogenarians, dead people love Queen Anne North as well, as the Mt. Pleasant Cemetery's booming business conclusively proves.

$ Banks

· **US Bank** · 301 W Nickerson St [3rd Ave W]

Car Washes

· **Brown Bear Car Wash** · 3435 15th Ave W [W Bertona St]

Coffee

· **Q Café** · 3223 15th Ave W [W Dravus St]

❋ Community Gardens

Gas Stations

· **76** · 1517 W Dravus St [15th Ave W]

Schools

· **Coe Elementary** · 2424 7th Ave W [W McGraw St]
· **Seattle Pacific University** ·
  3307 3rd Ave W [W Cremona St]

Map 12 · **Queen Anne (North)**

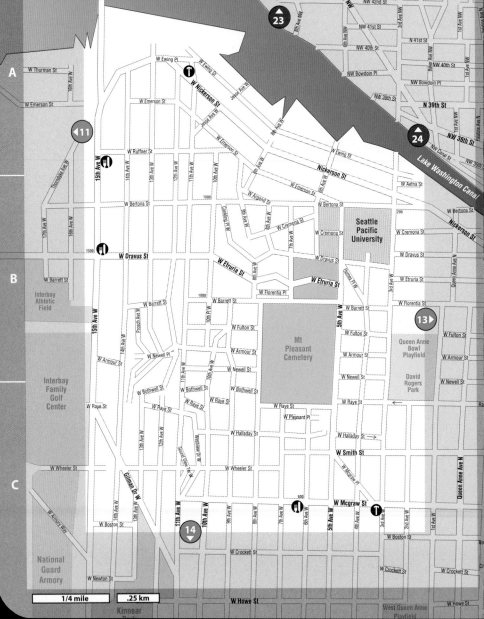

As a primarily residential locale, Queen Anne North doesn't offer much in the way of action. You can find Mexican food at La Palma or teriyaki at Yasuko's. Don't forget, Seattle Pacific University has a pretty campus with vending machines full of sodas and snacks, so get out and take a walk, for Pete's sake.

Hardware Stores

- **Five Corners Hardware ·**
  305 W McGraw St [3rd Ave W]
- **Home Builders' Center ·**
  1110 W Nickerson St [11th Ave W]

Restaurants

- **La Palma ·** 3456 15th Ave W [W Ruffner St]
- **Macrina Bakery & Café ·** 615 W McGraw St [6th Ave W]
- **Yasuko's Teriyaki ·** 3200 15th Ave W [W Dravus St]

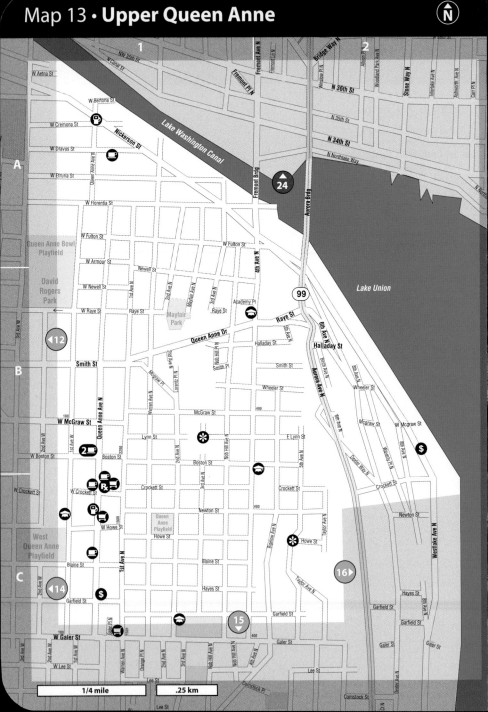

Map 13 · **Upper Queen Anne**

When the young urban professionals of LQA decide to marry and breed, they buy a house here. When you're deep inside this little suburban chimera, you can easily forget how close you are to the unsavory big city. There aren't many ways for kids or adults to get into trouble in these parts, unless your idea of trouble is having one-too-many mimosas with brunch. Make sure to grab a Mexican hot chocolate from the lovely ladies at El Diablo.

 Banks

- **Bank Of America** • 2200 Westlake Ave N [Crockett St]
- **Wells Fargo** • 1600 Queen Anne Ave N [Garfield St]

 Coffee

- **Caffe Ladro** • 2205 Queen Anne Ave N [W Boston St]
- **El Diablo Coffee** •
  1811 Queen Anne Ave N [W Blaine St]
- **The Grinder** • 41 Dravus St [Queen Anne Ave N]
- **Starbucks** • 2135 Queen Anne Ave N [W Crockett St]
- **Teacup** • 2207 Queen Anne Ave N [W Boston St]
- **Tully's** • 2128 Queen Anne Ave N [Crockett St]

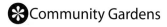 Community Gardens

 Gas Stations

- **76** • 1929 Queen Anne Ave N [W Howe St]
- **Shell** • 3 W Nickerson St [Queen Anne Ave N]

 Pharmacies

- **Safeway Pharmacy** •
  2100 Queen Anne Ave N [W Crockett St]

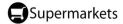 Schools

- **Hay Elementary** • 201 Garfield St [2nd Ave N]
- **McClure Middle** • 1915 1st Ave W [W Howe St]
- **Seattle Country Day** • 2619 4th Ave N [Queen Anne Dr]
- **Secondary Bilingual Ortn Ctr** •
  411 Boston St [4th Ave N]

Supermarkets

- **Metropolitan Market** •
  1908 Queen Anne Ave N [W Howe St]
- **Safeway** • 2100 Queen Anne Ave N [Crockett St]
- **Trader Joe's** • 112 W Galer St [1st Ave W]

Map 13 • **Upper Queen Anne**

This neighborhood is designed for people who plan to be in bed by 11 and like to pay too much for groceries. The Hilltop Ale House is decent and your only real nightlife option. How to Cook a Wolf will blow you away at dinner time, and for breakfast you can't do better than the 5 Spot.

Gyms

• **Curves** • 101 Nickerson St [Dravus St]

## Liquor Stores

• **McCarthy & Schiering Wine Merchants** •
2401 Queen Anne Ave N [W McGraw St]

Nightlife

• **Bricco Della Regina Anna** •
1525 Queen Anne Ave N [W Galer St]
• **Hilltop Ale House** •
2129 Queen Anne Ave N [W Crockett St]

Pet Shops

• **All the Best Pet Care** •
2127 Queen Anne Ave N [W Crockett St]

Restaurants

• **5 Spot** • 1502 Queen Anne Ave N [Galer St]
• **Canlis** • 2576 Aurora Ave N [6th Ave N]
• **Chinoise Café** • 12 Boston St [Queen Anne Ave N]
• **Hilltop Ale House** •
2129 Queen Anne Ave N [W Crockett St]
• **How to Cook a Wolf** •
2208 Queen Anne Ave N [W Boston St]
• **Kaosamai Thai** • 3 W Nickerson St [Queen Anne Ave N]
• **Opal** • 2 Boston St [Queen Anne Ave N]
• **Orrapin Thai Cuisine** • 10 Boston St [Queen Anne Ave N]
• **Ototo Sushi** • 7 Boston St [Queen Anne Ave N]
• **Pasta Bella** • 1530 Queen Anne Ave N [Galer St]
• **Pasta & Co** • 2109 Queen Anne Ave N [W Crockett St]
• **Ponti Seafood Grill** • 3014 3rd Ave N [Florentia St]
• **Queen Anne Café** •
2121 Queen Anne Ave N [W Crockett St]
• **Zeek's Pizza** • 41 Dravus St [Queen Anne Ave N]

Shopping

• **A & J Meats & Seafood** •
2401 Queen Anne Ave N [W McGraw St]
• **Oslo's A Men's Store** •
1519 Queen Anne Ave N [W Galer St]

Video Rental

• **Blockbuster** • 1630 Queen Anne Ave N [Garfield St]
• **Video Isle** • 2213 Queen Anne Ave N [W Boston St]

Map 14 · **Queen Anne (West)**

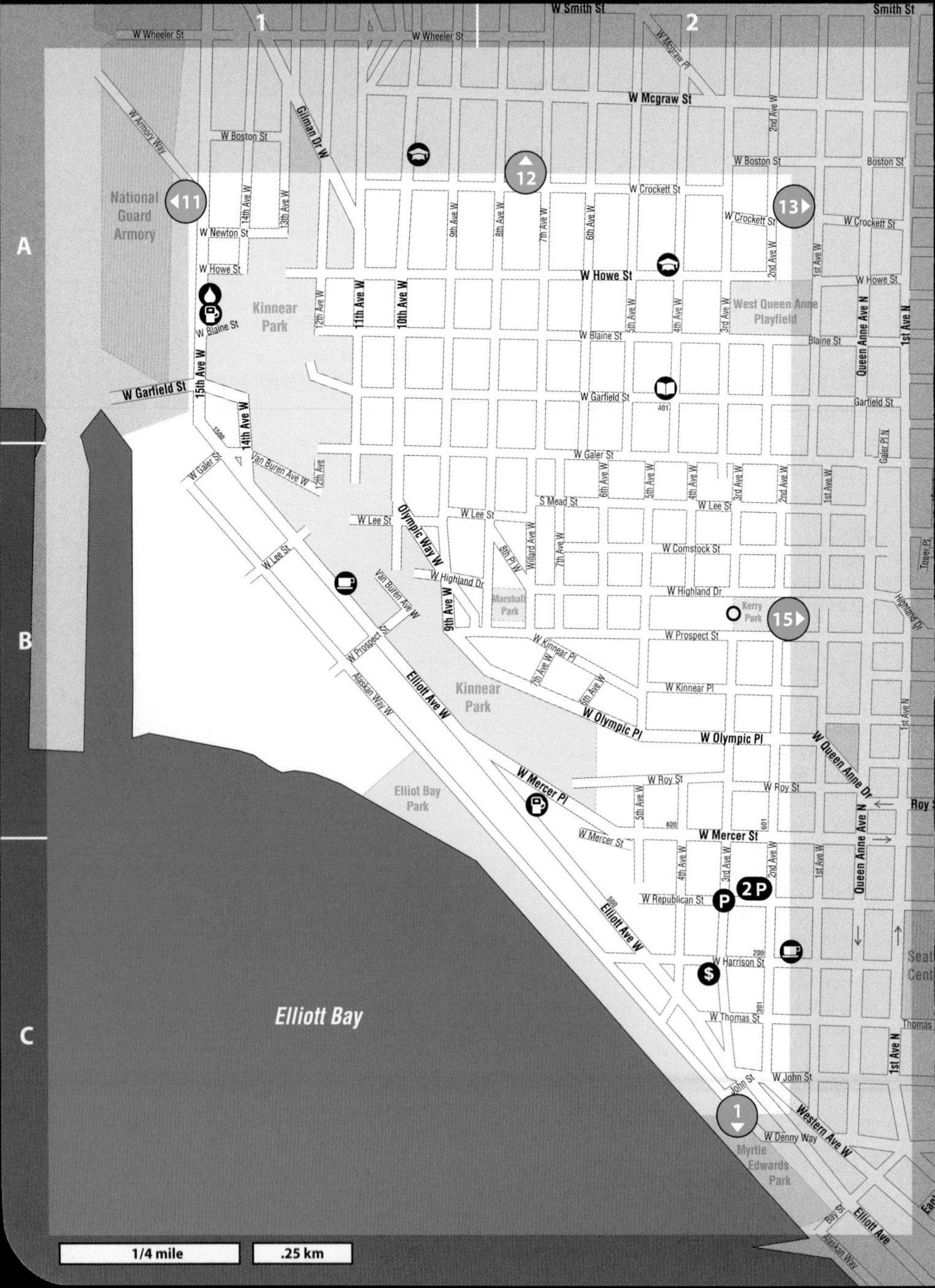

N

W Smith St

W Wheeler St

1

2

W McGraw St

W Boston St

National Guard Armory

◄11

Kinnear Park

West Queen Anne Playfield

13►

12

W Crockett St

W Newton St

W Howe St

W Blaine St

W Garfield St

W Galer St

Kinnear Park

Marshall Park

Kerry Park

15►

W Highland Dr

W Prospect St

Elliot Bay Park

W Kinnear Pl

W Olympic Pl

W Mercer Pl

W Roy St

W Mercer St

W Republican St

2 P

P

$

Elliott Bay

W Harrison St

W Thomas St

W John St

1

Myrtle Edwards Park

W Denny Way

Western Ave W

Elliott Ave

| 1/4 mile | .25 km |

Like the rest of Queen Anne, this section caters to the upwardly-mobile—meaning condos and attractive views. Speaking of which, Kinnear Park provides fine views of the Seattle skyline and Puget Sound from its upper tier, while the lower section appears welcoming until you stumble upon overgrown shrubs and the makeshift hobo camp.

Banks

• **Bank of America (ATM)** •
305 W Harrison St [3rd Ave W]

Car Washes

• **Brown Bear Car Wash** • 1800 15th Ave W [W Blaine St]

Coffee

• **Starbucks** • 1144 Elliott Ave W [W Prospect St]
• **Tully's** • 150 W Harrison St [W Harrison St]

Gas Stations

• **Chevron** • 1800 15th Ave W [W Blaine St]
• **Shell** • 630 Elliot Ave W [W Roy St]

oLandmarks

• **Kerry Park** • 211 W Highland Dr [2nd Ave W]

Libraries

• **Queen Anne Branch** • 400 W Garfield St [4th Ave W]

Parking

Schools

• **Matheia** • 414a W Howe St [4th Ave W]
• **Residential Consortium** •
2142 10th Ave W [W Crockett St]

Map 14 · Queen Anne (West)

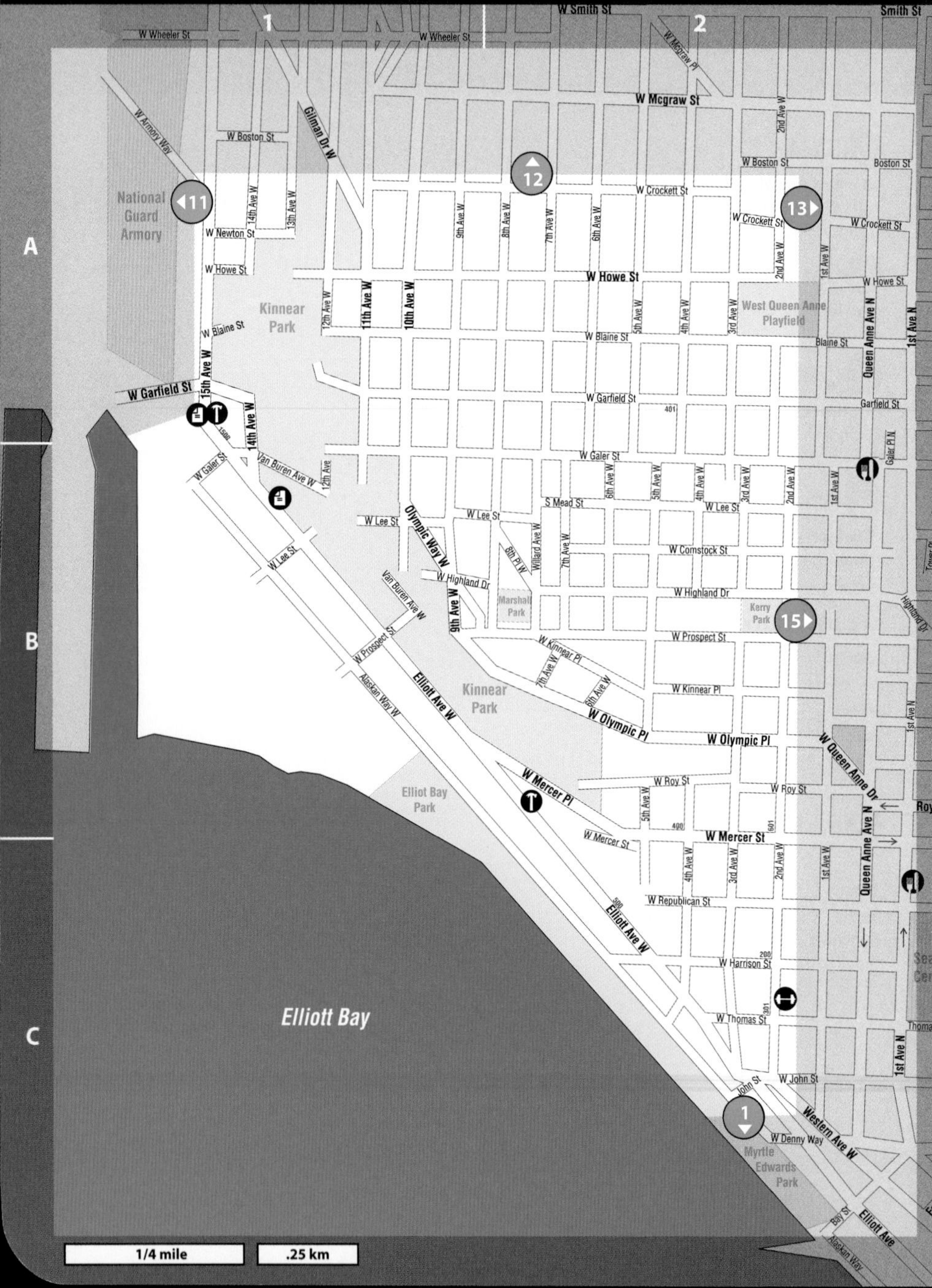

N

1
2

W Smith St
Smith St

W Wheeler St
W Wheeler St

W McGraw Pl
W McGraw St

Gilman Dr W

W Boston St
W Boston St
Boston St

W Armory Way

11

National
Guard
Armory

14th Ave W
13th Ave W

9th Ave W
8th Ave W
7th Ave W
6th Ave W

W Crockett St

12

W Crockett St
W Crockett St

13

2nd Ave W
1st Ave W

Kinnear
Park

W Newton St

W Howe St

W Howe St

5th Ave W
4th Ave W
3rd Ave W

Queen Anne Ave N
1st Ave W

West Queen Anne
Playfield

12th Ave W
11th Ave W
10th Ave W

W Blaine St

W Blaine St

Blaine St

W Garfield St

15th Ave W
14th Ave W

W Garfield St

Garfield St

401

Galer Pl N

12th Ave W

Van Buren Ave W

W Galer St

6th Ave W
5th Ave W
4th Ave W
3rd Ave W
2nd Ave W

W Galer St

S Mead St

W Lee St
W Lee St

Olympic Way W

9th Ave W

W Lee St

W Comstock St

Marshall
Park

8th Pl W
Willard Ave W

W Highland Dr
W Highland Dr

Kerry
Park

15

Van Buren Ave W

W Prospect St

W Prospect St

Elliott Ave W

Kinnear
Park

Alaskan Way W

7th Ave W
6th Ave W
5th Ave W

W Kinnear Pl
W Kinnear Pl

Queen Anne Dr

Highland Dr

1st Ave N

W Olympic Pl

W Olympic Pl

Elliot Bay
Park

W Mercer Pl

W Roy St
W Roy St

Roy

1st Ave N

W Mercer Pl

5th Ave W
4th Ave W
3rd Ave W
2nd Ave W

W Mercer St

W Mercer St

401

Elliott Ave W

W Republican St

Elliott Bay

W Harrison St

200

Sea
Ce

1st Ave N

W Thomas St

Thomas

W John St
W John St

1

Western Ave W

Myrtle
Edwards
Park

W Denny Way

Elliot Wa

Alaskan Way

| 1/4 mile | .25 km |

Most of the businesses on this side of town sell real estate or craft computer software, which is valuable to the local economy but doesn't do much good on a dull Thursday night. Betty and Moxie make fine dining options. Grab a drink with the locals at Targy's.

Copy Shops
- **Legal Copy Inc** · 1426 Elliott Ave W [W Lee St]
- **Staples** · 1541 15th Ave W [W Garfield St]

Gyms
- **All Star Fitness** · 330 2nd Ave W [W Thomas St]

Hardware Stores
- **Builders Hardware & Supply** ·
  1516 15th Ave W [W Garfield St]
- **Tool Town** · 652 Elliott Ave W [W Roy St]

Nightlife
- **Targy's** · 600 W Crockett St [6th Ave W]

Restaurants
- **Betty** · 1507 Queen Anne Ave N [W Galer St]
- **Moxie** · 530 1st Ave N [Republican St]

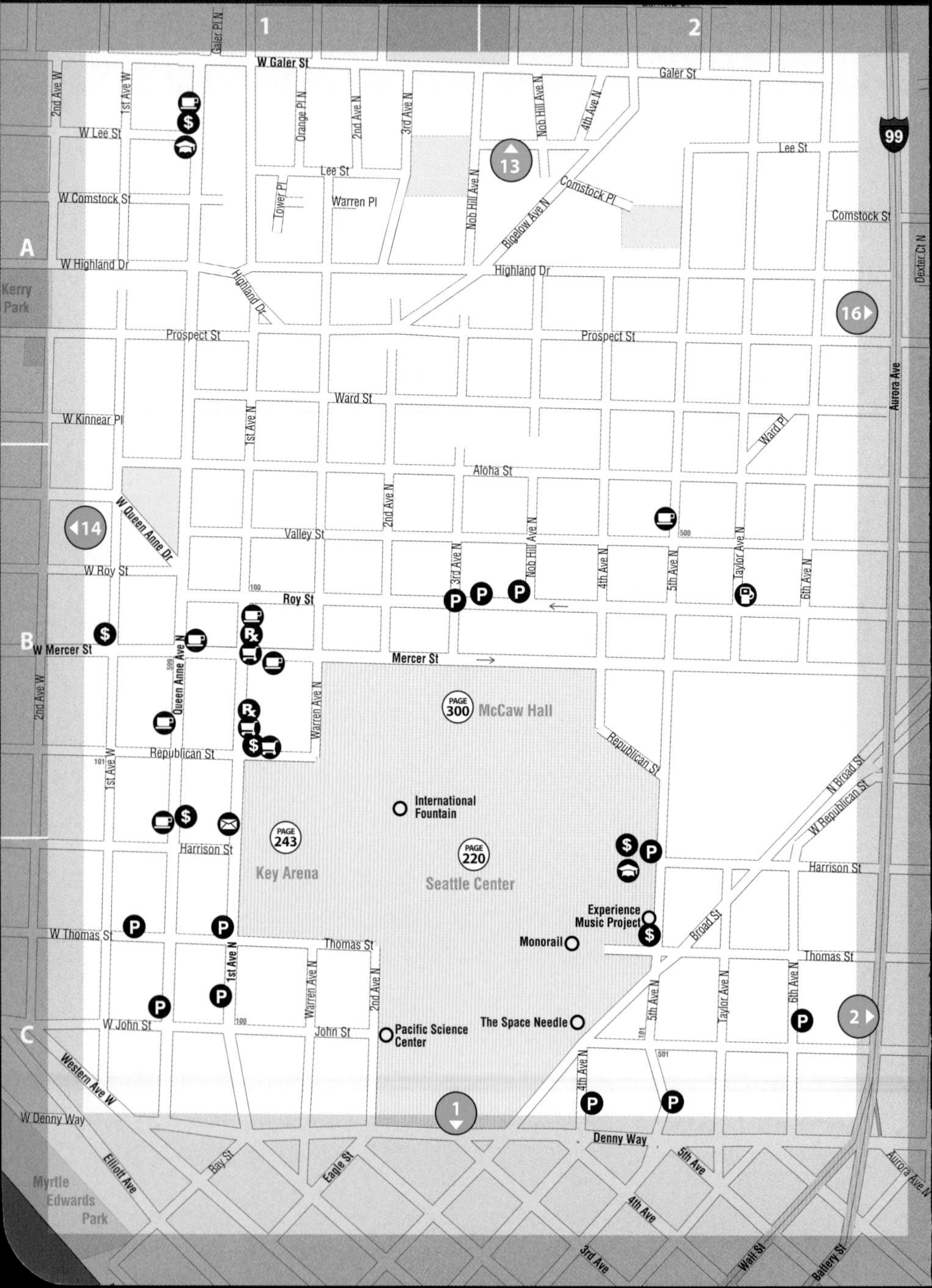

Map 15 • **Lower Queen Anne / Seattle Center**

N

2nd Ave W
1st Ave W
W Galer St
W Lee St
W Comstock St
Orange Pl N
2nd Ave N
3rd Ave N
Lower Pl
Lee St
Warren Pl
Nob Hill Ave N
4th Ave N
Galer St
Lee St
Comstock Pl
Comstock St

1

2

13

A

Kerry Park

W Highland Dr
Highland Dr
Bigelow Ave N
Highland Dr

16

Prospect St
1st Ave N
Prospect St

Aurora Ave N

Dexter Ct N

99

W Kinnear Pl
Ward St

W Queen Anne Dr
Aloha St

14

Valley St
2nd Ave N
3rd Ave N
Nob Hill Ave N
4th Ave N
5th Ave N
Taylor Ave N
6th Ave N
500

W Roy St
Roy St

B
W Mercer St
2nd Ave W
Queen Anne Ave N
Warren Ave N
Mercer St
McCaw Hall
PAGE 300
Republican St
N Broad St
W Republican St

1st Ave W
Republican St
International Fountain

Harrison St
Key Arena
PAGE 243
Seattle Center
PAGE 220
Experience Music Project
Harrison St

W Thomas St
1st Ave N
Thomas St
2nd Ave N
Monorail
Broad St
5th Ave N
Taylor Ave N
6th Ave N
Thomas St

C
W John St
Warren Ave N
2nd Ave N
John St
100
Pacific Science Center
The Space Needle
4th Ave N
5th Ave N
501
2

1

Western Ave W
W Denny Way
Elliott Ave
Bay St
Eagle St
Denny Way
5th Ave
4th Ave
Aurora Ave N

Myrtle Edwards Park

3rd Ave
Wall St
Battery St

Essentials

The residents of the LQA are mostly single, urban professionals in their mid-twenties to early thirties who enjoy a healthy nightlife and unassuming upscale residences. The neighborhood retains a slightly more economical Belltown vibe. Plus, sometimes they have an express train (some call it a monorail) to Westlake Center. Check for flames and smoke before boarding.

Map 15

Banks

- **Bank of America** • 100 W Mercer St [1st Ave W]
- **Bank of America (ATM)** •
  100 Republican St [1st Ave N]
- **Key Bank** • 434 Queen Anne Ave N [Harrison St]
- **Key Bank (ATM)** • 305 Harrison St [5th Ave N]
- **Key Bank (ATM)** • 325 5th Ave N [Thomas St]
- **Washington Mutual** •
  1417 Queen Anne Ave [W Lee St]

Coffee

- **Café Zingaro** • 127 Mercer St [1st Ave N]
- **Caffe Appassionato** •
  1417 Queen Anne Ave N [W Lee St]
- **Caffe Ladro** • 600 Queen Anne Ave N [W Mercer St]
- **Caffe Vita** • 813 5th Ave N [Valley St]
- **Peet's Coffee & Tea** • 100 Mercer St [1st Ave N]
- **Starbucks** • 425 Queen Anne Ave N [W Harrison St]
- **Uptown Espresso** •
  525 Queen Anne Ave N [W Republican St]

Gas Stations

- **Shell** • 720 Taylor Ave N [Roy St]

○ Landmarks

- **Experience Music Project** • 325 Fifth Ave N [Thomas St]
- **International Fountain** • 305 Harrison St [5th Ave N]
- **Monorail** • Seattle Ctr & Broad St [5th Ave N]
- **Pacific Science Center** • 200 2nd Ave N [John St]
- **The Space Needle** • 400 Broad St [John St]

P Parking

Rx Pharmacies

- **Bartell Drug Store** • 600 1st Ave N [Mercer St] ♿
- **Safeway Pharmacy** • 516 1st Ave W [W Republican St]

✉ Post Offices

- **Queen Anne** • 415 1st Ave N [Harrison St]

Schools

- **The Center School** • 305 Harrison St [5th Ave N]
- **St Anne** • 101 W Lee St [1st Ave W]

Supermarkets

- **Metropolitan Market** • 100 Mercer St [1st Ave N]
- **Quality Food Center** • 100 Republican St [1st Ave N]
- **Safeway** • 516 1st Ave W [W Republican St]

Map 15 · **Lower Queen Anne / Seattle Center**   (N)

1

2

99

W Galer St

Galer St

2nd Ave N

1st Ave N

W Lee St

Orange Pl N

Lee St

Nob Hill Ave N

4th Ave N

Lee St

13

2nd Ave N

3rd Ave N

Comstock Pl

Comstock St

W Comstock St

Tower Pl

Warren Pl

Bigelow Ave N

A

W Highland Dr

Highland Dr

Highland Dr

16▶

Kerry
Park

Prospect St

Prospect St

Dexter Ave N

Aurora Ave N

W Kinnear Pl

1st Ave N

Ward St

Ward Pl

Aloha St

2nd Ave N

3rd Ave N

Nob Hill Ave N

4th Ave N

5th Ave N

Taylor Ave N

6th Ave N

◀14

Valley St

2

500

W Queen Anne Dr

W Roy St

100

Roy St

3rd Ave N

2

B

W Mercer St

100

Queen Anne Ave N

Mercer St

Mercer St

399

2

Warren Ave N

PAGE
300   McCaw Hall

Republican St

N Broad St

101

Republican St

1st Ave N

Republican St

W Republican St

Harrison St

Harrison St

PAGE
243

PAGE
220

Broad St

Key Arena

Seattle Center

W Thomas St

Thomas St

Thomas St

5th Ave N

Taylor Ave N

6th Ave N

1st Ave N

Warren Ave N

2nd Ave N

4th Ave N

C

W John St

John St

2 ▶

Western Ave W

100

551

Aurora Ave

W Denny Way

1

Denny Way

5th Ave

Elliott Ave

Bay St

Eagle St

4th Ave

Wall St

Myrtle
Edwards
Park

W Denny Way

3rd Ave

Battery St

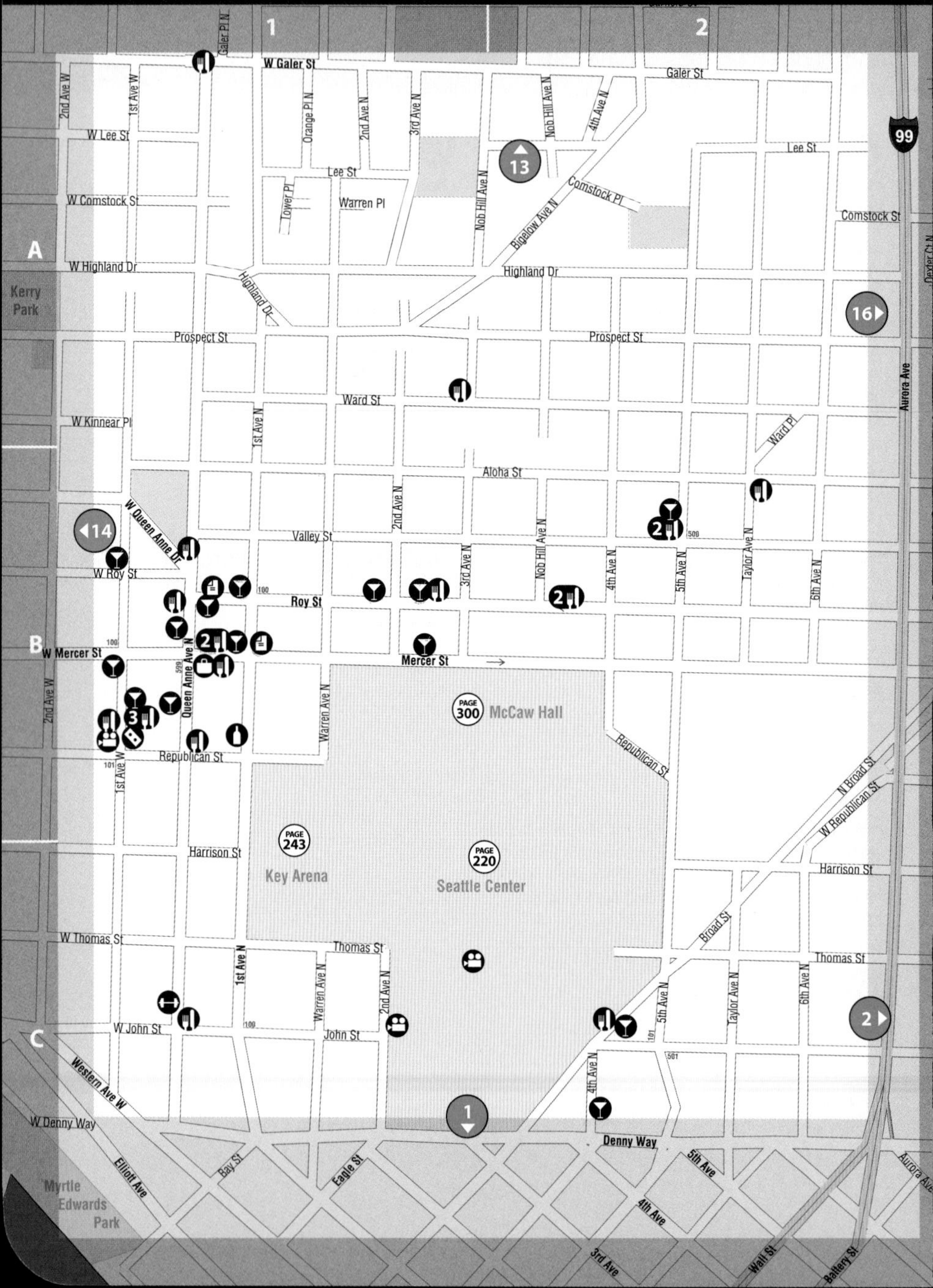

Map 15

The hub of LQA is contained in the several blocks near the Seattle Center that are packed with restaurants and bars. In terms of nightlife, Ozzie's and Peso's draw the biggest crowds and chiefly deal in meat-marketing. Start or end your night at the classic dive Mecca Cafe. Relish delectable Indian at Roti. Beware of depressed Sonic fans still mourning the impending loss of their beloved team.

Copy Shops

- **FedEx Kinko's** • 606 1st Ave N [Mercer St]
- **UPS Store** • 24 Roy St [Queen Anne Ave N]

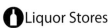Gyms

- **24 Hour Fitness** • 229 Queen Anne Ave N [W John St] ☾

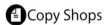Liquor Stores

- **Washington State Liquor Store** •
  515 1st Ave N [Republican St]

Movie Theaters

- **AMC Loews Uptown 3** •
  511 Queen Anne Ave N [W Republican St]
- **AT&T Outdoor Cinema -**
  Seattle Center Mural Stage •
  Thomas St & 3rd Ave N
- **Pacific Science Center IMAX** •
  200 2nd Ave N [John St]
- **SIFF Cinema** • 321 Mercer St [3rd Ave N]

Nightlife

- **10 Mercer** • 10 Mercer St [Queen Anne Ave N]
- **Chopstix Dueling Piano Bar** •
  11 Roy St [Queen Anne Ave N]
- **Crow Restaurant and Bar** • 823 5th Ave N [Valley St]
- **Fun House** • 206 5th Ave N [John St]
- **Jabu's Pub** • 174 Roy St [2nd Ave N]
- **Mecca Café** • 526 Queen Anne Ave N [Republican St]
- **Ozzie's Restaurant and Lounge** •
  105 W Mercer St [1st Ave W]
- **Peso's Kitchen and Lounge** •
  605 Queen Anne Ave N [W Mercer St]
- **The Sitting Room** • 108 W Roy St [1st Ave W]
- **Solo Bar** • 200 Roy St [2nd Ave N]
- **Sport** • 140 4th Ave N Ste 130 [Denny Wy]
- **Teatro Zinzanni Dinner and Dreams** •
  222 Mercer St [2nd Ave N]

Restaurants

- **Bamboo Garden** • 364 Roy St [Nob Hill Ave N]
- **Blue Water Taco Grill** •
  515 Queen Anne Ave N [W Republican St]
- **Crow Restaurant and Bar** • 823 5th Ave N [Valley St]
- **Dick's Drive-In** •
  500 Queen Anne Ave N [Republican St]
- **Gorditos** • 1507 Queen Anne Ave N [W Galer St]
- **Kidd Valley** • 531 Queen Anne Ave N [Republican St]
- **Mecca Café** • 526 Queen Anne Ave N [Republican St]
- **Mediterranean Kitchen** • 366 Roy St [Nob Hill Ave N]
- **The Melting Pot** • 14 Mercer St [Queen Anne Ave N]
- **Pagliacci Pizza** • 550 Queen Anne Ave N [Republican St]
- **Peso's** • 605 Queen Anne Ave N [W Mercer St]
- **Racha** • 23 Mercer St [Queen Anne Ave N]
- **Roti Cuisine of India** •
  530 Queen Anne Ave N [Republican St]
- **Shiki Japanese** • 4 W Roy St [W Roy St]
- **SkyCity at the Space Needle** • 400 Broad St [John St]
- **Solo Bar** • 200 Roy St [2nd Ave N]
- **Sushi Land** • 803 5th Ave N [Valley St]
- **Ten Mercer** • 10 Mercer St [Queen Anne Ave N]
- **Troiani** • 1001 3rd Ave N [Ward St]
- **Uptown China** • 200 Queen Anne Ave N [John St]
- **Veil** • 555 Aloha St [Taylor Ave N]

Shopping

- **Easy Street Records** • 20 Mercer St [Queen Anne Ave N]
- **Twice Sold Tales** • 7 Mercer St [Queen Anne Ave N]

Video Rental

- **Blockbuster** • 522 Queen Anne Ave N [Republican St]

Map 16 · **Westlake / South Lake Union**

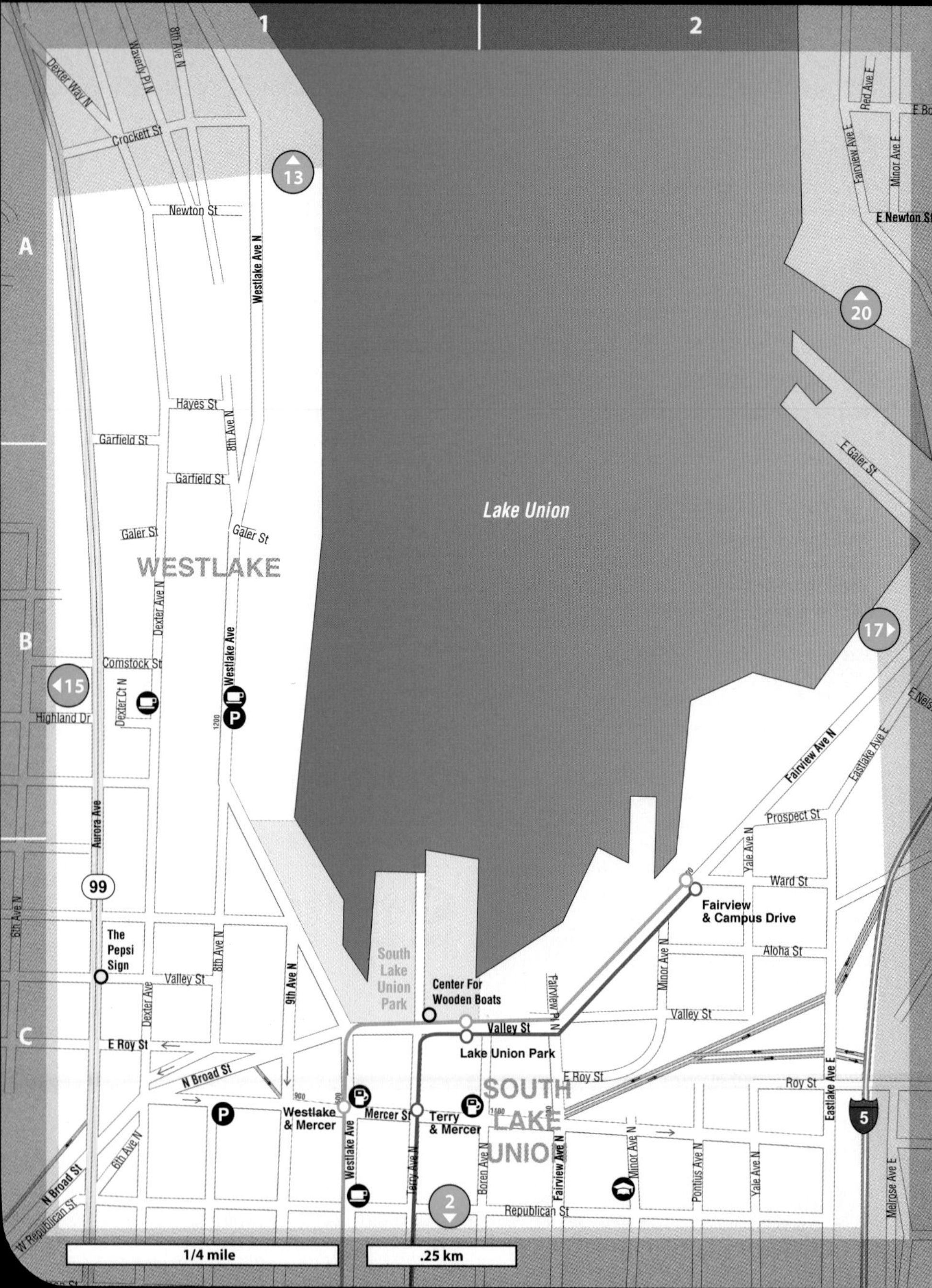

Ⓝ

Dexter Way N

Warren Pl N

8th Ave N

Crockett St

1

2

13

Newton St

Westlake Ave N

Fairview Ave E

Minor Ave E

Red Ave E

E Bo

E Newton St

A

20

Hayes St

8th Ave N

Garfield St

Garfield St

Galer St

Galer St

WESTLAKE

Lake Union

E Galer St

Dexter Ave N

Dexter Ct N

B

15

Highland Dr

Comstock St

Westlake Ave

P

17

E Ne

Eastlake Ave E

Fairview Ave N

Prospect St

Aurora Ave N

8th Ave N

99

Ward St

Fairview & Campus Drive

Yale Ave N

The Pepsi Sign

9th Ave N

Dexter Ave N

8th Ave N

Valley St

South Lake Union Park

Center For Wooden Boats

Fairview Ave N

Aloha St

Minor Ave N

Valley St

C

E Roy St

Valley St

Lake Union Park

SOUTH LAKE UNION

E Roy St

Roy St

Eastlake Ave E

Melrose Ave E

N Broad St

P

900

Westlake & Mercer

Mercer St

Westlake Ave N

Terry Ave N

P

Terry & Mercer

Boren Ave N

Fairview Ave N

Minor Ave N

Pontius Ave N

Yale Ave N

5

8th Ave N

N Broad St

W Republican St

2

Republican St

| 1/4 mile | .25 km |

Once a light industrial area on small, sweet Lake Union, South Lake Union is undergoing massive development with high-rise condos and a biotech corridor. The jewel at the center promises to be the new 12-acre waterfront park, originally proposed 100 years ago. Seattleites apparently don't like to rush into anything. Beware the useless novelty of the Seattle Streetcar (also known as the S.L.U.T.).

Coffee

- **Starbucks** • 1200 Westlake Ave N [Highland Dr]
- **Starbucks** • 1211 Dexter Ave N [Dexter Ct N]
- **Uptown Espresso** • 500 Westlake Ave N [Republican St]

oLandmarks

- **Center for Wooden Boats** • 1010 Valley St
- **The Pepsi Sign** • Aurora Ave N & Valley St

Gas Stations

- **76** • 600 Westlake Ave N
- **Shell** • 601 Boren Ave N [Mercer St]

PParking

Schools

- **Hutch** • 527 Minor Av N [Minor Ave N]

Map 16 · **Westlake / South Lake Union**

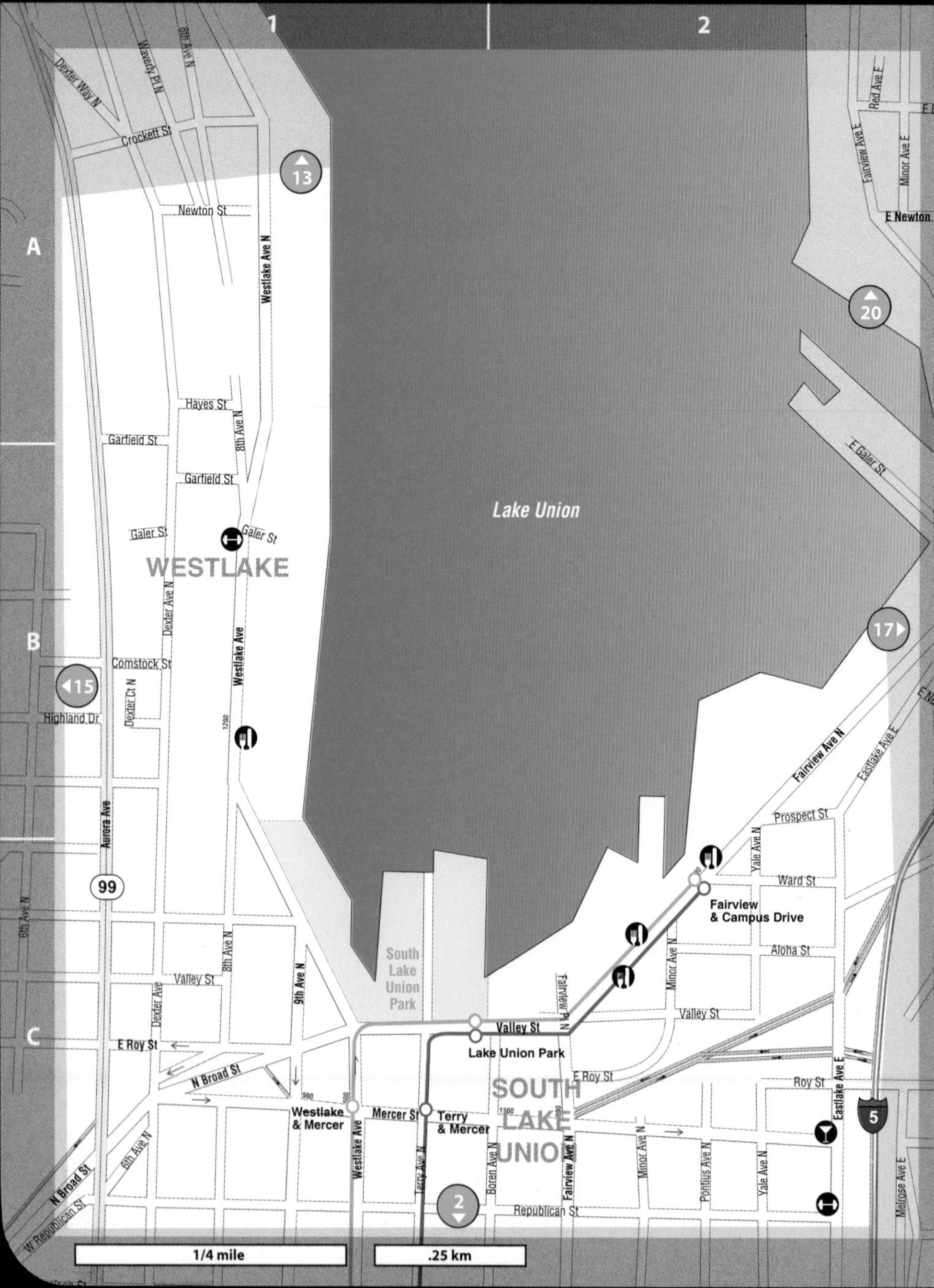

N

1   2

13

A

E Newton

20

Newton St

Westlake Ave N

8th Ave N

Waverly Pl N

Dexter Way N

Crockett St

Hayes St

Garfield St

Garfield St

Galer St   Galer St

WESTLAKE

Dexter Ave N

Westlake Ave

E Galer St

Lake Union

Fairview Ave E

Red Ave E

Minor Ave E

Comstock St

B

15

Highland Dr

Dexter Ct N

1700

Westlake Ave

17

Eastlake Ave E

E N

Aurora Ave

8th Ave N

99

Fairview Ave N

Prospect St

Yale Ave N

Ward St

Fairview
& Campus Drive

Valley St

Dexter Ave N

8th Ave N

9th Ave N

Fairview Ave N

Minor Ave N

Aloha St

South
Lake
Union
Park

C

E Roy St

Valley St

Valley St

N Broad St

Lake Union Park

E Roy St

Roy St

5

Westlake
& Mercer

Westlake Ave

Mercer St

Terry
& Mercer

Terry Ave N

900

**SOUTH
LAKE
UNION**

Boren Ave N

Fairview Ave N

Minor Ave N

Pontius Ave N

Yale Ave N

Eastlake Ave E

Melrose Ave E

N Republican St

N Broad St

8th Ave N

2

Republican St

| 1/4 mile | .25 km |

Once you've navigated the construction zone, partake in some lake-gazing—kayaks and seaplanes and boats, oh my!—from the windows of I Love Sushi or Chandler's Crabhouse. Or just get a view of fellow drinkers and local bands at Mars Bar.

Gyms

- **PRO Sports Club** · 501 Eastlake Ave E [Republican St]
- **Pure Fitness** · 1275 Westlake Ave N [Galer St]

Nightlife

- **Mars Bar/Café Venus** · 609 Eastlake Ave E [Mercer St]

Restaurants

- **Chandler's Crabhouse** ·
  901 Fairview Ave N [Minor Ave N]
- **Daniel's Broiler** · 809 Fairview Ave N [Minor Ave N]
- **I Love Sushi** · 1001 Fairview Ave N [Ward St]
- **McCormick & Schmick's Harborside** ·
  1200 Westlake Ave N [Highland Dr]

Map 17 · **Capitol Hill (West)**

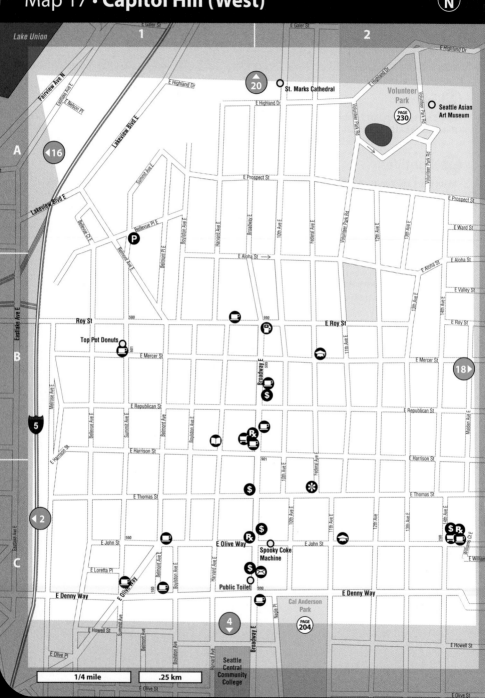

Lake Union

E Galer St

E Galer St

1

2

Fairview Ave N

Eastlake Ave E

E Nelson Pl

E Highland Dr

E Highland Dr

Lakeview Blvd E

20

St. Marks Cathedral

E Highland Dr

Volunteer
Park
**PAGE
230**

Seattle Asian
Art Museum

A

16

Lakeview Blvd N

Lakeview Blvd E

Summit Ave E

Bellevue Ct E

E Prospect St

Voluntary Park Rd

E Prospect St

E Ward St

P

Belmont Pl E

Belmont Ave E

Boylston Ave E

Harvard Ave E

Broadway

10th Ave E

Federal Ave E

Volunteer Park Rd

12th Ave E

13th Ave E

14th Ave E

E Aloha St

E Aloha St

E Valley St

E Aloha St

Eastlake Ave E

Roy St

500

900

E Roy St

E Roy St

B

Top Pot Donuts

E Mercer St

Broadway E

599

E Mercer St

18

Melrose Ave

Bellevue Ave E

Summit Ave E

Belmont Ave E

Boylston Ave E

11th Ave E

Malden Ave E

E Republican St

$

E Republican St

5

E Harrison St

901

E Harrison St

E Harrison St

$

※

E Thomas St

E Thomas St

2

E John St

500

10th Ave E

11th Ave E

12th Ave E

13th Ave E

14th Ave E

E John St

$

E Olive Way

$

E John St

E Williams

E Loretta Pl

Spooky Coke
Machine

E Williams

C

E Denny Way

E Olive Way

Belmont Ave E

Boylston Ave E

Harvard Ave

$

Public Toilet

900

E Denny Way

E Howell St

Summit Ave

Belmont Ave

Boylston Ave

Naglee Pl

Cal Anderson
Park
**PAGE
204**

E Howell St

4

E Olive Pl

Broadway E

E Williamstown

| 1/4 mile | | .25 km |

E Olive St

Harvard Ave

Broadway E

Seattle
Central
Community
College

E Olive St

Essentials

Map 17

Seattle's a gay-friendly city, and there's no neighborhood pinker than this, particularly along the main drag, Broadway. Rainbow flags festoon the lampposts, bold displays of affection are commonplace, and leather daddies can be spotted strolling grocery store aisles in full regalia. Meanwhile, runaway street urchins make themselves at home and new condos are beginning to sprout up on every corner. Get an espresso at Joe Bar and contemplate it all.

$ Banks

- **Bank of America** • 230 Broadway E [E John St]
- **US Bank (ATM)** • 133 Broadway E [E Denny Wy]
- **Washington Mutual** • 301 Broadway E [W Thomas St]
- **Wells Fargo** • 1410 E John St [14th Ave E]
- **Wells Fargo (ATM)** • 512 Broadway E [E Republican]

Coffee

- **B & O Espresso** • 204 Belmont Ave E [E Olive Wy]
- **Espresso Vivace** • 530 E Broadway [E Mecer St]
- **Joe Bar** • 810 E Roy St [Harvard Ave E]
- **Online Coffee Company** •
  1720 E Olive Wy [Boylston Ave E]
- **Starbucks** • Safeway • 1410 E John St [14th Ave E]
- **Starbucks** • 1600 E Olive Wy [E Loretta Pl]
- **Starbucks** • QFC • 417 Broadway E [E Harrison St]
- **Starbucks** • 434 Broadway E [E Harrison St]
- **Top Pot Donuts** • 609 Summit Ave E [E Mercer St]

✳ Community Gardens

Gas Stations

- **76** • 915 E Roy St [Broadway E]

o Landmarks

- **Public Toilet on Broadway** •
  near Dick's at 115 Broadway E [E Denny Wy]
- **Seattle Asian Art Museum** •
  1400 E Prospect St [E Highland Dr]
- **Spooky Coke Machine** • E John St b/w
  Broadway E & 10th Ave E
- **St Marks Cathedral** • 1245 10th Ave E [E Highland Dr]
- **Top Pot Donuts** • 609 Summit Ave E [E Mercer St]

📖 Libraries

- **Capitol Hill Branch** • 425 Harvard Ave E [E Harrison St]

P Parking

℞ Pharmacies

- **Quality Food Center** • 417 Broadway E [E Harrison St]
- **Rite Aid** • 201 Broadway E [E Olive Wy]
- **Safeway Pharmacy** • 1410 E John St [14th Ave E]

✉ Post Offices

- **Broadway** • 101 Broadway E [E Denny Wy]

Schools

- **Lowell Elementary** • 1058 E Mercer St [Federal Ave E]
- **Puget Sound Primary** • 1122 E John St [11th Ave E]

Supermarkets

- **Quality Food Center** • 417 Broadway E [E Harrison St]
- **Safeway** • 1410 E John St [14th Ave E]

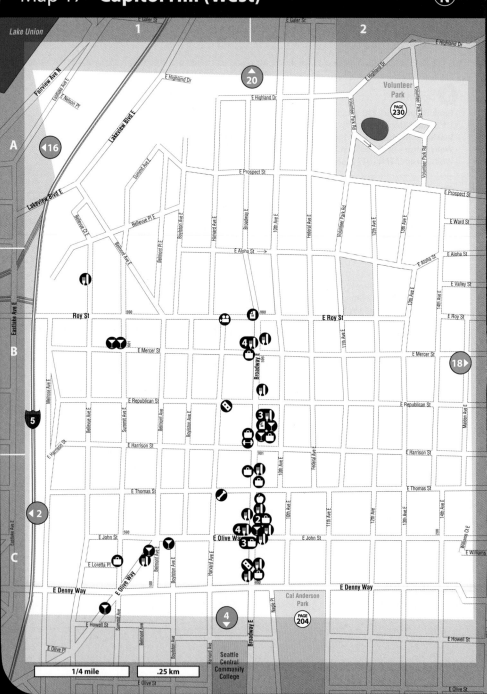

Map 17 · **Capitol Hill (West)**

Lake Union

E Galer St

1

E Galer St

2

E Highland Dr

E Highland Dr

E Highland Dr

20

Volunteer Park

E Highland Dr

PAGE 230

Fairview Ave N

Eastlake Ave E

E Nelson Pl

Lakeview Blvd E

16

A

Volunteer Park Rd

Volunteer Park Rd

E Prospect St

E Prospect St

Lakeview Blvd E

Summit Ave E

Bellevue Pl E

Belmont Pl E

Boylston Ave E

Harvard Ave E

Broadway E

10th Ave E

Federal Ave E

Volunteer Park Rd

12th Ave E

13th Ave E

E Ward St

E Aloha St

Bellevue Ct E

E Aloha St

E Aloha St

13th Ave E

14th Ave E

E Valley St

Belmont Ave E

Roy St

990

E Roy St

E Roy St

E Roy St

B

901

E Mercer St

4

11th Ave E

E Mercer St

18

Eastlake Ave E

Melrose Ave E

Bellevue Ave E

Summit Ave E

Belmont Ave E

Boylston Ave E

Broadway E

E Republican St

995

Maiden Ave E

5

E Republican St

E Harrison St

3

E Harrison St

E Harrison St

E Harrison St

991

Federal Ave E

E Thomas St

10th Ave E

E Thomas St

E Thomas St

2

E John St

2

4

10th Ave E

11th Ave E

12th Ave E

13th Ave E

14th Ave E

Williams Ct E

E John St

E Olive Way

3

E John St

E Williams

C

E Loretta Pl

986

E Olive Way

Belmont Ave E

Boylston Ave E

Harvard Ave E

E Denny Way

E Denny Way

Cal Anderson Park

PAGE 204

E Denny Way

E Howell St

E Olive Way

Summit Ave

Belmont Ave

Boylston Ave

986

Harvard Ave E

Broadway E

4

Naple Pl

Seattle Central Community College

E Howell St

E Olive St

E Olive Pl

| 1/4 mile | | .25 km |

E Olive St

Chompin' on a burger at Dick's Drive-In is the place to be on a late Friday night, but the Deluxe Grill pours generous drinks and serves big sandwiches when there's time and money to burn. The Stumbling Monk is a comfy spot for Belgian beers and good conversation. Glo's is the place for breakfast, but be prepared to wait. For your literary needs, Bailey-Coy Books never fails to satisfy.

Copy Shops
- **FedEx Kinko's** · 700 Broadway E [E Roy St]
- **UPS Store** · 410 Broadway E [E Harrison St]

Farmers Markets
- **Broadway (Sun, 11 am–3 pm, May–Nov)** · 230 Broadway E [E John St]

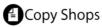Gyms
- **Gold's Gym** · 401 Broadway E [E Harrison St]

Liquor Stores
- **Washington State Liquor Store** · 400 Broadway E [E Harrison St]

Movie Theaters
- **Landmark Harvard Exit** · 807 E Roy St [Harvard Ave E]

Nightlife
- **Bleu Bistro** · 202 Broadway E [E John St]
- **Café Metropolitain** · 1701 E Olive Wy [E Olive Wy]
- **Dilettante** · 416 Broadway E [E Harrison St]
- **Elite Tavern** · 1520 E Olive Wy [E Denny Wy]
- **The Stumbling Monk** · 1635 E Olive Wy [E John St]
- **Summit Public House** · 601 Summit Ave E Ste 102 [E Mercer St]
- **Sun Liquor** · 607 Summit Ave E [E Mercer St]

Pet Shops
- **Mud Bay** · 815 E Thomas St [Harvard Ave E]

Restaurants
- **Aoki Japanese Grill & Sushi Bar** · 621 Broadway E [E Mercer St]
- **Artemis** · 757 Bellevue Ave E [Bellevue Pl E]
- **Bleu Bistro** · 202 Broadway E [E John St]
- **Broadway Grill** · 314 Broadway E [E Thomas St]
- **Café Septieme** · 214 Broadway E [E Olive Wy]
- **Charlie's on Broadway** · 217 Broadway E [E Olive Wy]
- **Deluxe Bar & Grill** · 625 Broadway E [E Mercer St]
- **Dick's Drive-In** · 115 Broadway E [E Denny Wy]
- **Dilettante Chocolates** · 416 Broadway E [E Harrison St]
- **Table 219** · 219 Broadway E [E Olive Wy]
- **Galerias** · 611 Broadway E [E Mercer St]
- **Glo's** · 1621 E Olive Wy [Belmont Ave E]
- **Jai Thai** · 235 Broadway E [E Olive Wy]
- **Noah's Bagels** · 220 Broadway E [E John St]
- **Pagliacci Pizza** · 426 Broadway E [E Harrison St]
- **Pho Cyclo** · 406 Broadway E [E Harrison St]
- **Pho Thân Brothers'** · 516 Broadway E [E Republican]
- **Piroshki on Broadway** · 128 Broadway E [E Denny Wy]
- **Queen Sheba** · 916 E John St [E Olive Wy]
- **Rom Mai Thai** · 613 Broadway E [E Mercer St]
- **Siam on Broadway** · 616 Broadway E [E Mercer St]
- **Table 219** · 219 Broadway E [E Olive Wy]
- **Taqueria Guaymas** · 213 Broadway E [E Olive Wy]

Shopping
- **American Apparel** · 200 Broadway E [E Olive Wy]
- **Bailey-Coy Books** · 414 Broadway E [E Harrison St]
- **Broadway News** · 605 Broadway E [E John St]
- **Castle Superstore** · 206 Broadway E [E John St]
- **Crossroads Trading Co** · 325 Broadway E [E Thomas St]
- **Everyday Music** · 112 Broadway E [E Denny Wy]
- **Metro Clothing** · 231 Broadway E [E Olive Wy]
- **Pretty Parlor** · 119 Summit Ave E [E Loretta Pl]
- **Red Light Vintage Clothing** · 312 Broadway E [E Thomas St]
- **Twice Sold Tales** · 905 E John St [E Olive Wy]
- **Urban Outfitters** · 401 Broadway E [E Harrison St]

Video Rental
- **Broadway Video** · 813 E Republican St [Harvard Ave E]
- **Hollywood Video** · 129 Broadway E [E Denny Wy]

Map 18 · **Capitol Hill (East) / Madison Valley**

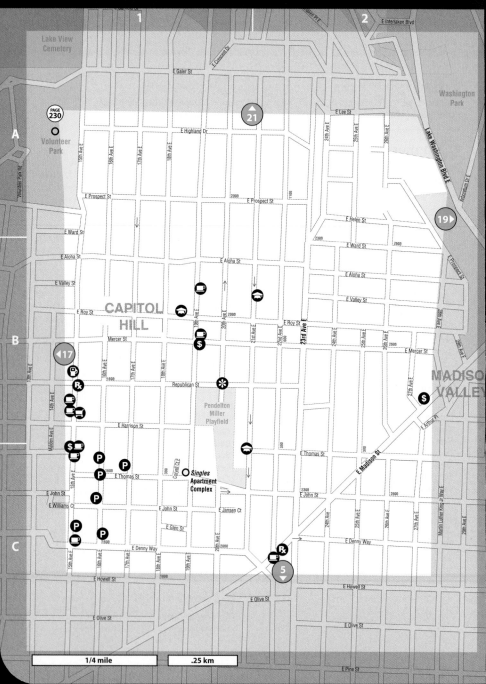

While the western side of Capitol Hill caters directly to the young and decadent, the eastern portion of the neighborhood is more of a, well, neighborhood. Still, there's no shortage of pink pride or night life, so it's not an utter culture shock. Nearby Madison Valley is even homier, with numerous parks, public schools, and escalating real estate values—a far cry from the down-and-out neighborhood it used to be a mere decade ago.

Banks

- **Key Bank** · 321 15th Ave E [E Thomas St]
- **US Bank (ATM)** · 2720 E Madison St [27th Ave E]

Coffee

- **Caffe Ladro** · 435 15th Ave E [E Harrison St]
- **Coffee Pronto** · 312 15th Ave E [E Thomas St]
- **Fuel** · 610 19th Ave E [E Mercer St]
- **Insomniax Coffee** · 102 15th Ave E [15th Ave E]
- **Starbucks** · 2201 E Madison St [22nd Ave E]
- **Starbucks** · 328 15th Ave E [E Thomas St]
- **Tully's** · 746 19th Ave E [E Roy St]
- **Victrola Coffee & Art** · 411 15th Ave E [E Harrison St]

Community Gardens

Gas Stations

- **Hilltop Service Station/ no brand** ·
  523 15th Ave E [E Republican St]

Landmarks

- *Singles* **Apartment Complex** ·
  1820 E Thomas St [19th Ave E]
- **Volunteer Park** · 1247 15th Ave E

Parking

Pharmacies

- **Safeway Pharmacy** · 2201 E Madison St [22nd Ave E]
- **Walgreens** · 500 15th Ave E [E Republican St]

Schools

- **Holy Names Academy** · 728 21st Ave E [E Roy St]
- **Meany Middle** · 301 21st Ave E [21st Ave E]
- **St Joseph** · 700 18th Ave E [E Roy St]
- **Stevens Elementary** · 1242 18 Ave E [E Thomas Ave]

Supermarkets

- **Quality Food Center** · 416 15th Ave E [E Harrison St]

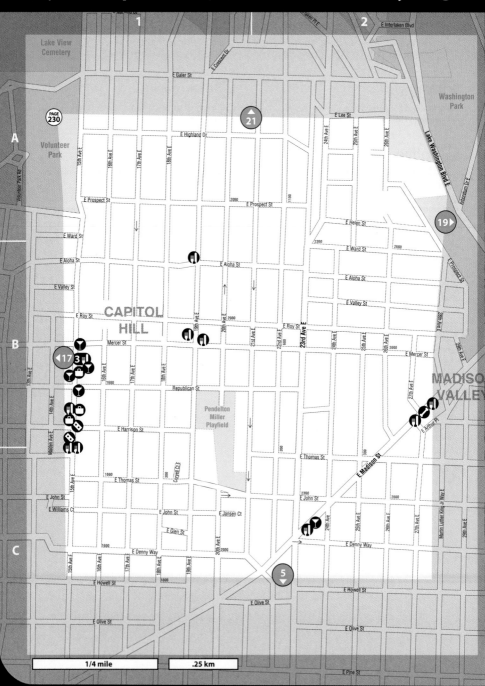

Map 18 · **Capitol Hill (East) / Madison Valley**

Capitol Hill East is home to plenty of laid-back restaurants and pubs. The Canterbury is a peculiar old tavern with shuffleboard and a loyal band of regulars. Linda recently revived 15th with her dark gastropub named Smith. The Kingfish Café serves up tasty soul food and fries a mean chicken. Madison Valley is known for fancy four-star eateries for folks in ties and polished shoes like Crush and Harvest Vine. Shoprite has all your deluxe dollar goods, while music junkies score the newest tunes at Sonic Boom.

Nightlife

- **Bottleneck Lounge** • 2328 E Madison St [23rd Ave E]
- **Canterbury Ales and Eats** •
  534 15th Ave E [E Mercer St]
- **Hopvine Pub** • 507 15th Ave E [E Republican St]
- **Liberty** • 517 15th Ave E [E Republican St]
- **Smith** • 332 15th Ave E [E Harrison St]

Pet Shops

- **All the Best Pet Care** • 2713 E Madison St [27th Ave E]

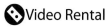Restaurants

- **22 Doors** • 405 15th Ave E [E Harrison St]
- **Coastal Kitchen** • 429 15th Ave E [E Harrison St]
- **Crush** • 2319 E Madison St [23rd Ave E]
- **Essential Baking Company** •
  2719 E Madison St [27th Ave E]
- **The Harvest Vine** • 2701 E Madison St [27th Ave E]
- **Karam's Lebanese Cuisine** •
  340 15th Ave E [E Thomas St]
- **Kingfish Café** • 602 19th Ave E [E Mercer St]
- **Monsoon** • 615 19th Ave E [E Mercer St]
- **Remedy Teas** • 345 15th Ave E [E Harrison St]
- **Samui Thai Cuisine** • 524 15th Ave E [E Republican St]
- **Smith** • 332 15th Ave E [E Harrison St]
- **Vios Café & Marketplace** • 903 19th Ave E [E Aloha St]

Shopping

- **Rainbow Natural Remedies** •
  409 15th Ave E [E Harrison St]
- **Shoprite** • 432 15th Ave E [E Harrison St]
- **Sonic Boom Records** • 514 15th Ave E [E Republican St]

Video Rental

- **On 15th Video** • 400 15th Ave E [E Harrison St]
- **Video Connection** • 345 15th Ave E [E Thomas St]

Map 19 · **Madison Valley / Denny Blaine**

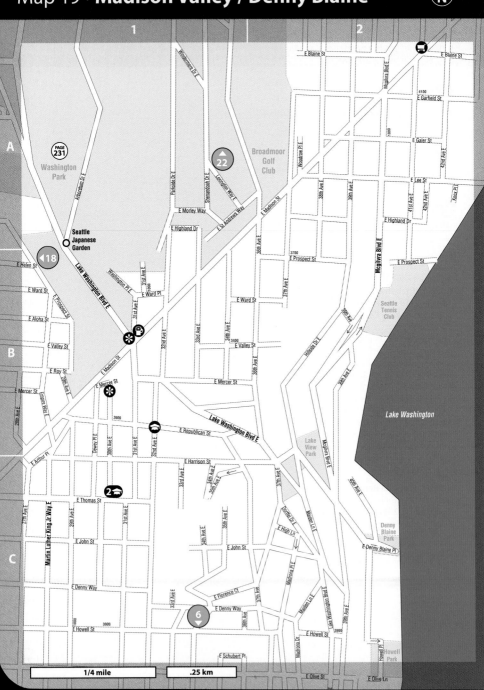

Polar opposite extremes of wealth and health. Families living in mansions on Lake Washington recreate at the Seattle Tennis Club's waterfront courts and privately educate prodigal youth at the elite Bush School. Nearby, at a gritty city intersection, Seattle's Bailey-Bouche provides housing for people living with terminal diseases and public schools get the axe due to budget cuts. Gotta love the commonalities— Seattle Tennis Club, Bush School, and Bailey-Bouche House all have exclusive admission criteria.

 Community Gardens

Gas Stations

- **Shell** · 3100 E Madison St [31st Ave E]

o Landmarks

- **Seattle Japanese Garden** ·
  1075 Lake Washington Blvd E [Arboretum Dr]

 Schools

- **Bush** · 405 36th Ave E [E Thomas St]
- **Martin Luther King Elementary** ·
  3201 E Republican St [E Republican St]
- **Valley** · 310 30th Ave E [E Thomas St]

Supermarkets

- **Red Apple** · 1801 41st Ave E [E Madison St]

Map 19 • **Madison Valley / Denny Blaine**

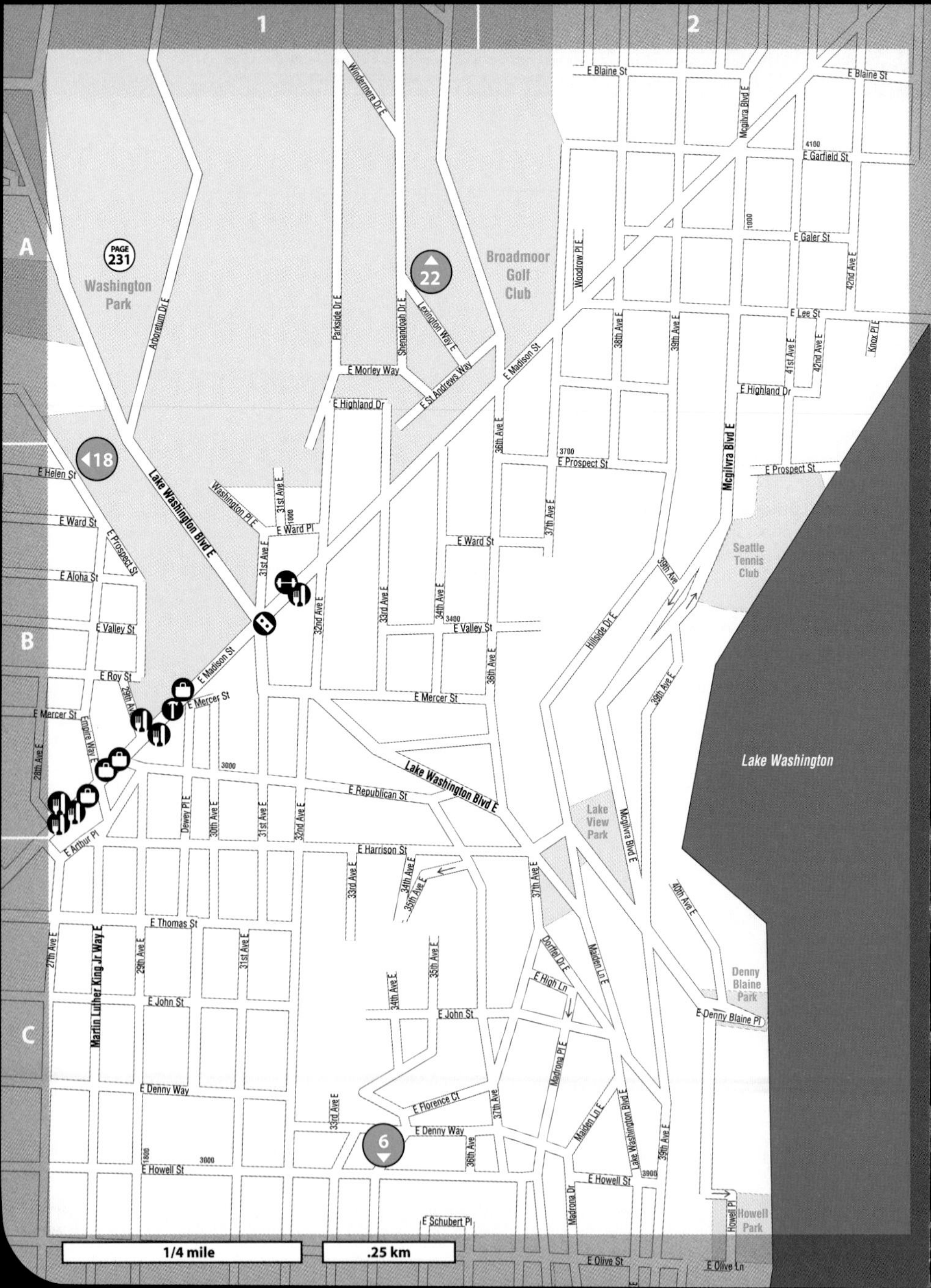

N

1

2

E Blaine St

E Blaine St

Woodmere Dr E

E Garfield St

4100

Mcgilvra Blvd E

1000

38th Ave E

39th Ave E

E Galer St

42nd Ave E

A

PAGE
231

Broadmoor
Golf
Club

Woodrow Pl E

E Lee St

41st Ave E

42nd Ave E

Kona Pl E

Washington
Park

Arboretum Dr E

22

Parkside Dr E

Shenandoah Dr E

Lexington Way E

E Morley Way

Madison St

E Highland Dr

E St Andrews Way

E Highland Dr

38th Ave E

E Prospect St

E Prospect St

Mcgilvra Blvd E

18

E Helen St

Washington Pl E

31st Ave E

E Ward Pl

37th Ave E

Seattle
Tennis
Club

E Ward St

E Prospect St

Lake Washington Blvd E

E Ward St

34th Ave E

B

E Aloha St

E Valley St

31st Ave E

Madison St

32nd Ave E

33rd Ave E

3400

E Valley St

36th Ave E

Hillside Dr E

38th Ave E

E Roy St

E Mercer St

38th Ave E

T

E Mercer St

E Mercer St

E Republican St

Lake Washington Blvd E

37th Ave E

Denny Pl E

30th Ave E

31st Ave E

32nd Ave E

3000

Mcgilvra Blvd E

Lake Washington

Lake
View
Park

E Arthur Pl

Empire Way E

28th Ave E

E Harrison St

33rd Ave E

34th Ave E

35th Ave E

37th Ave E

36th Ave E

E Thomas St

27th Ave E

29th Ave E

31st Ave E

31st Ave E

34th Ave E

Pacific Dr E

Madison Ln E

E High Ln

40th Ave E

Denny
Blaine
Park

Martin Luther King Jr Way E

E John St

E John St

35th Ave E

38th Ave E

Madison Pl E

E Denny Blaine Pl

C

E Denny Way

33rd Ave E

E Florence Ct

E Denny Way

36th Ave E

37th Ave E

Madison Ln E

Lake Washington Blvd E

39th Ave E

6

1800

3000

E Howell St

Madrona Dr

E Howell St

Howell
Park

E Schubert Pl

E Olive St

E Olive Ln

| 1/4 mile | .25 km |

Browse myriad unique shops and cafés to inspire your muse, delight your eye, and thin your wallet. Redecorate her beautifully at Fury and him handsomely at Gentlemen's Consignment. Sushi craving? Nishino or Chinoise. French? Try world-renowned Rover's or rustic Voilà. Café Flora defines gourmet vegetarian. Love life in a rut? Stroll through Washington Park whilst pondering the virtues of celibacy.

Gyms

- **Denali Fitness** · 3130 E Madison St [32nd Ave E]

Hardware Stores

- **City People's Garden Store True Value** ·
2939 E Madison St [29th Ave E]

Restaurants

- **Café Flora** · 2901 E Madison St [29th Ave E]
- **Chinoise Café** · 2801 E Madison St [28th Ave E]
- **Nishino** · 3130 E Madison St [32nd Ave E]
- **Rover's** · 2808 E Madison St [28th Ave E]
- **Voilà! Bistrot** · 2805 E Madison St [28th Ave E]

Shopping

- **City People's Garden Store** ·
2939 E Madison St [29th Ave E]
- **Fury Extraordinary Consignment** ·
2810 E Madison St [29th Ave E]
- **Gentlemen's Consignment** ·
2809 E Madison St [29th ave E]
- **The Lavender Heart** · 2812 E Madison St [29th Ave E]

Video Rental

- **Island Video** · 3109 E Madison St [Lake Washington Blvd E]

Map 20 · **Eastlake / Montlake / Portage Bay**

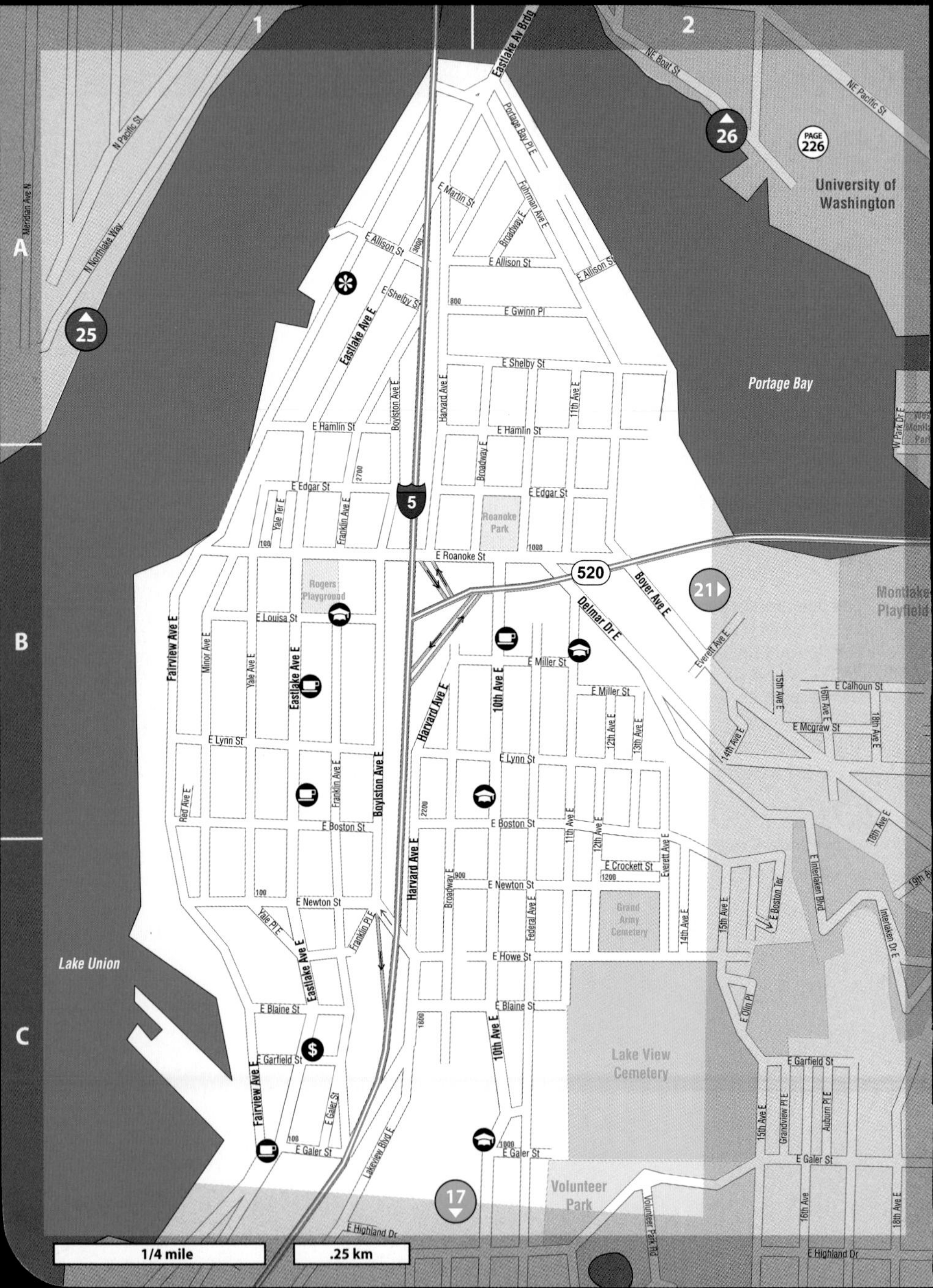

N

1 2

25 26 PAGE 226

University of Washington

Eastlake Ave Brdg

N Pacific St

NE Boat St

NE Pacific St

Meridian Ave N

N Northlake Way

Portage Bay Pl E

E Martin St

Fairview Ave E

Broadway E

E Allison St E Allison St

E Shelby St

E Gwinn Pl

800

E Shelby St

Portage Bay

Eastlake Ave E

Boylston Ave E

Harvard Ave E

11th Ave E

E Hamlin St E Hamlin St

E Edgar St

Broadway E

E Edgar St

2700

Yale Ter E

Franklin Ave E

1000

Roanoke Park

5

E Roanoke St

520 Boyer Ave E

1000

Delmar Dr E

21 Montlake Playfield

Fairview Ave E

Minor Ave E

Yale Ave E

Rogers Playground

E Louisa St

Eastlake Ave E

Everett Ave E

15th Ave E

16th Ave E

E Calhoun St

E Miller St

E Miller St

12th Ave E

13th Ave E

E McGraw St

14th Ave E

Reid Ave E

Franklin Ave E

Boylston Ave E

Harvard Ave E

10th Ave E

E Lynn St

E Boston St

2200

E Lynn St

E Boston St

10th Ave E

12th Ave E

Everett Ave E

E Boston Ter

15th Ave E

16th Ave E

Interlaken Blvd

E Interlaken Blvd

Interlaken Dr E

100

E Newton St

900

Broadway E

E Newton St

E Crockett St
1200

Federal Ave E

E Clark St

Grand Army Cemetery

14th Ave E

E Howe St

Lake Union

Eastlake Ave E

Franklin Pl E

E Blaine St

10th Ave E

1600

E Blaine St

Lake View Cemetery

E Garfield St

Grandview Pl E

15th Ave E

Auburn Pl E

$

E Garfield St

E Galer St

Fairview Ave E

Galer St

100

E Galer St

E Galer St

1000

16th Ave E

18th Ave E

17

Volunteer Park

Volunteer Park Rd

E Highland Dr

Lakeview Blvd E

E Highland Dr

1/4 mile .25 km

Eastlake is one gem of a neighborhood with an ideal location—a short bus ride from the U District and a hop-skip-jump from downtown. Being nuzzled up to Lake Washington makes the 'hood that much more desirable. It's old, funky, and a touch European, with its brightly painted homes and homespun shops. Once a more industrial section of town, residential buildings have sprung up near Eastlake's idyllic and thriving houseboat community.

Map 20

Banks

• **Bank of America** • 1600 Eastlake Ave E [E Garfield St]

Coffee

• **Café Dharwin** • 2406 10th Ave E [E Miller St]
• **Cuppa Jo On the Go** •
  1500 Fairview Ave E [Eastlake Ave E]
• **Sitka and Spruce** • 2238 Eastlake Ave E [E Boston St]
• **Starbucks** • 2344 Eastlake Ave E [E Lynn St]

Community Gardens

Schools

• **Bertschi** • 2227 10th Ave E [E Boston St]
• **Bright Water** • 1501 10th Ave, E #100 [E Galer St]
• **Seattle Prep** • 2400 11th Ave E [E Miller St]
• **Tops K-8** • 2500 Franklin Ave E [E Louisa St]

Map 20 · **Eastlake / Montlake / Portage Bay**

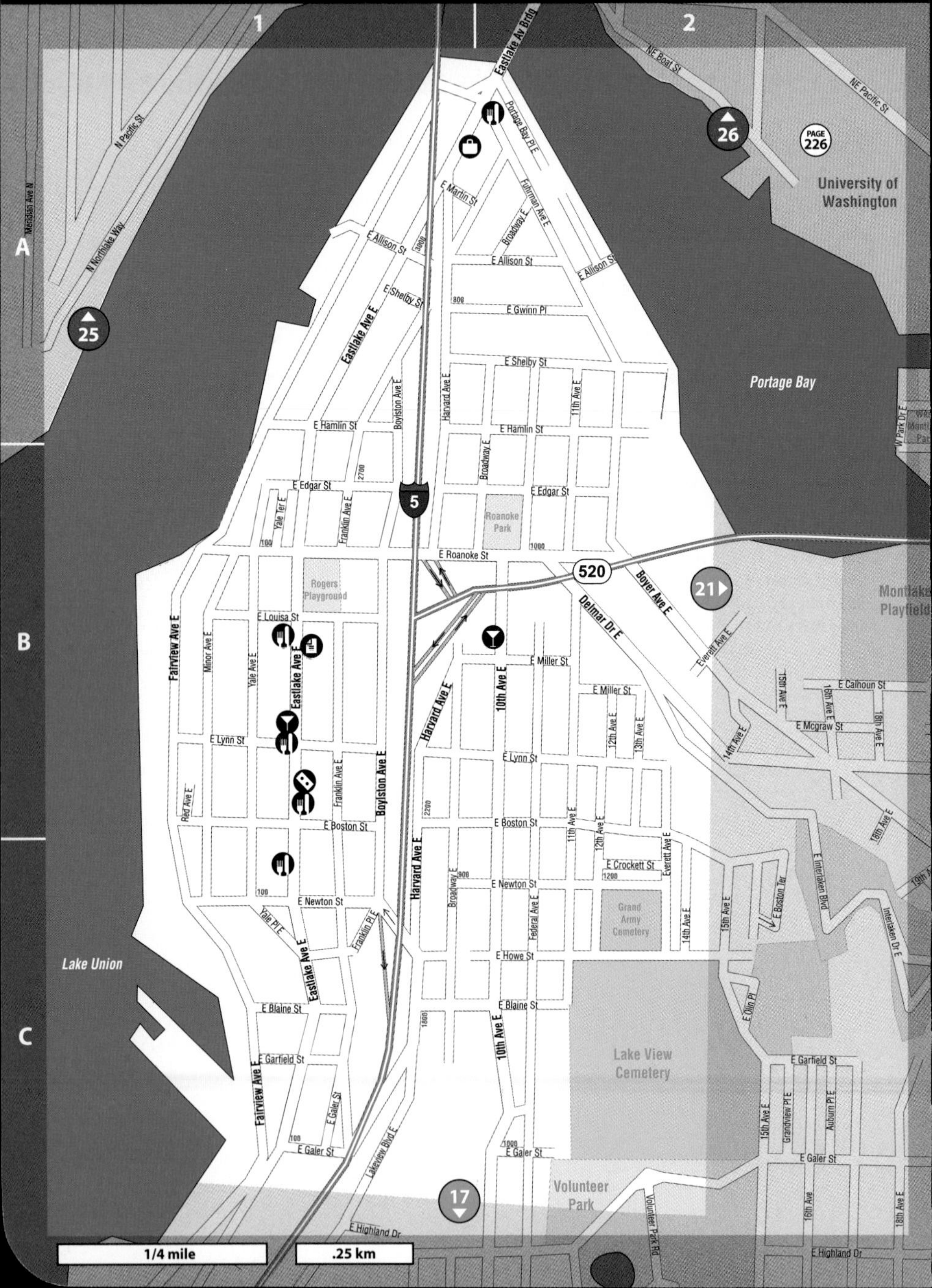

N

1
2

Eastlake Av Brdg

Portage Bay Pl E

NE Boat St

NE Pacific St

26

PAGE 226

University of Washington

E Martin St

Broadway E

Fairview Ave E

E Allison St

E Allison St

E Allison St

A

25

E Shelby St

1900

E Gwinn Pl

Eastlake Ave E

E Shelby St

Harvard Ave E

Boylston Ave E

E Shelby St

10th Ave E

Portage Bay

E Hamlin St

E Hamlin St

E Hamlin St

2700

Broadway E

W Park Dr E
W Montlake Par

E Edgar St

Franklin Ave E

Yale Ter E

E Edgar St

5

1100

Roanoke Park

2900

1000

E Roanoke St

Rogers Playground

520

Boyer Ave E

21

Montlake Playfield

Delmar Dr E

Fairview Ave E

Minor Ave E

Yale Ter E

E Louisa St

Eastlake Ave E

Everett Ave E

10th Ave E

E Miller St

E Miller St

Harvard Ave E

12th Ave E

13th Ave E

14th Ave E

15th Ave E

16th Ave E

17th Ave E

E Calhoun St

E McGraw St

B

E Lynn St

Riad Ave E

Franklin Ave E

Boylston Ave E

E Lynn St

E Boston St

2200

10th Ave E

E Boston St

11th Ave E

12th Ave E

13th Ave E

Everett Ave E

14th Ave E

15th Ave E

19th Ave E

E Boston Ter

E Boston St

Broadway E

E Newton St

E Crockett St

1200

Interlaken Blvd

100

Yale Pl E

E Newton St

Federal Ave E

E Howe St

Grand Army Cemetery

Lake Union

Eastlake Ave E

Franklin Pl E

E Blaine St

Harvard Ave E

E Blaine St

C

E Garfield St

10th Ave E

Lake View Cemetery

E Garfield St

15th Ave E

Grandview Pl E

Auburn Pl E

Fairview Ave E

Galer St

E Galer St

E Galer St

E Galer St

16th Ave E

18th Ave E

1800

Lakeview Blvd E

100

2000

17

Volunteer Park

Volunteer Park Rd

E Highland Dr

E Highland Dr

| 1/4 mile | .25 km |

Map 20

Living up to Eastlake's quaint and quirky reputation, Eastlake Avenue is crowded with inventive yet homey cafés and bistros like Sitka & Spruce and 14 Carrot Café. Seattle institutions like the original Red Robin outpost are also nearby. The nightlife scene is decidedly more mature and quiet—most locals opt to partake of restaurant happy hours (Serafina is a favorite) or, if they're feeling a little more raucous, head to the Eastlake Zoo for some pool and darts.

Copy Shops

- **G & H Printing** · 2370 Eastlake Ave E [E Louisa St]

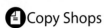Nightlife

- **Eastlake Zoo Tavern** · 2301 Eastlake Ave E [E Lynn St]
- **Roanoke Park Place** · 2409 10th Ave E [E Miller St]

Restaurants

- **14 Carrot Café** · 2305 Eastlake Ave E [E Lynn St]
- **Louisa's Café & Bakery** ·
  2379 Eastlake Ave E [E Louisa St]
- **Red Robin Gourmet Burgers** ·
  2815 Eastlake Ave E [E Hamlin St]
- **Serafina** · 2043 Eastlake Ave E [E Newton St]
- **Sitka & Spruce** · 2238 Eastlake Ave E [E Boston St]

Shopping

- **The Flower Lady** · 3230 Eastlake Ave E [Furhman Ave E]

Video Rental

- **Video Quest** · 2234 Eastlake Ave E [E Boston St]

Map 21 · **Montlake**

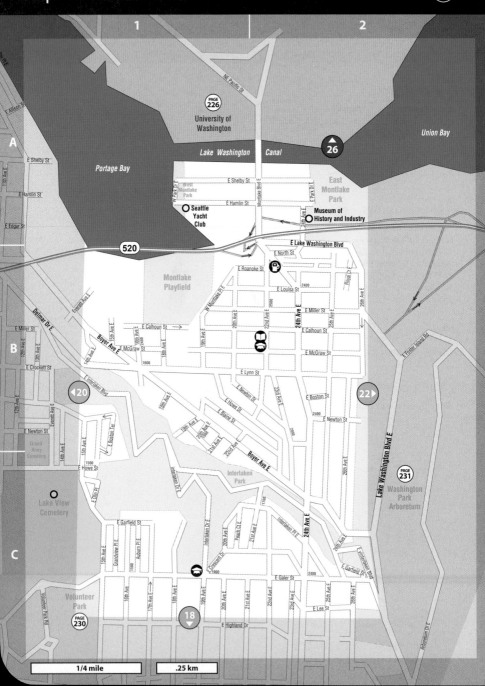

This classy, educated neighborhood borders the bucolic Arboretum, the wooded ravines of Interlaken Park, and the Montlake Cut connecting Lake Union and Lake Washington. The venerable Seattle Yacht Club presides west of the bridge; to the east is the Museum of History and Industry. The spiffy new Montlake Library branch attracts local brainiacs, and regattas draw rowers to May's raucous first day of boating season. Beware—traffic chokes Montlake on Husky game days and during drawbridge openings.

Gas Stations

- **76** • 2625 E Montlake Pl E [E Roanoke St]
- **Texaco** • 2625 E Montlake Pl E [E Roanoke St]

oLandmarks

- **Lake View Cemetery** • 1554 15th Ave E [E Garfield St]
- **Museum of History & Industry** •
  2700 24th Ave E [E Hamlin St]
- **Seattle Yacht Club** • 1807 E Hamlin St [E Republican St]

Libraries

- **Montlake Branch** • 2401 24th Ave E [E McGraw St]

Schools

- **Montlake Elementary** • 2409 22nd Ave E [E McGraw St]
- **Seattle Hebrew Academy** •
  1617 Interlaken Dr E [E Galer St]

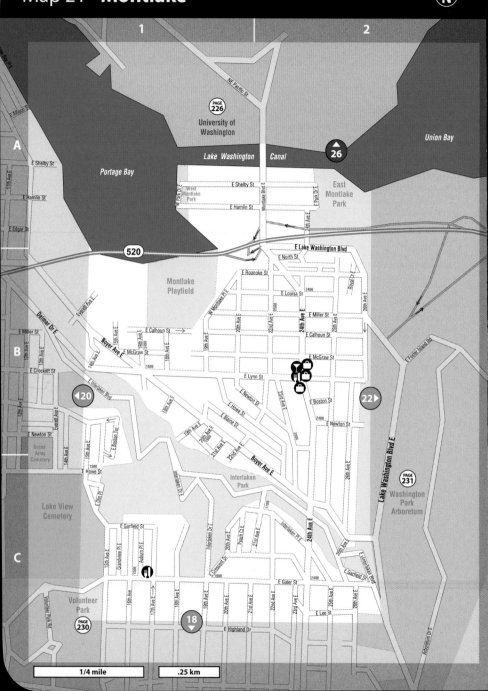

Map 21 · Montlake

1 | 2

A

PAGE 226

University of Washington

Union Bay

Lake Washington Canal

Portage Bay

Portage Bay

E Shelby St

E Hamlin St

E Edgar St

West Montlake Park

E Shelby St

E Hamlin St

East Montlake Park

26

520

B

Delmar Dr E

E Miller St

E Crockett St

E Interlaken Blvd

E Newton St

Grand Army Cemetery

Montlake Playfield

E North St

E Roanoke St

E Louisa St

E Miller St

E Calhoun St

E McGraw St

E Lynn St

E Newton St

E Howe St

E Blaine St

E Boston St

E Newton St

20

22

E Lake Washington Blvd

Boyer Ave E

Lake Washington Blvd E

PAGE 231

Washington Park Arboretum

C

Lake View Cemetery

Volunteer Park

PAGE 230

Interlaken Park

E Garfield St

E Galer St

E Lee St

E Highland Dr

E Garfield St

18

1/4 mile | .25 km

Little wonder no one leaves Montlake—we could live happily ever after being charmed by the Café Lago family, drinking wine and devouring blissfully delicious rustic Italian fare. Montlake Ale House draws the college crowd, Mont's Market provides champagne, and with the Montlake Bicycle Shop for gear and Mr. Johnson's Antiques for funk, it's pretty darn sweet!

 Nightlife

- **Montlake Ale House** · 2307 24th Ave E [E Lynn St]

 Restaurants

- **Café Lago** · 2305 24th Ave [E Lynn St]
- **Volunteer Park Cafe and Marketplace** · 1501 17th Ave E [E Galer St]

 Shopping

- **Mont's Market** · 2350 24th Ave E [E McGraw St]
- **Montlake Bicycle Shop** · 2223 24th Ave E [E Lynn St]
- **Mr Johnson's Antiques** · 2315 24th Ave E [E Lynn St]

Map 22 · **Madison Park**

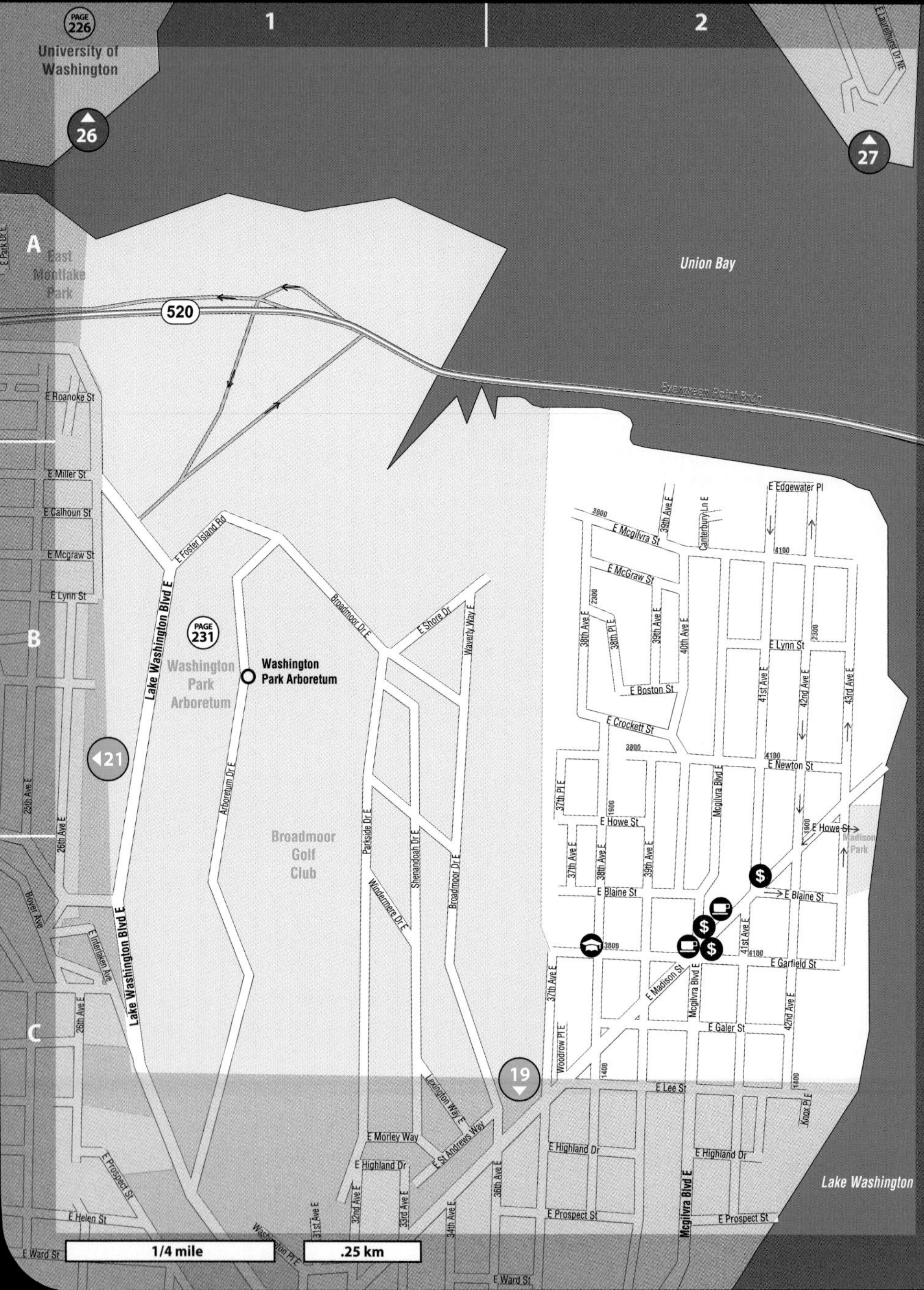

N

PAGE 226
University of
Washington

26

27

1

2

A

East Montlake Park

Union Bay

520

Evergreen Point Blvd

E Roanoke St

E Miller St

E Calhoun St

E Mcgraw St

E Lynn St

E Foster Island Rd

Broadmoor Dr E

E Shore Dr E

Waverly Way E

E Edgewater Pl

3800

E Mcgilvra St

Canterbury Ln E

4100

E McGraw St

36th Ave E

38th Ave E

39th Ave E

40th Ave E

E Lynn St

41st Ave E

42nd Ave E

43rd Ave E

3900

B

PAGE 231

Washington
Park
Arboretum

○ Washington
Park Arboretum

Lake Washington Blvd E

Arboretum Dr E

2300

E Boston St

E Crockett St

3800

Mcgilvra Blvd

4100

E Newton St

21

26th Ave E

Broadmoor
Golf
Club

Parkside Dr E

Shenandoah Dr E

Broadmoor Dr E

Woodmont Dr E

37th Pl E

1900

E Howe St

37th Ave E

37th Ave E

38th Ave E

Mcgilvra Blvd

E Howe St

Madison Park

$

E Blaine St

$

E Blaine St

C

Lake Washington Blvd E

24th Ave E

28th Ave E

Enterprise Rd E

$
$

🖥

🖥

🖥

3800

E Madison St

41st Ave E

42nd Ave E

Knox Pl E

4100

E Garfield St

E Galer St

37th Ave E

Mcgilvra Blvd

Woodrow Pl E

19

1400

E Lee St

Lake Washington Blvd E

Lengston Way E

E Sq Andrews Way

36th Ave E

E Morley Way

E Highland Dr

E Highland Dr

1600

E Highland Dr

E Helen St

E Prospect St

31st Ave E

32nd Ave E

33rd Ave E

34th Ave E

E Prospect St

Mcgilvra Blvd E

E Prospect St

Lake Washington

Washington Pl E

E Ward St

E Ward St

1/4 mile	.25 km

Transferred here from Connecticut and miss the East Coast? Move to Madison Park and fork over serious dough for a cozy bungalow. Or for a few million more, you'll feel right at home in Broadmoor, a gated community established long before anyone knew gates from Gates. Waterfront condos have mountain and lake views, and the Madison Park hub will offer you those trendy little shops and cliquey, smug, safe neighborhood feel you've been missing since moving from Darien.

Banks

- **Bank of America** • 4112 E Madison St [41st Ave E]
- **Washington Mutual** •
  4020 E Madison St [Mcgilvra Blvd E]
- **Wells Fargo** • 4009 E Madison St [E Garfield St]

Coffee

- **Starbucks** • 4000 E Madison St [Mcgilvra Blvd E]
- **Tully's** • 4036 E Madison St [Mcgilvra Blvd E]

○ Landmarks

- **Washington Park Arboretum** •
  2300 Arboretum Dr E [E Foster Island Rd]

Schools

- **McGilvra Elementary** • 1617 38th Ave E [38th Ave E]

Map 22 · **Madison Park**

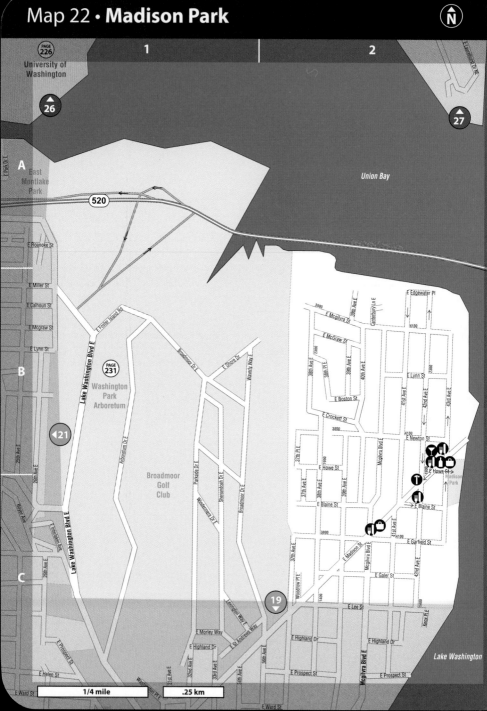

Sundries / Entertainment

Map 22

Spa salons, wine cellars, clothing, jewelry, hardware, and gift shops in Madison Park are high quality and high priced. But for pocket change you'll devour custard doughnuts at the Madison Park Café and tasty burgers and ice cream at Scoop du Jour. The mojitos at Cactus are deservedly legendary. Sostanza offers fine dining and respite from Seattle's famed rainy nights.

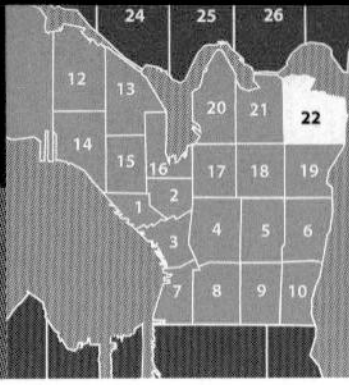

Hardware Stores
- **McKee's Hardware True Value** ·
  1837 42nd Ave E [E Madison St]

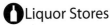Liquor Stores
- **Madison Park Cellars** · 4227 E Madison St [E Howe St]

Nightlife
- **Impromptu Wine Bar Café** ·
  4235 E Madison St [E Howe St]

Restaurants
- **Cactus** · 4220 E Madison St [E Howe St]
- **Madison Park Café** · 1807 42nd Ave E [E Blaine St]
- **Scoop du Jour** · 4029 E Madison St [Mcgilvra Blvd]
- **Sostanza Trattoria** · 1927 43rd Ave E [E Madison St]

Shopping
- **Madison Park Cellars** · 4227 E Madison St [E Howe St]
- **Scoop du Jour** · 4029 E Madison St [Mcgilvra Blvd]

Map 23 · **Ballard**

A Scandinavian fishing village at the turn of the 20th century, and still considered a neighborhood for senior citizens when we struck 21, Ballard has reinvented and reinvigorated itself as one of Seattle's most admired 'nabes. Life's necessities are never hard to track down in this triangle-shaped hub hugging Salmon Bay, and a recent boom in condo development certainly doesn't hurt.

$ Banks

- **Frontier Bank** • 5602 15th Ave NW [NW 56th St]
- **Key Bank** • 1536 NW Market St [15th Ave NW]
- **Sterling Savings Bank** •
  5512 22nd Ave NW [NW Market St]
- **US Bank** • 6100 15th Ave NW [NW 61st St]
- **US Bank (ATM)** • 6100 NW 15th Ave [NW 61st St]
- **Washington Federal Savings** •
  2020 NW Market [Russell Ave]
- **Washington Mutual** •
  5511 22nd Ave NW [NW Market St]
- **Washington Mutual** • 915 NW 45th St [9th Ave NW]

◯ Car Washes

- **Brown Bear Car Wash** •
  5111 15th Ave NW [NW 51st St]

🖥 Coffee

- **Caffe Fiore** • 5405 Leary Ave NW [NW Vernon Place]
- **Cupcake Royale/Verite Coffee** •
  2052 NW Market St [Russell Ave NW]
- **Java Jahn** • 1428 NW Leary Wy [14th Ave NW]
- **Java Jazz** • 5905 15th Ave NW [NW 59th St]
- **Javabean Inc Ballard** • 5819 24th Ave NW [NW 58th St]
- **Mr Spot's Chai House** •
  5463 Leary Ave NW [NW Market St]
- **Nervous Nellie's Espresso Co** •
  1556 NW 56th St [17th Ave NW]
- **Starbucks** • Safeway •
  1423 NW Market St [14th Ave NW]
- **Starbucks** • 2204 NW Market St [22nd Ave NW]
- **Starbucks** • 4400 11th Ave NW [NW 44th St]
- **Tully's** • 2060 NW Market St [Russell Ave NW]
- **Tully's** • 915 NW 45th St [9th Ave NW]

ⓟ Gas Stations

- **76** • 5715 15th Ave NW [NW 57th St]
- **Shell** • 4600 Leary Wy NW [NW 46th St]
- **Texaco** • 5500 15th Ave NW [NW Market St]

➕ Emergency Rooms

- **Swedish Medical Center / Ballard** •
  5300 Tallman Ave NW [17th Ave NW]

◑ Landmarks

- **Archie McPhee's** • 2428 NW Market St [24th Ave NW]

📖 Libraries

- **Ballard Branch** • 5614 22nd Ave NW [NW 56th St]

ⓟ Parking

℞ Pharmacies

- **Bartell Drug** • 5605 22nd Ave NW [NW 56th St]
- **Fred Meyer** • 915 NW 45th St [9th Ave NW]
- **Lafferty's Pharmacy** • 5312 17th Ave NW [NW 53rd St]
- **Market Street Pharmacy** •
  1723 NW Market St [17th Ave NW]
- **Safeway** • 1423 NW Market St [14th Ave NW]
- **Walgreens** • 5409 15th Ave NW [NW 54th St]

✉ Post Offices

- **Ballard** • 5706 17th Ave NW [NW 57th St]

🏫 Schools

- **St Alphonsus** • 5816 15th Ave NW [NW 58th St]

🛒 Supermarkets

- **Fred Meyer** • 915 NW 45th St [9th Ave NW]
- **Safeway** • 1423 NW Market St [14th Ave NW]

Map 23 • **Ballard**

Spots like Hattie's Hat, Tractor Tavern, King's Hardware, and the People's Pub have the bases covered for great neighborhood nightlife. The two main and navigable drags—vibrant Market Street and historic Ballard Avenue—feature lots of restaurants. La Carta de Oaxaca is well worth the wait, while Vera's is one of the last true old-school dining spots left in the city. And don't miss the Ballard Market every Sunday.

Copy Shops
• **FedEx Kinko's** • 1740 NW Market St [Barnes Ave NW]

Gyms
• **Ballard Health Club** • 2208 NW Market St [22nd Ave NW]

Hardware Stores
• **Ballard Hardware & Supply** •
4749 Ballard Ave NW [NW 48th St]
• **Tool Trader** • 1149 NW 52nd St [11th Ave NW]

Liquor Stores
• **Portalis Wine Shop & Wine Bar** •
5205 Ballard Ave NW [20th Ave NW]

Movie Theaters
• **Majestic Bay Theatres** •
2044 NW Market St [Russell Ave NW]

Nightlife
• **DiVino** • 5310 Ballard Ave NW [NW Vernon Place]
• **Hattie's Hat** • 5231 Ballard Ave NW [20th Ave NW]
• **Hazelwood** • 2311 NW Market St [Ballard Ave NW]
• **Jolly Roger Taproom** • 1514 NW Leary Wy [15th Ave W]
• **King's Hardware** • 5225 Ballard Ave NW [20th Ave NW]
• **Matador** • 2221 NW Market St [Ballard Ave NW]
• **Ocho** • 2325 NW Market St [24th Avenue NW]
• **People's Pub** • 5429 Ballard Ave NW [22nd Ave NW]
• **The Sunset Tavern** • 5433 Ballard Ave NW [22nd Ave NW]
• **Tractor Tavern** • 5213 Ballard Ave NW [20th Ave NW]
• **Zayda Buddy's** • 5404 Leary Ave NW [20th Avenue NW]

Pet Shops
• **Ballard Pet Store** • 6115 15th Ave NW [NW 61st St]
• **Bark Natural Pet Care** •
5338 Ballard Ave NW [NW Vernon Pl]
• **The Tweetery** • 8541 15th Ave NW [NW 57th St]

Restaurants
• **Anne's Teriyaki** • 2246 NW Market St [24th Avenue NW]
• **Ballard Mandarin Chinese Restaurant** • 5500   8th
Ave NW [NW Market St]
• **Café Besalu** • 5909 24th Ave NW [59th St NW]
• **Dandelion** • 5809 24th Ave NW [NW 58th St]
• **The Dish** • 4358 Leary Wy NW [8th Ave NW]

• **Hale's Ales Pub** • 4301 Leary Wy NW [7th Ave NW]
• **The Hi-Life** • 5425 Russell Ave NW [20th Ave NW]
• **India Bistro** • 2301 NW Market St [Ballard Ave NW]
• **Isla Seattle** • 2320 NW Market St [Ballard Ave NW]
• **Jolly Roger Taproom** • 1514 NW Leary Wy [15th Ave W]
• **La Carta de Oaxaca** • 5431 Ballard Ave NW [22nd Ave NW]
• **Louie's Cuisine of China** • 5100 15th Ave NW [NW 51st St]
• **Madam K's Pizza Bistro** • 5327 Ballard Ave NW [NW Vernon Pl]
• **Market Street Grill** • 1744 NW Market St [Barnes Ave NW]
• **Matt's Famous Chili Dogs** •
2325 NW Market St [Ballard Ave NW]
• **Matador** • 2221 NW Market St [Ballard Ave NW]
• **The Other Coast Café** • 5315 Ballard Ave NW [NW Vernon Pl]
• **Pasta Bella** • 5909 15th Ave NW [NW 59th St]
• **Pho Thân Brothers'** • 2021 NW Market St [Russell Ave NW]
• **Senor Moose** • 5242 Leary Ave NW [NW Lone Pl]
• **Tall Grass Bakery** • 5907 24th Ave NW [NW 59th St]
• **Thaiku** • 5410 Ballard Ave NW [22nd Ave NW]
• **Vera's** • 5417 22nd Ave NW [Ballard Ave NW]
• **Volterra** • 5411 Ballard Ave NW [22nd Ave NW]
• **Zayda Buddy's** • 5404 Leary Ave NW [20th Avenue NW]

Shopping
• **Anchor Tattoo** • 2313 NW Market St [Ballard Ave NW]
• **Archie McPhee** • 2428 NW Market St [24th Ave NW]
• **Ballard Farmers Market** • 5330 Ballard Ave NW [NW Vernon Pl]
• **Bop Street Records** • 5219 Ballard Ave NW [20th Ave NW]
• **Damsfly** • 5346 Ballard Ave NW [NW Vernon Pl]
• **Epilogue Books** • 2001 NW Market St [20th Ave NW]
• **Fred Meyer** • 915 NW 45th St [9th Ave NW]
• **Greener Lifestyles** • 5317 Ballard Ave NW [NW Vernon Pl]
• **JoAnn Fabrics** • 2217 NW 57th St [22nd Ave NW]
• **La Tienda Folk Art Gallery** •
2050 NW Market St [Russell Ave NW]
• **Ok Ok** • 5107 Ballard Ave NW [NW Dock Pl]
• **Olsen's Scandinavian Foods** •
2248 NW Market St [22nd Ave NW]
• **Re-Soul** • 5319 Ballard Ave NW [NW Vernon Pl]
• **The ReStore** • 1440 NW 52nd St [14th Ave NW]
• **Rudy's Barbershop** • 5512 20th Ave NW [NW Market St]
• **Second Ascent** • 5209 Ballard Ave NW [20th Ave NW]
• **Sonic Boom Records** • 2209 NW Market St [22nd Ave NW]
• **Velouria** • 2205 NW Market St [22nd Ave NW]

 Video Rental
• **Blockbuster** • 5900 15th Ave NW [NW 59th St]
• **Hollywood Video** • 5314 15th Ave NW [NW 53rd St]

Map 24 · **Fremont**

Once a haven for counterculture in Seattle, Fremont has gentrified in recent years. Getty Images, Adobe, and Google all have offices near the ship canal and the famous naked cyclists of the Solstice Parade now bike past high-end boutiques and a Peet's Coffee. Vladimir Lenin still glowers in mute disdain over yuppies and hippies alike.

Banks

- **Bank of America** • 3601 Stone Wy N [N 36th St]
- **Frontier Bank** • 601 N 34th St [Evanston Ave N]
- **US Bank (ATM)** • 5500 Phinney Ave N [N 55th St]

Car Washes

- **Brown Bear Car Wash** •
  3977 Leary Wy NW [NW 40th St]

Coffee

- **Caffe Ladro** • 452 N 36th St [Francis Ave N]
- **Candles Café** • 1060 N 39th St [Woodland Park Ave N]
- **Diva Espresso** • 4615 Stone Wy N [Stone Ave N]
- **Espresso Splendido** • 4110 Stone Wy N [N 41st St]
- **Espresso To Go** • 3512 Fremont Pl N [N 35th St]
- **Fremont Coffee** • 459 N 36th St [Francis Ave N]
- **Icon Coffee** • 4301 Fremont Ave N [N 43rd St]
- **Lighthouse Roasters** • 400 N 43rd St [Phinney Ave N]
- **Peet's Coffee & Tea** • 3401 Fremont Ave N [N 34th St]
- **Shortstop Espresso** • 4013 Leary Wy NW [NW 40th St]
- **Starbucks** • 3415B Fremont Ave N [N 34th St]

Community Gardens

Gas Stations

- **76** • 4600 Fremont Ave N [N 46th St]
- **Chevron** • 1420 N 45th St [Interlake Ave N]
- **Shell** • 3950 Leary Wy NW [NW Bowdoin Pl]
- **Shell** • 4605 Fremont Ave N [N 46th St]

Landmarks

- **Aurora Bridge** • Aurora Ave N & N 34th St
- **Fremont Rocket** • 601 N 35th St [Evanston Ave N]
- **Fremont Troll** • N 36th St & Troll Ave N
- **Statue of Vladimir Lenin** •
  600 N 36th St [Evanston Ave N]
- **Waiting for the Interurban** •
  N 34th St & Fremont Ave N

Libraries

- **Fremont Branch** • 731 N 35th St [Fremont Ave N]

Parking

Post Offices

- **Wallingford** • 1329 N 47th St [Stone Wy N]

Schools

- **Bf Day** • 3921 Linden Ave N [N 39th St]
- **Garfield High** • 4400 Interlake Ave N [N 44th St]
- **Hazel Wolf High** • 1310 N 45th St [Stone Wy N]
- **Northwest Montessori** •
  4910 Phinney Ave N [N 49th St]
- **Pacific Crest** • 600 NW Bright St [6th Ave NW]

Map 24 · **Fremont**

N

Woodland Park Loop

N 56th St

N Argyle Pl

N 55th St

N 55th St

NW 54th St

N 54th St

N 54th St

N 54th St

N 53rd St

NW 52nd St

N 53rd St

30

Woodland Park

PAGE **234**

N 55th St

N 54th St

N 53rd St

N 52nd St

N 51st St

7th Ave NW

6th Ave NW

5th Ave NW

4th Ave NW

NW 56th St

N 57th St

2nd Ave NW

1st Ave NW

N 54th St

N 53rd St

N 52nd St

Baker Ave NW

3rd Ave NW

2nd Ave NW

Palatine Ave N

Phinney Ave N

Aurora Ave N

Ashworth Ave N

A

NW 51st St

NW 50th St

N 50th St

N 50th St

99

N 51st St

8th Ave NW

NW Market St

NW 49th St

NW 47th St

NW 47th St

NW 46th St

Greenwood Ave N

Dayton Ave N

Evanston Ave N

Fremont Ave N

Linden Ave N

N Phinney Way

N 45th St

N 50th St

Whitman Ave N

Green Lake Way N

N Midvale Pl

N 49th St

N 48th St

N 47th St

N 46th St

N 45th St

Stone Way N

2

123

N 45th St

NW 44th St

N 45th St

25

8th Ave NW

7th Ave NW

6th Ave NW

5th Ave NW

4th Ave NW

3rd Ave NW

2nd Ave NW

1st Ave NW

Baker Ave NW

Palatine Ave N

N Allen Pl

N 44th St

N 44th St

Winslow Pl N

N 43rd St

N Allen Pl

N 44th St

B

NW 43rd St

NW 42nd St

NW 41st St

NW 40th St

NW Bowdoin Pl

Leary Way NW

Francis Ave N

N 43rd St

N 42nd St

N 41st St

N Motor Pl

N 43rd St

N 42nd St

Dayton Ave N

Evanston Ave N

Phinney Ave N

Aurora Ave N

N Allen Pl

Whitman Ave N

Woodland Park Ave N

Midvale Ave N

Stone Way N

Interlake Ave N

Ashworth Ave N

N Menford Pl

N 42nd St

N Lucas Pl

N 40

N Dorothy Pl

NW 39th St

NW Bowdoin Pl

N Bowdoin Pl

Francis Ave N

Greenwood Ave N

Dayton Ave N

Evanston Ave N

Fremont Ave N

Fremont Way N

Linden Ave N

N 40th St

N 39th St

Winslow Pl N

Bridge Way N

Stone Way N

Interlake Ave N

Ashworth Ave N

Carr Pl N

N 38th St

N 38th Ct

N 37th St

C

W Cremona St

W Aetna St

13

NW Canal St

W Bertona St

N 34th St

N 34th St

Palatine Ave N

Fremont Ave N

Fremont Ln N

2

3

2

3

3

5

3

NW 35th St

NW 36th St

Albion Pl N

Woodland Park Ave N

Stone Way N

Interlake Ave N

Ashworth Ave N

NW 35th St

Lake Washington Canal

W Cremona St

W Dravus St

W Etruria St

W Fiorentia St

W Cremona St

W Cremona Ave W

Queen Anne Ave N

3rd Ave N

Nickerson St

Fremont Brdg

Aurora Brdg

N Northlake Way

N Northlake Way

N Northlake Pl

Lake Union

W Barrett St

W Barrett St

W Fiorentia St

Florentia St

3rd Ave N

W Fulton St

| 1/4 mile | .25 km |

Though it lacks quite a few practical amenities, Fremont has more cool shops than you have fingers and possibly more Thai restaurants per capita than Bangkok. Rare and precious, however, are the meaty Cuban sandwiches at Paseo and the low-brow Britishness of the George & Dragon. Beware of Fremont nightlife: the classiness of a bar is often inversely proportional to that of its clientele.

 Copy Shops
- **University Reprographics** •
  3806 Woodland Park Ave N [N 38th St]
- **UPS Store** • 3518 Fremont Ave N [N 35th St]

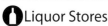 Hardware Stores
- **Hard Hat Tool & Supply** • 3506 Stone Wy N [N 35th St]
- **Stoneway Hardware & Supply** •
  4318 Stone Wy N [NW 43rd St]

Liquor Stores
- **Washington State Liquor Store** • 1300 N 45th St [Stone Wy N]

Movie Theaters
- **Fremont Original Outdoor Cinema (May–Sept)** •
  N 35th St & Phinney Ave N

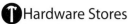 Nightlife
- **Brouwer's Café** • 400 N 35th St [Phinney Ave N]
- **The Buckaroo Tavern** • 4201 Fremont Ave N [N 42nd St]
- **El Camino** • 607 N 35th St [Evanston Ave N]
- **George & Dragon Pub** • 206 N 36th St [Palatine Ave NW]
- **High Dive** • 513 N 36th St [Dayton Ave N]
- **Nectar Lounge** • 412 N 36th St [1st Ave NW]
- **Norm's Eatery and Ale House** • 460 N 36th St [Palatine Ave NW]
- **The Pacific Inn** • 3501 Stone Wy N [N 35th St]
- **Smash** • 1401 N 45th St [Interlake Ave N]
- **Triangle Lounge** • 3507 Fremont Pl N [Evanston Ave N]]
- **Tost Lounge** • 513 N 36th St Space E [Dayton Ave N]

Pet Shops
- **Railey's Leash & Treat** • 513 N 36th St [Dayton Ave N]

Restaurants
- **35th Street Bistro** • 709 N 35th St [Freemont Ave N]
- **Art of the Table** • 1054 N 39th St [Whitman Ave N]
- **Asteroid Café** • 3601 Fremont Ave N [N 36th St]
- **Bizzarro Italian Café** • 1307 N 46th St [Stone Wy N]
- **Blue C Sushi** • 3411 Fremont Ave N [N 34th St]
- **Brad's Swingside Café** • 4212 Fremont Ave N [N 42nd St]
- **Brouwer's Café** • 400 N 35th St [Phinney Ave N]
- **Chillies Paste** • 119 N 36th St [1st Ave NW]
- **Chiso** • 3520 Fremont Ave N [N 35th St]
- **Costa's Opa Greek Restaurant** •
  3400 Fremont Ave N [N 34th St]
- **Dad Watson's** • 3601 Fremont Ave N [N 36th St]
- **Eggs Cetera's Blue Star Café** • 4512 Stone Wy N [N 45th St]
- **El Camino** • 607 N 35th St [Evanston Ave N]

- **Jai Thai** • 3423 Fremont Ave N [N 34th St]
- **Kidd Valley** • 4910 Green Lake Way N [Stone Ave N]
- **Kwanjai Thai** • 469 N 36th St [Francis Ave N]
- **Le Gourmand** • 425 NW Market St [5th Ave NW]
- **Musashi's** • 1400 N 45th St [Interlake Ave N]
- **Paseo** • 4225 Fremont Ave N [N 42nd St]
- **Persimmon** • 4256 Fremont Ave N [N 43rd St]
- **Postmark Gelato** • 3526 Fremont Pl N [N 35th St]
- **The Red Door** • 3401 Evanston Ave N [N 34th St]
- **Perche No Pasta & Vino** •
  1319 N 49th St [Green Lake Way N]
- **Pontevecchio** • 710 N 34th St [Fremont Ave N]
- **Rocking Wok** • 4301 Interlake Ave N [N 43rd St]
- **Roxy's Deli** • 462 N 36th St [Francis Ave N]
- **Silence-Heart-Nest** • 3508 Fremont Pl N [N 35th St]
- **Simply Desserts** • 3421 Fremont Ave N [N 34th St]
- **Tawon Thai** • 3410 Fremont Ave N [N 34th St]
- **Tutta Bella Neopolitan Pizzeria** •
  4411 Stone Wy N [N 44th St]

 Shopping
- **Bliss** • 3501 Fremont Ave N [Freemont Pl N]
- **Blue Video** • 4100 Aurora Ave N [N 41st St]
- **Deluxe Junk** • 3518 Fremont Pl N [N 35th St]
- **Desteenation Shirt Co.** • 3412 Evanston Ave N [N 34th St]
- **Electric Vehicles Northwest** • 110 N 36th St [1st Ave NW]
- **Enexile** • 611 N 35th St [Evanston Ave N]
- **Fremont Antique Mall** • 3419 Fremont Pl N [Freemont Ave]
- **Fremont News** • 3416 Fremont Ave N [N 34th St]
- **Fremont Sunday Market** • N 34th St & Phinney Ave
- **Fusion Beads** • 3830 Stone Wy N [N 38th St]
- **Goodwind's Kites** • 3420 Stone Wy N [N 34th St]
- **The Indoor Sun Shoppe** • 160 N Canal St [Phinney Ave N]
- **The Industry** • 3516 Fremont Pl N [N 35th St]
- **Jive Time Records** • 3506 Fremont Ave N [Freemont Pl N]
- **PCC Natural Markets** • 600 N 34th St [Evanston Ave N]
- **Portage Bay Goods** • 706 N 34th St [Freemont Ave N]
- **Private Screening** • 3504 Fremont Pl N [N 35th St]
- **Rudy's Barbershop** • 475 N 36th St [Dayton Ave N]
- **Sonic Boom Records** • 3414 Fremont Ave N [N 34th St]
- **Twice Sold Tales** • 3504 Fremont Ave N [Freemont Pl N]

Video Rental
- **Rain City Video** • 464 N 36th St [Francis Ave N]
- **Rain City Video** • 719 NW Market St [7th Ave NW]
- **Video Isle** • 4459 Fremont Ave N [N 45th St]

Map 25 • **Wallingford**

Thanks to the enormous sign atop the local QFC supermarket (a nod to the old Food Giant sign), visitors know when they reach Wallingford. With Woodland Park and Green Lake to the north and Gas Works Park to the south, the neighborhood has a Sunday afternoon vibe all week long. This somewhat sleepy residential neighborhood hosts multiple summer food festivals and is home to the original Dick's Drive-In.

Banks
• **Washington Mutual** • 1919 N 45th St [Burke Ave N]
• **Wells Fargo** • 1701 N 45th St [Densmore Ave N]

Coffee
• **Chocolati Cafe** • 1716 N 45th St [Densmore Ave]
• **Essential Baking Company** •
  1604 N 34th St [Woodlawn Ave N]
• **Palazzo** • 1906 N 34th St [Burke Ave N]
• **Starbucks** • 2110 N 45th St [Meridian Ave N]
• **Tea House Kuan Yin** • 1911 N 45th St [Burke Ave N]
• **Tully's** • 2100 N 45th St [Meridian Ave N]

Community Gardens

Gas Stations
• **Shell** • 210 NE 45th St [2nd Ave NE]

Landmarks
• **The Blue Moon Tavern** • 712 NE 45th St [7th Ave NE]
• **Dick's Drive-In** • 111 NE 45th St [1st ave NE]
• **Gas Works Park** • 2101 N Northlake Wy [Meridian Ave N]
• **Sadako and the Thousand Cranes Peace Park** •
  NE Pacific St & NE 40th St

Libraries
• **Wallingford Branch** • 1501 N 45th St [Woodlawn Ave N]

Pharmacies
• **Bartell Drugs** • 1820 N 45th St [Wallingford Ave N]
• **Bartell Drugs** • 4700 4th Ave NE [NE 47th St]

Schools
• **Hamilton Int'L Middle** • 1610 N 41 St [Woodlawn Ave N]
• **J Stanford International Elementary** •
  4057 5th Ave NE [NE 42nd St]
• **The Meridian** • 4649 Sunnyside Ave N [NE 50th St]
• **St Benedict Elementary and Middle** •
  4811 Wallingford Ave N [NE 48th St]

 Supermarkets
• **Quality Food Center** •
  1801 N 45th St [Wallingford Ave N]

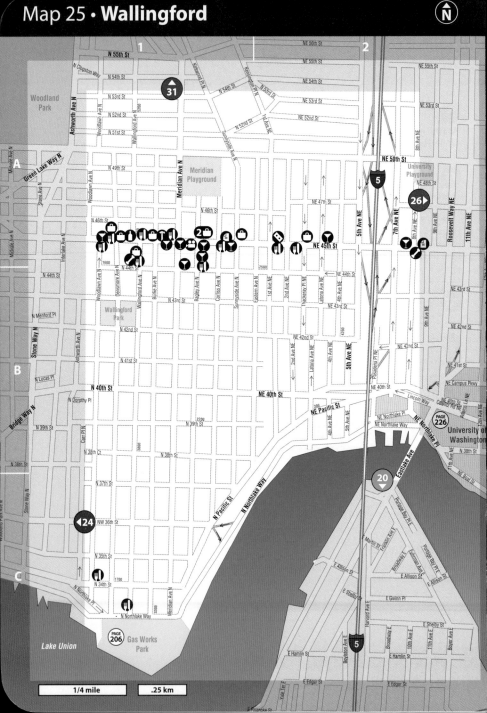

Map 25 · Wallingford

While Wallingford's portion of 45th Street isn't much of a weekend destination, there are more than enough bars, restaurants, and cafés to make a night of it. Al's is our favorite little hole in the wall with Moon Temple running a close second. Happily spend your entire paycheck at Bottleworks—the beer selection is incredible. Or fill your backpack at Wide World of Books & Maps, a Seattle institution since the '70s.

Copy Shops
- **FedEx Kinko's** • 810 NE 45th St [8th Ave NE]
- **UPS Store** • 2311 N 45th St [Corliss Ave N]

Hardware Stores
- **Tweedy & Popp Ace Hardware** • 1916 N 45th St [Burke Ave N]

Liquor Stores
- **City Cellars Fine Wines** • 1710 N 45th St, Ste 1 [Densmore Ave N]

Movie Theaters
- **Landmark Guild 45th** • 2115 N 45th St [Meridian Ave N]

Nightlife
- **Al's Tavern** • 2303 N 45th St [Corliss Ave N]
- **Blue Moon Tavern** • 712 NE 45th St [7th Ave NE]
- **Goldie's on 45th** • 2121 N 45th St [Meridian Ave N]
- **Kate's Pub** • 309 NE 45th St [Latona Ave NE]
- **May Restaurant and Lounge** • 1612 N 45th St [Woodlawn Ave N]
- **Moon Temple** • 2108 N 45th St [Meridian Ave N]
- **Murphy's Pub** • 1928 N 45th St [Burke Ave N]
- **Sea Monster Lounge** • 2202 N 45th St [Bagley Ave N]

Pet Shops
- **Four Legs Good** • 4411 Wallingford Ave N [N 44th St]
- **Petco - Seattle** • 809 NE 45th St [8th Ave NE]

Restaurants
- **Boulangerie** • 2200 N 45th St [Bagley Ave N]
- **Chinoise Café** • 1618 N 45th St [Woodlawn Ave N]
- **Chutney's Bistro** • 1815 N 45th St [Wallingford Ave N]
- **Dick's Drive-In** • 111 NE 45th St [1st Ave NW]
- **Elemental@Gasworks** • 3309 Wallingford Ave N [N Northlake Wy]
- **Essential Baking Company** • 1604 N 34th St [Woodlawn Ave N]
- **Joule** • 1913 N 45th St [Burke Ave N]
- **Julia's** • 4401 Wallingford Ave N [N 44th St]
- **Kabul Afghan Cuisine** • 2301 N 45th St [Corliss Ave N]
- **May Restaurant and Lounge** • 1612 N 45th St [Woodlawn Ave N]
- **Molly Moon's** • 1622 N 45th St [Woodlawn Ave N]
- **Rancho Bravo Tacos** • 211 NE 45th St [2nd Ave NE]

Shopping
- **Bottleworks** • 1710 N 45th St [Densmore Ave N]
- **Comics Dungeon** • 250 NE 45th St [Thackeray Pl NE]
- **The Erotic Bakery** • 2323 N 45th St [Corliss Ave N]
- **I Do Bridal** • 2206 N 45th St [Bagley Ave N]
- **Open Books: A Poem Emporium** • 2414 N 45th St [Sunnyside Ave N]
- **Trophy Cupcakes** • 1815 N 45th St [Wallingford Ave]
- **Wide World Books & Maps** • 4411 Wallingford Ave N [N 44th St]

Video Rental
- **Hollywood Video** • 118 NE 45th St [1st Ave NW]

Map 26 · **U District**

N

NE 60th St

2

NE 59th St
NE 58th St
NE 57th St
NE 56th St
NE 55th St

NE Ravenna Blvd

Twin Maple Ln NE

NE 58th St

NE Park Rd

18th Ave NE

NE 58th Ave NE

Ravenna Park

25th Ave NE

NE 57th St

26th Ave NE

30th Ave NE

31st Ave NE

33rd Ave NE

34th Ave NE

Cowen Pl

NE 57th St

NE 55th Pl

Ravenna Ave NE

NE 55th St

NE 55th St

NE 54th St

NE 54th St

31

32

A

NE 53rd St

Scarecrow Video

50th Ave NE

NE 52nd St

22nd Ave NE

NE 53rd Pl
NE 53rd St
52nd Ave NE
NE 51st St

24th Ave NE

NE Blakeley St

NE 53rd St
NE 52nd St

30th Ave NE

Calvary Catholic Cemetery

NE 50th St

12th Ave NE

Brooklyn Ave NE

16th Ave NE

17th Ave NE

18th Ave NE

19th Ave NE

20th Ave NE

21st Ave NE

NE 50th St

NE 48th St

P

NE 49th St

University Village

NE University Village

NE 48th St

University View PL NE

University View Pl NE

32nd Ave NE

34th Ave NE

NE 50th St

NE 48th St

NE 50th St

NE 47th St

NE University Village

NE 47th St

Union Bay Pl NE

NE Blakeley St

NE 45th St E

11th Ave NE

9th Ave NE

Roosevelt Way NE

NE 47th St

NE 46th St

NE 45th St

Union Bay Pl NE

University Way NE

NE 45th St

Mary Gates Memorial Dr NE

NE 44th St

NE 43rd St

25th Ave NE

$

NE 43rd St

NE 42nd St

25

P

NE 42nd St

Memorial Way

NE 42nd St

7th Ave NE

8th Ave NE

B

NE Campus Pkwy

12th Ave NE

NE 41st St

$

$

Red Square

PAGE 226

$

27

Cowlitz Rd NE

Lincoln Way

NE 40th St

University Way NE

NE 38th St

$

11th Ave NE

Wall of Death

University of Washington

NE Boat St

NE Northlake Way

University Brdg

Montlake Blvd NE

NE Pacific St

Stevens Way

Union Bay

NE Boat St

NE Pacific St

NE Pacific Pl

Husky Stadium

PAGE 242

Portage Bay PL E

Franklin Ave E

Roosevelt Ave E

10th Ave E

E Allison St

E Allison St

Gwinn Pl

C

20

2 $

Lake Washington Canal

Portage Bay

Montlake Brdg

21

22

Broadway E

10th Ave E

11th Ave E

Boyer Ave E

E Shelby St

E Edgar St

Montlake Blvd E

24th Ave E

E Shelby St

E Hamlin St

26th Ave E

E Park Dr E

NE Pacific St

520

E North St

E University Blvd

E Roanoke St

| 1/4 mile | .25 km |

The U-Dub boasts an impeccable reputation as a bastion of higher learning—after all, Bruce Lee once studied here. The campus is as charming as enrollment brochures suggest, but the surrounding area is an unlikely collision of thug-lifers, rah-rah collegiate types, meth-damaged street hustlers, and stubborn eccentrics. The U District has been designated an "alcohol impact zone," banning certain types of beverages from package stores, so plan ahead if you need some fortified wine for a sorority party.

Banks

- **Bank of America** • 4701 University Wy NE [NE 47th St]
- **Key Bank** • 1300 NE 45th St [Brooklyn Ave NE]
- **Key Bank** • 4501 27th Ave NE [University Village Pl NE]
- **Key Bank (ATM)** •
  2690 NE University Vlg [University Village Pl NE]
- **US Bank** • University of Washington, HUB Bldg
- **US Bank (ATM)** • 1959 NE Pacific St [NE Pacific Pl]
- **US Bank (ATM)** • 3900 Montlake Blvd NE [25th Ave NE]
- **US Bank (ATM)** • 4245 Roosevelt Wy NE [NE 42nd St]
- **US Bank (ATM)** • University of Washington–
  Odegaard Undergraduate Library
- **US Bank (ATM)** • University of Washington–
  South Campus Ctr Bldg
- **Washington Federal Savings** •
  1200 NE 45th St [12th Ave NE]
- **Washington Mutual** • 4300 Brooklyn Ave NE [NE 43rd St]
- **Washington Mutual** • 4907 25th Ave NE [NE 49th St]
- **Wells Fargo** • 4100 University Wy NE [NE 41st St]
- **Wells Fargo** • 4500 University Wy NE [NE 45th St]

 Coffee

- **Bean & Bagel** • 1410 NE 40th St [University Wy NE]
- **Café Allegro Expresso Bar** •
  4214 University Wy NE [NE 42nd St]
- **Café on the Ave** • 4201 University Wy NE [NE 42nd St]
- **Caffe Appassionato** • 4518 University Wy NE [NE 45th St]
- **Starbucks** • 2650 NE 49th St [25th Ave NE]
- **Starbucks** • 4147 University Wy NE [NE 41st St]
- **Starbucks** • 4555 University Wy NE [NE 45th St]
- **Sureshot Espresso** • 4505 University Wy NE [NE 45th St]
- **Trabant Coffee & Chai** • 1309 NE 45th St [Brooklyn Ave NE]
- **Tully's** • 3042 NE 45th St [Union Bay Pl NE]
- **Tully's** • 4507 Brooklyn Ave NE [NE 45th St]
- **Tully's** • 4700 University Wy NE [NE 47th St]
- **Yunnie Bubble Tea** • 4511 University Wy NE [NE 45th St]

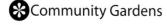 Community Gardens

Gas Stations

- **76** • 5100 25th Ave NE [NE Blakely St]
- **Chevron** • 4700 Brooklyn Ave NE [NE 47th St]
- **Shell** • 1013 NE 45th St [Roosevelt Wy NE]

Emergency Rooms

- **University of Washington Medical Center** •
  1959 NE Pacific St [NE Pacific Pl]

Landmarks

- **Red Square** • University of Washington
- **Scarecrow Video** • 5030 Roosevelt Wy NE [NE 50th St]
- **Wall of Death** •
  Burke Gilman Trail Under the University Bridge

 Libraries

- **University Branch** • 5009 Roosevelt Wy NE [NE 50th St]

Parking

Pharmacies

- **Bartell Drug Store** •
  2700 NE University Vlg [University Village Pl NE]
- **Bartell Drug Store** • 4344 University Wy NE [NE 45th St]
- **QFC** • 2746 NE 45th St [Union Bay Pl NE]
- **Rite Aid Pharmacies** • 4535 University Wy NE [NE 45th St]
- **Walgreens** • 1205 NE 50th St [12th Ave NE]

Post Offices

- **University** • 4244 University Wy NE [NE 43rd St]

Schools

- **Experimental Education Unit** •
  1959 NE Pacific St [NE Pacific Pl]
- **La Escuelita Billingual** • 2500 NE 49th St [25th Ave NE]
- **Menachem Mendel Seattle Cheder** •
  4541 19th Ave NE [NE 45th St]
- **University Child Development** •
  5062 9th Ave NE [NE 53rd St]
- **University Of Washington** • NE 45th St & 15th Ave NE

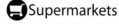 Supermarkets

- **Safeway** • 3020 NE 45th St [Union Bay Place NE]
- **Safeway** • 4732 Brooklyn Ave NE [NE 47th St]
- **Trader Joe's** • 4555 Roosevelt Wy NE [N 45th St]

Map 26 · U District

N

31
32
25
27
20
21
22

NE 59th St
Cowl Pl
NE 58th St
NE Ravenna Blvd
NE 57th St
NE 56th St
NE 55th St
NE 55th Pl
Ravenna Park
NE 55th St
NE 54th St
NE 53rd St
NE 52nd St
NE 50th St
NE 48th St
NE 47th St
NE 45th St

Twin Maple Ln NE
NE 60th St
NE 57th St
NE 57th St
NE 55th St
NE 54th St
NE 53rd St
NE Blakeley St

Calvary Catholic Cemetery

NE 49th St
NE 48th St
NE University Village
University Village
NE 50th St

Union Bay Pl NE
NE 45th St

Mary Gates Memorial Dr NE
Union Bay Pl NE

NE 43rd
NE 42nd

Roosevelt Way NE
11th Ave NE
12th Ave NE
Brooklyn Ave NE
15th Ave NE
16th Ave NE
17th Ave NE
18th Ave NE
19th Ave NE
20th Ave NE
21st Ave NE

7th Ave NE
8th Ave NE
9th Ave NE

NE 53rd St
NE 52nd St
NE 50th St
NE 48th St

NE 43rd St
NE 42nd St
NE 42nd St
NE 41st St
NE Campus Pkwy
NE 40th St
Cowlitz Rd NE
Lincoln Way
NE 38th St

University Way NE
Memorial Way
Stevens Way

PAGE 226

University of Washington

NE Pacific St
NE Pacific Pl

Husky Stadium
PAGE 242

Union Bay

NE Boat St
NE Boat St
11th Ave NE
12th Ave NE

University Bdg
NE Northlake Way

Portage Bay

Lake Washington Canal
Montlake Blvd E
Montlake Bdg
Montlake Blvd NE

Portage Bay Pl E
Franklin Ave E
Broadway E
Harvard Ave E
E Allison St
E Allison St

E Shelby St
E Hamlin St
E Shelby St
E Park Dr
W Park Dr

E Edgar St
E Roanoke St
Gwinn Pl
E University Bdg
E North St

520

Boyer Ave E

1/4 mile   .25 km

25th Ave NE
30th Ave NE
31st Ave NE
33rd Ave NE
34th Ave NE
35th Ave NE
University View Pl NE
32nd Ave NE
NE Blakeley St

22nd Ave NE
Ravenna Ave NE

Kai's makes the best Manhattan in the city, but for serious drinking, head over to Earl's, that place with the black facade and chicken wire instead of windows. During happy hour, a PINT of well booze is $3. Thai food reigns supreme, with seemingly dozens of joints on every block varying wildly in quality and price. Thai Tom is worth the long wait for a seat, but check out the slightly less delicious Thai 65 if you're in a hurry. Memo's slings burritos 24/7. Pho Thân Brothers' blows away the copious competition.

Copy Shops

- **Avenue Copy Center** •
  4141 University Wy NE [NE 41st St]
- **FedEx Kinko's** • 3042 NE 45th St [Union Bay Pl NE]
- **Minuteman Press** •
  1006 NE 50th St [Roosevelt Wy NE]
- **Office Depot** • 4900 25th Ave NE [NE 49th St]
- **Rams Copy Center** •
  4144 University Wy NE [NE 42nd St]
- **UPS Store** • 4616 25th Ave NE [Ne 45th St]

Farmers Markets

- **University District**
  (Sat, 9 am–2 pm, May–Dec) •
  University Wy NE & NE 50th St

Gyms

- **Curves** • 4530 Union Bay Pl NE [NE 45th St]
- **University Fitness** •
  4511 Roosevelt Wy NE [NE 45th St]

Hardware Stores

- **Hardwick's** • 4214 Roosevelt Wy NE [NE 42nd St]
- **University Hardware True Value** •
  4731 University Wy NE [NE 47th St]

Liquor Stores

- **Dawgpound** •
  5201 University Wy NE [NE 52nd St]
- **Washington State Liquor Store** •
  2746 NE 45th St [Union Bay Pl NE]

Movie Theaters

- **Grand Illusion Cinema** •
  1403 NE 50th St [NE 50th St]
- **Landmark Metro Cinemas** •
  4500 9th Ave NE [NE 45th St]
- **Landmark Neptune Theatre** •
  1303 NE 45th St [Brooklyn Ave NE]
- **Landmark Seven Gables Theatre** •
  911 NE 50th St [9th Ave NE]
- **Landmark Varsity Theatre** •
  4329 University Wy NE [NE 43rd St]

Nightlife

- **Big Time Brewery & Alehouse** •
  4133 University Wy NE [NE 41st St]
- **College Inn Pub** •
  4006 University Wy NE [NE 40th St]
- **Dante's** • 5300 Roosevelt Wy NE [NE 53rd St]
- **Earl's on the Ave** •
  4333 University Wy NE [NE 45th St]
- **Flowers Bar & Restaurant** •
  4247 University Wy NE [NE 43rd St]
- **Galway Arms** •
  5257 University Wy NE [NE 52nd St]

- **Monkey Pub** •
  5305 Roosevelt Wy NE [NE 53rd St]

Pet Shops

- **Mud Bay - University Village** •
  4612 25th Ave NE [NE 45th St]

Restaurants

- **Agua Verde** • 1303 NE Boat St [Brooklyn Ave NE]
- **Aladdin Gyrocery** •
  4541 University Wy NE [NE 45th St]
- **Araya's Vegetarian Place** •
  1121 NE 45th St [11th Ave Ne]
- **Atlas Foods** •
  2675 NE Village Ln [University Village Pl NE]
- **Blue C Sushi** • 4601 26th Ave NE [NE Blakeley St]
- **Burger & Kabob Hut** •
  4142 University Wy NE [NE 41st St]
- **Cedars** • 4757 12th Ave NE [NE 50th St]
- **Chaco Canyon Café** •
  4759 Brooklyn Ave NE [NE 50th St]
- **Ciao Bella** • 3626 NE 46th St [NE 38th St]
- **Delfino's Chicago Style Pizzeria** •
  2631 NE University Vlg [NE 47th St]
- **Flowers Bar & Restaurant** •
  4247 University Wy NE [NE 43rd St]
- **Hillside Quickie's** •
  4106 Brooklyn Ave NE [NE 41st St]
- **Jimmy John's** •
  4141 University Wy NE [NE 41st St]
- **Kai's Bistro & Lounge** •
  1312 NE 43rd St [Brooklyn Ave NE]
- **La Casa Del Mojito** •
  5253 University Way NE [NE 52nd St]
- **Mamma Melina** •
  4759 Roosevelt Wy NE [NE 50th St]
- **Matt's Famous Chili Dogs** •
  1301 NE 45th St [Brooklyn Ave NE]
- **Memo's Mexican Food** •
  4743 University Wy NE [NE 47th St]
- **Orange King** • 1411 NE 42nd St [University Wy NE]
- **Pagliacci Pizza** •
  4529 University Wy NE [NE 45th St]
- **Pam's Kitchen** •
  5000 University Wy NE [NE 50th St]
- **Paoli's Pizza and Pasta** •
  4510 University Wy NE [NE 45th St]
- **Pasta & Co** • 4622 26th Ave NE
  [NE University Village]
- **Pho Thân Brothers'** •
  4207 University Wy NE [NE 42nd St]
- **Pho Vietnam 2** •
  4235 University Wy NE [NE 42nd St]
- **Portage Bay Café** •
  4130 Roosevelt Wy NE [NE 42nd St]
- **Ruby** • 4241 University Wy NE [NE 42nd St]
- **Shultzy's Sausage** •
  4114 University Wy NE [NE 41st St]
- **Tandoor Indian Restaurant** •
  5024 University Wy NE [NE 50th St]
- **Thai 65** • 4214 University Wy NE [NE 42nd St]

- **Thai Tom** • 4543 University Wy NE [NE 45th St]
- **Thaiger Room** •
  4228 University Wy NE [NE 42nd St]

Shopping

- **American Apparel** •
  4345 University Wy NE [NE 45th St]
- **Anthropologie** •
  2520 NE University Village [25th Ave NE]
- **Buffalo Exchange** •
  4530 University Wy NE [NE 45th St]
- **Bulldog News** •
  4208 University Wy NE [NE 42nd St]
- **Cellophane Square** •
  4538 University Wy NE [NE 45th St]
- **Cinema Books** •
  4753 Roosevelt Wy NE [NE 50th St]
- **Fireworks** •
  2617 NE Village Ln [University Village Pl NE]
- **Gargoyles Sanctuary** •
  4550 University Wy NE [NE 45th St]
- **Half Price Books** •
  4709 Roosevelt Wy NE [NE 47th St]
- **Hardwick's** • 4214 Roosevelt Wy NE [NE 42nd St]
- **Magus Bookstore** •
  1408 NE 42nd St [University Wy NE]
- **Recycled Cycle** • 1007 NE Boat St [11th Ave NE]
- **Red Light Vintage Clothing** •
  4560 University Wy NE [NE 45th St]
- **Rudy's Barbershop** •
  4738 University Wy NE [NE 47th St]
- **Scarecrow Video** •
  5030 Roosevelt Wy NE [NE 50th St]
- **Sephora** • 2618 NE University Village
  [University Village Pl NE]
- **Shiga's Imports** •
  4306 University Wy NE [NE 43rd St]
- **Something Silver** •
  4628 Village Ct NE [University Place NE]
- **Tiger Tiger** • 4321 University Wy NE [NE 43rd St]
- **Trader Joe's** •
  4555 Roosevelt Wy NE [NE 47th St]
- **Twice Sold Tales** •
  4501 University Wy NE [NE 45th St]
- **University Bookstore** •
  4326 University Wy NE [NE 43rd St]
- **University True Value Hardware** •
  4731 University Way NE [NE 47th Street]
- **University Village** • 2624 NE University
  Village [University Village Pl NE]
- **Weaving Works, Inc** •
  4717 Brooklyn Ave NE [NE 47th St]
- **Wooly Mammoth** •
  4303 University Wy NE [NE 43rd St]
- **Zanadu Comics** •
  1307 NE 45th St [Brooklyn Ave NE]

Video Rental

- **Blockbuster** • 4715 25th Ave NE [24th Ave NE]
- **Scarecrow Video** •
  5030 Roosevelt Wy NE [NE 50th St]

Map 27 · **Laurelhurst / Wedgwood / Sand Point** Ⓝ

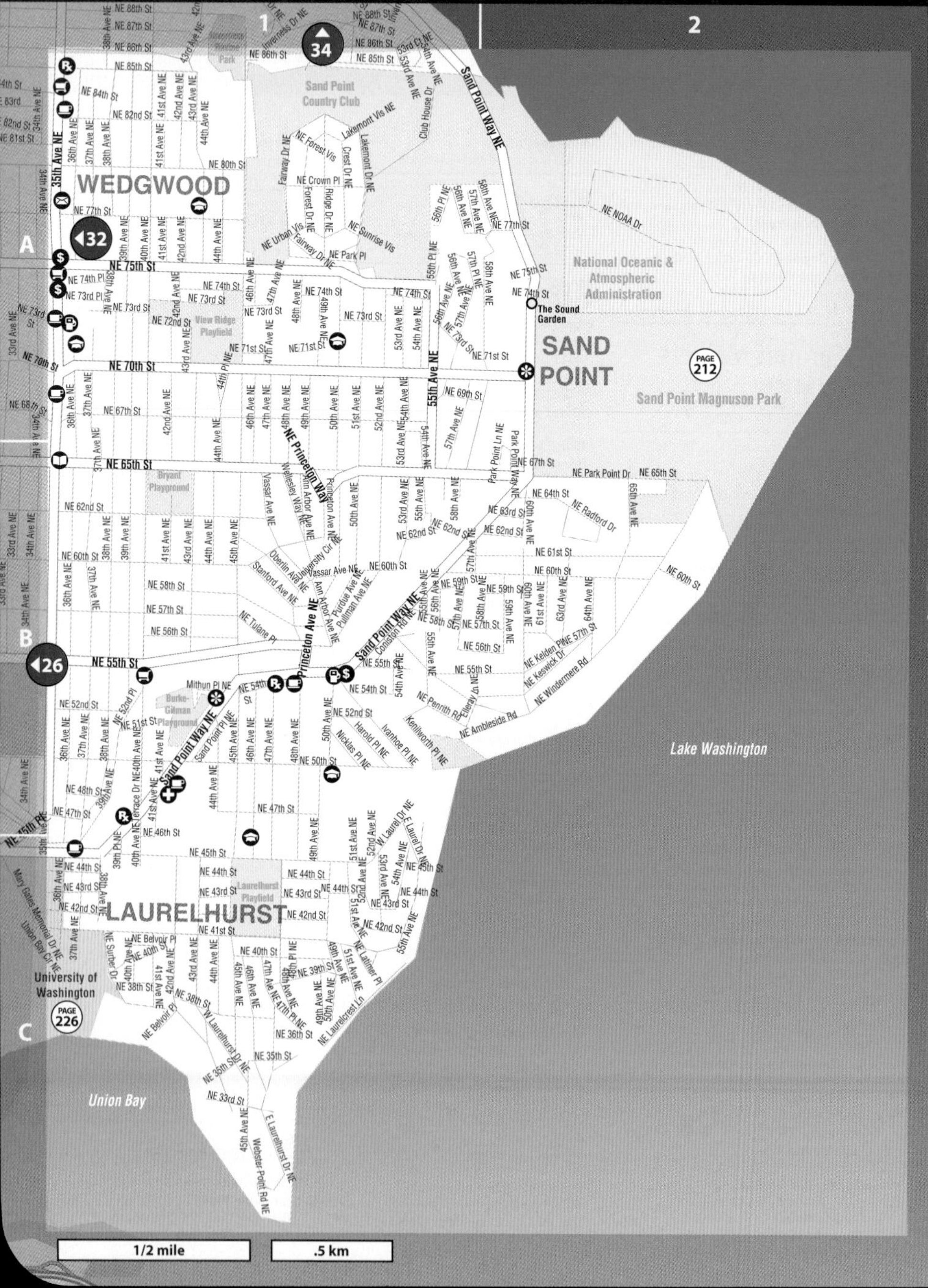

WEDGWOOD

SAND POINT

LAURELHURST

Sand Point Country Club

National Oceanic & Atmospheric Administration

Sand Point Magnuson Park

The Sound Garden

University of Washington

Lake Washington

Union Bay

View Ridge Playfield

Bryant Playground

Burke-Gilman Playground

Laurelhurst Playfield

Mary Gates Memorial Dr NE

PAGE 212

PAGE 226

1/2 mile

.5 km

The half-dozen 'hoods northeast of UW make up "Seattle's First Suburb": a nice, quiet place that's good for, um, raising kids. Its identity mimics the UW profs who live here: homogenous, overly-intellectual, and passive. Seattle's second-largest Jewish community (after Rainier Beach) dwells in Wedgwood/ View Ridge, which explains the synagogues, temples, Jewish Library, Jewish Community Center, bagels, and Universalist Unitarians.

Banks

- **Washington Federal Savings** •
  7334 35th Ave NE [NE 73rd St]
- **Washington Mutual** •
  5464 Sand Point Wy NE [Ivanhoe Pl NE]
- **Washington Mutual** • 7512 35 Ave NE [NE 75th St]

Coffee

- **Café Van Gogh** • 8210 35th Ave NE [NE 82nd St]
- **The Coffee Crew** • 3614 NE 45th St [37th Ave NE]
- **Gretchens Place** •
  5432 Sand Point Wy NE [Princeton Ave NE]
- **Starbucks** • 7303 35th Ave NE [NE 73rd St]
- **Top Pot Donuts** • 6855 35th Ave NE [NE 70th St]
- **Tully's** • 4800 Sand Point Wy NE [41st Ave NE]

Community Gardens

Gas Stations

- **Chevron** • 7300 35th Ave NE [NE 73rd St]
- **76** • 5450 Sand Point Wy NE [Ivanhoe Pl NE]

Emergency Rooms

- **Children's Hospital and Regional Medical Center** •
  4800 Sand Point Wy NE [41st Ave NE]

Landmarks

- **The Sound Garden** •
  7400 Sand Point Wy NE [NE 74th St]

Libraries

- **North East Branch** • 6801 35th Ave NE [NE 65th St]

Pharmacies

- **Katterman's Sand Point Pharmacy** •
  5400 Sand Point Wy NE [47th Ave NE]
- **Rite Aid** • 8500 35th Ave NE [NE 85th Ave]
- **Sand Point Clinic Pharmacy** •
  4575 Sand Point Wy NE [40th Ave NE]

Post Offices

- **Wedgwood** • 7724 35th Ave NE [NE 77th St]

Schools

- **Alternative Elementary #2 (Decatur)** •
  7711 43rd Ave NE [NE 77th St]
- **Concordia Lutheran** • 7040 36th Ave NE [NE 70th St]
- **Laurelhurst Elementary** •
  4530 46th Ave NE [NE 45th St]
- **View Ridge Elementary** •
  7047 50th Ave NE [NE 70th St]
- **Villa Academy** • 5001 NE 50th St [50th Ave NE]

Supermarkets

- **Metropolitan Market** • 5250 40th Ave NE [NE 52nd Pl]
- **Quality Food Center** • 8400 35th Ave NE [NE 84th St]
- **Safeway** • 7340 35th Ave NE [NE 75th St]

Map 27 · Laurelhurst / Wedgwood / Sand Point ⓝ

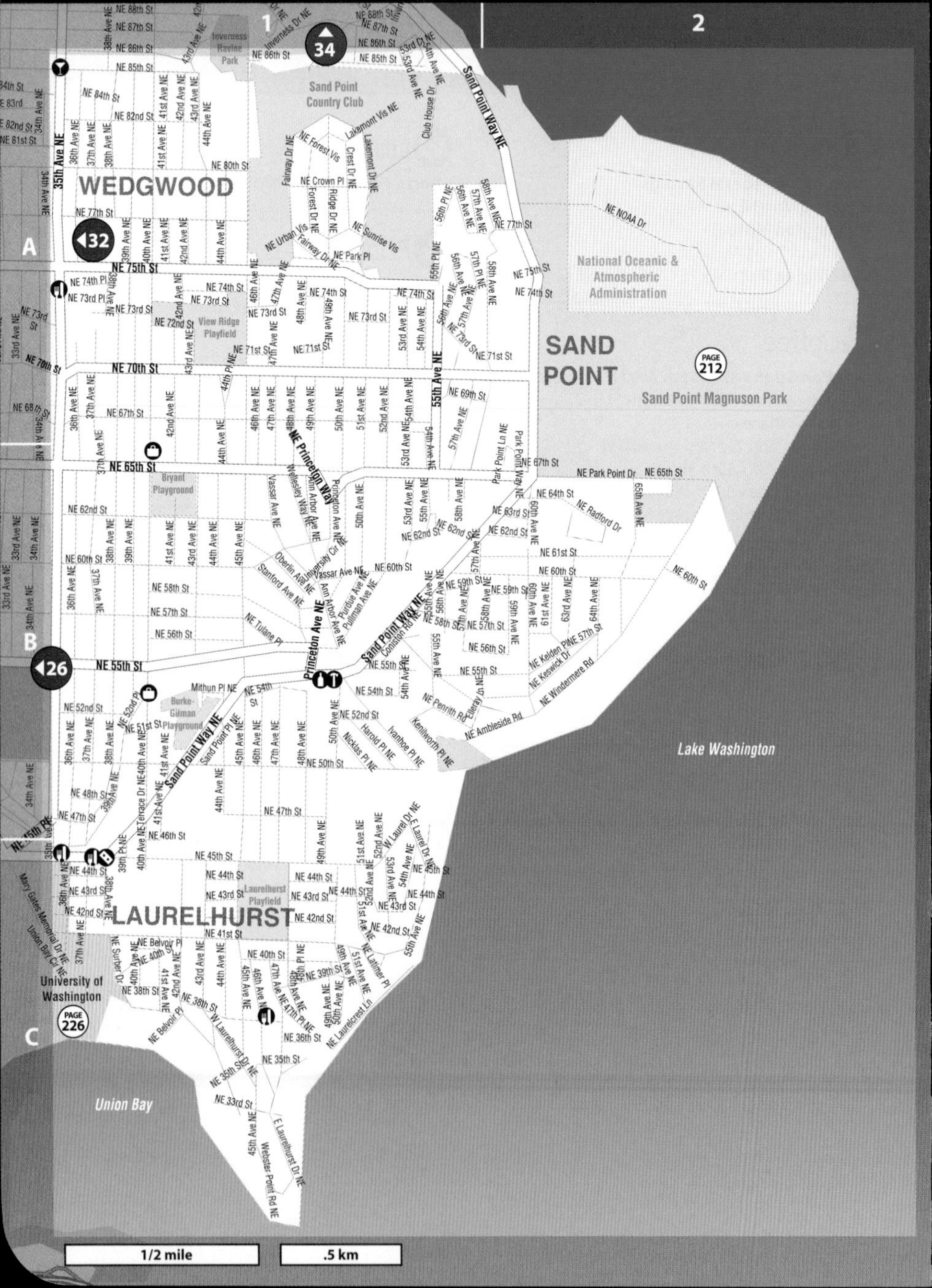

WEDGWOOD

SAND POINT

LAURELHURST

National Oceanic & Atmospheric Administration

Sand Point Country Club

Sand Point Magnuson Park

Inverness Ravine Park

View Ridge Playfield

Bryant Playground

Burke-Gilman Playground

Laurelhurst Playfield

University of Washington

Lake Washington

Union Bay

PAGE 212

PAGE 226

34

132

26

Sand Point Way NE

Princeton Ave NE

35th Ave NE

55th Ave NE

NE 88th St
NE 87th St
NE 86th St
NE 85th St
NE 84th St
NE 82nd St
NE 80th St
NE 77th St
NE 75th St
NE 74th St
NE 73rd St
NE 70th St
NE 67th St
NE 65th St
NE 62nd St
NE 60th St
NE 58th St
NE 57th St
NE 56th St
NE 55th St
NE 54th St
NE 52nd St
NE 48th St
NE 47th St
NE 46th St
NE 45th St
NE 44th St
NE 43rd St
NE 42nd St
NE 41st St
NE 40th St
NE 38th St
NE 36th St
NE 35th St
NE 33rd St

NE NOAA Dr

NE Park Point Dr
NE Radford Dr
Park Point Way NE
NE Windermere Rd
NE Keswick Dr
NE Kelden Pl NE
NE Ambleside Rd
Kenmonth Pl NE
Ivanhoe Pl NE
Niclas Pl NE
Harold Pl NE
Kenwood Pl NE

E Laurelhurst Dr NE
Webster Point Rd NE

Burke-Gilman Trail

1/2 mile   .5 km

The shops on Sand Point Way peter out leaving U Village, as do those on 35th. PCC and Metropolitan Market, both on 40th, battle for the chance to provide your overpriced organic and gourmet foods. Entertainment? There are several decent daycares for those of you with kids. If you insist on going out locally, you have one option: the greasy Wedgwood Ale House. For nature enthusiasts, Magnuson Park offers a universe of entertainment.

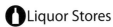Hardware Stores
• **City People's Sandpoint True Value** •
5440 Sand Point Wy NE [Princeton Ave NE]

Liquor Stores
• **La Cantina Wine Merchants** •
5436 Sand Point Wy NE [Princeton Ave NE]

Nightlife
• **Wedgwood Ale House** •
8515 35th Ave NE [NE 85th Ave]

Restaurants
• **Black Pearl** • 7347 35th Ave NE [NE 75th St]
• **Jak's Grill** • 3701 NE 45th St [37th Ave NE]

Shopping
• **Metropolitan Market** • 5250 40th Ave NE [NE 52nd Pl]
• **PCC Natural Markets** • 6514 40th Ave NE [NE 65th St]

Video Rental
• **Island Video** • 3711 NE 45th St [37th Ave NE]

Map 28 · **Ballard (West)**

N

1 2

PAGE
207

Golden
Gardens
Park

Puget Sound

NW 85th St

NW 83rd St

NW 80th St

NW 77th St

Loyal Ave NW

A

33

29

23

11

Seaview Ave NW

32nd Ave NW

33rd Ave NW

33rd Pl NW

30th Ave NW

29th Ave NW

28th Ave NW

Earl Ave NW

27th Ave NW

26th Ave NW

25th Ave NW

24th Ave NW

Jones Ave NW

23rd Ave NW

22nd Ave NW

NW 75th St

NW 74th St

NW 73rd St

NW 73rd St

NW 72nd St

NW 71st St

NW 70th St

B

NW 69th St

NW 68th St

NW 68th St

NW 67th St

NW 67th St

NW 67th St

NW 66th St

NW 66th St

NW 65th Ct

NW 65th St

NW 64th St

NW 64th St

NW 63rd St

NW 62nd St

NW 62nd St

NW 61st St

NW 61st St

Ballard
Playground

NW 60th St

← NW 60th St

NW Brygger Pl

NW 59th St

NW 59th St

NW 58th St

NW 57th St

NW 54th St

NW 54th St

34th Ave NW

35th Ave NW

35th Pl NW

36th Ave NW

37th Ave NW

38th Ave NW

Parker Ct NW

32nd Ave NW

28th Ave NW

26th Ave NW

24th Ave NW

22nd Ave NW

*Shilshole
Bay*

C

58th Ave W

W Hooker St

39th Ave W

42nd Ave W

41st Ave W

40th Ave W

W Sheridan St

W Cramer St

PAGE
208

Discovery
Park

NW Market St

NW Market St

NW 54th St

W Commodore Way

Hiram M. Chittenden Locks

Salmon Bay

Seaview Ave NW

Shilshole Ave NW

Ballard Ave NW

Leary Ave NW

1/4 mile   .25 km

This 'hood is on the rise, as newfangled restaurants and merchants have begun to hobnob with austere industrial firms and revered maritime showrooms. What has remained unchanged are two of Seattle's trademark hotspots: the Hiram M. Chittenden Locks, where a canal joins the city's freshwater lakes with the saltwater of Puget Sound, and the waterside Golden Gardens Park, with its sandy beaches, bonfires, and sunsets over the Olympics.

Coffee

- **Caffe Fiore Coffee Roasting Company •**
  3125 NW 85th St [31st Ave NW]
- **Karma Coffee** • 2817 NW Market St [28th Ave NW]
- **The Purple Cow** • 6301 Seaview Ave NW
- **Walter's Café** • 6408 32nd Ave NW [NW 64th St]

Community Gardens

Landmarks

- **Hiram M Chittenden Locks •**
  3015 NW 54th St [32nd Ave NW]

Schools

- **Adams Elementary •**
  6110 28th Ave NW [NW 61st St]
- **Loyal Heights Elementary •**
  2511 NW 80th St [25th Ave NW]
- **Wexford** • 7317 26th Ave NW [NW 73rd St]

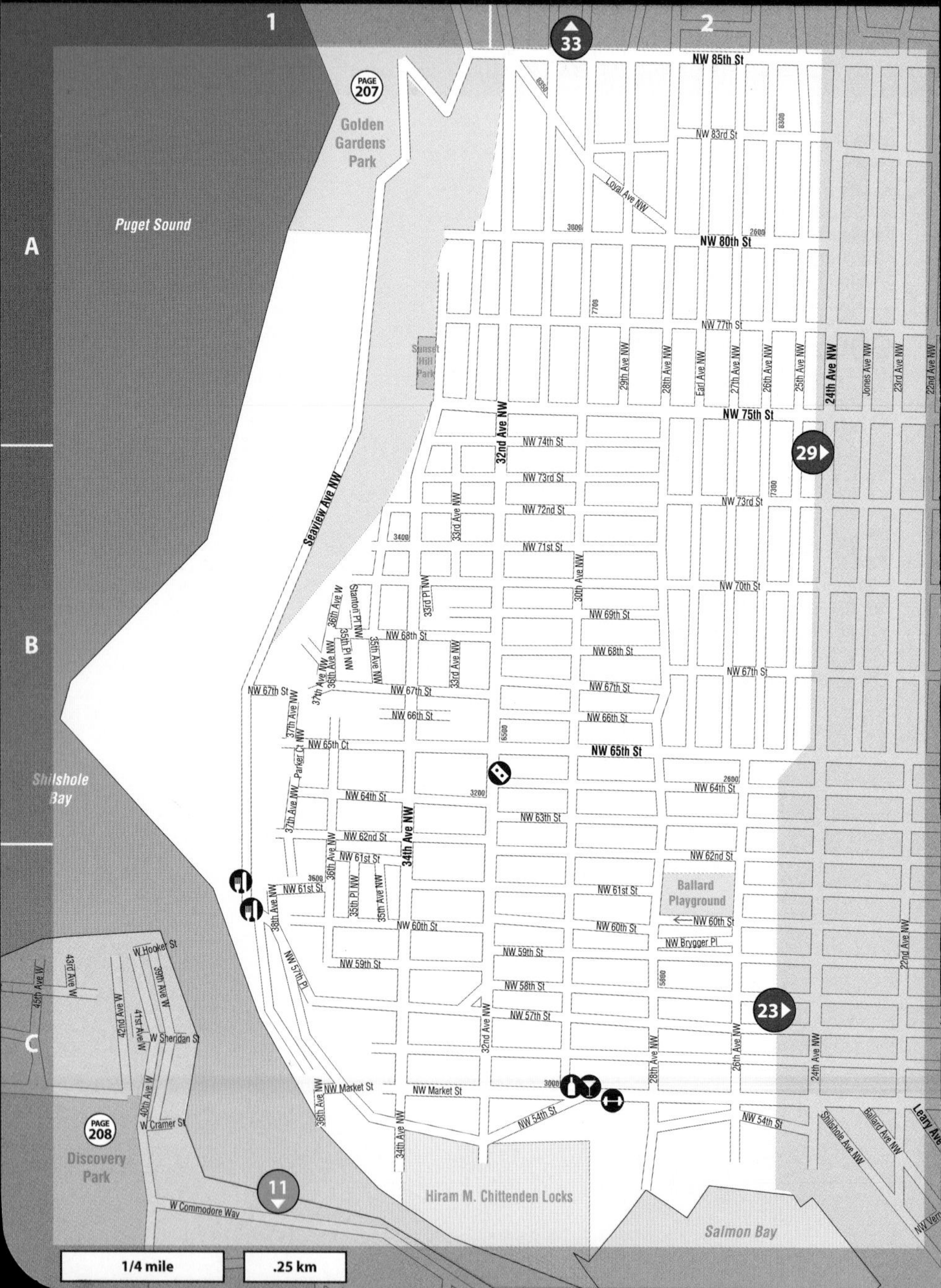

Map 28 · **Ballard (West)**

Puget Sound

Golden
Gardens
Park

PAGE
207

Summit
Hill
Park

Shilshole
Bay

Discovery
Park

PAGE
208

Hiram M. Chittenden Locks

Salmon Bay

NW 85th St
NW 83rd St
Loyal Ave NW
NW 80th St
NW 77th St
NW 75th St
NW 74th St
NW 73rd St
NW 73rd St
NW 72nd St
NW 71st St
NW 70th St
NW 69th St
NW 68th St
NW 68th St
NW 67th St
NW 67th St
NW 67th St
NW 66th St
NW 66th St
NW 65th St
NW 65th Ct
NW 64th St
NW 64th St
NW 63rd St
NW 62nd St
NW 62nd St
NW 61st St
NW 61st St
NW 60th St
NW 60th St
NW Brygger Pl
NW 59th St
NW 59th St
NW 58th St
NW 57th St
NW Market St
NW Market St
NW 54th St
NW 54th St
W Hooker St
W Sheridan St
W Cramer St
W Commodore Way

Ballard
Playground

Seaview Ave NW

32nd Ave NW
33rd Ave NW
34th Ave NW
30th Ave NW

29th Ave NW
28th Ave NW
Earl Ave NW
27th Ave NW
26th Ave NW
25th Ave NW
24th Ave NW
Jones Ave NW
22nd Ave NW
Seaview Ave NW
Leary Ave NW

33
29
23
11

1/4 mile   .25 km

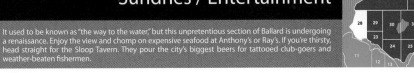

It used to be known as "the way to the water," but this unpretentious section of Ballard is undergoing a renaissance. Enjoy the view and chomp on expensive seafood at Anthony's or Ray's. If you're thirsty, head straight for the Sloop Tavern. They pour the city's biggest beers for tattooed club-goers and weather-beaten fishermen.

Gyms

• **Curves** • 2821 NW Market St [28th Ave NW]

Liquor Stores

• **Washington State Liquor Store** •
2840 NW Market St [NW 54th St]

Nightlife

• **Sloop Tavern** • 2830 NW Market St [NW 54th St]

Restaurants

• **Anthony's HomePort** •
6135 Seaview Ave NW [NW 61st St]
• **Ray's Boathouse Café** •
6049 Seaview Ave NW [38th Ave NW]

Video Rental

• **Rain City Video** • 6412 32nd Ave NW [NW 64th St]

Map 29 • **Ballard / Loyal Heights**

NW 89th St
NW 88th St
NW 87th St
NW 86th St

24th Ave NW
22nd Ave NW
21st Ave NW
20th Ave NW
18th Ave NW
17th Ave NW
15th Ave NW
14th Ave NW
13th Ave NW
12th Ave NW
11th Ave NW
10th Ave NW

NW 87th St
NW 86th St
NW 85th St

33

Rx
Rx
$

Baker
Park

A
NW 84th St
NW 83rd St
NW 82nd St
NW 81st St

NW 83rd St

8th Ave NW

NW 80th St
NW 79th St
NW 78th St
NW 77th St
NW 76th St

27th Ave NW
26th Ave NW
25th Ave NW

NW 77th St

28
Loyal
Heights
Playfield

16th Ave NW
Mary Ave NW
14th Ave NW

NW 75th St

B
**LOYAL
HEIGHTS**

NW 74th St

30

24th Ave NW
Jones Ave NW
23rd Ave NW
22nd Ave NW
21st Ave NW

NW 73rd St

15th Ave NW
Mary Ave NW
Alonzo Ave NW
14th Ave NW
13th Ave NW
12th Ave NW
11th Ave NW
10th Ave NW

Cleopatra Pl NW

NW 73rd St

NW Canoe Pl
Salmon
Bay
Park
NW Sloop Pl

NW 70th St

N 70th St

7th Ave NW

NW 67th St

Mary Ave NW
Alonzo Ave NW
14th Ave NW
13th Ave NW
12th Ave NW
11th Ave NW
10th Ave NW

19th Ave NW
18th Ave NW

Ballard
High School
Playground

Mary Ave NW

Dibble Ave NW
Division Ave NW

C
BALLARD
NW 65th St

NW 64th St
NW 63rd St

26th Ave NW
22nd Ave NW
20th Ave NW
17th Ave NW
15th Ave NW

$

14th Ave NW
11th Ave NW
9th Ave NW

8th Ave NW

NW 62nd St
NW 62nd St
NW 61st St

23

NW 59th St

NW 58th St

7th Ave NW
6th Ave NW

| 1/4 mile | .25 km |

The residential focus of Loyal Heights means family green areas like Salmon Bay and Baker Parks and a half-dozen learning institutions, including Seattle's coolest, Ballard High School. But one blockbuster drive from 85th Street (where Mt. Rainier looms over the city like a giant ice cream cone) down the ever-active 15th Avenue Northwest, and Ballard's long-lost neighborhood brother is found again.

Banks

- **First Mutual Bank** • 6301 15th Ave NW [NW 63rd St]
- **Washington Federal Savings** •
  8318 15th Ave NW [NW 83rd St]

Car Rental

- **Enterprise** • 7301 15th Ave NW [NW 73rd St]

Coffee

- **Starbucks** • Safeway • 8340 15th Ave NW [NW 83rd St]

Pharmacies

- **Bob Johnson's Pharmacy** •
  1407 NW 85th St [14th Ave NW]
- **Safeway Pharmacy** • 8340 15th Ave NW [NW 83rd St]
- **Walgreens** • 8500 15th Ave NW [NW 85th St]

Schools

- **Ballard High** • 1418 NW 65th St [14th Ave NW]
- **Cinquegranelli Montessori** •
  1405 NW 85th St [14th Ave NW]
- **Salmon Bay Schoo** • 1810 NW 65th St [18th Ave NW]
- **Whittier Elementary** • 1320 NW 75th St [13th Ave NW]

Supermarkets

- **Safeway** • 8340 15th Ave NW [NW 83rd St]

Map 29 · **Ballard / Loyal Heights**

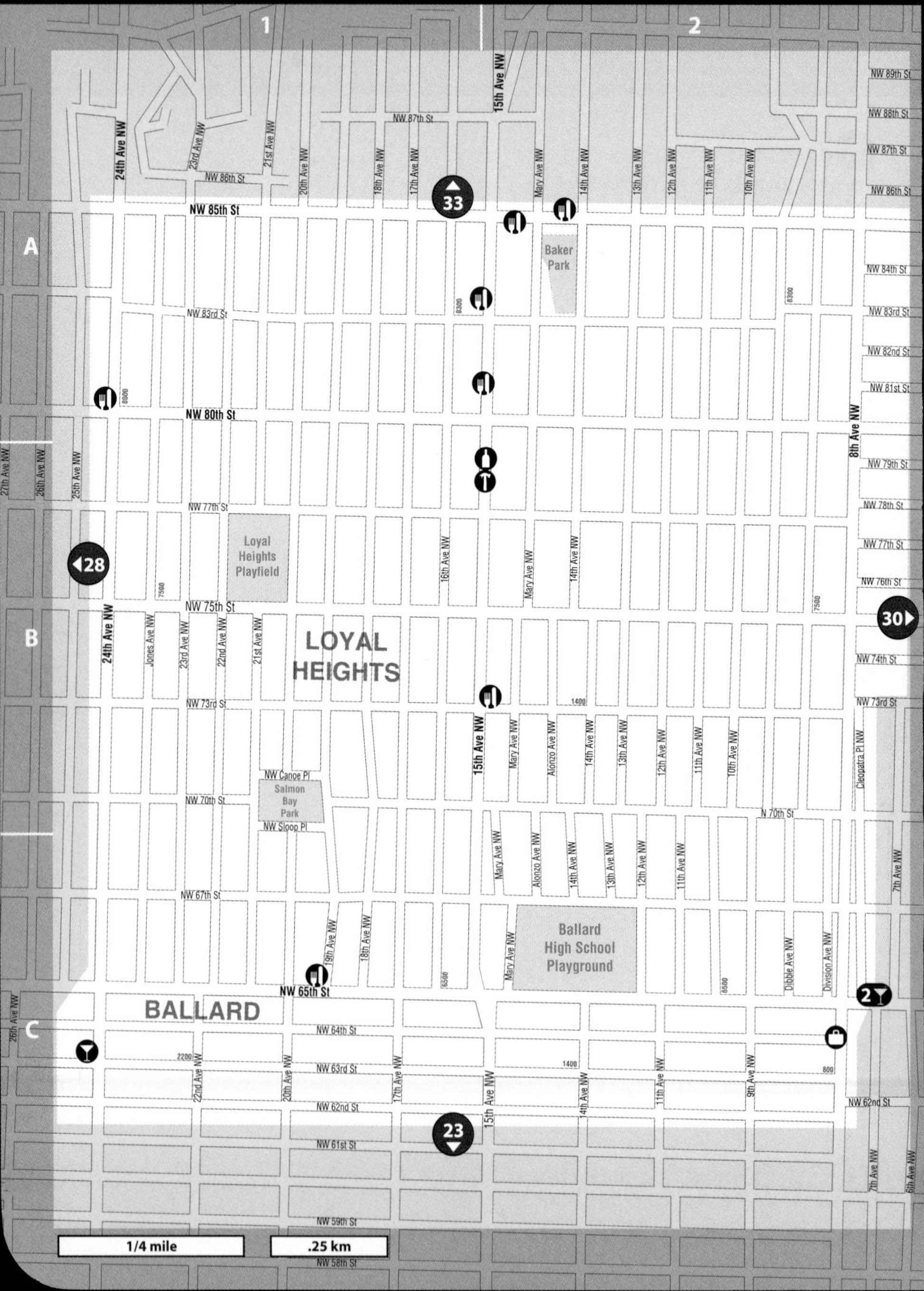

N

1

2

NW 89th St

NW 88th St

NW 87th St

NW 86th St

NW 87th St

15th Ave NW

24th Ave NW

23rd Ave NW

21st Ave NW

20th Ave NW

18th Ave NW

17th Ave NW

14th Ave NW

13th Ave NW

12th Ave NW

11th Ave NW

10th Ave NW

NW 86th St

A

NW 85th St

33

NW 84th St

Baker
Park

NW 83rd St

NW 83rd St

NW 82nd St

NW 81st St

8th Ave NW

NW 80th St

NW 79th St

27th Ave NW

26th Ave NW

25th Ave NW

NW 78th St

NW 77th St

NW 77th St

28

Loyal
Heights
Playfield

16th Ave NW

Mary Ave NW

14th Ave NW

NW 76th St

30

B

NW 75th St

24th Ave NW

Jones Ave NW

23rd Ave NW

22nd Ave NW

21st Ave NW

**LOYAL
HEIGHTS**

NW 74th St

NW 73rd St

NW 73rd St

15th Ave NW

Mary Ave NW

Alonzo Ave NW

14th Ave NW

13th Ave NW

12th Ave NW

11th Ave NW

10th Ave NW

Cleopatra Pl NW

NW Canoe Pl

Salmon
Bay
Park

NW 70th St

NW Sloop Pl

N 70th St

7th Ave NW

NW 67th St

Mary Ave NW

Alonzo Ave NW

14th Ave NW

13th Ave NW

12th Ave NW

11th Ave NW

9th Ave NW

18th Ave NW

Ballard
High School
Playground

NW 65th St

Mary Ave NW

Dibble Ave NW

Division Ave NW

2

BALLARD

C

NW 64th St

20th Ave NW

NW 63rd St

22nd Ave NW

20th Ave NW

17th Ave NW

15th Ave NW

14th Ave NW

11th Ave NW

9th Ave NW

NW 62nd St

NW 62nd St

NW 61st St

23

7th Ave NW

6th Ave NW

NW 59th St

NW 58th St

1/4 mile

.25 km

The eateries here are as eclectic as anywhere in town: Zagi's authentic big-slab pizzeria, Smokin' Pete's BBQ, and Thai Siam, one of Seattle's best Thai restaurants. Both 15th and 24th Avenues are main drags, the latter thoroughfare just blocks from exquisite Puget Sound views (and million-dollar homes).

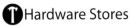Hardware Stores

- **Crown Hill Hardware** • 7759 15th Ave NW [NW 80th St]

Liquor Stores

- **Washington State Liquor Store** •
  7740 15th Ave NW [NW 80th St]

Nightlife

- **Copper Gate** • 6301 24th Ave NW [NW 63rd St]
- **The Dray** • 708 NW 65th St [8th Avenue NW]
- **Lunchbox Laboratory** • 7302 15th Ave NW
- **Tigertail** • 704 NW 65th St [7th Avenue NW]

Restaurants

- **Kasbah Authentic Moroccan** •
  1471 NW 85th St [NW 85th St]
- **Lunchbox Laboratory** •
  7302 15th Ave NW [NW 73rd St]
- **The Original Pancake House** •
  8037 15th Ave NW [NW 80th St]
- **Smokin' Pete's BBQ** • 1918 NW 65th St [19th Ave NW]
- **Thai Siam** • 8305 15th Ave NW [NW 83rd St]
- **Wild Mountain Café** • 1408 NW 85th St [NW 85th St]
- **Zagi's Pizza** • 2408 NW 80th St [24th Ave NW]

Shopping

- **Goodwill** • 6400 8th Ave NW [NW 64th St]

Map 30 · **Greenwood / Phinney Ridge**

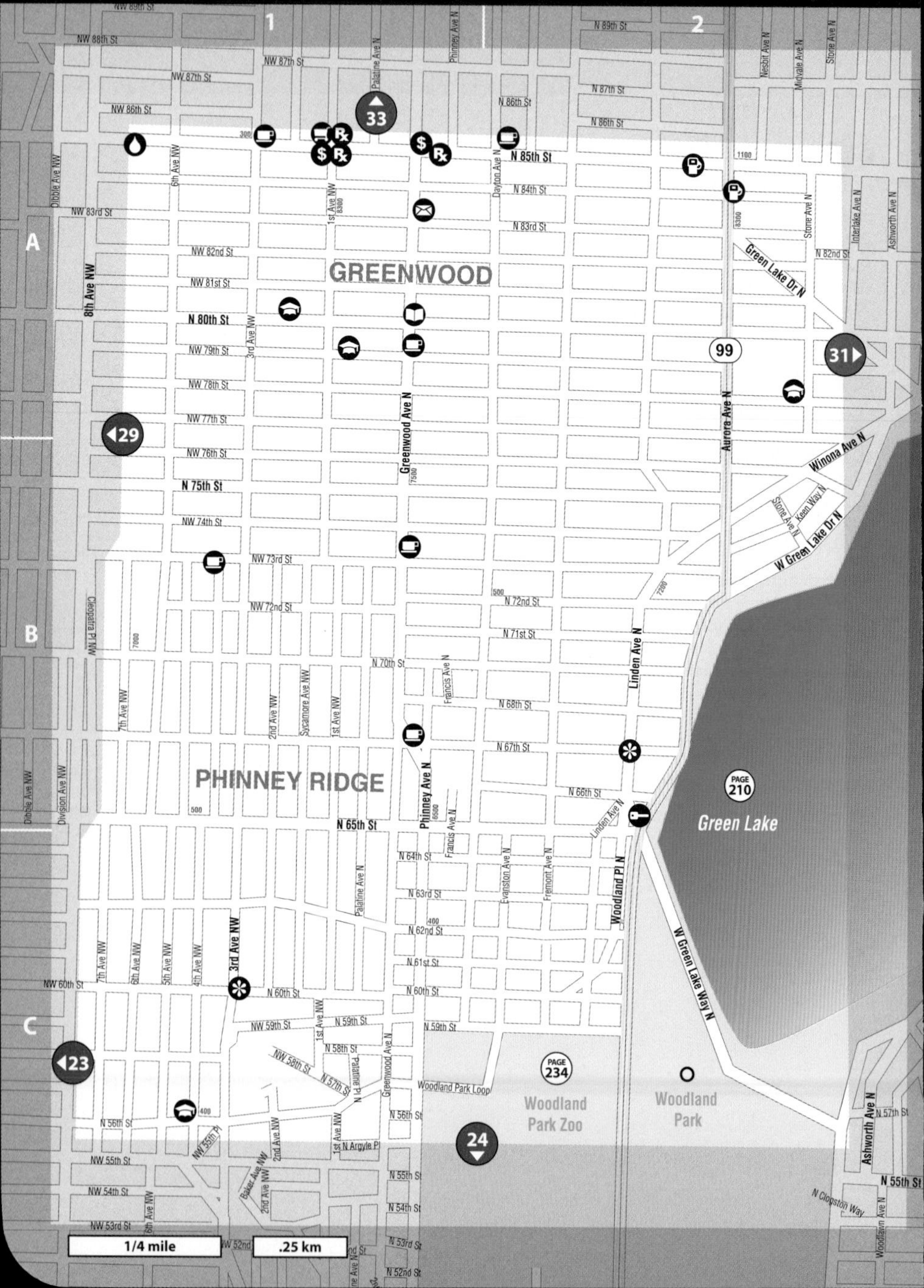

1
2

NW 89th St
NW 88th St
N 89th St
NW 87th St
NW 87th St
NW 86th St
N 86th St
N 87th St
N 86th St
NW 86th St
N 85th St
33
NW 83rd St
N 84th St
N 83rd St
A
NW 82nd St
NW 81st St
GREENWOOD
N 80th St
NW 79th St
NW 78th St
99
NW 77th St
31
NW 76th St
29
N 75th St
NW 74th St
Aurora Ave N
Winona Ave N
NW 73rd St
B
NW 72nd St
N 72nd St
N 71st St
W Green Lake Dr N
N 70th St
N 68th St
N 67th St
PHINNEY RIDGE
N 66th St
PAGE 210
N 65th St
N 64th St
Green Lake
N 63rd St
N 62nd St
N 61st St
N 60th St
NW 60th St
NW 59th St
N 59th St
C
N 59th St
23
N 58th St
NW 58th St
NW 57th St
NW 56th St
PAGE 234
N 56th St
NW 55th St
Woodland Park Zoo
Woodland Park
NW 54th St
N 55th St
24
NW 53rd St
N 53rd St
N 55th St
NW 52nd St
N 52nd St

1/4 mile | .25 km

The tree-lined corridor at Phinney and Greenwood Avenues is one of the better places to raise a family in Seattle, while the blocks along Aurora will show your kids what will happen to them if they don't stay in school. Right around Green Lake the area turns downright affluent, but all the best shopping, eating, and drinking can be found where the regular folk live.

Banks

- **US Bank (ATM)** • 100 NW 85th St [1st Ave NW]
- **Washington Mutual** •
  8500 Greenwood Ave N [N 85th St]

Car Rental

- **Best Rent-A-Car** • 6501 Aurora Ave N [N 66th St]

⬤Car Washes

- **Car Wash Palace** • 655 NW 85th St [6th Ave NW]

⬛Coffee

- **Café Bambino** • 405 NW 65th St [4th Ave NW]
- **Diva Espresso** • 7916 Greenwood Ave N [NW 79th St]
- **Herkimer Coffee** •
  7320 Greenwood Ave N [NW 73rd St]
- **Javabean Inc Greenwood** •
  8500 3rd Ave NW [3rd Ave NW]
- **Monkey Grind Espresso Bar** •
  518 N 85th St [Dayton Ave N]
- **Starbucks** • 316 N 67th St [NW 67th St]

✳Community Gardens

Gas Stations

- **76** • 8408 Aurora Ave N [N 84th St]
- **Arco** • 950 N 85th St [Aurora Ave NW]

○Landmarks

- **Woodland Park** • Aurora Ave N & 59th St

🏛Libraries

- **Greenwood Branch** •
  8016 Greenwood Ave N [N 80th St]

℞Pharmacies

- **Bartell Drugs** • 120 N 85th St [1st Ave NW]
- **Fred Meyer** • 100 NW 85th St [1st Ave NW]
- **Medicine Man** • 323 N 85th St [Greenwood Ave N]

✉Post Offices

- **Greenwood** • 8306 Greenwood Ave N [N 83rd St]

Schools

- **Daniel Bagley Elementary** •
  7821 Stone Ave N [N 78th St]
- **Greenwood Elementary** •
  144 NW 80th St [3rd Ave NW]
- **St John** • 120 N 79th St [1st Ave NW]
- **West Woodland Elementary** •
  5601 4th Ave NW [NW 56th St]

🛒Supermarkets

- **Fred Meyer** • 100 NW 85th St [1st Ave NW]

Map 30 · **Greenwood / Phinney Ridge**

Ⓝ

1 **2**

NW 89th St
NW 88th St
NW 87th St
NW 86th St
NW 87th St
N 89th St
N 87th St
N 86th St
N 86th St
N 85th St
N 84th St
N 83rd St

33
2

Meridian Ave N
Midvale Ave N
Stone Ave N
Interlake Ave N
Ashworth Ave N

Dibble Ave NW
8th Ave NW
6th Ave NW
1st Ave NW
3rd Ave NW
Palatine Ave N
Phinney Ave N
Dayton Ave N

A

NW 83rd St
NW 82nd St
NW 81st St
N 80th St
NW 79th St
NW 78th St
NW 77th St
NW 76th St
N 75th St
NW 74th St
NW 73rd St
NW 72nd St

GREENWOOD

Green Lake Dr N

99

31

29

Greenwood Ave N
Aurora Ave N
Winona Ave N
Stone Ave N
Kirkwood Pl N
Linden Ave N

Green Lake Dr N
W Green Lake Dr N

3

N 72nd St
N 71st St
N 70th St
N 68th St
N 67th St
N 66th St

B

Clopidine Pl NW
7th Ave NW
2nd Ave NW
Sycamore Ave NW
1st Ave NW
Francis Ave N
Phinney Ave N

PHINNEY RIDGE

PAGE 210

Green Lake

Dibble Ave NW
Division Ave NW
5th Ave NW

N 65th St

N 64th St
N 63rd St
N 62nd St
N 61st St
N 60th St
N 59th St

Palatine Ave N
Fremont Ave N
Evanston Ave N
Linden Ave N
Woodland Pl N

W Green Lake Way N

PAGE 234

C

23

7th Ave NW
6th Ave NW
5th Ave NW
4th Ave NW
3rd Ave NW
Greenwood Ave N
N Ardsley Pl
N Argyle Pl

NW 60th St
N 60th St
NW 59th St
NW 59th St
N 59th St
NW 58th St
N 58th St
N 57th St
NW 58th St
N 56th St
N 55th St
NW 55th St
NW 54th St
NW 53rd St
NW 52nd St

24

Woodland Park Loop
N 56th St
N 55th St
N 54th St
N 53rd St
N 52nd St

**Woodland
Park Zoo**

**Woodland
Park**

Ashworth Ave N
N 57th St
N Clopston Way
N 55th St

1/4 mile	.25 km

Bistros Carmelita and Stumbling Goat bring casual elegance to the neighborhood, while Gordito's, Beth's Café, and Red Mill feed the happy masses. The crack-house chic of Aurora gives way to two of the most comprehensive beer bars in Seattle——Duck Island Ale House and Über Tavern. Wash your pint down with some good eats at 74th Street Ale House. The younger, grungier crowd is at Tin Hat.

 Farmers Markets

- **Phinney (Fridays, 3pm–7pm, mid-May through early October)** • Phinney Ave N & N 67th St

Hardware Stores

- **Greenwood Hardware** •
  7201 Greenwood Ave N [N 72nd St]

Liquor Stores

- **Vineyard Wine Shop** •
  8218 Greenwood Ave N [N 82nd St]

Nightlife

- **Barking Dog Alehouse** •
  705 NW 70th St [7th Ave NW]
- **Duck Island Ale House** •
  7317 Aurora Ave N [Winona Ave N]
- **El Chupacabra** •
  6711 Greenwood Ave N [N 67th St]
- **Kangaroo & Kiwi Pub** •
  7305 Aurora Ave N [N 73rd St]
- **Prost!** • 7311 Greenwood Ave N [N 73rd St]
- **St Andrew's Bar & Grill** •
  7406 Aurora Ave N [Winona Ave N]
- **Sully's Snow Goose Saloon** •
  6119 Phinney Ave N [N 61st St]
- **Tin Hat Bar & Grill** •
  512 NW 65th St [5th Ave NW]
- **Über Tavern** • 7517 Aurora Ave N [N 75th St]

Pet Shops

- **Mud Bay - Greenwood** •
  8221 Greenwood Ave N [N 82nd St]

Restaurants

- **74th Street Ale House** •
  7401 Greenwood Ave N [N 74th St]
- **Barking Dog Alehouse** • 705 NW 70th St [7th Ave NW]
- **Beth's Café** • 7311 Aurora Ave N [N 73rd St] ⚑
- **Carmelita** • 7314 Greenwood Ave N [N 73rd St]
- **El Chupacabra** • 6711 Greenwood Ave N [N 67th St]
- **Gordito's** • 213 N 85th St [Palatine Ave N]
- **Mae's Phinney Ridge Café** •
  6412 Phinney Ave N [N 65th St]
- **Molly Maguire's** • 610 NW 65th St [7th Avenue NW]
- **Olive You** • 8516 Greenwood Ave N [N 85th St]
- **Pho Thân Brothers'** • 7714 Aurora Ave N [N 77th St]
- **Red Mill Burgers** • 312 N 67th St [N 67th St]
- **Santa Fe Café** • 5910 Phinney Ave N [N 59th St]
- **Stacia's** • 305 NW 85th St [1st Ave NW]
- **Stumbling Goat Bistro** •
  6722 Greenwood Ave N [N 68th St]
- **Yanni's** • 7419 Greenwood Ave N [N 74th St]
- **Zeek's Pizza** • 6000 Phinney Ave N [N 60th St]

Shopping

- **Couth Buzzard Used Books** •
  7221 Greenwood Ave N [N 72nd St]
- **Fred Meyer** • 100 NW 85th St [1st Ave NW]
- **Greenwood Hardware** •
  7201 Greenwood Ave N [N 72nd St]
- **Ken's Market** • 7231 Greenwood Ave N [N 72nd St]
- **PCC Natural Markets** • 7504 Aurora Ave N [N 75th Ave]
- **Rudy's Barbershop** • 6415 Phinney Ave N [N 64th St]
- **The Sneakery** • 612 NW 65th St [7th Avenue NW]

Video Rental

- **Blockbuster** • 100 N 85th St [1st Ave NW]
- **Island Video Greenwood Store** •
  7120 Greenwood Ave N [N 71st St]

Map 31 · **Green Lake / Roosevelt**

GREEN LAKE

Green Lake

ROOSEVELT

Green Lake Park

Green Lake Reservoir

Maple Leaf Reservoir

Maple Leaf Playground

Froula Playground

Cowen Park

Woodland Park

Bettie Page Mural

1/4 mile   .25 km

Map 31

Seattle's singletons and families alike flock to Green Lake on rare sunny days for outdoor fun and frolic, jogging, rollerblading, and paddle boat rentals. The pedestrian-friendly lake and surrounding park are true gems for those without private waterfront access or million dollar houseboats. Nearby Roosevelt, smaller and less popular than its sister 'hood, is a quiet, tree-lined residential enclave on the outskirts of Ravenna Park.

$ Banks

- **Key Bank** • 426 NE 70th St [Oswego Pl NE]
- **Key Bank (ATM)** • 400 NE Ravenna Blvd [NE 70th St]
- **US Bank** • 1023 NE 63rd St [Roosevelt Wy NE]
- **US Bank (ATM)** • 1023 NE 63rd St [Roosevelt Wy NE]

Car Rental

- **Budget** • 6000 Roosevelt Wy NE [NE 60th St]
- **Enterprise** • 5715 Roosevelt Way NE [NE 55th St]

Coffee

- **Bus Stop Espresso** • 800 NE 65th St [8th Ave NE]
- **Café Javasti** • 8410 5th Ave NE [NE 84th St]
- **Café Lulu** • 6417 Latona Ave NE [NE 64th St]
- **Cafe Racer** • 5828 Roosevelt Way NE [NE 59th St]
- **Peet's Coffee & Tea** •
  6850 E Green Lake Wy N [4th Ave NE]
- **Revolutions Espresso** •
  7012 Woodlawn Ave NE [Woodlawn Ave NE]
- **Starbucks** • 6417 Roosevelt Wy NE [NE 64th St]
- **Starbucks** • 7100 E Green Lake Dr N [NE 71st St]
- **Zoka Coffee Roaster & Tea Company** •
  2200 N 56th St [N 56th St]

Community Gardens

Gas Stations

- **Shell** • 7501 Roosevelt Wy NE [NE 75th St]

○ Landmarks

- **Bettie Page Mural** • 700 NE 59th St [NE 7th St]

Libraries

- **Green Lake Branch** •
  7364 E Green Lake Dr N [4th Ave NE]

P Parking

Rx Pharmacies

- **Bartell Drugs** • 6401 12th Ave NE [NE 64th St]
- **Park's** • 401 NE Ravenna Blvd [Woodlawn Ave NE]
- **Safeway Pharmacy** •
  7300 Roosevelt Wy NE [NE 73rd St]

 Schools

- **Billings Middle** • 7217 Woodlawn Ave NE [NE 72nd St]
- **Bishop Blanchet High** •
  8200 Wallingford Ave N [N 82nd St]
- **Evening School (Marshall)** •
  520 NE Ravenna Blvd [NE 68th St]
- **Fairview Christian** • 844 NE 78th St [8th Ave NE]
- **Green Lake Elementary** •
  2400 N 65th St [Sunnyside Ave N]
- **Hawthorn** • 6414 Latona Ave NE [NE 64th St]
- **John Marshall Middle** •
  520 NE Ravenna Blvd [NE 68th St]
- **Montessori Garden** • 8301 5th Ave NE [NE 83rd St]
- **St Catherine** • 8524 8th Ave NE [8th Ave NE]

Supermarkets

- **Quality Food Center** •
  6600 Roosevelt Wy NE [NE 66th St]
- **Safeway** • 7300 Roosevelt Wy NE [NE 73rd St]
- **Whole Foods** • 1026 NE 64th St [Roosevelt Wy NE]

Map 31 • **Green Lake / Roosevelt**

Before enjoying a lap or three around the lake, the avid cyclist should check out Gregg's Greenlake Cycle for expert service and superior selection. After all that exercise, enjoy an affordable meal and stiff drinks at Luau Polynesian Lounge. By contrast, Roosevelt offers a less athletic and more hippie vibe for those of the mellower persuasion. Establishments like East West Bookshop and Sunlight Café, Seattle's oldest vegetarian restaurant, define the neighborhood's shopping district.

Copy Shops
• **UPS Store** • 1037 NE 65th St [Roosevelt Wy NE]

Gyms
• **Anderson's Nautilus Fitness Center** •
7203 Woodlawn Ave NE [NE 72nd St]

Nightlife
• **Die Bierstube** • 6106 Roosevelt Wy NE [Ne 61st St]
• **Elysian Tangletown** • 2106 N 55th St [Kenwood Pl N]
• **La Casa Del Mojito** •
7545 Lake City Way NE [11th Ave NE]
• **Little Red Hen** • 7115 Woodlawn Ave NE [NE 71st St]
• **Luau Polynesian Lounge** •
2253 N 56 St [Kirkwood Place N]
• **Pies and Pints** • 1215 NE 65th St [12th Ave NE]
• **Teddy's Tavern** • 1012 NE 65th St [Roosevelt Wy NE]

Pet Shops
• **Animal Talk** • 6514 Roosevelt Wy NE [NE 65th St]

Restaurants
• **Blue Onion Bistro** •
5801 Roosevelt Wy NE [NE 59th St]
• **Duke's Chowder House** •
7850 Green Lake Dr N [Densmore Ave N]
• **Eva** • 2227 N 56th St [Keystone Pl N]
• **Krittika Noodles & Thai Cuisine** •
6411 Latona Ave NE [64th St]
• **Latona Pub** • 6423 Latona Ave NE [NE 65th St]
• **Mighty-O Donuts** • 2110 N 55th St [Kenwood Pl N]
• **Mona's Bistro & Lounge** •
6421 Latona Ave NE [64th St]
• **Nell's** • 6804 E Green Lake Wy N [2nd Ave NE]
• **Pies and Pints** • 1215 NE 65th St [12th Ave NE]
• **Primo Burgers** • 6501 Roosevelt Wy NE [NE 65th St]
• **Salvatore Ristorante** • 6100 Roosevelt Wy NE [NE 61st St]
• **Spud Fish & Chips** • 6860 E Green Lake Wy N [4th Ave NE]
• **Sunlight Café** • 6403 Roosevelt Wy NE [NE 64th St]
• **Sushi Tokyo** • 6311 Roosevelt Wy NE [NE 63rd St]
• **Taqueria Guaymas** • 6808 E Green Lake Wy N [2nd Ave NE]

• **Taste of India** • 5517 Roosevelt Wy NE [NE 55th St]
• **Wayward Café** • 901 NE 55th St [9th Ave Pl]

Shopping
• **Arnie's Vintage Costumers** •
7011 Roosevelt Wy NE [Roosevelt Wy NE]
• **East West Bookshop** •
6500 Roosevelt Wy NE [NE 65th St]
• **Fish Store** • 6109 Roosevelt Wy NE [Ne 61st St]
• **Gregg's Greenlake Cycle** •
7007 Woodlawn Ave NE [NE Ravenna Blvd]
• **J n S Phonograph Needles** •
1028 NE 65th St [Roosevelt Wy NE]
• **The Last White Elephant** • 902 NE 65th St [9th Ave NE]
• **Mamo Jewelry Design** •
6317 Roosevelt Way NE [NE 63rd St]
• **Pop Tots** • 6405 Roosevelt Wy NE [NE 64th St]
• **Science, Art and More** •
6417 Roosevelt Wy NE [NE 64th St]
• **Trading Musician** •
5908 Roosevelt Wy NE [NE Ravenna Blvd]

Video Rental
• **Hollywood Video** • 6415 12th Ave NE [NE 72nd St]
• **Videophile Inc** • 1028 NE 65th St [Roosevelt Wy NE]

Map 32 · **Ravenna**

N

1

2

34

NE 92nd St

NE 91st St

NE 90th St

NE 90th St

NE 89th St

NE 89th St

NE 88th St

NE 88th St

35th Ave NE

Maple Leaf Reservoir

NE 86th St

23rd Ave NE

NE 86th St

NE 87th St

25th Ave NE

27th Ave NE

NE 87th St

NE 86th St

A

Maple Leaf Playground

NE 85th St

NE 85th St

14th Ave NE

15th Ave NE

16th Ave NE

Lake City Way NE

17th Pl NE

20th Ave NE

NE 83rd St

21st Ave NE

NE 83rd St

Ravenna Ave NE

NE 83rd St

NE 84th St

NE 83rd St

NE 82nd St

31st Ave NE

34th Ave NE

36th Ave NE

NE 82nd St

NE 82nd St

22nd Ave NE

23rd Pl NE

24000

NE 81st Pl

NE 81st Pl

NE 81st St

27th Ave NE

28th Ave NE

NE 81st St

37th Ave NE

39th Ave NE

Brooklyn Ave NE

12th Ave NE

NE 81st St

NE 80th St

23rd Ct NE

NE 80th St

29th Ave NE

31

NE 79th St

1600

NE 77th St

11th Ave NE

14th Ave NE

Brooklyn Ave NE

NE 77th St

NE 76th St

Waldo J Dahl Playfield

28th Ave NE

29th Ave NE

30th Ave NE

31st Ave NE

32nd Ave NE

NE 77th St

34th Ave NE

NE 77th St

27

9th Ave NE

NE Banner Pl

522

NE 74th St

11th Ave NE

12th Ave NE

Perkins Pl

NE 73rd St

NE 72nd St

Green Lake Reservoir

Froula Playground

NE 75th St

Ravenna Ave NE

24th Ave NE

NE 74th St

NE 74th St

The Wedgwood Rock

NE 72nd St

NE 72nd St

31st Ave NE

32nd Ave NE

33rd Ave NE

NE 74th Pl

NE 73rd St

NE 73rd St

38th Pl NE

NE 73rd St

NE 73rd St

B

NE 71st St

Roosevelt Way NE

14th Ave NE

Brooklyn Ave NE

20th Pl NE

NE 73rd St

NE 70th St

NE 70th St

15th Ave NE

16th Ave NE

17th Ave NE

20th Ave NE

21st Ave NE

23rd Ave NE

25th Ave NE

28th Ave NE

27th Ave NE

29th Ave NE

30th Ave NE

31st Ave NE

NE 70th St

34th Ave NE

36th Ave NE

37th Ave NE

NE 70th St

NE 69th St

NE 68th St

NE 68th St

NE 68th St

NE 67th St

37th Ave NE

NE 66th St

Ravenna Eckstein Park

NE 62nd St

NE 65th St

NE 65th St

14th Ave NE

NE 65th St

21st Ave NE

NE 65th St

NE 63rd St

NE Naomi Pl

21st Ave NE

22nd Ave NE

6200

NE 62nd St

NE 62nd St

30th Ave NE

31st Ave NE

32nd Ave NE

33rd Ave NE

35th Ave NE

38th Ave NE

9th Ave NE

12th Ave NE

NE 64th St

NE 62nd St

21st Ave NE

NE 62nd St

NE 61st St

NE 60th St

Cowen Park

Brooklyn Ave NE

NE 61st St

NE Ravenna Blvd

Cowen Pl NE

Ravenna Park

24th Ave NE

NE 81st St

Twin Maple Ln NE

25th Ave NE

3000

NE 60th St

30th Ave NE

31st Ave NE

32nd Ave NE

33rd Ave NE

34th Ave NE

NE 60th St

C

NE 58th St

NE 57th St

11th Ave NE

University Way NE

15th Ave NE

16th Ave NE

17th Ave NE

18th Ave NE

NE 58th St

NE 56th St

NE 55th Pl

26th Ave NE

27th Ave NE

NE 57th St

NE 58th St

NE Blakeley St

NE 55th St

1600

NE 55th St

Ravenna Ave NE

NE 55th St

NE 54th St

NE 54th St

30th Ave NE

26

NE 53rd St

NE 52nd St

18th Ave NE

19th Ave NE

20th Ave NE

21st Ave NE

22nd Ave NE

Ravenna Ave NE

NE 53rd St

NE 52nd St

Calvary Catholic Cemetery

NE 52nd St

9th Ave NE

NE 51st St

NE 50th St

1/4 mile   .25 km

Ravenna is a residential wasteland that lies just north of the U District. It is populated largely by grad students and young families. However, the densely green surroundings and the amazing woodland bubble of Ravenna Park lend a refreshing, non-suburban ambiance to the area.

Coffee

- **Blue Dog Kitchen** •
  5509 University Wy NE [NE 55th St]
- **Diva Espresso** • 8014 Lake City Wy NE [NE 80th St]
- **Espresso Express** • 6500 15th Ave NE [NE 65th St]
- **Muddy Waters Coffee Company** •
  2258 NE 65th St [23rd Ave NE]
- **Rooster's Espresso Inc** •
  7809 Lake City Wy NE [12th Ave NE]

Gas Stations

- **Chevron** • 2424 NE 65th St [24th Ave NE]

○Landmarks

- **The Wedgwood Rock** • 28th Ave NE & NE 72nd St

Schools

- **Assumption St Bridget** •
  6220 32nd Ave NE [NE 62nd St]
- **Bryant Elementary** • 3311 NE 60th St [33rd Ave NE]
- **Eckstein Middle** • 3003 NE 75th St [30th Ave NE]
- **Northwest Montessori** • 7400 25th Ave NE [NE 74th St]
- **Roosevelt High** • 1410 NE 66th St [14th Ave NE]
- **Seattle Jewish Community** •
  2618 NE 80th St [25th Ave NE]
- **University Cooperative** •
  5601 University Wy NE [NE 56th St]
- **University Prep** • 8000 25th Ave NE [NE 80th St]
- **Wedgwood Elementary** •
  2720 NE 85th St [28th Ave NE]

Map 32 • **Ravenna**

Sundries / Entertainment

Entertainment-wise, Ravenna isn't a destination. But if you live there, and feel complacent, you have some options. Board games and wood decor at The Pub at Third Place will make you feel snowed in at a ski lodge. The Ravenna Alehouse is an inoffensive neighborhood pub. Knarr is a comfortable dive. The restaurant scene is looking good with the excellent Pair leading the way, and Gaudi.

Liquor Stores

- **McCarthy & Schiering Wine Merchants** •
  6500 Ravenna Ave NE [Ravenna Ave NE]
- **Vesta Wine Cellars** • 8016 15th Ave NE [NE 80th St]

Nightlife

- **Knarr Tavern** • 5633 University Wy NE [NE 56th St]
- **The Pub at Third Place** • 6504 20th Ave NE [NE 65th St]
- **Ravenna Alehouse** • 2258 NE 65th St [23rd Ave NE]

Pet Shops

- **All the Best Pet Care** •
  8050 Lake City Wy NE [15th Ave NE]

Restaurants

- **Bagel Oasis** • 2112 NE 65th St [21st Ave NE]
- **Blue Dog Kitchen** •
  5509 University Wy NE [NE 55th St]
- **Gaudi** • 3410 NE 55th St [34th Ave NE]
- **Hot Dish** • 2255 NE 65th St [23rd Ave NE]
- **Kidd Valley** • 5502 25th Ave NE [NE 55th St]
- **Mr Villa** • 8064 Lake City Wy NE [15th Ave NE]
- **Nana's Soup House** • 3418 NE 55th St [34th Ave NE]
- **Pair** • 5501 30th Ave NE [NE 55th St]
- **Pizza Pi Vegan Pizzaria** •
  5500 University Wy NE [NE 55th St]
- **Queen Mary Tea Room** • 2912 NE 55th St [30th Ave NE]
- **Tempero do Brasil** •
  5628 University Wy NE [NE 56th St]
- **Zeek's Pizza** • 2108 NE 65th St [21st Ave NE]

Shopping

- **3rd Place Ravenna** • 6504 20th Ave NE [NE 65th St]
- **Sidecar for Pigs Peace** •
  5270 University Wy NE [NE 55th St]

Map 33 · **Northwest Seattle**

Like its NE counterpart, NW Seattle contains a blight (Aurora), a hidden corner of wanna-be elitists (Broadview), and a few funky neighborhoods that defy sensibilities of affordability. It isn't as dull as NE, but that's not saying much. It's slightly more developed and neighborhoody than the other side of I-5, but still nothing to get excited about.

Banks

- **Key Bank** • 9735 Holman Rd NW [6th Ave NW]
- **Key Bank (ATM)** • 10504 Aurora Ave N [N Northgate Wy]
- **Key Bank (ATM)** • 14424 Greenwood Ave N [N 144th St]
- **US Bank** • 13050 Aurora Ave N [N 130th St]
- **Washington Mutual** • 8555 15th Ave NW [NW 87th St]

Car Rental

- **A&S Rent-A-Car** • 10501 Greenwood Ave N [N 105th St]
- **Enterprise** • 12001 Aurora Ave N [N 125th St]
- **EZ Auto Rent** • 14135 Aurora Ave N [N 141st St]
- **Hertz** • 14333 Aurora Ave N [Roosevelt Wy N]

Coffee

- **Diva Espresso** • 14419 Greenwood Ave N [N 144th St]
- **Starbucks** • 10002 Aurora Ave N [N 102nd St]
- **Starbucks** • 13035 Aurora Ave N [N 130th St]
- **Starbucks** • 13050 Aurora Ave N [N 130th St]
- **Starbucks** • 2137 N Northgate Wy [Meridian Ave N]
- **Starbucks** • Safeway • 8704 Greenwood Ave N [N 87th St]
- **Starbucks** • 9999 Holman Rd NW [4th Ave NW]
- **Tully's** • 8551 Greenwood Ave N [N 87th St]
- **Tully's** • 9000 Holman Rd NW [NW 90th St]

Community Gardens

Gas Stations

- **76** • 14056 Greenwood Ave N [N 143rd St]
- **Arco** • 10504 Aurora Ave N [N Northgate Wy]
- **Chevron** • 2150 N Northgate Wy [Meridian Ave N]
- **Shell** • 1935 N Northgate Wy [Meridian Ave N]
- **Shell** • 9796 Holman Rd NW [6th Ave NW]

Emergency Rooms

- **Northwest Hospital and Medical Center** •
  1550 N 115th St [Meridian Ave N]

Landmarks

- **The Elephant on Aurora** • 8808 Aurora Ave N [N 88th St]
- **Granite Curling Club** • 1440 N 128th St [Ashworth Ave N]

Libraries

- **Broadview Branch** •
  12755 Greenwood Ave N [N 130th St]

 Pharmacies

- **Lowry's Prescriptions** • 10330 Meridian Ave N [N 103rd St]
- **Quality Food Center** • 8532 15th Ave NW [NW 85th St]
- **Quality Food Center** • 9999 Holman Rd NW [4th Ave NW]
- **Rite Aid** • 13050 Aurora Ave N [N 130th St]
- **Rite Aid** • 13201 Aurora Ave N [N 130th St]
- **Safeway Pharmacy** • 8704 Greenwood Ave N [N 87th St]
- **Walgreens** • 14510 Aurora Ave N [N 145 St]
- **Walgreens** • 8701 Greenwood Ave N [N 87th St]

Police

- **North Precinct** • 10049 College Wy N [N 103rd St]

Post Offices

- **Bitter Lake** • 929 N 145th St [Aurora Ave N]

Schools

- **Broadview-Thomson Elementary** •
  13052 GreeNWood Ave N [N 130th St]
- **Christ the King Elementary** • 415 N 117th St [Phinney Ave N]
- **Home School Resource** • 9250 14th Ave NW [NW 92nd St]
- **Ingraham High** • 1819 N 135th St [Wallingford Ave N]
- **Middle College High** • 1330 N 90th St [Stone Ave N]
- **Montessori for Kids** • 14410 Greenwood Ave N [N 144th St]
- **North Beach Elementary** • 9018 24th Ave NW [NW 90th St]
- **North Seattle Community College** •
  9600 College Wy N [N 97th St]
- **Northgate Christian Academy** •
  10510 Stone Ave N [N Northgate Wy]
- **Small Faces Child Dev Center** •
  9250 14th NW [NW 92nd St]
- **Viewlands Elementary** • 10525 3rd Ave NW [NW 105th St]
- **Whitman Middle** • 9201 15th Ave NW [NW 92nd St]

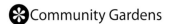 Supermarkets

- **Quality Food Center** • 9999 Holman Rd NW [4th Ave NW]
- **Safeway** • 8704 Greenwood Ave N [N 87th St]

Map 33 · **Northwest Seattle**

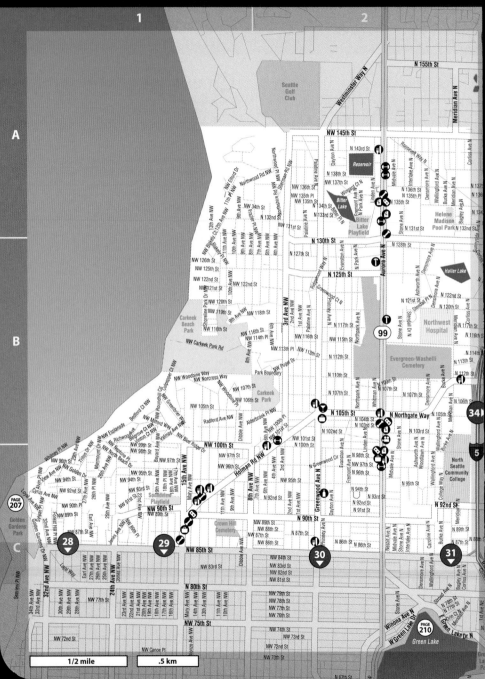

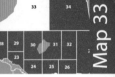
NW has a few pockets of commercial activity that contain life, most notably along 85th and north on Greenwood. The further north you go, the more suburban the setting. Sticking to Aurora, you'll find an abundant selection of $2 beers, pull tabs, used cars and meth heads, with the occasional hooker waiting to reveal her "hidden neighborhood treasure."

Copy Shops

- **Minuteman Press** • 10308 Aurora Ave N [N 103rd St]
- **Office Depot** • 13501 Aurora Ave N [N 135th St]
- **Staples** • 13240 Aurora Ave N [N 135th St]
- **UPS Store** • 10002 Aurora Ave N [N 100th St]

Gyms

- **Bally** • 13201 Aurora Ave N [N 135th St]
- **Curves** • 10033 Holman Rd NW [3rd Ave NW]
- **Gold's Gym** • 9701 Aurora Ave N [NW 97th St]
- **Ideal Exercise** • 13754 Aurora Ave N [N 140th St]
- **Ideal Exercise** • 14032 Aurora Ave N [N 140th St]

Hardware Stores

- **Home Depot** • 11616 Aurora Ave N [N 115th St]
- **Lowe's** • 12525 Aurora Ave N [N 125th St]

Liquor Stores

- **Washington State Liquor Store** •
  9218 Greenwood Ave N [N 92nd St]

Movie Theaters

- **AMC Loews Oak Tree 6** •
  10006 Aurora Ave N [N 102nd St]

Nightlife

- **Rickshaw** • 322 N 105th St [Greenwood Ave N]

Pet Shops

- **All the Best Pet Care** • 13510 Aurora Ave N [N 135th St]
- **Crown Hill Pet Supply** •
  9053 Holman Rd NW [NW 92nd St]
- **Little Amazon Fish & Pet** •
  10316 Aurora Ave N [N 103rd St]
- **Petco - Seattle** • 8728 Holman Rd NW [NW 87th St]
- **PETsMART** • 13000 Aurora Ave N [N 130th St]
- **The Tweetery** • 8541 15th Ave NW [NW 85th St]

Restaurants

- **Acorn Eatery & Bar** •
  9041 Holman Rd NW [Mary Ave NW]
- **Baranof** •
  8549 Greenwood Ave N [85th St]
- **Bick's Broadview Grill** •
  10555 Greenwood Ave N [N 107th St]
- **Burgermaster** • 9820 Aurora Ave N [N 98th St]
- **Burrito Loco** • 9211 Holman Rd NW [13th Ave NW]
- **Cyndy's House of Pancakes** •
  10507 Aurora Ave N [N 105th St]
- **Dick's Drive-In** • 9208 Holman Rd NW [13th Ave NW]
- **Kidd Valley** • 14303 Aurora Ave N [N 143rd St]
- **Patty's Eggnest** • 9749 Holman Rd NW [6th Ave NW]
- **Taqueria la Pasadita #2** •
  2143 N Northgate Way [Meridian Ave N]

Shopping

- **Lenny's Fruits & Vegetables** •
  10410 Greenwood Ave N [N 104th St]
- **The Maltese Falcon** • 9921 Aurora Ave N [N 100th St]
- **Value Village** • 8700 15th Ave NW [NW 87th St]

Video Rental

- **Blockbuster** • 10002 Aurora Ave N [N 100th St]
- **Blockbuster** • 13500 Aurora Ave N [N 135th St]
- **Blockbuster** • 9000 Holman Rd NW [NW 90th St]
- **Top Video** • 10318 Aurora Ave N [N 103rd St]

Map 34 · **Northeast Seattle**

Like its NW counterpart, NE Seattle is a smattering of obscure neighborhoods and a horrid blight (Lake City Way). The neighborhood's defining monstrosity, Northgate Mall—the nation's first—should probably be avoided unless you're nostalgic for Sears. On the upside, the neighborhoods are quaint and hide a few gems. The libraries are good and the parks clean and it's…um, a nice place to raise kids? If it's any consolation, it gets worse in Shoreline.

$ Banks

- **Frontier Bank** • 2825 NE 125th St [28th Ave NE]
- **Key Bank** • 353 NE Northgate Wy [3rd Ave NE]
- **Sterling Savings Bank** • 828 NE Northgate Wy [8th Ave NE]
- **US Bank** • 815 NE Northgate Wy [8th Ave NE]
- **US Bank** • 8702 35th Ave NE [NE 87th St]
- **Washington Federal Savings** • 14360 15th Ave NE [N 145th St]
- **Washington Mutual** • 12360 Lake City Wy NE [31st Ave NE]
- **Washington Mutual** • 520 NE Northgate Wy [5th Ave NE]

Car Rental

- **Enterprise** • 11717 Lake City Wy NE [NE 117th St]

Car Washes

- **Bigfoot Car Wash** • 11310 Lake City Wy NE [NE 113th St]
- **Brown Bear Car Wash** • 12506 15th Ave NE [N 125th St]
- **Jet Car Wash** • 1513 NE 145th St [15th Ave NE]

Coffee

- **Cloud City Coffee** • 8801 Roosevelt Wy NE [NE 88th St]
- **Starbucks** • QFC • 11100 Roosevelt Wy NE [NE 112th St]
- **Starbucks** • 12001 Lake City Wy NE [NE 120th St]
- **Starbucks** • 14330 Lake City Wy NE [NE 143rd St]
- **Starbucks** • 14359 15th Ave NE [N 145th St]
- **Starbucks** • 301 NE Northgate Wy [3rd Ave NE]
- **Starbucks** • 540 NE Northgate Wy [5th Ave NE]

Community Gardens

Gas Stations

- **76** • 11001 Roosevelt Wy NE [NE Northgate Wy]
- **76** • 11346 Lake City Wy NE [NE 113th St]
- **Arco** • 11611 8th Ave NE [NE 117th St]
- **Chevron** • 11750 Lake City Wy NE [NE 117th St]
- **Chevron** • 13001 Lake City Wy NE [N 130th St]
- **Exxon** • 14312 Lake City Wy NE [NE 143rd St]
- **Mobil** • 11310 Lake City Way NE [NE 113th St]
- **Shell** • 9500 35th Ave NE [NE 95th St]

○ Landmarks

- **Rick's** • 11332 Lake City Wy NE [NE 113th St]

Libraries

- **Lake City Branch** • 12501 28th Ave NE [N 130th St]
- **Northgate Branch** • 10548 5th Ave NE [N 105th St]

P Parking

Rx Pharmacies

- **Bartell Drugs** • 3018 NE 125th St [Lake City Wy NE]
- **Fred Meyer** • 13000 Lake City Wy NE [N 130th St]
- **Maple Leaf** • 8830 Roosevelt Wy NE [NE 88th St]
- **Northaven Pharmacy** • 531 NE 112th St [5th Ave NE]
- **Quality Food Center** • 11100 Roosevelt Wy NE [NE 112th St]
- **Safeway Pharmacy** • 12318 15th Ave NE [N 123rd St]
- **Target** • 302 NE Northgate Wy [3rd Ave NE]
- **Walgreens** • 14352 Lake City Wy NE [NE 145th St]
- **Walgreens** • 859 NE Northgate Wy [8th Ave NE]

Post Offices

- **Lake City** • 3019 NE 127th St [30th Ave NE]
- **Northgate** • 11036 8th Ave NE [NE Northgate Wy]

Schools

- **AS#1 (Pinehurst) K-8** • 11530 12th Ave NE [Pinehurst Wy NE]
- **The Clearwater** • 11006 34th Ave NE [N 110th St]
- **Dartmoor** • 9618 Roosevelt Wy NE [NE 96th St]
- **Educational Advancement Academy** • 9750 3rd Ave NE, Ste 102 [NE 100th St]
- **Haller Lake Childrens Center** • 13305 1st Ave NE [N 133rd St]
- **John Rogers Elementary** • 4030 NE 109th St [Alton Ave NE]
- **Lakeside** • 14050 1st Ave NE [N 143rd St]
- **Middle College High** • 401 NE Northgate Wy [5th Ave NE]
- **Nathan Hale High** • 10750 30th Ave NE [N 110th St]
- **Northgate Elementary** • 11725 1st Ave NE [N 117th St]
- **Olympic Hills Elementary** • 13018 20th Ave NE [N 130th St]
- **Olympic View Elementary** • 504 NE 95th St [5th Ave NE]
- **Our Lady of the Lake** • 3520 NE 89th St [35th Ave NE]
- **The Perkins** • 9005 Roosevelt Wy NE [NE 90th St]
- **Sacajawea Elementary** • 9501 20th Ave NE [NE 96th St]
- **Seattle Waldorf** • 2728 NE 100th St [27th Ave NE]
- **St Matthew Elementary** • 1230 NE 127th St [14th Ave NE]
- **Summit K-12** • 11051 34th Ave NE [N 110th St]

Supermarkets

- **Fred Meyer** • 13000 Lake City Wy NE [N 130th St]
- **Quality Food Center** • 11100 Roosevelt WY NE [NE 112th St]
- **Quality Food Center** • 3020 NE 127th St [30th Ave NE]
- **Quality Food Center** • 1531 NE 145th St [15th Ave NE]
- **Safeway** • 12318 15th Ave NE [N 123rd St]

Map 34 · Northeast Seattle

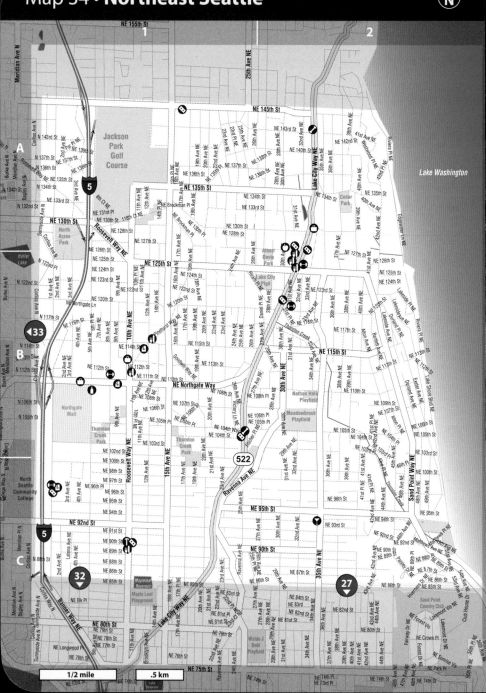

You'll be hard pressed to find a riveting night out in the whole NE. "Noteworthy" bars on this page can be counted on half a hand (translation: Fiddler's Inn). If your luck has really run out, try one of the crusty pubs along Lake City Way. The beer is cheap and the conversation priceless. For less discouraging fare, turn to another page.

Copy Shops

- **FedEx Kinko's** • 831 NE Northgate Wy [8th Ave NE]
- **Pip Printing** • 11325 Pinehurst Wy NE [NE 114th St]
- **UPS Store** • 9594 1st Ave NE [NE 95th St]

Farmers Markets

- **Lake City (Thurs, 3 pm–7 pm, May to October)** •
  Behind fire station • 127th St & 30th Ave NE

Gyms

- **24 Hour Fitness** • 11030 8th Ave NE [NE Northgate Wy] ♿
- **Curves** • 12520 Lake City Wy NE [N 125th St]
- **Curves** • 9580 1st Ave NE [NE 95th St]
- **Mieko's Fitness** • 12015 31st Ave NE [NE 120th St]

Hardware Stores

- **Maple Leaf Ace Hardware** •
  9000 Roosevelt Wy NE [NE 90th St]

Liquor Stores

- **Washington State Liquor Store** •
  10744 5th Ave NE [NE Northgate Wy]

Nightlife

- **Fiddler's Inn** • 9219 35th Ave NE [NE 93rd St]

Pet Shops

- **The Best Little Rabbit Rodent & Ferret House** •
  14317 Lake City Wy NE [N 143rd St]
- **Pet Pros - Seattle** •
  10304 Lake City Wy NE [NE 104th Wy]

Restaurants

- **Café Long** • 12517 Lake City Wy NE [N 125th St]
- **Café Weini** • 1510 NE 117th St [Pinehurst Wy NE]
- **Dick's Drive-In** • 12325 30th Ave NE [Lake City Wy NE]
- **Enat Ethiopian** • 11546 15th Ave NE [NE 111th St]
- **Judy Fu's Snappy Dragon** •
  8917 Roosevelt Wy NE [NE 89th St]
- **Toyoda Sushi** • 12543 Lake City Wy NE [N 127th St]

Shopping

- **Display & Costume** •
  11201 Roosevelt Wy NE [Pinehurst Wy NE]
- **Fred Meyer** • 13000 Lake City Wy NE [N 130th St]
- **The Northgate Mall** •
  401 NE Northgate Wy [5th Ave NE]

Video Rental

- **Blockbuster** • 3050 NE 127th St [Lake City Wy NE]
- **Reckless Video Inc** •
  9020 Roosevelt Wy NE [NE 90th St]
- **Silver Platters** • 9560 1st Ave NE [NE 95th St]
- **Video Factory** • 1557 NE 145th St [15th Ave NE]
- **Video Theater** • 12320 Lake City Wy NE [N 123rd St]
- **Video Videos No 2** •
  10326 Lake City Wy NE [NE 104th Wy]
- **World Wide Video of Washington** •
  12708 Lake City Wy NE [N 127th St]

Map 35 · **Alki / West Seattle / North Admiral**

Many Seattleites believe West Seattle is on the other side of the world. The monstrous West Seattle Freeway Bridge connects this area with the rest of the city. The California Avenue and Alaska Way intersection---known as The Junction---feels like a small, hip town of its own, littered with fabulous restaurants, shops, and historical landmarks. Similarly, west-facing Alki Avenue feels like a California beach town---with little sunshine, snowcapped mountains, and ferry boats.

Banks

- **Bank of America** • 4323 SW Admiral Wy
- **First Mutual Bank** • 4102 California Ave SW [SW Dakota St]
- **Key Bank** • 4701 California Ave SW [SW Alaska St]
- **Key Bank (ATM)** • 4712 44th Ave SW [SW Alaska St]
- **US Bank** • 4200 SW Edmunds St [42nd Ave SW]
- **Washington Federal Savings** •
  4700 42nd Ave SW [SW Alaska St]
- **Washington Mutual** • 2610 California Ave SW [SW Admiral Wy]
- **Washington Mutual** • 4501 California Ave SW [SW Oregon St]
- **Wells Fargo** • 2358 California Ave Sw, [SW College St]
- **Wells Fargo** • 4314 SW Alaska St [California Ave SW]

Coffee

- **Alki Mail and Dispatch** •
  4701 SW Admiral Way [47th Ave SW]
- **C&P Coffee Company** • 5612 California Ave SW [SW Findlay St]
- **Coffee To A Tea With Sugar** •
  4541 California Ave SW [SW Oregon St]
- **Cupcake Royale/Verite Coffee** •
  4556 California Ave SW [SW Oregon St]
- **Easy Street Records** •
  4559 California Ave SW [SW Oregon St]
- **Freshy's** • 2735 California Ave SW [SW Lander St]
- **Hotwire Online Coffeehouse** •
  4410 California Ave SW [SW Genesee St]
- **Revolution Coffee** • 4217 SW Admiral Wy [42nd Ave SW]
- **Starbucks** • Safeway • 2622 California Ave SW [SW Admiral Wy]
- **Starbucks** • 2742 Alki Ave SW [61st Ave SW]
- **Starbucks** • Safeway • 4754 42nd Ave SW [SW Alaska St]
- **Tully's** • 2676 Alki Ave SW [60th Ave SW]
- **Uptown Espresso** • 4301 SW Edmunds St [California Ave SW]

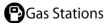 Community Gardens

 Gas Stations

- **Chevron** • 2347 California Ave SW [SW College St]
- **Exxon** • 4001 California Ave SW [SW Andover St]

Landmarks

- **Alki Beach** • Alki Ave SW & Bonair Dr SW
- **Birthplace of Seattle Monument** •
  62nd Ave SW & Alki Ave SW
- **Schmitz Park** • 5551 SW Admiral Wy
- **Statue of Liberty** • 61st Ave SW & Alki Ave SW
- **Whale Tail Park** • 58th Ave SW & SW Lander St

Libraries

- **West Seattle Branch** • 2306 42nd Ave SW [SW College St]

Parking

Pharmacies

- **Bartell Drugs** • 2345 42nd Ave SW [SW College St]
- **Bartell Drugs** • 4706 42nd Ave SW [SW Alaska St]
- **Morton's** • 4707 California Ave SW [SW Alaska St]
- **Rite Aid** • 5217 California Ave SW [SW Dawson St]
- **Safeway Pharmacy** •
  2622 California Ave SW [SW Admiral Wy]
- **Westside Pharmacy** •
  5401 California Ave SW [SW Brandon St]

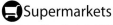 Post Offices

- **West Seattle** • 4412 California Ave SW [SW Genesee St]

Schools

- **Alki Elementary** • 3010 59 Ave SW [SW Stevens St]
- **Holy Rosary** • 4142 42nd Ave SW [SW Dakota St]
- **Hope Lutheran** • 4446 42nd Ave SW [SW Genesee St]
- **Lafayette Elementary** •
  2645 California Ave SW [SW Admiral Wy]
- **Madison Middle** • 3429 45th Ave SW [SW Hinds St]
- **Pathfinder K-8** • 5012 SW Genesee St [50th Ave SW]
- **Schmitz Park Elementary** •
  5000 SW Spokane St [50th Ave SW]
- **Seattle Lutheran High** • 4141 41st Ave SW [SW Dakota St]
- **West Seattle Christian** • 4401 42nd Ave SW [SW Genesee St]
- **West Seattle High** • 3000 California Ave SW [SW Stevens St]

Supermarkets

- **Metropolitan Market** • 2320 42nd Ave SW [SW College St]
- **Safeway** • 2622 California Ave SW [SW Admiral Wy]
- **Safeway** • 4754 42nd Ave SW [SW Alaska St]

Map 35 • **Alki / West Seattle / North Admiral** Ⓝ

Park free in lots around The Junction and start roaming. With no Starbucks in sight, you'll have to get caffeinated at—believe it or not—Easy Street Records. Ama Ama Oyster Bar and Lee's Asian Restaurant stand out for unique, fresh meals, while the historic Husky Deli serves homemade ice cream. Head downhill and west to Alki beach for a Celtic Swell Guinness and explore what's referred to as the birthplace of Seattle.

Copy Shops

- **Alki Mail and Dispatch** • 4701 SW Admiral Wy [47th Ave SW]
- **UPS Store** • 4742 42nd Ave SW [SW Alaska St]

Farmers Markets

- **West Seattle (Sun, 10 am–2 pm, April–Dec)** •
  SW Alaska St & California Ave SW

Gyms

- **Curves** • 3280 California Ave SW [SW Hinds St]
- **Fitness for Women** • 5908 California Ave SW [SW Juneau St]

Hardware Stores

- **Junction True Value Hardware** •
  4747 44th Ave SW [SW Alaska St]

Liquor Stores

- **Washington State Liquor Store** •
  4513 California Ave SW [SW Oregon St]

Movie Theaters

- **Admiral Theater** • 2343 California Ave SW [SW College St]
- **West Seattle Walk-In Theater** •
  California Ave SW & SW Alaska St

Nightlife

- **Bamboo Bar & Grill** • 2806 Alki Ave SW [62nd Ave SW]
- **Celtic Swell Irish Pub** • 2722 Alki Ave SW [61st Ave SW]
- **Elliot Bay Brewpub** • 4720 California Ave SW, [SW Alaska St]
- **The Matador** • 4546 California Ave SW [SW Oregon St]
- **Poggie Tavern** • 4717 California Ave SW [SW Alaska St]
- **West 5 Lounge & Restaurant** •
  4539 California Ave SW [SW Oregon St]

Pet Shops

- **Mud Bay Granary** • 2611 California Ave SW [SW Admiral Wy]
- **Next To Nature** • 4543 California Ave SW [SW Oregon St]
- **Petco - Seattle** • 4732 California Ave SW [SW Alaska St]

Restaurants

- **Alki Bakery** • 2738 Alki Ave SW [62nd Ave SW]
- **Alki Café** • 2726 Alki Ave SW [62nd Ave SW]
- **Alki Homestead** • 2717 61st Ave SW [Alki Ave SW]
- **Ama Ama Oyster Bar** •
  4752 California Ave SW [SW Edmonds St]
- **Angelina's Trattoria** • 2311 California Ave SW [SW College St]
- **Bakery Nouveau** • 4737 California Ave SW [SW Alaska St]
- **Blackbird Bistro** • 2329 California Ave SW [SW College St]
- **Cactus** • 2820 Alki Ave [SW 63rd Avenue SW]
- **Christo's on Alki** • 2508 Alki Ave SW [57th Ave SW]
- **Circa Neighborhood Grill and Alehouse** •
  2605 California Ave SW [SW Admiral Wy]
- **Duke's Chowder House** • 2516 Alki Ave SW [57th Ave SW]
- **Easy Street Records** • 4559 California Ave SW [SW Oregon St]
- **Elliott Bay Brewery & Pub** • 4720 California Ave SW [SW Alaska St]
- **Jak's Grill** • 4548 California Ave SW [SW Oregon St]
- **La Rustica** • 4100 Beach Dr SW [SW Carroll St]
- **Lee's Asian Restaurant** • 4510 California Ave [SW Oregon St]
- **Mashiko** • 4725 California Ave SW [SW Alaska St]
- **The Mission Tapas and Bar** •
  2325 California Ave SW [SW College St]
- **Pagliacci Pizza** • 4449 California Ave SW [SW Oregon St]
- **Pailin Thai** • 2223 California Ave SW [SW Walker St]
- **Pegasus Pizza** • 2758 Alki Ave SW [62nd Ave SW]
- **Pepperdock's Restaurant** • 2618 Alki Ave SW [59th Ave SW]
- **Pho Thân Brothers'** • 4822 California Ave SW [SW Edmunds St]
- **Shadowland** • 4458 California Ave SW [SW Oregon St]
- **Spud Fish & Chips** • 2666 Alki Ave SW [60th Ave SW]
- **Sunfish Seafood** • 2800 Alki Ave SW [62nd Ave SW]
- **Talarico's** • 4718 California Ave SW [SW Alaska St]
- **Taqueria Guaymas** • 4719 California Ave SW [SW Alaska St]
- **Zatz A Better Bagel** • 2348 California Ave SW [SW College St]

Shopping

- **Capers** • 4521 California Ave SW [SW Oregon St]
- **Click! Design that Fits** • 2210 California Ave SW [SW Walker St]
- **Coastal Surf Boutique** • 2532 Alki Ave SW [58th Ave SW]
- **Curious Kidstuff** • 4740 California Ave SW [SW Alaska St]
- **Easy Street Records** • 4559 California Ave SW [SW Oregon St]
- **Husky Deli** • 4721 California Ave SW [SW Alaska St]
- **Metropolitan Market** • 2320 42nd Ave SW [SW College St]
- **Northwest Art & Frame** • 4733 California Ave SW [SW Alaska St]
- **PCC Natural Markets** • 2749 California Ave SW [SW Lander St]
- **Seattle Fish Company Inc** •
  4435 California Ave SW [SW Genesee St]
- **Small Clothes** • 3236 California Ave SW [SW Hanford St]
- **Square One Books** • 4724 42nd Ave SW [SW Alaska St]
- **West Seattle Farmers Market** •
  SW Alaska St & California Ave SW
- **Zamboanga** • 4531 California Ave SW [SW Oregon St]

Video Rental

- **Blockbuster** • 2222 California Ave SW [SW Walker St]

Map 36 · **North Delridge**

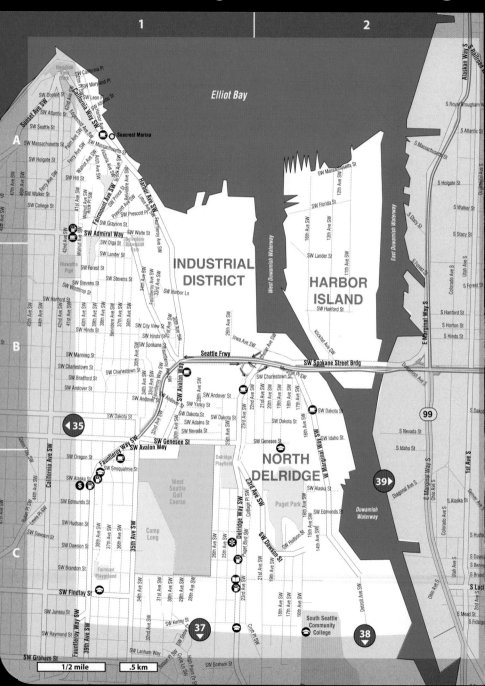

1

2

Elliot Bay

Hamilton
View Park

SW California Pl
SW Maryland Pl

SW Donald St
SW Leon St

SW Seattle St
SW Atlantic St
SW Harbor St
SW Massachusetts St

Seacrest Marina

A

SW Massachusetts St

S Atlantic St

S Massachusetts St

SW Holgate St

S Holgate St

SW Hill St

SW Walker St

S Walker St

SW College St

S Stacy St

SW Prince St

SW Belvidere Pl SW

SW Prince

Procaut Ave SW

SW Prescott Pl

SW Admiral Way

Belvidere
Viewpoint
Park

SW Waite St

SW Olga St

Hiawatha
Plgd

SW Lander St

SW Forest St

**INDUSTRIAL
DISTRICT**

SW Massachusetts St

12th Ave SW

SW Florida St

13th Ave SW

16th Ave SW

SW Lander St

11th Ave SW

SW Stevens St

SW Stevens St

SW Winthrop St

SW Hanford St

SW City View St

SW Harbor Ln

**HARBOR
ISLAND**

SW Hanford St

East Duwamish Waterway

S Forest St

S Hanford St

S Horton St

S Hinds St

SW Hinds St

SW Hinds St

SW Spokane St

Seattle Frwy

26th Ave SW

Iowa Ave SW

Cedar Ave SW

West Duwamish Waterway

Klickitat Ave SW

E Marginal Way S

B

SW Manning St

SW Charlestown St

SW Charlestown St

SW Bradford St

SW Andover St

SW Spokane Street Brdg

Marginal Pl SW

SW Charlestown St

22nd Ave SW
21st Ave SW
20th Ave SW
19th Ave SW
18th Ave SW
17th Ave SW

SW Dakota St

16th Ave SW

SW Idaho St

Diagonal Ave S

Dawson St

Duwamish Ave S

99

S Nevada St

S Idaho St

SW Avalon Way

SW Andover St

SW Yancy St

SW Andover St

28th Ave SW

23rd Ave SW

SW Dakota St

SW Dakota St

35

SW Nevada St

SW Adams St

SW Nevada St

SW Genesee St

39

SW Genesee St

SW Avalon Way

Fauntleroy Way SW

SW Oregon St

Delridge
Playfield

**NORTH
DELRIDGE**

SW Alaska St

S Alaska St

S Hudson St

SW Alaska St

SW Snoqualmie St

**West
Seattle
Golf
Course**

SW Edmunds St

16th Ave SW

Puget Park

SW Edmunds St

15th Ave SW

14th Ave SW

Duwamish
Waterway

SW Hudson St

SW Dawson St

**Camp
Long**

SW Dawson St

35th Ave SW

37th Ave SW
36th Ave SW

C

SW Brandon St

SW Hudson St

Fairmont
Playground

Delridge Way SW

Puget Blvd SW

SW Dawson St

Detroit Ave SW

S Hudson

S Dawson St

S Benne

S Brand

S Luci

SW Findlay St

26th Ave SW
25th Ave SW

23rd Ave SW

SW Juneau St

SW Raymond St

31st Ave SW
30th Ave SW
29th Ave SW
28th Ave SW

21st Ave SW

18th Ave SW
17th Ave SW
16th Ave SW

S Mead St

S Fidalgo

**South Seattle
Community
College**

37

38

Croft Pl SW

SW Kenny St

SW Lanham Way

SW Graham St

SW Graham St

Fauntleroy Way SW
39th Ave SW

California Ave SW

47th Ave SW

1/2 mile

.5 km

The charm of this part of town is that they seem to have one foot in the 1950s while the other foot steps bravely into the 21st century. A large elderly population thrives amongst a strong influx of young families seeking kid-friendly goods and services. Snap the ideal panoramic photograph of Seattle's skyline from Harbor Avenue or up steep Admiral Way. There's really nothing pretentious in this neck of the woods. A coffee stop at Javabean in Luna Park is worth the detour.

Banks

- **Bank of America** • 4001 SW Alaska St [40th Ave SW]

Coffee

- **Bubbles** • 1619 Harbor Ave SW [Ferry Ave SW]
- **Diva Espresso** • 4480 Fauntleroy Wy SW [SW Oregon St]
- **Javabean Inc West Seattle** •
  2920 SW Avalon Wy [Fauntleroy Wy SW]
- **Jun's Espresso** •
  4100 W Marginal Wy SW [SW Dakota St]
- **Starbucks** • 4101 SW Admiral Wy [41st Ave SW]
- **Uptown Espresso** • 3845 Delridge Wy SW [23rd Ave SW]

Community Gardens

Gas Stations

- **76** • 4580 Fauntleroy Wy SW [SW Alaska St]
- **Exxon** • 5235 Delridge Wy SW [SW Dawson St]
- **Shell** • 3901 SW Alaska St [Fauntleroy Wy SW]
- **Shell** • 4100 SW Admiral Wy [41st Ave SW]
- **Shell** • 5441 Delridge Wy SW [SW Brandon St]

oLandmarks

- **Seacrest Marina** • 1660 Harbor Ave SW [Ferry Ave SW]

Libraries

- **Delridge Branch** • 5423 Delridge Wy SW [SW Brandon St]

Schools

- **Cleveland High (Temporary location)** •
  5950 Delridge Wy SW [SW Juneau St]
- **Cooper Elementary** •
  1901 SW Genesee St [19th Ave SW]
- **Fairmount Park Elementary** •
  3800 SW Findlay St [38th Ave SW]
- **South Seattle Community College** •
  6000 16th Ave SW [SW Juneau St]
- **West Seattle Montessori** •
  4536 38th Ave SW [Fauntleroy Wy SW]

Map 36 · **North Delridge**

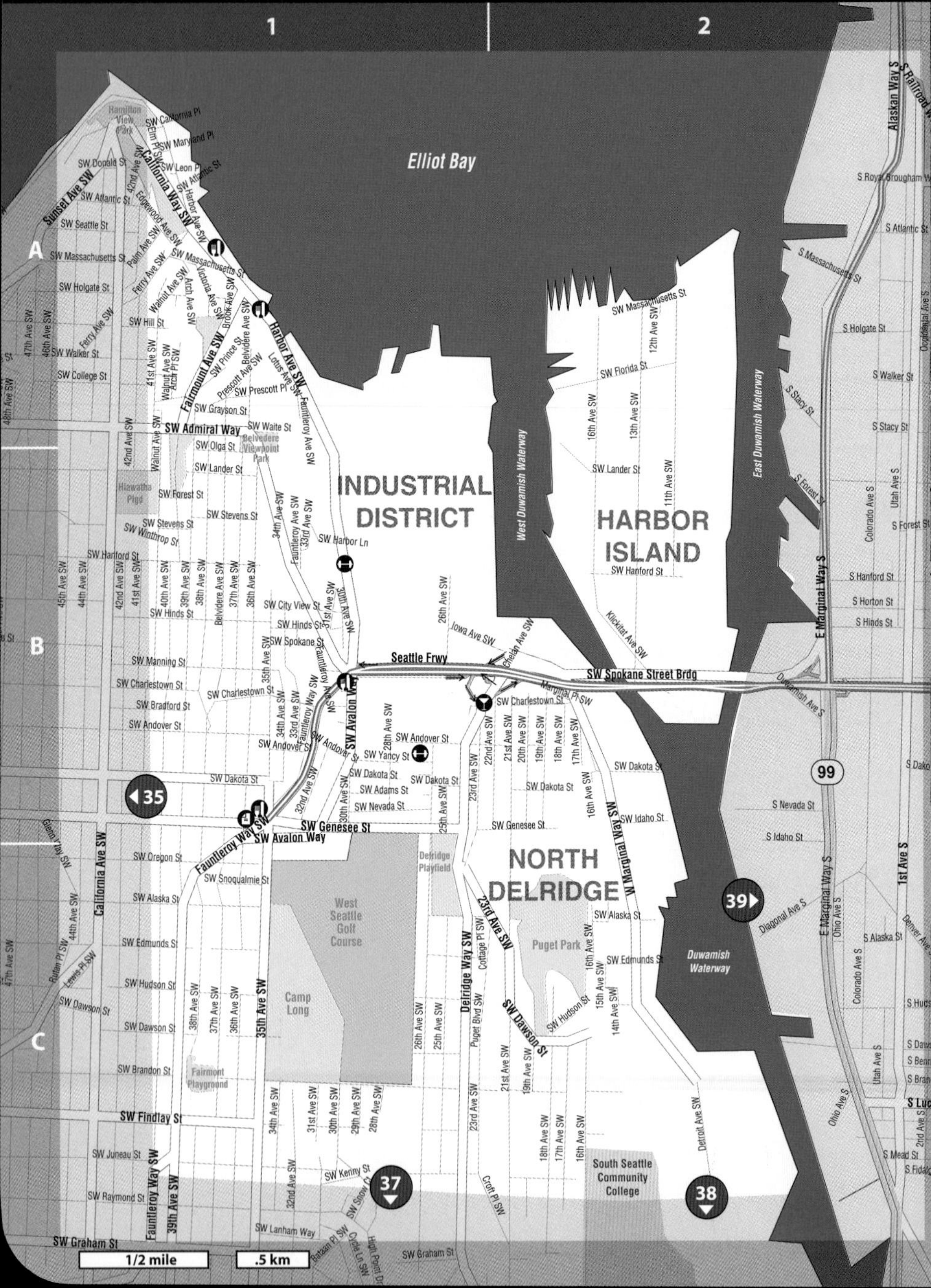

Ⓝ

1 | **2**

Elliot Bay

Hamilton View Park

SW Donald St
SW California Pl
SW Leon Pl
SW Maryland Pl
SW Atlantic St
California Way SW
California Ave SW
Sunset Ave SW

SW Seattle St

A

SW Massachusetts St
SW Massachusetts St
SW Massachusetts St
12th Ave SW

47th Ave SW
46th Ave SW
SW Holgate St
SW Holgate St
Pearl Ave SW
Ferry Ave SW
Walnut Ave SW
Arch Ave SW
Duroc Ave SW
Harbor Ave SW

SW Hill St
41st Ave SW
SW Walker St
40th Ave SW
SW Florida St
16th Ave SW
13th Ave SW
SW College St
SW Prince St
SW Prince St
Fauntleroy Way SW
Prescott Ave SW
Belvidere Ave SW
SW Prescott Pl
Fairmount Ave SW
Harbor Ave SW

SW Grayson St

East Duwamish Waterway
West Duwamish Waterway

SW Admiral Way
SW Waite St
SW Lander St
11th Ave SW
42nd Ave SW
Walnut Ave SW
SW Olga St
Belvidere Viewpoint Park
SW Lander St
NS SW

**INDUSTRIAL
DISTRICT**

Hiawatha Plgd

SW Forest St
SW Forest St
SW Stevens St
SW Stevens St
34th Ave SW
33rd Ave SW

SW Wintrop St
SW Harford St
SW City View St
SW Harbor Ln

**HARBOR
ISLAND**

45th Ave SW
44th Ave SW
42nd Ave SW
41st Ave SW
40th Ave SW
38th Ave SW
36th Ave SW
SW Hinds St
SW Hinds St
SW Hinds St
26th Ave SW
28th Ave SW
Iowa Ave SW
SW Hanford St

SW Spokane St
SW Spokane St
Sixian Ave SW
Klickitat Ave SW

B

SW Manning St
SW Charlestown St
SW Bradford St
SW Andover St

Seattle Frwy
SW Charlestown St
SW Charlestown St
35th Ave SW
34th Ave SW
33rd Ave SW
Marginal Pl SW

SW Spokane Street Brdg
Duwamish Ave S

99

SW Andover St
SW Andover St
22nd Ave SW
21st Ave SW
20th Ave SW
19th Ave SW
18th Ave SW
17th Ave SW
SW Avalon Way
28th Ave SW
SW Yancy St
SW Dakota St
SW Dakota St
SW Dakota St
SW Dakota St
16th Ave SW
SW Dakota St
SW Nevada St
S Nevada St
S Idaho St

SW Adams St
SW Nevada St
25th Ave SW
23rd Ave SW
SW Genesee St
SW Genesee St

◀ **35**
SW Genesee St
Fauntleroy Way SW
SW Avalon Way

SW Oregon St
SW Snoqualmie St
Delridge Playfield
**NORTH
DELRIDGE**
Puget Park

S Idaho St
SW Idaho St

39 ▶

SW Alaska St
California Ave SW
46th Ave SW
44th Ave SW
SW Edmunds St
SW Hudson St
West Seattle Golf Course
SW Alaska St
Delridge Way SW
23rd Ave SW
Cottage Pl SW
16th Ave SW
SW Edmunds St
Duwamish Waterway

47th Ave SW
Lexs Pl SW
44th Pl SW
SW Dawson St
SW Dawson St
Camp Long
SW Hudson St
Puget Blvd SW
21st Ave SW
19th Ave SW
15th Ave SW
14th Ave SW
Detroit Ave SW

C

SW Brandon St
38th Ave SW
37th Ave SW
36th Ave SW
35th Ave SW
28th Ave SW
25th Ave SW

Fairmont Playground
SW Dawson St
SW Findlay St
Delridge Way SW
SW Dawson St

SW Juneau St
SW Raymond St
Fauntleroy Way SW
39th Ave SW
34th Ave SW
32nd Ave SW
31st Ave SW
30th Ave SW
SW Kenny St
23rd Ave SW
19th Ave SW
17th Ave SW
16th Ave SW

37
38

SW Graham St
SW Lanham Way
Croft Pl SW
Puget Blvd SW
Croft Ln SW
SW Graham St

**South Seattle
Community
College**

S Royal Brougham Way
Alaskan Way S
Klickitat Ave S
S Atlantic St
S Massachusetts St
S Holgate St
S Walker St
S Stacy St
S Stacy St
Colorado Ave S
Utah Ave S
S Forest St
S Hanford St
S Horton St
S Hinds St
E Marginal Way S

1st Ave S
Denver Ave S
Ohio Ave S
Colorado Ave S
S Alaska St
S Hudson St
S Dawson St
S Brandon St
S Luc

1/2 mile | .5 km

Most tourists head straight for pricey Salty's on Alki, with its stunning city view. Locals get fish and chips with the same view for a fraction of the price at Alki Crab Company. Skylark Café and Club packs them in on the weekend and serves up the ultimate combination of tater tots with a side of rock n' roll.

Copy Shops

• **Sudden Printing** •
4151 Fauntleroy Wy SW [SW Genesee St]

Gyms

• **All-Star Fitness** • 2629 SW Andover St [26th Ave SW]
• **X Gym** • 3213 Harbor Ave SW [SW Harbour Ln]

Nightlife

• **Skylark Café & Club** •
3803 Delridge Wy SW [SW Charlestown St]

Restaurants

• **Alki Crab & Fish Company** •
1660 Harbor Ave SW [Ferry Ave SW]
• **Buddha Ruksa** • 3520 SW Genesee St [35th Ave SW]
• **Luna Park Cafe** • 2918 SW Avalon Way [SW Spokane St]
• **Salty's on Alki Beach** •
1936 Harbor Ave SW [Fairmount Ave SW]

Map 37 • **Fauntleroy / Arbor Heights**

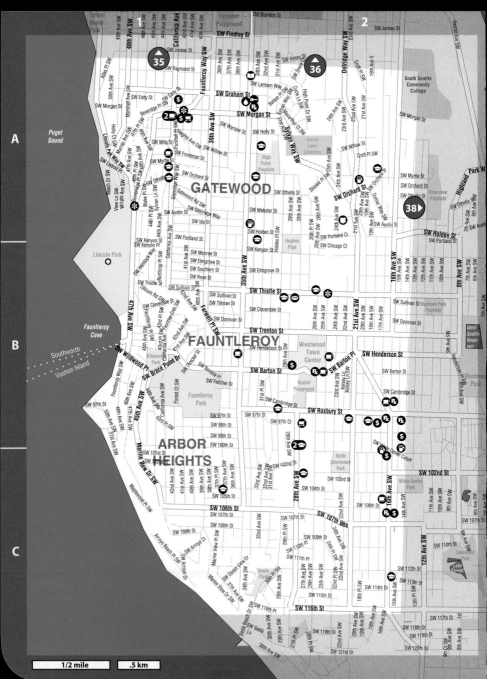

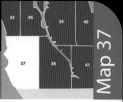
Fauntleroy Way, the street from which this area gets its name, can be thought of as the "Gateway to Vashon Island," with its direct route through quaint, garden-lush, old neighborhoods bordering Lincoln Park to the Vashon Ferry Terminal. Arbor Heights and communities east of Fauntleroy, including White Center, reflect populations struggling to keep afloat as well as young families who can't afford to live closer to the water or in one of Seattle's pricier, more central neighborhoods.

Banks

- **Key Bank** • 9655 17th Ave SW [SW Roxbury St]
- **US Bank** • 9800 15th Ave SW [SW 98th St]
- **US Bank (ATM)** • 10616 16th Ave SW [SW 106th St]
- **Washington Federal Savings** •
  6428 California Ave SW [SW Eddy St]
- **Washington Mutual** • 1616 SW 100th St [16th Ave SW]
- **Washington Mutual** • 2890 SW Barton St [29th Ave SW]
- **Washington Mutual** • 4201 SW Morgan St [42nd Ave SW]

Car Rental

- **Enterprise** • 6313 35th Ave SW [SW Graham St]

Car Washes

- **Car Wash Palace** • 6301 35th Ave SW [SW Graham St]

Coffee

- **Bird On A Wire Espresso** •
  3509 SW Henderson St [35th Ave SW]
- **Café Rozella** • 9434 Delridge Wy SW [17th Ave SW]
- **Caffe Ladro** • 7011 California Ave SW [SW Frontenac St]
- **First Choice Espresso** • 10439 16th Ave SW [SW 104th St]
- **Starbucks** • QFC • 2500 SW Barton St [25th Ave SW]
- **Starbucks** • 6501 California Ave SW [Fauntleroy Wy SW]
- **Starbucks** • 9023 25th Ave SW [SW Henderson St]
- **Tully's** • 4205 SW Morgan St [42nd Ave SW]

Community Gardens

Gas Stations

- **Arco** • 7301 Delridge Wy SW [Sylvan Wy SW]
- **Chevron** • 1520 SW 100th St [15th Ave SW]
- **Chevron** • 7580 35th Ave SW [SW Ida St]
- **Exxon** • 9857 17th Ave SW [SW 100th St]

Landmarks

- **Lincoln Park** • 8011 Fauntleroy Wy SW [SW Monroe St]

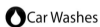 Libraries

- **Southwest Branch** •
  9010 35th Ave SW [SW Henderson St]
- **High Point Branch** • 3411 SW Raymond St [34th Ave SW]

Pharmacies

- **Albertson's** • 10616 16th Ave SW [SW 106th St]
- **Bartell Drugs** • 9600 15th Ave SW [SW Roxbury St]
- **Rite Aid** • 2600 SW Barton St [26th Ave SW]
- **Walgreens** • 6330 35th Ave SW [SW Graham St]
- **Walgreens** • 9456 16th Ave SW [SW Cambridge St]
- **White Center Pharmacy** • 9601 16th Ave SW [SW Roxbury St]

Police

- **Southwest Precinct** • 2300 SW Webster St [24th Ave SW]

Post Offices

- **Westwood** • 2721 SW Trenton St [28th Ave SW]

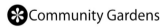 Schools

- **Arbor Heights Elementary** • 3701 SW 104th St [37th Pl SW]
- **Denny Middle** • 8402 30th Ave SW [SW Thistle St]
- **Explorer West Middle** • 10015 28th Ave SW [SW 99th St]
- **Gatewood Elementary** • 4320 SW Myrtle St [California Ave SW]
- **Gatewood Private** • 4316 SW Othello St [44th Ave SW]
- **High Point Elementary** • 6760 34th Ave SW [SW Willow St]
- **Holy Family** • 9615 20th Ave SW [SW Roxbury St]
- **Learning Way** • 9421 18th Ave SW [SW Cambridge St]
- **New Start** • 11216 16th Ave SW [SW 112th St]
- **Our Lady of Guadalupe** • 3401 SW Myrtle St [34th Ave SW]
- **Roxhill Elementary** • 9430 30th Ave SW [SW Roxbury St]
- **Sanislo Elementary** • 1812 SW Myrtle St [18th Ave SW]
- **Sealth High** • 2600 SW Thistle St [26th Ave SW]
- **Shorewood Christian** • 10300 28th Ave SW [SW 102nd St]
- **South Lake High** • 7740 34th Ave SW [SW Holden St]
- **Westside** • 10015 28th Ave SW [SW 99th St]

 Supermarkets

- **Safeway** • 9620 28th Ave SW [SW Roxbury St]
- **Thriftway** • 4201 SW Morgan St [42nd Ave SW]

Map 37 · **Fauntleroy / Arbor Heights**

Not much nightlife around these parts, but when you're done shopping at Westwood Town Center, Mother Nature can show you a spectacular time at Lincoln Park. A labyrinth of easy trails lead to a saltwater community pool and wild beaches. Just up from the Fauntleroy Ferry Terminal at the park's south entrance, Endolyne Joe's offers a divine, ever-changing menu. Salvadorean Bakery is beyond delicious and 88 Restaurant offers fat bahn mi and fragrant pho. If you really need a beer, dive right in with the colorful locals at The Tug Tavern.

Copy Shops

• **Staples** • 2501 SW Trenton St [25th Ave SW]

Gyms

• **24 Hour Fitness** • 2500 SW Barton St [25th Ave SW] ♿
• **Curves** • 11001 16th Ave SW [SW 110th St]

Hardware Stores

• **Home Depot** • 7345 Delridge Wy SW [Sylvan Wy SW]
• **McLendon Hardware Inc** •
  10210 16th Ave SW [SW 102nd St]

Liquor Stores

• **Washington State Liquor Store** •
  6527 California Ave SW [Fauntleroy Wy SW]
• **Washington State Liquor Store** •
  9822 15th Ave SW [SW 98th St]
• **West Seattle Cellars** •
  6026 California Ave SW [SW Raymond St]

Movie Theaters

• **Kenyon Hall** • 7904 35th Ave SW [SW Kenyon St]

Nightlife

• **The Tug Tavern** • 2216 SW Orchard St [Sylvan Way SW]

Restaurants

• **88 Restaurant** • 9418 Delridge Wy SW [SW Roxbury St]
• **Eats Market Café** • 2600 SW Barton St [26th Ave SW]
• **Endolyne Joe's** • 9261 45th Ave SW [SW Wildwood Pl]
• **Salvadorean Bakery** •
  1719 SW Roxbury St [17th Ave SW]
• **Taqueria Guaymas** •
  1622 SW Roxbury St [Delridge Wy SW]
• **Zippy's Burgers** • 1513 SW Holden St [15th Ave SW]

Video Rental

• **Blockbuster** • 10640 16th Ave SW [SW 106th St]
• **Blockbuster** • 6451 Fauntleroy Wy SW [42nd Ave SW]
• **Hollywood Video** • 2500 SW Barton St
• **Minh Quang Video** • 9819 16th Ave SW [SW 98th St]
• **Seoul Video (Korean)** •
  1515 SW Roxbury St [15th Ave SW]
• **Your Choice Video** • 9811 16th Ave SW [SW 98th St]

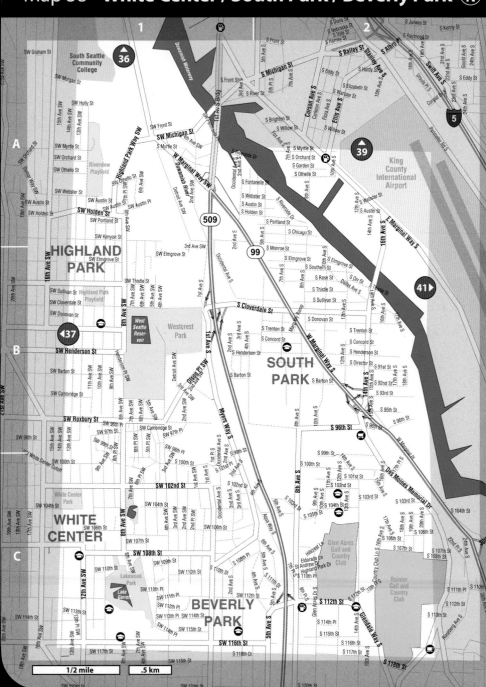

Map 38 · White Center / South Park / Beverly Park

Where can you find two spacious, members-only country clubs poised over an industrial waterway area rivaling the worst of North Jersey and a town hub thick with ethnic markets and seedy tattoo parlors? Step right up folks—it's all here! Yup, life in White Center (a.k.a Rat City for reasons best left to urban legend) means never having to leave the 'hood for fun.

Coffee

- **Java Express** •
  11600 Des Moines Memorial Dr [S 116th St]

Gas Stations

- **Arco** • 7200 E Marginal Wy S [Ellis Ave S]
- **Chevron** • 5940 E Marginal Wy S [S Fidalgo St]
- **Chevron** • 805 S 112th St [8th Ave S]

Schools

- **Beverly Park Elementary at Glendale** •
  1201 S 104th St [12th Ave S]
- **Cascade Middle** • 11212 10th Ave SW [SW 112th St]
- **Concord Elementary** • 723 S Concord St [7th Ave S]
- **Evergreen High** • 830 SW 116th St [8th Ave SW]
- **Hamlin Robinson** • 10211 12th Ave S [S 102nd St]
- **Highland Park Elementary** •
  1012 SW Trenton St [10th Ave SW]
- **Mount View Elementary** •
  10811 12th Ave SW [SW 108th St]
- **Southern Heights Elementary** •
  11249 14th Ave S [Glendale Wy S]
- **White Center Heights Elementary** •
  11427 3rd Ave S [S 116th St]

Supermarkets

- **Red Apple** • 9627 Des Moines Memorial Dr [S 96th St]

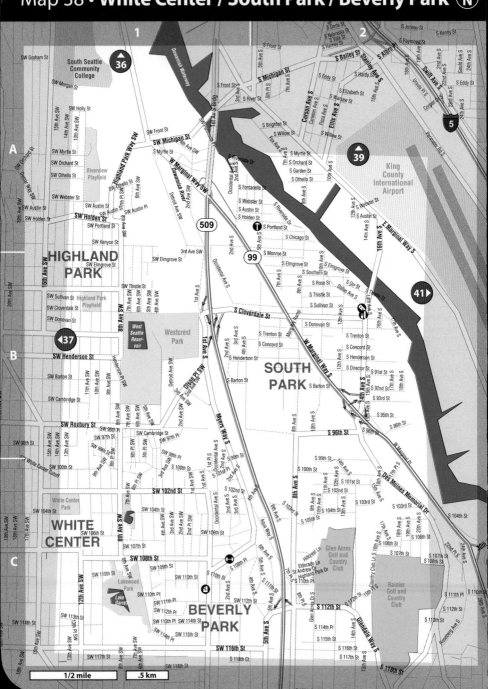

Map 38 • White Center / South Park / Beverly Park Ⓝ

With all the factories and industrial parks, this area lacks a bit in good dining and nightlife options. But South Park (the 'hood, not the TV show) is home to Muy Macho, the best authentic Mexican restaurant in Seattle. When the sun goes locals flock to Loretta's, a great addition to the neighborhood. Even if you don't live here, Loretta's is well worth planning a night out in South Park. Who ever thought you'd hear us say that?

Copy Shops

• **Sudden Printing** • 11009 1st Ave S [S 112th St]

Gyms

• **United Gym** • 10778 Myers Wy S [S 108th St]

Hardware Stores

• **Pacific Industrial Supply** •
  1231 S Director St [12th Ave S]
• **Swift Tool** • 7709 5th Ave S [S Holden St]

Nightlife

• **Loretta's** • 8617 14th Ave S [S Cloverdale St]

Restaurants

• **Muy Macho** • 8515 14th Ave S [Dallas Ave S]

Video Rental

• **Video Mart** • 8525 14th Ave S [S Sullivan St]

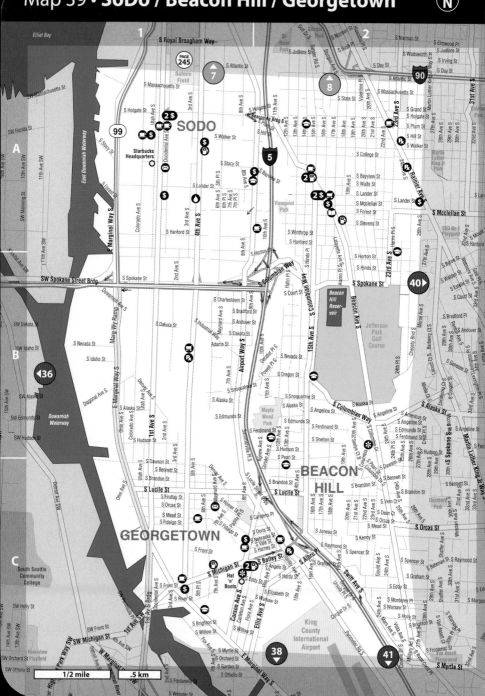

Map 39 • SoDo / Beacon Hill / Georgetown

Remember the town in the sitcom Roseanne? In case you forgot, it was an industrial community consisting of burger, barbeque, and Mexican food loving folks. Locals gathered in dive bars for a few cold ones or hung around at the only gas station to talk about the latest fashions. That's sort of like this part of town, only divided by I-5 and the gas station is a hat and pair of boots made of steel.

$ Banks

- **Bank of America** • 2555 Beacon Ave S [15th Ave S]
- **Bank of America** • 2764 1st Ave S [S Lander St]
- **Bank Of America (ATM)** •
  2707 Rainier Ave S [S Lander St]
- **Key Bank** • 1920 1st Ave S [S Holgate St]
- **Key Bank (ATM)** • 1900 1st Ave S [S Holgate St]
- **US Bank** • 2401 3rd Ave S [S Stacey St]
- **US Bank** • 303 S Michigan St [E Marginal Wy S]
- **US Bank (ATM)** • 2401 Utah Ave S [S Stacey St]
- **Washington Federal Savings** •
  2800 Beacon Ave S [S McClellan St]
- **Wells Fargo** • 1763 4th Ave S [S Holgate St]
- **Wells Fargo** • 5963 Corson Ave S, Ste 140 [S Vale St]
- **Wells Fargo (ATM)** • 2701 Beacon Ave S [S Lander St]

Car Washes

- **Elephant Car Wash** • 2763 4th Ave S [S Lander St]

Coffee

- **All City Coffee** • 1205 S Vale St [Airport Wy S]
- **Detour Expresso** • 2006 Rainier Ave S [S Plum St]
- **Espresso By Design** • 511 S Mead St [S Fidalgo St]
- **Java Love Café** • 2414 Beacon Ave S [14th Ave S]
- **Perfect Cup Espresso** • 6185 4th Ave S [S Michigan St]
- **Starbucks** • 1962 1st Ave S [S Holgate St]
- **Starbucks** • 2962 1st Ave S [S Walker St]
- **Starbucks** • 2401 Utah Ave S [S Stacey St]
- **Starbucks** • 5963 Corson Ave S [S Vale St]
- **Tully's** • 3100 Airport Wy S [S Hanford St]

❋ Community Gardens

Ⓟ Gas Stations

- **76** • 2415 Beacon Ave S [14th Ave S]
- **Arco** • 2200 4th Ave S [S Walker St]
- **Exxon** • 3002 Beacon Ave S [S Stevens St]
- **Shell** • 2424 Beacon Ave S [14th Ave S]
- **Shell** • 600 S Michigan St [6th Ave S]
- **Shell** • 6200 Corson Ave S [S Bailey St]
- **Texaco** • 6200 Corson Ave S [S Bailey St]

○ Landmarks

- **Hat 'n' Boots** • 6400 Carson Ave S [S Eddy St]
- **Starbucks Headquarters** •
  2401 Utah Ave S [S Stacey St]

📖 Libraries

- **Beacon Hill Branch** •
  2821 Beacon Ave S [S McClellan St]

℞ Pharmacies

- **Bartell Drugs** • 2345 Rainier Ave S [S College St]
- **Costco** • 4401 4th Ave S [S Industrial Wy]
- **Georgetown Pharmacy** •
  6111 13th Ave S [Airport Wy S]
- **Nguyen's Pharmacy** • 2120 Rainier Ave S [S Hill St]

✉ Post Offices

- **Georgetown** • 620 S Orcas St [6th Ave S]
- **Terminal Finance Station** •
  2420 4th Ave S [S Stacey St]

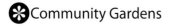 Schools

- **Aviation High** •
  6770 E Marginal Wy S, Bldg B [S River St]
- **Beacon Hill Elementary** • 2025 14 Ave S [S Plum St]
- **Career Link** • 2445 3rd Ave S [S Stacey St]
- **Kimball Elementary** • 3200 23rd Ave S [S Hanford St]
- **Maple Elementary** • 4925 Corson Ave S [S Ferdinand St]
- **Mercer Middle** • 1600 S Columbian Wy [16th Ave S]
- **St George** • 5117 13th Ave S [S Pearl St]

Supermarkets

- **Costco** • 4401 4th Ave S [S Industrial Wy]
- **Red Apple** • 2701 Beacon Ave S [S Lander St]

Map 39 • SoDo / Beacon Hill / Georgetown

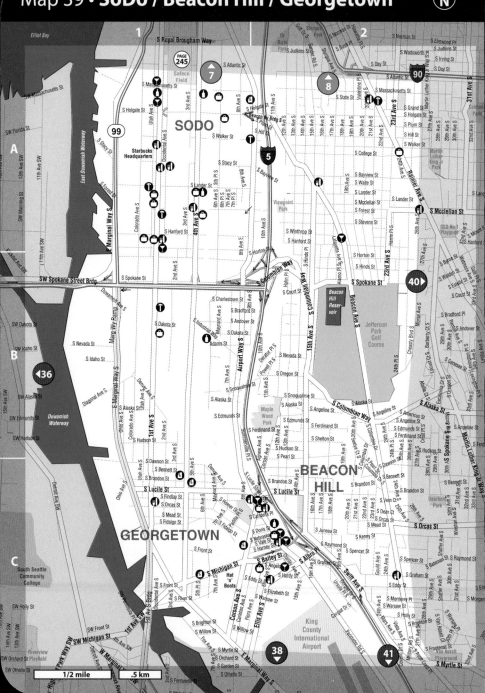

SoDo is great for pork lovers (Pecos Pit BBQ), those who worship at the temple of the mermaid (Starbucks corporate headquarters is located here), and hardware store junkies. Georgetown is for the urban cowboy/girl. It contains a planet (a.k.a Uncle Moe's Watering Hole), a Nine Pound Hammer (a biker/punk hangout), a George (gallery), a Stellar pizza joint, and a Liquor Company. Beacon Hill has La Cabana Café and Beacon Pub, and beauty salons occupy every corner for the hair and nail enthusiast.

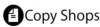Copy Shops

- **Custom Printing** • 317 S Bennett St [3rd Ave S]
- **FedEx Kinko's** • 5963 Corson Ave S [S Vale St]
- **Minuteman Press** • 401 S Brandon St [4th Ave S]
- **Office Depot** • 1751 Airport Wy S [S Massachusetts St]
- **Sudden Printing** • 6505 5th Pl S [S Michigan St]

Hardware Stores

- **Compton Lumber Hardware** • 3847 1st Ave S [S Dakota St]
- **Home Depot** • 2701 Utah Ave S [S Lander St]
- **Rejuvenation** • 2910 1st Ave S [S Forest St]
- **Stellar Industrial Supply** • 915 S Walker St [5th Ave S]
- **Stewart Lumber & Hardware Co** • 1761 Rainier Ave S [S State St]

Liquor Stores

- **Esquin Wine Merchant** • 2700 4th Ave S [S Lander St]
- **Georgetown Brewing Company** • 5840 Airport Wy S [S Homer St]
- **Washington State Liquor Store** • 1702 4th Ave S [S Massachusetts St]
- **Western Washington Beverage** • 4201 6th Ave S [S Industrial Wy]
- **Wine Outlet** • 1701 1st Ave S [S Massachusetts St]

Nightlife

- **Beacon Pub** • 3057 Beacon Ave S [S Hanford St]
- **Georgetown Liquor Company** • 5501 Airport Way S [S Lucile St]
- **Hooverville Bar** • 1721 1st Ave S [S Massachusetts St]
- **Jules Maes Saloon** • 5919 Airport Wy S [S Nebraska St]
- **Nine Pound Hammer** • 6009 Airport Wy S [S Vale St]
- **Showbox SoDo** • 1700 1st Ave S [S Massachusetts St]
- **Studio Seven** • 110 S Horton St [1st Ave S]
- **Uncle Moe's Watering Hole (aka Planet Georgetown)** • 6266 13th Ave S [S Albro Pl]

Restaurants

- **By's Drive-In** • 2901 4th Ave S [S Forest St]
- **Calamity Jane's** • 5701 Airport Way S [St Carstens Pl]
- **Dahlak Eritrean Cuisine** • 2007 S State St [20th Ave S]
- **Georgetown Liquor Company** • 5501 Airport Way S [S Lucile St]
- **Jones Barbeque** • 2454 Occidental Ave S [S Stacey St]
- **La Cabana Café** • 2532 Beacon Ave S [15th Ave S]
- **Matt's Famous Chili Dogs** • 6615 E Marginal Wy S [S River St]
- **Pecos Pit BBQ** • 2260 1st Ave S [S Walker St]
- **Pho Cyclo** • 2414 1st Ave S [S Stacey St]
- **Pig Iron Bar-B-Q** • 5602 1st Ave S [S Findlay St]
- **Smarty Pants** • 6017 Airport Wy S [S Vale St]
- **SODO Deli** • 3228 1st Ave S [S Hanford St]
- **Squid & Ink** • 1128 S Albro Pl [Ellis Ave S]
- **Stellar Pizza, Ale & Cocktails** • 5513 Airport Wy S [S Lucile St]
- **Viengthong** • 2820 Martin Luther King Jr Way S [S McClellan St]
- **Willie's Taste of Soul BBQ** • 6305 Beacon Ave S [S Graham St]

Shopping

- **Daniel Smith** • 4150 1st Ave S [S Dakota St]
- **Esquin Wine Merchants** • 2700 4th Ave S [S Lander St]
- **George** • 5633 Airport Wy S [Corson Ave S]
- **Georgetown Records/Fantagraphics** • 1201 S Vale St [Airport Wy S]
- **Goodwill Outlet** • 1765 6th Ave S [S Massachusetts St]
- **JC Marble & Granite** • 2735 1st Ave S [S Lander St]
- **Maruta** • 1024 S Bailey St [Flora Ave S]
- **Moe's Home Collection** • 1926 6th Ave S [S Holgate St]
- **Northwest Shower Door** • 3223 1st Ave S [S Hanford St]
- **Remo Borracchini's** • 2307 Rainier Ave S [S College St]
- **Seattle Pottery Supply** • 35 S Hanford St [Colorado Ave S]
- **Visions Espresso Service** • 2737 1st Ave S [S Lander St]

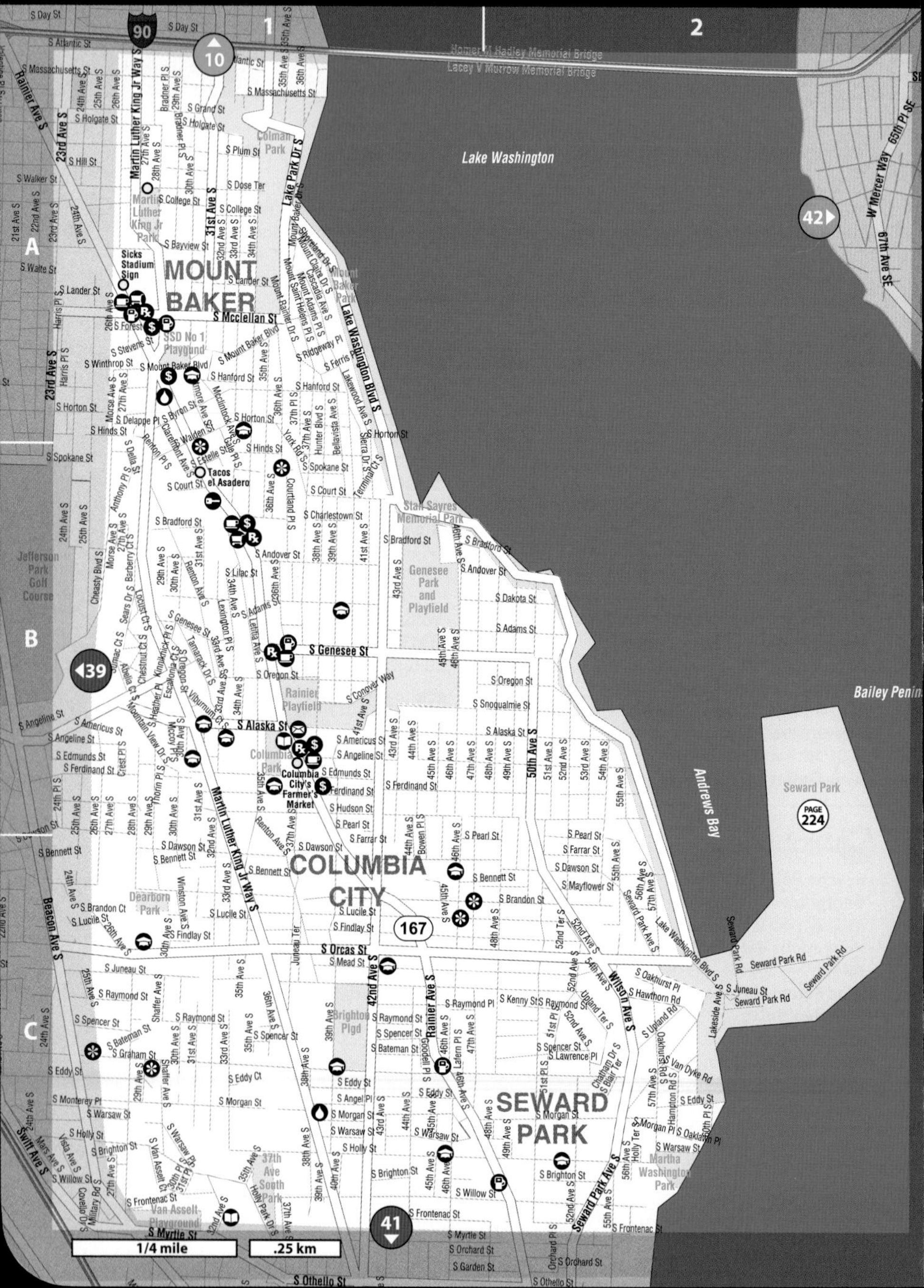

Map 40 · **Mount Baker / Seward Park / Columbia City** (N)

90

I-90

1 2

10

S Day St
S Day St
S Atlantic St
S Massachusetts Ave S
S Holgate St
S Grand St
S Holgate St
S Plum St
S Hill St
S College St
S College St
S Bayview St

Colman Park

Lake Washington

Lake Park Dr S

42

W Mercer Way · 65th Pl SE
6th Ave SE

Martin Luther King Jr Way S
31st Ave S

Sicks Stadium Sign

MOUNT BAKER

S Walker St
S Walte St
S Lander St
Harris St
Harris Pl S

SSD No 1 Playground

S McClellan St
S Winthrop St
S Mount Baker Blvd
S Hanford St
S Hanford St
S Horton St
S Hinds St
S Hinds St

Mount Baker Park

Tacos el Asadero

S Spokane St
S Court St

23rd Ave S

S Bradford St
S Charlestown St
S Bradford St
S Andover St

Stan Sayres Memorial Park

Genesee Park and Playfield

S Lilac St
S Adams St
S Dakota St
S Andover St

S Genesee St

Jefferson Park Golf Course

39

Rainier Playfield

S Oregon St
S Oregon St
S Snoqualmie St

S Alaska St
S Alaska St

Columbia Park

S Americus St
S Angeline St
S Edmunds St
S Ferdinand St

Columbia City's Farmer's Market

S Hudson St
S Pearl St
S Farrar St

S Pearl St
S Farrar St
S Dawson St

Seward Park

PAGE 224

Andrews Bay

Bailey Penin

COLUMBIA CITY

Dearborn Park

S Bennett St
S Brandon St
S Lucile St
S Findlay St

S Bennett St
S Mayflower St

167

S Orcas St
S Mead St

Brighton Pigd

42nd Ave S
Rainier Ave S
Wilson Ave S

S Raymond St
S Spencer St
S Bateman St
S Graham St
S Eddy St
S Morgan St

SEWARD PARK

S Angel Pl
S Morgan St
S Warsaw St
S Holly St

S Brighton St

Martha Washington Park

Seward Park Rd
Seward Park Rd
Lake Washington Blvd S

41

S Myrtle St
S Orchard St
S Othello St

1/4 mile   .25 km

Wanna change in race, creed, and color? Head south to the increasingly desirable Mount Baker, Seward Park, and Columbia City 'hoods. Orthodox Jews mingle with Vietnamese Presbyterians; folks fishing from lake piers make way for Mount Baker's rowing crews. Potters, joggers, and picnickers frequent Seward Park. Warning: Seattle's answer to NASCAR, the Seafair Hydroplane and Blue Angel extravaganza takes over in early August. Locals exit while 300,000+ party hearty.

$ Banks

- **Bank of America** • 4825 Rainier Ave S [S Edmunds St]
- **US Bank** • 2910 Rainier Ave S [S Forest St]
- **Washington Federal Savings** •
  4800 Rainier Ave S [S Angelina St]
- **Washington Mutual** • 3820 Rainier Ave S [S Charlestown St]
- **Wells Fargo** • 3100 Rainier Ave S [S Mt Baker Blvd]

Car Rental

- **Enterprise** • 3711 Rainier Ave S [S Court St]

Car Washes

- **National Pride Car Wash** • 3151 Rainier Ave S [S Mt Baker Blvd]
- **Suds City Car Wash** •
  6500 Martin Luther King Jr Wy S [S Morgan St]

Coffee

- **Starbucks** • 2707 Rainier Ave S [S McClellan St]
- **Starbucks** • 2921 Martin Luther King Jr Wy S [Rainier Ave S]
- **Starbucks** • 3820 Rainier Ave S [S Charlestown St]
- **Starbucks** • 4824 Rainier Ave S [S Angelina St]
- **Tully's** • 4400 Rainier Ave S [S Genesee St]

Community Gardens

Gas Stations

- **76** • 2801 Martin Luther King Jr Wy S [S McClellan St]
- **76** • 6230 Rainier Ave S [S Graham St]
- **Chevron** • 2802 Rainier Ave S [S McClellan St]
- **Exxon** • 6815 Rainier Ave S [S Willow St]
- **Shell** • 3611 S Genesee St [36th Ave S]

o Landmarks

- **Columbia City Farmers Market** •
  4801 Rainier Ave S [S Angelina St]
- **Martin Luther King Jr Memorial Park** •
  2200 Martin Luther King Jr Wy S [S Walker St]
- **Sicks Stadium Sign** • 2700 Rainier Ave S [S McClellan St]
- **Tacos el Asadero** • 3513 Rainier Ave S [S Estelle St]

Libraries

- **Columbia Branch** • 4721 Rainier Ave S [S Alaska St]
- **NewHolly Branch** • 7058 32nd Ave S [S Myrtle St]

Pharmacies

- **Columbia Pharmacy** • 4741 Rainier Ave S [S Angelina St]
- **Rite Aid** • 2707 Rainier Ave S [S McClellan St]
- **Safeway Pharmacy** • 3820 Rainier Ave S [S Charlestown St]
- **Walgreens** • 4412 Rainier Ave S [S Genesee St]

Post Offices

- **Columbia** • 3727 S Alaska St [Rainier Ave S]

Schools

- **Aki Kurose Middle** • 3928 S Graham St [39th Ave S]
- **Brighton Elementary** • 6725 45th Ave S [S Holly St]
- **Dearborn Park Elementary** • 2820 S Orcas St [26th Ave S]
- **Franklin High** • 3013 S Mt Baker Blvd [30th Ave S]
- **Graham Hill Elementary** • 5149 S Graham St [52nd Ave S]
- **Hawthorne Elementary** • 4100 39th Ave S [S Dakota St]
- **Interagency Programs** • 3100 S Alaska St [31st Ave S]
- **John Muir Elementary** • 3301 S Horton St [33rd Ave S]
- **Maxine Mimms High** • 3019 St Angeline St [30th Ave S]
- **Orca Elementary (Columbia)** •
  3528 S Ferdinand St [35th Ave S]
- **St Edward** • 4212 S Mead St [42nd Ave S]
- **Whitworth Elementary** • 5215 46th Ave S [S Dawson St]
- **Zion Preparatory Academy** • 4730 32nd Ave S [S Alaska St]

Supermarkets

- **Quality Food Center** • 2707 Rainier Ave S [S McClellan St]
- **Safeway** • 3820 Rainier Ave S [S Charlestown St]

Map 40 • **Mount Baker / Seward Park / Columbia City** Ⓝ

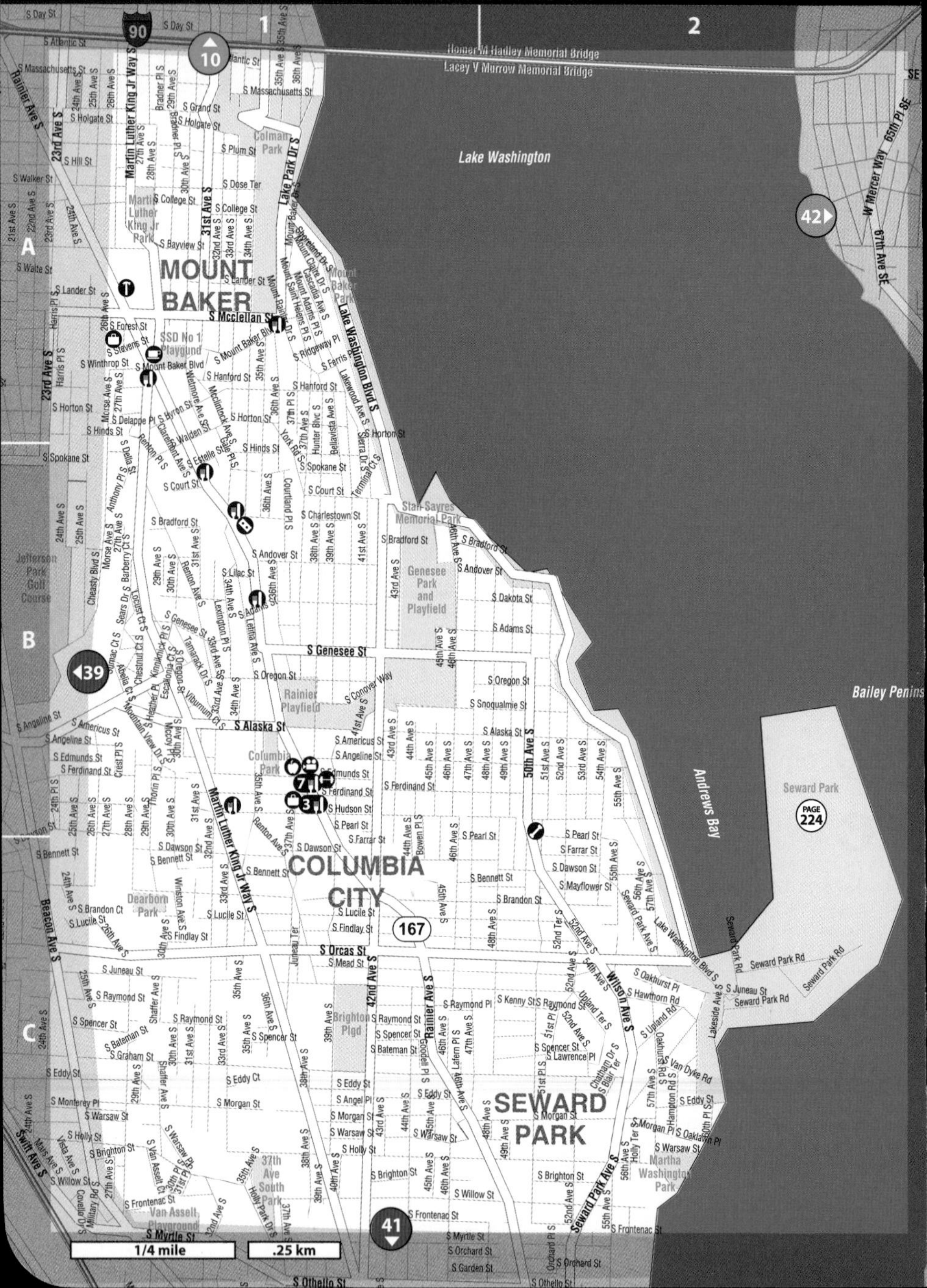

1

2

90

S Day St

S Atlantic St

Homer M Hadley Memorial Bridge
Lacey V Morrow Memorial Bridge

S Massachusetts St

S Holgate St

Lake Washington

S Grand St

Colman Park

S Plum St

S Dose Ter

S College St

S College St

Martin Luther King Jr Park

S Bayview St

A

S Waite St

MOUNT BAKER

S Lander St

S McClellan St

S Forest St

SSD No 1 Playgrnd

S Stevens St

S Mount Baker Blvd

S Winthrop St

S Hanford St

S Horton St

S Hanford St

S Hinds St

S Horton St

S Hinds St

S Spokane St

S Court St

S Court St

Stan Sayres Memorial Park

S Bradford St

S Bradford St

Genesee Park and Playfield

S Andover St

S Lilac St

S Dakota St

S Adams St

B

S Genesee St

S Oregon St

Rainier Playfield

S Oregon St

S Snoqualmie St

Bailey Penins

S Alaska St

S Alaska St

S Americus St

Columbia Park

S Angeline St

S Edmunds St

S Ferdinand St

S Hudson St

S Pearl St

Andrews Bay

Seward Park

PAGE 224

S Farrar St

S Dawson St

COLUMBIA CITY

S Bennett St

S Mayflower St

S Brandon St

Dearborn Park

S Lucile St

S Lucile St

S Findlay St

167

S Orcas St

S Mead St

S Oakhurst Pl

S Hawthorn Rd

Seward Park Rd

Brighton Plgd

S Raymond St

S Kenny St

S Juneau St
Seward Park Rd

C

S Spencer St

S Bateman St

S Lawrence Pl

SEWARD PARK

S Eddy St

S Morgan St

S Warsaw St

S Brighton St

Martha Washington Park

S Willow St

S Myrtle St

41

S Orchard St

1/4 mile   .25 km

Columbia City's tiny triangular hub on Rainier Avenue between Orcas and Alaska keeps increasing in popularity and packing in the eateries and condos. Our fave cafe is La Medusa—they concoct edible miracles and we happily eat 'em. For BBQ, try Jones or Roy's, Columbia City Bakery for artisan fare, Tutta Bella for family pizza, Geraldine's Counter anytime, and Lottie's Lounge for those mornings you need a stiff one to get rolling.

Farmers Markets

- **Columbia City (Wed, 3 pm–7 pm, May–Oct)** •
  4801 Rainier Ave S [S Angelina St]

Gyms

- **Bull Stewart Fitness Center** •
  4860 Rainier Ave S [S Hudson St]

Hardware Stores

- **Lowe's** • 2700 Rainier Ave S [S McClellan St]

Movie Theaters

- **Columbia City Cinema** •
  4816 Rainier Ave S [S Angelina St]

Pet Shops

- **Ideal Pet Stop** • 5044 Wilson Ave S [S Hudson St]

Nightlife

- **Lottie's Lounge** • 4900 Rainier Ave S [S Ferdinand St]

Restaurants

- **Cafe Ibex** •
  3218 Martin Luther King Jr Way S [S Hanford St]
- **Columbia City Ale House** •
  4914 Rainier Ave S [S Ferdinand St]
- **Columbia City Bakery** • 4865 Rainier Ave S [S Edmunds St]
- **Da Pino's** • 4225 Rainier Ave S [S Adams St]
- **El Asadero Taco Truck** • 3517 Rainier Ave S [S Estelle St]
- **Geraldine's Counter** • 4872 Rainier Ave S [S Edmunds St]
- **Jones Barbeque** •
  3216 S Hudson St [Martin Luther King Wy S]
- **Jones Barbeque** • 3810 S Ferdinand St [Rainier Ave S]
- **La Medusa** • 4857 Rainier Ave S [S Edmunds St]
- **Mioposto** • 3601 S McClellan St [S Mt Baker Blvd]
- **Roy's BBQ** • 4903 Rainier Ave S [S Ferdinand St]
- **Silver Fork** • 3800 Rainier Ave S [S Charlestown St]
- **Tutta Bella Neopolitan Pizzeria** •
  4918 Rainier Ave S [S Ferdinand St]
- **Verve Wine Bar and Cellar** •
  3820 S Ferdinand St [39th Ave S]
- **Wellington Tea Room** •
  4869 Rainier Ave S [S Edmunds St]

Shopping

- **Bike Works!** • 3709 S Ferdinand St [37th Ave S]
- **Grocery Outlet** • 2929 27th Ave S [S Forest St]
- **PCC Natural Market** • 5041 Wilson Ave S [50th Ave S]

Video Rental

- **Hollywood Video** • 3820 Rainier Ave S [S Charlestown St]

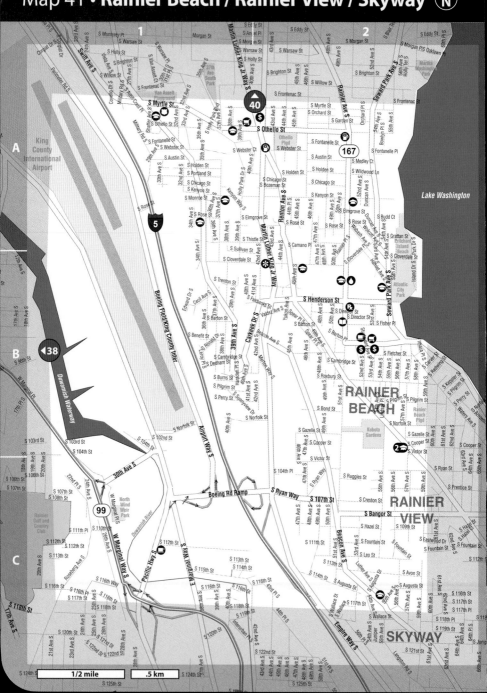

Map 41 • Rainier Beach / Rainier View / Skyway

Real estate prices are truly insane when few can afford homes in this predominately low- to middle-income area (except the beaucoup bucks waterfront homeowners). Kubota Gardens and the Rainier Beach Library are lovely and the public boat launch is handy, but the crime rate here will make insurance costlier than your car. Rainier Beach High School is filled with talent, strife, multiple ethnicities, and awards. RBHS alums include NBA star Jamal Crawford, who donated "Crawford Court" in 2005.

Banks

- **Key Bank** • 9255 Rainier Ave S [Sturtevant Ave S]
- **Washington Federal Savings** •
  9325 Rainier Ave S [52nd Ave S]
- **Washington Mutual** •
  7100 Martin Luther King Jr Wy S [S Myrtle St]

Car Washes

- **Jet Car Wash** • 8808 Rainier Ave S [S Cloverdale St]

Coffee

- **Jet Fuel Espresso** •
  11234 Tukwila International Blvd [S 112th St]
- **Starbucks** • Safeway • 9262 Rainier Ave S [S Fisher Pl]

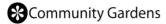 Community Gardens

Gas Stations

- **Exxon** • 7500 Martin Luther King Jr Wy S [S Webster St]
- **Shell** • 7301 Rainier Ave S [S Othello St]

Libraries

- **Rainier Beach Branch** • 9125 Rainier Ave S [S Fisher Pl]

Pharmacies

- **Rite Aid** • 9000 Rainier Ave S [S Henderson St]

Police

- **South Precinct** • 3001 S Myrtle [Beacon Ave S]

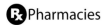 Schools

- **Academy for Excellence** •
  7930 Rainier Ave S [S Kenyon St]
- **African American Academy K-8** •
  8311 Beacon Ave S [S Rose St]
- **Amazing Grace Christian** •
  10056 Renton Ave S [57th Ave S]
- **Dunlap Elementary** •
  4525 S Cloverdale St [45th Ave S]
- **The New School at South Shore** •
  8825 Rainier Ave S [S Cloverdale St]
- **Rainier Beach High** •
  8815 Seward Park Ave S [Hamlet Ave S]
- **Rainier View Elementary** •
  11650 Beacon Ave S [55th Ave S]
- **Seattle Urban Academy** •
  3800 S Othello St [38th Ave S]
- **St Paul** • 10001 57th Ave S [Renton Ave S]
- **Van Asselt Elementary** •
  7201 Beacon Ave S [S Othello St]
- **Wing Luke Elementary** •
  3701 S Kenyon St [37th Ave S]

Supermarkets

- **Safeway** • 3900 S Othello St [39th Ave S]
- **Safeway** • 9262 Rainier Ave S [Sturtevant Ave S]

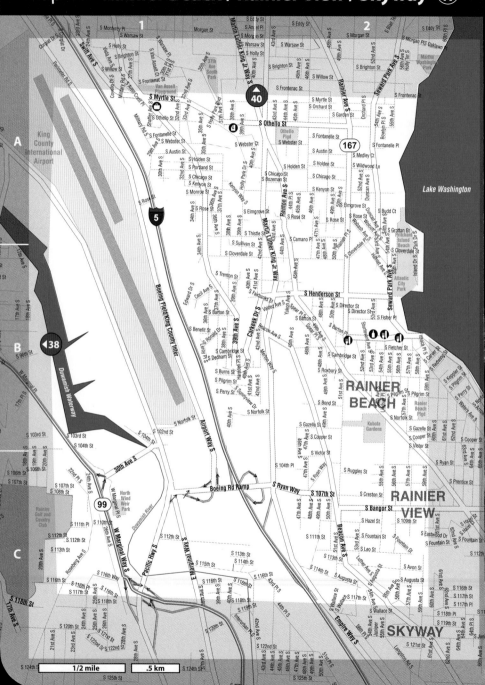

Map 41 · **Rainier Beach / Rainier View / Skyway** Ⓝ

The multicultural Rainer Beach Safeway offers everything from posole to matzoh to gyoza wrappers. Nearby is a King Donut, a mind-boggling combo of a teriyaki joint, doughnut shop, and laundromat all under one roof! Maya's Mexican Restaurant slow cooks borrego (lamb shanks wrapped in banana leaves) and across the street, Hong Kong Seafood offers daily dim sum until 3 pm and a righteous version of Singapore fried rice noodles.

Copy Shops

• **UPS Store** • 3815 S Othello St [38th Ave S]

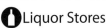Liquor Stores

• **Washington State Liquor Store** •
9258 Rainier Ave S [Sturtevant Ave S]

Restaurants

• **Hong Kong Seafood Restaurant** •
9400 Rainier Ave S [54 Ave S]
• **King Donut** • 9170 Rainier Ave S [51st Ave S]
• **Maya's Mexican Restaurant** •
9447 Rainier Ave S [56th Ave S]

Shopping

• **Van Asselt Beauty Salon** •
7136 Beacon Ave S [S Myrtle St]

Map 42 · **Mercer Island**

While back in olden times it was a mild-mannered dairy farm community, Mercer Island has long been associated with wealth, so do we need to tell you that boating is popular? This is the neighborhood where Paul Allen sleeps, dreaming up new ways to show off his money. Regular folks are welcome, too, as long as they know their place.

Banks

- **Bank of America** • 2830 80th Ave SE [SE 28th St]
- **Bank of America** • 8421 SE 68th St [84th Ave SE]
- **Bank of America (ATM)** • 7823 SE 28th St [78th Ave SE]
- **Key Bank** • 2731 77th Ave SE [SE 27th St]
- **Sterling Savings Bank** • 7803 SE 27th St [78th Ave SE]
- **US Bank** • 2737 78th Ave SE [SE 27th St]
- **US Bank (ATM)** • 2755 77th Ave SE [SE 27th St]
- **Washington Mutual** • 7900 SE 28th St [78th Ave SE]
- **Wells Fargo** • 3001 78th Ave SE [SE 30th St]
- **Wells Fargo (ATM)** • 8435 SE 68th St [84th Ave SE]

Coffee

- **Starbucks** • 7620 SE 27th St [76th Ave SE]
- **Starbucks** • 7695 SE 27th St [77th Ave SE]
- **Starbucks** • 7823 SE 28th St [78th Ave SE]
- **Starbucks** • 8415 SE 68th St [84th Ave SE]
- **Starbucks** • QFC • 8421 SE 68th St [84th Ave SE]
- **Tully's** • 7810 SE 27th St [78th Ave SE]

Gas Stations

- **76** • 2411 76th Ave SE [SE 24th St]
- **Chevron** • 7725 Sunset Hwy [77th Ave SE]
- **Chevron** • 8407 SE 68th St [84th Ave SE]
- **Shell** • 2903 78th Ave SE [SE 29th St]
- **Shell** • 7655 Sunset Hwy [77th Ave SE]
- **Shell** • 7833 SE 28th St [78th Ave SE]

Libraries

- **Mercer Island Library** • 4400 88th Ave SE [SE 44th St]

Pharmacies

- **Albertson's** • 2755 77th Ave SE [SE 27th St]
- **Rite Aid** • 8441 SE 68th St [84th Ave SE]
- **Rite Aid** • 3023 78th Ave SE [SE 30th St]
- **Walgreens** • 7707 SE 27th St [77th Ave SE]

Police

- **Mercer Island Police Dept** •
  9611 SE 36th St [E Mercer Wy]

Post Offices

- **Mercer Island** • 3040 78th Ave SE [SE 30th St]

Schools

- **American Academy** •
  7834 SE 32nd St # 204 [80th Ave SE]
- **Child School/New Heights** •
  4030 86th Ave SE, Ste F [SE 40th St]
- **Children's Institute for Learning Differences (Child)** • 4030 86th Ave SE, Ste F [SE 40th St]
- **Crest Learning Center** • 4150 86th Ave SE [SE 42nd St]
- **Etc Preparatory Academy** •
  8005 SE 28th St [80th Ave SE]
- **French-American School** •
  3795 E Mercer Wy [SE 40th St]
- **Island Park Elementary** •
  5437 Island Crest Wy [SE 54th St]
- **Islander Middle** • 8225 SE 72nd St [82nd Ave SE]
- **Lakeridge Elementary** • 8215 SE 78th St [84th Ave SE]
- **Mercer Island HS** • 9100 SE 42nd St [91st Ave SE]
- **Northwest Yeshiva High** •
  5017 90th Ave SE [SE 51st Pl]
- **St Monica** • 4320 87th Ave SE [SE 44th St]
- **West Mercer Elementary** •
  4141 81st Ave SE [SE 40th St]

Supermarkets

- **Quality Food Center** • 7823 SE 28th St [78th Ave SE]
- **Quality Food Center** • 8421 SE 68th St [84th Ave SE]

Map 42 · **Mercer Island**

Whether you're rich or not, there isn't a whole lot to do on Mercer Island, which is part of its charm and the main draw for locals. Roanoke Inn has been pouring suds and serving classic bar fare since 1914, making it a Washington State Historical Landmark as well as the best place to grab a drink. Try Roberto's for pizza, Seven Star for Chinese, and Bennett's Pure Food Bistro for health food.

Copy Shops

- **Sudden Printing** • 2690 76th Ave SE [SE 27th St]
- **The UPS Store** • 7683 SE 27th St [77th Ave SE]

Gyms

- **Club Emerald** • 3028 78th Ave SE [SE 30th St]

 Hardware Stores

- **True Value Hardware** • 2615 76th Ave SE [SE 27th St]

Pet Shops

- **Denise's Parrot Place** • 7641 SE 27th St [77th Ave SE]

Restaurants

- **Bennett's Pure Food Bistro** •
  7650 SE 27th St [77th Ave SE]
- **Pon Proem** • 3039 78th Ave SE [SE 30th St]
- **Roanoke Inn** • 1825 72nd Ave SE [N Mercer Wy]
- **Roberto's** • 7605 SE 27th St [76th Ave SE]
- **Seven Star** • 2775 78th Ave SE [SE 27th St]
- **Thai on Mercer** • 7691 27th St [77th Ave SE]

Video Rental

- **Hollywood Video** • 2750 77th Ave SE [SE 27th St]

Map 43 • Bellevue (Southwest)

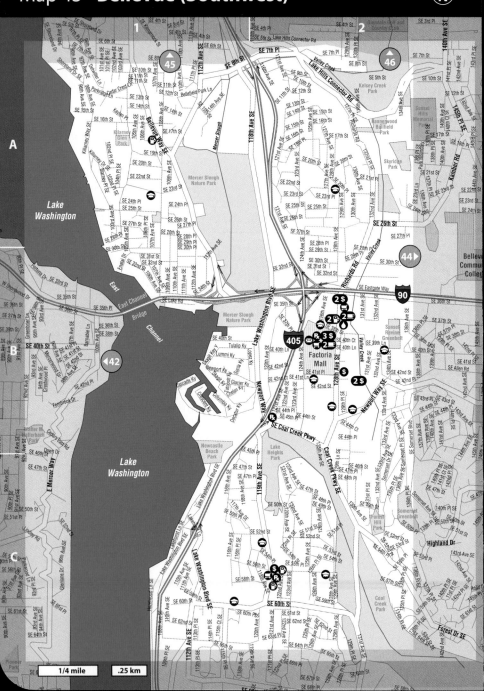

Bellevue is home to a ton of smart teenagers, with three of the finest high schools in the nation as ranked by Newsweek. These Bellevue braniacs will probably be your boss one day. When not studying, you can find them hanging out at the food court in the Factoria Mall.

Banks

- **Bank of America** • 11905 SE 56th St [119th Ave SE]
- **Bank of America** • 12727 SE 38th St [128th Ave SE]
- **Bank of America (ATM)** •
  3505 Factoria Blvd SE [SE 36th St]
- **Bank of America (ATM)** •
  3550 128th Ave SE [SE 36th St]
- **Bank of America (ATM)** •
  3919 Factoria Sq Mall SE [SE 40th Ct]
- **Key Bank** • 4122 Factoria Blvd SE [SE 41st Pl]
- **US Bank** • 4040 Factoria Blvd SE [SE 40th Pl]
- **Washington Mutual** •
  3919 Factoria Blvd SE [SE 40th Ct]
- **Wells Fargo** • 4020 Factoria Blvd SE [SE 40th Ln]

Car Washes

- **Brown Bear Car Wash** •
  3724 Factoria Blvd SE [SE 38th St]

Coffee

- **Jitters Coffee** • 4004 Factoria Blvd SE [SE 40th Ct]
- **Seattle's Best Coffee** •
  4004 Factoria Blvd SE [SE 40th Ct]
- **Starbucks** • 3560 128th Ave SE [SE 36th St]
- **Starbucks** • 3720 128th Ave SE [SE 38th St]

Gas Stations

- **76** • 3724 Factoria Blvd SE [SE 38th St]
- **76** • 3727 Factoria Blvd SE [SE 38th St]
- **76** • 5804 119th Ave SE [SE 58th St]
- **Chevron** • 11919 SE 56th St [119th Ave SE]
- **Chevron** • 1649 Bellevue Wy SE [107th Ave SE]

Pharmacies

- **Newport Hills Drug** • 5620 119th Ave SE [SE 56th St]
- **Rite Aid** • 3905 Factoria Sq Mall SE [SE 40th Ct]
- **Safeway** • 6911 Coal Creek Pkwy SE [119th Ave SE]

Post Offices

- **CPU Factoria** • 4020 Factoria Sq Mall SE [SE 40th Ct]

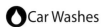Schools

- **Eastside Catholic High** •
  11650 SE 60th St [116th Ave SE]
- **Educational Advancement Academy** •
  12600 SE 38th St, Ste 111 [126th Ave SE]
- **Enatai Elementary** • 10615 SE 23rd St [108th Ave SE]
- **Kelsey Creek Home School** •
  5225 119th Ave SE [SE 52nd St]
- **Kindercare 12415 #946** •
  12415 SE 41st Pl [124th Ave SE]
- **Newport Children's** •
  12930 SE Newport Wy [129th Pl SE]
- **Newport Heights Elementary** •
  12635 SE 56th St [126th Ave SE]
- **Newport High** • 4333 Factoria Blvd SE [SE Newport Wy]
- **Puesta del Sol Elementary** •
  3810 132nd Ave SE [SE 41st St]
- **Woodridge Elementary** •
  12619 SE 20th Pl [126th Ave SE]

Supermarkets

- **Quality Food Center** • 3550 128th Ave SE [SE 36th St]
- **Red Apple** • 5606 119th Ave SE [SE 56th St]
- **Safeway** • 3903 Factoria Sq Mall SE [SE 40th Ct]

Map 43 · **Bellevue (Southwest)**

There are a couple of restaurant gems including Shanghai Café, known for their own hand-shaven noodles, and Top Gun Seafood for their excellent dim sum. If you're really desperate for non-Chinese food, try Grazie Ristorante Italiano. Other entertainment options revolve around catching a flick at Factoria Mall.

Copy Shops

- **CCS Digital Printing** • 13312 SE 30th St [Richards Rd SE]
- **FedEx Kinko's** • 3900 Factoria Blvd SE [SE 38th St]
- **The UPS Store** • 12819 SE 38th St [Factoria Blvd SE]
- **Zebra Printing** • 2930 Richards Rd [SE 30th St]

Gyms

- **Pure Fitness** • 12600 SE 38th St [126th Ave SE]

Liquor Stores

- **Washington State Liquor Store** •
  6927 Coal Creek Pkwy SE [119th Ave SE]

Movie Theaters

- **AMC Loews Factoria 8** •
  3505 Factoria Blvd SE [SE 36th St]

Pet Shops

- **Sierra Fish & Pets - Factoria** •
  3710 Factoria Blvd SE [SE 38th St]

Restaurants

- **Grazie Ristorante Italiano** •
  3820 124th Ave SE [SE 38th St]
- **Shanghai Café** • 12708 SE 38th St [Factoria Blvd SE]
- **Top Gun Seafood** • 12450 SE 38th St [126th Ave SE]

Video Rental

- **Blockbuster** • 3640 128th Ave SE [SE 36th St]
- **Southgate Video Rentals** •
  3900 Factoria Blvd SE [SE 38th St]

Map 44 · **Bellevue (South)**

1/2 mile   .5 km

As the third largest institution of higher education in Washington, Bellevue Community College sends more transfer students to four-year universities than any other community college in the state. At first glance the region appears to be quiet residential suburbs, but the proximity of I-90 and I-405 can make this area hell during traffic hours, so WSDOT's "South Bellevue Widening" project, expected to be completed by late 2009, should help relieve the headache a little bit.

Banks

- **Bank of America** •
  14440 SE Eastgate Wy [142nd Pl SE]
- **Bank of America** •
  15550 Lake Hills Blvd [156th Ave SE]
- **Bank of America (ATM)** •
  1510 145th Pl SE [SE Lake Hills Blvd]
- **Bank of America (ATM)** •
  4989 Lakemont Blvd SE [Village Park Dr SE]
- **Washington Federal Savings** •
  3712 150th Ave SE [SE 37th St]

Coffee

- **Starbucks** • 3181 156th Ave SE [SE 30th Pl]
- **Starbucks** • 4851 Lakemont Blvd SE [Village Park Dr SE]
- **Tully's** • 3080 148th Ave SE [SE Eastgate Wy]

Gas Stations

- **Chevron** • 1607 145th Pl SE [SE 16th St]

Libraries

- **Lake Hills Library** •
  15228 Lake Hills Blvd [154th Ave SE]
- **Newport Way Library** •
  14250 SE Newport Wy [142nd Pl SE]

Pharmacies

- **Rite Aid** • 15100 SE 38th St [150th Ave SE]

Schools

- **Bellevue Community College** •
  3000 Landerholm Cir SE [Coal Creek Rd]
- **Cambridge College** •
  14432 SE Eastgate Wy [142nd Pl SE]
- **Cougar Mountain Montessori** •
  4442 158th Ave SE [SE 44th St]
- **Cougar Ridge Elementary** •
  4630 167th Ave SE [SE 46th St]
- **Eastgate Elementary** • 4355 153rd Ave SE [SE 44th Pl]
- **Eastside Christian** • 14615 SE 22nd St [146th Pl SE]
- **Forest Ridge** • 4800 139th Ave SE [SE 47th St]
- **Hillside Student Community** •
  5027 159th Pl SE [159th Pl SE]
- **Lake Hills Elementary** •
  14310 SE 12th St [143rd Ave SE]
- **Lakemont Academy** •
  5015 Lakemont Blvd SE [Village Park Dr SE]
- **Open Window** • 6128 168th Pl SE [SE 60th St]
- **Phantom Lake Elementary** •
  1050 160th Ave SE [158th Pl SE]
- **Robinswood High/Middle** •
  14844 SE 22nd St [148th Ave SE]
- **Somerset Elementary** •
  14100 SE Somerset Blvd [140th Ave SE]
- **Spiritridge Elementary** •
  16401 SE 24th St [166th Ave SE]
- **Sunset Elementary** •
  4229 W Lake Sammamish Pkwy SE [179th Ln SE]
- **Tillicum Middle** • 16020 SE 16th St [160th Ave SE]
- **Tyee Middle** • 13630 SE Allen Rd [SE Newport Wy]

Supermarkets

- **Quality Food Center** •
  1510 145th Pl SE [SE Lake Hills Blvd]
- **Thriftway** • 4989 Lakemont Blvd SE [Village Park Dr SE]

Map 44 · Bellevue (South)

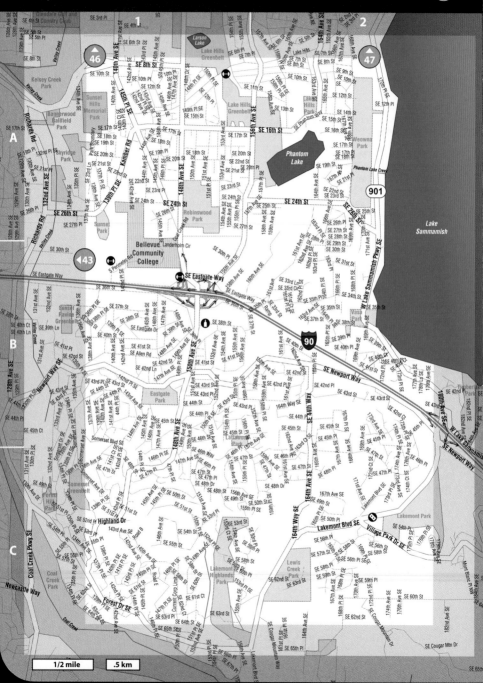

People sleep here. That's about it. With mostly little eateries and fast food chains, people looking for more variety in eating and entertainment head for downtown Bellevue or east to Issaquah. That's a bummer.

Gyms

- **Bally Total Fitness** •
  3235 148th Ave SE [SE Eastgate Wy]
- **Samena Swim & Recreation Club** •
  15231 Lake Hills Blvd [154th Ave SE]
- **Sunset North Fitness Center** •
  3060 139th Ave SE [SE 32nd St]

Liquor Stores

- **Washington State Liquor Store** •
  15100 SE 38th St

Video Rental

- **Blockbuster** •
  4851 Lakemont Blvd SE

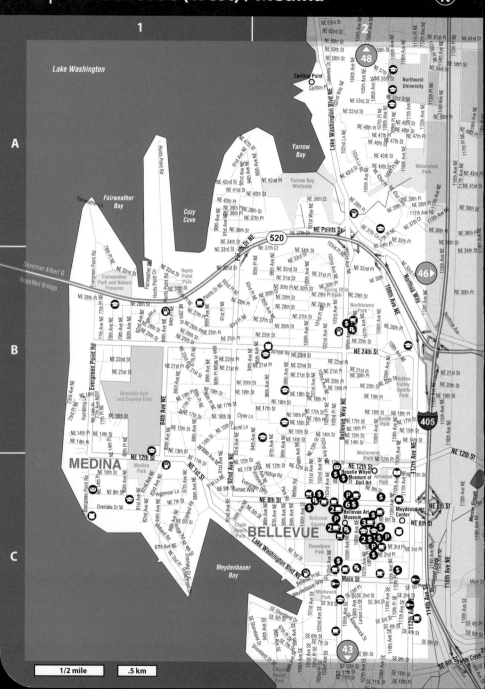

Map 45 · **Bellevue (West) / Medina**

Shiny skyscrapers, properties, and retail spaces are continually developing, and cranes seem to be a permanent fixture as more construction is expected in downtown Bellevue to accommodate the booming business and technology industries. Bellevue Way becomes "Snowflake Lane" during the holiday season with nightly parades and Christmas lights on display. Upscale and strictly residential Medina is known for its homes right on the shoreline of Lake Washington.

Banks

- **Bank of America** •
  10116 NE 8th St [102nd Ave NE]
- **Bank of America** •
  10555 NE 8th St [106th Ave NE]
- **Bank of America** •
  415 106th Ave NE [NE 4th St]
- **Bank of America (ATM)** •
  10500 NE 8th St [Bellevue Wy NE]
- **Bank of America (ATM)** •
  2636 Bellevue Wy NE [NE 26th St]
- **Evergreen Bank** •
  110 110th Ave NE [Main St]
- **First Mutual Bank** •
  10001 NE 8th St [100th Ave NE]
- **First Mutual Bank** •
  400 108th Ave NE [NE 4th St]
- **Key Bank** •
  1055 Bellevue Wy NE [NE 10th St]
- **Key Bank** •
  10655 NE 4th St [106th Pl NE]
- **Key Bank** •
  601 108th Ave NE [NE 6th St]
- **Sterling Savings Bank** •
  500 108th Ave NE [NE 4th St]
- **US Bank** •
  10800 NE 8th St [108th Ave NE]
- **US Bank (ATM)** •
  10425 NE 8th St [Bellevue Wy NE]
- **Washington Mutual** •
  10550 NE 8th St [106th Ave NE]
- **Washington Mutual** •
  123 Bellevue Wy NE [NE 1st St]
- **Wells Fargo** •
  1130 Bellevue Wy NE [NE 12th St]
- **Wells Fargo** •
  225 108th Ave NE [NE 2nd Pl]

Car Rental

- **Avis** • 300 112th Ave SE [NE 10th St]
- **Budget** • 21 Bellevue Wy SE [Main St]
- **Hertz** • 11211 Main St [112th Ave SE]

Coffee

- **Belvi Coffee & Tea Exchange** •
  900 108th Ave NE [NE 10th St]
- **Café Habits** • 550 106th Ave NE [NE 6th St]
- **Koots Green Tea** •
  700 Bellevue Way NE [NE 8th St]
- **Seattle's Best Coffee** •
  226 Bellevue Sq [NE 6th St]
- **Starbucks** • 10214 NE 8th St [102nd Ave NE]
- **Starbucks** • 11010 NE 8th St [110th Ave NE]
- **Starbucks** • 255 108th Ave NE [NE 2nd Pl]
- **Starbucks** • 44 Bellevue Wy NE [Main St]
- **Starbucks** • 500 108th Ave NE [NE 4th St]
- **Starbucks** • 545 Bellevue Wy SE [SE 6th St]
- **Starbucks** • 601 108th Ave NE [NE 6th St]
- **Starbucks** • 626 106th Ave NE [NE 6th St]
- **T'Latte** • 37 103rd Ave NE [NE 1st Pl]
- **Tully's** • 10500 NE 8th St [Bellevue Wy NE]
- **Tully's** • 10812 Main St [108th Ave NE]
- **Tully's** • 2002 Bellevue Sq Mall [NE 8th St]
- **Tully's** • Hilton • 300 112th Ave SE [SE 4th St]
- **Tully's** • 302 Bellevue Sq [NE 6th St]
- **Tully's** • 700 Bellevue Wy NE [NE 8th St]
- **Tully's** • 8805 Points Dr NE [NE 28th St]

Gas Stations

- **Chevron** • 10011 Main St [100th Ave NE]
- **Chevron** • 2626 Bellevue Wy NE [NE 26th St]
- **Chevron** • 8401 NE 12th St [84th Ave NE]
- **Shell** •
  3828 Lake Washington Blvd NE [NE 38th Pl]
- **76** • 2724 84th Ave NE [NE 28th St]

Landmarks

- **Bellevue Art Museum** •
  510 Bellevue Wy NE [NE 6th St]
- **Carillon Point** •
  3240 Carillon Point [Lake Washington Blvd NE]
- **Meydenbauer Center** •
  11100 NE 6th St [110th Ave NE]
- **Rosalie Whyel Museum of Doll Art** •
  1116 108th Ave NE [NE 12th St]

Libraries

- **Bellevue Regional Library** •
  1111 110th Ave NE [NE 11th St]

Parking

Pharmacies

- **Bartell Drugs** • 10116 NE 8th St [102nd Ave NE]
- **Bartell Drugs** • 424 Bellevue Wy NE [NE 4th St]
- **Quality Food Centers Pharmacy** •
  2636 Bellevue Wy NE [NE 26th St]
- **Rite Aid** • 120 106th Ave NE [NE 2nd St]

Police

- **Bellevue Police Dept** •
  450 110th Ave NE [NE 4th St]
- **Clyde Hill Police Dept** •
  9605 NE 24th St [96th Ave NE]
- **Medina Police Dept** •
  501 Evergreen Point Rd [Overlake Dr W]

Post Offices

- **Bellevue** • 1171 Bellevue Wy NE [NE 12th St]
- **Medina** • 816 Evergreen Point Rd [NE 8th St]

Schools

- **Bellevue Christian High/Junior High** •
  1601 98th Ave NE [NE 16th St]
- **Bellevue High** •
  10416 Wolverine Wy [Bellevue Wy NE]
- **Bellevue Montessori** •
  2411 112th Ave NE [NE 24th St]
- **BEST High** • 10903 NE 53rd St [108th Ave NE]
- **Chinook Middle** • 2001 98th Ave NE [NE 20th St]
- **Clyde Hill Elementary** •
  9601 NE 24th St [96th Ave NE]
- **De Vry University** • 500 108th Ave NE [NE 4th St]
- **Eastside Preparatory** •
  10635 NE 38th Pl [NE 37th Cir]
- **Kirkland SDA** • 5320 108th Ave NE [NE 53rd St]
- **Learning Garden** • 505 106th Ave NE [NE 6th St]
- **Medina Elementary** •
  8001 NE 8th St [80th Ave NE]
- **Northwest University** •
  5520 108th Ave NE [NE 55th St]
- **Sacred Heart** • 9450 NE 14th St [94th Ave NE]
- **St Thomas** • 8300 NE 12th ST [84th Ave NE]
- **Three Points Elementary** •
  7800 NE 28th St [79th Ave NE]

Supermarkets

- **Quality Food Center** •
  10116 NE 8th St [102nd Ave NE]
- **Quality Food Center** •
  2636 Bellevue Wy NE [NE 26th St]
- **Safeway** • 410 Bellevue Wy NE [NE 4th St]

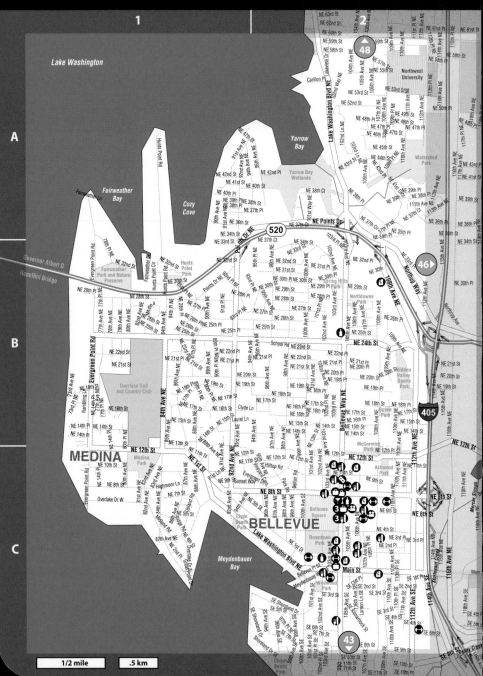

Map 45 · **Bellevue (West) / Medina**

Lake Washington

Fairweather Bay

Cozy Cove

Yarrow Bay

Yarrow Bay Wetlands

Northwest University

Watershed Park

Fairweather Park and Nature Preserve

Hunts Point Park

Spring Hills Park

Northtowne Park

Hidden Valley Sports Park

Overlake Golf and Country Club

Evergreen Point Park

MEDINA

Medina Park

McCormick Park

Ashwood Park

Bower Park

BELLEVUE

Bellevue Square

Downtown Park

Clyde Beach Park

Wildwood Park

Meydenbauer Bay

Chismore Beach Park

Governor Albert D. Rosellini Bridge

1/2 mile   .5 km

Be forewarned: expect crowds and long waits at every nice restaurant within walking distance of Bellevue Square. Skip the lines at the Lincoln Square Cinemas and get tickets at the various kiosks in Bellevue Square. If you've got the dough, the membership-only Bellevue Club is recognized for its vast athletic facilities, which include an Olympic-size swimming pool and indoor track. Carillon Point is a perfect place to stroll and watch the sunset after dinner.

Copy Shops

- **Belgate & Printing Copy** •
  1035 103rd Ave NE [NE 10th St]
- **FedEx Kinko's** • 10635 NE 8th St [106th Ave NE]
- **FedEx Kinko's** • 40 Bellevue Wy NE [Main St]
- **Minuteman Press** • 1101 106th Ave NE [NE 12th St]
- **Office Depot** • 100 108th Ave SE [Main St]
- **Print Inc** • 3015 112th Ave NE [Northup Wy]
- **The UPS Store** • 227 Bellevue Wy NE [NE 2nd St]

Gyms

- **Bellevue Club** • 11200 SE 6th St [112th Ave SE]
- **Bellevue Place Club** •
  800 Bellevue Wy NE, Ste 200 [NE 8th St]
- **Curves** • 102 Bellevue Way NE [NE 1st Pl]
- **Elite Fitness Training** • 136 102nd Ave SE, Ste 101 [Main St]
- **First St Fitness** • 10001 NE 1st St [100th Ave NE]
- **LA Fitness Sports Clubs** • 550 106th Ave NE [NE 6th St]
- **Skyline Tower Fitness Center** •
  10900 NE 4th St, Ste 120 [110th Ave NE]
- **YMCA** • 777 108th Ave NE [NE 8th St]

Liquor Stores

- **Vino 100** • 700 Bellevue Wy NE [NE 8th St]
- **Washington State Liquor Store** •
  10307 NE 1st St [103rd Ave NE]
- **Washington State Liquor Store** •
  2616 Bellevue Wy NE [NE 26th St]

Nightlife

- **Parlor** • 700 Bellevue Way NE [NE 8th St]

Movie Theaters

- **Bellevue Galleria Stadium 11** •
  550 106th Ave NE [NE 6th St]
- **Lincoln Square Cinemas** •
  700 Bellevue Wy NE [NE 8th St]

Restaurants

- **Bamboo Garden Restaurant** •
  202 106th Ave NE [NE 2nd St]
- **Bis on Main** • 10213 Main St [102nd Ave SE]
- **Cheesecake Factory** • 401 Bellevue Sq [NE 6th St]
- **Daniel's Broiler** • 10500 NE 8th St [106th Ave NE]
- **Facing East Taiwanese Restaurant** •
  1075 Bellevue Way NE [10th Street]
- **Mediterranean Kitchen** • 103 Bellevue Wy NE [NE 1st St]
- **The Melting Pot** • 302 108th Ave NE [NE 4th St]
- **Moghul Palace** • 10303 NE 10th St [103rd Ave NE]
- **Pagliacci Pizza** • 563 Bellevue Sq [NE 6th St]
- **Pasta & Co** • 10218 NE 8th St [102nd Ave NE]
- **PF Chang's China Bistro** • 525 Bellevue Wy SE [SE 6th St]
- **Ruth's Chris Steak House** • 565 Bellevue Sq [NE 6th St]
- **Seastar Restaurant and Raw Bar** •
  205 108th Ave NE [NE 2nd St]
- **Tap House Grill** • 550 106th Ave NE [NE 6th St]

Shopping

- **Bellevue Square** • Bellevue Wy NE & NE 8th St
- **Fireworks** • 196 Bellevue Sq [NE 6th St]
- **Lincoln Square** • Bellevue Wy NE & NE 8th St
- **Made In Washington** • 190 Bellevue Sq [NE 6th St]
- **Rudy's Barbershop** • 5 Bellevue Wy NE [Main St]
- **Sephora** • 141 Bellevue Sq [NE 6th St]

Video Rental

- **Blockbuster** • 939 Bellevue Wy NE [NE 10th St]

Map 46 • Bellevue (Central)

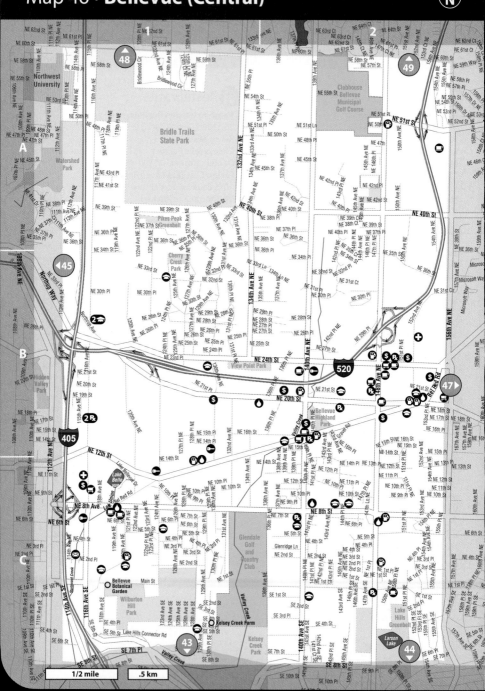

The latest census reported Bellevue to have the highest percentage of non-white residents in the state, with the Chinese and Indian populations having increased twofold since 2000. Despite the materialistic air of the "SoCal of Puget Sound," Bellevue was ranked #21 in Money magazine's 100 Best Places to Live in 2006.

$ Banks

- **Bank of America** • 2245 Bel Red Rd [NE 24th St]
- **Bank of America (ATM)** • 1035 116th Ave NE [NE 8th St]
- **Key Bank** • 15110 NE 24th St [151st Pl NE]
- **Key Bank (ATM)** • 12903 Northup Wy St [130th Ave NE]
- **US Bank** • 13830 NE 20th St [136th Pl NE]
- **US Bank** • 15000 NE 24th St [151st Pl NE]
- **Washington Federal Savings** •
  14801 NE Bellevue Redmond Rd [148th Ave NE]
- **Wells Fargo** • 1645 140th Ave NE [NE Bellevue Redmond Rd]

Car Rental

- **Enterprise** • 12200 NE 12th St [124th Ave NE]
- **Enterprise** • 2233 140th Ave NE [NE 24th St]
- **Hertz** • 1405 130th Ave NE [NE 14th Pl]
- **Thrifty** • 655 116th Ave NE [NE 8th St]

Car Washes

- **Bellevue Car Wash** • 14008 NE 8th St [140th Ave NE]
- **Brown Bear Car Wash** • 14801 NE 8th St [148th Ave NE]
- **Brown Bear Car Wash** • 15248 Bel Red Rd [NE 21st St]
- **Elephant Car Washes** • 12900 Bel Red Rd [130th Ave NE]
- **Genesis Wash & Detail** • 13421 NE 20th St [136th Pl NE]
- **TIKI Car Wash & Food Mart** • 11909 NE 8th St [120th Ave NE]

Coffee

- **Bellisimo Espresso** • 11909 NE 8th St [120th Ave NE]
- **Blue Cow Espresso** • 2201 140th Ave NE [NE 24th St]
- **Jitters Coffee** • 2200 148th Ave NE [NE 22nd St]
- **Starbucks** • 15000 NE 24th St [151st Pl NE]
- **Starbucks** • 15015 Main St [150th Ave NE]
- **Starbucks** • 1645 140th Ave NE [NE Bellevue Redmond Rd]
- **Starbucks** • 2020 148th Ave NE [NE 20th St]
- **Starbucks** • Safeco • 4854 NE 154th Pl [NE 51st St]
- **Starbucks** • 661 120th Ave NE [NE 8th St]

Gas Stations

- **76** • 106 148th Ave NE [NE 1st St]
- **76** • 14014 Bel Red Rd [140th Ave NE]
- **76** • 14801 NE 8th St [148th Ave NE]
- **76** • 15248 Bel Red Rd [NE 21st St]
- **76** • 2421 148th Ave NE [NE 24th St]
- **Chevron** • 12900 Bel Red Rd [130th Ave NE]
- **Chevron** • 13948 NE 20th St [140th Ave NE]
- **Chevron** • 5040 148th Ave NE [NE 51st St]
- **Chevron** • 11 148th Ave SE [Main St]
- **Texaco** • 15248 Bel Red Rd [NE 20th St]

+ Emergency Rooms

- **Eastside Hospital** • 2700 152nd Ave NE [NE 24th St]
- **Overlake Hospital** • 1035 116th Ave NE [NE 8th St]

○ Landmarks

- **Bellevue Botanical Garden** • 12001 Main St [118th Ave SE]
- **Kelsey Creek Farm** • 410 130th Ave SE [SE 4th St]

Rx Pharmacies

- **65 Plus** • 14339 NE 20th St [140th Ave NE]
- **Bellegrove Pharmacy** • 1535 116th Ave NE [NE 12th St]
- **Fred Meyer** • 2041 148th Ave NE [NE 20th St]
- **Rite Aid** • 14880 NE 24th St [148th Ave NE]
- **Rxtra Care Pharmacy U & I-Bellevue** • 29 148th Ave SE [Main St]
- **Safeway** • 1645 140th Ave NE [NE Bellevue Redmond Rd]
- **United Drugs** • 1535 116th Ave NE [NE 12th St]
- **Walgreens** • 647 140th Ave NE [NE 8th St]

✉ Post Offices

- **Midlakes** • 11405 NE 2nd Pl [116th Ave NE]

Schools

- **Americas Child Montessori** • 14340 NE 21st St [140th Ave NE]
- **BSD Vocational Education/Career Educ Options** •
  12111 NE 1st St [Main St]
- **Cherry Crest Elementary** • 12400 NE 32nd St [124th Ave NE]
- **Chestnut Hill Academy** • 2610 116th Ave NE [Northup Wy]
- **City University** • 11900 NE 1st St [Main St]
- **Early World Childrens** • 13831 Bel Red Rd [NE 16th St]
- **Highland Middle** • 15027 NE Bellevue Redmond Rd [152nd Ave NE]
- **International** • 445 128th Ave SE [SE 4th Pl]
- **Kindercare 2060 #903** • 2060 152nd Ave NE [NE 21st St]
- **Learning Garden** • 2320 130th Ave NE [NE 24th St]
- **The Little School** • 2612 116th Ave NE [Northup Wy]
- **Neighborhood Christian** • 625 140th Ave NE [NE 8th St]
- **Odle Middle** • 14401 NE 8th St [144th Ave Ne]
- **Sammamish HS** • 100 140th Ave SE [SE 1st St]
- **Stevenson Elementary** • 14220 NE 8th St [143rd Ave NE]
- **Three Cedars** • 556 124th Ave NE [NE 6th Pl]

Supermarkets

- **Fred Meyer** • 2041 148th Ave NE [NE 20th St]
- **Safeway** • 15000 NE 24th St [151st Pl NE]
- **Safeway** • 1645 140th Ave NE [NE Bellevue Redmond Rd]
- **Trader Joe's** • 15400 NE 20th St [NE Bellevue Redmond Rd]
- **Whole Foods** • 888 116th Ave NE [NE 8th St]

Map 46 · **Bellevue (Central)**

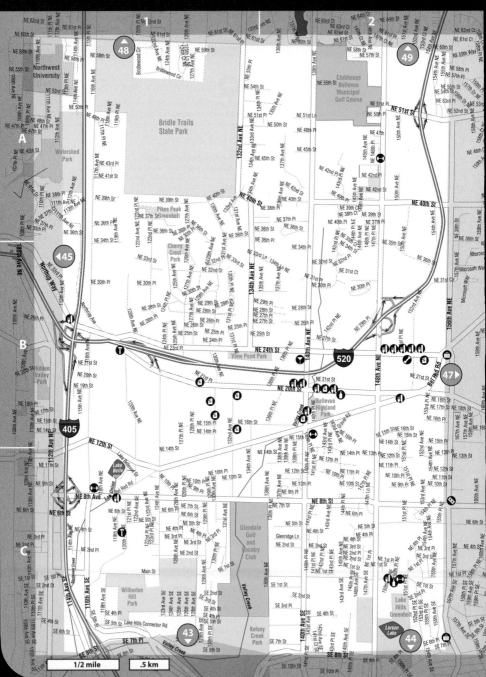

Creative I Love Sushi fashions and names their own sushi rolls—including an "I Love Roll." Head for college-budget friendly Trader Joe's for affordable groceries and the best snacks to help you through that all-nighter—peanut-butter filled pretzels and dark chocolate covered espresso beans. Asians would go nuts without Asian specialty grocery stores: Japanese-established Uwajimaya carries everything from basic Western essentials to durian and pig feet, while Paldo World specializes in Korean food and has tasty, throat-burning kimchee to go.

Copy Shops

- **Digital Reprographic Services** •
  12880 NE 21st Pl [Northup Wy]
- **Gateway Printing** • 12890 NE 15th Pl [130th Ave NE]
- **Minuteman Press** • 1817 130th Ave NE [NE 20th St]
- **Office Depot** • 15301 NE 24th St [152nd Ave NE]
- **Olympic Reprographics** •
  1555 132nd Ave NE [NE 16th St]
- **Perfect Press** • 1910 132nd Ave NE [NE 20th St]
- **Staples** • 1645 140th Ave NE [NE Bellevue Redmond Rd]
- **The UPS Store** • 14150 NE 20th St [140th Ave NE]

Gyms

- **24 Hour Fitness - Bellevue** •
  1505 140th Ave NE [NE Bellevue Redmond Rd] ♿
- **Curves** • 15015 Main St, Ste 105 [150th Pl NE]
- **PRO Sports Club** • 4455 148th Ave NE [NE 43rd Pl]
- **Sportzal Inc** • 800 118th Ave NE [NE 8th St]

Hardware Stores

- **The Home Depot** • 325 120th Ave NE [NE 5th St]
- **Lowe's** • 11959 Northup Wy [120th Ave NE]

Liquor Stores

- **Washington State Liquor Store** •
  14315 NE 20th St [140th Ave NE]
- **Washington State Liquor Store** •
  15015 Main St [150th Pl NE]

Nightlife

- **Skate King** • 2301 140th Ave NE [NE 24th St]

Pet Shops

- **Wild Birds Unlimited** • 15155 NE 24th St [152nd Ave NE]

Restaurants

- **Andre's Eurasian Bistro** •
  14125 NE 20th St [140th Ave NE]
- **Blue Ginger Korean Grill and Sushi** •
  14045 NE 20th St [140th Ave NE]
- **Dixie's BBQ** • 11522 Northup Wy [116th Ave NE]
- **I Love Sushi** • 11818 NE 8th St [NE Bellevue Redmond Rd]
- **Jeem Asian Restaurant** •
  14850 NE 24th St [148th Ave NE]
- **Malay Satay Hut** • 15230 NE 24th St [152nd Ave NE]
- **Noble Court** • 1644 140th Ave NE [NE Bellevue Redmond Rd]
- **Pho Hoa** • 15169 NE 24th St [151st Pl NE]
- **Regent Bakery & Cafe** •
  15159 NE 24th St [152nd Ave NE]
- **Saigon City** • 15045 Bel Red Rd [152nd Ave NE]
- **Sichuanese Cuisine** • 15005 NE 24th St [148th Ave NE]
- **Szechuan Chef** • 15015 Main St [148th Ave NE]
- **Thai Kitchen** • 14115 NE 20th St [140th Ave NE]
- **Tosoni's** • 14320 NE 20th St [140th Ave NE]

Shopping

- **Paldo World** • 549 156th Ave SE [SE Lake Hines Blvd]
- **Uwajimaya** • 15555 NE 24th St [NE Bellevue Redmond Rd]

Video Rental

- **Blockbuster** • 15600 NE 8th St [156th Ave NE]

Map 47 • **Bellevue (East) / Redmond**

Essentials

Trees and scattered parks with numerous sports camps surround the quiet residential areas, keeping the moms and soccer vans busy. An ideal location for picnics and water sports, Idylwood Beach Park on Lake Sammamish is a popular hangout for teenagers eager (and wishing) for the sun and warm weather. Rural farmland less than sixty years ago, Redmond is now a pricey city and home to a certain corporation you may have heard of----Microsoft.

$ Banks
- **Bank of America (ATM)** •
  15751 NE 15th St [156th Ave NE]
- **Bank of America (ATM)** •
  15800 NE 8th St [Crossroads Pl]
- **First Mutual Bank** • 15635 NE 8th St [156th Ave NE]
- **Key Bank** • 1350 156th Ave NE [NE 13th Pl]
- **US Bank** • 1128 156th Ave NE [NE 11th St]
- **Washington Mutual** • 15600 NE 8th St [156th Ave NE]
- **Washington Mutual** • 1955 156th Ave NE [NE 20th St]
- **Wells Fargo** • 2201 156th Ave NE [NE 24th St]
- **Wells Fargo (ATM)** • 15600 NE 8th St [156th Ave NE]

Coffee
- **Starbucks** • 15600 NE 8th St [156th Ave NE]

Gas Stations
- **76** • 15615 NE 8th St [156th Ave NE]

Landmarks
- **Microsoft Corporate Headquarters** •
  1 Microsoft Wy [NE 36th St]

Pharmacies
- **Bartell Drugs** • 653 156th Ave NE [NE 6th St] ♿
- **Clark's Pharmacy** • 15615 Bel Red Rd
- **Pharmacy Plus** • 1299 156th Ave NE [NE 13th Pl]
- **Top Food & Drug** • 15751 NE 15th St [156th Ave NE]

Post Offices
- **Crossroads** • 15731 NE 8th St [156th Ave NE]

Schools
- **Ardmore Elementary** •
  16616 NE 32nd St [167th Ave NE]
- **Audubon Elementary** •
  3045 180th Ave NE [NE 30th St]
- **Bellevue Children's Academy** •
  15061 Bel Red Rd [NE 20th St]
- **Bennett Elementary** • 17900 NE 16th St [179th Ave NE]
- **Calvary Lutheran** • 16231 NE 6th St [164th Ave NE]
- **Cascadia Montessori** •
  4239 162nd Ave NE [NE 44th Ct]
- **Eton School** • 2701 Bel Red Rd [SE 4th St]
- **Family Learning Center
  (Grades K-12 Homeschool Support)** •
  2315 173rd Ave NE [NE 24th St]
- **Interlake HS** • 16245 NE 24th St [162nd Ave Ne]
- **Jewish Day** • 15749 NE 4th St [157th Ave NE]
- **Marymoor Spanish Montessori** •
  4244 Bel Red Rd [NE 40th St]
- **Sherwood Forest Elementary** •
  16411 NE 24th St [164th Ave NE]
- **Spectrum Learning Community** •
  16230 NE 4th St [164th Ave NE]
- **St Louise** • 133 156th Ave SE [SE 4th St]
- **Veladare** • 15617 Bel Red Rd [156th Ave NE]

Supermarkets
- **Quality Food Center** •
  15600 NE 8th St, K-1 [156th Ave NE]

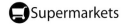

Map 47 • **Bellevue (East) / Redmond**

Sundries / Entertainment

The food court at the aging Crossroads Bellevue shopping center is more popular than the stores themselves, but the mall provides important community services including a mini police department, city hall, and even a library. Plus, all the public areas have free Wi-Fi. Come watch locals duke it out on the giant public chess board.

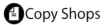Copy Shops

- **FedEx Kinko's** • 1313 156th Ave NE [NE 13th Pl]
- **The UPS Store** • 15600 NE 8th St [156th Ave NE]

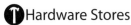Hardware Stores

- **Crossroads Ace Hardware** •
  653 156th Ave NE [NE 8th St]

Movie Theaters

- **Regal Crossroads 8 Cinemas** •
  1200 156th Ave NE [NE 12th St]

Restaurants

- **Firenze Ristorante Italiano** •
  15600 NE 8th St [156th Ave NE]

Shopping

- **Crossroads Bellevue** • NE 8th St & 156th Ave NE

Map 48 · **Kirkland**

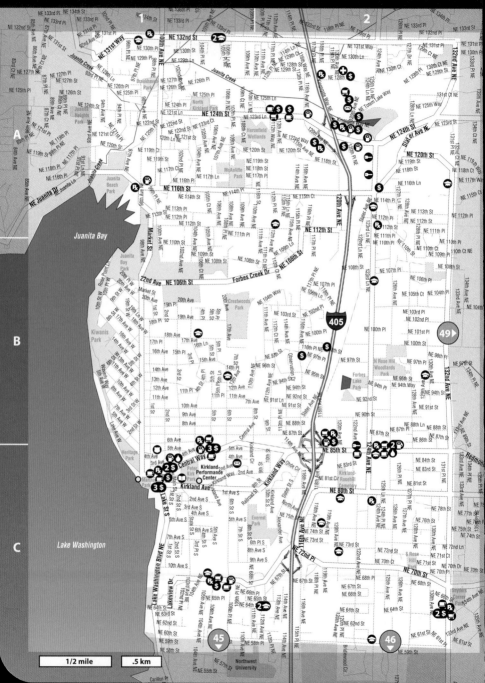

With a landscape view of the Seattle skyline, apartments and condos here are costly. With a waterfront downtown, the quiet, romantic lifestyle here attracts retirees. Kirkland's pedestrian-friendly (translation: major traffic), village-like character is maintained by the assortment of little consignment boutiques, art galleries, coffee shops, and restaurants. The home of the original headquarters of Costco (hence the Kirkland Signature brand), Kirkland is also the host of the Junior League Softball World Series, the Seattle Thunderbirds Hockey Team, and the Seattle Seahawks training facility.

 Banks

- **Bank of America** • 101 Kirkland Ave [Lake St]
- **Bank of America** •
  10623 NE 68th St [106th Ave NE]
- **Bank of America** • 11617 97th Ln [16th Ave NE]
- **Bank of America** •
  12424 Totem Lake Blvd NE [120th Ave NE]
- **Bank of America (ATM)** •
  11224 NE 124th St [113th Ave NE]
- **Bank of America (ATM)** •
  11831 124th Ave NE
- **Bank of America (ATM)** •
  211 Park Pl Ctr [Central Wy]
- **Bank of America (ATM)** •
  8629 120th Ave NE [NE 85th St]
- **First Mutual Bank** • 278 Central Wy [3rd St]
- **Frontier Bank** •
  12507 116th Ave NE [NE 124th St]
- **Frontier Bank** • 132 Kirkland Ave [Lake St]
- **Key Bank** •
  12604 Totem Lake Blvd NE [120th Ave NE]
- **Key Bank** • 327 Parkplace Ctr [Central Wy]
- **Key Bank (ATM)** •
  12040 NE 128th St [120th Ave NE]
- **Sterling Savings Bank** •
  230 Main St [Central Wy]
- **US Bank** • 177 Central Wy [Lake St]
- **Washington Federal Savings** •
  116 Kirkland Ave [Lake St]
- **Washington Mutual** •
  12080 NE Totem Lake Wy [120th Ave NE]
- **Washington Mutual** •
  12221 120th Ave NE [NE 124th St]
- **Washington Mutual** •
  6625 132nd Ave NE [NE 66th St]
- **Wells Fargo** •
  12560 120th Ave NE [NE Totem Lake Wy]
- **Wells Fargo** • 460 Central Wy [5th St]
- **Wells Fargo** • 6615 132nd Ave NE [NE 66th St]
- **Wells Fargo** • 9750 117th Pl NE [NE 98th St]

 Car Rental

- **Enterprise** • 12047 124th Ave NE [NE 124th St]
- **Enterprise** • 8514 122nd Ave NE [NE 85th St]
- **Hertz** • 11709 124th Ave NE [NE 116th St]

 Car Washes

- **Rose Hill Car Wash** •
  12633 NE 85th St [126th Ave NE]
- **White Swan Car Wash** •
  324 Central Wy [3rd St]

 Coffee

- **Caffe Ladro** •
  104 Central Way [1st Street]
- **Kahili Coffee** • 105 Lake St S [Kirkland Ave]

- **Starbucks** • QFC • 11224 NE 124th St [113th Ave NE]
- **Starbucks** • 11400 NE 124th St [113th Ave NE]
- **Starbucks** • 12209 NE 85th St [122nd Ave NE]
- **Starbucks** • Safeway •
  12519 NE 85th St [126th Ave NE]
- **Starbucks** • 208 Park Pl Ctr [5th Street]
- **Starbucks** • 6617 132nd Ave NE [NE 66th St]
- **Starbucks** • 6733 108th Ave NE [NE 68th St]
- **St. James Espresso** •
  355 Kirkland Ave [State St S]
- **Terra Bite Lounge** •
  219 Kirkland Ave [Main St]

 Gas Stations

- **76** • 11848 NE 85th St [120th Ave NE]
- **76** • 12302 NE 124th St [124th Ave NE]
- **76** • 12412 116th Ave NE [NE 124th St]
- **76** • 9800 NE 116th St [98th Ave NE]
- **Chevron** • 12500 Totem Lake Blvd NE [120th Ave NE]
- **Chevron** • 12607 NE 85th St [126th Ave NE]
- **Chevron** • 324 Central Wy [3rd St]
- **Shell** • 10801 NE 68th St [108th Ave NE]
- **Shell** • 12221 NE 124th St [120th Pl NE]
- **Shell** • 12520 NE 85th St [126th Ave NE]
- **Shell** • 406 Central Wy [4th St]

 Emergency Rooms

- **Evergreen Hospital Medical Center** •
  12040 NE 128th St [120th Ave NE]

 Landmarks

- **Kirkland Performance Center** •
  350 Kirkland Ave [3rd St]
- **Marina Park** • 25 Lake Shore Plz [Market St]

 Libraries

- **Kirkland Library** • 308 Kirkland Ave [3rd St]

 Pharmacies

- **Assured Pharmacy** •
  12071 124th Ave NE [NE 124th St]
- **Bartell Drugs** • 10625 NE 68th St [106th Ave NE]
- **Bartell Drugs** • 6619 132nd Ave NE [NE 66th St]
- **Costco** • 8629 120th Ave NE [NE 85th St]
- **Evergreen Professional Center Pharmacy** •
  11800 NE 128th St [Totem Lake Blvd NE]
- **Fred Meyer** • 12221 120th Ave NE [NE 124th St]
- **Lakeshore Pharmacy** •
  134 Central Wy [Lake St]
- **Quality Food Centers Pharmacy** •
  11224 124th Ave NE [NE 112th Pl]
- **Quality Food Centers Pharmacy** •
  211 Park Pl Ctr [Central Wy]
- **Rite Aid** •
  12530 Totem Lake Blvd NE [120th Ave NE]

- **Rite Aid** • 9820 NE 132nd St [100th Ave NE]
- **Safeway** • 12519 NE 85th St [126th Ave NE]
- **Walgreens** • 11607 98th Ave NE [NE Juanita Dr]
- **Walgreens** • 12405 NE 85th St [124th Ave NE]

 Police

- **Kirkland Police Dept** • 123 5th Ave [1st St]

 Post Offices

- **Cpu Totem Lake** •
  12556 120th Ave NE [NE Totem Lake Wy]
- **Kirkland** • 721 4th Ave [6th St]

 Schools

- **Bell Elementary** •
  11212 NE 112th St [112th Ave NE]
- **Community School** •
  11133 NE 65th St [111th Ave NE]
- **Franklin Elementary** •
  12434 NE 60th St [125th Ln NE]
- **Futures** • 10601 NE 132nd St [105th Pl NE]
- **Holy Family** • 7300 120th Ave NE [NE 73rd St]
- **International Community** •
  11144 NE 65th St [111th Ave NE]
- **Juanita Elementary** •
  9635 NE 132nd St [97th Ave NE]
- **Juanita HS** • 10601 NE 132nd St [105th Pl NE]
- **Kindercare 11404 #1024** •
  11404 Slater Ave NE [124th Ave NE]
- **Kirkland Junior High** • 430 18th Ave [4th St]
- **Lake Washington HS** •
  12033 NE 80th St [120th Ave NE]
- **Lake Washington Technical College** •
  11605 132nd Ave NE [NE 117th St]
- **Lakeview Elementary** •
  10400 NE 68th St [104th Ave NE]
- **Northstar Junior High** •
  11822 NE 75th St [118th Ave NE]
- **Peter Kirk Elementary** • 1312 6th St [13th Ave]
- **Rose Hill Elementary** •
  8110 128th Ave NE [NE 81st Pl]
- **Springhurst** • 10737 124th Ave NE [NE 107th Pl]
- **Twain Elementary** •
  9525 130th Ave NE [NE 95th St]

 Supermarkets

- **Costco** • 8629 120th Ave NE [NE 85th St]
- **Quality Food Center** •
  11224 NE 124th St [113th Ave NE]
- **Quality Food Center** • 211 Park Pl Ctr [Central Wy]
- **Red Apple** • 6625 132nd Ave NE [NE 66th St]
- **Safeway** • 12519 NE 85th St [126th Ave NE]
- **Thriftway** • 10611 NE 68th St [106th Ave NE]
- **Trader Joe's** •
  12632 120th Ave NE [NE 128th St]

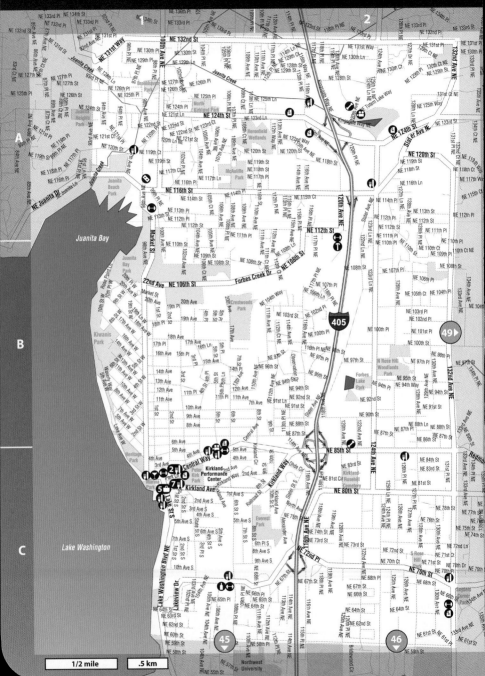

Map 48 · **Kirkland**

1/2 mile   .5 km

Your Sunday plans: grab a newspaper and a latte at Kahili's Coffee or Caffe Ladro, take a walk with your dog and feed the ducks at Marina Park, satisfy your stomach with a juicy burger at The Slip, catch a musical performance at the Kirkland Performance Center, then grab dinner at one of the many Thai restaurants. For the most authentic Japanese food on this side of the lake, it has to be Izumi, while Third Floor Fish Café and Anthony's dish out the best seafood. If you must make a fool of yourself, there's karaoke at Pegasus Pizza and the "classy" Tiki Joe's Wet Bar.

Copy Shops

- **FedEx Kinko's** • 518 Central Wy [5th St]
- **Minuteman Press** • 12700 NE 124th St [128th Ln NE]
- **The Print Factor-E** • 12330 120th Ave NE [NE 124th St]
- **The UPS Store** • 11410 NE 124th St [116th Ave NE]
- **The UPS Store** • 218 Main St [Park Ln]
- **The UPS Store** • 6513 132nd Ave NE [NE 66th St]

Gyms

- **24 Hour Fitness** • 529 Parkplace Centre [6th Street] ⊛
- **Bally Total Fitness** • 6601 132nd Ave NE [NE 66th St]
- **Columbia Athletic Clubs** •
  11400 98th Ave NE [NE 116th St]
- **Curves** • 10633 NE 68th St [106th Ave NE]
- **Gold's Gym - Kirkland** •
  11133 120th Ave NE [NE 112th St]
- **X Gym** • 126 Central Wy [Lake St]

Hardware Stores

- **Plasker John C & Associates** •
  11001 120th Ave NE [NE 112th St]

Liquor Stores

- **Washington State Liquor Store** •
  10609 NE 68th St [106th Ave NE]

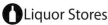

Movie Theaters

- **Kirkland Parkplace Cinema** • 404 Parkplace Ctr
- **Totem Lake Cinemas** •
  12232 NE Totem Lake Wy [120th Ave NE]

Nightlife

- **The Shark Club** • 52 Lake Shore Plz [Market St]
- **Tiki Joe's Wet Bar** • 106 Kirkland Ave [Lake St S]

Pet Shops

- **Denny's Pet World** •
  12534 120th Ave NE [NE Totem Lake Wy]
- **Petco - Kirkland** • 12040 NE 85th St [120th Ave NE]

Restaurants

- **21 Central Steakhouse** • 21 Central Wy [Market St]
- **Anthony's** • 135 Lake St S [Kirkland Ave]
- **Blue Fish Sushi Bar & Grill** • 166 Lake St S [2nd Ave S]
- **Boston Wood Fired Pizza** •
  13200 Old Redmond Rd [132nd Ave NE]
- **Cactus** • 121 Park Ln [Lake St]
- **Café Juanita** • 9702 NE 120th Pl [97th Ave NE]
- **Calabria Ristorante Italiano** •
  132 Lake St S [Kirkland Ave]
- **Hanuman Thai Cafe** • 115 Central Way [Lake St S]
- **Izumi** • 12539 116th Ave NE [NE 124th St]
- **Lynn's Bistro** • 214 Central Wy [2nd Pl S]
- **The Original Pancake House** •
  130 Parkplace Ctr [Central Wy]
- **Pegasus Pizza** • 12669 NE 85th St [126th Ave NE]
- **Purple Café & Wine Bar** • 323 Park Pl Ctr [5th Street]
- **Ristorante Paradiso** • 120A Park Ln [Lake St]
- **Shamiana** • 10724 NE 68th St [108th Ave NE]
- **Thai Kitchen** • 11701 124th Ave NE [NE 116th St]
- **The Slip** • 80 Kirkland Ave [Lake St S]
- **Thin Pan Siam Bistro** • 170 Lake St S [Kirkland Ave]
- **Third Floor Fish Café** • 205 Lake St S [2nd Ave S]
- **Wing Dome** • 232 Central Wy [2nd Pl S]

Shopping

- **Champagne Taste** • 147 Park Ln [Lake St]
- **PCC Natural Market** • 10718 NE 68th St [106th Ave]
- **Reasons to Believe** • 92 Kirkland Ave [Lake St]
- **Rebekah's** • 117 Lake St S [Lake St]
- **Simplicity Décor** • 126 Park Ln [Lake St]
- **Tim's Seafood** • 224 Park Ln [Main St]

Video Rental

- **Blockbuster** • 11636 98th Ave NE [NE 116th St]

Map 49 · **Redmond**

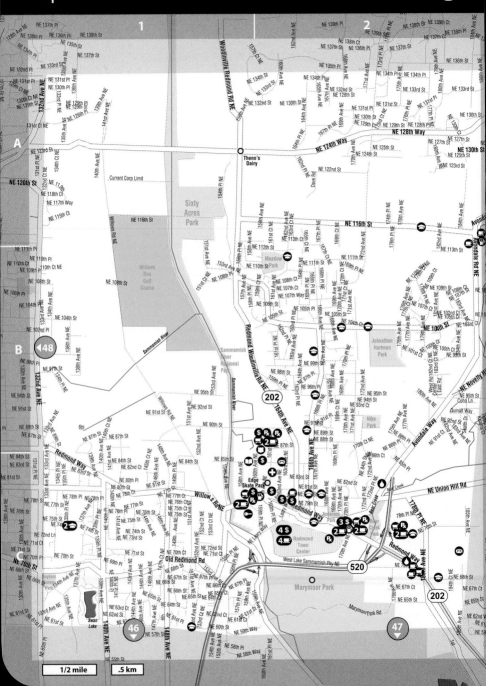

Essentials

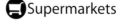

Map 49

Easily accessible to and from the surrounding Eastside cities and to Seattle, Redmond claims the title "Bicycle capital of the Northwest"—the eleven-mile Sammamish River Trail takes cyclists to the Burke Gilman Trail ending in Seattle. With a dozen Starbucks locations (and counting) within a five mile radius, the daily mocha will help you dwell less on the rain. For rich and real homemade ice cream, head for family-run Theno's Dairy, open since 1944. Catch a summer concert or even the Cirque de Soleil at Marymoor Park.

Banks

- **Bank of America** • 7450 170th Ave NE [NE 76th St]
- **Bank of America** • 8867 161st Ave NE [NE 90th St]
- **Bank of America (ATM)** • 15800 Redmond Wy NE [159th Pl NE]
- **Bank of America (ATM)** • 16517 NE 74th St [164th Ave NE]
- **Bank of America (ATM)** • 16550 NE 74th St [166th Ave NE]
- **Bank of America (ATM)** • 7320 170th Ave NE [NE 76th St]
- **First Mutual Bank** • 16900 Redmond Wy [Avondale Wy NE]
- **Frontier Bank** • 17000 Avondale Wy NE [NE 79th St]
- **Key Bank** • 16401 Redmond Wy [164th Ave NE]
- **US Bank** • 17020 Redmond Wy [170th Ave NE]
- **US Bank** • 8005 161st Ave NE [Redmond Wy]
- **Washington Federal Savings** • 16200 Redmond Wy [Brown St]
- **Wells Fargo** • 8502 160th Ave NE [NE 85th St]

Car Rental

- **Enterprise** • 7809 159th Pl NE [Redmond Wy]

Car Washes

- **Brown Bear Car Wash** • 17809 Redmond Wy [NE 70th St]
- **Super Bright Carwash** • 8296 Avondale Wy NE [NE 80th St]

Coffee

- **Java Junction** • 11440 Avondale Rd NE [NE 116th St]
- **Jerzy's Coffee** • 16727 Redmond Wy [168th Ave NE]
- **Mercurys Coffee Co** • 17980 Redmond Wy [180th Ave NE]
- **Peet's Coffee and Tea** • 17887 Redmond Way [NE 70th St]
- **Starbucks** • 11523 Avondale Rd NE [NE 116th St]
- **Starbucks** • 15738 Redmond Wy [159th Pl NE]
- **Starbucks** • QFC • 15800 Redmond Wy [159th Pl NE]
- **Starbucks** • 16495 NE 74th St [164th Ave NE]
- **Starbucks** • 16500 NE 74th St [164th Ave NE]
- **Starbucks** • 17196 Redmond Wy [170th Ave NE]
- **Starbucks** • Safeway • 17246 Redmond Wy [170th Ave NE]
- **Starbucks** • Fred Meyer • 17667 NE 76th St [Redmond Wy]
- **Starbucks** • Target • 17700 NE 76th St [Redmond Wy]
- **Starbucks** • 7625 170th Ave NE [NE 76th St]
- **Starbucks** • 8867 161st Ave NE [NE 90th St]
- **Tully's** • 8862 161st Ave NE [NE 87th St]
- **Tully's** • 16349 NE 74th St [164th Ave NE]
- **Victor's Celtic Coffee** • 7993 Gilman St [164th Ave NE]

Gas Stations

- **Chevron** • 16010 Redmond Wy [160th Ave NE]
- **Shell** • 11520 Avondale Rd NE [NE 116th St]
- **76** • 16909 Redmond Wy [Cleveland St]

Emergency Rooms

- **Evergreen Hospital Medical Center** •
  8301 161st Ave NE [NE 83rd St]

Landmarks

- **Edge Skate Park** • NE 83rd St & 161st Ave NE
- **Marymoor Park** • 6046 W Lake Sammamish Pkwy NE
- **Theno's Dairy** • NE 124th St & WA-202 (Redmond Woodinville Rd)

Libraries

- **Redmond Regional Library** • 15990 NE 85th St [160th Ave NE]

Pharmacies

- **Bartell Drugs** • 7370 170th Ave NE [NE 76th St]
- **Bartell Drugs** • 8862 161st Ave NE [NE 90th St]
- **Fred Meyer** • 17667 NE 76th St [Redmond Wy]
- **Lakeside Drug** • 15840 Redmond Wy [159th Pl NE]
- **Quality Food Centers Pharmacy** • 8867 161st Ave NE [NE 90th St]
- **Rite Aid** • 17220 Redmond Wy [170th Ave NE]

Police

- **Redmond Police Dept** • 8701 160th Ave NE [NE 85th St]

Post Offices

- **Redmond** • 16135 NE 85th St [161st Ave NE]
- **Redmond Carrier Annex** • 7241 185th Ave NE [NE 76th St]

Schools

- **19-21 Transition Academy** • 16642 Cleveland St [166th Ave NE]
- **Einstein Elementary** • 18025 NE 116th St [179th Ct NE]
- **Faith Lutheran** • 9041 166th Ave NE [NE 91st St]
- **Horace Mann Elementary** • 17001 NE 104th St [170th Ave NE]
- **Little Folks Christian** • 16601 NE 95th St [166th Ave NE]
- **Medina Academy** • 16600 NE 80th St, Rm 206 [166th Ave NE]
- **Redmond Elementary** • 16800 NE 80th St [168th Ave NE]
- **Redmond High** • 17272 NE 104th St [172nd Ave NE]
- **Redmond Junior High** • 10055 166th Ave NE [NE 100th St]
- **Rockwell Elementary** • 11125 162nd Ave NE [NE 112th St]
- **Rose Hill Junior High** • 13505 NE 75th St [135th Pl NE]
- **Rush Elementary** • 6101 152nd Ave NE [NE 60th St]
- **Sammamish Montessori** • 7655 178th Pl NE [NE 76th St]
- **Stella Schola** • 13505 NE 75th St [135th Pl NE]
- **WA Academy of Performing Arts** •
  18047 NE 68th St #b130 [180th Ave NE]

Supermarkets

- **Fred Meyer** • 17667 NE 76th St [Redmond Wy]
- **Quality Food Center** • 15800 Redmond Wy [159th Pl NE]
- **Quality Food Center** • 8867 161st Ave NE [NE 90th St]
- **Safeway** • 17246 Redmond Wy [170th Ave NE]
- **Whole Foods** • 17991 Redmond Wy [180th Ave NE]

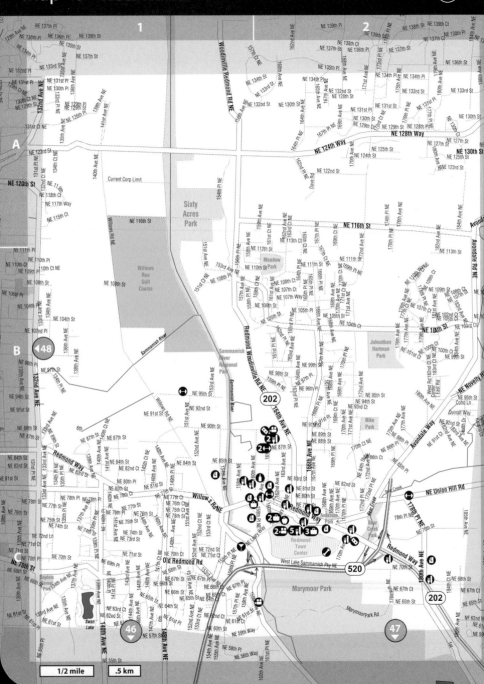

Map 49 · Redmond

People grimace when they hear the words "Redmond" and "nightlife" in the same sentence. Don't count on much being open after 10 pm. With the exception of two movie theaters and a few restaurants with decent happy hours, people head for downtown Seattle. Organic grocery stores Whole Foods (correctly dubbed Whole Paycheck) and PCC Natural Markets are good shopping option, but make sure to support local farmers at the Redmond Saturday Market.

Copy Shops

- **Alegra Print & Imaging** •
  8447 154th Ave NE [NE 85th St]
- **FedEx Kinko's** • 16815 Redmond Wy [Cleveland St]
- **Hot Off The Press** • 7114 180th Ave NE [NE 68th St]
- **Pip Printing** • 8040 161st Ave NE [Redmond Wy]
- **Precision Press** • 7635 159th Pl NE [Redmond Wy]
- **Staples** • 15790 Redmond Wy [159th Pl NE]
- **The UPS Store** • 16625 Redmond Wy [166th Ave NE]

Farmers Markets

- **Redmond Saturday Market (Sat, 9 am–3 pm, May–Oct)** • 7730 Leary Wy NE [NE 76th St]

Gyms

- **Curves** • 8052 161st Ave NE [Redmond Wy]
- **Eastside Gym** • 15040 NE 95th St [151st Ave NE]
- **Fitness Together** • 16130 NE 87th St [161st Ave NE]
- **Gold's Gym** • 7956 178th Pl NE [NE 80th St]
- **Redmond Athletic Club** •
  8709 161st Ave NE [NE 87th St]

Liquor Stores

- **Washington State Liquor Store** •
  8215 160th Ave NE [NE 83rd St]

Movie Theaters

- **AMC Loews Redmond Town Center 8** •
  16451 NE 74th St [164th Ave NE]
- **AT&T Outdoor Cinema** • Marymoor Park •
  6046 W Lake Sammamish Pkwy NE [NE Marymoore St]
- **Big Picture Redmond** • 7411 166th Ave NE [NE 74th St]
- **Regal Bella Bottega 11** • 8890 161st Ave NE [NE 90th St]

Nightlife

- **Celtic Bayou Brewpub** •
  7281 W Lake Sammamish Pkwy NE [NE Leary Wy]

Pet Shops

- **Petco** • 7215 170th Ave Ne [168th Ave NE]

Restaurants

- **Desert Fire Southwestern Grill** •
  7211 166th Ave NE [166th Ave NE]
- **Family Pancake House** •
  17621 Redmond Wy [NE 70th St]
- **Frankie's Pizza and Pasta** •
  16630 Redmond Wy [166th Ave NE]
- **Kikuya** • 8105 161st Ave NE [Redmond Wy]
- **Matt's Rotisserie & Oyster Lounge** •
  16651 NE 74th St [166th Ave NE]
- **Nara Japanese Restaurant** •
  16564 Cleveland St, # M [166th Ave NE]
- **Ooba's Mexican Grill** • 15802 NE 83rd St [158th Ave NE]
- **Pasta & Co** • 7625 170th Ave NE [NE 76th St]
- **Pizza Schmizza** • 16552 NE 74th St [166th Ave NE]
- **Pho Thân Brothers'** • 7844 Leary Wy NE [Cleveland St]
- **Pomegranate Bistro** • 18005 NE 68th St [180th Ave NE]
- **Sages Restaurant** • 15916 NE 83rd St [160th Ave]
- **Sushi Land Marinepolis** •
  8910 161st Ave NE [NE 90th St]
- **Taste the Moment** • 8110 164th Ave NE [NE 81st St]
- **Thai Ginger** • 16480 NE 74th St [164th Ave NE]
- **Todai Redmond** • 7548 164th Ave NE [NE 76th St]
- **Typhoon!** • 8936 161st Ave NE [NE 90th St]
- **Yummy Teriyaki** •
  17218 Redmond Wy [Bear Creek Crossing]

Shopping

- **Bergman Travel Shop** •
  16516 NE 74th St [166th Ave NE]
- **Half Price Books** • 7805 Leary Wy NE [NE 76th St]
- **PCC Natural Market** •
  11435 Avondale Rd NE [NE 116th St]
- **Redmond Saturday Market** •
  7730 Leary Wy NE [NE 76th St]
- **Redmond Town Center** •
  16495 NE 74th St [166th Ave NE]
- **REI** • 7500 166th Ave NE [NE 76th St]
- **Tree Top Toys** • 15752 Redmond Wy [158th Ave NE]

Video Rental

- **Blockbuster** • 17209 Redmond Wy [Bear Creek Crossing]
- **Hollywood Video** • 8867 161st Ave NE [NE 90th St]

Parks & Places · **Bainbridge Island**

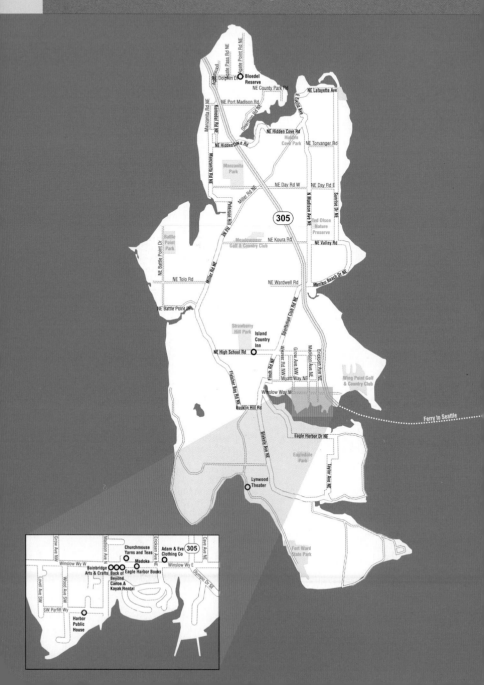

Overview

Over the centuries, Bainbridge has seen a little of everything—Native American battlefields, logging camps, strawberry farms, artist colonies, and more. Fort Ward and Battlepoint Park were two important military outposts. Battlepoint was the first place to receive the signal that Pearl Harbor had been bombed. No longer a sleepy little bohemian enclave, Bainbridge Island's recent growth has been tremendous, with condos sprouting like fungus and a highly affluent population flocking to live in them. Today, it's an upscale bedroom community, with the majority of its working citizens commuting across the Puget Sound to Seattle. And remember that old Pearl Jam song about the boy who played show and tell with a gun and his head? Yeah, he was a real kid from Bainbridge.

Attractions

In addition to a nice main street, where an excellent Fourth of July parade happens every year, Bainbridge enjoys a lively arts scene. The Island Theater produces free play readings every two months and Bainbridge Arts and Crafts (www.bainbridgeartsandcrafts.org) features local artists in their gift shop (no crocheted toilet paper covers here!). Bainbridge Performing Arts (www.theplayhouse.org) hosts theater, dance, and musical performances with a lower rate of Guffmanesque amateurism than most communities. The Lynnwood Theater (206-842-3080), Bainbridge's arty movie house, just celebrated its 75th anniversary with a new Art Deco style marquee. The Strawberry Farms are still around and deliver delectable fruit in the state, which can be sampled at the festival held every July. Stars are hard to come by on the mainland but Bainbridge can bring the skies back to you. Battlepoint has a Hubble lens in its observatory tower that is open to the public.

The Bloedel Reserve (206-842-7631; www.bloedel reserve.org) is an immaculately kept wildlife and garden sanctuary. Reservations are necessary, so call ahead or reserve online. The waterfront park behind the main street offers tennis courts, a playground, and a dock for the nautically-minded. Canoes and kayaks can be rented seasonally from Back of Beyond Canoe and Kayak Rentals (206-842-9229).

Shopping

Not exactly bargain territory, Bainbridge shops are upscale but casual. Adam and Eve (400 Winslow Wy E) carries trendy designer clothes for men and women. For the sewing crowd, Churchmouse Yarns and Teas (118 Madrone Ln; www. churchmouseyarns.com) carries the finest yarns available, and Esther's Fabrics (285 Winslow Wy E ; www.esthersfabrics. com) stocks cloth that is expensive and worth every cent. With peaceful surroundings, frequent readings, and a fine selection, Eagle Harbor Books (157 Winslow Wy E; www. eagleharborbooks.com) is everything a bookstore should be.

Restaurants

Oddly enough for an island, there aren't many restaurants with a water view. Worth noting, however, is the Harbor Public House (231 Parfitt Wy SW, 206-842-0969; www. harbourpub.com) with exceptional pub grub and a bar stocked with choice Washington State wines and beers. More noteworthy is Edna's Beach Café (4738 Lynwood Center Rd NE, 98110, 206-855-0820), set atop a hill in an amazing historical building far removed from the downtown area, it possesses the island's most breathtaking aquatic view. Café Nola (101 Winslow Wy E, 206-842-3822; www.cafenola. com) is a European style café with an excellent, reasonably priced menu. The upscale but overrated Four Swallows (481 Madison Ave, 206-842-3397; www.fourswallows.com) is a tourist trap which the locals steer clear of. Madoka (241 Winslow Wy; www.madokaonbainbridge.com) serves a Pan-Pacific menu and while pricier than most, it's worth it. For a casual breakfast or lunch, try Streamliner Diner (397 Winslow Wy E, 206-842-8595), or check out Pegasus Coffee (131 Parfitt Wy, 206-842-6725; www.pegasuscoffeehouse.org) for great java in a rustic, ivy-covered brick structure.

Lodgings

The Island's two hotels, Best Western and Island Country Inn, which can be found next to the Safeway strip mall, both provide reasonably priced lodging. A better choice is selecting from one of the many bed-and-breakfast establishments on the Island, where all the amenities of home make an extended visit to Bainbridge a lot more inviting (find a comprehensive list at www.bainbridgelodging.com/ list.html).

How to get there

By Ferry

Washington State Ferries leave from Coleman Dock at Pier 52 on Alaskan Way every 50 minutes or so, but make sure to double check the schedule (www.wsdot.wa.gov/ferries). The round trip walk-on fare is $6.70 for adults and $5.40 for children. Cars are $14.45 each way; each passenger is additional. There are buses that meet the boats during commuter hours; check Kitsap Transit (1-800-501-RIDE; www.kitsaptransit.org) for details.

By Car

Driving to Bainbridge Island from Seattle without using the ferry is inconvenient, but not impossible. Take I-5 through Tacoma, then follow Highway 16 north through Bremerton. From there take Highway 3 to 305 and cross the Agate Pass Bridge. Depending on traffic, the whole trip takes about an hour and forty-five minutes and is recommended only for those desperate to get to or from the airport when the ferries aren't running.

General Information

NFT Map   4
Address: 1635 11th Ave
           Seattle, WA 98102
Phone: 206-684-4075
Website: www.seattle.gov/parks/Parkspaces/
           anderson.htm
Hours: 4 am–11:30 pm

Overview

Cal Anderson Park, named after Washington's first openly gay state legislator, is located in the heart of Capitol Hill and includes the Lincoln Reservoir and the Bobby Morris Playfield. Formerly Lincoln Park, (no relation to Linkin Park) Cal Anderson has had numerous, and regrettably appropriate, nicknames over the years such, as "Hobo Park" and "Heroin Park." However, in 2005, Cal Anderson was the recipient of a major overhaul that transformed the strung-out little duckling into a beautiful countercultural swan.

Many doubted the renovations would do any good, but the success was undeniable when the park reopened on September 24th, 2005. The makeover included lush, manicured grass, new paths and benches, a wading pool, a reflecting pool, a fountain, a giant chess board, and a small playground.

Not a hint remains of its former desolate state. Cal Anderson is now a joyful, welcoming place. People from all walks of life come to relax and partake in their favorite outdoor activities, from dog-walking to sun-bathing, Live Action Role Playing to chillin' with their didgeridoo. It is a glimpse into a utopian society wherein hipsters, yuppies, and punks can all come together on a warm summer day and play kickball. Just be careful what you decide to smoke on a sunny day. The city recently installed cameras in their noble and oh-so-effective efforts to win the war on drugs.

Attractions

Between the wading pool, the reflecting pool, the fountain, and the reservoir, water features abound. And luckily, Cal Anderson is a park for the people, so none of these enticing fixtures are off limits. Adults climb to the top of the volcano-esque fountain. Kids splash each other in the reflecting pool or play on the jungle gym. It's also one of the best places to people-watch in Capitol Hill. Where else can you see a goth couple read under matching black parasols whilst a group of hippies fly their homemade kites several yards away?

The Shelterhouse is available to rent for small parties and gatherings. Call 206-684-4753 for more information.

Sports

Bobby Morris Playfield is mostly used for soccer, baseball, tennis, and the occasional kickball practice. The Underdog Sports League also uses it for their amateur league games which include a dodgeball division. In other parts of the park, the word "sports" is used a bit more loosely. There are always joggers, skaters, and cyclists, but you can also find such alternative sports as lawn bowling, urban golf, Frisbee golf, kung-fu, tai chi, and hula hooping. Capitol Hillites are nothing if not creative about their means for exercise.

General Information

NFT Map: 3
Address: 700 Seneca St
           Seattle, WA 98101
Website: www.seattle.gov/parks/parkspaces/
           freewaypark.htm
Phone: 206-684-4075
Hours: 6 am–11:30 pm daily

Overview

Freeway Park was an oh-so-lovely idea back in the day. In the '60s, city and state officials thought that a park spanning the recently-completed Seattle portion of I-5 would brighten up the area and add a little something green to downtown. They enlisted the genius of Lawrence Halprin, a prolific landscape architect, to make it extra-snazzy. And indeed, when unveiled in 1976, Freeway Park deftly combined elements of city and nature and was deemed a triumph of urban landscaping. That is, until people started getting stabbed and assaulted left and right. You see, Halprin's artistic stylings created a lot of maze-like and shadowy areas that seemed to call out to criminals, "Come! Do your evil deeds here!"

And so they did. An endless stream of seedy and downright scary events went down in Freeway's dark nooks and zigzagging pathways. The violent murder of a deaf and mute woman in 2002 finally got people talking about redesigning the park. A neighborhood group, the Freeway Park Neighborhood Association (FPNA), sprung up to lead the cause, advocating better lighting, increased security, and the removal of particularly obscuring shrubbery. The City has even designated the park as a Wi-Fi Hot Spot to lure laptop-toting professionals from the nearby Convention Center instead of knife-wielding ruffians from who-knows-where. The "New Vision for Freeway Park" seems to be working, with crime down a reported 90% compared to three years ago. So go forth, enjoy the lovely fountains and water features (when they're operating), and pull up a newly sun-kissed spot to enjoy your take-out lunch.

But you may still want to mosey on out before the sun goes down.

Wi-Fi

Freeway Park is one of a few parks and districts being tested for the City of Seattle's Wi-Fi pilot project (www.seattle.gov/html/citizen/wifi.htm). What that means to you—absolutely free wireless Internet! Some have griped about its spotty nature, but it *is* a pilot and the kinks are still being worked out. You can log on by using the log-in "seattlewifi."

Activities & Events

In light of the park's rather unsavory past, community leaders are trying to encourage community activities in the park (apparently, bingo is not only fun but also wards off the criminal element). For example, there's a walking group that meets at 10:30 am daily near the bathrooms. For your own walking pleasure, there are various trails and paths that wind through the park. But it is advisable to have a buddy along.

The summer months (July–August) usher in some fun Freeway events, like free lunchtime music concerts, public theater performances, and "intergenerational" activities that are geared towards children and seniors.

What the Future Holds

Freeway Park is undergoing a definite makeover, although it has yet to be determined how that will actually pan out. Some ideas include a skating rink, a dog run, and a coffee stand. In the meantime, maintenance projects that are underway include the removal of trees to increase light exposure and the restoration of the park's four fountains, which never seem to be working.

How to Get There

There are tons of Metro buses that will take you almost directly to the park. Routes 16, 255, and 358 are a few from downtown; it's advisable to check out Metro's website (transit.metrokc.gov) for the best ones from your neighborhood. There is no designated parking lot for the park; you'll have to try your luck on the street or pay for a parking garage.

General Information

NFT Map: 25
Address: 2101 N Northlake Wy
Seattle, WA 98103
Phone: 206-684-4075
Website: www.seattle.gov/parks/parkspaces/
gasworks.htm
Hours: 4 am–11:30 pm daily

Overview

If ever you feel disenchanted with Seattle, head directly to Gas Works Park and stand at the top of the kite-flying hill. Even on a dreary day, the strange combination of water, sky, and rusted metal is dramatic, and the juxtaposition of natural beauty and urban architecture should be sufficient to remind you why you live here. The 20-acre park juts out into the north shore of Lake Union, creating a panoramic view of the downtown skyline framed by the hills of Queen Anne and Eastlake. On the water, seaplanes launch at regular intervals over a serene flotilla of kayaks, sailboats, and yachts. On a quiet afternoon, the proclamations of those dreadful Ride the Ducks tour guides are clearly audible from shore, but at least they don't wave at you from that distance.

The city first cleared this land in 1906 for use by the Seattle Gas Light Company. The Lake Station Plant, as it was known, converted coal into methane gas until 1956, when natural gas became available via interstate pipeline. The City of Seattle purchased the gas works six years later and opened the public park in 1975. The gargantuan ruins of the plant have been left standing, now fenced off and scrubbed of decades of graffiti. Exhauster-compressor machinery has been converted into a children's play area. The former boiler house now houses picnic tables, barbecue grills, and a concession stand that operates sporadically during the summer months. The picnic area can be reserved by calling 206-684-4081, but keep in mind that this part of the park tends to double as a homeless shelter.

For some Seattle residents, the large quantities of benzene and other goodies left behind by the gasification plant raise the question, "Will picnicking at Gas Works shave precious years off of my life?" According to the Washington State Department of Ecology—no. The site underwent a massive, $3-million cleanup project in 2001 to remove contaminants from the soil, and chemical levels remain under constant observation. Nevertheless, visitors are still advised not to eat the dirt. Swimming, wading, and fishing are also at-your-own-risk activities.

Sports

Conveniently located along the Burke-Gilman Trail, Gas Works Park receives its share of bicycle traffic, though trails within the park are relatively few. The park's abundance of concrete and freestanding metal is a draw for skate boarders, and the city is considering building a skate park there. Yoga and tai chi classes are also known to congregate on the lawns. However, the most numerous enthusiasts at the park seem to be the kite flyers that flock to the landscaped hill, faces tilted to the sky, fists holding tight to the strings of their kites. Should you find yourself kiteless on a windy day, the nearby Goodwind's Kites (3420 Stone Wy N, 206-633-4780) can set you up in no time.

Festivals & Events

Gas Works Park leads Seattle in events for naked people. The annual Solstice Parade, featuring the famous (and fabulous) naked cyclists, pedals its way from Fremont to Gas Works where the pageant continues into the evening. The park is also the starting point of Seattle's World Naked Bike Ride, an event that protests oil dependency and suggests better living through nudity.

The Independence Day festivities at Gas Works are an all-day affair, complete with food vendors, a beer garden, and loud music. Though the fireworks over Lake Union are spectacular, sitting in the squalor beneath a giant inflatable Statue of Liberty head is likely to make you feel like a huddled mass.

How to Get There

By car: From I-5, take the 45th Street exit and go west on NE 45th Street. Turn left on Meridian Avenue N and continue to the end of the street. Turn right on N Northlake Way and turn into the parking lot. Parking lot hours: 6 am–9 pm.

By bus: Metro bus 26, connecting downtown and east Green Lake, stops on N 40th Street and Burke Avenue N, over half a mile from the park. Other nearby routes include the 31, 74, 45, and 46.

General Information

NFT Map: 33
Address: 8498 Seaview Pl NW
Seattle, WA 98117
Website: www.seattle.gov/parks/parkspaces/
golden.htm
Hours: 6 am–11:30 pm

Overview

Originally designed as a destination at the end of an electric car line for folks to escape hectic city life, Golden Gardens is just that, minus the electric car line.

Hidden from (or hiding) the city behind immense bluffs, Golden Gardens is Puget Sound at its finest and then some—romantic vistas of the Olympics, tranquil waters, barking sea lions locked in a floating cage, an occasional thundering train, and heaps of hippies drumming randomly around bonfires. On any given day you'll find a black-tie wedding, a Mexican barbeque, Chinese karaoke, beach volleyball, the ubiquitous drum circle, a pick-up soccer game, and young lovers smooching in the tall grass.

The park is divided by train tracks into lower and upper sections. The lower section features sandy beaches, picnic areas, fire pits, restored wetlands, a renovated bathhouse for rent (206-684-7254), beached logs, and lots and lots of bonfires. The upper portion is a maze of trails zigzagging up the bluffs, a 2.2 acre off-leash dog area, and tons of blackberry bushes.

The park has overcome "problems" of the past—namely, excessive drinking, loud music, and out-of-control bonfires. The city took efforts to get things under control (you'd think that people would know not to burn things like futons and wooden crates, but alas the police had to intervene to reinforce that rule). Now sentries are present on the summer weekends to make sure you're burning firewood and that you don't have any alcohol (try keeping a straight face when you say "no," and they'll try to believe you).

Long gone are the days when you could cavort with friends around a toasty fire late into the evening. Park officials promptly come by at 10:30 pm and without saying a word, douse all bonfires with a large bucket of water. At 11:30 pm the park closes and the gates are locked.

Getting There

By Car

Take Market Street through Ballard and beyond the locks, where it turns into Shilshole Avenue. Another mile past the marina sits the entrance to the park; a public boat launch is at the south end (next to Coney's, a generic burger/shake/fish joint), and the first of several parking lots. The road turns right and winds up the bluffs to 85th Street. There is parking at the south end of the park, in the middle of the park, and just across under the railroad tracks.

By Bus

Take the 46 bus from the U District or take the 18 from downtown.

By Bike

Golden Gardens should be the natural end of the Burke-Gilman Trail, though planners haven't yet put those pieces together.

Shilshole Bay

Salmon Bay Waterway

W Sheridan St

W Crafter St

W Sheridan St

Picnic Area

Daybreak Star Cultural-Education Center

Lawtonwood Rd

Illinois St

Wolf Tree Nature Trail

W Commodore Way

Picnic Area

Picnic Area

P

Army Reserve (No Trespassing)

Picnic Area

Kansas Ave

Loop Trail

Texas Way

North Beach

Coast Guard Lighthouse

West Point Wastewater Treatment Facility

Hidden Valley Trail

South Beach

Military Housing (No Trespassing)

Stables

Utah St

Teamster's Quarters

Band House

Post Exchange

Guardhouse

Military Housing (No Trespassing)

Headquarters

Authorized Vehicles Only

Vermont Ave

Fort Lawton Cemetery

Washington Ave

NIKE Warehouse

Visitors Center

W Govern

Texas Way W

South Beach Trail

Loop Trail

Military Housing (No Trespassing)

Discovery Park Environmental Learning Center

Picnic Area

Tennis Courts

Iowa St

Chapel Picnic Area

Oregon Ave

P

Playground

Maintenance Facility

Carolina St

W Emerson St

Puget Sound

45th Ave W

Perkins Ln W

Magnolia Blvd W

43rd Ave W

41st Ave W

Arapahoe Pl W

40th Ave W

39th Ave W

W Ruffner St

W Viewmont Way W

38th Ave W

37th Ave W

W Bertona St

W Prosper St

W Dravus St

MAP 11

General Information

NFT Map: 11
Address: 3801 W Government Wy
          Seattle, WA 98199
Phone: 206-386-4236
Website: www.cityofseattle.net/parks/
          environment/discovparkindex.htm

Overview

Discovery Park is by far Seattle's largest park, covering over 530 acres. On the Magnolia bluffs, occupying most of the former Fort Lawton military base. Discovery offers the most extensive hiking trails within the city, just under 12 miles worth of trails, making it the perfect destination for those times when you've just had enough of the city, but don't want to go too far away.

You will find that Discovery has an amazing amount of natural diversity. On a single trail you will encounter open meadows, breathtaking sea cliffs (don't get too close!), forested areas, thickets, streams, and even an active sand dune. There is a short hike down to two miles of protected tidal beaches with tree houses along the way for scenic views of the Puget Sound and a resting place for the brutal hike back. All of the trails are well marked, but be sure to remember which parking lot you left your car in, because it's easy to get lost. You can print out a map of the trails from the Discovery Park website.

The views you'll find at Discovery are phenomenal. You can see Puget Sound spread out before you, framed by the majestic Olympic Mountains. On a clear day, there is also the opportunity to gaze upon Mt Rainier, which true Seattleites never get sick of seeing. Stroll by the Coast Guard Lighthouse or look for the enormous West Point Treatment Facility located just next to Discovery Park.

Park History

Discovery's history is an interesting one. The city of Seattle originally donated this land to the Federal Government to use as a military base. In 1938 the US Army offered to give all of Fort Lawton back to Seattle for the bargain price of one dollar. The city actually refused this sweet deal because they weren't sure they could afford the upkeep. Then in 1964, the US Secretary of Defense decided that 85% of Fort Lawton was to be surplus and Seattle would have to cough up 50% of fair market value (whoops). Luckily, in 1965, legislation was passed that said Seattle could have it for free because it was given as a donation in the first place (phew). Then the United Indians of All Tribes jumped into the mix in 1970, claiming that all lands might be declared surplus, so they were allowed to lease 17 acres. You can now find the Daybreak Star Cultural-Education Center on those 17 acres.

How to Get There—Driving

Discovery is huge, and if you stray from the main path, it is easy to get lost in the maze of homes surrounding the park. When all else fails, just keep heading west. However, if you follow these directions, you can't miss it.

From I-5 take the 45th Street exit and head west. 45th Street becomes 46th Street then turns into Market Street. From Market, turn left onto 15th Avenue NW and take the first right after the bridge onto Emerson Street. Turn right onto West Gilman, which becomes West Government Way. Follow that until you come to the east entrance of the park. Go straight and you will find the Visitor Center to your left.

Parking

Once you get to the east entrance of the park from West Government Way, you can go straight to find several parking lots or turn left and head towards the south parking lot.

How to Get There—Mass Transit

If you don't mind a long bus ride, the 33, 24, and 994 will take you to Discovery Park.

N 79th St

N 78th St

N 80th St

5

N 77th St

MAP
30

N 76th St

Green Lake Dr N

Winona Ave N

E Green Lake Dr N

N 75th St

West
Beach

Bathhouse
Theatre

P

Tennis
Courts

P

Community C
& Evans Pool

East
Beach

Aurora Ave N

Green Lake

E Green Lake Way N

N 65th St

N 64th St

N 63rd St

N 63rd St

N 62nd St

MAP
31

N 60th St

N 59th St

W Green Lake Way N

N 58th St

N 57th St

Green Lake Way N

N 56th St

Aurora Ave N

General Information

NFT Map: 31
Address: 7201 E Green Lake Dr N
               Seattle, WA 98103
Phone: 206-684-4075
Website: www.seattle.gov/parks/parkspaces/
               greenlak.htm
Hours: Open 24 hours a day

Overview

For over a century, Seattleites have enjoyed the cool tranquility of Green Lake Park, a popular destination for joggers, dog walkers, bikers, roller skaters, and more. This is one of Seattle's loveliest parks, which sometimes means crowds on pleasant weekends, but the calming vibe of the water and the woods tends to ease everyone's need for personal space. A paved trail of 2.8 miles circles the lake, providing two separate tracks for those on foot and those on wheels, and another unpaved trail for joggers meanders a bit longer at 3.2 miles. A stroll around Green Lake is a painless way to grab some exercise in the city without an overdose of auto exhaust or having to dodge panhandlers.

As for wildlife, waterfowl abound, from ducks to Canadian Geese to majestic herons, and they're not only unafraid of the constant human traffic, they're nearly confrontational about it. Don't feed these birds, no matter how adorable they seem—it's not allowed. New visitors to Green Lake will remark on the robust rabbit population, the result of certain short-sighted folks letting their domesticated pet bunnies free in the foliage by the water. Many generations hence, great fat rabbits infest the area, breeding and burrowing and wreaking havoc on native plant life. As with the waterfowl, do not feed these cuddly-yet-feral beasts.

Activities

The lake's moniker stems from its susceptibility to algae blooms, a picturesque affliction that the city has fought often during the park's history, leading to a number of beach closures throughout the years. While some brazen water-worshippers insist that Green Lake is the best swimming hole in Seattle, the city's official website warns of the possibility of contracting swimmer's itch. Consider dipping instead into the chlorine-fueled Evans Pool, a large indoor swimming facility on the lakeshore, or take the kids to the outdoor wading pool, which writhes every summer with the kinetic energy of splashing toddlers.

Green Lake's Small Craft Center offers classes for young and old alike in the arts of kayaking, canoeing, sweep rowing, and sculling (don't forget to pass your "float test" first—it's required). For private paddleboat rentals, the Green Lake Boat Rental company is at your service, and there's no nicer way to share the lake with someone special. Three annual rowing regattas invade the lake each year for exhibition-style water sports, sponsored by the local Rowing Advisory Council.

Or you could ignore the water altogether. Work out on one of the park's tennis courts, try a few holes of mild golfing at the Green Lake Pitch & Putt, or just laze beneath a shady pine and take in some people-watching. The park draws groups of tai chi and martial arts devotees, novice tightrope walkers, and even medieval faire types practicing their swordplay in full costume. The strains of bagpipes and plaintive guitar strummers float among the Frisbee tossers and sunbathers, and if you're lucky you'll see the guy who walks around the lake with "Spanish Lessons" emblazoned on his shirt (it's no gag—he'll tutor you on the spot).

How to Get There

By Bus
The 48 rolls past Green Lake on an average of every fifteen minutes during the day, servicing the University District, Montlake, Greenwood, and Loyal Heights among other neighborhoods. The 16 stops about every twenty minutes and will cart you up from downtown or down from the Northgate Mall. The 26 is slightly less frequent and a longer ride, starting off downtown, threading up through Fremont and Wallingford until reaching the end of the line on Green Lake Way.

By Car
If coming by Aurora Avenue, take the Green Lake Way exit and follow it until you're circling the lake.

If coming by I-5 southbound, take exit 171 toward NE 71st Street/NE 65th Street, merge onto 6th Avenue NE, turn right on NE 71st Street and follow it to East Green Lake Drive N.

If coming by I-5 northbound, take exit 170 toward NE 65th Street, merge onto NE Ravenna Boulevard and follow it to E Green Lake Drive N.

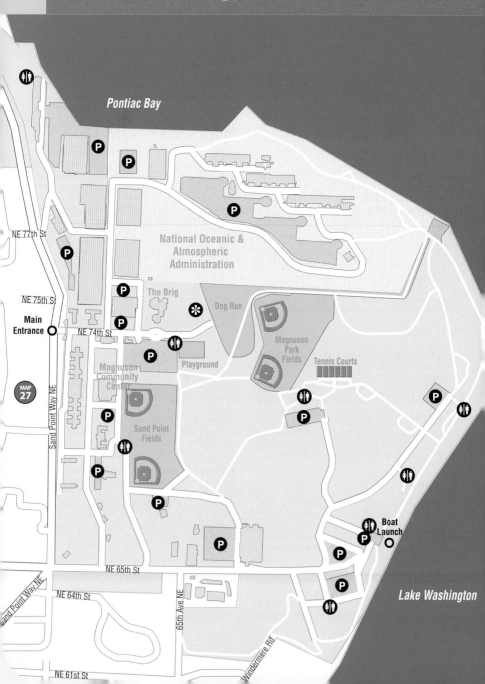

Pontiac Bay

NE 77th St

National Oceanic & Atmospheric Administration

NE 75th St

The Brig

Dog Run

Magnuson Park Fields

Tennis Courts

Main Entrance

NE 74th St

Playground

MAP 27

Magnuson Community Center

Sand Point Way NE

Sand Point Fields

Boat Launch

NE 65th St

NE 64th St

65th Ave NE

Sand Point Way NE

Lake Washington

NE 61st St

Windermere Rd

General Information

NFT Maps: 27
Address: 7400 Sand Point Wy NE
                Seattle, WA 98115
Website: www.seattle.gov/parks/magnuson
Phone: 206-684-4946
Hours: May 1 to Labor Day: 4 am–11:30 pm
                Labor Day to April 30: 4 am–10 pm

Overview

There are parks, and then there are parks. Magnuson, 350 acres on the shores of Lake Washington, is Seattle's second largest park and is a recreational wonderland. That wasn't always the case, though. The park was purchased by the government at the turn of the century and given to the federal government to turn into a naval base. Over the years, parts of the park were relinquished to the public and became Warren G. Magnuson Park, so named for the senator dude who advocated that the land be used for the community, rather than for a noisy airfield. The Navy continued to use part of the park all the way until 1990, when it was officially closed for military purposes and handed over to the city.

The park is crammed full of things to do. The historic Art Deco and Colonial Revival buildings are now home to a variety of non-profit community groups, ranging from sailing enthusiasts to an organization dedicated to protecting bats (nocturnal, not wooden). There's a boat launch, playground, basketball courts, tennis courts, picnic facilities, trails, windsurfing areas, and a huge off-leash dog park. Then there's the public art. And the community garden. And the butterfly garden. And…well, a million other things. It doesn't end there—even more features and renovations are being planned.

If you've exhausted all the possibilities of the park's resident features, there are a multitude of events throughout the year, like the Fall Wild Mushroom Show (www.psms.org) and an antiques market. Check out the Seattle Parks website for an updated events calendar.

Magnuson Community Center
7110 62nd Ave NE, 206-684-7026
The Community Center has always been a recreational hub and meeting ground, even during its military years, during which there was a library, swimming pool, and a bowling alley, all integral to Navy training exercises. Nowadays, one may find amenities no less entertaining, such as a 560-seat auditorium, gymnasium, racquetball court, and meeting room. Still, bringing back the bowling alley would be pretty cool.

The Brig
6344 NE 74th St, 206-684-7026
The Brig is another community center that's had a colorful past, from its original purpose as a jail for holding military prisoners and its more recent use as a set for several episodes of the X-Files. It's adjacent to the community garden and has been renovated with large, wood-floored activity spaces and meeting rooms.

Warren G. Magnuson Off-Leash Dog Area
7400 Sand Point Wy NE, 206-684-4946;
www.seattle.gov/parks/magnuson/ola.htm
This is absolute dog heaven, stretching for nine acres and including several varied environments such as dirt hills, flat gravel for fetch, tall brush, and a mud pit. The highlight is the accessible shoreline on Lake Washington—dogs go crazy for it, and Magnuson boasts the only dog park with water access within city limits. To get to the shore, there's a winding fenced-in trail so you can get some walking in while Rover is permitted to roam and

sniff off-leash alongside. Small and shy dogs will appreciate their own separate and spacious pen. As always, be sure your pooch is properly vaccinated and that you clean up after him.

Magnuson Community Garden
7400 Sand Point Wy NE, 206-684-4946;
www.cityofseattle.net/magnusongarden/
This former parking lot has been converted into a thriving garden with the purpose of serving the community of Seattle. There's the outdoor amphitheatre, which hosts various performances and events during the year, a garden tailored to gardeners with disabilities, and orchards and P-patches growing food for local food banks. It's a nice little oasis that just warms your heart.

NOAA Art Walk and Sound Garden
7400 Sand Point Wy NE, 206-526-6163 (NOAA facility manager);
www.wasc.noaa.gov
Right in the park's backyard is a bunch of outdoor art installations made by some pretty well-known artists (at least in the outdoor art installation crowd). The National Oceanic and Atmospheric Administration (NOAA) campus is located at the northern end of the Sand Point Peninsula. Though it's not technically included in the park, its close proximity invites a lot of park visitors to come check out the half-mile trail that passes by six outdoor artworks. The most popular is the Sound Garden, from which a certain Seattle grunge band lifted its own moniker. Per its self-descriptive name, the installation is composed of pipes that generate different tones that vary with the changing wind. Apparently even artwork is not immune from the security scares generated by 9/11; the facility was put on threat level Yellow (no weekends; no cars; backpack searches). Whatever.

Sail Sand Point
7777 62nd Ave NE #107, 206-525-8782; www.sailsandpoint.org
Sail Sand Point is Seattle's new community sailing center. It's located on the north shore of the park on Lake Washington. There are programs and classes for both youth and adults.

How to Get There

Bus
Metro bus routes 74 and 75 serve the park along Sand Point Way NE. Connections are in the University District (Routes 74 and 75) and Northgate (Route 75).

Bike
The Burke-Gilman Trail is approximately 1/4 mile west of Warren G. Magnuson Park. With a traffic signal and crosswalks, the NE 65th Street crossing is the safest point to enter the park. Once on the east side of Sand Point Way NE bicyclists can continue either east along NE 65th Street, or north along 62nd Avenue NE. Note that bicycle riding is limited to paved surfaces within Warren G. Magnuson Park. There are no designated bike trails in the park.

Driving
From I-5 you can exit at either NE 45th Street (Exit 169) or NE 65th Street (Exit 171). From the NE 45th Street exit, go east on 45th, past the UW campus, and down the 45th Street ramp. Continue east past University Village Shopping Center. Bear left and continue about 2 miles. From the I-5 NE 65th Street exit, head east approximately four miles on 65th (stay on the arterial!) until you have crossed Sand Point Way NE into the NE 65th Street entrance.

Parking

Parking is free and ample. There are two lots—one on 65th with parallel parking, and a larger lot on 77th.

213

Overview

Plopped between Puget Sound and Lake Washington, Lake Union is the baby bear of the waterways in Seattle. On the east, it has a watery arm that stretches to Lake Washington—Portage Bay—and another to the west that connects it to Puget Sound.

Lake Union itself is riddled with marinas and a vibrant, eclectic houseboat community (eclectic in this instance means high-end homes as well as scows). The area around the lake was fairly neglected and somewhat industrial until recently. It's got a rapidly growing biotechnology corridor along the east side; the south side is undergoing rapid development (www.discoverslu.com) which will include the usual stuff—condos, coffee shops, spas, and lots of cash for the developers. The north side has Gas Works Park, an old gas manufacturing plant that has a playground, trails and well, gas works. The Seattle Streetcar is now open, connecting South Lake Union to downtown (www.seattlestreetcar.org).

Attractions

As you'd expect for a lake, most of the attractions have at least something to do with water. At the south end of Lake Union, located at Valley Street and Fairview Avenue North, is the Center for Wooden Boats (www.cwb.org). There is a small museum, of sorts, and you can rent both sailboats and rowboats. Moving up the west side of the lake, on aptly named Westlake Avenue N, catch a scenic tour of Seattle in a seaplane for $75 with Kenmore Air. (866-435-9524; www.kenmoreair.com) It's also possible to fly to Vancouver, Victoria, or the San Juan Islands from here.

Shopping

Unless you're in the market for a yacht, there's not much shopping around the lake. REI's flagship store (222 Yale Ave N, 206-223-1944; www.rei.com), is the exception. For all your outdoor needs, which, in Seattle, are considerable.

Restaurants

What Lake Union does have plenty of, other than water, is restaurants. There's Daniel's Broiler, a steak house with a view (809 Fairview N, 206-621-8262). Nearby is Chandler's Crabhouse and Fish Market (901 Fairview N, 206-223-2722). As the name implies they rely heavily on fresh fish dishes. While we're on fresh fish, there's I Love Sushi (1001 Fairview N, 206-625-9604). Try to overlook the silly name; it's a great sushi place with more spectacular views. And of course we can't overlook Hooters (901 Fairview Ave N, 206-625-0555) for wings and breasts. If you want to spend big money (and here you actually do get what you pay for), try Canlis (2576 Aurora Ave N, 206-283-3313). It features the absolute best of Northwest cuisine.

Lodging

Silver Cloud Inn
www.silvercloud.com
1150 Fairview N, 206-447-9500

Residence Inn
800 Fairview N, 206-624-6000

Marriott Courtyard
925 Westlake Ave N, 206-213-0100

How to Get There   Driving

Lake Union is immediately off I-5 at exit 167. Turn right off the exit onto Fairview Avenue N, then left on Valley Street. Lake Union is bound by Valley Street on the south, Westlake Avenue N on the west, N Northlake Way on the north, and on the east is Eastlake and Fairview Avenue N. You can pretty much circumnavigate it in roughly 20 minutes. On a good traffic day. With no construction anywhere. This, of course, never happens.

How To Get There-Mass Transit

Metro bus routes 70, 71, 72, and 73 will all deliver you to the south end of the lake. The 25, 66, and 74 all run up the east side.

General Information

NFT Map: 1
Website: www.seattleartmuseum.org/visit/osp
Entry: Free

Overview

Seattle Art Museum's 8.5-acre waterfront sculpture park opened in January 2007. The sculpture includes a massive piece by Richard Serra, *Wake*, as well as pieces by Claes Oldenburg, Alexander Calder, and Louise Bourgeois. There's also a *Vivarium* by Mark Dion featuring a nurse log and its attendant nurslings—in all, 22 pieces of phenomenal sculpture.

If you like a little controversy with your art, check out *Father and Son*. A popular target for those whose mantra is 'Think of the children!', it depicts a man and a boy, both nude, facing each other with arms outstretched as water from a fountain rises and falls around them.

Art is only part of the attraction. As well as monumental sculpture, the park has meadows, forests, and stunning views. The other reason to visit the park is the setting. Walking on the z-path from the Pavilion, as you come through a recreated Northwest native trees forest, the view is, well, ok, breathtaking...an unobstructed view of the Olympics and Puget Sound. Seattle's chronic rainfall can't mess with that. Even if you hate museums, maybe especially if you hate museums, this place will afford you an entirely different experience of art—art like it's s'posed to be.

How To Get There-Driving

The park occupies 8.5 acres between Western Avenue and Elliott Avenue at Eagle and Broad Streets. Take exit 167 at Mercer Street, turn right on Fairview, left on Valley. Valley becomes Broad Street. (The Space Needle should appear on your right.) Turn right on Western Avenue. There is parking under the Pavilion at the park.

How To Get There-Mass Transit

Metro routes 1, 2, 13, 15, 18, and 19 heading north from downtown.

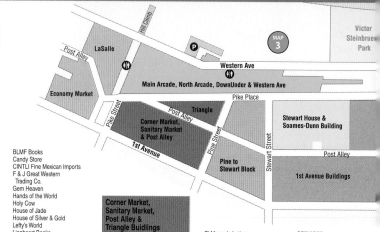

Economy Market & LaSalle Buildings

SHOPS
Art Stall Gallery
Ed Newbold Wildlife Artist
Studio Solstone
J&J Gifts & Sportswear
Pike Place Outfitters
Best Flowers
First & Pike News
Raven's Nest Treasures
Rings 'n Things
Tenzing Momo
The Great Wind Up

RESTAURANTS & TAKE-OUT
Alibi Room
Belle Epicurean
Crepe de France
Danny's Wonder Freeze
Deluxe BBQ
Il Bistro
La Vaca Burrito Express
Maximilien Bistro
Place Pigalle
Soul Food Stop
World Class Chili

SERVICES & ENTERTAINMENT
Chapel of Sts. Martha & Mary
Market Foundation
Pike Place Dental
Pike Place Market Merchants Assoc.
Pike Place Market Preservation & Development Authority
Ticket Ticket
Top of the Market
Unexpected Productions/Market Theater
Washington Wine Commission

SPECIALTY FOOD & BEVERAGE
Bottega Italiana
Daily Dozen Donuts
DeLaurenti Specialty Food & Wine
Don & Joe's Meats
Garlic Garden
Market Cellar Winery
MarketSpice
Pike Place Fish
Pike Place Nuts
Simply the Best

Main Arcade, North Arcade, DownUnder & Western Ave

SHOPS
Antique Touch
Charlotte's Web
Golden Age Collectables
Grandma's Attic
Miniature Car Dealer
Old Friends Antiques
Old Seattle Paperworks
Pen & Ink Drawings by Patrick T. Kerr
Pike's Asian Art
Portraits by Nick Elizar
Twilight Artist Collective
Two Angels Antiques & Interiors
Yesterdaze
Afghani Crafts
Cibola
Marakesh Leathers
Mobeta Shoes
Yazdi Imports
All Things Lavender
Animal Gifts & Collectibles
At Random Productions
Baja Bath Salts
Benavi's
Big Boys Toys
Black Creek Botanicals

BLMF Books
Candy Store
CINTLI Fine Mexican Imports
F & J Great Western Trading Co.
Gem Heaven
Hands of the World
Holy Cow
House of Jade
House of Silver & Gold
Lefty's World
Lionheart Books
Market Coins
Market Magic & Novelty Shop
Mastercraft Leather
Moon Valley Honey
Outback Opal
Pharaoh's Treasures
Pike Discount Camera and Electronics
Pike Place Bags
Pike Place Gifts
Pike Place Nutrition
Pipe Palace
Polish Pottery Place
Ruby's Seattle Gifts
Sunshine Jewelry
Swanberg Gifts
Sweeties Candy
Taj Mahal
The Bead Zone
The Giving Tree
Women's Hall of Fame

RESTAURANTS & TAKE-OUT
Athenian Inn
Lowell's Restaurant
Market Grill
Pike Place Chinese Cuisine
Sestos Café & Coffee House
Soundview Café

SERVICES
Balcony Barber Shop
Christopher's Lamp
Downtown Food Bank
Heritage Center
Heritage House
Madame Lazonga Tattoo
Pike Market Childcare & Preschool
Public Market Parking Garage

SPECIALTY FOOD & BEVERAGE
Catanzaro & Sons
Chicken Valley
Chukar Cherries
City Fish
Constantino's Produce
Manzo Bros. Produce
Mick's Peppourri
Pike Place Bakery
Pure Food Fish
Rotary Grocery
Sosio's Produce
Uli's Famous Sausage
Woodring Orchards

Corner Market, Sanitary Market, Post Alley & Triangle Buildings

SHOPS
Milagros Mexican Folk Art
Earth, Wind & Fire
Etruscan Design
Old Duffers Stuff
African Treasures
Dar Salaam
Dog Alley
Dragon's Toy Box
House of Woks
Kitchen Basics
Lamplight Used Books
Left Bank Books
Made in Washington
Metsker Maps
Pike Place Flowers

RESTAURANTS & TAKE-OUT
Café Mimosa
Café Yarmarka
Chez Shea
Copacabana Restaurant
Falafel King
Jasmine
La Buona Tavola Truffle Café & Specialty Foods
Lee's Corner
Lo Priore Brothers
Matt's in the Market
Mee Sum Pastries
Mr. D's Greek Deli
Pan Africa Café & Market
Pike Place Bagel Bakery
Pike Place Bar & Grill
Pike Place Chowder
Shea's Lounge
Sisters Café
Three Girls Bakery
The Vaudeville

SERVICES
Bohemia Therapeutic Massage
Matchmaker in the Market
New Mark Tailor
Paul Souders World Foto
Pike Place Barber
Pike Place Naturopathic
Rummage Hall
Tony Puma
US Bank

SPECIALTY FOOD & BEVERAGE
Choice Produce
Cinnamon Works
Corner Produce
Confectional Cheesecakes
Crumpet Shop

El Mercado Latino
Emerald Kettle
Fero's Meat Market
Frank's Quality Produce
Jack's Fish Spot
Oriental Mart
Pike Place Market Creamery
Quality Cheese
Seattle's Best Coffee
Shy Giant Frozen Yogurt
Sotto Voce
Stewart's Meats
The Juice Emporium

Pine to Stewart Block

SHOPS
Orca Bay Gallery
Fini
Sur La Table
Watson Kennedy Fine Living

RESTAURANTS & TAKE-OUT
Bacco
Campagne
Café Campagne

LODGING
Inn at the Market

SERVICES
Arne Bystrom, Architect
New London Salon

SPECIALTY FOOD & BEVERAGE
Beecher's Handmade Cheese
Dilettante Chocolate
Local Color Art, Coffee & More

Stewart House & Soames-Dunn Building

SHOPS
Lisa Harris Gallery
Little Shanghai
Lungu Gifts
Market Tobacco Patch
Paper Moon
Seattle Cutlery
The Soap Box

RESTAURANTS & TAKE-OUT
Emmett Watson's Oyster Bar
Japanese Gourmet
Michou
Piroshky-Piroshky
Sabra Mediterranean
Saigon Restaurant
The Pink Door

SERVICES
Market Optical
Sergio's Barbershop
Wagner Architects
Wanderers Mail Service

SPECIALTY FOOD & BEVERAGE
Bavarian Meats
Chocolate & Ice Cream Delight
Le Panier
Mexican Grocery
Starbucks Coffee
The Souk
Totem Smokehouse

1st Avenue Buildings

SHOPS
Antiques at Pike Place
Market Graphics
Boston St. Children's Everything Store
Isadora's Antique Clothing
Maggie's Shoes
Zebra Club

LODGING
Pensione Nichols

RESTAURANTS & TAKE-OUT
Caffe Lieto
Kell's Irish Restaurant & Pub
Le Pichet
94 Stewart
Sonya's
Starlite Lounge
Taxi Dogs
Turkish Delight
Virginia Inn

SERVICES
American Institute of Architects
Coupe Rokei
Pike Market Medical Clinic
Pike Market Senior Center
Site Workshop

SPECIALTY FOOD & BEVERAGE
Perennial Tea Room
Pike and Western Wine
Pike Place Grocery & Deli
Rose's Chocolate Treasures
The Tasting Room/ Wines of Washington
White Horse Trading Co

General Information

NFT Map:	3
Manager:	Pike Place Market Preservation & Development Authority
Address:	85 Pike St, Rm 500 Seattle, WA 98101
Phone:	206-682-7453
Website:	www.pikeplacemarket.org
Hours:	10 am–6 pm daily; many fish and produce stands open by 8 am or earlier; some store and restaurant hours may vary so make sure to call ahead; closed Thanksgiving, Christmas, and New Year's

Overview

While it doesn't share the Space Needle's phallic elegance, Pike Place Market matches the monument's importance as a symbol of Seattle. The oldest farmers market in the country has experienced myriad changes over its past century of operation, but still exists primarily for the purpose of bringing farmers and consumers together without the sticky fingers of the middleman.

Early on a weekday morning is the best time to hit the Market if sustenance-shopping is the goal. Perusing the bounty of ripe fruit, crisp root vegetables, and tender greens while contending with the bovine rush of tourists isn't always an attractive option for the average city dweller. But sometimes the Pike Place Market is worth a little hassle—supporting local farmers is easy when the produce is this fresh and priced better than the average supermarket. Especially worth seeking out is the organic Wednesday market from June to October.

Fresh Fish

A Seattle-centric trope as strong as coffee, rain, and dot-coms, the flashy flying fish of the imaginatively-named **Pike Place Fish** pack in gawking yokels from around the world every day with their zany antics. A crew of handsome (but smelly) fishmongers engage their shoppers in boisterous banter and throw fish corpses to each other (and potential buyers) all day long, usually with uncanny accuracy. Other fishmongers at the market feel obliged to compete with such flamboyance, so you'll find most white-smocked fin-handlers at **Pure Food Fish** and **City Fish** to be fairly gregarious, handing out samples, and glad-handing their prey. But **Jack's Fish Spot** isn't trying to impress anybody, so choose them to buy fresh flounder, live crabs, or grab a quick snack of fried salmon at Pike Place Market without all the jive.

Fresh Meat

The old-school butcher shop is quickly disappearing in Seattle (and everywhere else for that matter). Even at Pike Place there used to be dozens of great little meat markets back in the day. Luckily, there are still a few high quality shops left. **Don & Joe's** prides itself on good quality and personal service. Don't see it? They'll order it for you. **Fero's Meat Market** has affordable prices and offers halal meats. For your next Oktoberfest party, head to **Bavarian Meats** for all kinds of brats and wursts. And for the best sausage in Seattle, **Uli's Famous Sausage** will hook you up.

Arts & Crafts

Buskers can apply for a performer's badge, which allows them to entertain the shopping throng for up to an hour at a time at one of twelve designated points. A variety of music flows forth as a result, from ham-fingered folk strummers to electrifying doo-wop vocalists. Remember the Spoonman of Soundgarden fame? He's there too. It's not just music—puppeteers, dancers, and sleight-of-hand artists pass the hat at Pike Place Market, as well as the "cat guy" who wears modified cat suits and brings his feline pets along as visual aids as he solicits funds for a local animal shelter.

Most of the art hawked on the upper level of the market falls into the tie-dyed, air-brushed, pastel-colored variety, of interest only to those who feel compelled to buy something to commemorate their dream vacation in Seattle. Want a generic pink or teal souvenir t-shirt festooned with a cartoon salmon or the Space Needle? You got it, along with wind chimes, dream catchers, belt buckles, incense burners, and

"specialty pipes." But if you look hard and long enough, you'll find some good and interesting art hidden amongst the kitsch. Plenty of Mother Nature's art is on hand too, in the form of gorgeous fresh floral bouquets available for very reasonable prices every few steps, so take your time when picking out that perfect arrangement.

Unique Shops

The lower levels and hidden corners of the market hold plenty of weird little shops that vary from stupid-to-start fleecing joints to truly eccentric stands that couldn't exist anywhere else. Choose **Market Magic** when shopping for the professional magician, clown, or ventriloquist in your life—card tricks, collapsible canes, juggling clubs, and vintage magic ephemera. Antique stores like **Yesterdaze** and **Charlotte's Web** run the gamut from treacly porcelain figurines to hip pop culture artifacts. A handful of shops offer upscale kitchen equipment, with **Sur La Table** being the most ostentatious, and there's a plethora of unique boutiques dedicated to eclectic fashions for all.

One could spend hours sifting through the vintage posters, advertisements, and postcards available at **Old Seattle Paperworks**. Readers can peruse used books at **Lamplight Books** or **BLMF Books**, grab specialty magazines at **First and Pike News**, or study rabble-rousing political screeds from **Left Bank Books**. Speaking of which, **Lefty's World** serves Seattle's overlooked left-handed community with specialty products and some long-overdue dignity. Imported art, clothing, and products from Africa, Mexico, China, and other exotic climes can also be had. And if you just happen to need a haircut, head straight to **Sergio's Barber Shop** in the Stewart House.

Restaurants & Bars

Pike Place is an eating and drinking wonderland. Hungry shoppers can grab a quick snack of French pastries from **Le Panier**, Italian gelato at **Bottega Italiana**, Russian fare at **Piroshky-Piroshky**, amazing African cuisine at **Pan Africa**, free cheese samples at **Beecher's**, Greek food from **Mr. D's**, and almost anything else you can think of. If you have more time, grab a seat at **Matt's in the Market**, **Le Pichet**, or **Japanese Gourmet**. Gluttons for punishment are welcome to visit the purported site of the "first" **Starbucks** store—actually the beast was born on Western Avenue in 1971 and didn't relocate to the market until 1976, but whatever.

Say, who needs a drink? **Lowell's** is a homely three-floor operation that still looks as scruffy as it probably did when it opened in 1957. But the food is cheap and plentiful, and you'll get a fine eyeful of the Puget Sound. **The Athenian Inn** is the requisite old-school hang-out complete with great views and colorful locals. Head there for the best Market gossip. If the **Alibi Room** is too cool for school, head to **Zig Zag** for a classic drink or to **Copacabana** for a Bolivian beer on the deck to check out the real scenery at the market—the people.

How to Get There—Driving

Pike Place Market Parking Garage Address: *1531 Western Ave* Parking at Pike Place Market can be a big'ol pain in the butt. People expect to drive right down the ever packed Pike Place and find a spot right next to Rachel the Pig. It's not gonna happen. And if it does, you'll probably get a ticket. Try your luck on the metered spots downtown or head to the main parking garage on Western Avenue for the best deals.

From I-5 northbound, take exit #165, turn left on Madison Street and follow to Western Avenue. Turn right on Western, follow for five blocks to the parking garage.

From I-5 southbound, take exit #166 toward Stewart Street, follow to 1st Avenue and turn right. After two blocks turn left onto Lenora Street, then left onto Western Avenue, follow three blocks to the parking garage.

How To Get There—Bus

Many Metro bus lines go right past Pike Place Market. The 1 starts at 5th Avenue S and passes the market on its way to Queen Anne. The 10 originates downtown and goes on up to Capitol Hill. The 15 and 18 both pass by the market on their way to the northern part of Seattle. The 21, 22, and 36 come from way down south and land you right on 1st and Pike.

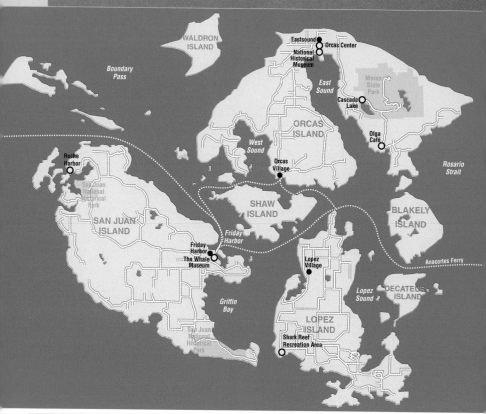

Overview

The San Juan Islands provide an idyllic escape from the city and a memorable excursion into pristine wilderness, with abundant whale-watching opportunities to boot. Situated in the San Juan Channel between the Strait of Juan de Fuca and the Georgia Strait, there are more than 700 islands in the archipelago; of those, 450 have been named, and most are uninhabited. Only 80 miles northwest of Seattle, the San Juans are an excellent weekend getaway to relax and have fun in the outdoors.

Lopez Island

City slickers might find themselves questioning whether they've got long lost relatives here, as nearly every person who passes waves at visitors. It's a bit like the "Twilight Zone" until one realizes that inhabitants of this small, exceedingly friendly island are just genuinely nice.

Lopez Village

This street is the meeting place for island folk, filled with cafés, antique shops, a bookstore, and small grocery store. Take a stroll along the nearby hiking trail on a weekend morning, and don't miss the summer farmers market.

Shark Reef Recreation Area

A popular hiking spot noted for its beautiful bluff, Shark Reef will delight any nature enthusiast.

Orcas Island

The largest of the islands, Orcas Island maintains a tranquil balance of creature comforts and natural outdoor adventures. You know you're entering someplace special as you cruise the winding streets beneath Calder mobiles hanging from the lush trees.

Eastsound

The epitome of quaint, Eastsound is a place to lose yourself in the many restaurants, spa services, and bookstores bordering the water. Stock up on essentials at the natural food store or the larger supermarket, or catch a performance at Orcas Center (917 Mt. Baker Rd, Eastsound, 360-376-2281; www.orcascenter.org) Don't miss the Orcas Island Historical Museum (181 N Beach Rd, Eastsound, 360-376-4849; www.orcasisland.org/~history) for a recreated glimpse into the island's past.

Olga

Olga Café (11 Point Lawrence Rd, Olga, 360-376-5098) is a homey place with good food and a local art gallery. The last commercial business in the bend in the road which is the tiny town of Olga, the café is located within an old strawberry packing plant. It's definitely worth the drive and the perfect place for a quiet dinner away from the more populous Eastsound and Orcas Village. Be cautious when driving its winding roads, especially at night, since many deer graze close to the roadsides.

Orcas Village

This tourist trap is the central hub of activity as passengers load and depart the ferries at the harbor. The elegant Orcas Hotel (888-672-2792; www.orcashotel.com), overlooking the waterfront is a nice place for a relaxing beverage on the wrap-around porch while waiting for the ferry.

Cascade Lake

Family fun abounds at this wilderness lake, located between Eastsound and Olga. Swimming, paddle boats, a nature trail, and a wooded picnic area are just some of the ways to enjoy this day use area situated at the base of Mt. Moran.

Moran State Park/Mt. Constitution

www.parks.wa.gov/parkpage.sp?selectedpark=moran
Moran State Park is a nature lover's dream, with camping and 30 miles of hiking trails. Those who challenge themselves to climb from base to summit of Mt. Constitution, the highest point in the San Juan Islands, should come well-equipped with a compass, plenty of water, good hiking shoes, and a cell phone for emergencies. Look across to distant Vancouver, BC from atop the stone observation tower at the peak of the mountain.

San Juan Island

San Juan Island is the most commercial and the second-largest of all the islands. It was originally inhabited by Native Americans before sailors arrived in the 1850s and transformed the area into a busy seaport by the end of the century.

Friday Harbor

The only incorporated town in the islands, Friday Harbor has something for everyone, especially the shopping-inclined. Enjoy the Whale Museum (62 First St N, Friday Harbor, 360-378-4710) for an education about the area's native underwater inhabitants. Or, spend an afternoon browsing the local art galleries, cafés, and a multitude of specialty shops.

Roche Harbor

This resort and marina on the northwest tip of the island provides a quiet retreat from the bustling tourism of Friday Harbor. Explore the nearby English Camp on West Valley Road, part of the San Juan Island National Historical Park (360-378-2902; www.nps.gov/sajh).

Shaw Island

If Shaw Island had a motto, it would be, fittingly, "Not For Tourists." The least-welcoming of the four ferry-accessible islands, its residents prefer their remote isolation and have chosen to avoid the commercialism of their island sisters. Expect to find a primitive campsite and not much else.

Island Activities

There's a plethora of things to do and see in the San Juans, and more businesses that provide sightseeing excursions, vehicle rentals, and adventure packages than there's room to print. Here's a sample:

Bicycling

Island Bicycles
380 Argyle Ave
Friday Harbor, WA 98250
360-378-4941
www.islandbicycles.com

Wildlife Cycles
350 North Beach Rd
Orcas Island, WA 98245
360-376-4708
www.wildlifecycles.com

Lopez Bicycle Works
2847 Fisherman Bay Rd
Lopez Island, WA 98261
360-468-2847
www.lopezbicycleworks.com

Camping

San Juan Island County Parks
www.co.san-juan.wa.us/parks/

Moran State Park Camping
www.camis.com/wa/camping/maps.asp?loc=203

Kayaking

Lopez Island Sea Kayak
2845 Fisherman Bay Rd
Lopez Island, WA 98261
360-468-2847
www.lopezkayaks.com

Outdoor Odysseys Inc.
86 Cedar St
Friday Harbor, WA 98250
800-647-4621
360-378-3533
www.outdoorodysseys.com

Orcas Outdoors Inc.
P.O. Box 284
Orcas Island, WA 98280
360-376-4611
www.orcasoutdoors.com

Lodging

www.guidetosanjuans.com
www.orcasisland.org
www.orcasisle.com
www.orcas-lodging.com

www.san-juan-island.net
www.sanjuanweb.com
www.sanjuansites.com
www.visitsanjuans.com

Ferries

The islands are only accessible by air and water. By far the most popular way to travel to there, for those without private planes and boats, is via the Washington State Ferry system (www.wsdot.wa.gov/ferries). Plan to arrive in Anacortes extra early in the summer, at least two hours before your scheduled ferry departs. Bring books, playing cards, or other amusements, as a minimum of three-hour-long waits are not unusual during the busy season.

Two ways to avoid the long lines is to walk on or bring a bike rather than a car onto the ferry; there are peak and off-season parking rates if you choose to leave your car behind. Ferries from Anacortes travel to the four largest and most populated islands: Lopez, Orcas, San Juan, and Shaw.

Fares vary depending on the island destinations. During the peak season, be prepared to pay an average of $40 per vehicle and driver, and an additional $12 per passenger. Discounted rates are available for seniors and children. Bicycle surcharge rates are only $4 during the peak season.

Directions to Anacortes Ferry Terminal: Anacortes is about two hours north of Seattle. Take I-5 North for approximately 85 miles to SR 20. Take exit 230, turn left at the light and follow the signs into downtown Anacortes. Turn left on 12th Street and follow the signs to the terminal.

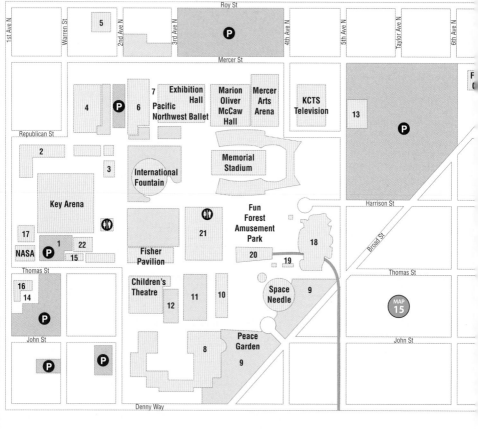

1 South Court Secured Parking
2 Northwest Rooms
3 Northwest Craft Center
4 Seattle Repertory Theater
5 Color Craft Building
6 Intiman Theatre
7 Founder's Court
8 Pacific Science Center / IMAX
9 Sculpture Garden
10 Fun Forest Pavilion
11 Mural Amphitheater
12 Children's Garden
13 Nate McMillian Basketball Court

14 Pottery Northwest
15 Blue Spruce
16 Park Place
17 Seattle Sonics / Storm Team Shop
18 Experience Music Project / Sci-Fi Museum
19 Frontier Galllery
20 Seattle Center Monorail
21 Seattle Center House / The Children's Museum
22 Seattle Center Pavilion

General Information

NFT Map: 15
Address: 305 Harrison St
             Seattle, WA 98109
Phone: 206-684-7202
Website: www.seattlecenter.com

Overview

Seattle Center is the hub of tourism in the city, but it also provides a number of interesting pursuits for the locals. While the out-of-towners flock to the Space Needle, Monorail, and EMP (or board those damned Ducks across the street), Seattleites attend concerts or sporting events at the Key Arena, see a play at one of several theaters, or hang out at Bumbershoot, Folklife, or Beerfest. Each year on New Year's Eve, the Space Needle is lit up by an impressive fireworks display.

But Seattle Center isn't just about partying and tourism. It's also about getting your learn on. The Children's Museum and the Pacific Science Center have interactive exhibits year-round. The IMAX Theater provides the typical educational fare as well as some new releases in 3D. And of course, each weekend you can rock out to your favorite psychedelic band at the Laser Dome.

There have been a few news-making events at Seattle Center. After his suicide in 1994, Nirvana fans came out in droves for a candlelight vigil memorializing Kurt Cobain. It has also been the site of several protests. In 2006, the annual Gay Pride Parade was moved from Broadway in Capitol Hill to the Seattle Center.

Space Needle

The Space Needle (800-937-9582; www.spaceneedle.com) is categorically the most overrated and over-photographed landmark in Seattle. The view might be impressive, but it's not the best one in the city, and it's certainly not worth the price of admission. There may be a modicum of charm in eating a meal in a rotating restaurant, but it's rarely a recipe for a quality meal.

Experience Music Project

Seattleites widely regard the EMP (877-367-5483; www.emplive.org) as an eyesore. Furthermore, no one but designer Frank Gehry and owner Paul Allen think it looks like a smashed guitar (the phrase "psychedelic clown poop" comes to mind). But if you're a music fan, you're in for a treat. That is, if you're *really* into Jimi Hendrix and looking at famous sweaters. In short, visiting the EMP is like paying $19.95 to go to the Hard Rock Café.

Science Fiction Museum

By and large, the Sci-Fi Museum (206-724-3428; www.sfhomeworld.org) is more like a visit to Paul Allen's walk-in closet of books and memorabilia than a legitimate exhibit on the history of the genre. But there are a few really cool pieces of sci-fi history such as Dr. Zaius from *Planet of the Apes*, a Cylon Commander from the original *Battlestar Galactica* series, and the Alien Queen and Power Loader from *Aliens*. A devotee (read: SF geek) would mostly agree these things are worth the $12.95 price of admission… Mostly.

Monorail

Like the Space Needle, the Monorail (206-448-3481; www.seattlemonorail.com) is a novelty that was built for the World's Fair. It runs about a mile from the Seattle Center to Westlake Center Mall. Round-trip fare for adults is $4 and $1.50 for children under 12. Seniors are $2 and kids under 5 are free. If this sounds like a rip-off for a two-minute trip, you aren't wrong.

No Seattle resident has ever used the Monorail as public transportation. Don't let any film or TV show set in Seattle convince you otherwise. It is nothing but a tourist trap. And lately, it has also been a bit of a death trap. In recent years, collisions, de-railings, and fires have repeatedly put the Monorail out of commission. But it sure does look cool on camera!

Children's Museum

Located on the first floor of the Center House, the Children's Museum (206-441-1768; www.thechildrensmuseum.org) features several child-sized environments designed for education, including a mountain forest, a global village, a mini-Seattle neighborhood, and Cog City. They also offer the typical gambit of youth programs and workshops. Admission is $7.50 for adults and children and $6.50 for grandparents. Children under 1 are free.

INTIMAN Theatre

The INTIMAN (206-269-1906; www.intiman.org) provides thought-provoking, Pulitzer Prize winning plays like *Angels in America* and the occasional Shakespeare work.

Center House Stage

Located on the first floor of the Center House, it encompasses the administrative offices of the Seattle Shakespeare Company and the Book-It Repertory Theatre (206-684-7200). Zounds!

Seattle Children's Theatre

Comprised of the Charlotte Martin Theatre and the Eve Alvord Theatre, the Seattle Children's Theatre (206-441-3322; www.sct.org) naturally offers a season of family-oriented plays as well as classes, workshops, and even birthday parties.

Seattle Repertory Theatre

The Seattle Rep (206-443-2222; www.seattlerep.org) includes the Bagley Wright Theatre, the Leo Kreielsheimer Theatre, and the PONCHO Forum. They perform classic and contemporary plays as well as original works and adaptations of novels.

Center House

The Center House is occupied by the Children's Museum and their very own theater. They also have various exhibits, dance exhibitions, and choral concerts throughout the year. Looking for an alternative to expensive fair food and Honey Buckets during Bumbershoot? Duck into the food court for a more reasonable meal and an actual restroom.

Fun Forest

The Fun Forest (206-728-1586; www.funforest.com) is another Center attraction that films tend to sensationalize. Perhaps at one time it was a groovy teenage date night. These days, however, it is a dilapidated affair that is more KISS Ghost Mystery than Fun for the Whole Family. Rickety roller coasters, a dubious Ferris wheel, and a Tin Can Alley staffed by bored high school students with Blackberries and Sidekicks all help to round out the ramshackle ambiance. The "Entertainment" Pavilion is pure 1987 with a few video games, bumper cars, Lazer Tag, a small climbing wall, and the sparsest mini-golf course you ever did see. If you have a death wish, or you just enjoy creepy urban landmarks, Fun Forest is for you. But get your thrills while the gettin's good. The Fun Forest has just been sold and will finally be refurbished when the contract ends in late 2009. They are still debating what to replace it with but the way development has been going around here lately, we're guessing it will be more condos. FUN condos!

McCaw Hall

The $127 million McCaw Hall (206-684-7200) is to home to the Pacific Northwest Ballet, the Seattle Opera, and the SIFF Cinema. A lecture hall and an array of meeting rooms are available for rent for your next grandiose function.

Key Arena

The fate of the Key Arena (206-684-7200) is somewhat uncertain at the moment, since the SuperSonics no longer belong to Seattle. However, it will still be used for the women's basketball team, the Seattle Storm, and the hockey team, the Thunderbirds. Besides, every city needs a Key Arena so that Neil Diamond has a place to perform.

Pacific Science Center/IMAX

The Pacific Science Center (206-443-2001; www.pacsci.org) houses a very good collection of science-related entertainment. From the dinosaur exhibit to the Butterfly House, the Insect Playground to the interactive Science Playground, adults and children alike owe it to themselves to explore the grounds at least once. Don't miss the Planetarium. In addition to the usual documentaries and nature films at the IMAX, they also present the odd theatrical release (such as *Harry Potter* and *Superman Returns*) in giant wrap-around screen splendor, and, occasionally 3D. And, of course, there's always *Laser Floyd*.

Art & Fountains

As you stroll through the Seattle Center, you will notice a multitude of abstract sculptures and unusual fountains. Many of them, such as the whale-esque Neototem Series, and the can't-miss-because-it's-a-giant-ball-in-the-center-of-the-grounds International Fountain, double as jungle gyms for the kids. The Olympic Iliad, a series of orange tubes intertwined, sits on the lawn of the Pacific Science Center. The Reeds, a row of 30-foot, well, reeds, divide the walkway and parking lot outside of the EMP. The Vortex Fountain aptly swirls between the INTIMAN Theatre and McCaw Hall.

Getting There

By Car: From I-5, take the Mercer Street/Seattle Center Exit #167. At the first light, turn right onto Fairview and follow the flow of traffic to the left, turning onto Broad Street. Take a right onto Fifth Avenue and a left onto Roy Street. From there you can find on-street parking, or use one of the lots or garages.

By Bus:
From Downtown, catch routes 1, 2, 3, 4, 8, 13, 15, 16, 18, 19, 24, or 33.
From Queen Anne, catch the 1, 2, 3, 4, 8, or 13.
From First Hill, catch the 2, 3, or 4.
From Capitol Hill, catch the 8.
From Wallingford/Northgate, catch the 16.
From Ballard, catch the 15 or 18.
From Magnolia, catch the 19, 24, 33 or 45.
From the Fremont/U-District, catch the 74.

By Monorail: Don't be a chump. Take the bus.

General Information

NFT Map	3
Address:	1000 Fourth Ave
	Seattle, WA 98104
Phone:	206-386-4636
Website:	www.spl.org
Hours:	Mon-Thurs: 10 am–8 pm, Fri-Sat:
	10 am–6 pm, Sun: 12 pm–6 pm

Overview

Opened to the public in May 2004 to much fanfare, the Seattle Central Library has helped to rescue the city from its growing reputation as an architectural vacuum. The stunning, avant-garde glass and steel structure designed by Dutch architect Rem Koolhaas is the third incarnation of the Central Library, with over 160,000 more square footage of program space than its dingy 1960s predecessor. The new building's diamond-grid "glass skin" makes the most of Seattle's scarcest resource—sunlight—filling the library's vast open spaces with light and framing 360-degree views of the surrounding buildings. The interior combines striking, modern decor with more serene touches. Polished steel surfaces abut scrap wood floors; fluorescent yellow escalators lead to grass-patterned carpeting. Particularly eccentric are the blood red hallways of the Meeting Level on the fourth floor. The place is downright trippy. But unlike other new buildings around town (sorry EMP), this architectural gem actually lives up to the hype.

True to Seattle ideals, the building is energy efficient, earthquake safe, and unbelievably high-tech, with self-checkout terminals, an automated book-sorting system, and wireless communication devices for staff members. The library's nonfiction stacks are housed in an innovative "books spiral," which, much like the Guggenheim Museum in New York, allows uninterrupted progress through the collection. Other highlights include the 400-seat Betty Jane Narver Reading Room featuring views of Elliot Bay, a wall of audio booths for language study, several video art installations, and the 275-seat Microsoft Auditorium where free author events are a regular occurrence.

Internet

The Central Library, housing nearly 400 public computers, was designed with access to technology in mind. A valid library card or a temporary guest pass is required for internet use on a library PC. Free Wi-Fi access is available throughout the building. Most seating in reading rooms and in the stacks is equipped with electrical outlets for laptops.

For the Kids

Kid-sized bookshelves and a toddler play area can be found in the cheerfully rubberized Faye G. Allen Children's Center on Level 1. The Anne Marie Gault Story Hour Room hosts children's activities almost every day of the week. On Level 3, discernable by its bright orange flooring, is the Starbucks Teen Center, complete with young adult books and graphic novels, a special teen reference desk, and computers and workstations exclusively for teen use.

Food and Gifts

The FriendShop on Level 3 near the Fifth Avenue entrance sells an assortment of trendy gift items and is one of the better places to buy a greeting card downtown. Espresso, pastries, and sandwiches can be purchased in the adjacent Fare Start Café. Snacks should be consumed in the cafe area, but feel free to roam the stacks with your lidded latte—ah, Seattle.

How to Get There—Driving

From the north take I-5 exit 165B at Union Street. Follow Union three blocks west to Fifth Avenue, then turn left and go south three blocks to Spring Street.

From the south, take I-5 exit 165 at Seneca Street. Follow Seneca one block west. Turn left on Fifth Avenue and go south one block to Spring Street.

From the east, drive to the end of I-90 and take the ramp toward northbound I-5. Take the second exit at Madison Street. Turn left on Madison Street and go west two blocks to Fifth Avenue.

Parking

Underground parking is accessible on Spring Street between Fourth and Fifth Avenues. The first 20 minutes are free; 20 to 40 minutes cost $3; 40 to 60 minutes, $5; then gradually increasing for each additional hour. The Sunday rate is $5 for up to four hours and $2 for each additional hour. Bike racks are located at all major entrances and inside the parking garage.

How to Get There—Mass Transit

Most downtown buses stop within walking distance of the Central Library.

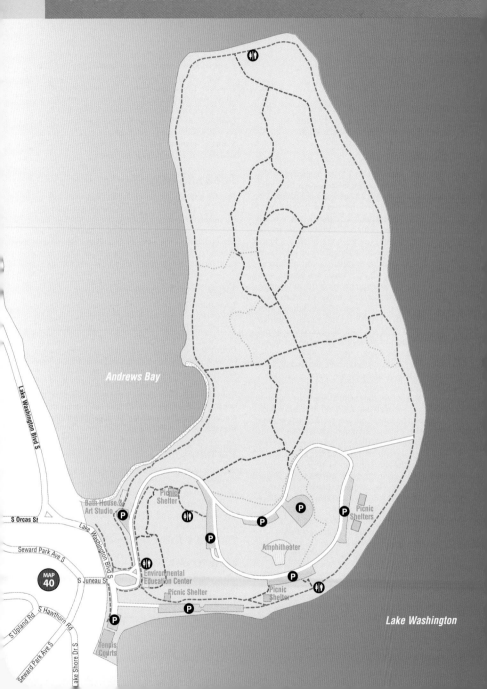

Andrews Bay

Lake Washington Blvd S

S Orcas St

Seward Park Ave S

MAP
40

S Juneau St

S Hawthorn Rd

S Upland Rd

Seward Park Ave S

Lake Shore Dr S

Bath House &
Art Studio

Lake Washington Blvd S

Picnic
Shelter

Environmental
Education Center

Picnic Shelter

Amphitheater

Picnic
Shelters

Picnic
Shelter

Tennis
Courts

Lake Washington

General Information

NFT Map: 40
Address: 5920 Lake Washington Blvd S
                 Seattle, WA 98118
Park Hours: 6 am–11 pm
Phone: Environmental Learning Center
                 206-684-4396;
                 Art Studio 206-722-6342
Seattle City Park Website:
                 www.seattle.gov/parks/parkspaces/
                 sewardpark.htm
Friends of Seward Park:
                 www.sewardpark.org

Overview

Seward Park was purchased by the city in 1910 for $322,020, less than today's price for a tiny home in south Seattle's nearby neighborhoods. It is a gigantic 300-acre thumb of land jutting into the (relatively) fresh water of Lake Washington, and much of the acreage encompasses old growth forest. Thanks to the ongoing work of Friends of Seward Park and city staff weeding out invasive non-indigenous plants, the park retains much of its splendid original habitat and native flora and fauna. On a clear day, walking around the peninsula's 2.4-mile lakefront loop allows views of Mount Rainier to the south, the Cascade Mountain range to the east, Mount Baker to the north, and a glimpse of the Olympic Mountain range to the west. You won't find a better walking trail in Seattle for a 360-degree vista of the glories of the Pacific Northwest, but the park does attract some unsavory characters—don't leave valuables in your car or send your children into the restrooms alone. Located amid the ethnically and income diverse neighborhoods of Mount Baker, Leschi, Seward Park, and Rainier Beach, you are as likely to see joggers in spandex pushing high-tech baby strollers as men in yarmulkes walking arm in arm or Muslim women cloaked in traditional garb. The park hosts many community events, from running and bicycle races to charity pet walks—check the park calendar for the schedule of evening hayrides, concerts in the spacious outdoor amphitheater, and the listing of classes offered by park naturalists.

How to Get There

Car, bike, bus, boat, or kayak will all get you there from here. Parking lots are plentiful and usually only crowded on summer weekends and sunny days. Driving south along Lake Washington Boulevard is scenic—if the route is open. From May to September, the stretch of road along the lakeshore from Mount Baker to Seward Park is closed two days a month for bicycle use on weekends. When the road is open to car

traffic, you may be tempted to cut in front of the hordes of cyclists, but bear in mind that bicycles have the right of way. If you can't beat 'em, hop on an expensive Klein racing bike or a beat up Schwinn, and join 'em. Metro Bus Routes 34 and 39 stop at Seward Park Avenue S and S Juneau Street.

Activities

This 300-acre park packs a wallop. Stay all day and you'll see the sun rise over Mount Rainier and set over downtown Seattle's Columbia Tower. In between, fish off the dock, swim in the lake, study lichens and mushrooms, add diving ducks to your life list of birds, use the Art Studio to fire your pottery, overhear a half dozen different languages, and glaze over watching a tai chi class on the beach. Your Aunt Mildred (or Jonathan Franzen if you happen to be entertaining famous authors for the weekend) can focus her binoculars on the bald eagle nests in the old growth forest, while your nephews play tennis on the waterfront courts. After catching his day's quota of fish, Dad can relax with a cool one in the picnic shelters overlooking the lake and he'll enjoy the same views as Lake Washington's multi-millionaire waterfront homeowners. There is anchorage for your uncle's yacht in protected Andrews Bay; in the summer he can row ashore to buy a hotdog and a sno-cone from the park's snack truck. If your family includes canine members, they are welcome, but keep them on a leash—if your rambunctious Airedale runs off you can (and will) be ticketed by park rangers intent on keeping the grebes, herons, and cormorants in the lake and the dogs out. There are hiking trails through the woods, grassy playfields for Frisbee tossing, and a small but well-used playground for the kids. Best of all, you can paddle off from the whole fam-damily in your kayak without anyone knowing you've slipped away.

Future

Big plans and the required multi-million dollar fundraising are in the works to finance "The Seward Park Environmental & Audubon Center," a joint venture of Audubon Washington and Seattle Parks & Recreation Department. Once the renovation is completed, the old Tudor-style brick building at the entrance to the park will be transformed into an environmental education center. Some neighbors fear that the already heavily-used park will become even more crowded (although birding isn't *quite* as popular with Americans as, say, football), but most welcome the opportunity to teach Seattle's next generation of REI shoppers why they need to leave no tracks behind when they trek off into Washington's wilderness.

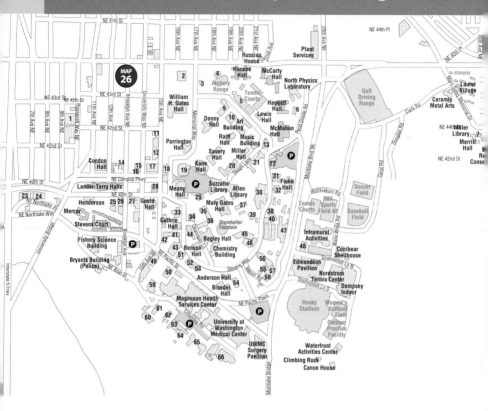

1. UWMC Roosevelt
2. Burke Memorial Museum
3. Theodor Jacobsen Observatory
4. Hughes Penthouse Theatre
5. Hutchinson Hall
6. Cyclotron Shop
7. NorthWest Horticultural Society Hall
8. Issacson Hall
9. Balmer Hall
10. Mackenzie Hall
11. Eagleson Hall
12. Social Work/Speech and
    Hearing Sciences Building
13. Clark Hall
14. Brooklyn Building
15. Playhouse Theater
16. Staff HR Center
17. Schmitz Hall
18. Henry Art Gallery
19. Odegaard Undergrad Library
20. Smith & Gowen Halls
21. Thomson Hall/Communications Building
22. Padelford Hall
23. Research & Technology Building

24. Publications Services Building
25. Child Care Center
26. Ethnic Cultural Center
27. Instructional Center/Theater
28. Commodore-Duchess Apartments
29. Gerberding Hall
30. Student Union Building (HUB)
31. Hall Health Center
32. The University of Washington Club
33. Architecture Hall
34. Cunningham Hall
35. Johnson Hall
36. Atmospheric Sciences-Geophysics
37. Sieg Hall
38. Engineering Library
39. Kirsten Aeronautical Lab
40. Loew Hall
41. Physics/Astronomy Building
42. Physics/Astronomy Tower
43. Physics/Astronomy Auditorium
44. Chemistry Library Building
45. Electrical Engineering Building
46. Paul G. Allen Center for Computer Science
    & Engineering

47. Power Plant
48. Graves Hall
49. W.H. Foege Bioengineering
    & Genome Sciences Building
50. Hitchcock Hall
51. Kincaid Hall
52. Botany Greenhouse
53. Plant Lab
54. Winkenwerder Forest Lab
55. Roberts Hall
56. More Hall
57. Wilcox Hall
58. Wilson Ceramic Lab
59. Ocean Sciences Building
60. Marine Sciences Building
61. Oceanography Teaching
62. Harris Hydraulics Lab
63. South Campus Center
64. Oceanography Building
65. Fisheries Center
66. Experimental Education Unit

General Information

NFT Map:	26
Address:	1410 NE Campus Pkwy
	Seattle, WA 98105
Phone:	206-543-2100
Website:	www.washington.edu

Overview

Founded November 4, 1861, the University of Washington, or UW (pronounced U-Dub) is the oldest university on the west coast and the largest in the Pacific Northwest. There are three campuses—Tacoma, Bothell, and Seattle—Seattle being the main one and largest of the three. It is a public research school of almost 40,000 students with many of its programs ranked in the top ten, including a #1 ranking for both the medical and nursing schools by *US News and World Report*. *Newsweek* recently rated it 26th in the world. It doesn't hurt that UW gets a great deal of funding from—yeah, those guys again—Microsoft masterminds Paul Allen and Bill Gates. It also boasts one of the most beautiful campuses in the country, with dramatic views of Mt. Rainier. It's well worth a stroll, even if you're not the studious type.

The 643-acre Seattle campus is home to 218 buildings and contains a courtyard full of cherry trees that are in the shape of a W when viewed from the sky. Unfortunately, they always seem to be in bloom when school is out of session for spring break. Although UW is best known for its medical programs, the Creative Writing Department recently received $15 million from the S. Wilson and Grace M. Polluck Foundation, the largest donation ever made to the College of Arts and Sciences.

Tuition

For the 2007–2008 academic school year, tuition for the University of Washington is $6,385 for residents and $22,131 for non-residents. On campus room and board will run you $8,337; for books and supplies you will need to get about $1,008 together.

Sports

Students and Seattle citizens are extremely proud of their Huskies and flock to the football games at Husky Stadium. You'll find die hard fans tailgating on their boats on Lake Washington during games, even in miserable weather. The Huskies participate in the NCAA Division I-A and the PAC 10. The football team may not be setting the world on fire like the old days, but the girl's volleyball team definitely is, recently becoming NCAA Division 1 national champions. Men's basketball is nothing to sniff at either thanks to a resurgence under head coach Lorenzo Romar, who frequently leads them to the NCAA tournament. Rowing is where the Huskies really shine. Men's Crew has won eleven national titles and 15 Olympic gold medals, while the women have won ten national titles and two gold medals. The Marching Band of UW is also well known, using a traditional high step, one of very few marching bands left to use this strategy of hyping up the already excited crowds.

Culture on Campus

The University of Washington's Seattle campus has culture up the wazoo. If you're into museums, try the Burke, which is the state museum of natural and cultural history. There is also the Henry Art Gallery, the first public art museum in the state of Washington, which features contemporary art (including the trippy *Skyspace* by James Turrell). Meany Hall is the place for performing arts and home to UW's School of Drama performances, recently ranked as one of the top five theater programs in the country. They put on at least seven shows per year, but you can also catch performances from the Schools of Dance, Music, Digital Arts, and Experimental Media Program. If you're more into the outdoors, head over to the Botanic Gardens, otherwise known as the arboretum. You will run out of time and energy before you run out of land to explore. The university also runs the RainyDawg Radio, a student run internet radio station and UWTV which is broadcast state-wide and is available to cable television viewers.

Departments

Undergraduate Admissions	206-543-9686
College of Arts and Sciences	206-543-5340
Business School	206-543-4750
School of Dentistry	206-543-5982
College of Education	206-616-4805
College of Engineering	206-543-0340
College of Forest Resources	206-685-1928
The Graduate School	206-543-5900
Information School	206-685-9937
School of Law	206-543-4550
School of Medicine	206-543-2100
School of Nursing	206-543-8736
College of Ocean and Fishery Sciences	206-543-6605
School of Pharmacy	206-543-2030
Daniel J Evans School of Public Affairs	206-543-4900
Henry M Jackson School of International Studies	206-543-4370
School of Public Health and Community Medicine	206-543-1144
School of Social Work	206-543-5640

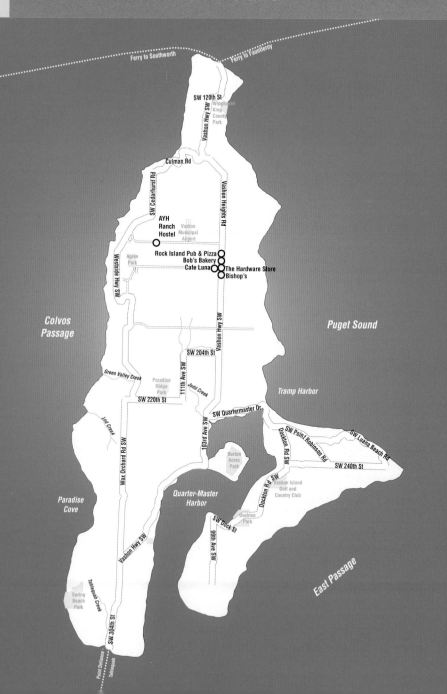

Ferry to Southworth

Ferry to Fauntleroy

SW 120th St

Wingehaven King County Park

Vashon Hwy SW

Culman Rd

SW Cedarhurst Rd

Vashon Heights Rd

AYH Ranch Hostel

Vashon Municipal Airport

Westside Hwy SW

Agren Park

Rock Island Pub & Pizza
Bob's Bakery
Cafe Luna
The Hardware Store
Bishop's

Colvos Passage

Puget Sound

SW 204th St

Green Valley Creek

Paradise Ridge Park

11th Ave SW

Judd Creek

Tramp Harbor

SW 220th St

Jird Creek

103rd Ave SW

SW Quartermaster Dr

SW Point Robinson Rd

Dockton Rd SW

SW Luana Beach Rd

SW 240th St

Wax Orchard Rd SW

Burton Acres Park

Paradise Cove

Quarter-Master Harbor

Vashon Island Golf and Country Club

Dockton Rd SW

Dockton Park

SW Dock St

Vashon Hwy SW

99th Ave SW

East Passage

Spring Beach Park

Tahlequah Creek

IS WS 304th SW

Point Defiance

Tahlequah

Overview

Vashon Island plays the role of that forgotten, odd-ball, self-isolated community populated with eccentric characters and legendary landmarks only locals can appreciate (a bike in a tree, a strawberry festival without strawberries, and so on). Vashon is less a destination than Bainbridge or the San Juans. In fact, with no hotels, only a dozen-ish B&Bs, and virtually no camping allowed anywhere on the island, Vashon doesn't exactly encourage tourism.

Roughly the same size as Seattle, but with only 10,000 inhabitants, Vashon is rural and decentralized—perfect for the organic farmers and radical GW-hating liberals (no, not like the ones in Seattle but the *really* radical ones) who call it home. Vashon is great for a short visit, especially if you have friends on the island or a purpose.

Lacking any stoplights, "Downtown Vashon" at Vashon Highway and Bank Road lies two miles from the ferry. There you'll find independent cafés, bookshops, art galleries, and restaurants. Bishop's is *the* center of nightlife (and that's not a snotty, emphatic "the," but a singular "the" as in "only place"). The locals go to Thriftway to hobnob and gossip about each other. Among restaurants, The Hardware Store was just that for over 100 years until 2005 when it was turned into a happening eatery.

Art Night

The rural, getaway nature of Vashon has attracted a flock of artists and galleries. A few of them have banded together for the First Friday Gallery Cruise. Also, twice a year (May, December) over 40 artists open their studios to the public. Information on both can be found at www.vashonalliedarts.org.

Strawberries?

The famed Vashon Island Strawberry Festival happens every July. It's much like small town fairs all over the country—elephant ears, nauseating rides, creepy carnies—but oddly, no strawberries. To the lament of the island's hippies, it occurs the same weekend as the venerated Oregon Country Fair. A highlight for car enthusiasts is the classic car parade which attracts gear heads from all over the state to show off their retro beauties that spend the rest of the year hiding under tarps

Earth Island

The Vashon Earth Island Fair (www.islandearthfair. org) happens every August and features a variety of alterna-activities, focusing on speakers and workshops on sustainability, renewable energy, healing arts, and healthy living, as well as musicians and legalized camping.

Where to Eat and Drink

The Hardware Store, 17601 Vashon Hwy SW, 206-463-1800. Serving lunch and dinner, plus breakfast on Sundays, the menu features straightforward café fare that includes buttermilk fried chicken and a nice selection of salads. Don't miss the bar area, a perfect perch for watching the ferry traffic stream into town while you sip some good vino from their wine list.

Rock Island Pub & Pizza, 23319 Vashon Hwy SW, 206-463-6814. A good range of pies and pastas. Take it outside to the patio with a pitcher of beer on a nice day or sidle up to the stone fireplace in the winter.

Bob's Bakery, 17506 Vashon Hwy SW, 206-463-1441. Bob bakes up a great selection of breads and sweet things, chief among them a slab of a maple bar that's not to be missed

Café Luna, 9924 SW Bank Rd, 206-463-0777. Serves up the best mocha on the island and offers a range of teas, baked goods, and grilled paninis.

Bishop's Pub & Grill, 17618 Vashon Hwy SW, 206-463-5959. The local dive bar that frequently has live music on the weekends.

Getting There

By Car: Take I-5 south to the West Seattle Bridge, keep to your left toward Alaska Junction to Fauntleroy and follow the signs to the ferry.

Ferries leave from the Fauntleroy terminal in West Seattle seven days a week. On weekdays, you can take a passenger-only ferry from Pier 50 in Seattle. Bus 54 will take you directly to the Fauntleroy ferry terminal from downtown. Bus 560 will take you there from the airport. To get to Fauntleroy by car, take I-5 to exit 163 to the West Seattle bridge to Fauntleroy Way SW. Follow Fauntleroy Way SW to the end, and look for signs for the ferry.

Where to Stay

AYH Ranch Hostel
12119 SW Cove Rd
Vashon, WA 98070
206-463-2592
www.vashonhostel.com

General Information

NFT Map: 17 & 20
Address   1247 15th Ave E
            Seattle, WA 98112
Phone: 206-684-4555
Website: www.seattle.gov/parks/parkspaces/
            volpark.htm
Hours: 6 am–11 pm daily

Overview

By day, Volunteer Park is another jewel in Seattle's crown of gorgeous public spaces. This 48.3-acre park features a museum, a conservatory, and many fine public art pieces. However, locals whisper that at night, Volunteer Park becomes a seedier place, where the randier citizens of Seattle lurk in the underbrush in search of anonymous partnerships. NFT cannot confirm or deny this rumor, only assist in spreading it. What is sure is that Volunteer Park (so named in 1901 to honor Spanish-American War recruits) suffers not a whit from these purported nocturnal dalliances—it's still a peaceful place to stroll away from the city with assorted trails and paths that allow one to gently meander or stretch the legs in a vigorous jog. A children's wading pool draws countless tykes all summer long, a quartet of tennis courts welcomes the net set, and the band stand provides a stage for regular outdoor music performances.

Seattle Asian Art Museum & Volunteer Park Conservatory

Volunteer Park has long been a popular destination for lovers of art and botany. Abstract sculptures and statues honoring local pioneers, military heroes, and public servants distinguish the grounds. The park is also home to the Seattle Asian Art Museum, an extensive collection of historical and modern art with ever-changing exhibits. The nearby Volunteer Park Conservatory has been here since 1912, featuring five different habitats for a wild assortment of exotic plants from around the world.

The Water Tower

The water tower on the south side of Volunteer Park is a popular landmark for those planning to meet up for a little Frisbee golf or friendly dog-walking. If you can handle 106 steps, you can visit the tower's observation deck, which automatically puts you at the highest point of Capitol Hill and affords a beautiful view. While there, take the time to peruse the historical exhibit that celebrates the Olmsted brothers, early-20th-century pioneers in establishing the park system in Seattle, including Volunteer Park.

Lake View Cemetery

Volunteer Park borders the Lake View Cemetery, a historical spot filled with graves of the many founding fathers and mothers of Seattle. Those who know names like Denny, Mercer, and Yesler only from street signs will come face to face with the resting places of the fabled men themselves. Lake View also boasts the graves of the mighty Bruce Lee and his son Brandon, both charismatic martial arts action heroes who died mysteriously. Sorry Mr. Mercer, but being in the eternal presence of Kato and the Crow is a bigger thrill, even if you did clear the trees to make way for the University of Washington.

How To Get There—Bus

The 10 hits Volunteer Park nearly every fifteen minutes with service from downtown.

How to Get There—Driving

From I-5 northbound, take exit 166 and turn right on E Olive Way, following until it merges with E John Street. Turn left on 15th Avenue E, then enter Volunteer Park after 3/4 mile.

From I-5 southbound, take exit 168A and turn left on E Roanoke Street. Turn right at 10th Avenue E, turn left onto E Boston Street until it becomes 15th Avenue E. Volunteer Park will be on the left.

General Information

NFT Map:	22 & 19
Address:	2300 Arboretum Dr E
	Seattle, WA 98122
Phone:	206-543-8800
Website:	www.depts.washington.edu/wpa/

Overview

The Washington Park Arboretum is 230 acres of sprawling beauty that contains more than 5,000 different plant species. You will find a large collection of sorbus and maple as well as an abundance of wildlife. The Arboretum is huge. It is difficult to see it all in one day, but definitely fun to try. There are many meandering trails with few hills, so it's perfect for jogging (just look out for people taking pictures!). You will find a strange combination of the beauty and serenity in the view in front of you and the constant din of traffic from the nearby freeway. However, once you push that out of your head, it is a wonderful place to get away from it all. And speaking of traffic, it can be pretty bad surrounding the park, so give yourself extra time to navigate it. Once there, take a stroll to Foster Island, where the floating bridges provide extra fun when boats go by and create a wake. Here especially, keep your eye out for birds and turtles. But don't go too quickly! The fragile earth under your feet wishes you to walk not run. If you really love the plants and desperately want to take them home with you, seedlings are available for purchase. Your only shot is on Tuesday's 10 am–12 pm at the Pat Calvert Greenhouse located just south of the Graham Visitor Center.

Japanese Gardens

Address:	1075 Lake Washington Blvd E
	Seattle, WA 98122
Phone:	206-684-4725
Website:	www.seattle.gov/tour/gardens.htm
Hours:	March–Apr: Tues-Sun 10 am–6 pm
	May–Aug 28th: Daily 10 am–8 pm
	Aug 29th–Sep 30th: Daily 10 am–7 pm
	Oct 1st–Oct 28th: Tues–Sun 10 am–6 pm
	Oct 29th–Nov 30th: Tues–Sun 10 am–4 pm
Admission:	18-64 $5; youths 6-17, seniors 65+, college students with ID, and disabled $3; children 0-5 free.

This 3.5-acre, formal garden was dreamed up by world-renowned Japanese garden designer Juki Iiada in 1960. He oversaw all construction of this garden, which includes a koi pond and a traditional tea house. The Garden is exceptionally beautiful and unique as it incorporates both plants traditionally found in a Japanese garden and plants native to the Northwest. It can be a welcome sanctuary from busy city life and well worth the admission fee. Try to catch a tea ceremony, which is periodically offered in the tea house.

Guided Tours

To better appreciate the diversity of the different plant species at the arboretum, take a free guided tour on the 1st and 3rd Sunday of each month. Guides will expertly highlight the plant collections, different seasonal displays of beauty, and the history of the arboretum in 60–90 minutes. Tours start at the Graham Visitor Center, and it's best to call ahead to ensure availability.

Scheduled guided tours are offered for groups of ten or more. These, however, are not free. Choose between whatever seasonal tour is being offered, the Foster Island Ecology tour, or the Native Plants and Ethnobotany tour. These tours require three weeks advance notice.

Address:	Graham Visitor Center
	2300 Arboretum Drive E
	Seattle, WA 98122
Phone:	free tours 206-543-8800;
	guided tours 206-543-8801
Website:	www.depts.washington.edu/wpa/ adulttours.htm

Boating

The arboretum now includes three public, non-motorized boat-launching sites and is a part of the Lakes to Locks Water Trail which starts in Lake Sammamish and ends at Puget Sound. Since it used to be illegal to land your boat at a public park, it's a welcome addition. If you don't own a boat or kayak, you can rent one from the Washington Activities Center (206-543-9433; H2ofront@u.washington.edu) just across the lake from the park. Once you're on the water, paddle around the water lilies and under the famous "ramp to nowhere" as you head over to Foster Island to explore its watery corridors. You will be treated to excellent bird watching, and the chance to see otters, turtles, or perhaps even a beaver dam. Once again, you'll come face to face with a thriving eco-system next to a busy freeway, giving you renewed hope for the future of planet Earth.

How to Get There—Driving

From Downtown: Go east on Madison Street to Lake Washington Boulevard E then turn left into the arboretum.

From I-5: Take exit 168 onto highway 520. Take the first exit to Lake Washington Boulevard E and follow it into the arboretum.

How to Get There—Bus

The 11, 43, and 48 will get you close to the park.

Deception Pass
State Park

Ala
Spit

*Skagiit
Bay*

Ault Field Rd

20

Oak Harbor

Fort Nugent Rd

*Crescent
Harbor*

West Beach Rd

Ebey's
Landing

Penn Cove

Coupeville

Fort Ebey
State Park

Engle Rd

20

Wannamaker Rd

Port Townsend - Keystone Ferry

525

*Admiralty
Bay*

Greenbank
Farm

Greenbank

S Smuggler's Cove Rd

Saratoga Rd

SE Harbor Rd

Langley

Double Bluff
Beach

525

Cultus Bay Rd

Clinton

Clinton - Mukilteo Ferry

*Useless
Bay*

General Information

Phone: 888-747-7777 x 22
Website: www.whidbeycamanoislands.com

Overview

One of Seattle's biggest perks is its proximity to an endless variety of retreats and getaways. Just miles from the hustle and bustle lay idyllic islands that can wipe away any memory of hellish downtown traffic. One of the prettiest and closest of these is Whidbey Island, known for its scenic shores, quaint island communities, and increasingly-precious real estate.

As with most of the territory in North America, Whidbey was once occupied by several local Native American tribes until those pesky Europeans came over. A guy named Joseph Whidbey came along and circumnavigated the whole island, which apparently was impressive enough for it to be named after him. Full colonization of the island took its sweet time, though. The first permanent arrival was murdered and beheaded by some unhappy natives, and understandably there was a bit of healthy skepticism on the part of would-be immigrants. Nowadays Whidbey is a thriving agricultural community as well as home to a naval station, a healthy tourism industry, and the most visited state park in Washington. Despite all that Whidbey's got goin' on, it's an extremely laid-back kind of place.

Activities

Though the island's motto of "Do Nothing Here" might imply a lazy sort of attitude on the part of Whidbey residents, that's certainly not the case. If you feel compelled to do more than skipping rocks on the bay or snuggling in your cottage (both more-than-acceptable activities), the island teems with things to do for all tastes and energy levels. There are no fewer than ten public beaches on the island where you can go clamming, watch gray whales in season, or, if you're brave, go swimming. A few favorites include Ala Spit (popular with birdwatchers) and Double Bluff (with an off-leash area for your pup).

Adults can check out the different wineries and pubs, like the Whidbey Island Winery (www.whidbeyislandwinery.com), or go treasure-hunting at the scores of antique shops. There are also several farmers markets during the peak of the season where you can buy local loganberries and homemade ice cream. And if you *really* want to do something instead of nothing, there are sites for almost every type of outdoorsy activity, from hiking to fishing to kayaking. Basically, Whidbey's got it all.

Towns

One of the biggest draws is the quaint postcard towns scattered across the island. Visitors and residents alike enjoy spending an entire day strolling and soaking up the charm. Towards the south and only a few miles from the Clinton ferry dock is Langley, an artists' village with the highest concentration of boutique lodgings in the state. Further north, historic Coupeville is situated on Penn Cove (home to the famously delectable mussels of the same name) and is the second oldest town in the entire state. It's loved for its charming shops and B&Bs, the Historical Society Museum, and the town ice cream parlor (yum).

Tours

The lovely Garden Isles Guest Cottages in Coupeville (www.gardenislecottages.com/tours.html) offers tours to some of Whidbey's highlights, like Ebey's Landing (the very first National Historic Reserve in the country), Deception Pass, the Greenbank Farm, and Langley. The Whidbey Island Garden Tour (www.wigt.org) is an extremely popular once-yearly event. Tickets are limited, so reserve well in advance in early summer.

Deception Pass State Park

360-675-9438; www.deceptionpassvisitorcenter.com
Deception Pass State Park is a 4,134-acre marine and camping park just north of Oak Harbor with amazing stretches of saltwater shoreline, as well as freshwater shoreline on three lakes. The park is the most popular in the state, and for good reason. There are breath-taking views, rugged cliffs, old-growth forests, and abundant wildlife. The park is open year-round for camping and day use, although select campgrounds are closed during the winter.

How to Get There—Driving

There's only one way to go if you're choosing to drive all the way to Whidbey—the breathtaking entrance to the north end of the island otherwise known as Deception Pass Bridge. Take the Anacortes exit off I-5, just north of Mt. Vernon. There are pull-outs and several points along the way where you can get out and take it all in. Trust us, it's stunning.

How to Get There—Ferry

Ferries are probably the most popular way to get to the island and the easiest from Seattle. The Mukilteo-Clinton ferry departs every 30 minutes from Mukilteo. Take I-5 north from Seattle and follow the Mukilteo/Whidbey Island exit (#189), which will take you straight to the ferry dock. At peak times there can be a significant wait, so check the current wait times before you go (www.wsdot.wa.gov/ferries). The ride takes about 20 minutes and will take you to the town of Clinton on the southern end of the island.

The Pt. Townsend-Keystone ferry also takes about 30 minutes and connects the Olympic Peninsula to Keystone Landing in Ebey's National Historical Reserve on the island. From the Peninsula, head east on Highway 101 and take the SR20 East exit. The highway will turn into Sims Way and then Water Street, which will take you to the ferry dock.

How to Get There—Plane

Seaplanes are a fun and incredibly scenic way to go, departing from Lake Union. If you want to bypass the whole ferry trip (which, on a bad day, can take hours), Kenmore Air (www.kenmoreair.com) will fly you for $29-$49 each way.

How to Get There—Bus

If you're up further north, the Island Transit system will take you between Mt. Vernon and the island for absolutely nothing. Check out the schedules at www.islandtransit.org.

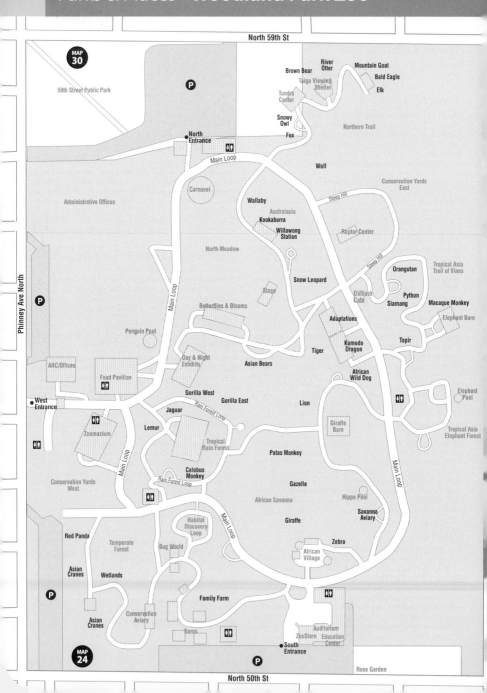

North 59th St

MAP 30

59th Street Public Park

Brown Bear
River Otter
Mountain Goat
Bald Eagle
Taiga Viewing Shelter
Elk
Tundra Center
Snowy Owl
Northern Trail
Fox
North Entrance
Main Loop
Wolf
Carousel
Conservation Yards East
Administrative Offices
Wallaby
Steep Hill
Australasia
Kookaburra
Willawong Station
Raptor Center
North Meadow
Phinnie Ave North
Main Loop
Steep Hill
Tropical Asia Trail of Vines
Orangutan
Snow Leopard
Stage
Outback Café
Python
Siamang
Macaque Monkey
Butterflies & Blooms
Adaptations
Elephant Barn
Penguin Pool
Tapir
Komodo Dragon
ARC/Offices
Day & Night Exhibits
Tiger
Asian Bears
African Wild Dog
Food Pavilion
Elephant Pool
West Entrance
Gorilla West
Gorilla East
Lion
Rain Forest Loop
Jaguar
Giraffe Barn
Tropical Asia Elephant Forest
Zoomazium
Lemur
Tropical Rain Forest
Patas Monkey
Main Loop
Colobus Monkey
Conservation Yards West
Rain Forest Loop
Gazelle
Main Loop
African Savanna
Hippo Pool
Habitat Discovery Loop
Savanna Aviary
Giraffe
Red Panda
Bug World
Temperate Forest
Zebra
African Village
Asian Cranes
Wetlands
Family Farm
Asian Cranes
Conservation Aviary
Barns
MAP 24
Auditorium Education Center
ZooStore
South Entrance
Rose Garden
North 50th St

General Information

NFT Map:	24 & 30
Address:	5500 Phinney Ave N
	Seattle, WA 98103
Phone:	206-684-4800
Website:	www.zoo.org
Hours:	Open 365 days a year;
	Sep 18–Oct 15: 9:30 am–5 pm;
	Oct 16–Apr 30: 9:30 am–4 pm
Admission:	Oct 1–April 30 $11 adult, $8 kids;
	May 1–Sep 30 $15 adult, $10 kids.

Overview

It may not be the biggest, it may not have the rarest animals, but what the Woodlawn Park Zoo lacks in size, it makes up for with style. There is a strong focus on education and conservation and the exhibits themselves will not leave you feeling depressed like some other zoos can. It's easy to tell why this zoo is world-renowned for its animal exhibits and education programs.

Zoomazium

Geared to kids eight and younger, this all-weather facility is the coolest indoor playground ever. You will find a stage, a project place, and an active space where parents let their kids loose to tire them out before the drive home. It's a great place for kids to learn as they play. There is a 20-foot tree to climb, caves to explore, and a watering hole that reflects an animal face when you look into it.

Jaguar Cove

The zoo's Jaguar Cove exhibit contains a large pool and waterfall as jaguars are the only large cat willing to get their tootsies wet. Even more impressive, this is the only zoo to boast a cross-section for underwater viewing of an enormous hungry jaguar coming right at you.

Other Interesting Zoo Offerings

As if their exhibits weren't amazing enough, here are some other highlights:

Rose Garden: This is technically located outside of the zoo, but admission is free, so don't miss a quick stroll through the 2.5-acre garden. This is a popular and affordable spot for weddings, making the photographer's job a no brainer. There are 280 varieties of roses and over 5,000 individual plants. It is one of only 24 All American Rose Selections Test Gardens in the US. You can smell it before you even walk in.

ZooTunes: Summer concerts at the zoo!

Zoo Overnight Adventure: If you just can't get enough of the zoo, you can stay there overnight. Small groups can reserve overnight accommodations that include private tours and breakfast. Approximately $39 per person.

Eating at the Zoo

When you get hungry like the wolf:

Naturally Untamed Grill: Burgers and fries, vegetarian friendly.

Cucina Rosso: Fast Italian food.

Bamboo Hut: Asian fare.

Rain Forest Deli: Soups and sandwiches.

Dreyers Ice Cream: Just what it sounds like.

Rain Forest Express: Hot dogs, nachos, and other deliciously guilty pleasures.

Jungle Java: When you just can't make it to the jaguar without your java.

Tortilla Express: Mexican food.

Outback Café: BBQ, hotdogs, and "bear necessities."

Picnic tables are also available for food brought from home.

How to Get There

By Car: From I-5 take the 50th Street exit (#169) west for 1.3 miles to the south gate located on N 50th Street and Fremont Avenue N.

By Bus: From downtown take the MT 5 from 3rd Avenue and Pine Street to the west gate at N 55th Street & Phinney Avenue N.

Parking: $4, but try for free street parking first.

When it comes to biking, Seattle is kind of like your earnest, hard-working yet clueless teenager. Sure, it tries hard, and overall it's a good kid—much better than the average city—but it's nothing like those pesky neighbors, Vancouver and Portland. And sometimes it just screws up so badly in the simplest, most obvious of ways, it makes a biker rather frustrated.

All this being said, the city is actually quite bike-friendly. Overly-environmentally-conscious Seattleites are supportive of bikers and most drivers are aware and cautious. There's a large network of trails and good bike lanes and plenty of good bike shops around town. Many Seattle employers even have incentives for bike commuters.

Recently, though, criticism has grown about some of the unfriendly realities. Some of those trails end abruptly in the middle of nowhere, or worse, are interrupted by very bike-unfriendly elements (like trucking lanes). Paths and routes are poorly marked. Major arteries have no bike lanes. Whole sections of the city are difficult to navigate by bike. There's only one southbound route into downtown and zero from the north. And let's not forget The Ballard Bridge which is a particularly notorious deathtrap.

The city recently started the processes of correcting some of these pitfalls. In the meantime, if you commute by bike, it's fairly easy to establish a route, just as it's easy to leisurely bike around on the good trails. Seattle and King County publish free and extensive bike maps—available at most libraries.

Although biking in Seattle can be a little frustrating at times, it's still worth it to get out of your car and hop on a bicycle. You'll be fitter, happier, and, best of all, not stuck in traffic like everyone else. All this is moot, however, if you can't handle the rain or the hills—which are nearly impossible to avoid.

Burke-Gilman Trail

Seattle's been heralding its crown jewel of bike trails, the Burke-Gilman, for nearly 20 years. Starting from Lake Sammamish on the Eastside (with recent extensions to Issaquah), the trail runs 25 miles around the north of Lake Washington to the University of Washington. But beware! Even the official bike map warns about neglected stretches along the north Seattle section. From the UW, the BGT traces the ship canal and Lake Union through Wallingford and Fremont to the edge of Ballard, where it mysteriously disintegrates into a gravel-strewn truck route.

Many commuters from north Seattle cross the Fremont Bridge onto Dexter, the unofficial bike highway that two miles further, um, ends abruptly at Denny. It's not difficult to cut across to Second Avenue, a one-way south-bound artery with bike lanes, but don't look for such luxury returning north. The city is currently debating how to solve that issue.

Elliot Bay Trail

This is another nice, yet incomplete, trail. Starting from Golden Gardens, a short trail leads you to the Ballard Locks. After walking across the locks (or paying the $25 fine for riding) you can either follow the truck lane to the left or go straight uphill on the dead-end street to one hell of a suspension bridge. Take the bridge across some railroad tracks before turning onto a proper bike lane on Government Way/Gilman Avenue. The lane turns into a bike trail that cuts right through the rail yard, with some harrowing and extremely narrow sections, before blossoming into the **Elliot Bay Trail**. The trail empties into downtown, where it is sprinkled with tourists under the Alaska Way Viaduct. Ostensibly, this is a designated bike route that leads to the West Seattle Bridge, but the potholes and trucks flooding in from the port make it an unpleasant journey. If you can make it to the West Seattle Bridge, things get much better, quieter, and easier to navigate. Turn north for the **Alki Trail** or south on yet another missing link before reaching the **Duwamish Trail** to South Park. From there, a spotty connection of side roads connects you to W Marginal Way S before smoothing out to the **Green River Trail**, which takes you all the way to Kent.

Lake Washington Loop

You can also use a combination of the Burke-Gilman to make a less frustrating trip circling Lake Washington. Depart the BGT at Montlake, cross the Montlake Bridge, and wind through the Arboretum (a nice ride, even with all the cars). From there, a route leads to Lake Washington Boulevard, one of Seattle's more pleasant and peaceful rides that continues all the way to Renton. A series of other trails bring you up the east side of the lake. Neither of southeast Seattle's main arteries, Rainier Avenue or Martin Luther King Way, are known for being bike-friendly, with the latter currently torn up for the construction of the light rail.

Coming to/from the Eastside, the I-90 Trail makes for an interesting ride along side eight lanes of traffic. Luckily, the trail has its own tunnel and connects to downtown.

General Information

Seattle Bike Club: www.seattlebike.org
Critical Mass: www.seattlecriticalmass.org
Seattle Biking Blog: www.bikeseattle.org
King County Bike Page:
www.metrokc.gov/kcdot/roads/bike/index.cfm
City of Seattle Bike Maps:
www.seattle.gov/transportation/bikemaps.htm
Bike Alliance: www.bicyclealliance.org
Cascade Bike Club: www.cascade.org
Reload Messenger Bags: www.reloadbags.com

A Few Bike Shops

Bike Works: 3709 S Ferdinand St, 206-725-9408;
www.bikeworks.org
Elliot Bay Bicycles: 2116 Western Ave, 206-441-8144;
www.elliotbaybicycles.com
Gregg's: 7007 Woodlawn Ave NE, 206-523-1822;
www.greggscycles.com
Montlake Bicycle Shop: 2223 24th Ave E, 206-329-7333;
www.montlakebike.com
Second Ascent: 5209 Ballard Ave NW, 206-545-8810;
www.secondascent.com
Velo Bike Shop: 1535 11th Ave, 206-325-3292;
www.velobikeshop.com

Face it. In a city where it's fashionable to commute to work by kayak, Seattle's traffic problems aren't isolated to the Mercer mess; they spill over into the area's multiple salt and fresh waterways. Everyone and their sister owns some sort of boat in Seattle, and many Seattleites have more boats than kids. After all, you need different kinds of boats for salmon fishing, river kayaking, sculling, cruising the San Juans, racing Vic-Maui, or rounding the buoys on a Wednesday night Duck Dodge. Plus, you gotta have a Zodiac or a dinghy to row into shore when your yacht is anchored out in Andrews Bay during Seafair. And of course it takes a little Boston Whaler to buzz over from Portage Bay on a summer night to have a beer and a bowl of steamed clams in a waterfront joint on Lake Union.

In Elliott Bay, Seattle's main harbor, tugboats, barges, container ships, fishing vessels, ferries, sailboats, powerboats, and cruise ships as big as football fields all vie for the same waterway space. Floating homes with deepwater boat moorage on Lake Union are more highly coveted than a landlubber's three-car garage, and if you have room to tie up your float plane, so much the better. Seattle's boating scene can be as silly as it can be serious—more than one yacht club has a tavern as its clubhouse, but Seattle has produced world class rowers, some of the America Cup's best crews, and Olympic-class kayakers.

Of course, there are rivalries between the "stinkpotters" and vessels powered by sails, oars, or paddles. Hydroplanes? Love 'em or get out of town the first weekend of August, when the gas guzzling, engine whining hydros churn up Lake Washington at Seafair, Seattle's answer to NASCAR, and the lake fills up with log booms of yachts, festooned with bikini clad women and beer guzzling men intent on partying hearty. All of this is in stark contrast to Lake Washington's typical bucolic scene of rowers and scullers practicing for the next regatta. Many local universities, private schools, city parks, non-profit rowing clubs, and kayaking organizations teach water skills and advocate to preserve Seattle's precious waterways for future generations.

Like the human body, Seattle is made up primarily of water—so find your boat of choice and get out there—you'll have lots of company.

Small Boats Centers	Address	Phone
The Center for Wooden Boats	1010 Valley St	206-382-2628
Green Lake Boat Rental	7351 E Green Lake Dr N	206-527-0171
Moss Bay Rowing, Kayaking, and Sailing Center	1001 Fairview Ave N	206-682-2031
Washington Activities Center	Behind Husky Stadium at the University of Washington	206-543-9433

Yacht and Cruising Clubs	Address	Phone
Corinthian Yacht Club - Shilshole	7755 Seaview Ave NW	206-789-1919
Corinthian Yacht Club - Leschi	106 Lakeside Ave	206-322-7877
Hidden Harbor Yacht Club - Seattle	319 Nickerson St	206-284-1047
Meydenbauer Yacht Club - Bellevue	9927 Meydenbauer Wy SE, Bellevue	425-454-8880
Puget Sound Yacht Club - Lake Union	2321 North Northlake Wy	206-634-3733
Queen City Yacht Club - Portage Bay	2608 Boyer Ave E	206-709-2000
Rainier Yacht Club - Lake Washington	9094 Seward Park Ave S	206-722-9576
Seattle Yacht Club - Montlake	1807 E Hamlin St	206-325-1000
Sloop Tavern Yacht Club - Ballard	2830 NW Market St	206-782-3330
Tyee Yacht Club - Lake Union	3229 Fairview Ave E	206-324-0200
University of Washington Yacht Club - Campus Boat Club	University of Washington Activities Center	

Rowing Clubs and Centers	Address	Phone
Lake Washington Rowing Club	910 N Northlake Wy	206-547-1583
Green Lake Crew	5900 W Greenlake Wy N	206-684-4074
Green Lake Small Craft Center	5900 W Greenlake Wy N	206-684-4074
Lake Union Crew	11 E Allison St	206-860-4199
Mount Baker Rowing and Sailing Center	3800 Lake Washington Blvd S	206-386-1913
Pocock Rowing Center	3320 Fuhrman Ave E	206-328-7272

Kayaking Clubs and Centers	Address	Phone
Kayak Academy	11801 188th Ave SE, Issaquah	206-527-1825
Mountaineers Club	300 Third Ave W	206-284-6310
Northwest Outdoor Center	2100 Westlake Ave N	206-281-9694
Seattle Canoe and Kayak Club	5900 W Greenlake Wy N	206-684-4074
University of Sea Kayaking	PO Box 12249, Mill Creek	425-741-0960
Washington Water Trails Association	4649 Sunnyside Ave N #305	206-545-9161

Bowling alleys have not quite gone the way of the drive-in theater yet, but sophisticated, urbane Seattle seems to have little use for them. Over the years bowling spots have declined in the heart of the city, leaving downtown-bound hipsters dry, but on Capitol Hill a billiards hall called the **Garage (Map 4)** filled the gap in 2003 by adding fourteen swanky lanes for metrosexual pin pals. By contrast **Imperial Lanes (Map 40)** is old-school bowling at its finest. The popular Underdog Sports League (www.underdogseattle.com) holds their team competitions here while locals hang out at the no-frills bar. Aside from that, Seattle bowlers are forced to seek their sport in outlying townships and unfashionable parts of the city proper.

ACME Bowling, Billiards, and Events houses the newest, shiniest lanes in the greater Seattle area, adjacent to the Southcenter Mall in Tukwila and decked out in a sleek faux-retro fashion. This is the bowling alley for people who are afraid to go to bowling alleys. It's an open, well-lit place that serves gourmet pizzas and portobello mushroom sandwiches directly to your lane. Private bowling with cool blue neon lighting and projection screens is available, the perfect spot for bachelorette parties or an ironic evening out with co-workers.

For those after a more traditional bowling experience, South Seattle can satisfy. The **Skyway Park Bowl** tore out their indoor miniature golf course to expand the casino, but retained its warmth and old-school appeal. **Magic Lanes (Map 37)** is open 24 hours a day and looks a little tired, but there's a great bar and TV sets next to the scoring screens. The nearby **Roxbury (Map 37)** advertises "saloon and casino" in the same breath as "family-friendly" and that's about the size of it—expect exuberant children on the lanes and enthusiastic drinkers in the bar.

West Seattle Bowl (Map 36) strikes a nice compromise between the sterility of ACME and the earthier tones of the older bowling alleys, with a Chinese restaurant on site, comfy booths on the lanes, and a video bowling game if you really are that lazy. And to the north, **Lynnwood Bowl & Skate** brings pins and wheels together for all-ages action, or check out **Spin Alley** in Shoreline, which opened in 1997 as a smoke-free bowling emporium (a fine sentiment rendered moot by Initiative 901, which banned smoking in public places statewide eight years later). For information on tournaments and other bowling-related news, check out the Greater Seattle Bowling Association (www.seattlebowling.org).

Bowling

	Address		Phone	Map	Fees
Garage Billiards & Bowl	1130 Broadway	Seattle	206-322-2296	4	$14.00/hr, $3.00/shoes.
West Seattle Bowl	4505 39th Ave SW	Seattle	206-932-3731	36	$3.67/game, $2.50/shoes.
Magic Lanes	10612 15th SW	Seattle	206-244-5060	37	$3.50/game, $2.50/shoes.
Roxbury	2823 Roxbury St	Seattle	206-935-7400	37	$3.95/game, $3.50/shoes.
Imperial Lanes	2101 22nd Ave S	Seattle	206-325-2525	40	$4/game, $3.25 for shoes.
AMF Sun Villa Lanes	3080 148th SE	Bellevue	425-455-8155	44	$5.25/game, $4.50/shoes.
Lucky Strike Lanes	700 Bellevue Wy NE	Bellevue	425-453-5137	45	
TechCity Bowl	13033 NE 70th Pl	Kirkland	425-827-0785	48	$5.60/game, $3.75/shoes.
ACME Bowling	100 Andover Park W	Tukwila	206-340-2263	n/a	$5.50/game, $3 for shoes.
Brunswick Majestic Lanes	1222 164th SW	Lynnwood	425-743-4422	n/a	$4.39/game, $3.69/shoes.
Chalet Bowl	3806 N 26th St	Tacoma	253-752-5200	n/a	$4.00/game, $3.25/shoes.
Daffodil Entertainment Center	1624 E Main	Puyallup	253-845-9166	n/a	$4.00/game, $3.00/shoes.
Evergreen Lanes	5111 Claremont Wy	Everett	425-259-7206	n/a	$2.35/game, $2.25/shoes.
Glacier Bowling Lanes	9630 Evergreen Wy	Everett	425-353-8292	n/a	$3.25/game, $2.25/shoes.
Hi-Line Lanes	15733 Ambaum Blvd SW	Burien	206-244-2272	n/a	$4.25/game, $3.25/shoes.
Hillcrest Family Bowling Center	2809 NE Sunset Blvd	Renton	425-226-1600	n/a	$4.95/game, $3.95/shoes.
Kenmore 50 Lanes & Casino	7638 NE Bothell Wy	Bothell	425-486-5555	n/a	$2.50/game, $2.50/shoes.
Kent Bowl	1234 N Central	Kent	253-852-3550	n/a	$4.25.game, $3.00/shoes.
Lynnwood Bowl and Skate	6210 200th St SW	Lynnwood	425-778-3133	n/a	$4.50/game, $3 for shoes.
Melady Lanes	420 N Olympic Ave	Arlington	360-435-2466	n/a	$15.00/hr, $1.00/shoes.
Mt Si Bowl	3740 Railroad Ave SE	Snoqualmie	425-888-1377	n/a	$4.50/game, $2.50/shoes.
Pacific Lanes	7015 S D St	Tacoma	253-474-0594	n/a	$2.75/game, $2.50/shoes.
Paradise Village Bowl	12505 Pacific Ave S	Tacoma	253-537-6012	n/a	$3.50/game, $3.00/shoes.
Secoma Lanes	34500 Pacific Hwy S	Federal Way	253-927-0611	n/a	$3.50/game, $2.50/shoes.
Skyway Park Bowl Casino	11819 Renton Ave S	Seattle	206-772-1220	n/a	$3.50/game, $2.99/shoes.
Spin Alley Bowling Center	1430 NW Richmond Beach Rd	Shoreline	206-533-2345	n/a	$3.50/game, $2.50/shoes.
Strawberry Lanes	1067 Columbia Ave	Marysville	360-659-7641	n/a	$3.25/game, $2.00/shoes.
Tower Inn & Lanes	6323 6th Ave	Tacoma	253-564-8853	n/a	$2.50/game, $3.00/shoes.
Twin City Lanes	27120 92nd Ave NW	Stanwood	360-629-3001	n/a	$3.00/game, $1.50/shoes.

Golf

	Address	Phone	Map	Fees	Par, Holes
Interbay Golf Center	2501 15th Ave W	206-285-2200	12	Mon–Fri$13, Sat–Sun $15	Par-28, 9 holes
Green Lake Pitch & Putt	5701 E Green Lake Wy N	206-632-2280	30		
Battle Creek Golf Course	6006 Meridian Ave N	360-659-7931	31	Mon–Fri $25, Sat–Sun $32	Par-73, 18 holes
Jackson Park Golf Course	1000 NE 135 St	206-363-4747	34	Mon–Fri $28, Sat–Sun $33	Par-71, 18 holes
Jefferson Park Golf Course	4101 Beacon Ave S	206-762-4513	34	Mon–Fri $28, Sat–Sun $33	Par-70, 18 holes
West Seattle Golf Course	4470 35th Ave SW	206-935-5187	36	Mon–Fri $28, Sat–Sun $33	Par-72, 18 holes
Bellevue Municipal Golf Course	5500 140th Ave NE	425-452-7250	46	Mon–Thurs $27, Fri–Sun $31	Par-71,18 holes
Foster Golf Links	13500 Interurban Ave S, Tukwila	206-242-4221	n/a	Mon–Fri $21, Sat–Sun $23	Par-69, 18 holes

Tennis	Address	Phone	Map	
Bobby Morris PF	1635 11th Ave	206-684-4062	4	2 courts, Lighted
Garfield PF	23rd Ave & E Cherry St	206-684-4062	5	3 courts, Lighted
Madrona Playfield	34th Ave E & E Spring St	206-684-4062	6	2 courts, Lighted
I-90 Lid/Sam Smith	1400 Martin Luther King Jr Wy S	206-684-4062	10	2 courts
Leschi Park	201 Lakeside Ave S	206-684-4062	10	1 court
Discovery Park	3801 W Government Wy	206-684-4062	11	2 courts
Magnolia Park	1461 Magnolia Blvd W	206-684-4062	11	2 courts
Magnolia PF	2518 34th Ave W	206-684-4062	11	4 courts
David Rodgers Park	2800 1st Ave W	206-684-4062	13	3 courts, Backboard
Kinnear Park	899 W Olympic Pl	206-684-4062	14	1 court
Miller PF	400 19th Ave E	206-684-4062	18	2 courts, Lighted
Volunteer Park	1247 15th Ave E	206-684-4062	18	4 court, Lighted, Backboard
Rogers PG	Eastlake Ave E & E Roanoke St	206-684-4062	20	3 courts
Madison Park	2300 43rd Ave E	206-684-4062	22	2 courts, Lighted
Gilman PG	923 NW 54th St	206-684-4062	24	2 courts
Woodland Park (Lower)	5851 West Green Lake Wy N	206-684-4062	24	10 courts
Woodland Park (Upper)	Midvale Ave N & N 50th St	206-684-4062	24	4 courts
Wallingford PF	4219 Wallingford Ave N	206-684-4062	25	2 courts
University PG	9th Ave NE & NE 50th St	206-684-4062	26	2 courts, Backboard
Bryant PG	4103 NE 65th St	206-684-4062	27	2 courts
Laurelhurst PF	4544 NE 41st St	206-684-4062	27	4 courts, Lighted, Backboard
Magnuson Park	6500 Sand Point Wy NE	206-684-4062	27	6 courts
Froula PG	7200 12th Ave NE	206-684-4062	31	2 courts
Green Lake Park	7201 E Green Lake Dr N	206-684-4062	31	5 courts
Cowen Park	5849 15th Ave NE	206-684-4062	32	3 courts
Ravenna Park	5520 Ravenna Ave NE	206-684-4062	32	2 courts, Backboard
Ravenna-Eckstein	6535 Ravenna Ave NE	206-684-4062	32	1 court
Bitter Lake PF	13030 N Park Ave N	206-684-4062	33	4 courts, Lighted
Soundview PF	1590 NW 90th St	206-684-4062	33	2 courts
Meadowbrook PF	10533 35th Ave NE	206-684-4062	34	6 courts, Lighted
Victory Heights PG	1737 NE 106th St	206-684-4062	34	1 court
Alki PG	5817 SW Lander St	206-684-4062	35	1 court, Lighted
Hiawatha PF	2700 California Ave SW	206-684-4062	35	3 courts, Lighted, Backboard
Delridge PF	4458 Delridge Wy SW	206-684-4062	36	2 courts
Jefferson Park	4165 16th Ave SW	206-684-4062	36	2 courts, Lighted
High Point PF	6920 34th Ave SW	206-684-4062	37	2 courts
Lowman Beach Park	7017 Beach Dr SW	206-684-4062	37	1 court
Solstice Park	8603 Fauntleroy Wy SW	206-684-4062	37	6 courts, Lighted, Backboard
Highland Park PG	1100 SW Cloverdale St	206-684-4062	38	1 court
Riverview PF	7226 12th Ave SW	206-684-4062	38	2 courts
South Park PG	738 S Sullivan St	206-684-4062	38	2 courts
Beacon Hill PG	1902 13th Ave S	206-684-4062	39	2 courts, Backboard
Cleveland High	5511 15th Ave S	206-684-4062	39	2 courts
Georgetown PF	750 S Homer St	206-684-4062	39	1 court
Amy Yee Tennis Center	2000 Martin Luther King Jr Wy S	206-684-4764	40	4 courts
Beer Shiva Park	55th Ave S	206-684-4062	40	1 court
Brighton PF	6000 39th Ave S	206-684-4062	40	2 courts
Dearborn Park	2919 S Brandon St	206-684-4062	40	2 courts
Mount Baker Park	2521 Lake Park Dr S	206-684-4062	40	2 courts, Lighted
Rainier PF	3700 S Alaska St	206-684-4062	40	4 courts, Lighted
Seward Park	5902 Lake Washington Blvd S	206-684-4062	40	1 court
Hutchinson PG	S Norfolk St & 59th Ave S	206-684-4062	41	2 courts
Rainier Beach PF	8802 Rainier Ave S	206-684-4062	41	4 courts, Lighted
Homestead Park	82nd Ave SE & SE 40th St	206-236-3545	42	4 courts
Luther Burbank Park	2040 84th Ave SE	206-236-3545	42	3 courts
Park on the Lid	I-90 & W Mercer Wy	206-236-3545	42	4 courts
Robinswood Tennis Center	2400 151st Pl SE	425-452-7690	44	6 indoor, 2 outdoor
Everest Park	500 8th Ave S	425-587-3347	48	1 outdoor
Heritage Park	111 Waverly Wy	425-587-3342	48	2 outdoor
Juanita Beach Park	9703 NE Juanita Dr	425-587-3340	48	2 outdoor
Peter Kirk Park	202 3rd St	425-587-3342	48	2 outdoor
Grass Lawn Park	7031 148th Ave NE	425-556-2311	49	2 outdoor

Overview

The Northwest is famous for its mountainous terrain, so finding a trail to hike in these parts is not difficult. But if you don't have a car, or don't feel like venturing outside of King Country, there are plenty of urban hikes to keep your Nalgene bottle dust-free.

The Burke-Gilman is the most popular urban trail. Parks like Carkeek, Lincoln, and Magnuson have trails along the waterfront as well as beautiful vistas that will make you forget you're a stone's throw from civilization. If it's communing with nature you're after, visit the Arboretum or the Schmitz Park Reserve. If you are in need of a real endorphin-kicker, you still need only drive a few minutes east to the switchbacks of Tiger Mountain. Since none of the parks are very expansive, it's difficult to lose your way, but if you're the type who could get lost in their own museum, never fear. All of these parks have kiosks with trail maps.

If most of your friends consider lifting pint glasses exercise, you can meet other hiking enthusiasts by means of the Seattle Mountaineers (www.mountaineers.org). They offer regularly scheduled hikes as well as other outdoor activities.

Carkeek Park

950 NW Carkeek Park Rd • 6 miles • Easy • Map 29-30
Carkeek is most famous for the salmon preserve in Pipers Creek. In the late fall, you can follow the Piper's Creek trail to catch a glimpse of the fish-filled waters. Year-round, North Bluff Trail provides fantastic views of the Olympic Mountains and Puget Sound. The Wetland Trail leads you down to the beach.

Burke-Gilman Trail

60th Place NE and Bothell Wy to 8th NW •
14 miles • Easy-Moderate • Map 23-27, 34
This multi-purpose trail covers over 14 miles from 11th Ave NW to Tracy Owen Station in Kenmore. It allows bikers and joggers as well as hikers, so it can sometimes be a bit too crowded for a contemplative, woodsy walk. But it is the longest urban trail around, so no matter what neighborhood you live in, there is most likely an access point near you. Among the many entrances to the trail are Ballard, Fremont, Sand Point, and Matthews Beach Park. The trail also runs through the University of Washington campus. They are constantly renovating it and adding new trail segments. For a complete map of the trail please visit www.seattle.gov.

Lincoln Park

8011 Fauntleroy Wy SW • 5 miles •
Easy-Moderate • Map 37
If you're after a mostly water-vista for your hike, Lincoln Park is the place for you. The 100-foot high Bluff Loop trail provides a stunning view of Puget Sound. The South Beach trail borders Fauntleroy Cove. Those trails are fantastic in the warm weather, but the wind can make them unpleasant during the off-season. The North Beach Trail is slightly more shielded by trees, so it is ideal for a hike on those blustery winter days. In the summer, you can conclude your hike by taking a dip in the heated saltwater Coleman Pool.

Schmitz Park Preserve

5551 SW Admiral Wy • 2 miles • Easy • Map 35
One of the few urban areas to boast old growth forest, the Schmitz Park Preserve (www.schmitzpark.org) is a great place to stroll in quiet contemplation amidst the majesty of nature. Despite its diminutive size (a mere 53 acres), it isn't difficult to feel secluded as you stroll along the often-empty figure 8 trail that curves through the area. Be on the lookout for foxes, bats, and coyotes.

Seward Park

5900 Lake Washington Blvd • 3 miles • Easy • Map 40
Like Schmitz Park, Seward Park possesses the splendor of old growth forest: 250 acres of impressively ancient Douglas Firs and Western Red Cedars. The perimeter path, popular with joggers and bikers, runs along the beach and presents views of the Seattle skyline, Lake Washington, Mercer Island, and Mount Rainier. The interior path, which breaks off into several shorter trails, runs through the thick of the forest. Despite being surrounded by urban sprawl, the area is often dead quiet, particularly in the winter.

Discovery Park

3801 W Government Wy • 7 Miles • Easy-Moderate • Map 11
The city's largest public park was built on an old Army base. This urban oasis is a veritable checklist of habitats including forest, meadow, saltwater beach, and sand dunes. Aptly named, Discovery Park is a versatile dominion in which you can take a quick 30-minute jaunt or play "Blair Witch" and get lost in the wilderness. The grounds are rife with fruit during blackberry season, providing a delectable mid-hike snack. The main trail is the 3-mile Loop Trail, which meanders through many of the aforementioned habitats and past the abandoned army barracks. Several steep trails will take you down to the beach and to the West Point lighthouse, which was built in 1881. Off of West Point, you can sometimes spot sea lions, seals, orcas, or porpoises. While the water is never quite warm enough to swim in, people often sunbathe on the beaches during those scorching 75-degree summer days. Some of the less-modest park visitors have deemed the beach clothing-optional. The South Bluff Trail will lead you to spectacular views of Mount Rainier and the city skyline. For a short but interesting jaunt, the half-mile Wolf Tree nature trail brings you through the dwellings of coyotes, river otters, muskrats, and bobcats. Additionally, 253 species of birds dwell within the park.

Washington Park Arboretum

2300 Arboretum Dr E • 4 miles • Easy • Map 22
Stroll through the 250 acres of one of the Northwest's largest collections of plants and trees, numbering upwards of 5,500 species. The Arboretum Waterfront Trail starts at the parking lot and leads to Marsh and Foster Islands. In the warm seasons, this trail is ideal for bird watching. From Foster Island, you can hike to the north tip and enjoy a stunning view across Union Bay. Azalea Way is an easy-going ¾-mile walk through the—you guessed it—azaleas. To get there from downtown Seattle, drive east on Madison Street to Lake Washington Boulevard and turn left into the Arboretum.

Sand Point Magnuson Park

7400 Sandpoint Wy NE • 4 miles • Easy • Map 27
Magnuson Park is a 350-acre area located in the middle of a former Navy facility. Parts of it are paved and crowded, but you can also find secluded grass and wetland habitats to wander through. The trailhead to the Cross-Park Trail, located next to the playground, will take you through the grasslands. Promontory Point meanders through a restored wildlife habitat. You can find that trail at the south end of the park.

Tiger Mountain

Issaquah • Moderate
If the above-mentioned urban hikes aren't extreme enough for your lifestyle, but you still don't want to travel far from the city, Tiger Mountain affords the perfect temporary wilderness retreat. It's also a good alternative for hardcore hikers who can't get their cars over the snowy passes in the wintertime. The West Tiger 3 provides a 2,000-foot elevation stretched over five miles. Its switchback-heavy path will definitely make you feel worthy of your fleece. For a less-strenuous wander through the woods, try the Around The Lake Tradition Trail. The Tradition Plateau and Bus Trail are moderate hikes. Look for the skeleton of an abandoned Greyhound bus that gives the latter trail its name. To get there, take exit 20 off I-90 East and follow the signs.

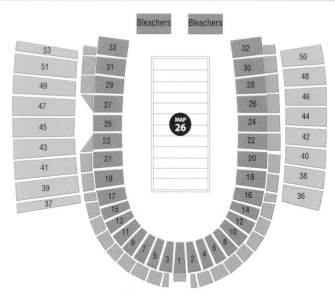

General Information

NFT Map: 26
Address: University of Washington, 315 Hec Edmundson
Pavilion, Seattle, WA 98195
Tickets: 206-543-2200
Website: www.gohuskies.com

Overview

Husky Stadium, home to the University of Washington Huskies, is recognized as one of the nation's most scenic football stadiums. From the upper deck on the stadium's north side, fans have views of downtown Seattle, the Olympic Mountains, and Mt. Rainier (when it's clear, that is). Built in 1920, the stadium seats 72,500 fans—more than 70 percent between the end zones—and ranks among the nation's loudest venues. Game days have turned into ten-hour events, thanks to the pre- and post-game tailgating, which takes place in automobiles, RVs, and boats that dock in special moorings. 1991 saw the peak of Husky football glory with its first and only National Championship. In 2001 the Huskies won the Rose Bowl, and things were looking good for the future. Tickets were almost impossible to come by, and Husky pride was near an all time high. But in the coming years, former head coach Rick Neuheisel became embroiled in a seemingly harmless NCAA betting scandal that took down the athletic director and signaled a downward spiral in the team's fortunes. Despite a few coaching changes, the Huskies have been floundering near the bottom of the Pac-10 ever since. A word of advice: Unless you are on foot, bike or segue, get a copy of the Husky schedule and avoid the U-District at all costs during game times lest it quadruple your travel time

How to Get Tickets

Individual game tickets can be purchased from the Huskies' website, by calling 206-543-2200, or in person at the ticket office (3910 Montlake Blvd, Graves Building 101). The office is open Monday through Friday from 8:30 am–5 pm.

How to Get There—Driving

From I-5 north or south, take the Highway 520 exit toward Bellevue-Kirkland, then exit on Montlake Boulevard. Turn left and cross the bridge. Husky Stadium is on the right. From Highway 405 north or south, take Highway 520 exit toward Seattle and cross the Evergreen Point Floating Bridge heading west. Exit on Montlake Boulevard. Turn left and cross the bridge. Husky Stadium is on the right.

Parking

Parking in adjoining neighborhoods is prohibited. Public parking lots on the east side of the UW campus generally fill 30–60 minutes before kick-off. Parking is on a first-come, first-served basis.

How to Get There—By Bus

The UW offers all ticket holders free bus rides to and from games when they present their game ticket to the driver. Seattle Metro buses offer dozens of routes from throughout the Puget Sound region.

General Information

NFT Map: 15
Address: 305 Harrison St, Seattle, WA 98109
Tickets: 206-283-DUNK
Basketball Websites:
www.seattlesonics.com; www.wnba/storm
Arena Website: www.seattlecenter.com

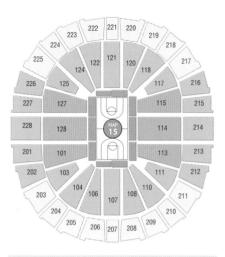

Overview

The 17,000-seat Key Arena is home (at least for now) to the Seattle Supersonics of the NBA and the Seattle Storm of the WNBA. It also hosts events such as circuses, ice skating exhibitions, professional wrestling, NCAA basketball, and concerts. Located in Seattle Center under the Space Needle, the arena opened in 1962 and has served as the host of Seattle's professional sports championships—the 1979 Sonics and the 2004 Storm. In 1995 the arena received a $75-million renovation, leaving the exterior as is, but dropping the playing court 22 feet underground to provide 3,000 additional seats. A 15-year naming rights deal with a bank has provided TV announcers endless pun opportunities such as "the Key to tonight's game" and "the defense is really Keyed in right now." The Key also provides an intimate setting to watch a game, especially when compared to the new NBA palaces being built (see The Staples Center in LA). With great sightlines and the ability to get really loud, it's a fun place to spend an evening. Just don't get too comfortable. First Mr. Sonic (Nate McMillan) defected to Portland, and then Mr. Starbucks (Howard Schultz) sold the team to the two-timing Clay Bennett of Oklahoma City. Bennett promised to try to keep the Sonics in Seattle then promptly got permission from the NBA to move them to his hometown. Then the City of Seattle sued Bennett to keep the team in Key Arena through 2010. Hopefully this epic soap opera will end with the Sonics sticking in Seattle. But don't hold your breath.

How to Get Tickets

Individual game tickets can be purchased through Ticketmaster (www.ticketmaster.com), by calling 206-283-DUNK, or in person at the Key Arena box office. If you're feeling brave, scalpers are known to wander the grounds of Seattle Center looking to unload tickets before a game.

How to Get There—Driving

From the north or south on I-5, take the Mercer Street exit and follow the signs to Seattle Center. Key Arena is on the northwest corner of the Seattle Center grounds, with street access along First Avenue North and cross streets Thomas and Republican.

Parking

Public lot, meter, and street parking are available along First Avenue and Fifth Avenue North, Mercer Street, and throughout the lower Queen Anne neighborhood.

How to Get There—By Ferry

Boats arrive hourly at Colman Dock on the waterfront. Key Arena is about 1-1/2 miles north of the ferry terminal, best reached by Seattle Metro busses.

How to Get There—By Bus

Seattle Metro buses offer dozens of routes from throughout the Puget Sound region. For routes and schedules, visit www.metrokc.gov.

How to Get There—By Monorail

Even if the 'ol heap of tourist metal is actually running, it's still not worth the $4 roundtrip ticket price.

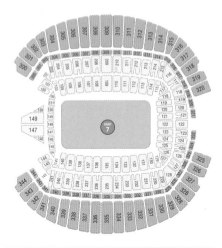

General Information

NFT Map:	7
Address:	800 Occidental Ave. S
	Seattle, WA 98134
Mariners Office Phone:	206-346-4000
Tickets:	888-635-4295
Football Website:	www.seahawks.com
Soccer Website:	www.seattlesounders.net
Stadium Website:	www.qwestfield.com

Overview

The Seattle Seahawks finally play football as it is meant to be played—outdoors and in the elements—after abandoning the Kingdome for the newfangled Seahawk Stadium (now called Qwest Field) for the start of the 2002 season. With more than 67,000 seats and a sloping roof design that covers 70 percent of the seating area, Qwest Field is both comfortable and loud. Fans enjoy wide seats that, in the front rows, are only 40–50 feet from the playing field. If you can't afford the primo tickets, grab a metal bleacher seat in the Hawk's Nest on the north side of the field and bond with the diehards. This fantastic atmosphere has provided the Seahawks with one of the National Football League's top home field advantages, one that helped lead the team to its first Super Bowl in 2006. Qwest Field also also hosts the home games of the other football—er, soccer—team in town, the Seattle Sounders, who play in the A-

League division. While the couple of thousand loyal Sounder fans won't rival Manchester United any time soon, it's a cheap and fun way to experience the stadium, especially when arch rival Portland comes to town.

How to Get Tickets

Tickets sell out fast, so buy them early from the Seahawks website, by calling 888-635-4295, or in person at the Qwest Field box office when they go on sale. Children aged two and up require tickets.

How to Get There

From the north and south, exit I-5 at James Street, Fourth Avenue or Airport Way. From the east, exit I-90 where it ends at Fourth Avenue and turn right. Then turn right at Royal Brougham Way.

Parking

For Sunday afternoon games, street parking can be had for free if you get there at least three hours early to snag a space. It can be found in Pioneer Square, SoDo, and the International District. Three parking lots near the stadium open three hours prior to game time, however many of these spaces are sold in advance so be aware of limited status. Private lots are available on First and Fourth Avenues surrounding the stadium.

How to Get There—By Ferry

Boats arrive hourly at Colman Dock on the waterfront, just a 10-minute walk from the stadium. Walk east on Occidental Avenue and turn right.

How to Get There—By Bus

Most Seattle Metro buses swing through downtown close to the stadium.

How to Get There—By Light Rail

Sound Transit runs special trains on Sundays from Tacoma and Everett when the Seahawks are playing. Check the website for details (www. soundtransit.org).

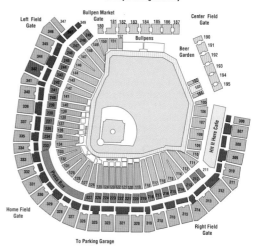

Legend:
- Lower Box
- Field
- Terrace Club INF
- Terrace Clun OF
- View Box
- Lower Outfield Reserved
- Lower Outfield Reserved (Sec 103)
- View Reserved
- View Reserved Family (Sec 103)
- Left Field Bleachers
- Center Field Bleachers

General Information

NFT Map: 7
Address: 1250 First Ave S,
                  Seattle, WA 98134
Mariners Office Phone: 206-346-4000
Tickets: 206-622-HITS
Website: www.seattlemariners.com

Overview

Mariners fans like to revel in the glory days of 1995, when the team played in the Kingdome and almost (yeah, almost) made it to the World Series. But baseball purists point to the opening of Safeco Field on July 16, 1999, as the real crowning achievement for the Mariners. Finally, Seattle fans had a real ballpark with real grass, real sky, and real natural light. Since then, Safeco Field has become the city's summer cathedral, a gathering place for families, friends, couples, and singles to watch baseball, nosh on fancy baseball fare, and socialize in the ballpark's many congregation areas—all of which offer unobstructed views of the field. And in case the rain clouds come rushing in, a mechanical roof can cover the ballpark in just 12 minutes to keep the faithful dry. More than 3 million people jammed into Safeco annually during the early 2000s, especially during the Mariners' record-setting 116-win season in 2001. But thanks to the traitor trifecta (Ken Griffey, Randy Johnson, and Alex Rodriguez) and clueless ownership, a million or so have been whittled from that attendance figure. Luckily, they were smart enough to sign Ichiro to keep local Japanese fans flocking to right field to watch him work his magic. The crowd is one of the most polite in baseball (except when Pay-Rod is in town) which makes for a fun-for-the-whole-family type of environment. If you like your games a little rowdier, head for the beer garden in center field. They have a bunch of micro brews on tap to ensure an eventful and entertaining evening, even if the Mariners' bullpen gives up the lead in the eighth inning again. Accompany your overpriced beer with a basket of their inexplicably delicious nachos. Damn, those things are tasty.

How to Get Tickets

Individual game tickets can be purchased from the Mariners' website by calling 206-822-HITS, or in person at Mariners Team Stores at Safeco Field and downtown Seattle. You can also buy tickets at the Safeco Field Box Office, open weekdays from 9 am–5 pm and weekends from 10 am–4 pm. You can also try your luck with a variety of scalpers that troll Occidental Avenue before the games. Bargains can be had, but beware of scams. Tickets are required for children older than two.

How to Get There—Driving

Seattle is notorious for its freeway traffic, so travel with care and patience on the way to weeknight games. From the south, exit I-5 at Spokane Street and turn right on First Avenue. From the north, exit I-5 at James Street, and turn left on First Avenue. From the east, exit I-90 where it ends at Fourth Avenue and turn right. Then turn right at Royal Brougham Way.

Parking

Street parking can be found in Pioneer Square, SoDo, and the International District. The Mariners operate a parking garage across Edgar Martinez Way. In addition, dozens of parking lots within ten blocks of Safeco Field provide game day parking for anywhere from $10 to $30, depending on convenience and location.

How to Get There—By Ferry

Ferryboats arrive hourly at Colman Dock on the waterfront, just a 10-15 minute walk from the ballpark. Walk two blocks east to First Avenue and turn right.

How to Get There—By Bus

Any bus that goes downtown will get you close, since Safeco is only a 10-minute walk from downtown. Seattle Metro buses 15 and 18 stop closest to Safeco Field but can get packed on game days.

General Information

Directions and hours for beaches, pools, and parks: www.seattle.gov

Overview

Since there are only 1-2 months out of the year when the water in Seattle becomes warm enough to swim in without the threat of hypothermia, there are not a great deal of favorable options for swimming. Even when it's been hot for a while, the water rarely heats up enough to entice most people, particularly in the open water areas. Still, on any given sunny day, many Seattleites adorn their ashen bodies with bathing suits and take to the beaches and pools. Options may be slightly deficient, but they are numerous nonetheless.

Beaches

The water in Lake Washington remains frigid year round, but that can feel pretty good on those rare stiflingly hot summer days. Of course, everyone in town has the same idea, so most of the beaches get crowded fast. **Magnuson Park (Map 27)** and **Madison Park (Map 22)** are by far the most popular, followed by **Madrona (Map 6)** and **Mount Baker (Map 40) Parks**. They are more for waders and sunbathers. **Matthews Beach Park (Map 34)**, **Seward Park (Map 40)**, and **Prichard Island Beach (Map 41)** tend to be less crowded and a bit more pleasant overall. All of the beach parks have rafts, diving boards, picnic areas, and lifeguards on duty. If you are looking for open water swimming, you can find it off the beaten path at Matthews and Seward. Matthews Beach is a welcome end to a hike along the Burke-Gilman Trail.

Golden Gardens (Map 33), which overlooks the Puget Sound, is by far the most beautiful swimming location. Unfortunately, the water is almost always unbearably cold, but the nice sandy beach is good for sunbathing, strolling, and BBQs.

The water in Green Lake is notoriously filthy (swimmer's itch anyone?), but that doesn't appear to deter people on a hot day. There are two beaches on Green Lake, **East Beach (Map 31)** and **West Beach (Map 30)**. They both have rafts, diving boards, and lifeguards.

Pools

If you want to swim in clean water that isn't just warmed by the urine of children, Coleman and Mounger pools are another option. They both heat their water to 85 degrees. **Coleman (Map 37)** is an Olympic-sized pool which overlooks the beach and is filled with saltwater. It also boasts a giant tube slide. **Mounger (Map 11)** has a large pool with a corkscrew slide and a smaller pool for wading and children's swimming lessons. Both of these outdoor pools are only open during the summer.

If you are dying for a dip in the off-season, you can always pay a visit to one of Seattle's warm-water indoor pools which offer lap swimming and water aerobics. There are nominal admission fees.

Wading Pools & Water Features

If you just want to cool off your feet, there are numerous shallow wading pools in parks and playfields around the city. They are, of course, usually crawling with children. Wading pools are drained in the off-season.

For that invigorating, running-through-the-sprinklers sensation, check out the water features at **Judkins Park (Map 9)** and **Pratt Park (Map 9)**. **The International Fountain (Map 15)** (the giant, water-spewing ball) in Seattle Center is usually full of tourists, but if you find yourself sweltering at the Bite, Folklife, or Bumbershoot, it can be welcome refreshment. It's also great fun to play in the volcano fountain at **Cal Anderson Park (Map 3)**.

Beaches	Address	Phone	Map
Madrona Park Beach	853 Lake Washington Blvd	206-684-4075	6
Madison Park Beach	E Madison St & E Howe St	206-684-4075	22
Warren G Magnuson Park	7400 Sand Point Wy NE	206-684-4946	27
Green Lake Park West Beach	7312 W Green Lake Dr N	206-684-4075	30
Green Lake Park East Beach	7201 E Green Lake Dr N	206-684-4075	31
Golden Gardens	8099 Seaview Ave NW	206-684-4075	33
Matthews Beach Park	NE 95th St & 45th Ave NE	206-684-4075	34
Mount Baker Park Beach	2301 Lake Washington Blvd	206-684-4075	40
Seward Park Beach	5902 Lake Washington Blvd S	206-684-4075	40
Prichard Island Beach	8400 55th Ave S	206-684-4075	41
Calkins Landing	SE 28th St & 60th Ave SE	206-236-3545	42
Clark Beach	E Mercer Wy	206-236-3546	42
Groveland Beach	W Mercer Wy	206-236-3547	42
Luther Burbank Park	2040 84th Ave SE	206-236-3548	42
Enatai Beach Park	3519 108th Ave SE	425-452-4448	43
Newcastle Beach Park	4400 Lake Washington Blvd SE	425-452-4450	43
Chesterfield Beach Park	2501 100th Ave SE	425-452-4445	45
Chism Beach Park	1175 96th Ave SE	425-452-4446	45
Clyde Beach Park	2 92nd Ave NE	425-452-4447	45
Medina Beach Park	501 Evergreen Pt Rd	425-233-6400	45
Meydenbauer Beach Park	419 98th Ave NE	425-452-4449	45

Pools	Address	Phone	Map		Fees
Medgar Evers Pool	500 23rd Ave	206-684-4766	5	Indoor	Ages 1–17 & over 64: $2.75, 18–64: $3.75
Mounger Pool	2535 32nd Ave W	206-684-4708	11	Outdoor	Ages 1–17 & over 64: $2.75, 18–64: $3.75
Queen Anne Pool	1920 1st Ave W	206-386-4282	13	Indoor	Ages 1–17 & over 64: $2.75, 18–64: $3.75
Ballard Pool	1471 NW 67th St	206-684-4094	29	Indoor	Ages 1–17 & over 64: $2.75, 18–64: $3.75
Evans Pool	7201 E Green Lake Dr N	206-684-4961	31	Indoor	Ages 1–17 & over 64: $2.75, 18–64: $3.75
Madison Pool	13401 Meridian Ave N	206-684-4979	33	Indoor	Ages 1–17 & over 64: $2.75, 18–64: $3.75
Meadowbrook Pool	10515 35th Ave NE	206-684-4989	34	Indoor	Ages 1–17 & over 64: $2.75, 18–64: $3.75
Coleman Pool	8603 Fauntleroy Wy SW	206-684-7494	37	Outdoor	Ages 1–17 & over 64: $2.75, 18–64: $3.75
Southwest Pool	2801 SW Thistle St	206-684-7440	37	Indoor	Ages 1–17 & over 64: $2.75, 18–64: $3.75
Rainier Beach Pool	8825 Rainier Ave S	206-386-1944	41	Indoor	Ages 1–17 & over 64: $2.75, 18–64: $3.75
Bellevue Aquatic Center	601 143rd Ave NE	425-452-4444	46	Indoor	Adults: $4.75, under 12: $3.75
Redmond Pool	17535 NE 104 St	425-233-3031	49	Indoor	$3.50, Seniors $3.25

Wading and Sprinklers	Address	Phone	Map	Type
Cal Anderson Park	1635 1st Ave	206-684-7796	3	Wading
Judkins Park	2150 S Norman St	206-684-7796	9	Wading, Sprinkler
Pratt Park	1800 S Mainv St	206-684-7796	9	Sprinkler
Peppi's Playground	3233 E Spruce St	206-684-7796	10	Wading
Powell Barnett Park	352 Martin Luther King Jr Wy	206-684-7796	10	Wading
E Queen Anne Playfield	160 Howe St	206-684-7796	13	Wading
International Fountain	305 Harrison St	206-684-7200	15	Sprinkler
Miller Playfield	330 19th Ave E	206-684-7796	18	Wading
Volunteer Park	1247 15th Ave E	206-684-7796	18	Wading
Ballard Commons Park	5701 22nd Ave NW	206-684-7796	23	Sprinkler
Gilman Playground	923 NW 54th St	206-684-7796	23	Wading
Wallingford Playfield	4219 Wallingford Ave N	206-684-7796	25	Wading
View Ridge Playfield	4408 NE 70th St	206-684-7796	27	Wading
Warren G Magnuson Park	7400 Sand Pointt Wy NE	206-684-7796	27	Wading
Green Lake Park	N 73rd St & W Green Lake Dr N	206-684-7796	31	Wading
Dahl Playfield	7700 25th Ave NE	206-684-7796	32	Wading
Ravenna Park	5520 Ravenna Ave NE	206-684-7796	32	Wading
Bitter Lake	13035 Linden Ave N	206-684-7796	33	Wading
Sandel Playground	9053 1st Ave NW	206-684-7796	33	Wading
Soundview Playfield	1590 NW 90 St	206-684-7796	33	Wading
Northacres Park	12800 1st Ave NE	206-684-7796	34	Wading
Hiawatha Playfield	2700 California Ave SW	206-684-7796	35	Wading
Delridge Playfield	4501 Delridge Wy SW	206-684-7796	36	Wading
EC Hughes Playground	2805 SW Holden St	206-684-7796	37	Wading
Lincoln Park	8011 Fauntleroy Wy SW	206-684-7796	37	Wading
Highland Park Playfield	1100 SW Cloverdale St	206-684-7796	38	Wading
South Park Playground	8319 8th Ave S	206-684-7796	38	Wading
Beacon Hill Playfield	1820 13th Ave S	206-684-7796	39	Wading
Georgetown Playfield	750 S Homer St	206-684-7796	39	Wading
Van Asselt Playground	2820 S Myrtle St	206-684-7796	41	Wading

General Information

Amtrak Reservations:	1-800-USA-RAIL (872-7245)
Amtrak Website:	www.amtrak.com
King Street Station Address:	303 S Jackson St 98104
King Street Station Phone:	206-382-4125
Hours:	6 am–10:30 pm daily

Overview

Some travelers hate to fly. Others just hate the airlines. And don't even mention Greyhound. When the fear and anger become too profound, there's always Amtrak. Amtrak is hardly a perfect substitute—because of geographic and commercial concerns, train routes can't match the flexibility of flying, and the bureaucracy can get just as snarled and inefficient as any airline. However, there's a sweet Zen to the experience of sitting still for hours as the train chugs towards its destination, with nothing to do but read or stare out the windows as America flies by.

Located in Pioneer Square on the cusp of the International District, King Street Station services Seattle Amtrak traffic. It's a handsome rust brick building complete with a clock tower; it was the city's tallest structure when erected in 1906. Clueless mid-century renovations dulled the station's luster, and travelers dwindled over the years, leading to a certain defeated quality in the air as one waits for a train. While a renovation project is finally underway to restore King Street Station's original stateliness, progress has been sluggish, so don't get there too early.

Fares

Amtrak prices tend to fluctuate wildly, so like airlines, it's best to book your trip early. Bargain hunters with sufficient lead time can find promotional discounts. Last minute types may find themselves paying near airline prices for a trip that takes ten times as long. Student and senior discounts are available, so consider lying about your age. Amtrak coach seats are very comfortable, and many passengers elect to sleep sitting up (or hunched over) on red-eye trips. But it's a rare voyager who can take that kind of punishment more than one night in a row, so contemplate a sleeping car for marathon train sessions. It's not cheap—a private car can easily double the price of a ticket, and they're hardly deluxe accommodations (imagine a closet with bunk beds). But lying prone behind a locked door is a dream shared by every coach passenger after the first 24 hours of travel.

Service

Amtrak doesn't own the tracks their trains roll on, giving freight trains the right of way. This can occasionally lead to frustrating delays. If you need to get there fast, it is advisable to find alternate means. Rail travel is as much about the journey as the destination. Speaking of which, alcohol is available in the club car at airport bar prices. Luckily, they don't have that 3oz rule, so sneaking your own adult beverages on board is a piece of delicious cake.

Carry a stash of food along, adjusting quantities to suit the length of the trip. Even if you spring for expensive meals in the dinner car, the food can be lousy and there isn't enough of it. The prices of snacks in the club car are inflated as a courtesy to Amtrak's captive clientele, so bring your own pretzels.

Going to Portland

Stumptown is a fun place to visit, and the Amtrak Cascades takes you there in style. The Spanish-designed Talgo trains provide comfy seats with big windows for great views of Puget Sound. They thankfully discourage the use of cell phones on board, and they even offer a free film (just make sure to bring your own headphones). And once you dig into some Ivar's clam chowder and sip on a Black Butte Porter in the dining car, you'll never take Greyhound to Portland again.

Going to Vancouver, BC

The Amtrak Cascades departs Seattle every morning for a four hour trip to "the poor man's Amsterdam." Be advised that Vancouver, British Columbia is located in the sovereign nation of Canada—make sure to bring your passport and remember that all Amtrak trains are subject to random searches by border officials. It's a beautiful journey up along the coast, but pesky freight train traffic will inevitably cause delays. For a fun Friday night getaway, Amtrak also offers a very un-Greyhound like bus from King Street Station for a good price.

Going to Los Angeles

The Coast Starlight leaves Seattle every morning headed south and makes Los Angeles in about 35 hours. Prices for a one-way fare range between $89 and $180, depending on what time of year and how far in advance you are buying your tickets. Popular stops along the way include Portland, OR (although take the Cascades if you can) and Emeryville, CA (about 23 hours of travel, and only an hour's bus ride from San Francisco).

Going to Chicago

The Empire Builder leaves Seattle daily and reaches the Windy City in a mere 45 hours for a one-way fare between $134 and $294. That's a long ride with two guaranteed nights sleeping upright in coach and not bathing, but such asceticism can sometimes lead to spiritual fulfillment. So think of it as time to get to know yourself. Among the cities the Empire Builder services are Whitefish, MT, Fargo, ND, Minneapolis, MN, and Milwaukee, WI. Plus, there's no better way to appreciate the scenery of the heartland than through the window of a train.

General Information

Address:	811 Stewart St
	Seattle, WA 98101
Main Phone:	206-628-5526
Baggage:	206-628-5555
Greyhound	
Package Express:	206-628-5555
Customer Service:	206-628-5561
Greyhound Charter:	800-454-2487
Greyhound Website:	www.greyhound.com
Hours:	6:00 am–11:30 am daily
Greyhound	
Package Express:	6:00 am–11:30 am daily
Ticketing:	6:00 am–11:30 pm daily
Food Service:	Monday–Sunday: 6 am–9 pm
	Holiday: 6 am–9 pm

Overview

Nothing epitomizes a "long day's journey into night" like traveling on a bus full of folks bridging the many miles between Los Angeles and Vancouver. Sure, Amtrak is cleaner, faster, and more scenic, but where else can you experience traveling in close quarters amongst more parolees than voting-eligible citizens? Ah, the smells, the stories, the uniquely gritty perspective you get only from traveling Greyhound. Of course it's dirt cheap, considering current eye-gouging gas prices. What could be better than a weekend jaunt to Oly and a show at Capitol Theater for only $22 round-trip, or check out some of Tacoma's up-and-coming talent at Hell's Kitchen for only $12 (round-trip from Seattle).

Station

Seattle's Greyhound station is not the most awe-inspiring public space in town. In fact, it makes King Street Station look downright Grand Central-esque. It's located in one of the last truly sketchy parts of downtown at 811 Stewart Street (at 8th Ave). It's a short walk east from the Westlake Center shopping nucleus, where many cross-city Metro buses travel. Or take the 66 or 545 to be deposited closer to the Greyhound terminal.

Tickets

Tickets may be purchased in person at the terminal, online at www.greyhound.com, or over the phone at 1-800-231-2222. The first option is the least convenient due to the long and disorderly lines at the Seattle station; advance reservations are not necessary.

Fares

The Greyhound website offers special e-fares, including eSavers, Companion Fares, and Go Anywhere Fares. Discounted fares are also available for students, seniors, children, and military personnel.

Baggage

Passengers are allowed two pieces of checked baggage and two carry-on items per person. An additional fee will be charged for baggage over the 50 pound weight limit. Baggage insurance is available, but as with any type of travel (especially Greyhound), it's wise to keep your most valuable items on your person or leave them at home.

Other Services

Greyhound Package Xpress is available for fast shipping on oversized or overweight items, or as a shipping alternative to USPS, FedEx, and UPS. They offer door-to-door and online service. For more information about Package Xpress call 1-800-739-5020.

General Information

Zipcar Website: www.zipcar.com
Phone: 866-4ZIPCAR

Seattle is a walkable city with fairly adequate public transportation, so it's feasible for denizens to live comfortably without owning a car. In fact, the freedom that comes with removing that albatross from around the neck can be quite exhilarating. Farewell to high insurance and fuel costs, the travails of big city parking, and the constant threat of mechanical breakdown—hello to the smug satisfaction of reducing one's ecological impact on the tender earth. Still, schlepping laundry, groceries, and children around the city on the bus isn't always ideal, and sooner or later, a private conveyance becomes temporarily necessary. Hence the concept of "car sharing" catching on in nearly fifty American cities, including Seattle.

Zipcar provides customers with access to a fleet of autos parked in dozens of convenient parking spots throughout the area. For an annual subscription fee, users can reserve a vehicle up to fifteen minutes in advance (on the phone or through their website) and drive for $8–9.50 an hour. A membership card and a PIN unlocks the car, which is programmed to start only for the particular subscriber holding the reservation. Frequent drivers can choose various monthly packages that include pre-paid road time and reduced hourly rates. Zipcar covers gas, insurance and maintenance costs, and well over 100 cars, trucks, SUVs and hybrids are available— even a few sporty convertibles for a spontaneous joy ride.

Zipcar took over Flex Car, a Seattle-based company with a similar business plan, which was partly funded by the King County government. Flex Car suffered some growing pains which caused grief to its customers in the early days. Of course there were customer complaints about Zipcar at first as well. How many Seattleites does it take to change a light bulb? Five: One to change it and four to complain about how the old one was better. Nonetheless, most citizens of the Emerald City agree that car sharing is an excellent idea in light of current affairs.

General Information

City of Seattle Department of Transportation (DOT)

Address:	PO Box 34996
	Seattle, Wa 98124
Phone:	206-684-ROAD (7623)
Website:	www.seattle.gov/transportation/
Webcams:	www.seattle.gov/trafficcams/

Orientation

The bad news is, Seattle is not an easy city to drive in without getting lost or frustrated. There are tons of one-way streets, dead ends, windy roads, and many bridges. Sometimes a street will disappear for awhile, then reappear blocks later. In fact, it was listed by Sterling as one of the top-ten most difficult cities to navigate, clocking in at number eight. On top of all that, traffic, especially on I-5, is absolutely horrendous, with no cure on the horizon. This is all due to the fact that Seattle keeps growing at furious pace and is split between large bodies of water and I-5, making it nearly impossible to get from point A to point B via a straight line. The good news is, once you do figure out how to get around, there are many alternative routes to take to avoid traffic. Just get out there, strap on your seatbelt, and force yourself to learn the roads. Once you get a route down, try changing it up. Sometimes it can be as simple as going one street over to avoid traffic. Generally, only streets that run more or less east-west are called "streets." Only streets that run for the most part north-south are called "avenues." However, roads, boulevards, and ways can go any direction they please. In other words, good luck. Also, Seattle is full of bold cyclists, but if you just keep reminding yourself that they mean one less car on the road, you'll find your patience for them will increase.

Bridges

Seattle is surrounded by water, so get used to dealing with lots of bridges. Drawbridges are enemy number one for the hurried driver. There is no way to know when a bridge is going to go up, unless you are in a really big hurry. Then it's guaranteed. Other drawbridge hyjinks include the Ballard, University District, and Montlake bridges. And that's when someone hasn't decided to make stopping traffic their final act, by leaping off of it. The other drawbridges you will have to deal with are the Ballard, University District, and Montlake Bridges. If you get stuck when a bridge is going up, all you can do is turn off your engine (idling cars are bad for the environment) and wait it out. Another notable bridge that serves I-90 and connects Seattle to Mercer Island is the Lacey V. Murrow Memorial Bridge—the second longest floating bridge in the world. If you just have to experience the longest floating bridge in the world, don't despair—the Evergreen Point Floating Bridge (a.k.a. Bridge 520) is just a few miles north. Both of these get you to I-405, and one is usually busier than the other, so pay close attention to traffic reports before you make your choice. Either way, you will be treated to a beautiful view on your way across. Also important to water-body navigation are the West Seattle Bridge and the George Washington Memorial Bridge (a.k.a. the Aurora Bridge).

Dealing with Highway 99

Highway 99, the original superhighway of Seattle, runs parallel to I-5. It can be a useful route when I-5 is congested (which is almost always). However, it can be difficult to navigate. You may find yourself heading north on the stretch from Greenlake Avenue N to Denny and you need to be going south or vice versa. Well, that's too bad. Sometimes you just have to stick it out until you find an exit or risk turning off into the black hole that is Queen Anne Hill. Also, the Alaskan Way Viaduct (part of Highway 99) is currently being evaluated for structural safery regarding a dreaded earthquake. In the meantime drive over it fast, before it comes crumbling down on top you. Stay tuned to find out what happens to Seattle's version of the Big Dig.

Major Expressways

I-5, Seattle's main freeway, running north/south, is almost always congested. From I-5 you can access either I-90 or SR520 running east/west parallel to each other. One is often busier than the other, so pay attention to traffic reports. Running parallel to I-5 is Highway 99, which will go no farther than five miles west of it, and I-405 running on the other side of Lake Washington. I-5 has expressways in the center of the freeway that anyone can access, but be careful because exits are limited and you may end up going farther than you would have liked. The city provides real-time traffic and web cameras at their website listed above.

DMVs

Visits to the Seattle DMV are relatively painless, especially if you go on a weekday morning. If you must go on a Saturday, be prepared to wait. However, try saving yourself a trip by visiting their website at www.dmv.org to find out what can be done online.

Seattle DMVs	Address	Phone
Greenwood	320 N 85th St	206-706-4269
	Seattle, WA 98103	
Seattle-North	907 N 135th St	206-368-7261
	Seattle, WA 98133	
Seattle-Downtown Limited Service Office	380 Union St	206-464-6845
	Seattle, WA 98101	
Seattle-East	5811 Rainier Ave S	206-721-4560
	Seattle, WA 98118	
Seattle-West	8830 25th Ave SW	206-764-4143
	Seattle, WA 98106	

General Information

Parking Ticket Payments
In Person: 600 5th Ave
                   Seattle, Wa 98104
Phone: 206-233-7000
Website: www.seattle.gov/courts/ticket/
                   ticketinformation.htm

Parking Meters

Seattle has installed green computerized meters throughout the city that accept credit cards. You simply pick the amount of time you want, slide your credit card, and a sticker will be printed for you to place on the inside of the window closest to the sidewalk. This is truly amazing for those striving for a cashless society. It's also handy because the sticker is valid at any location, so any unused time can be used somewhere else. However, if for whatever reason, the machine is not accepting your credit card or is broken, you can't park there! The city, of course, apologizes for the inconvenience, but who is going to apologize to your boss? The machines also accept change but not dollar bills.

Residential Parking Zone Program

Many Seattle neighborhoods (usually those near commercial strips) participate in a permit program. It is meant to discourage long-term parking by non-residents. Look for the green and white signs which limit you to two hour parking except by permit. Permits cost $35 and are good for two years. Permits can only be issued to residents who live on a block with signs installed or within the boundaries of the RPZ. In order to apply, you must have proof of residency and current Washington State vehicle registration. One permit is issued per vehicle and one guest permit can be issued per household. Temporary permits may be issued for up to sixty days for construction, out of state, new, and student vehicles. You may obtain a permit by mail or in person. Call 206-684-5086 Monday through Friday 8 am to 5 pm for more information.

Mail requests to:

Seattle Department of Transportation
Residential Parking Zone Program, 37th Floor
700 Fifth Ave, Suite 3900
PO Box 34996
Seattle, WA 98124

Curbs

It is important to understand Seattle's curb color system. After searching for a parking spot on Capitol Hill for two hours, you finally find the perfect one right in front of your apartment. Too good to be true, right?

Well, it probably is. If the curb is painted white, it is either a three-minute loading zone or police and fire department parking. If the curb is yellow, it is a thirty-minute loading zone. Red means no parking anytime and they mean it. You will get towed so fast it'll make your head spin. Alternating yellow and red makes it a bus zone, so don't even think about parking there.

Parking Tickets and Impound

Parking tickets issued by the Seattle Police Department are handled by the Seattle Municipal Court. You can pay them online at www.seattle.gov or over the phone at 206-684-5600. If you fail to pay your ticket within 15 days, the fine will automatically double. Unpaid parking tickets will result in a hold on your vehicle registration tabs.

To contest a parking ticket, you can request a hearing before a Municipal Court Magistrate to gently explain why they should shove their fines where the sun doesn't shine. You can contact them at 206-684-5600.

If your car gets towed, call the Seattle Police Department (206-682-2869), although it may take a few hours for it to show up in their system. Towed cars are taken to one of three impound lots in Seattle, ABC Towing (206-682-2869), E T Towing (206-622-9188), or Lincoln Towing (206-364-2000). In order to get your vehicle free, you will be required to pay the fine to the impound lot immediately, and the registered owner must be present with appropriate documentation. Under special circumstances, arrangements can be made for someone other than the registered owner to retrieve the vehicle. Vehicles in storage for over 21 days may be put up for auction and/or shipped to Albania.

Extra Parking Tips:

It is legal to park facing any direction on either side of the street. Well, within reason of course; you can't veer across three lanes into oncoming traffic to catch that that perfect spot on the other side of the street.

There are signs all over that say No Parking north/south/east/west of here. It just means, don't park past that sign, so keep an eye out for those sneaky little things.

Street parking is free after 6 pm on Sundays and holidays.

It is illegal to park a car in the same spot for more than 72 hours. Failure to move your car around the block for no good reason will result in a ticket or towing. It is also illegal to let your car bumper hang even a millimeter over the driveway (including your own) into the sidewalk. If a traffic cop is bored, they will slap you with a $38 fine with no apologies

General Info

Mailing Address: 201 S Jackson St
                     KSC-TR-0415
                     Seattle, WA 98104

Website: transit.metrokc.gov
Main Phone: 206-553-3000
Customer Service: 206-553-3060
Lost and Found: 206-553-3090

Overview

Anyone who isn't convinced that Seattle is a colorful town of eccentrics and madmen needs to ride the bus. This could be true about many American cities, but Seattle's lost souls take to public transportation in a major way, and it won't be a week before any newly-transplanted citizen starts collecting stories that begin with, "There was this crazy guy on the bus…" This is not to dissuade the timid rider, but one should always expect the unexpected when facing so much humanity within an enclosed space.

Many city dwellers who lack wheels for ideological or financial reasons find getting around Seattle on Metro buses a necessity. Service is extensive, reaching throughout the city, but the quality and comfort of the ride varies from one line to the next. Buses between Capitol Hill and the University District run reliably every ten minutes or so for most of the day. A fleet of buses that connect the downtown area with northern 'hoods like Wedgwood and Ravenna can be counted on. And the express buses that rocket passengers to outlying suburbs are always on time. However, like any modern urban transit system, the city faces unique geographic challenges (in this case hills, water, and bridges) that can lead to trouble. Some Metro routes are chronically late, crowded with standing passengers, or peppered with anti-social types, and woe be to the rider who depends on such a bus to get to work every day. Check Metro's website for alternate (if inconvenient) itineraries.

The downtown area is a free zone between the hours of 6 am and 7 pm, so any daytime journey that begins and ends in the heart of the city is on Metro. Here's where it can get confusing. The fare system changes depending on which way the ride is going and when—daytime buses headed for downtown require payment upon entrance, while daytime buses leaving the area collect the cash as you exit. And after 7 pm all buses require the fare up front. Standard adult fare is $1.50, but during peak hours (weekdays 6 to 9am and 3 to 6pm) it's an extra quarter. It's exact change only and drivers and riders alike are impatient to people fiddling in their pockets, so make sure you have your money and pass ready when you step on board. The price rises depending on how far out of the city limits the ride takes you. Discounts for students, seniors, and the disabled cut the cost, and buses are fully equipped to handle those with mobility challenges. Transfers allow re-entry for up to two hours on most lines, and for dedicated (or resigned) daily Metro users, the PugetPass offers savings when you pony up in advance.

Bicyclists can stash their machines on racks attached to the front of the bus, although putting them on or taking them off is prohibited in the Downtown free zone. Car owners can leave their vehicles at a number of Park & Ride locations available through King County, so those with longer commutes can avoid the snarl of inner-city traffic. At press time, the vintage streetcars that roll along the waterfront have been halted while Metro builds their new maintenance center, but they're scheduled to be back on track carting tourists around sometime in 2007. At press time, the vintage streetcars that roll along the waterfront have been halted but there are restoration plans pending a decision about the Alaskan Way Viaduct. In 2008, the downtown bus tunnel reopened after undergoing retrofitting for the new Light Rail, (scheduled to start running in 2009). The bus tunnel whisks express buses underneath downtown Seattle while suckers in cars sit motionless above ground. Sadly, it is only open weekdays from 5 am to 7pm.

A charming custom in Seattle is the bus rider's habit of thanking the driver as he/she disembarks. Most Metro bus drivers deserve this simple courtesy—it must be a stressful, monotonous task hauling tired, sullen strangers to their jobs every day—so don't forget to give your driver the benefit of the doubt.

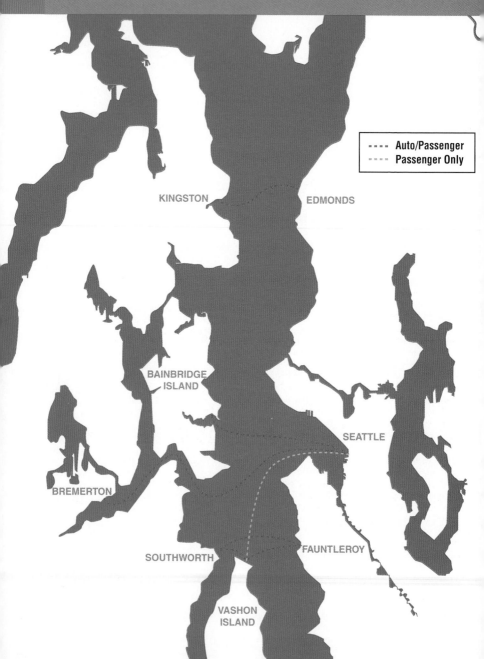

KINGSTON   EDMONDS

---- Auto/Passenger
---- Passenger Only

BAINBRIDGE
ISLAND

SEATTLE

BREMERTON

SOUTHWORTH   FAUNTLEROY

VASHON
ISLAND

General Information

Webiste: www.wsdot.wa.gov/ferries
Phone: 206-464-6400

Overview

The largest ferry system in the country, Washington State Ferries can actually make commuting pleasurable—once you're actually on the boat. The entire ferry system encompasses a total of ten routes and twenty terminals, so be sure you know where you want to go. The boats running to Bainbridge, Bremerton, and a passenger-only boat to Vashon Island are located at Colman Dock at Alaskan Way and Marian Street. The most popular route, from Seattle to Bainbridge, sails every 50 minutes or so during peak hours and approximately every hour at other times until 2 am. Check the website for exact schedules, and note that there is a slight variation at the end of the day on weekends and holidays. The ferries run in all weather, but the Port Townsend and Vashon runs are occasionally limited by extreme low tides. The web site will have current information as well as real-time web cams on the docks. Bikes and motorcycles load through the auto gates and are given preference over cars at loading time. Colman Dock has recently added several food and coffee vendors as well as a small wine bar. (Commuter Comforts is the best of the lot.) There is food, beer, and wine available on the boats (hooray!) until about 8 pm, but don't get too excited since the food is abysmal and overpriced. Once you're actually on the boat, settle in and enjoy the ride. There's an open deck upstairs for viewing. The scenery on a good day is awe-inspiring—the Cascades to the east, Mt. Rainier to the south, the Olympic mountain range to the west, and Puget Sound is, obviously, everywhere. It's a good guess that there are frequent proposals (of one kind or another) on the ferries.

Parking

Parking? Oh please. Your choices are to take your car on—expensive and time-consuming (the auto line at peak hours can be a wait of several boats) or find a lot, a garage, or on-street parking near the terminals. In Seattle, cars left on street between 3 and 6 pm are towed, so a lot or a garage is a safer bet. There are a number of them sprinkled on Western Avenue between Yesler Way and Spring Street. There are also buses that stop in front of Coleman Dock. Check Metro's website (http://transit.metrokc.gov) for details.

Fares

Fares can vary depending on where and when you'll be going, so make sure to check the website before heading out. Of course, bringing a car always drives up the price and in the peak season (May 1 to the second Saturday in October) you'll have to pay more. Thankfully, the ferry system accepts all major credit cards, so you won't have to abandon your car and make a run for an ATM. Round trip fare for passengers from Seattle to Bainbridge/Bremerton and from Edmonds to Kingston is now $6.70 for adults and $5.40 for children. $3.35 for seniors and disabled. Car and driver is $14.45. Walk on from Seattle Pier 50 to Vashon is $8.70. Fauntleroy to Vashon is $4.30 for adults, $3.45 for children and $2.15 for seniors/disabled. Car and driver is $18.50. When possible, leave the car at home and pay an extra buck to bring your bicycle aboard. Your wallet and body will thank you. Finally, for those who ride the boats often, commuter books are available and will save you a bunch of dough.

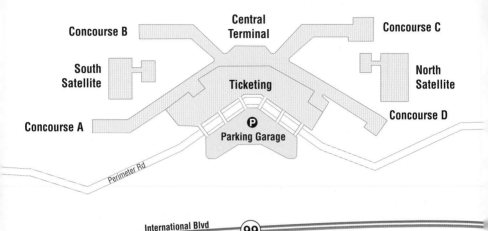

General Information

Address:	17801 International Blvd
	Seattle, WA 98158
Phone:	206-433-5388
Websites:	www.seatac.org
Airport Police:	206-431-3490
Ground Transportation:	Various providers.
	Please check website.
Lost & Found:	206-443-5312
Customer Service:	800-508-1705

Overview

Prior to 1944, Boeing Field was Seattle's main passenger airport. When the U.S. Military took it over for use in World War II, we needed a new commercial airport. Thus, Sea-Tac International Airport was born.

Though in the top 30 of the world's busiest airports, Sea-Tac isn't a terribly harrowing travel experience. It consists of a main terminal with four concourses and two satellite terminals, which are connected to the main terminal via an underground tram. Trains run every 5–10 minutes, so it never takes long to get from one terminal to another. Overall, Sea-Tac is a well-run and organized airport, which is impressive when you consider that it catered to 31 million passengers in 2007.

As with most airports these days, it is advisable to either check in online or at a self check-in station. However, our TSA agents seem to have a handle on security checks, as the line moves fairly quickly most of the time. Of course, in terms of airport travel, it is always advisable not to temp fate.

The one area in which Sea-Tac needs improvement is baggage handling. Even before the ban on liquids forced everyone to check their bags, it took forever for a flight to bring the luggage back to their owners. It is not unheard of for travelers to wait over an hour to collects their bags from a direct and on-time flight.

If you find yourself with some time, you can grab a bite to eat in the new food court or take your chances with the inevitable Starbucks or gift shops in your terminal. For a decent sit-down meal, Anthony's in the Central terminal is your best bet for quality. For a good, stiff (albeit pricy) cocktail, try Cascade's right off the Central terminal.

How to Get There—Driving

From the north or south, take I-5 to Exit 154 B and drive west on State Route 518 to the Sea-Tac Airport Exit. Heading east, take I-405, which turns into State Route 518, to the Sea-Tac Airport Exit. Signs are clearly marked from that point on.

Parking

With cost-effective alternatives available, choosing to drive to Sea-Tac is akin to burning money, but there are many options for those willing to lighten their wallet. The top four floors of the garage offer hourly parking ($4 for the first and up to $30 a day). Long-term parking is also available for $22 a day with a "special weekly rate" of $130. Don't forget to bring your parking ticket with you for use in the exitxpress pay stations.

If you've managed to bribe a friend into picking you up, they can wait for you in the Cell Phone Waiting Lot. To get there, take the 170th/Air Cargo exit from the Airport Expressway. Turn right and take an immediate left into the clearly marked lot. To get to Baggage Claim from the lot, take a right out of the lot and then an immediate left at the To Terminal sign. Follow the signs to Arrivals.

How to Get There—Mass Transit

While many world-class cities have rail connections to their airports (see San Francisco, Chicago, Portland, everything in Europe and Asia, and so on), Seattleites dependent on public transit still rely on the bus to schlep them out to Sea-Tac. Metro is by far the most economical way to travel to and from Sea-Tac. But it's also the most unglamorous, with no space to put your baggage and a guaranteed cast of colorful characters to make your journey memorable. Seriously, if you can convince friends or family to pick you up, you'll save time and your sanity. Coaches stops at the far end of the baggage claim drive and run until midnight. Look for route numbers 194 (about 30 minutes) or 174 (about 45 mintutes) to and from downtown Seattle. You can also take route numbers 140 and 560 to Burien and West Seattle and route number 574 to Lakewood. Metro also has route 180 to service Auburn, Kent, and Burien. If you are traveling during rush hour, you'll be trapped for a few hours in cramped quarters with surly Seattleites. You'll get enough of that on the airplane. For Metro schedules and trip planning, visit www.metrokc.gov. In 2009, look for the new light rail system that will run to and from downtown Seattle. If all goes according to plan, Seattle will finally have a civilized way of getting to the airport. It can't happen soon enough.

How to Get There—Shuttle

For shared rides, Shuttle Express (800-487-7433) services areas within a 30 mile radius. Pick-up and drop-off is on the third floor of the Airport Garage. The check-in for scheduled Airporter services is on the Baggage Claim level. Airporter Shuttle (866-235-5247) serves Western Washington. Capital Aerporter serves Seattle (253-838-7431), Olympia (360-754-7113), Tacoma (253-927-6179), and outside of Western Washington (800-962-3579). Gray Line Downtown Airporter (800-426-7532) departs twice an hour until 11 pm to major downtown Seattle hotels. Check the website for Airport Express schedules and other service areas.

Car Rentals

Avis	800-331-1212
Budget	800-527-7000
Enterprise	206-248-9013
Hertz	800-654-3131
Alamo	800-462-5266
National	800-328-4567
Dollar	206-433-5825
Thrifty	206-246-7566
Advantage	800-777-5500

(Off Airport)

U Save	206-242-9778
Century/Rent Rite	206-246-5039
EZ Rent-A-Car	800-277-5171
Fox Rent-A-Car	800-225-4369

Hotels

Airport Plaza Hotel • 18601 International Blvd • 206-433-0400
Best Western Airport Executel • 20717 Pacific Hwy S • 206-878-3300
Clarion Sea-Tac Airport Hotel • 3000 S 176th St • 206-242-0200
Coast Gateway Hotel • 18415 Pacific Hwy S • 206-248-8200
Comfort Inn at Sea-Tac • 19333 Pacific Hwy S • 206-878-1100
Courtyard by Marriott • 16038 W Valley Hwy • 800-321-2211
Days Inn Sea-Tac • 19015 International Blvd • 206-244-3600
Doubletree Inn Sea-Tac • 18740 Pacific Hwy S • 206-246-8600
Econo Lodge • 19255 Pacific Hwy S • 206-824-1350
Econo Lodge • 13910 Pacific Hwy S • 206-244-0810
Fairfield Inn by Marriott • 19631 International Blvd • 206-824-9909
Hampton Inn Sea-Tac • 19445 International Blvd • 206-878-1700
Heritage Inn • 16838 Pacific Hwy S • 206-248-0901
Hilton Seattle Airport • 17620 Pacific Hwy S • 206-244-4800
HoJo Inn by Howard Johnson • 20045 Pacific Hwy S • 206-878-3310
Holiday Inn Express Hotel & Suites • 19621 International Blvd • 206-824-3200
Holiday Inn Sea-Tac • 17338 International Blvd • 206-248-1000
Homewood Suites • 6955 Fort Dent Wy • 206-433-8000
Jet Motel • 17300 Pacific Hwy S • 206-244-6255
La Quinta Inn • 2824 S 188th St • 206-241-5211
Marriott Sea-Tac • 3201 S 176th St • 206-241-2000
Motel 6 • 20651 Military Rd S • 206-824-9902
Motel 6 • 16500 Pacific Hwy S • 206-246-4101
Radisson Hotel Gateway • 18118 Pacific Hwy S • 206-244-6666
Red Lion Seattle Airport • 18220 Pacific Hwy S • 206-246-5500
Roadway Inn • 2930 S 176th St • 206-246-9300
Sea-Tac Crest Motor Inn • 18845 Pacific Hwy S • 206-433-0999
Sea-Tac Super 8 Motel • 3100 S 192nd St • 206-433-8188
Silver Cloud Inn • 13050 48th Ave S • 206-241-2200
Sleep Inn Sea-Tac Airport • 20406 International Blvd • 206-878-3600
South City Motel • 14242 Pacific Hwy S • 206-243-0222
Travel Lodge • 2900 S 192nd St • 206-241-9292

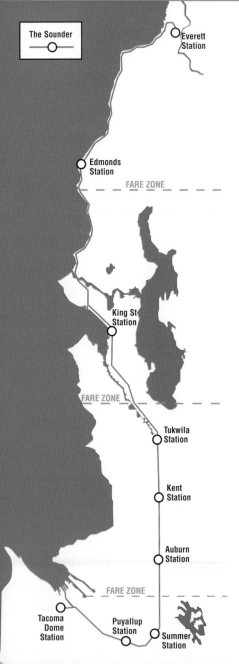

The Sounder

Everett Station

Edmonds Station

FARE ZONE

King St Station

FARE ZONE

Tukwila Station

Kent Station

Auburn Station

FARE ZONE

Tacoma Dome Station

Puyallup Station

Summer Station

General Information

Sound Transit Address: 401 S Jackson St,
Seattle, WA 98104
Phone: 206-398-5000
Website: www.soundtransit.org

Overview

Sound Transit was created by the Washington State Legislature to build a mass transit system that connects regional employment with population centers in King, Pierce, and Snohomish Counties. The organization has the Central Puget Sound region covered with a broad range of bus, light rail, and commuter rail services.

ST Express

The Sound Transit Regional Bus line connects Seattle, Bellevue, Everett, and Tacoma with the largest urban centers in the region. Transit centers, park-and-ride lots, and HOV access projects throughout the region have improved transit service for all bus riders and provide some help to the daily commute. The line connects more than 30,000 people each day throughout the three counties

Fares: Adults ages 19–64 pay $1.50 for one zone, $2.50 for two zones, and $3 for three zones. Youth ages 6–18 pay $1, $1.75, and $2.50. Senior citizens and disabled pay 50 cents, $1.25, and $1.50. Children under 6 ride free.

The Sounder

Sounder commuter trains run 75 miles every weekday (Monday to Friday only) between Everett and Tacoma. The Sounder North train connects Everett and Edmonds with Seattle (with a Mukilteo station scheduled to open in 2007). The Sounder South train runs from Tacoma to Puyallup, Sumner, Auburn, Kent, Tukwila, and downtown Seattle.

The Sounder also runs special trains for Seahawk home games and for select Mariners games. Check the website for more details.

Fares: Adults ages 19–64 pay $2 for one zone, $3 for two zones and $4 for three zones. Youth ages 6–18 pay $1.50, $2.25 and $3. Senior citizens and disabled pay $1, $1.50 and $2. Children under 6 ride free.

Tacoma Link Light Rail

The Tacoma Link light rail line began operating in August 2003 and quickly became a major factor in the renaissance of downtown Tacoma. The 1.6-mile route connects downtown Tacoma with the Tacoma Dome Station, where connections can be made to ST Express regional bus and Sounder commuter rail. Construction on another 15.6-mile Central Link light rail line is underway, which will connect downtown Seattle with Sea-Tac International Airport when it opens in 2009.

Fares: There is no charge for the Tacoma Link light rail. No pass or ticket is required.

Seattle Streetcar

General Info

NFT Maps:	2 & 16
Address:	Seattle Department of Transportation
	P.O. Box 34996
	Seattle, WA 98124
Phone:	206-553-3000
Lost and Found:	206-553-3090
Route and Schedule Information:	206-553-3000
Other Inquiries:	206-684-ROAD
Website:	www.seattlestreetcar.org

Overview

If the Metro bus is the faithful plain Jane of Seattle's public transportation system, then the streetcar is her much more glamorous yet vapid younger sister. Eleven stops are scattered along a 2.6-mile loop around the Denny Triangle and South Lake Union neighborhoods, with pretty purple streetcars zooming by every fifteen minutes. Honesty rules since riders hop on and off without anyone checking their fares, although supposedly you may be asked at anytime to present your proof of payment. PugetPass, bus transfers, and Metro cards are accepted or you can purchase tickets from machines located at the stations and on the streetcar itself. Strangely, the station ticketing machines don't accept bills but those on the cars do. Seattle being bike friendly, bicyclists can store their wheels in the open center section of the streetcars. Originally named the South Lake Union Trolley until city officials realized the unfortunate acronym this creates, the moniker was changed but Seattleites still delight in referring to it as the SLUT. Considering that the route doesn't really service any major points of interest, it has become a one-time novelty thing for residents just so they can say, "Yeah, I rode the SLUT."

Taxis

For its size, Seattle has much fewer taxis than some might expect. It seems that most of the residents here simply prefer hoofing, biking, or bussing it around town (if they're not cruising in their hybrids). Thus, hailing a cab can be a bit dicey, and it's dang near impossible to find one outside downtown. Your best bet is to call ahead—Puget Sound Dispatch will quickly hook you up with either a Yellow (206-622-6500) or a Redtop cab (206-789-4949). Normally, you won't be kept waiting much longer than 10–15 minutes. If you're cabbing it home after a night at the bars, try to leave before last call or you'll be waiting at least an hour for a ride home.

If you're milling about downtown, there are a couple designated taxi stands. There's one outside the Westin Hotel (on 5th Ave) and another at the Washington State Convention & Trade Center (on Pike St). If cabs are cruising at all, hotels are a good place to spot one. The standard drop rate for two is $2.50 plus $2.00 per mile and $.50 per extra passenger. And with our fun and fluctuating oil market, some cab companies might hit you with an additional $1.00 gas surcharge—but make *sure* this is posted clearly on the dash before going anywhere. And on top of that, a 10–15% tip is expected. If you don't happen to have wads of cash on you to pay for all that, most cabs do come equipped with credit card devices, although some driver get pretty surly if you use plastic for a short trip.

Should you be heading to SeaTac, the Metro bus system (www.transit.metrokc.gov) will take you right to the terminal for a crazy-cheap $1.50 (the 194 is a good one). But should you be toting an obscene amount of baggage or are extremely averse to the idea of public transit, taxis will chauffeur you gladly for about $28 from downtown. Coming back to Seattle from the airport is a whole 'nother ballgame, as prices mysteriously shoot up to about $35. There appears to be no satisfying explanation for this. Can we say "light rail?"

Yellow Cab	206-622-6500
Redtop	206-789-4949
Farwest Taxi	206-622-1717
Orange Cab	206-522-8800

January

Martin Luther King Jr. Day
March for peace, equality, or both—it's your choice. www.mlkseattle.org
Northwest Asian-American Film Festival
Specialty showcase for Asian-American filmmakers nationwide. www.nwaff.org

February

Mardis Gras
Head to Pioneer Square, if that's your scene.

March

Seattle Moisture Festival
A twisted cabaret with the scope of vaudeville. www.moisturefestival.com
The Seattle Center Irish Festival
Celebrating true Irish heritage, not simple stereotypes of shamrocks and whiskey.
Seattle Erotic Art Festival
Promotes freedom of sexuality, speech, and creativity. www.seattleerotic.org

April

Seattle Cherry Blossom & Japanese Cultural Festival
Martial arts, kites, and tea at Seattle Center.

May

U District Street Fair
First of the big summer festivals, crowded with art and dripping with funnel cake grease.
www.udistrictchamber.org/streetfair
Seattle International Children's Festival
Kid-centric music and arts festival. www.seattleinternational.org
Folklife Festival
Keeping traditional art and music alive. www.folklife.org
Seattle Cheese Festival
From mozzarella to manchego. www.seattlecheesefestival.org
Seattle International Film Festival
Largest film fest in the US. Really. www.seattlefilm.org

June

Fremont Solstice Parade
The wildest art party in the city. And yes, lots of naked people, for better or worse. www.fremontfair.com
Pike Place Market Street Fair
Self-explanatory. www.pikeplacemarketstreetfestival.com
Seattle Pride
Gay pride, that is. www.seattlepride.org
Juneteenth
A celebration of freedom from slavery in Pratt Park. www.scacc.net

July

Washington Mutual Family Fourth
Fireworks over Lake Union. No better way to celebrate America's independence than a big fireworks bash thrown by a bank. www.wamufamily4th.org
Ivar's Fourth of July
Fireworks over Elliot Bay. Same as above but replace bank with a local seafood restaurant chain.

July–*continued*

Seafair
A month-long tribute to Seattle's nautical heritage, with loud fighter jets and boat races. Beware of grown men dressed like pirates roaming the streets. www.seafair.com
I.D. Summer Festival
The International District parties at Hing-Hay Park.
Bite of Seattle
A showcase for local culinary excellence. www.biteofseattle.com
Capitol Hill Block Party
Who's who of Cap Hill rock culture. If you pay to get in, you're not really "in." www.capitolhillblockparty.com
Ballard Seafood Fest
Who knew fishermen still live in Ballard? www.seafoodfest.org
Wooden Boat Festival
Take a boat ride on Lake Union. www.cwb.org

August

Sunset Supper
Chow down and drink up at Pike Place Market for a good cause. www.pikeplacemarket.org
Seattle Music Fest at Alki
An alternative to alternative music festivals. www.northwestarts.org/smf/aboutsmf.htm
Hempfest
Rick-Steves-approved pro-legalization really, but who can think about politics after a few of those brownies? www.hempfest.org
Arab Festival
Authentic Arabic food and strong coffee! www.arabcenter.net
Central Area Festival & Parade
Fostering community pride and cultural diversity. www.cacf.com

September

Bumbershoot
The granddaddy of all Seattle festivals, with big stars and long lines. www.bumbershoot.org
Do the Puyallup!
Two words: mutton bustin'. www.thefair.com
Fremont Oktoberfest
Squeeze two weeks of beer tasting into one bleary-eyed weekend. www.fremontoktoberfest.com

October

Earshot Jazz Festival
Bringing top jazzers to the Emerald City since 1989. www.earshot.org
Fremont Troll-a-go-go
The annual masquerade ball thrown by the Fremont Arts Council. www.fremontartscouncil.org/events/trollagogo.html
Turkfest
Indulge your senses with a strong dose of Turksih culture. www.turkfest.org

November

Seattle Marathon
Burn off some of the previous year's holiday gorging. www.seattlemarathon.org

December

Christmas Ships Festival
Big boats in bright lights, and vice-versa. www.argosycruises.com/themecruises/xmas.cfm

General Information

Website: www.seattle.gov/parks/parkspaces/
yodogs.htm

Overview

Seattleites aren't just tree-huggers; they're dog lovers, too. Animals are dear to their hearts (if the plentitude of vegetarians/vegans is any indication) and dogs bound and abound here. And with the gorgeous backdrop that is the Emerald City, Seattle's dog parks are a far cry from most of the drab, chain-link gravel pits you'll find in other large cities. The eleven dog areas in Seattle are usually well-maintained, spacious, and just as much fun for man as it is for his best friend. Of course, there are a few obvious rules to follow. Keep your dog on a leash outside of the off-leash area (duh), make sure he or she has had all of the proper shots and licensing, and please, for heaven's sake, scoop the dang poop. The Citizens for Off-Leash Areas (COLA) is a community of dog owners committed to everything dog-park, so check out their site (www.coladog.org) for all you need to know. If you're not a good little doggie owner, beware—you could be slapped with a fine up to $150. Now, that's ruff! (Sorry.)

Off Leash Areas:

Genesee Park (Map 40)
4316 S Genesee St
Genesee Park and Playfield is a broad, rough meadow stretching for about five blocks north from Genesee Street to Stan Sayres Memorial Park on Lake Washington Boulevard. There is a separate fully-fenced off-leash area, complete with a doggie drinking fountain (aw!). It's gravelly and not all that interesting, but is flat and open—perfect for playing fetch.

Golden Gardens (Map 33)
8498 Seaview Pl NW
This waterfront park is huge, running alongside Puget Sound. There are hiking trails for a nice little walk, restored wetlands, sandy beaches, fishing, boating, picnic tables—you name it, Golden's got it. The icing on the cake is the stunning view of the Olympics along the rugged coastline. Uphill to the east is a moderately-sized off-leash area for your doggie. Just be sure to bring your galoshes if there's a hint of rain, as it can get extremely mucky.

I-5 Colonnade (Map 20)
Beneath I-5, south of E Howe St b/w Lakeview Blvd & Franklin Ave E
This is a weird, creepy park underneath roaring I-5 on Capitol Hill. It's a huge, maze-like gravel pit with lots of chain-link fence, no open areas, and concrete blocks everywhere, their function mysterious. Not the best for fancy-free frolicking with your dog, but if you're just taking Fido out to do his business, it works. There is however a cool mountain bike course under construction and an art installation by John Roloff.

Magnuson Park (Map 27)
7400 Sand Point Wy NE
The absolute crème de la crème of dog parks in Seattle. The park itself is 40 acres, with a whopping *nine* of them dedicated to an off-leash pooch area. It's a veritable Disneyland for dogs, with several different scenic areas (dirt hills, grassy brush, mud pit), an exclusive shy/older dog pen, and a flat gravel area for fetch. The highlight is a long winding trail leading down to the shores of Lake Washington— Magnuson is the only dog park within city limits with water access. It's also a great park for socializing with other owners.

Northacres Park (Map 34)
12718 1st Ave NE
Tucked away next to some athletic fields, this park is small but lots of fun. It's an intimate maze-like affair with lots of short trails through dense, well-kept foliage. Small open areas spring up along the way with benches for a quick rest while your dog bounds through the brush.

Blue Dog Pong (Map 9)
Martin Luther King Jr Wy S & S Massachusetts

Dr. Jose Rizal Park (Map 8)
1008 12th Ave S

Plymouth Pillars Park (Map 3)
Boren Ave b/w Pike St & Pine St

Regrade Park (Map 1)
2251 3rd Ave

Westcrest Park (Map 38)
8806 8th Ave SW

Woodland Park (Map 31)
W Greenlake Wy N

Best Rainy Day Activities

Here are a couple of places to help you and your kids battle cabin fever and keep your sanity during those long, rainy months of winter.

International District: Yes, honey, those ducks are for eating.

Waterfront/Piers: Fish n' chips! Seagulls! An arcade! Pirates!

Pacific Science Center: Giant insects.

Seattle Central Library: Holy cow, this place is huge!!!

Ballard Library: The roof is alive and growing!

Experience Music Project: Mommy, what's that man doing to his guitar?

Burke Museum: Dinosaurs!

Seattle Center: A big, urban park with museums, food courts, a tiny amusement park, and a huge fountain.

Seattle Children's Museum: Kid-centered museum.

Seattle Aquarium: Pretty fish.

Woodlawn Park Zoo: Yes, it's mostly outside, but those animals sure are cool.

The Best of the Best

Rock on, Dude

The Vera Project is a long-time all-ages music venue and teen-centered non-profit recently relocated to the Seattle Center's Snoqualmie Room. Kids rock out to Seattle bands big and small while parents go to the opera. They also have volunteer projects for kids and host a variety of classes including breakdancing and punk rock.

Feed the Seagulls:

Take your kids to Ivar's on the pier, munch on fish and chips while watching the ferries come and go, then fend off the seagulls with those crusty, hard leftover bits at the bottom.

Ice Cream Cruise:

Yeah, kids like ice cream. But what's better than ice cream? Ice cream on a boat! Sip on a classic root beer float and enjoy the scenery. Departs hourly 11 am to 5 pm, every Sunday from under the Aurora Bridge (801 N Northlake Wy, 206 713-8446; www.seattleferryservice.com)

Learn to Build a Bike:

At Bike Works, kids can learn how to build a bike. And after working eight hours, that bike is theirs to take home.

Coolest Park:

The giant iron wrought structures of Gasworks Park make this a great kid-friendly destination. Fly a kite at the top of the hill, watch the seaplanes land on Lake Union, or look for unrefined oil ooze out of the ground (and if you find some, please contact the authorities).

Ferries:

Did you see that? Was that a Whale? They say 90 orcas (once known by the killer nickname, killer whales) live in Puget Sound, so if you take a ferry ride you should see one, right? Wait! What's that? Is that a whale? Maybe it's a shark? Or a sturgeon? Can you see sturgeons from the ferries? Ride the ferries and find out.

Year-Round Trick-or-Treating:

Quirky Fremont is a kid-like, permanently silly place. Start the tour off at 36th and Fremont Place at the Lenin Statue, and ponder the future of communism in Seattle. Head across the street towards the water a block to The Rocket, which traveled to the moon thirty-five times before retiring in 1986. From there, take a left to the other end of the block and you'll be standing at the actual Center of the Universe. Pretty cool, huh? But don't stand too long or you'll cause an imbalance. Next, cross the street and head downhill until you see those people Waiting for the Interurban. They've been waiting so long, they've turned to stone. Head under the Aurora Bridge to find the infamous Fremont Troll. This troll wandered the thick forests of north Seattle, merciless devouring all those who dared to cross the water, until a group of kids turned him to stone in a grueling 22-day battle in 1950. Unfortunately, the troll destroyed their VW Bug in the process.

Let's Go Sledding:

It rarely snows in Seattle—bummer, eh? But when it does, boy is it fun. The entire city shuts down with the thought of three inches of snow—businesses cut their hours, downtown office workers play hooky, buses take alternate routes, and best of all, schools close. Actually, that's second best. The best part about snow in Seattle is that all these huge hills turn into giant, carless sledding runs. Grab a cardboard box, wrap yourself in cellophane, and hit the slopes! Be sure to supervise the kids and have hot chocolate ready upon the return to home.

Shopping Essentials

Magic Mouse Toys • 603 1st Ave • 206-682-8097 • We think it's run by elves.

Archie McPhee • 2428 NW Market St • 206-297-0240 • All the greatest pleasures in life—rubber lizards, fake spiders-in-ice, and boxing nun puppets.

Top Ten Toys • 104 N 85th St • 206-782-0098 • Educational toys for kids of all ages.

Gasworks Park Kite Shop • 3420 Stone Wy N • 206-633-4780 • Get your kite!

Math N Stuff • 8926 Roosevelt Wy NE • 206-522-8891 • Fun Math?! No Way?!

Izilla Toys • 2840 E Madison •206-322-8697 • A house full of cool toys.

Elliot Bay Books • 101 S Main St • 206-624-6600 • Great kids section.

Schmancy • 1932 2nd Ave • 206-728-8008 • Super quirky "toy shop," more for the childish adult or the mature minded child.

All for Kids Books & Music • 2900 NE Blakeley St • 206-526-2768 • www.allforkidsbooks.com • They will find the perfect book for your child.

Map 1 • Belltown

Self-Service	2101 4th Ave	5:10 pm
FedEx Kinko's	2500 2nd Ave	5 pm
Self-Service	2401 4th Ave	4:30 pm
Self-Service	2601 4th Ave	4:30 pm
Self-Service	2815 2nd Ave	4:30 pm
Self-Service	2701 1st Ave	4 pm

Map 2 • Downtown/Denny Triangle

Self-Service	402 Pontius Ave N	5:10 pm
Self-Service	2201 6th Ave	5:10 pm
Self-Service	1100 Olive Wy	5 pm
Self-Service	1730 Minor Ave	5 pm
Self-Service	600 Stewart St	5 pm
Self-Service	234 Dexter Ave N	5 pm
Self-Service	2033 6th Ave	5 pm
Self-Service	2001 6th Ave	5 pm

Map 3 • Downtown

FedEx Kinko's	1200 6th Ave	5:30 pm
Self-Service	701 5th Ave	5:25 pm
FedEx Kinko's	735 Pike St	5:15 pm
Self-Service	600 University St	5:15 pm
Self-Service	1601 5th Ave	5:10 pm
Self-Service	700 5th Ave	5:10 pm
Self-Service	1501 4th Ave	5:10 pm
Self-Service	1325 4th Ave	5:05 pm
Self-Service	1215 4th Ave	5:05 pm
Mail Boxes Etc	800 5th Ave #101	5 pm
Mail Boxes Etc	800 5th Ave #101	5 pm
FedEx Kinko's	816 3rd Ave	5 pm
FedEx Kinko's	816 3rd Ave	5 pm
Self-Service	1191 2nd Ave	5 pm
Self-Service	520 Pike St	5 pm
Self-Service	1111 3rd Ave	5 pm
Self-Service	1301 5th Ave	5 pm
Self-Service	1420 5th Ave	5 pm
Self-Service	1201 3rd Ave	5 pm
Self-Service	816 3rd Ave	5 pm
Self-Service	999 3rd Ave	5 pm
Self-Service	2025 1st Ave	5 pm
Self-Service	1000 2nd Ave	5 pm
Self-Service	801 2nd Ave	5 pm
Self-Service	506 2nd Ave	5 pm
Self-Service	1001 4th Ave	5 pm
Self-Service	720 Olive Wy	4:55 pm
Wanderers' Mail Service	1916 Pike Pl Ste 12	4:45 pm
Self-Service	1809 7th Ave	4:45 pm
Self-Service	911 Western Ave	4:45 pm
Self-Service	1424 4th Ave	4:45 pm
Self-Service	719 2nd Ave	4:45 pm
Self-Service	900 4th Ave	4:45 pm
Self-Service	2003 Western Ave	4:40 pm
Self-Service	1402 3rd Ave	4:30 pm
Self-Service	1904 3rd Ave	4:30 pm
Self-Service	1511 3rd Ave	4:15 pm
Self-Service	1932 1st Ave	4:15 pm
Self-Service	915 2nd Ave	4:15 pm

Map 4 • First Hill / Pike / Pine

Post Option	1122 E Pike St	5 pm
Self-Service	600 Broadway	5 pm
Self-Service	801 Broadway	5 pm
Self-Service	1201 Marion St	5 pm
Quality Copy & Business Center	714 12th Ave	4 pm

Map 6 • Madrona

Self-Service	1421 34th Ave	4:15 pm

Map 7 • Pioneer Square / SoDo

Self-Service	316 Occidental Ave S	5 pm
Self-Service	1201 1st Ave S	5 pm
Self-Service	505 5th Ave	4:45 pm
Self-Service	101 Yesler Wy	4:45 pm
Self-Service	411 1st Ave S	4:45 pm
FedEx Kinko's	418 S Jackson St	4:30 pm
Self-Service	401 2nd Ave S	4:30 pm
Self-Service	418 S Jackson St	4:30 pm

Map 8 • International District

Opas Express	710 6th Ave S	5 pm

Map 10 • Leschi

Self-Service	102 Lakeside Ave	4:45 pm

Map 11 • Magnolia / Interbay

Self-Service	1900 W Nickerson St	5 pm
Self-Service	1600 W Dravus St	4:45 pm
The Mailbox	3213 W Wheeler St	3:45 pm
Self-Service	3215 W Lynn St	3:45 pm

Map 13 • Upper Queen Anne

Self-Service	180 Nickerson St	4:30 pm
Self-Service	2100 Queen Anne Ave N	3:45 pm

Map 14 • Queen Anne (West)

Self-Service	220 W Mercer St	4:45 pm
Self-Service	1201 Amgen Ct W	4:30 pm

Map 15 • Lower Queen Anne / Seattle Center

FedEx Kinko's	606 1st Ave N	5 pm
Self-Service	415 1st Ave N	4:45 pm
Self-Service	100 W Harrison St	4:45 pm
Self-Service	18 W Mercer St	4:45 pm
Self-Service	221 1st Ave W	4:45 pm
The Mail Box	300 Queen Anne Ave N	4 pm
Self-Service	550 Mercer St	4 pm

Map 16 • Westlake / South Lake Union

Self-Service	1200 Westlake Ave N	5 pm
Self-Service	823 Yale Ave N	5 pm
Aaron's Mini Storage	2030 Dexter Ave N	4:45 pm
Self-Service	1818 Westlake Ave N	4:45 pm
Self-Service	701 Dexter Ave N	4:45 pm

Map 17 • Capitol Hill (West)

FedEx Kinko's	700 Broadway E	4:45 pm
Self-Service	401 Broadway E	4:30 pm
Postal Plus	1463 E Republican St	4 pm

Map 19 • Madison Valley / Denny Blaine

Self-Service	2801 E Madison St	4 pm

Map 20 • Eastlake / Montlake / Portage Bay

Self-Service	2825 Eastlake Ave E	5 pm
Self-Service	1910 Fairview Ave E	4:30 pm
Self-Service	2366 Eastlake Ave E	4:15 pm
Eastlake Mail	2226 Eastlake Ave E	4 pm
Lake Union Mail	117 E Louisa St	4 pm

Map 23 • Ballard

Self-Service	5706 17th Ave NW	5 pm
Self-Service	1135 NW Leary Wy	4:45 pm
Ballard Mail & Dispatch	1752 NW Market St	4:30 pm
FedEx Kinko's	1740 NW Market St	4:30 pm
Ballard Mailbox & Shipping	2442 NW Market St	4 pm

Map 24 • Fremont

Self-Service	400 N 34th St	5 pm
Natco	4509 Interlake Ave N	4:30 pm
Self-Service	1329 N 47th St	4:30 pm
Self-Service	3420 Fremont Ave N	4:15 pm

Map 25 • Wallingford

FedEx Kinko's	810 NE 45th St	5 pm
Self-Service	810 NE 45th St	5 pm
Self-Service	400 NE 45th St	4 pm

Map 26 • U District

FedEx Kinko's	3042 NE 45th St	4:45 pm
Self-Service	3042 NE 45th St	4:45 pm
Self-Service	1107 NE 45th St	4:45 pm
Self-Service	1959 NE Pacific St	4:45 pm
Self-Service	4311 11th Ave NE	4:30 pm
Self-Service	4700 University Village Pl NE	4:30 pm
University Photo & Mail	4203 University Wy NE	4 pm
Mail Etc	4739 University Wy NE	4 pm

Map 27 • Laurelhurst / Wedgwood / Sand Point

Self-Service	4500 Sand Point Wy NE	4:30 pm
Self-Service	7724 35th Ave NE	4 pm

Map 29 • Ballard / Loyal Heights

The Mailbox In Ballard	6201 15th Ave NW	4:45 pm
The Mailbox & Bus Service Center	2400 NW 80th St	4:30 pm

Map 30 • Greenwood / Phinney Ridge

Greenwood Postal Center	8314 Greenwood Ave N	4:30 pm

Map 31 • Green Lake / Roosevelt

Self-Service	7110 E Green Lake Dr N	4:15 pm
Econo-mini Storage	6920 Roosevelt Wy NE	3:45 pm

Map 33 • Northwest Seattle

Self-Service	10700 Meridian Ave N	5 pm
Self-Service	8532 15th Ave NW	4:45 pm
Self-Service	1155 N 130th St	4:45 pm
Highland Mailbox Services	14419 Greenwood Ave N	4:30 pm
Self-Service	929 N 145th St	4 pm

Map 34 • Northeast Seattle

FedEx Kinko's	831 NE Northgate Wy	5 pm
Self-Service	9709 3rd Ave NE	5 pm
Self-Service	831 NE Northgate Wy	5 pm
Self-Service	11036 8th Ave NE	5 pm
Longs Drugs	818 NE Northgate Wy	4:45 pm
Self-Service	9725 3rd Ave NE	4:45 pm
Self-Service	3019 NE 127th St	4:15 pm
Pony Express	12345 Lake City Wy NE	4 pm

Map 35 • Alki / West Seattle / North Admiral

Self-Service	4700 42nd Ave SW	5 pm
Alki Mail & Dispatch	4701 SW Admiral Wy	4:30 pm
Self-Service	4412 California Ave SW	4:15 pm
Admiral Junction Mailing	2701 California Ave SW	4 pm

Map 36 • North Delridge

Self-Service	1001 SW Klickitat Wy	4:45 pm
Self-Service	4025 Delridge Wy SW	4:15 pm

Map 37 • Fauntleroy / Arbor Heights

Self-Service	2721 SW Trenton St	3 pm

Map 38 • White Center / South Park / Beverly Park

Self-Service	309 S Cloverdale St	4:45 pm
Westcoast Postal Services	9620 14th Ave SW	3 pm

Map 39 • SoDo / Beacon Hill / Georgetown

Federal Express	651 S Alaska St	6 pm
Self-Service	620 S Orcas St	5:30 pm
FedEx Kinko's	5963 Corson Ave S	5:15 pm
Self-Service	5963 Corson Ave S Ste 176	5:15 pm
Self-Service	5601 6th Ave S	5 pm
Self-Service	5950 6th Ave S	4:45 pm
Self-Service	2420 4th Ave S	4:30 pm
Self-Service	4735 E Marginal Wy S	3:45 pm

Map 40 • Mount Baker / Seward Park / Columbia City

Longs Drugs	3820 Rainier Ave S Ste B	3:30 pm
Columbia City Parcel	3703 S Edmunds St	3:30 pm

Map 41 • Rainier Valley / Rainier Beach / Skyway

Self-Service	3315 S 116th St	5:15 pm
Rainier Mailbox	8334 Rainier Ave S Ste 101	3 pm

Map 42 • Mercer Island

Self-Service	7525 SE 24th St	5 pm
Self-Service	7900 SE 28th St	4:45 pm
Self-Service	9725 SE 36th St	4:45 pm
Self-Service	3040 78th Ave SE	3:45 pm

Map 43 • Bellevue (Southwest)

Self-Service	11400 SE 8th St	4:45 pm
Self-Service	14205 SE 36th St	4:45 pm
Self-Service	915 118th Ave SE	4:30 pm
Self-Service	13555 SE 36th St	4:15 pm
FedEx Kinko's	3900 Factoria Blvd SE	4 pm
Self-Service	1309 114th Ave SE	4 pm
Self-Service	3900 Factoria Blvd SE	4 pm
Self-Service	3605 132nd Ave SE	4 pm
Newport Hills Mailboxes	5806 A 119th Ave SE	2 pm

Map 44 • Bellevue (South)

Mail Plus	15100 SE 38th St, Ste 101	4:45 pm
Self-Service	13810 SE Eastgate Wy	4:45 pm
Self-Service	3633 136th Pl SE	4:30 pm
Eastgate Postal Center	14644 SE Eastgate Wy	3:30 pm

Map 45 • Bellevue (West) / Medina

FedEx Kinko's	40 Bellevue Wy NE	5:15 pm
Self-Service	40 Bellevue Wy NE	5:15 pm
Self-Service	1171 Bellevue Wy NE	5:15 pm
Self-Service	601 108th Ave NE	5 pm
Self-Service	500 108th Ave NE	5 pm
Self-Service	10900 NE 4th St	5 pm
Self-Service	777 108th Ave NE	5 pm
Self-Service	10800 NE 8th St	5 pm
Self-Service	2025 112th Ave NE	4:45 pm
FedEx Kinko's	10635 NE 8th St	4:30 pm
Self-Service	10500 NE 8th St	4:30 pm
Self-Service	3015 112th Ave NE	4:30 pm
Self-Service	11225 SE 6th St	4:30 pm
Self-Service	10900 NE 8th St	4:30 pm
Self-Service	10885 NE 4th St	4:30 pm
Self-Service	411 108th Ave NE	4:15 pm
Self-Service	600 108th Ave NE	4:15 pm
Self-Service	1750 112th Ave NE	4:15 pm
Self-Service	11100 NE 8th St	4:15 pm
Self-Service	110 110th Ave NE	4:15 pm
Self-Service	10655 NE 4th St	4 pm
Self-Service	2959 Northup Wy	4 pm
Self-Service	205 108th Ave NE	3:45 pm
Self-Service	155 108th Ave NE	3:45 pm
Self-Service	4030 Lake Washington Blvd NE	3:45 pm
Pak Mail	2620 Bellevue Wy NE	3 pm

Map 46 • Bellevue (Central)

Self-Service	1 Lake Bellevue Dr	4:45 pm
Self-Service	1239 120th Ave NE	4:45 pm
PostNet	677 120th Ave NE Ste 2A	4:30 pm
Self-Service	2331 130th Ave NE	4:30 pm
Self-Service	13201 NE 20th St	4:30 pm
Self-Service	11811 NE 1st St	4:30 pm
Self-Service	2525 151st Pl NE	4:30 pm
Self-Service	11820 Northup Wy	4:15 pm
Goin Postal	14725 NE 20th St	4 pm
Pony Express Mail	15127 NE 24th St	4 pm
Self-Service	14800 NE 40th St	4 pm
Self-Service	14811 NE 2nd Pl	3:45 pm
Longs Drugs	15400 NE 20th St	3:30 pm

Map 47 • Bellevue (East) / Redmond

FedEx Kinko's	1313 156th Ave NE	4 pm
Self-Service	1313 156th Ave NE Ste 200	4 pm
Self-Service	15731 NE 8th St	3:45 pm
Self-Service	2010 156th Ave NE	3:15 pm

Map 48 • Kirkland

Self-Service	733 7th Ave	4:30 pm
Self-Service	11400 NE 120th St	4:30 pm
Self-Service	11411 NE 124th St	4:30 pm
Self-Service	2000 Carillon Pt	4:30 pm
Self-Service	411 Parkplace Ctr	4:30 pm
Self-Service	15 Lake St	4:15 pm
FedEx Kinko's	518 Central Wy	4 pm
Self-Service	610 Market St	4 pm
Self-Service	520 Kirkland Wy	4 pm
Self-Service	518 Central Wy	4 pm
Self-Service	12825 NE 126th Pl	4 pm
Mail Max	8554 122nd Ave NE	3:45 pm
Pony Express Juanita	9805 NE 116th St	3:45 pm
Self-Service	721 4th Ave	3:45 pm
Self-Service	11844 120th Pl NE	3:45 pm
Self-Service	9757 NE Juanita Dr	3:40 pm

Map 49 • Redmond

FedEx Kinko's	16815 Redmond Wy	4:40 pm
Self-Service	16815 Redmond Wy, Ste 220	4:40 pm
Pony Express	16541 Redmond Wy, Ste C	4:30 pm
Mailbox & Shipping Center	16149 Redmond Wy	4:30 pm
Self-Service	15110 NE 90th St	4:30 pm
Self-Service	15600 Redmond Wy	4:30 pm
Self-Service	8585 154th Ave NE	4:30 pm
Self-Service	14826 NE 95th St	4:30 pm
Self-Service	6675 185th Ave NE	4:15 pm
Self-Service	17519 NE 67th Ct	4:15 pm
Self-Service	7981 168th Ave NE	3:45 pm
Self-Service	16135 NE 85th St	3:30 pm
Ship-N-Shop	22310 NE Marketplace Dr Ste 10	12:30 pm

Emergency Rooms

	Address	Phone	Map
Children's Hospital and Regional Medical Center	4800 Sand Point Wy NE	206-987-2000	27
Eastside Hospital	2700 152nd Ave NE	425-883-5151	46
Evergreen Hospital Medical Center	12040 NE 128th St	425-899-1000	48
Evergreen Hospital Medical Center	8301 161st Ave NE	425-899-1000	49
Harborview Medical Center	325 9th Ave	206-731-3000	8
Northwest Hospital and Medical Center	1550 N 115th St	206-364-0500	33
Overlake Hospital	1035 116th Ave NE	425-688-5325	46
Swedish Medical Center / Ballard	5300 Tallman Ave NW	206-782-2700	23
Swedish Medical Center - First Hill	747 Broadway	206-386-6000	4
Swedish Medical Center - Providence	500 17th Ave	206-320-2000	5
University of Washington Medical Center	1959 NE Pacific St	206-598-3300	26
Virginia Mason Medical Center	1100 9th Ave	206-223-6600	4

Other Hospitals

City of Hope	1309 114th Ave SE	425-464-9530	43
Fairfax Hospital	10200 NE 132nd St	425-821-2000	48
Group Health Central Hospital	201 16th Ave E	206-326-3000	18
Kindred Hospital	10560 5th Ave NE	206-364-2050	34
The Polyclinic	1145 Broadway	206-329-1760	4

Sometimes you need a hotel room that's a step up from Aurora Avenue. Maybe you'd like to offer your visiting Aunt Mildred something more comfy than your futon. Maybe it's late and your condo on the Eastside seems intolerably far away. Maybe there are things you need to do in this hotel that you can't do at home. Whatever your business, here are the options.

Obscenely Expensive

Ranking as the only AAA five-diamond hotel in the Pacific Northwest, the **Georgian Fairmont Olympic (Map 3)** is in a class by itself, with single rooms starting around $300. The terrifying grandeur of the lobby is worth a peak, even if you have neither means nor motive to stay there. One baby step down in price ($200 and up) are the super-swank **W Hotel Seattle (Map 3)** and **The Westin Hotel (Map 1)** whose double 47-story towers are a difficult sight to miss. **The Grand Hyatt Seattle (Map 3)** offers luxury of the giant franchise sort. Or, for an Italianate flair, try the **Sorrento Hotel (Map 4)**, a bit more out of the way on First Hill.

Indulgent, but Not Ostentatious

Downtown Seattle is glutted with boutique hotels who make their names on style and service. Most rooms range between $130 and $200. **Hotel Max (Map 2)** doubles as an art gallery, and **Inn at El Gaucho (Map 1)** evokes a retro, boys' club glamour, while **Hotel Monaco (Map 3)** is more sumptuous and flamboyant. **The Paramount Hotel (Map 3)** and **Hotel Andra (Map 1)** are also popular for good reason. A fine choice north of Lake Union is the **Watertown Hotel (Map 26)** in the U District.

Just Trying to Avoid the Indignities of Motel 6

If you dare to lodge in Seattle without going broke, your first choice should be Belltown's **Ace Hotel (Map 1)**. Though the cheapest rates require a shared bathroom, that bathroom is the height of modern design. **The Moore Hotel (Map 3)** has clean, no-frills accommodation in a great location for downtown entertainment. For a total absence of style at a great price, there's the **Sixth Avenue Inn (Map 2)**. Lest we leave out our backpacking friends, the best bunks are at the friendly and inauspicious **Green Tortoise Hostel (Map 3)**. Whatever your budget, remember to ask the internet—sites such as Hotels.com, Expedia, Travelocity, Hotwire, and Seattle.com are invaluable for comparing prices and finding deals.

Map 1 • Belltown

	Address	Phone	Nightly Rate
Ace Hotel	2423 1st Ave	206-448-4721	85
Andra Hotel	2000 4th Ave	206-448-8600	200
The Edgewater	2411 Alaskan Wy	206-728-7000	210
Inn At El Gaucho	2505 1st Ave	206-728-1133	175
Kings Inn	2106 5th Ave	206-441-8833	79
Ramada Seattle Downtown	2200 5th Ave	206-441-9785	100
Warwick Hotel	401 Lenora St	206-443-4300	200
The Westin Seattle	1900 5th Ave	206-728-1000	250

Map 2 • Downtown / Denny Triangle

	Address	Phone	Nightly Rate
Best Western Loyal Inn	2301 8th Ave	206-682-0200	120
Days Inn Seattle Downtown	2205 7th Ave	206-448-3434	76
Days Inn Town Center	2205 7th Ave	206-448-3434	100
Eighth Avenue Inn	2213 8th Ave	206-624-6300	99
Holiday Inn	211 Dexter Ave N	206-728-8123	130
Holiday Inn Exp City Center	226 Aurora Ave N	206-441-7222	160
Hotel Max	620 Stewart St	206-728-6299	240
La Quinta Inn & Suites Seattle Downtown	2224 8th Ave	206-624-6820	110
Quality Inn & Suites	225 Aurora Ave N	206-728-7666	90
Seattle Pacific Hotel	325 Aurora Ave N	206-441-0400	69
Sixth Avenue Inn	2000 6th Ave	206-441-8300	129
Vance Hotel	620 Stewart St	206-441-4200	159

Map 3 • Downtown

	Address	Phone	Nightly Rate
Alexis Hotel	1007 1st Ave	206-624-4844	300
Crowne Plaza Downtown	1113 6th Ave	206-464-1980	136
Executive Hotel Pacific	400 Spring St	206-623-3900	180
Georgian-Fairmont Olympic Hotel	411 University St	206-621-1700	359
Grand Hyatt	721 Pine St	206-774-1234	375
Green Tortoise Backpackers Guesthouse	105 Pike St	206-340-1222	Dorm $24–29; Single $62
Hilton Seattle	1301 6th Ave	206-624-0500	190
Hotel 1000	1000 1st Ave	206-957-1000	225
Hotel Monaco	1101 4th Ave	206-621-1770	230
Hotel Seattle	315 Seneca St	206-623-5110	100
Inn at Harbor Steps	1221 1st Ave	206-748-0973	175
Inn at the Market	86 Pine St	206-443-3600	210
Madison Renaissance Hotel	515 Madison St	206-583-0300	210
Marriott Seattle Waterfront	2100 Alaskan Wy	206-443-5000	270
Mayflower Park Hotel	405 Olive Wy	206-382-6990	210
Moore Hotel	1926 2nd Ave	206-448-4851	65
The Paramount Hotel	724 Pine St	206-292-9500	169
Red Lion Hotel On Fifth Avenue	1415 5th Ave	206-971-8000	165
The Roosevelt Hotel	1531 7th Ave	206-621-1200	125
Sheraton Seattle Hotel	1400 6th Ave	206-621-9000	200
Vintage Park Hotel	1100 5th Ave	206-624-8000	270
W Seattle	1112 4th Ave	206-264-6000	330

Map 4 • First Hill / Pike / Pine

Baroness Hotel	1005 Spring St	206-624-0787	60
Seattle Suites	1400 Hubbell Pl	206-232-2799	130
Silver Cloud	1100 Broadway	206-325-1400	200
Sorrento Hotel	900 Madison St	206-622-6400	270
Summerfield Suites	1011 Pike St	206-682-8282	180

Map 7 • Pioneer Square / SoDo

Best Western Pioneer Square Hotel	77 Yesler Wy	206-340-1234	160

Map 8 • International District

Panama Hotel	605 1/2 S Main St	206-223-9242	85

Map 14 • Queen Anne (West)

Homewood Suites Seattle	206 Western Ave W	206-281-9393	150

Map 15 • Lower Queen Anne / Seattle Center

Best Western Executive Inn	200 Taylor Ave N	206-448-9444	140
Comfort Suites	601 Roy St	206-282-2600	150
Hampton Inn & Suites Downtown/ Seattle Center	700 5th Ave N	206-282-7700	170
Inn At Queen Anne	505 1st Ave N	206-282-7357	100
Marqueen Hotel	600 Queen Anne Ave N	206-282-7407	130
Mediterranean Inn	425 Queen Anne Ave N	206-428-4700	100
Travelodge By The Space Needle	200 6th Ave N	206-441-7878	130

Map 16 · Westlake / South Lake Union

Courtyard Seattle Downtown/Lake Union	925 Westlake Ave N	206-213-0100	170
Residence Inn Downtown Lake Union	800 Fairview Ave N	206-624-6000	170
Silver Cloud Inns	1150 Fairview Ave N	206-447-9500	180

Map 17 · Capitol Hill (West)

11th Avenue Inn	121 11th Ave E	206-669-4373	79
Shafer-Bailey Mansion Guest House	907 14th Ave E	206-322-4654	140

Map 20 · Eastlake / Montlake / Portage Bay

Eastlake Inn	2215 Eastlake Ave E	206-322-7726	65

Map 24 · Fremont

Bridge Motel	3650 Bridge Wy N	206-632-7835	55
Chelsea Station On The Park	4915 Linden Ave N	206-547-6077	110
Marco Polo Motel	4114 Aurora Ave N	206-633-4090	65
Park Plaza Motel	4401 Aurora Ave N	206-632-2101	45
Wallingford Inn	4450 Green Lake Wy N	206-632-3733	65

Map 26 · U District

Best Western University Tower Hotel	4507 Brooklyn Ave NE	206-634-2000	170
Chambered Nautilus Bed Breakfast Inn	5005 22nd Ave NE	206-522-2536	120
College Inn	4000 University Wy NE	206-633-4441	40
Silver Cloud Inns	5036 25th Ave NE	206-526-5200	200
Travelodge Seattle University	4725 25th Ave NE	206-525-4612	145
University Hotel Suites	4731 12th Ave Ne	206-522-4724	70
University Inn	4140 Roosevelt Wy NE	206-632-5055	99
Watertown Hotel	4242 Roosevelt Wy NE	206-826-4242	213

Map 30 · Greenwood / Phinney Ridge

Sun Hill Motel	8517 Aurora Ave N	206-525-1205	55
Travelodge Seattle North/Arurora	8512 Aurora Ave N	206-522-5000	90

Map 33 · Northwest Seattle

Ambassador Motel	12059 Aurora Ave N	206-362-6000	49
Aurora Nites Inn	11746 Aurora Ave N	206-365-3216	50
Aurora Seafair Inn	9100 Aurora Ave N	206-524-3600	65
Best Western Evergreen Inn	13700 Aurora Ave N	206-361-3700	90
Columbus Motor Inn	9613 Aurora Ave N	206-524-8880	55
Georgian Motel	8801 Aurora Ave N	206-524-1004	50
Green Lake Motel	8900 Aurora Ave N	206-523-4703	41
Holiday Inn Exp Ste Northgate	14115 Aurora Ave N	206-365-7777	110
Klose in Motel	9309 Aurora Ave N	206-527-0330	40
Orion Motel	12045 Aurora Ave N	206-364-6095	45
Seal's Motel	12035 Aurora Ave N	206-363-9009	46

Map 36 · North Delridge

Travelodge West Seattle	3512 SW Alaska St	206-937-9920	80

Map 37 · Fauntleroy / Arbor Heights

Wildwood Bed & Breakfast	4518 SW Wildwood Pl	206-819-9075	80

Map 38 · Delridge / White Center

Munson Motel	7060 E Marginal Wy S	206-762-6684	50

Map 39 · SoDo / Beacon Hill / Georgetown

Georgetown Inn	6100 Corson Ave S	206-762-2233	70
La Hacienda Motel	5414 1st Ave S	206-762-2460	50

Map 41 · Rainier Valley / Rainier Beach / Skyway

Red Lion Hotel	11244 Tukwila International Blvd	206-762-0300	120

Map 42 · Mercer Island

Travelodge Seattle	7645 Sunset Hwy	206-232-8000	79

Map 44 · Bellevue (South)

Days Inn Bellevue	3241 156th Ave SE	425-643-6644	90
Embassy Suites Hotel Seattle-Bellevue	3225 158th Ave SE	425-644-2500	130
Silver Cloud Inn-Eastgate	14632 SE Eastgate Wy	425-957-9100	180

Map 45 · Bellevue (West) / Medina

Bellevue Downtown Courtyard by Marriott	11010 NE 8th St	425-454-5888	140
Hilton Bellevue	300 112th Ave SE	425-455-1300	129
Hyatt Regency Bellevue	900 Bellevue Wy NE	425-462-1234	150
La Quinta Inn Seattle Bellevue	10530 Northup Wy	425-828-6585	100
La Residence Suite Hotel	475 100th Ave Ne	425-455-1475	135
Paragon Hotel Bellevue	818 112th Ave NE	425-455-1515	100
Red Lion Bellevue Inn	11211 Main St	425-455-5240	200
Silver Cloud Inn	10621 NE 12th St	425-637-7000	180
The Woodmark Hotel on Lake Washington	1200 Carillon Point	425-822-3700	260

Map 46 · Bellevue (Central)

Coast Bellevue Hotel	625 116th Ave NE	425-455-9444	100
Courtyard By Marriott - Bellevue	14615 NE 29th Pl	425-869-5300	120
Silver Cloud Inns	2122 152nd Ave NE	425-746-8200	180

Map 48 · Kirkland

Baymont Inn	12223 NE 116th St	425-822-2300	100
Clarion Inn At Totem Lake	12233 NE Totem Lake Wy	425-821-2202	165
Comfort Inn Kirkland	12202 NE 124th St	425-821-8300	100
Motel 6	12010 120th Pl NE	425-821-5618	60

Map 49 · Redmond

Redmond Inn	17601 Redmond Wy	425-883-4900	130

We've compiled a list of places (99% of them are cafés) where you can surf the Net. The following list does not include Starbucks, which have T-Mobile HotSpot Wi-Fi (translation: you gotta pay) at all their shops. See our coffee listings in the front of the book for specific Starbucks locations. Happy surfing.

Editor's Picks

	Address	Phone	Map
Central Library	1000 4th Ave	206-386-4636	3
Coffee Animals	550 12th Ave	206-726-9600	4
Capitol Hill Branch	425 Harvard Ave E	206-684-4715	17
Joe Bar	810 E Roy St	206-324-0407	17
Top Pot Donuts	609 Summit Ave E	206-323-7841	17

Internet

Online Coffee Company	1111 1st Ave	206-381-1911	3
Online Coffee Company	1404 E Pine St	206-323-7798	4
Uncle Elizabeth's Internet Café	1123 Pike St	206-381-1600	4
Q Café	3223 15th Ave W	206-352-2525	12
Online Coffee Company	1720 E Olive Wy	206-328-3731	17
Monkey Grind Espresso Bar	518 N 85th St	206-782-6100	30
Hotwire Online Coffeehouse	4410 California Ave SW	206-935-1510	35
Bubbles	1619 Harbor Ave SW	206-938-0153	36

Wi-Fi

Bellino Coffee	2421 2nd Ave	206-956-4237	1
Caffe Bella	2621 5th Ave	206-441-4351	1
Cherry St Coffee Belltown	2121 1st Ave	206-441-7176	1
Cherry Street Coffee House	2719 1st Ave	206-441-5489	1
Top Pot Donuts	2124 5th Ave	206-728-1966	1
Tully's	2929 1st Ave	206-441-9777	1
Uptown Espresso	2504 4th Ave	206-441-1084	1
World Cup Coffee	2819 2nd Ave	206-441-2967	1
Motore	1904 9th Ave	206-388-2803	2
Tully's	2326 6th Ave	206-443-0444	2
Ancient Grounds	1220 1st Ave	206-749-0747	3
Caffe Appassionato	801 Alaskan Wy	206-264-2500	3
Caffe D'Arte	1625 2nd Ave	206-728-4468	3
Caffe Ladro	108 Union St	206-267-0600	3
Caffe Ladro	801 Pine St	206-405-1950	3
Central Library	1000 4th Ave	206-386-4636	3
Cherry St Coffee House	103 Cherry St	206-621-9372	3
Cherry Street Coffee House	808 3rd Ave	206-442-9372	3
Online Coffee Company	1111 1st Ave	206-381-1911	3
Seattle's Best Coffee	1100 4th Ave	206-623-0104	3
Seattle's Best Coffee	400 Pike St	206-624-1635	3
Seattle's Best Coffee	621 2nd Ave	206-264-1020	3
Tully's	1015 3rd Ave	206-341-9488	3
Tully's	1015 3rd Ave	206-341-9488	3
Tully's	1222 Post Aly	206-624-6397	3
Tully's	1401 4th Ave	206-625-0600	3
Tully's	1601 5th Ave	206-405-3797	3
Tully's	2000 1st Ave	206-443-6871	3
Tully's	2001 Western Ave	206-443-1915	3
Tully's	601 Union St	206-292-5644	3
Tully's	701 5th Ave	206-682-6575	3
Tully's	821 2nd Ave	206-382-0533	3
Tully's	824 Pike St	206-328-6264	3

Wi-Fi–continued	Address	Phone	Map
Valdez Juan	1427 5th Ave	206-267-6770	3
Aurafice Internet and Coffee Bar	616 E Pine St	206-860-9977	4
Bauhaus Books & Coffee	301 E Pine St	206-625-1600	4
Caffe Vita	1005 E Pike St	206-709-4440	4
Chatterbox Café	1100 12th Ave	206-324-2324	4
Coffee Animals	550 12th Ave	206-726-9600	4
Crave	1621 12th Ave	206-388-0526	4
Online Coffee Company	1404 E Pine St	206-323-7798	4
Uncle Elizabeth's Internet Café	1123 Pike St	206-381-1600	4
Cupcake Royale/Verite Coffee	1101 34th Ave	206-709-4497	6
Verite Coffee	1101 34th Ave	206-709-4497	6
All City Coffee	125 Prefontaine Pl S	206-652-8331	7
Caffe Umbria Retail	320 Occidental Ave S	206-624-5847	7
Tully's	201 S Jackson St	206-332-0493	7
Tully's	408 2nd Ave S	206-332-0493	7
Zeitgeist Kunst And Kaffee	171 S Jackson St	206-583-0497	7
Panama Hotel Tea & Coffee House	607 S Main St	206-515-4000	8
The Gossip Espresso & Tea	651 S King St	206-624-5402	8
Tully's	625 5th Ave S	206-748-0140	8
Café Vega	1918 E Yesler Wy	206-322-0807	9
Tully's	3223 W McGraw St	206-282-3191	11
Macrina Bakery & Café	615 W McGraw St	206-283-5900	12
Q Café	3223 15th Ave W	206-352-2525	12
Caffe Ladro	2205 Queen Anne Ave N	206-282-5313	13
El Diablo Coffee	1811 Queen Anne Ave N	206-285-0693	13
Pat's on The Ave	1905 Queen Anne Ave N	206-284-0121	13
Teacup	2207 Queen Anne Ave N	206-283-5931	13
Tully's	2128 Queen Anne Ave N	206-282-7422	13
Hollys Espresso & Desserts	1907 10th Ave W	206-284-7144	14
Tully's	150 W Harrison St	206-378-1878	14
Café Zingaro	127 Mercer St	206-352-2861	15
Caffe Appassionato	1417 Queen Anne Ave N	206-270-8760	15
Caffe Ladro	600 Queen Anne Ave N	206-282-1549	15
Caffe Vita	813 5th Ave N	206-285-9662	15
Uptown Espresso	525 Queen Anne Ave N	206-285-3757	15
Uptown Espresso	500 Westlake Ave N	206-621-2045	16
Capitol Hill Branch	425 Harvard Ave E	206-684-4715	17
Joe Bar	810 E Roy St	206-324-0407	17
Online Coffee Company	1720 E Olive Wy	206-328-3731	17
Top Pot Donuts	609 Summit Ave E	206-323-7841	17
Caffe Ladro	435 15th Ave E	206-267-0551	18
Fargonian Coffee House	2328 E Madison St	206-709-2020	18
Fuel	610 19th Ave E	206-329-4700	18
Insomniax Coffee	102 15th Ave E	206-322-6477	18
Tully's	746 19th Ave E	206-568-1044	18
Victrola Coffee & Art	411 15th Ave E	206-325-6520	18
Café Dharwin	2406 10th Ave E	206-709-9452	20
Tully's	4036 E Madison St	206-329-6659	22
Ballard Branch	5614 22nd Ave NW	206-684-4089	23
Cupcake Royale/Verite Coffee	2052 NW Market St	206-782-9557	23
Java Jazz	5905 15th Ave NW	206-706-0772	23
Mr Spot's Chai House	5463 Leary Ave NW	206-297-2424	23
Tully's	2060 NW Market St	206-781-4887	23
Caffe Ladro	452 N 36th St	206-675-0854	24
Fremont Coffee	459 N 36th St	206-632-3633	24
Icon Coffee	4301 Fremont Ave N	206-632-3535	24
Lighthouse Roasters	400 N 43rd St	206-634-3140	24

Tea House Kuan Yin	1911 N 45th St	206-632-2055	25
Tully's	2100 N 45th St	206-632-5259	25
Café Allegro Expresso Bar	4214 University Wy NE	206-633-3030	26
Café on the Ave	4201 University Wy NE	206-632-6001	26
Caffe Appassionato	4518 University Wy NE	206-545-4865	26
QFC	2746 NE 45th St	206-729-3080	26
Sureshot Espresso	4505 University Wy NE	206-632-3100	26
Trabant Chai Lounge	1309 NE 45th St	206-675-0668	26
Tully's	3042 NE 45th St	206-525-5110	26
Tully's	4507 Brooklyn Ave NE	206-545-1375	26
Tully's	4700 University Wy NE	206-527-2373	26
Yunnie Bubble Tea	4511 University Wy NE	206-547-9648	26
Cafe Van Gogh	8210 35th Ave NE	206-523-1466	27
The Purple Cow	111 NE 45th St	206-784-1417	28
Café Bambino	405 NW 65th St	206-706-4934	30
Greenwood Branch	8016 Greenwood Ave N	206-684-4086	30
Herkimer Coffee	7320 Greenwood Ave N	206-784-0202	30
Javabean	8500 3rd Ave NW	206-782-7009	30
Monkey Grind Espresso Bar	518 N 85th St	206-782-6100	30
Bus Stop Espresso	800 NE 65th St	206-528-5997	31
Revolutions Espresso	7012 Woodlawn Ave NE	206-527-1908	31
Zoka Coffee Roaster & Tea Company	2200 N 56th St	206-545-4277	31
Blue Dog Coffehouse	5509 University Wy NE	206-523-1933	32
Espresso Express	6500 15th Ave NE	206-524-6326	32
Tully's	8551 Greenwood Ave N	206-788-0181	33
Cloud City Coffee	8801 Roosevelt Wy NE	206-527-5552	34
C&P Coffee Company	5612 California Ave SW	206-933-3125	35
Chevron	2347 California Ave SW	206-933-1100	35
Coffee To A Tea With Sugar	4541 California Ave SW	206-937-1495	35
Cupcake Royale/Verite Coffee	4556 California Ave SW	206-932-2971	35
Freshy's	2735 California Ave SW	206-937-4316	35
Hotwire Online Coffeehouse	4410 California Ave SW	206-935-1510	35
Infinity Espresso	4704 42nd Ave SW	206-923-2944	35
Revolution Coffee	4217 SW Admiral Wy	206-932-3661	35
Tully's	2676 Alki Ave SW	206-938-0732	35
Uptown Espresso	4301 SW Edmunds St	206-935-3753	35
Bubbles	1619 Harbor Ave SW	206-938-0153	36
Uptown Espresso	3845 Delridge Wy SW	206-933-9497	36
Bird On A Wire Espresso	3509 SW Henderson St	206-932-1143	37
Café Rozella	9434 Delridge Wy SW	206-763-5805	37
Caffe Ladro	7011 California Ave SW	206-938-8021	37
Tully's	4205 SW Morgan St	206-938-4450	37
Firstchoice Espresso	10801 Myers Wy S	206-901-9264	38
All City Coffee	1205 S Vale St	206-767-7146	39
Detour Expresso	2006 Rainier Ave S	206-709-4139	39
Tully's	3100 Airport Wy S	206-267-0101	39
Tully's	4400 Rainier Ave S	206-722-3830	40
Jet Fuel Espresso	11234 Tukwila International Blvd	206-764-4944	41
Tully's	7810 SE 27th St	206-236-2959	42
Tully's	3080 148th Ave SE	425-562-7030	44
Tully's	10812 Main St	425-646-3909	45
Tully's	2002 Bellevue Sq Mall	425-467-0247	45
Tully's	302 Bellevue Sq	425-467-0247	45
Tully's	700 Bellevue Wy NE	425-274-4600	45
Tully's	8805 Points Dr NE	425-456-0724	45
Kahili Coffee	105 Lake St S	425-576-5600	48
Jerzy's Coffee	16727 Redmond Wy	425-702-8575	49
Pony Express	16541 Redmond Wy	425-881-2449	49

Seattle is a city of few monuments and has little in the way of epic architecture (the **Central Library (Map 3)** notwithstanding). When other American cities were stockpiling marble and granite, Seattle was still a muddy outpost with wooden sidewalks. Today, post-boom, there remains an unfinished feeling to the landscape. Our most iconic landmark, the structure with which we are most often associated, **The Space Needle (Map 15)**, is largely ignored and sometimes reviled by Seattleites. Same goes for that useless hunk-o-metal better known as the **Monorail (Map 15)**. On the other hand, Seattle possesses no shortage of humorous, weird, sometimes misguided displays of civic pride and identity.

Historic Seattle

An obvious place to start is the **Pike Place Market (Map 3)**, which celebrated its 100th birthday in 2007. Beset though it is by tourists determined to see airborne fish, the market still has a lot to offer local residents. **Smith Tower (Map 7)** was the tallest building west of the Mississippi for nearly 50 years. Both the **Paramount (Map 3)** and **5th Avenue Theatres (Map 3)** take visitors back to vaudeville days. **The Seattle Asian Art Museum (Map 17)** is a 1933 Art Deco wonder in the middle of Volunteer Park. To go back even further, the **Birthplace of Seattle Monument (Map 35)**, an obelisk on Alki Point, marks the arrival of the first white folk in 1851.

Open Spaces

Though there have been a few missteps in the parks department (consider the scary, concrete wonderland of **Freeway Park (Map 3)** the out-of-doors is what Seattle does best. From the untouched to the intricately landscaped, you are never far away from a patch of green in the Emerald City. For complete respite from the urban din, **Discovery Park (Map 11)** is the largest, and perhaps wildest, park within city limits. If it's botany you're after, **Washington Arboretum (Map 22)** on Union Bay contains an herbarium, horticulture center, the **Seattle Japanese Garden (Map 19),** and it's accessible by kayak. The gardens at **Woodland Park (Map 30)** and the **Hiram M. Chittenden Locks (Map 28)** (a.k.a. the Ballard Locks) are gorgeous in season. Both **Gas Works Park (Map 24)** and **Kerry Park (Map 14)** afford postcard-worthy views of the skyline. Finally, **Volunteer Park (Map 18)** on the Hill is Seattle's ultimate urban oasis.

Public Art

Despite Seattle's reputation for lefty-leaning political attitudes, the existence of a mammoth statue of **Vladimir Lenin (Map 24)** in the heart of the Fremont neighborhood strikes most spectators as puzzling. Built in Slovakia and transported to the Emerald City after the fall of communism, this handsome piece now stands among Mexican restaurants, fashionable clothing boutiques, and other bastions of capitalism. Other public sculptures make for easier contextualization, such as Pioneer Square's life-size bronze **Fallen Firefighters' Memorial (Map 7)**, Fremont's six cast-aluminum **Waiting for the Interurban (Map 24)**, and the **Jimi Hendrix Statue (Map 4)** on Capitol Hill. The alluring **Bettie Page Mural (Map 31)** makes commuting interesting for those stuck on I-5, while **The Martin Luther King Jr. Mural (Map 5)** inspires contemplation and reflection each time you stroll by.

Lowbrow Landmarks

Be it the punny greetings of the **Lusty Lady's (Map 3)** marquee or the mammoth, hippy-eating **Fremont Troll (Map 24)**, Seattle's oddball landmarks expose the real character of the city. Not even Wikipedia can explain the existence of Post Alley's **Gum Wall (Map 3)** or the **Wall of Death (Map 26)**, a sculpture that pays homage to, of all things, a motorcycle stunt. The **Pepsi Sign (Map 16)** on Aurora and pink pachyderms of the **Elephant Carwash (Map 2)** offer a comment on the historic value of neon. **The Spooky Coke Machine (Map 17)** is a thirst-quenching mystery. Georgetown's **Hats 'n' Boots (Map 39)** is pure Americana—a roadside wonder built for a gas station now ensconced in a local park. As funky bars go, none is so well-steeped in grime and history as the **Blue Moon Tavern (Map 25)**, a former haunt of beat poets and other counterculture figures**.**

Map 1 • Belltown

Cinerama	2100 4th Ave	206-441-3080	One of three theaters in the world showing three-panel Cinerama films. Amazing.
Edgewater Hotel	2411 Alaskan Wy	206-728-7000	Yes, Virginia, you really can fish from your hotel window.
Olympic Sculpture Park	Western Ave & Broad St	206-332-1333	Ambitious new venue for the SAM's sculpture collection.
Seattle P.I. Globe	101 Elliott Ave W	800-542-0820	Is it the Post-Intelligencer or the Daily Planet?

Map 2 • Downtown / Denny Triangle

Elephant Car Wash	616 Battery St	206-441-6776	That giant pink elephant in the sky.

Map 3 • Downtown

5th Avenue Theatre	1308 5th Ave	206-625-1900	Lavish Chinese-inspired interior. Cheesy shows.
The Blade	Pike St & 2nd Ave		Used to be crack and coke. Now it's condos and coffee.
Columbia Center	701 5th Ave		Tallest building in Seattle with an observation deck on the 73rd floor.
Freeway Park	700 Seneca St		Unique urban park. Bonus points for making it out alive.
Giant Rotating Shuttlecock	Western Ave & Lenora St		Officially known as Angie's Umbrella.
Gum Wall	Lower Post Aly		The most unlikely public art, created by thousands of wads of masticated gum.
The Hammering Man	100 University St	206-654-3100	Jonathan Borofsky's mechanized sculpture looms over the SAM.
Lusty Lady	1315 1st Ave	206-622-2120	Putting the T & A in Seattle since the '70s. Happy Spanksgiving!
Paramount Theatre	911 Pine St	206-467-5510	Former vaudeville theater houses a rare Wurlitzer organ.
Pike Place Market	1501 Pike Pl # 510		So authentic even locals shop here!
Rachel the Pig	Pike Pl & Pike St		Meeting point for internet daters.
Rainier Tower	1301 5th Ave	206-628-5070	Architect Minoru Yamasaki also designed the World Trade Center in NYC.
Seattle Art Museum	100 University St		SAM gets more space and a facelift.
Seattle Central Library	1000 4th Ave	206-264-1120	Koolhaas-designed. Stunning inside and out. Free tours.
"Seattle Police Are Communists" Guy	6th Ave & Pine St		Year round, a man holds a cardboard sign and shouts his polemic about Seattle's finest.

Map 4 • First Hill / Pike / Pine

Egyptian Theatre	805 E Pine St	206-781-5755	Classic, old-style theatre with midnight movies.
Jimi Hendrix Statue	Broadway & E Pine St		Tribute to the wailing guitar god.

Map 5 • Central District (North)

AM/PM Gas Station	23rd Ave & E Cherry St		Panhandlers' address.
Black Panther Headquarters	2111 E Union St		Power to the people.
Martin Luther King, Jr Mural	2726 E Cherry St		A painting of his contemplation.

General Information • **Landmarks**

Map 5 • Central District (North)-continued

Medgar Evers Swimming Pool Mosaic Art	500 23rd Ave		Beautiful, child-like art.
Polish Home	1714 18th Ave	206-322-3020	Pierogies and bison grass vodka, every Friday night.

Map 6 • Madrona

Spectrum Dance Theater	800 Lake Washington Blvd	206-325-4161	Beautiful old brick building is a rare waterfront venue for dance performances.

Map 7 • Pioneer Square / SoDo

Elliott Bay Books	101 S Main St	206-624-6600	Flagship establishment of the Seattle literary scene.
Fallen Firefighters' Memorial	Occidental Park, Occidental Ave S & S Main St		Bronze firemen amid the pigeons and the homeless.
Russian Cobra	101 Alaskan Wy S, Pier 48	206-223-1767	Relive the cold war on a Russian submarine!
Safeco Field	Occidental Ave S & S Royal Brougham Wy	206-628-0888	Lovable M's keep losing here, but at least they have Ichiro and a beer garden.
Smith Tower	506 2nd Ave	206-622-4004	View from 1914 tower is cheaper (and maybe better) than the Space Needle.
The Underground Tour	610 1st Ave	206-682-4646	Entertaining walking tour of Seattle's forgotten bowels.
Waterfall Garden	2nd Ave S & S Main St		This tranquil urban haven commemorates the birth of UPS.

Map 8 • International District

Amazon.com Headquarters	1200 12th Ave S	206-266-1000	Former US Marine Hospital treated war veterans suffering from STDs.
The site of the former Wah Mee Club	Maynard Aly S & S King St		Site of 1983 gang massacre.
Wing Luke Asian Museum	719 S King St	206-623-5124	A gem of a museum in the heart of the ID.

Map 11 • Magnolia / Interbay

Discovery Park	3801 W Government Wy	206-386-4236	534 acres of honest-to-goodness nature.

Map 14 • Queen Anne (West)

Kerry Park	211 W Highland Dr	206-684-4075	All those scenic Seattle postcards? This is the vantage point.

Map 15 • Lower Queen Anne / Seattle Center

Experience Music Project	325 5th Ave N	206-367-5483	A billionaire's rock memorabilia collection and a public eyesore.
International Fountain	305 Harrison St	206-684-7200	Water show set to music.
Monorail	Seattle Ctr & Broad St	206-905-2600	90 thrilling seconds zipping through Seattle (if it's actually running).
Pacific Science Center	200 2nd Ave N	206-443-2001	You're never too old for a Floyd or Zeppelin laser show.
The Space Needle	400 Broad St	206-905-2100	Like so many things in life, it's not as big as you'd expect.

Map 16 • Westlake / South Lake Union

The Center for Wooden Boats	1010 Valley St	206382-2628	Free boat rides on Lake Union every Sunday.

| The Pepsi Sign | Aurora Ave N & Valley St | | Behold the power of neon. |

Map 17 • Capitol Hill (West)

Public Toilet on Broadway	near Dick's at 115 Broadway E		A crap capsule of sex and drugs.
Seattle Asian Art Museum	1400 E Prospect St	206-654-3100	Gorgeous Art Deco building with a superb collection of Asian art.
Spooky Coke Machine	E John St b/w Broadway E & 10th Ave E		Press the mystery button if you dare.
St Marks Cathedral	1245 10th Ave E	206-323-0300	Colossal cathedral on the hill; compline choir attracts yuppies, grannies, and street kids alike.
Top Pot Donuts	609 Summit Ave E	206-323-7841	The planet's best donut shop.

Map 18 • Capitol Hill (East) / Madison Valley

| *Singles* Apartment Complex | 1820 E Thomas St | | No, Matt Dillon doesn't live here anymore. |
| Volunteer Park | 1247 15th Ave E | 206-684-4555 | Climb to the top of this Victorian-era conservatory and water tower. |

Map 19 • Madison Valley / Denny Blaine

| Seattle Japanese Garden | 1075 Lake Washington Blvd E | 206-684-4725 | Renowned formal Japanese garden; check out the periodic tea ceremonies. |

Map 21 • Montlake

Lake View Cemetery	1554 15th Ave E	206-322-1582	Bruce Lee for Kung Fu enthusiasts. Brandon Lee for the Goths.
Seattle's Museum of History & Industry	2700 24th Ave E	206-324-1126	Experience the pre-Starbucks Seattle.
Seattle Yacht Club	1807 E Hamlin St	206-325-1000	Sorry little buddy, members only.

Map 22 • Madison Park

| Washington Park Arboretum | 2300 Arboretum Dr E | 206-543-8800 | A haven for tree-huggers, bird-watchers, and botanists. |

Map 23 • Ballard

| Archie McPhee's | 2428 NW Market St | 206-297-0240 | For all your plastic geoduck needs. |
| Sunset Bowl | 1420 NW Market St | 206-782-7310 | All-night fun: bowling, eating, gambling, and drinking. Is this really Seattle? |

Map 24 • Fremont

Aurora Bridge	Aurora Ave N & N 34th St		Affectionately known as "Suicide Bridge."
Fremont Rocket	601 N 35th St		1950s rocket fuselage bearing the motto, "De Libertas Quirkas," or "Freedom to Be Peculiar."
Fremont Troll	N 36th St & Troll Ave N		Monstrous public art, crushing a real VW.
Statue of Vladimir Lenin	600 N 36th St		The irony grows stronger with every new condo.
Waiting for the Interurban	N 34th St & Fremont Ave N		The 1979 sculpture of commuters is the victim of frequent "art attacks" by locals.

Map 25 • Wallingford

The Blue Moon Tavern	712 NE 45th St	206-675-9116	Countless artistic luminaries have passed out there.
Dick's Drive-In	111 NE 45th St	206-632-5125	A little bit nostalgia, a little bit cholesterol.
Gas Works Park	2101 N Northlake Wy	206-684-4075	Industrial site turned America's strangest park. Amazing view.
Sadako and the Thousand Cranes Peace Park	NE Pacific St & NE 40th St		A tribute to a young girl that died of leukemia after the atomic bombing of Nagasaki.

Map 26 · U District

Red Square	University of Washington		Home of the Barnett Newman's sculpture, *Broken Obelisk*.
Scarecrow Video	5030 Roosevelt Wy NE	206-524-8554	Best video store in the universe.
Wall of Death	Burke Gilman Trail Under the University Bridge		A tribute to the carnival motor domes of the early 20th century.

Map 27 · Laurelhurst / Wedgwood / Sand Point

The Sound Garden	7400 Sand Point Wy NE	Sonorous art installation from which a certain grunge band lifted its name.

Map 28 · Ballard (West)

Hiram M Chittenden Locks	3015 NW 54th St	206-783-7059	Industrial-age marvel; watch the local salmon populations dwindle before your very eyes!

Map 30 · Greenwood / Phinney Ridge

Woodland Park	Aurora Ave N & 59th St	206-684-4075	Here you'll find a zoo, a rose garden, and a veritable metropolis of bunny rabbits.

Map 31 · Green Lake / Roosevelt

Bettie Page Mural	700 NE 59th St	Giant Bettie seduces commuters from the side of a house.

Map 32 · Ravenna

The Wedgwood Rock	28th Ave NE & NE 72nd St	It's a bad sign when a neighborhood's major landmark is a rock.

Map 33 · Northwest Seattle

The Elephant on Aurora	8808 Aurora Ave N		The fate of this elephant is still unknown, so see it while you can.
Granite Curling Club	1440 N 128th St	206-362-2446	Only dedicated curling rink on the West Coast. Need we say more?

Map 34 · Northeast Seattle

Rick's	11332 Lake City Wy NE	206-362-4458	Taking down panties and politicians.

Map 35 · Alki / West Seattle / Admiral District

Alki Beach	Alki Ave SW & Bonair Dr SW	The closest Seattle gets to SoCal for two months a year.
Birthplace of Seattle Monument	62nd Ave SW & Alki Ave SW	Includes a piece of Plymouth Rock transported on the first cross-country road trip to Seattle.
Schmitz Park	5551 SW Admiral Wy	Old-growth forest paths wind along a creek.
Statue of Liberty	61st Ave SW & Alki Ave SW	In honor of the little New York that Alki never became.
Whale Tail Park	58th Ave SW & SW Lander St	Families come from all over Seattle to this little gem of a park. Close to the beach too!

Map 36 · North Delridge

Seacrest Marina	1660 Harbor Ave SW	Scuba divers galore. Elliot Bay Water Taxi to downtown leaves from here.

Map 37 · Fauntleroy / Arbor Heights

Lincoln Park	8011 Fauntleroy Wy SW	Bluff trails and a shoreline walk to salt-water filled Colman Public pool. Fun for the whole family.

Map 39 · SoDo / Beacon Hill / Georgetown

Hat 'n' Boots	6400 Carson Ave S	Former roadside attraction now safely ensconced in Oxbow Park.
Starbucks Headquarters	2401 Utah Ave S	Still waiting for that giant mermaid to jump out and go Godzilla on downtown.

Map 40 · Columbia City / Mount Baker / Seward Park

Columbia City Farmer's Market	4801 Rainier Ave S		Foodie heaven every Wednesday from May to October.
Martin Luther King Jr Memorial Park	2200 Martin Luther King Jr Wy S		A mountain of inspiration; words are inadequate.
Sicks Stadium Sign Rainier Valley	2700 Rainier Ave S	206-403-2080	Once, men hit homers and grounded out here. Now they buy drill bits and caulk.
Tacos el Asadero	3513 Rainier Ave S		The famous Taco Bus!

Map 45 · Bellevue (West) / Medina

Bellevue Art Museum	510 Bellevue Wy NE	425-519-0770	Across the street from Bellevue Square, exhibits arts and crafts from local artists.
Carillon Point	3240 Carillon Point	425-822-1700	Marina waterfront with carillons that ring every 30 minutes.
Meydenbauer Center	11100 NE 6th St	425-637-1020	Convention center featuring cultural, theater, and musical events.
Rosalie Whyel Museum of Doll Art	1116 108th Ave NE	425-455-1116	Mecca for doll lovers.

Map 46 · Bellevue (Central)

Bellevue Botanical Garden	12001 Main St	425-452-2750	Free guided tours on weekends through their 36 acres of gardens and woodlands.
Kelsey Creek Farm	410 130th Ave SE		Ponies and farm animals for the kids.

Map 47 · Bellevue (East) / Redmond

Microsoft Corporate Headquarters	1 Microsoft Wy	425-882-8080	Tiny software company named after that famous street in Redmond, Microsoft Way.

Map 48 · Kirkland

Kirkland Performance Center	350 Kirkland Ave	425-893-9900	400-seat theater hosting an array of performances.
Marina Park	25 Lake Shore Plz		Dig your toes into the sandy beach.

Map 49 · Redmond

Edge Skate Park	NE 83rd St & 161st Ave NE		Skateboard park and graffiti wall sponsored by the city. Cool.
Marymoor Park	6046 W Lake Sammamish Pkwy NE		640 acres for picnics, summer concerts, and chasing dogs.
Theno's Dairy	NE 124th St & WA-202 (Redmond Woodinville Rd)	425-885-2339	Old-fashioned, homemade ice cream with seasonal flavors. NFT fav.

Shortly after Stonewall's major breakthrough in 1969, Seattle's queer culture began to rally for its rights. Students of the University of Washington united to claim their existence and formed organizations. Political activists set up shop in Pioneer Square to protest discrimination. In 1973, the Seattle City Council passed the Fair Employment Practice Ordinance which protected gays and lesbians in the workforce. Eventually, 1977 gave birth to Gay Pride Week which paraded the streets of downtown and traveled up Capitol Hill's slope, where LGBT culture currently reigns. Throughout years of struggles and victories, the women and men of sexual diversities built a strong community for one another. And to this day their efforts thrive in every proud, queer Seattleite.

Seattle's rainy streets are willing and able to compassionately support you in many ways. Local newspapers and guides post listings of entertainment, organized groups, health centers, and gay friendly synagogues. Community publications are distributed to coffee bars, restaurants, clubs, bookstores, and well, just about anywhere dry. Flip through pages and pages of gay adventures for any night or day (both if you get lucky). You can find dykes to dance with and cowboys to ride. Whatever floats your boat, plenty of information can easily be found.

For the most part you can feel safe to publicly express gay affection. Not too many straight citizens express hatred when men grasp hands and women passionately embrace. Also, if your gaydar is finely tuned (or you're just obvious), then it's almost certain to acknowledge family anywhere in the city. Even though the rainy city is a bit introverted, Seattle queers are not too shy to engage in friendly chats. Yes indeed, it's a quaint little home for any ol' chap or dyke. In fact, many queer southerners venture north to saddle up here.

Publications/Media

Greater Seattle Business Association (GSBA) • Directory of businesses and community organizations that are owned, operated, and allies of LGBT.

Seattle Gay News • 1605 12th Ave, #31 • 206-324-4297 • www.sgn.org • Local newspaper featuring LGBT everything a gay community needs.

Seattle Treatment Education Project (STEP) • 206- 328-8979 • www.thebody.com/step/steppage.html • E-zine resource distributed to people affected by HIV/AIDS, case managers, front line workers, and other health professionals.

Capitol Hill Times • www.capitolhilltimes.com • Local newspaper covering Capitol Hill and First Hill news.

GO! • www.gonycmagazine.com • Woman loving women zine featuring national news, events, art, and culture.

Arts and Culture

clubdiversitytv/CPR • 800 Jefferson St, # 1620 • 206- 333-5958

Rainbow City Band • 12144 Shorewood Dr SW • 206- 431-9484 • www.rainbowcityband.com

Seattle Lesbian & Gay Chorus • PO Box 20729 • 206- 860-SLGC • www.slgc.org

Seattle Men's Chorus/ Seattle Women's Chorus • 319 12th Ave • 206- 323-0750 x212 • www.flyinghouse.org

Sports and Recreation

Different Spokes Bicycling Club • www.differentspokes.org

Emerald City Softball Association (Open Division) • 3828 Beach Dr SW Ste 202 • 206-938-7402 • www.seattlegaysoftball.com

Orca Swim Team • 1122 E Pike, PMB #869 • www.orcaswimteam.org

Seattle Frontrunners • www.seattlefrontrunners.org

Seattle Tennis Alliance Social Doubles • www.teamseattle.org/sta

Team Seattle Gay Sports Network • 206- 367-4064 • www.teamseattle.org

Social Groups / Organizations

BinNet Seattle · 206-728-4533 · www.binetseattle.org

Border Riders Motorcycle Club · 206-686-4176 · www.borderriders.com

Cookboys Potluck · 206-860-6969 · event for all ages

Ethyl Forever Car Club · 206-995-8833 · ethylforever@hotmail.com

Gay Fathers' Association of Seattle · www.gfas.org

Mature Friends · 206-781-7724 · www.maturefriends.org

Northwest Bears · 206-903-9288 · www.nwbears.com

Puddletown Dancers · 425-487-0219 · www.puddletowndancers.org

Queer Ladies Stitch & Bitch · queerladiesstichnbitch@yahoo.com

Queer Teen Ensemble Theatre (QUTET) · 608 19th Ave E · www.washingtonensemble.org

Seattle Bi-sexual Women's Network · 206-331-4810 · www.geocities.com/sbwn

Seattle Gay Couples · www.seattlegaycouples.com

Seattle Men in Leather · www.seattlemeninleather.org

Seattle Prime Timers · 206-329-0793 · www.seattleprimetimers.org

Trikone-Northwest: South Asian Queer Community · 1122 E Pike St, #1174 · 425-985-4376 · www.trikone-nw.org

Political Groups/Activism

Equal Rights Washington · PO Box 12216 · 206-324-2570 · www.equalrightswashington.org

Fighting for the Majority · 4329 1st Ave NE · 206-623-9949

Greater Seattle Business Association (GBSA) · 2150 N 107th St, Ste 205 · 206-363-9188 · www.thegsba.org

Greater Seattle Chamber of Commerce · 1301 15th Ave, #250 · 206-389-7215

National Gay and Lesbian Chamber of Commerce · 202-419-0440 · www.nglcc.org

National Gay & Lesbian Task Force · 202-393-5177 · www.thetaskforce.org

Pride Foundation · 1122 E Pike St, PMB 1001 · 206-323-3318 · www.pridefoundation.org

Seattle LGBT Community Center · 1122 E Pike St, #1010 · 206-323-2227 · www.seattlelgbt.org

Seattle Out and Proud (Seattle Pride) · 1605 12th Ave, Ste 2 · 206-322-9561 · www.seattlepride.org

Religious/ Spiritual Services

All Pilgrims Christian Church · 55 Broadway E · 206-322-0488 · www.allpilgrims.org

Broadview Community United Church of Christ · 325 N 125th St · 206-363-8060 · www.broadviewucc.org

Central Lutheran Church · 1710 11th Ave · 206-322-7500 · www.loveiscentral.org

Dharma Buddies/Seattle Gay Buddhist Fellowship · 303 17th Ave E · 206-329-4164 · www.dharmabuddies.org

Dignity/Seattle · 206-325-7314 · www.dignityseattle.org

Directions NW/Evangelicals Concerned · 206-781-6754 · www.ecwr.org

Findlay St. Christian Church (Disciples of Christ) · 4620 S Findlay St · 206-725-5067 · www.findlaystchurch.org

Metropolitan Community Church · 1122 E Pike St PMB 930 · 206-325-2421 · www.mccseattle.org

Plymouth Congregational Church · 1217 6th Ave · 206-622-4865 · www.plymouthchurchseattle.org

Temple De Hirschi Sinai · 1511 E Pike St · 206-315-7392 · www.tdhs-nw.org

University Congregational United Church of Christ · 4515 16th Ave NE · 206-524-2322 · www.universityucc.org

University Unitarian Church · 6556 35th Ave NE · 206-525-8400 · www.uuchurch.org

Wallingford United Methodist Church · 2115 N 42nd · 206-547-6945 · www.wallingfordumc.org

Health Centers and Support Organizations

4 the Moment • -2200 Rainier Ave S • 206- 322-7061 x 212 • Peer facilitated group open to LGBT dealing with both HIV and substance use. Must be abstinent to attend.

Domestic Violence & Sexual Assault:

Northwest Network • 206-568-7777 • 206-517-9670 (tty) • www.nwnetwork.org • Voice support & advocacy for bisexual, trans, lesbian & gay survivors of abuse & dating violence.

Dunshee House (formerly SASG) • 206-322-2437 • www.dunsheehouse.org

Gay City • 206-869-6969 • www.gaycity.org • Organizes events and activities for Gay and Bi men & offers anonymous and confidential HIV/STD testing.

Gay & Lesbian National Hotline (GLNH) • 1-888-843-4564 • Non-profit, peer counseling, information, and local resources.

HIV/AIDS Program, Seattle/King County Dept of Public Health • 206-205-7837 • Provides confidential/anonymous information about and testing for HIV/AIDS.

Ingersoll Gender Center • 206-329-6651• www.ingersollcenter.org • A service agency for the Transsexual, Transvestite, & Transgender community offering support groups, referrals to therapists, publications, and trainings.

Lifelong AIDS Alliance • 206-328-8979 • www.lifelongaidsalliance.org

PFLAG • 206-325-7724 • 1122 E Pike St PMB 620 • www.seattle-pflag.org • Seattle Parents/Families/ Friends of Lesbians and Gays

Project Neon • 511 E Pike • 206-323-1768 • www.crystalneon.org • Speed, sex, and sanity— information group about crystal meth and the gay community

Seattle Counseling Service for Sexual Minorities • 206-323-1768 • Offers support groups for men.

Verbana Health Clinic • 511 E Pike St • 206-299-1600 • A full-service clinic for Lesbians, bi women & transgendered people. Western and naturpathic care, gynecological services, transgender healthcare, fertility counseling, and allergy treatment. Sliding scale, no one turned away.

Women's Community Babes • 206- 720-5566 • Support groups for HIV + women.

Bars/Clubs

Changes • 2103 N 45th St • 206-545-8363

Crescent Lounge • 1413 E Olive Wy • 206-726-1774

Cuff Complex • 1533 13th Ave • 206-323-1525

Elite Tavern • 1520 E Olive Wy • 206-324-4470

Madison Pub • 1315 E Madison St • 206-325-6537

Manray Video Bar • 514 E. Pine St • 206-568-0750

Neighbours Nightclub • 1509 Broadway • 206-324-5358

PURR Cocktail Lounge • 1518 11th Avenue • 206-325-3112

RPlace • 19 E Pine St • 206-322-8828

The Seattle Eagle • 314 E Pike St • 206-621-7591

Thumper's • 1500 E Madison St • 206-328-3800

Wildrose • 1021 E Pike St • 206-324-9210

Youth & Families

American Friends Service Committee-GLBT Youth Program • 814 NE 40th St • 206- 632-0500 x13 • www.afsc.org

CampTen Trees • 1122 E Pike St #1488 • 206- 985-2864 • www.camptentrees.org

Diverse Harmony • 1111 Harvard Ave, #762 • www.diverseharmony.org

Family Works- Family Resource Center • 206- 694-6727 • www.familyworksseattle.org

Rainbow Families of Puget Sound • www.rainbowfamiliesps.org

Seattle Young People's Project • 2820 Cherry • 206-860-9606 • www.sypp.org

If you still associate the library with rubber date stamps and dusty card catalogues, you haven't made use of the Seattle Public Library lately. In keeping with our digital culture, the two-million-item catalogue and hold system are easily accessed online (www.spl.org). From the safety of your home computer you can have books, CDs, and DVDs delivered to your local branch. (Think of it as Netflix for really patient people.) The website also gives library card holders access to a collection of databases including periodical searches, phone and postal directories, and otherwise pricey reference sources such as the Oxford English Dictionary. Patrons can download digital media online and subscribe to library-related podcasts. Many of the 29 branches offer free Wi-Fi, and internet access is available on library PCs with a limit of one hour per patron per day. Audio books and large print editions can be found in most branches, but for a wider selection visit the **Washington Talking Book and Braille Library (Map 2)**.

Libraries

	Address	Phone	Map
Washington Talking Book & Braille Library	2021 9th Ave	206-615-0400	2
Central Library	1000 4th Ave	206-386-4636	3
Madrona-Sally Goldmark Branch	1134 33rd Ave	206-684-4705	6
International District / Chinatown Branch	713 8th Ave S	206-386-1300	8
Douglass-Truth Branch	2300 E Yesler Wy	206-684-4704	9
Magnolia Branch	2801 34th Ave W	206-386-4225	11
Queen Anne Branch	400 W Garfield St	206-386-4227	14
Capitol Hill Branch	425 Harvard Ave E	206-684-4715	17
Montlake Branch	2401 24th Ave E	206-684-4720	21
Ballard Branch	5614 22nd Ave NW	206-684-4089	23
Fremont Branch	731 N 35th St	206-684-4084	24
Wallingford Branch	1501 N 45th St	206-684-4088	25
University Branch	5009 Roosevelt Wy NE	206-684-4063	26
North East Branch	6801 35th Ave NE	206-684-7539	27
Greenwood Branch	8016 Greenwood Ave N	206-684-4086	30
Green Lake Branch	7364 E Green Lake Dr N	206-684-7547	31
Broadview Branch	12755 Greenwood Ave N	n/a	33
Lake City Branch	12501 28th Ave NE	206-684-7518	34
Northgate Branch	10548 5th Ave NE	206-386-1980	34
West Seattle Branch	2306 42nd Ave SW	206-684-7444	35
Delridge Branch	5423 Delridge Wy SW	206-733-9125	36
High Point Branch	3411 SW Raymond St	206-684-7454	37
Southwest Branch	9010 35th Ave S	n/a	37
Beacon Hill Branch	2821 Beacon Ave S	206-684-4711	39
Columbia Branch	4721 Rainier Ave S	206-386-1908	40
NewHolly Branch	7058 32nd Ave S	206-386-1905	40
Rainier Beach Branch	9125 Rainier Ave S	206-386-1906	41
Mercer Island Library	4400 88th Ave SE	206-236-3537	42
Lake Hills Library	15228 Lake Hills Blvd	425-747-3350	44
Newport Way Library	14250 SE Newport Wy	425-888-0554	44
Belluvue Regional Library	1111 110th Ave NE	425-450-1765	45
Kirkland Library	308 Kirkland Ave	425-822-2459	48
Redmond Regional Library	15990 NE 85th St	425-885-1861	49

General Information • **Media**

Television

4 (ABC) KOMO	www.komotv.com	**11 (CW) KSTW**	www.kstw.com
5 (NBC) KING	www.king5.com	**13 (FOX) KCPQ**	www.q13.trb.com
7 (CBS) KIRO	www.kirotv.com	**22 (My Q2)**	www.myq2.trb.com
9 (PBS) KCTS	www.kcts.org	**45 (Azteca America) KHCV**	www.tv45.tv

AM Stations

570 KVI	Talk
630 KCIS	Christian Talk
710 KIRO	Talk
770 KTTH	Talk
820 KGNW	Christian Talk
880 KIXI	Oldies
950 KJR	Sports Talk
1000 KOMO	Talk
1050 KBLE	Catholic Talk
1090 KPTK	Progressive Talk
1150 KKNW	Alternative Talk
1250 KKDZ	Radio Disney
1300 KOL	Talk
1360 KKMO	Spanish Language Programming
1420 KRIZ	Oldies
1560 KZIZ	Gospel
1590 KLFE	Christian Talk
1620 KYIZ	Urban

FM Stations

88.5 KPLU NPR	Don't forget to pledge.
89.5 KNHC	Top 40 • Operated by Nathan Hale High School students.
89.9 KGRG	Rock
90.3 KEXP	Alternative • Best station in town morning, noon, and night.
92.5 KLSY	Top 40
93.3 KUBE	R&B/Hip-Hop • Beyonce, Snoop Dogg, and Parliament unite.
94.1 KMPS	Country/Western
94.9 KUOW NPR	Mandatory blue state listening.
95.7 KJR	Oldies
96.5 KYPT	Oldies
97.3 KBSG	Oldies
98.1 KING	Classical
98.9 KWJZ	Smooth Jazz • Yes, Kenny G is from Seattle.
99.9 KISW	Rock
100.7 KQBZ	Talk
101.5 KPLZ	Rock
102.5 KZOK	Classic Rock • Sometimes you need to get the Led out.
103.7 KMTT	Rock
105.3 KCMS	Christian Music
106.1 KBKS	Top 40
106.9 KRWM	Soft Favorites • Perfect dental office soundtrack.
107.7 KNDD	Alternative • Grunge lives!

Print Media

Beacon Hill News & South District Journal

Belltown Messenger

Capitol Hill Times

Kirkland Courier

North Seattle Herald-Outlook

Madison Park Times

Magnolia News

Pacific Publishing Company
4000 Aurora Ave N, Ste 100
206-461-1300
Free neighborhood-specific newspapers including:

Pike Place Market News
93 Pike St, #312
206-251-2588
Monthly news and gossip from the market.

Queen Anne News

Real Change
2129 2nd Ave
206-441-3247
Raising awareness about local homeless issues.

Seattle's Conscious Choice
3600 15th Ave W, Ste 200
206-320-7788
Free alternative monthly. Socially-progressive news.

Seattle Daily Journal of Commerce
83 Columbia St
206-622-8272 • www.djc.com
Daily business news.

Seattle Gay News
1605 12th Ave, Ste 31
206-324-4297
Free LGBT weekly.

Seattle Magazine
1505 Western Ave, Ste 500
206-284-1750 • www.seattlemag.com
Monthly lifestyle magazine.

Seattle Post-Intelligencer
101 Elliott Ave W
206-448-8000 • www.seattlepi.com
Voice of the Northwest since 1863.

Seattle Sound
1201 1st Ave S, Ste 309
206-382-9220
Monthly local music and arts magazine.

Seattle Times
1120 John St
206-464-2111 • www.seattletimes.com
City's biggest daily. Happy 111th birthday.

Seattle Weekly
1008 Western Ave, Ste 300
206-623-0500 • www.seattleweekly.com
Free alternative weekly going strong for over three decades.

The Stranger
1535 11th Ave, 3rd Floor
206-323-7101 • www.thestranger.com
Seattle's best rag with entertaining political and arts news.

Where Magazine
1904 3rd Ave, Ste 623
206-826-2665
For tourists.

Police	Address	Phone	Map
West Precinct	810 Virginia St	206-615-1999	2
Seattle Police Headquarters	610 5th Ave	206-625-5011	3
East Precinct	1519 12th Ave	206-684-4300	4
North Precinct	10049 College Wy N	206-684-0850	33
Southwest Precinct	2300 SW Webster St	206-733-9800	37
South Precinct	3001 S Myrtle	206-386-1850	41
Mercer Island Police Dept	9611 SE 36th St	425-587-3400	42
Bellevue Police Dept	450 110th Ave NE	425-452-6917	45
Clyde Hill Police Dept	9605 NE 24th St	425-454-7187	45
Medina Police Dept	501 Evergreen Point Rd	425-233-6420	45
Kirkland Police Dept	123 5th Ave	425-587-3400	48
Redmond Police Dept	8701 160th Ave NE	425-556-2500	49

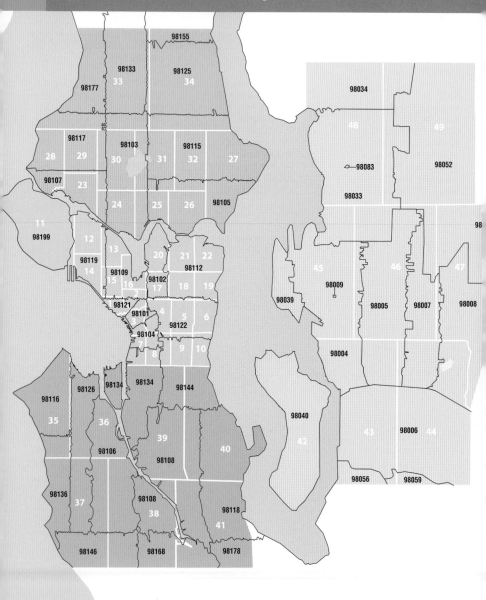

Post Offices

Post Offices	Address	Phone	Map
Cpu Harbor Heights 111	2512 5th Ave	206-448-9287	1
Columbia Center	701 5th Ave, Ste 306	206-625-2293	3
Federal Station	909 1st Ave, Ste 100	206-625-2293	3
Midtown	301 Union St	206-748-5417	3
Seafirst	1001 4th Ave	206-682-3958	3
East Union	1110 23rd Ave	800-ASK-USPS	5
Pioneer Square	91 S Jackson St	206-625-2293	7
International	414 6th Ave S	800-ASK-USPS	8
Magnolia	3211 W Mcgraw St	800-ASK-USPS	11
Queen Anne	415 1st Ave N	800-ASK-USPS	15
Broadway	101 Broadway E	800-ASK-USPS	17
Ballard	5706 17th Ave NW	800-ASK-USPS	23
Wallingford	1329 N 47th St	800-ASK-USPS	24
University	4244 University Wy NE	800-ASK-USPS	26
Wedgwood	7724 35th Ave NE	800-ASK-USPS	27
Greenwood	8306 Greenwood Ave N	800-ASK-USPS	30
Bitter Lake	929 N 145th St	800-ASK-USPS	33
Lake City	3019 NE 127th St	800-ASK-USPS	34
Northgate	11036 8th Ave NE	800-ASK-USPS	34
West Seattle	4412 California Ave SW	800-ASK-USPS	35
Westwood	2721 SW Trenton St	800-ASK-USPS	37
Georgetown	620 S Orcas St	800-ASK-USPS	39
Terminal Finance Station	2420 4th Ave S	800-ASK-USPS	39
Columbia	3727 S Alaska St	800-ASK-USPS	40
Mercer Island	3040 78th Ave SE	800-ASK-USPS	42
CPU Factoria	4020 Factoria Sq Mall SE	800-ASK-USPS	43
Bellevue	1171 Bellevue Wy NE	800-ASK-USPS	45
Medina	816 Evergreen Point Rd	800-ASK-USPS	45
Midlakes	11405 NE 2nd Pl	800-ASK-USPS	46
Crossroads	15731 NE 8th St	800-ASK-USPS	47
Cpu Totem Lake	12556 120th Ave NE	800-ASK-USPS	48
Kirkland	721 4th Ave	800-ASK-USPS	48
Redmond	16135 NE 85th St	800-ASK-USPS	49
Redmond Carrier Annex	7241 185th Ave NE	800-ASK-USPS	49

Useful Phone Numbers:

Emergencies:	911
Police Department:	206-625-5011
Fire Department:	206-386-1400
King County Medic One:	206-296-8550
Seattle Mayor's Office:	206-684-4000
Animal Control:	206-386-PETS (7387)

Websites:

www.exploitseattle.com · No nonsense Seattle events calendar.

www.pikepine.com · Seattle street fashion.

www.seattle.metblogs.com · All Seattle, all the time

www.seattlepi.com ·
The Voice of the Northwest Since 1863.

www.seattletimes.com · The largest daily newspaper in Washington State.

www.seattle.blogmob.org · More blogs.

www.seattle.gov · Official website of the City of Seattle.

www.seattle.gov/parks · Seattle Parks and Recreation.

www.seattle.craigslist.org · Find a job, join a band, buy a second-hand car, or fall in love.

www.spl.org · Seattle public library's website.

www.thestranger.com · Seattle's sharpest (and narrowest) alternative newsweekly.

www.supersonicsoul.com · The ultimate Sonic fansite.

www.sevennites.com · Search for happy hours in Seattle and drink all week.

www.seattle.net · Info on restaurants, shopping, hotels, and events (if NFT just ain't enough).

www.seattlest.com · A website about everything that happens in Seattle.

www.threeimaginarygirls.com · Seattle's sparkly indie-pop press. Local music news, reviews and commentary.

www.transit.metrokc.gov · Seattle Metro Bus website.

www.urbanspoon.com/seattle · Restaurant ratings and reviews.

Essential Seattle Movies

Tugboat Annie (1933)
It Happened At The World's Fair (1967)
Five Easy Pieces (1970)
Cinderella Liberty (1973)
McQ (1974)
WarGames (1983)
Streetwise (1984)
Trouble in Mind (1985)
Say Anything (1989)
My Own Private Idaho (1991)
The Hand That Rocks The Cradle (1992)
Singles (1992)
Sleepless in Seattle (1993)
Hype! (1996)
10 Things I Hate About You (1999)
The Ring (2002)
Police Beat (2005)

We're Number One!!!

· Seattleites buy more sunglasses per capita than any other American metropolis, because it's totally sunny here all the time.

· The Washington State Ferry system is the largest in the USA.

· The term "skid row" originated in Seattle, derived from the "skid road" that 19th-century loggers used to transport lumber through Pioneer Square—the area hit financial ruin during the Depression and the phrase became shorthand for any destitute neighborhood.

· Bertha Landes became the first female mayor of a large American city when she won the Seattle mayoral race in 1926.

· The world's first gas station opened in Seattle in 1907.

· The first publicized report of a flying saucer occurred in Lake City in 1947.

· The first radio station in America to play a Beatles song was in Seattle.

· Seattle is considered the nation's most literate city, and boasts the highest percentage of library card holders and college graduates in the country.

Essential Seattle Songs

"Seattle the Peerless City" — Official Song since 1909
"Seattle Ain't Bullshitting" — Sir Mix-A-Lot
"Seattle" — Public Image, Ltd.
"Seattle" — The Wailers
"Seattle" — Cop Shoot Cop
"Seattle" (from the Screen Gems TV Program Here Come the Brides) — Bobby Goldsboro, Perry Como, Connie Smith and others
"Seattle, WA" — Western Keys
"Seattle Hunch" — Jelly Roll Morton
"Seattle Was a Riot" — Anti-Flag
"Seattle Town" — Flatt & Scruggs
"Seattle Sonics Do It" — Luther Rabb
"Chief Seattle" — Gene Parsons
"Seattle Twist" — Rod McKuen
"Flight to Seattle" — DJ Magic Mike
"Seattle Shuffle" — Damo Suzuki's Network
"Seattle to Chicago" — Woody Guthrie
"The Day Seattle Died" — Cold
"Frances Farmer Will Have Her Revenge on Seattle" — Nirvana
"The Last One To Leave Seattle" — Waylon Jennings
"Sub Pop Rock City" — Soundgarden
"Viva! Sea-Tac" — Robyn Hitchcock
"Stranger" — The Presidents of the United States of America
"Nuke Seattle" — Quincy Punx

Essential Seattle Books

Sons of Profit, by William Speidel. Entertaining and honest look at Seattle's early history.

Buddy Does Seattle, by Peter Bagge. Classic slacker comics.

Eccentric Seattle: Pillars and Pariahs Who Made the City Not Such a Boring Place After All, by J. Kingston Pierce. The mavericks and misfits who shaped our city.

Never Mind Nirvana: A Novel, by Mark Lindquist. Former grunge rocker turns lawyer and experiences angst.

Loser: The Real Seattle Music Story, by Clark Humphrey. Indispensable guide to the city's rich rock and roll heritage.

The Kid: What Happened After My Boyfriend and I Decided to Go Get Pregnant, by Dan Savage. Openly gay Stranger editor/sex advice columnist adopts a young boy, then writes about it.

J.P. Patches, Northwest Icon, by Julius Pierpont Patches and Bryan Johnston. The story behind this beloved local kid's TV star.

Skid Road: An Informal Portrait of Seattle, by Murray Morgan. History of Seattle's rough-and-tumble frontier days.

Waxwings: A Novel, by Jonathon Raban. British-born UW prof finds his life falling apart in Seattle.

Madison House, by Peter Donahue. Novel about Seattle at the dawn of the 20th century.

Selling Seattle, by James Lyons. Academic exploration of Seattle's impact on American culture.

I Sing the Body Electronic: A Year With Microsoft on the Multimedia Frontier, by Fred Moody. A freelance writer goes inside the machine and lives to tell the tale.

The World of Chief Seattle: How Can One Sell the Air? by Warren Jefferson. All about the Suquamish tribe and the treaties that changed everything.

Rat City, by Curt Colbert. Mystery novel set in post-WWII Seattle.

Screaming Life, by Charles Peterson. This is what Seattle rock looks like.

21 Dog Years: Doing Time @ Amazon.com, by Mike Daisy. Hilarious account of Amazon culture during the boom years.

Seattle Timeline

1805: Lewis and Clark explore the Pacific Northwest, including the future state of Washington.

1851: Midwestern settlers led by David and Arthur Denny arrive and begin populating the area that will one day become Seattle.

1869: City of Seattle is incorporated.

1872: Earthquake measuring 7.4 on the Richter scale shakes Seattle.

1878: Seattle's first telephone service established.

1889: Great Seattle Fire destroys downtown.

1890: Bon Marche opens in Seattle as a dry goods store.

1891: Seattle University established.

1893: Transcontinental train line reaches Seattle.

1917: Boeing Airplane Company incorporated, and the Seattle Metropolitans hockey team wins Stanley Cup.

1919: Seattle General Strike begins; the first city-wide strike in the nation.

1928: Inventor/entrepreneur Don Ibsen spends the summer on Lake Washington trying to perfect water skis.

1933: Seattle Art Museum established.

1934: The Muzak corporation established.

1936: University of Washington rowing crew wins Olympic gold.

1938: World's first pressurized airliner, the Boeing Model 307 Stratoliner is launched.

1940: World's first floating bridge opens on Lake Washington.

1942: Jimi Hendrix born in Seattle.

1949: Seattle-Tacoma International Airport established. Also an earthquake measuring 7.1 on the Richter scale shakes Seattle.

1954: Dick's Drive-In serves its first hamburger.

1959: First documented sample of HIV-infected blood collected by University of Washington geneticist Dr. Arno Motulsky while working in the Congo.

1962: Seattle hosts the World's Fair. Science Center, Space Needle, and Monorail are erected for the celebration. Elvis Presley shoots *It Happened at the World's Fair* on location.

1965: Earthquake measuring 6.5 on the Richter scale shakes Seattle.

1970: Abortion legalized by state voters.

1979: Seattle SuperSonics win NBA Championship. Also, future indie-rock label Sub Pop is launched as a fanzine in nearby Olympia.

1980: Mount St. Helens erupts.

1983: Thirteen dead in the Wah Mee massacre in the International District.

1986: Microsoft goes public.

1991: Nirvana releases *Nevermind*, cementing Seattle's growing reputation as Rock City USA.

1995: Mariners almost make it to the World Series. Amazon.com founded.

1994: Nirvana's Kurt Cobain commits suicide, and major record companies start looking for "the next Seattle."

1998: The US Government sues Microsoft for antitrust violations.

1999: The World Trade Organization holds conferences in Seattle, leading to clashes between protesters and policemen downtown.

2000: Kingdome imploded.

2001: Boeing moves corporate offices to Chicago. Earthquake hits measuring 6.8 on the Richter scale.

2003: Green River Killer pleads guilty to 48 murders.

2004: New Seattle Central Library opens to global fanfare. Storm win WNBA championship. Ichiro sets record for most hits in a season (262).

2005: Citywide monorail plan falls apart (again), and Seattleites resigned to riding the bus for the next 2,000 years.

2007: The ultimate urban bible is published (NFT Seattle).

Gyms

	Address	Phone	Map
24 Hour Fitness	1827 Yale Ave		2
24 Hour Fitness	229 Queen Anne Ave N		15
24 Hour Fitness	11030 8th Ave NE		34
24 Hour Fitness	2500 SW Barton St		37
24 Hour Fitness	1505 140th Ave NE		46
24 Hour Fitness	529 Parkplace Centre		48
24 Hour Fitness	1207 N 152 St		n/a
24 Hour Fitness	20202 Ballinger Wy NE, Shoreline		n/a

Restaurants

Cafe Minnie's	101 Denny Wy	206-448-6263	1
Five Point Café	415 Cedar St	206-448-9993	1
13 Coins	125 Boren Ave N	206-243-9500	2
The Hurricane Café	2230 7th Ave	206-682-5858	2
Beth's Café	7311 Aurora Ave N	206-782-5588	30
Debby's Roadside Café	16708 Aurora Ave N	206-546-4144	n/a

Bail Bonds

Henry's Bail Bonds	600 1st Ave	206-332-0900	3
Lacey O'Malley Bail Bonds	601 3rd Ave	206-622-2666	3
All City Bail Bonds	601 6th Ave	206-622-9999	4
Seattle Bail Bonds	321 Yesler Wy	206-622-6633	7

Veterinarians

Animal Critical Care and Emergency Services	11536 Lake City Wy NE	206-364-1660	34

Pharmacies

Bartell Drugs	600 1st Ave N	206-284-1353	15
Bartell Drugs	653 156th Ave NE	425-641-9105	47

Locksmiths

24 Hour 1 Day Locksmith	206-774-9906
24 Hour A-1 Locksmith	206-762-5837
24 Hour A-1 Locksmith	206-363-1646
24 Hour Emergency Locksmith	206-219-9916
24 Hour Emergency Locksmith	206-774-1184
24 Hour Locksmith	206-282-0636
24 Hour Locksmith	206-297-8390
A Express Locksmith	253-815-0066
Bulger Safe & Lock	206-363-8797
Complete Locksmith	877-291-LOCK
Emergency A-1 Locksmith	206-774-9468
Emergency Locksmith	206-219-9953
Emergency Locksmith	206-774-9898
Lee's Keys & Locks	206-522-8840
Pop-A-Lock	253-333-7460
Seattle 5 Star Mobile Locksmith	206-587-4714
Ty's Locksmith	206-725-1997

Plumbers

All American Plumbing	425-489-0281
Best Rooter	206-633-1700
Quality Plumbing All City	206-789-7676

Towing

ABC Towing	206-682-2869
Arrow Towing	206-223-5566
Gerber Towing	206-542-9099
Jim's Northgate Towing	206-364-1500
Lang Towing	206-322-3383
Road Samaritan	206-767-6184

Overview

The city's art gallery epicenter has revolved around the architecturally traditional and not-so-funky Pioneer Square for many years. Perhaps it is the history of the place, the old cobblestones, and faded brick facades that make the neighborhood a natural backdrop for art. But lately the scene has been shifting to new neighborhoods, and Seattle's art scene is now spread out across the city. Make sure to get out and explore beyond Pioneer Square.

Although many neighborhood business associations offer monthly art walks, you'll have vastly differing experiences depending on which locale you choose. Head to Pioneer Square for more traditional art, such as abstract and still life paintings in oils and acrylics, paired with cheap wine and respectful crowds. In the summer months, Occidental Square is abuzz with tents of artists and crafts vendors selling unique jewelry, photography, and smaller works in the street until dark. Wander to Belltown for hip urban street art at **BLVD (Map 1)** or kitschy, lowbrow art at the nationally esteemed **Roq la Rue (Map 1)**. Recently opened to the public is the McLoed Residence, a unique community that domestic partnerships Burning Man with urban art sophisticate. Oh, and it becomes a bar at night. Ballard has a great art walk the second Saturday of each month. Check out the cool space of **OK OK Gallery (Map 23)** to see some of Seattle's newest talent. For an alternative to the refined gallery set, check out the personal studios at the **Tashiro-Kaplan Building (**115 Prefontaine Pl S) during public events, or climb the rickety five stories up **619 Western Avenue** to discover individual artists' lofts brimming with multi-media creativity and inspiration.

Glass Art

Thanks to the international fame and regional influence of local glass artist/corporation Dale Chihuly, Seattle goes wild for anything fragile and hand-blown. Along with area galleries like **William Traver (Map 3)** and **Foster/White (Maps 3 and 7)** that carry the famed Chihuly pieces, there are numerous galleries specializing in glass art from less-famous names, such as **Avalon Glassworks (Map 36)** or the **Seattle Glassblowing Studio (Map 1)**. Smaller local boutiques carry knockoffs that only the trained eye might be able to distinguish from so-called "fine art" pieces (or so we assume), proving the popularity of glass art among Seattle's hoi polloi as well as dot-com millionaires and other arbiters of taste.

Off the Beaten Path

Well worth seeking out is **Western Bridge** gallery **(Map 39)**, located in Seattle's industrial district**,** which exhibits local and international artists' work in a beautiful renovated warehouse setting. The non-profit Jack Straw Productions, founded in 1962, supports local audio arts first and foremost, providing recording studio assistance and performance space for its members. However, with the organization's **New Media Gallery (Map 26)**, the Straw extends the art of noise through combination with various disciplines, creating installations that are as visually arresting as they sound. Locally-based alternative comics press Fantagraphics recently opened a flagship store as well at **Georgetown Records (Map 39)**, not only to hawk its wares, but also to host showings of original artwork from renowned cartoonists**.**

Map 1 • Belltown

	Address	Phone
AT.31 Gallery	109 W Denny Wy	206-283-5253
BLVD	2316 2nd Ave	n/a
McLoed Residence	2209 2nd Ave	206-441-3314
Roq La Rue Gallery	2312 2nd Ave	206-374-8977
Seattle Glassblowing Studio	2227 5th Ave	206-448-2181
Solomon Fine Art	3131 Western Ave	206-297-1400
Suyuma Space	2324 2nd Ave	206-256-0810
Viveza	2604 Western Ave	206-956-3584

Map 2 • Downtown / Denny Triangle

Art Not Terminal Gallery	2045 Westlake Ave	206-233-0680
Patricia Cameron Fine Art	234 Dexter Ave N	206-343-9647
Winston Wachter Fine Art	203 Dexter Ave N	206-652-5855
Woodside/Braseth Gallery	2101 9th Ave	206-622-7243

Map 3 • Downtown

Benham Gallery	1216 1st Ave	206-622-2480
Carolyn Staley Fine Japanese Prints	2001 Western Ave	206-621-1888
Facere Jewelry Art Gallery	1420 5th Ave	206-624-6768
Foster/White Gallery	1331 5th Ave	206-583-0100
Friesen Gallery	1200 2nd Ave	206-628-9501
Gallery Mack	2003 Western Ave	206-448-1616
Isis on First	1100 1st Ave	866-628-9424
Jeffrey Moose Gallery	1333 5th Ave	206-467-6951
Kim Drew Studio and Gallery	1311 Post Aly	206-343-4101

Arts & Entertainment • **Art Galleries**

Map 3 • Downtown–continued

	Address	Phone
The Legacy Ltd	1003 1st Ave	206-624-6350
Lisa Harris Gallery	1922 Pike Pl	206-443-3315
Milagros Mexican Folk Art	1530 Post Aly	206-464-0490
Phoenix Rising Gallery	2030 Western Ave	206-728-2332
Vetri International Glass	1404 1st Ave	206-667-9608
William Traver Gallery	110 Union St	206-587-6501

Map 4 • First Hill / Pike / Pine

Ballard Fetherson Gallery	818 E Pike St	206-322-9440
Bluebottle Art Gallery	415 E Pine St	206-325-1592
Martin-Zambito Fine Art	721 E Pike St	206-726-9509
Photographic Center Northwest	900 12th Ave	206-720-7222
Pound Gallery	1216 10th Ave	206-323-0557
Warren Knapp Gallery	1530 Melrose Ave	206-381-3335

Map 7 • Pioneer Square / SoDo

Azuma Gallery	530 1st Ave S	206-622-5599
Corridor Gallery	306 S Washington St	206-856-7037
D'Amado/Woltz Gallery	307 Occidental Ave S	206-652-4414
Davidson Contemporary	310 S Washington St	206-624-7684
Davidson Galleries	313 Occidental Ave S	206-624-1324
Flury & Company Gallery	322 1st Ave S	206-587-0260
Foster/White Gallery	220 3rd Ave S	206-622-2833
G Gibson Gallery	300 S Washington St	206-587-4022
Gallery 110	110 S Washington St	206-624-9336
Gallery 4 Culture	101 Prefontaine Pl S	206-296-8674
Garde Rail Gallery	110 3rd Ave S	206-621-1055
Glasshouse Studio	311 Occidental Ave S	206-682-9939
Global Art Venue	314 1st Ave S	206-264-8755
Greg Kucera Gallery	212 3rd Ave S	206-624-0770
Grover/Thurston Gallery	309 Occidental Ave S	206-223-0816
Howard House Contemporary Art	604 2nd Ave	206-256-6399
James Harris Gallery	309A 3rd Ave S, Ste A	206-903-6220
Kagedo Japanese Art	520 1st Ave S	206-467-9518
Kibo Galerie	323 Occidental Ave S	206-442-2100
La Familia Gallery	117 Prefontaine Pl S	206-291-4608
Linda Hodges Gallery	316 1st Ave S	206-624-3034
NorthWest Fine Woodworking	101 S Jackson St	206-625-0542
Pacini Lubel Gallery	207 2nd Ave S	206-326-5555
Platform Gallery	114 3rd Ave S	206-323-2808
Punch Gallery	119 Prefontaine Pl S	206-621-1945
Soil Art Gallery	112 3rd Ave S	206-264-8061
Stonington Gallery	119 S Jackson St	206-405-4040
The Underground Gallery	214 1st Ave S, B-12	206-340-9395
Vision Gallery	312 S Washington St, Ste A	206-264-0609

Map 8 • International District

Lawrimore Project	831 Airport Wy S	206-501-1231

Map 12 • Queen Anne (North)

Fountainhead Gallery	625 W McGraw St	206-285-4467

Map 15 • Lower Queen Anne / Seattle Center

Pottery Northwest	226 1st Ave N	206-285-4421

Map 18 • Capitol Hill (East) / Madison Valley

Baas Art Gallery	2703 E Madison St	206-324-4742
Lewis/Wara Gallery	1121 15th Ave	206-405-4355
Miner Gallery	346 15th Ave E	206-568-7604

Map 23 • Ballard

Art By Fire Gallery	5465 Leary Ave NW	206-789-1490
Ok Ok	5107 Ballard Ave NW	206-789-6242

Map 24 • Fremont

Black Box Gallery	4911 Aurora Ave N	206-579-2662
Edge of Glass Gallery	513 N 36 St	206-632-7807
Gallery 154	154 N 35th St	206-632-4880
TimesInfinity Gallery	122 NW 36th St	206-973-4470

Map 26 • U District

Henry Art Gallery	4100 15th Ave NE	206-543-2280
Jack Straw / New Media Gallery	4261 Roosevelt Wy NE	206-634-0919
Kirsten Gallery	5320 Roosevelt Wy NE	206-522-2011

Map 28 • Ballard (West)

Sev Shoon Arts Center	2862 NW Market St	206-782-2415

Map 30 • Greenwood / Phinney Ridge

Francine Seders Gallery	6701 Greenwood Ave N	206-782-0355

Map 34 • Northeast Seattle

Snow Goose Associates	8806 Roosevelt Wy NE	206-523-6223

Map 36 • North Delridge

Avalon Glassworks	2914 SW Avalon Wy	206-937-6369

Map 39 • SoDo / Beacon Hill / Georgetown

Georgetown Records / Fantagraphics	1201 S Vale St	206-762-5638
Western Bridge	3412 4th Ave S	206-838-7444

Map 40 • Columbia City / Mount Baker / Seward Park

Columbia City Gallery	4864 Rainier Ave S	206-760-9843

Map 43 • Bellevue (Southwest)

East Shore Gallery	12700 SE 32nd St	425-747-3780

Map 45 • Bellevue (West) / Medina

Elements Gallery	10500 NE 8th St	425-454-8242
Ming's Asian Gallery	10217 Main St	425-462-4008

Map 48 • Kirkland

Gunnar Nordstrom Gallery	127 Lake St S	425-827-2822
Howard/Mandville Gallery	120 Park Ln, Ste D	425-889-8212
Patricia Rovzar Gallery	118 Central Wy	425-889-4627
Thomas D Mangelsen's Images of Nature Gallery	108 Central Wy	425-739-9118

With literary events cropping up all over Seattle—not just in libraries and bookstores, but in coffee houses, bars, art museums, and rock music venues—it's hardly a shock that we rank as the most literate city in the country. We love our libraries, devour our newspapers, and according to the 2005 CCSU study, only San Francisco has more booksellers than Seattle. Independent bookstores here, as everywhere, struggle to compete with the big conglomerates. But despite a chronic rash of Barnes & Nobles and Borders, as well as housing Amazon.com headquarters, privately owned bookstores in Seattle have maintained and strong presence and a loyal customer base.

Literary Treasures

Elliot Bay Book Company (Map 7) in Pioneer Square is the favorite son of Puget Sound literati. Established in 1973, the store long ago carved its niche as a cultural gathering place with frequent readings by big-name authors and book groups. It can be argued, however, that the only advantage Elliot Bay really has over the competition (besides all that exposed brick) is killer PR. Ask Seattleites to name the best local bookstore, and you'll rarely hear the same answer twice. Here are some contenders: **Bailey/Coy Books (Map 17)** is a popular favorite on Capitol Hill, known for its extensive gay and lesbian literature section and new and used editions. **Magus Books (Map 26)** in the U-District has a grandpa's attic feel. **Ravenna Third Place Books (Map 32)** offers excellent variety, as does Ballard's **Epilogue Books (Map 23)** and **Twice Sold Tales (Map 26)** on the Ave, which has several resident cats. **Wessel & Lieberman Booksellers (Map 7)** is ideal for more high-brow browsing, if you will, offering many antiquarian and out-of-print titles as well as prints.

Books by the Mile

If your true desire is to surround yourself with an immense acreage of reading material (no shame in that), check out **Barnes & Noble University Village (Map 26)**. With something like forty-thousand square feet of

retail space, you can browse until you fall down dead. **University Bookstore (Map 26)** also has an impressive collection of books including substantial technology, health science, and periodical sections (not to mention an art supply store), although a recent renovation dulled its independent spirit a few years ago. **Half Price Books (Maps 49, 17, 26)** is a regional chain with seven locations around Puget Sound and an ever-changing stock of used books, plus deals on CDs, DVDs, and magazines. To satiate your inner Comic Book Guy, check out their disorganized comics bin which is peppered with treasures cast off by boneheads who didn't know what they had.

Specialty

Open Books: A Poem Emporium (Map 25) bravely limits its stock to poetry—one of only two such bookstores in the US. **Cinema Books (Map 26)** is devoted solely to the silver screen. Collectors of art and architecture books should see **Peter Miller Books (Map 3)** downtown and **Art Books & Press (Map 23)** in Ballard. **Seattle Mystery Bookshop (Map 3)** is a paradise for readers of whodunits, thrillers, and true crime, but look to **Edge of the Circle Books (Map 4)** for your pagan and occult literature. **Left Bank Books Collective (Map 3)** is the place for all you lefty-commie-pinkos who still care about the world. May our numbers increase.

For travelers, **Wide World Books & Maps (Map 25)** has all manner of portable goodies in addition to an excellent selection of guidebooks and travel writing. **Metsker Maps of Seattle (Map 3)** in Pike Place Market also carries a variety of travel and recreational guidebooks, as well as carrying our favorite retail item—maps. Birders and botanists will love **Flora & Fauna Books (Map 12)**. Formerly of Pioneer Square, the naturalist bookstore has moved to Magnolia near Discovery Park. And for young minds, try **The Secret Garden Bookshop (Map 23)**, **Alphabet Soup (Map 24)**, and **All for Kids Books and Music (Map 26)**.

Map 2 • Downtown / Denny Triangle

Kaufer's Religious Supplies	320 9th Ave N	206-622-3100	Religious.

Map 3 • Downtown

A Literary Saloon - BLMF	1501 Pike Pl	206-621-7894	Used and rare.
Art of Illustration	1301 1st Ave	206-254-9100	Gallery of book illustrations/books about illustrators.
Arundel Books	1001 1st Ave	206-624-4442	New, used, and rare.
Barnes & Noble	600 Pine St	206-264-0156	Chain.
Borders	1501 4th Ave	206-622-4599	Chain.
Christian Science Downtown Reading Room	1215 2nd Ave	206-623-4034	Christian Science.

Map 3 • Downtown—*continued*

Eco-Elements	1530 1st Ave	206-467-7745	Mind-body-spirit-earth.
Left Bank Books Collective	92 Pike St	206-622-0195	Leftist slant.
M Coy Books & Espresso	117 Pine St	206-623-5354	Books and espresso.
Metsker Maps of Seattle	1511 1st Ave	206-623-8747	Maps and travel guides.
Peter Miller Books	1930 1st Ave	206-441-4114	Architecture and design.
Seattle Mystery Bookshop	117 Cherry St	206-587-5737	Mystery.
The White Horse Trading Co	1908 Post Aly	206-441-7767	Pub and bookstore.
Zanadu Comics	1923 3rd Ave	206-443-1316	Comics.

Map 4 • First Hill / Pike / Pine

Spine and Crown Books	413 E Pine St	206-322-1227	Neighborhood independent.
City Books	1305 Madison St	206-682-4334	Neighborhood independent.
Edge Of The Circle Books	701 E Pike St	206-726-1999	Paganism and the occult.
Revolution Books	1833 Nagle Pl	206-325-7415	Leftist slant.
Seattle University Bookstore	823 12th Ave	206-296-5820	Text books.

Map 7 • Pioneer Square / SoDo

Elliot Bay Books	101 S Main St	206-624-6600	New and used.
The Globe Bookstore	218 1st Ave S	206-682-6882	Theatre books.
Wessel & Lieberman	208 1st Ave S	206-682-3545	Rare books.

Map 8 • International District

Seattle Gospel Center Bookstore	667 S King St	206-624-0988	Spiritual.

Map 9 • Central District (South)

Jackson Street Books	2301 S Jackson St	206-324-7000	Neighborhood independent.

Map 12 • Queen Anne (North)

Flora & Fauna Books	3212 West Government Wy	206-623-4727	Natural history.

Map 13 • Upper Queen Anne

Armchair Sailor	2110 Westlake Ave N	206-283-0858	Nautical.
Queen Anne Avenue Books	1811 Queen Anne Ave N	206-283-5624	Contemporary literature and children's books.

Map 17 • Capitol Hill (West)

Bailey - Coy Books	414 Broadway E	206-323-8842	Neighborhood independent.
Half Price Books Records Magazines	115 Belmont Ave E	206-267-7777	New and used at half price.
Quest Bookshop	717 Broadway E	206-323-4281	Metaphysical.

Map 18 • Capitol Hill (East) / Madison Valley

Horizon Books	425 15th Ave E	206-329-3586	Used.

Map 20 • Eastlake / Montlake / Portage Bay

Vedanta Society of Western Washington	2716 Broadway E	206-323-1228	Hinduism and Vedanta.

Map 23 • Ballard

Arcane Comics and More	5809 15th Ave NW	206-781-4875	Comics, games, videos.
Art Books Press Bookstore & Gallery	4703 Ballard Ave NW	206-285-2665	Art books and gallery.
Epilogue Books	2001 NW Market St	206-297-2665	New and used.
Secret Garden Bookshop	2214 NW Market St	206-789-5006	Specilizes in kids books.

Arts & Entertainment • **Bookstores**

Map 24 • Fremont

Alphabet Soup	1406 N 45th St	206-547-4555	Kids books.
B Brown & Associates	3534 Stone Wy N	206-634-1481	Used and rare.
Episcopal Bookstore	3837 Stone Wy N	206-545-0500	Episcopal.
Fremont Place Book Co	621 N 35th St	206-547-5970	Neighborhood independent.
Laughing Elephant	3645 Interlake Ave N	206-447-9229	Family oriented religious.
Ophelia's Books	3504 Fremont Ave N	206-632-3759	An eclectic mix.
Sea Ocean Book Berth	3534 Stone Wy N	206-675-9020	Used maritime books.
Seattle Book Center	3530 Stone Wy N	206-547-7870	Used and rare.
Wit's End Bookstore & Tea Shop	4262 Fremont Ave N	206-547-2330	Neighborhood independent.

Map 25 • Wallingford

Comics Dungeon	250 NE 45th St	206-545-8373	Comics and comic-related items.
Open Books A Poem Emporium	2414 N 45th St	206-633-0811	Poetry and poetry related.
Wide World Books & Maps	4411 Wallingford Ave N	206-634-3453	Travel books.

Map 26 • U District

All for Kids Books & Music	2900 NE Blakeley St	206-526-2768	Kid's books.
Barnes & Noble	2675 NE University Village St	206-517-4107	Chain.
Cinema Books	4753 Roosevelt Wy NE	206-547-7667	Rare and collectable books on film.
Dreaming	5226 University Wy NE	206-525-9394	Comics.
Globe Books	5220 University Wy NE	206-527-2480	Used.
Half Price Books Records Magazines	4709 Roosevelt Wy NE	206-547-7859	New and used at half price.
Magus	1408 NE 42nd St	206-633-1800	Used.
Twice Sold Tales	4501 University Wy NE	206-545-4226	Used.
University Bookstore	4326 University Wy NE	206-634-3400	U of Washington.
Zanadu Comics	1307 NE 45th St	206-632-0989	Comics.

Map 28 • Ballard (West)

Abraxus Books	6335 Seaview Ave NW	206-297-6777	Used and rare.

Map 29 • Ballard / Loyal Heights

Crown Hill Stamp & Coin	8343 15th Ave NW	206-789-5363	Comics and collectables.

Map 30 • Greenwood / Phinney Ridge

Arundel Book Wearhouse	318 N 85th St	206-782-9470	New, used, and rare.
Couth Buzzard Books	7221 Greenwood Ave N	206-789-8965	Used.
Dreamstrands Comics & Such	115 N 85th St	206-297-3737	Comics.
Harvest Logos Bookstore	115 N 85th St	206-781-8725	Faith and religion.
Twelve Step Shop	6300 Phinney Ave N	206-789-6300	Health, addictions & abuse.

Map 31 • Green Lake / Roosevelt

East West Bookshop Of Seattle	6500 Roosevelt Wy NE	206-523-3726	Spiritual and metaphysical.
Horizon Books	6512 Roosevelt Wy NE	206-523-4217	Used.

Map 32 • Ravenna

Ravenna Rare Books	5639 University Wy NE	206-525-3737	Rare books.
Renaissance Books	5554 27th Ave NE	206-523-1712	Rare books.
Third Place Books Ravenna	6504 20th Ave NE	206-525-2347	Neighborhood independent.
Tree of Life Books & Judaica	2201 NE 65th St	206-527-1130	Books on Judaism.

Map 33 • Northwest Seattle

Balderdash Books & Art	8536 Greenwood Ave N	206-784-4660	Used.
Gary's Games & Hobbies	8539 Greenwood Ave N	206-789-8891	Books on chess, bridge, and other games.

Map 34 • Northeast Seattle

Barnes & Noble	401 NE Northgate Wy	206-364-5810	Chain.

Map 35 • Alki / West Seattle / North Admiral

Leisure Books	4537 California Ave SW	206-935-7325	New and used.
Pegasus Book Exchange	4553 California Ave SW	206-937-5410	Used.
Square One Books	4724 42nd Ave SW	206-935-5764	Neighborhood Independent.

Map 37 • Fauntleroy / Arbor Heights

Barnes & Noble	2600 SW Barton St	206-932-0328	Chain.

Map 40 • Columbia City / Mount Baker / Seward Park

Books4Cars	4850 37th Ave S	206-721-3077	Automotive books and manuals.
Bookworm Exchange	4860 Rainier Ave S	206-722-6633	New and used.

Map 41 • Rainier Valley / Rainier Beach

Aviation Book Company	7201 Perimeter Rd S	206-767-5232	Aviation.

Map 42 • Mercer Island

Island Books	3014 78th Ave SE	206-232-6920	Neighborhood independent.

Map 43 • Bellevue (Southwest)

Stargazers	12727 NE 20th St	425-885-7289	Spiritual.

Map 44 • Bellevue (South)

Deseret Book	3080 148th Ave SE	425-747-7475	Mormon.

Map 45 • Bellevue (West) / Medina

Barnes & Noble	626 106th Ave NE	425-451-8463	Chain.
University Book Store - Bellevue Store	990 102nd Ave NE	425-462-4500	UW text books and general.

Map 47 • Bellevue (East) / Redmond

Barnes & Noble	15600 NE 8th Ave	425-644-1650	Chain.
Lake Hills Book Exchange	523 156th Ave SE	425-746-0354	Used.

Map 48 • Kirkland

Family Christian Stores	12602 Totem Lake Blvd NE	425-821-1281	Christian.
Park Place Books	348 Central Wy	425-828-6546	Geared towards suburban families, selection is disappointing for an independent bookstore.
Stonehouse Bookstore & Growth Center	10600 NE 68th St	425-889-5106	Spiritual.

Map 49 • Redmond

Borders	16549 NE 74th St	425-869-1907	Chain.
Half Price Books	7805 Leary Wy NE	425-702-2499	Used.
Soulfood	15748 Redmond Wy	425-881-5309	Mind/body/spirit.

Outside our city walls, Seattle is probably best known in four different and very cliched capacities: the film *Sleepless in Seattle*, excessive rainfall, grunge music, and coffee. The first is a cheesy, yet strangely lovable, romantic comedy revealing little more about Seattle than the existence of some house boats and the Space Needle. The second is not an entirely accurate association, either (more inches fall on New York, people!). Grunge music has long vacated the premises (indie rock being the new tenant in town), but the last—sweet, sweet coffee—deserves its reputation as one of Seattle's reigning claims to fame. It is everywhere. It is on every city block. It is in every bookstore. Every grocery chain. You cannot escape the coffee.

The ubiquity is much owed, of course, to that little superchain known as Starbucks, which took our love of roasted goodness and dispatched it onto every street corner known to man. But one does not need to look much further than the green mermaid to find an overwhelming number of local coffee shops in the business of elevating the beverage into something of an art form. Some NFT neighborhood favorites: **Joe Bar (Map 17), Bauhaus Books & Coffee (Map 4), All City Coffee (Maps 7, 39), Zeitgeist (Map 7), Fuel (Map 18), Verite Coffee (Maps 6, 23, 35),** and **Caffe Vita (Maps 4, 15).**

So, with all these options, how does one choose the perfect percolated fix? Well, everyone's got their own cup of tricks. For ye seeking the double whammy caffeine-sugar combo to perk up your morning, get thee straight to **Top Pot (Maps 1, 17, 27)** for a double espresso and one of their legendary handcrafted donuts (the old-fashioned cake version is outlandish). The intellectual sipper will undoubtedly prefer the more cerebral draw of a "cupping" (that's a coffee tasting, for Folgers-minded folk), offered by the likes of **Caffe Appassionato (Maps 3, 15, 26)** and **Victrola (Maps 4, 18),** during which you'll be schooled—for free!—on coffee's more subtle nuances. Loyal followers trek regularly to the recently relocated **Espresso Vivace (Map 17),** one of the more serious players on the block. The proof is definitely in their crema—Vivace pours some of the most luscious espresso around, and they'll be happy to teach you the how-tos with a full line of their instructional DVDs. Perky pilgrims, from as far as South Korea, have come to be humbled by Vivace's gurus. Not to be outdone in the experience department, **Zoka Coffee Roasters & Tea (Map 31)** can lay claim to some lofty titles themselves, with a team of award-winning baristas and a qualified "Super Taster" (a person blessed with exceptional taste buds), plus industry honors aplenty. And now Portland-based **Stumptown Coffee (Map 4)** has entered the Seattle coffee frenzy with two new locations. Their shop on 12th Avenue houses a state-of-the art roasting facility where tastings are held everyday at 3 pm.

Saying Seattleites are obsessed with their coffee may be the most common cliche in the book, but an admitted one. When we've got it this good everywhere we go, we're allowed to be snobs. And that, our caffeinated birthright, is what allows us to say to all you East Coasters: whatever Dunkin Donuts serves, it is not good, and it is not coffee. Period.

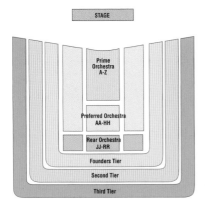

General Information

NFT Map: 3
Address: 200 University St
Seattle WA 98101
Website: www.seattlesymphony.org
Phone: 206-215-4800
Tickets: www.seattlesymphony.org; 206-215-4747
or www.ticketmaster.com; 206-292-2787

Overview

Rising up out of an entire city block in the heart of downtown, Benaroya Hall, home to the Seattle Symphony, opened in September 1998. The venue boasts the best balance between acoustic technology and luxurious ambience that 120 million dollars could provide. Taking full advantage of the astounding acoustics, local band Pearl Jam recorded and released *Live at Benaroya Hall* in 2004—but this is not the typical venue of rock musicians. In addition to the symphony, other art performances and lectures are offered in two halls, the S. Mark Taper Foundation Auditorium (capacity 2,500) and the Illsley Ball Nordstrom Recital Hall (capacity 540). Great glass flows of light and color fashioned by the renowned Dale Chihuly are featured in the lobby, which also houses a small café and a surprisingly good gift shop. Be forewarned when choosing your seat location—the front row seats in the upper tiers give the sensation that absolutely nothing is between you and the performance, including any protection from plunging over the edge. Nearby parking is plentiful, but if you arrive late, you can sip a glass of wine while you whisper to your fellow latecomers about the increasingly horrible Seattle traffic and watch the concert on a large screen television in the lobby until being seated at intermission.

How to Get Tickets

In addition to the cost of the ticket, you'll pay hefty fees for the dubious distinction of buying tickets through Ticketmaster at www.ticketmaster.com. Skip the fees, and buy your tickets directly from the Benaroya Box Office at the corner of Third Avenue and Union, visit their website at www.seattlesymphony.org, or call them at 206-215-4747. The ticket office is open 10 am to 6 pm weekdays, Saturday 1 pm to 6 pm, and 2 hours before performances begin.

How to Get There—Driving

Benaroya Hall occupies the block between 2nd and 3rd Avenue, and Union and University Streets. The main public entrances are on 3rd Avenue.

Southbound I-5: Take the Union Street exit (#165B) and proceed five blocks to 2nd Avenue. Turn left onto 2nd Avenue. The Benaroya Hall parking garage will be on your immediate left, with the garage entrance on 2nd Avenue just south of Union Street.

Northbound I-5: Exit left onto Seneca Street (exit #165). Proceed two blocks and turn right onto 4th Avenue. Continue two blocks and turn left onto Union Street. Continue two blocks and turn left onto 2nd Avenue. The Benaroya Hall parking garage will be on your immediate left, with the garage entrance on 2nd Avenue just south of Union Street.

Parking

Your best bet is the 430 car garage located beneath Benaroya Hall. The entrance is off of 2nd Avenue. If it is full, there is metered street parking and more garages nearby. Street parking is free after 6 pm and on Sundays.

How to Get There—Bus

Numerous bus routes serve Benaroya Hall. For details, call Metro Rider Information at 206-553-3000 (voice) or 206-684-1739 (TDD). Reach metro online at http://transit.metrokc.gov.

General Information

NFT Map: 15
Address: 321 Mercer St
Seattle WA 98109
Website: www.seattlecenter.com
Phone: 206-684-7200
Tickets: 206-684-7200; www.ticketmaster.com;
www.pnb.org; www.seattleopera.org;
www.seattlefilm.org

Overview

Marion Oliver McCaw Hall at Seattle Center, the state-of-the-art performance hall our reliance on cell phones helped finance, opened in June 2003. Of course, cell phones are strictly verboten during performances—there's just no place for your rap ringin', video camera of a cell phone during *Swan Lake* or *La Boheme*. Put the technology aside, relax, and enjoy yourself in this splendid venue. Besides being the home of the Pacific Northwest Ballet and Seattle Opera, McCaw Hall can be booked for weddings, conventions, and receptions if you have a pretty penny and need over-the-top accommodations. McCaw Hall houses a 2,900-seat auditorium, a 400-seat Lecture Hall, a café, a five-story serpentine glass Grand Lobby, and a 17,800-square-foot public plaza (the Kreielsheimer Promenade) that serves as an entry into McCaw Hall and the Seattle Center Campus. True to the eco-sensibilities of Seattle, McCaw Hall was built with green technology, featuring the use of recycled materials and energy-efficient theatrical lighting. Seattle opera and ballet-goers keep up the green theme—Dansko clogs are more common than Jimmy Choos, polar fleece wins out over cashmere. Even if you aren't an opera or ballet buff, it's worth a stroll through the promenade to experience just what money can buy, but if you want to be blown away by lavish productions in the extreme, splurge on the ballet and an opera and dress up—at least once. You might fall in love.

The Seattle International Film Festival recently opened a repertory movie house which, in addition to being a SIFF destination, programs retrospectives and cult films year round. In their first year they honored the great Stanley Kubrick by devoting a week to each of his films. Check out www.seattlefilm.org for more info.

How to Get Tickets

Pacific Northwest Ballet tickets can be purchased directly by calling 206-441-2424 or online at www.pnb.org. For the Seattle Opera call 206-389-7676 or visit www.seattleopera.org. You can also purchase tickets for performances at McCaw Hall online at www.ticketmaster.com or by calling the Ticketmaster Fine Arts Line at 206-292-2787. The box office for McCaw Hall events opens two hours before performances, and during normal weekday hours, but weekend hours vary, so call first. For a last minute option, you can also try the Craigslist tickets section. You might luck out, but beware of being scammed.

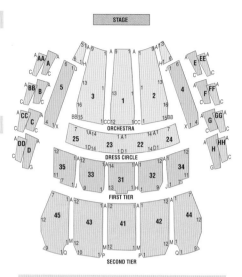

How to Get There—Driving

From I-5: Take the Mercer Street exit. At the first light, turn right. At the next light turn left on to Valley Street. Follow Valley Street as it turns into Broad Street, turn right immediately after the underpass. Take a right on 5th Avenue. Turn left on Roy Street, and then turn left onto 2nd Avenue. Turn left onto Mercer Street. McCaw Hall is directly on your right at 321 Mercer Street (Mercer & 3rd Ave N). If you think these directions sound confusing–you've understood them perfectly, it can be tricky to navigate around the perimeter of the Seattle Center. If you get lost, just head toward the Space Needle—McCaw Hall is located just north of the Space Needle on the grounds of the Seattle Center.

Parking

Your best bet is the parking garage located across Mercer Street from McCaw Hall. A skybridge connects the garage to the Hall. Or you can park in one of the several open-air lots surrounding the Seattle Center. Street parking is scarce and at night, Queen Anne neighborhood streets are reserved for residents with zone passes.

How to Get There— Bus or Monorail

Several Metro Transit bus routes provide service close to McCaw Hall, located on the north edge of Seattle Center. For the best route, call Metro's 24-hour Rider Information Line at 206-553-3000 or visit their website at transit.metrokc.gov. The Monorail? It's probably out of service, but you can try the information line at 206-905-2620 to see if it's back shuttling the short stretch of track between downtown and the Seattle Center.

BALCONY

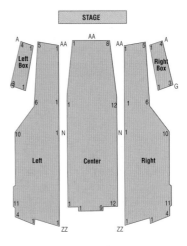

MAIN FLOOR

General Information

NFT Map: 3
Address: 1932 Second Ave
            Seattle, WA 98101
Website: www.themoore.com
Phone: 206-467-5510

Overview

The distinctive title of the country's oldest theater goes to Philadelphia's Walnut Street Theatre, but Seattle is quite proud of its own historic "walnut," the Moore Theatre. Celebrating its December 1907 centennial this year, the Moore was the culmination of effort and vision by developer James A. Moore, a Canadian who arrived in Seattle around 1886. The theater remains the oldest still operating within the city.

Its deceptively shoddy exterior and tacky marquee belie the grandeur and opulence within its walls, embellished with chandeliers, frescoes, mosaics, and marble. Its foyer was once noted for being the largest of any theater in the country. The majestic hall retains its striking elegance while continuing to be a relevant venue for music and other performances. Over the past two years, the old theater has hosted such diverse acts as Sonic Youth and Puppetry of the Penis. Its capacity is currently 1,419 seats, reduced from its original 2,436 after several remodels and renovations. Reservations are accepted for private parties in its lobby, theater, and downstairs bar.

How to Get Tickets

Box office hours are Tuesday to Friday from 11 am to 2:30 pm, 3:15 pm to 6 pm, and one hour prior to show time for that evening's performance. Cash, Visa, Master Card, and American Express are accepted; no personal checks. A $1.50 service charge per ticket will be added to the ticket price. Tickets may also be purchased through Ticketmaster for a higher service charge, with rates varying by performance. Season ticket packages are also available on the theater's website.

How to Get There—Driving

From I-5 North, take the Seneca Street exit; from I-5 South take the Stewart Street exit. Turn right onto First Avenue and head north to Virginia Street. Turn right onto Virginia Street and go one block to Second Avenue. Cross your fingers and hope to find parking.

From I-90 take the Madison Street exit. Turn left onto Madison, turn right onto Sixth Avenue, and head north to Stewart Street. Turn left onto Stewart Street, go down to First Avenue, turn right on First. Go north one block to Virginia Street, turn right onto Virginia, and go one block to Second Avenue.

Parking

The Moore Theatre is located downtown at the corner of Second Avenue and Virginia Street, four blocks from Pike Place Market, coincidentally celebrating its centennial this year as well. Parking is available in nearby pay lots and metered parking along the street, but is nearly impossible to find on a Friday or Saturday night. If you really must park, do your best to find street parking northeast of Fourth Avenue.

How to Get There—Bus

Take any Metro bus to the heart of downtown. The theater is just a short walk away.

BALCONY

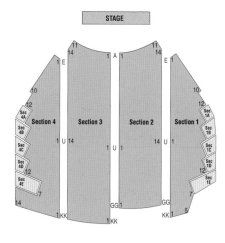

MAIN FLOOR

STAGE

A9 A7 A5 A3 A1 A A2 A4 A6 A8 A10

B7 B5 B3 B1 B B2 B4 B6 B8

C9 C7 C5 C3 C1 C C2 C4 C6 C8 C10

D11 D9 D7 D5 D3 D1 D D2 D4 D6 D8 D10 D12

E13 E11 E9 E7 E5 E3 E1 E E2 E4 E6 E8 E10 E12 E14

F15 F13 F11 F9 F7 F5 F3 F1 F F2 F4 F6 F8 F10 F12 F14 F16

G9 G7 G5 G3 G1 G G2 G4 G6 G8 G10

H15 H13 H11 H9 H7 H5 H3 H1 H H2 H4 H6 H8 H10 H12 H14 H16

J15 J13 J11 J9 J7 J5 J3 J1 J J2 J4 J6 J8 J10 J12 J14 J16

K13 K11 K9 K7 K5 K3 K1 K K2 K4 K6 K8 K10 K12 K14

L15 L13 L11 L9 L7 L5 L3 L1 L L2 L4 L6 L8 L10 L12 L14 L16

CABARET

General Information

NFT Map:	3
Address:	911 Pine St
	Seattle, WA 98101
Website:	www.theparamount.com
Phone:	206-467-5510
Tele-charge:	For art events, 206-292-ARTS (2787). For concert events call Ticketmaster, 206-628-0888 or visit www.tickemaster.com

Overview

In the 1920s, Paramount Pictures built a movie house in nearly every major city, and Seattle was no exception. To make up for the fact that the land they bought was less than prime, Paramount Pictures built the grandest movie house Seattle had ever seen. Modeled after the Palace of Versailles, it boasted a four-tiered lobby, a player piano, grand chandeliers, and original paintings in gilded frames. Those paintings have since been stolen, but nothing could steal the Paramount's dignity. Even after the Depression when people couldn't afford luxuries like movies, The Paramount employed ushers, including famous Seattle native Bruce Lee. In the early days, The Paramount hosted movies and vaudeville, then just first run movies, then second run movies and eventually, it was barely scraping by. It wasn't until 1971 when the Clise Corporation came along and recognized its potential as a live performance hall that things started to pick up again. After changing hands a few more times and undergoing some serious renovations, the Paramount stands again as a Seattle jewel. It even has a fully automated convertible floor system that can turn the theater into a ballroom. It was the first in the country to do so. Besides concerts, the Paramount also hosts a silent movie series on Mondays. The breathtaking lobby also has a bar to hide in when you realize you are the only person at the concert old enough to drink.

How to Get Tickets

You can get tickets at The Paramount box office Monday through Friday 10 am–6 pm. There is a $2.50 per ticket facility fee. You can also get tickets for art events by calling 206-292-ARTS (2787). For all concerts and any online purchases, it's all about Ticketmaster, and their ridiculous fees.

How to Get There—Driving

Coming north on I-5, take the Olive-Denny exit. Go one block to Melrose Street and turn right. The Paramount will be three blocks down on the corner of 9th Avenue and Pine Street.
Coming south on I-5, take the Stewart Street exit. Take Stewart to 9th Avenue and turn left. Follow 9th two blocks to Pine Street. The Paramount will be on your left.

Parking

The Paramount Theater does not have its own parking lot, so you are stuck with paying for an expensive lot or trying to find street parking. If it's after 6 pm or a Sunday, it's worth circling the blocks to find a spot on the street. If you don't have that kind of patience, try Pacific Place Mall parking (7th Ave & Pine St) which is the cheapest in the area. You can also try the Washington State Convention Center or the Grand Hyatt's garage (7th & Pike St). There is a loading zone on 9th Avenue and Pine Street to drop off passengers.

How to Get There—Mass Transit

From downtown, take MT 10, 11, 14, 43, 49, or 84. From the University District, MT 43 or 44. From Capitol Hill, MT 10. From Northgate, take the express MT 66. Because the Paramount Theater is so close to the Washington State Convention Center, and in a prime downtown location, there are over twenty bus routes that will get you within .1 miles of the theater. Your best bet is to http://visit transit.metrokc.gov or call 206-553-3000 to plan your route.

No doubt about it, Seattle is a cinephile's city. Cutting edge film from around the world screens daily, and even chain video stores stock adventurous fare. Each Spring for over thirty years the Seattle International Film Festival has summoned the best and brightest talent from Hollywood and beyond for a month-long movie binge to rival Sundance and Cannes. The non-profit organization Northwest Film Forum offers film production workshops, equipment rentals, and funding grants to local filmmakers. And while there's no shortage of mainstream multiplexes for the latest big-budget snooze, Seattle also boasts many moviehouses that are unique not only in architecture and ambience, but also in their programming choices. The result is a consistent flow of cult favorites, foreign cinema, and rarely-screened classics from the past.

Capitol Hill is home to the **Egyptian (Map 4)**, a large, ornate showroom built in 1915 as a Masonic Temple that runs bigger indie cinema titles and consistently surprising midnight movie selections on the weekends. Not far away is the **Northwest Film Forum (Map 4)**, where exciting, obscure cinema is the norm, and the **Harvard Exit (Map 17)**, with the most elegant lobby in town—complete with a grand piano, chandelier, and even a fireplace.

In the University District, the **Seven Gables (Map 26)** welcomes foreign film buffs with a bit of romantic atmosphere, aided and abetted by downstairs neighbor Mamma Melina Ristorante — a perfect first date package. **The Varsity (Map 26)** isn't as glamorous, but the sixty-year-old theater offers three screens on three floors connected by a staircase that claustrophobics should avoid. Rivaling the internal beauty of the Egyptian is the **Neptune Theatre (Map 26)**, with its majestic stained glass tribute to Roman god of the sea. Sure they only have one screen but they are almost always showing something cool. The employee-owned non-profit **Grand Illusion (Map 26)** (a dentist's office in a former life) only seats 70, but it's the best movie-going experience in the city—a cozy, intimate space to enjoy films handpicked by the cineastes on staff.

There are only two places left in the world equipped to properly show films shot in the Cinerama three-screen format, and we got one. A local billionaire (his name escapes us) saved the **Cinerama Theatre (Map 1)** from extinction in 1998 by kicking in for much-needed technological upgrades while preserving the retro charms of the house itself. Along with rare showings of 70mm classics, this is the place to experience big Hollywood special-effect spectaculars like *Indiana Jones* or *The Dark Knight* and classics like *Lawrence of Arabia*.

By contrast, the tiny **Jewel Box Theatre (Map 1)** seats even fewer than the Grand Illusion, but the advantage (or disadvantage, depending on one's attitude toward alcohol) is its location within a Belltown saloon called the Rendezvous—a speakeasy and burlesque stage during Prohibition. Now the Jewel Box features live bands and fringe theater events, as well as occasional special film presentations. Centrally located in the Central District, **Central Cinema (Map 5)** gives pizza, beer, and movies equal weight, serving hungry film fans who love their uniquely-themed programs, making it a better choice for regular drunken cinema binges. Central's more sophisticated sister is the **Big Picture (Maps 1, 49)**, accompanying first run films with high class cocktails to their downtown and Redmond locations. When you purchase your tickets, you can order a drink (or several) to be brought to you mid-movie.

The most recent addition to the movie theater scene is the **SIFF Cinema (Map 15)** at McCaw Hall in Seattle Center. Now the Seattle International Film Festival can show quality flicks year round.

Movie Theaters

Movie Theaters	Address	Phone	Map
Admiral Theater	2343 California Ave SW	206-938-3456	35
AMC Cinerama 1	2100 4th Ave	206-441-3080	1
AMC Loews Factoria 8	3505 Factoria Blvd SE	425-641-9206	43
AMC Loews Oak Tree 6	10006 Aurora Ave N	206-527-1748	33
AMC Loews Redmond Town Center 8	16451 NE 74th St	425-869-1800	49
AMC Loews Uptown 3	511 Queen Anne Ave N	206-285-1022	15
AMC Pacific Place 11	600 Pine St	206-652-2404	3
AT&T Outdoor Cinema	6046 W Lake Sammamish Pkwy NE	206-720-1058	49
AT&T Outdoor Cinema - Seattle Center Mural Stage	Thomas St & 3rd Ave N	206-720-1058	15
Bellevue Galleria Stadium 11	550 106th Ave NE	425-451-7161	45
Big Picture	2505 1st Ave	206-256-0572	1
Big Picture Redmond	7411 166th Ave NE	425-556-0565	49
Broadway Performance Hall	1625 Broadway	206-325-3113	4
Central Cinema	1411 21st Ave	206-328-3230	5
Columbia City Cinema	4816 Rainier Ave S	206-721-3156	40
Fremont Original Outdoor Cinema (May–Sept)	N 35th St & Phinney Ave N	206-767-2593	24
Grand Illusion Cinema	1403 NE 50th St	206-523-3935	26
Jewel Box Theatre	2322 2nd Ave	206-441-5823	1
Kenyon Hall	7904 35th Ave SW	206-937-3613	37
Kirkland Parkplace Cinema	404 Parkplace Ctr	425-827-9000	48
Landmark Egyptian Theatre	805 E Pine St	206-781-5755	4
Landmark Guild 45th	2115 N 45th St	206-781-5755	25
Landmark Harvard Exit	807 E Roy St	206-781-5755	17
Landmark Metro Cinemas	4500 9th Ave NE	206-781-5755	26
Landmark Neptune Theatre	1303 NE 45th St	206-781-5755	26
Landmark Seven Gables Theatre	911 NE 50th St	206-781-5755	26
Landmark Varsity Theatre	4329 University Wy NE	206-781-5755	26
Lincoln Square Cinemas	700 Bellevue Wy NE	425-454-7400	45
Majestic Bay Theatres	2044 NW Market St	206-781-2229	23
Northwest Film Forum	1515 12th Ave	206-267-5380	4
Pacific Science Center IMAX	200 2nd Ave N	206-443-4629	15
Regal Bella Bottega 11	8890 161st Ave NE	800-326-3264	49
Regal Crossroads 8 Cinemas	1200 156th Ave NE	800-326-3264	47
Regal Meridian 16	1501 7th Ave	206-223-9600	3
Totem Lake Cinemas	12232 NE Totem Lake Wy	425-820-5929	48
West Seattle Walk-In Theater	California Ave SW & SW Alaska St	206-767-2593	35

Arts & Entertainment • Museums

Art

The Seattle Art Museum (SAM) (Map 3) unveiled its expanded location in the spring of 2007 to rave reviews. The museum now has 70 percent more gallery space to show its extensive collections of Pacific Northwest art. It also opened a new and improved museum store along First Avenue. Its sister gallery, the **Seattle Asian Art Museum (SAAM) (Map 17)** is located in idyllic Volunteer Park, with its sweeping city, water, and mountain views and bad-boy reputation. The **Olympic Sculpture Park (Map 1)**, also a SAM project, showcases 22 monumental sculptures in a 9-acre park located on Seattle's waterfront. **The Frye Museum (Map 4)**, founded by a former meat packing executive, shows fairly traditional late 19th-, early 20th-century art in its elegant and contemporary building. Recently, they've brought in a new curator that shows more cutting edge work. Oh, and since Mr. Frye sold so much meat, it's always free admission.

The Henry Art Gallery (Map 26) is the University of Washington's gallery-cum-museum (or the other way around). On permanent display is James Turrell's *Skyspace*, a very cool enclosed light chamber. **Bellevue Art Museum (Map 45)** was once housed in a chi-chi mall, until it moved across the street into Steven Holl's architectural wonder where it promptly folded. BAM only reopened after reinventing itself as a crafts museum.

Historic Seattle

Wing Luke Museum (Map 8), located in the heart of the International District, is better than ever after its fantastic renovation. Its primary emphasis is on the cultural history of Asian Pacific Islanders, and the museum invites the community to participate in its exhibitions. **The Burke Museum (Map 26)** is the University of Washington's archeological and ethnographic museum. Here you can see the notorious Kennewick man. **The Nordic Heritage Museum (Map 28)** is dedicated to the history of immigrant Scandinavians—free your inner Norwegian. **The Museum of History and Industry (Map 21)** is a city history museum for Seattle aficionados.

Allentown

Ever wonder what billionaires keep in the basements of their mansions? Paul Allen puts his personal collection on display at two museums in the giant titanium blob at Seattle Center. **The Experience Music Project (Map 15)** invites you to free your inner-Jimi with lots of interactive music exhibits; it almost justifies the inflated admission when you get a little percussion or guitar time in. Right next to EMP, the **Science Fiction Museum (Map 15)** houses *Planet of the Apes* memorabilia and appeals to Seattle's geek-chic set (a.k.a former Microsoft executives).

Plane Fun

In Boeing-obsessed Seattle, airplanes are serious business and **The Museum of Flight (Map 41)** has this topic covered. This is the place to tour the now-defunct Concorde and JFK's Air Force One.

Museums	Address	Phone	Map
Burke Museum	17th Ave NE & NE 45th St	206-543-5590	26
The Center for Wooden Boats	1010 Valley St	206-382-2628	16
Center on Contemporary Art (CoCA)	6413 Seaview Ave NW	206-728-1980	2
The Children's Museum	305 Harrison St	206-441-1768	15
Experience Music Project (EMP)	325 5th Ave N	206-367-5483	15
Frye Art Museum	704 Terry Ave	206-622-9250	4
The Henry Art Gallery	15th Ave NE & NE 41st St	206-543-2280	26
Klondike Gold Rush Museum	319 Second Ave S	206-220-4240	7
Log House Museum	3003 61st Ave SW	206-938-5293	35
Museum of Flight	9404 E Marginal Wy S	206-764-5720	41
Nordic Heritage Museum	3014 NW 67th St	206-789-5707	28
Odyssey: The Maritime Discovery Center	2205 Alaskan Wy, Pier 66	206-374-4000	1
Pacific Science Center	200 2nd Ave N	206-443-2001	15
Science Fiction Museum & Hall of Fame	325 5th Ave N	206-770-2700	15
Seattle Art Museum Downtown	100 University St	206-654-3100	3
Seattle Asian Art Museum	1400 E Prospect St	206-654-3100	17
Seattle Metropolitan Police Museum	317 3rd Ave S	206-748-9991	7
Seattle's Museum of History & Industry	2700 24th Ave E	206-324-1126	21
Wing Luke Asian Museum	719 S King St	206-623-5124	8

Seattle may be a small dog, but our bite is as big as a New York or LA in terms of diverse nightlife offerings. From quaint dives to swanky Belltown wine bars, punk rock to hipster kitsch, in Seattle, anyone can find their scene.

The Hill Is Capitol

If you don't know what kind of scene you're in the mood for, Capitol Hill has a wide range of destinations. From the vintage Italian living room set of **Chez Gaudy (Map 4)** to the sexy red lighting of **Cha Cha (Map 4)**. From the welcoming party scene at **Neighbours (Map 4)** to the hunting lodge chic of **Redwood (Map 4)**, you'll find a cool place to hang out. The Hill is often pigeon-holed as a hipster/homo ghetto, but as long as you're open minded, it really can be all things to all people.

Live Music

The grunge days of flannel and hype may be long gone (thank goodness), but Seattle still has a thriving live music scene. **Fun House (Map 15)** specializes in punk rock of every stripe, from swaggering garage to freeform noise to stubbornly traditional 1977-style mohawk types. Plus, they feature a mini-basketball court for athletically-inclined drunks. Ground zero for alt-country and twang fans can be found at the **Tractor Tavern (Map 23)**, but if you prefer turntables over pedal steel, then make it over to **Chop Suey (Map 4)** for "live" music. Nearby, **Neumo's (Map 4)** rivals the **Showbox (Map 3)** for booking the latest indie rock sensations, but their sound is definitely more on the dirty side. Across the street from Neumo's, regality has risen in a formerly stabby night club spot. **King Cobra (Map 4)** has a hard rock and metal business plan for those of you with the blackest of hearts. **The Sunset Tavern (Map 23)** is Seattle's best small venue, a friendly joint with red velvet interior that consistently books great up and coming local acts plus a succession of superior touring rockers from abroad. **The Mars Bar (Map 16)** and the **High Dive (Map 24)** are other good spots to check out new (if not necessarily stellar) local talent.

Dive Right In

Whether ironic or earnest, one thing Seattle excels in is dive bars. **The Comet (Map 4)** is a Seattle staple in this regard. They have live music and karaoke, but the real show comes from the bartenders and clientèle. It was probably hit the hardest from the smoking ban a few years back, and the atmosphere isn't quite the same without the asphyxiation. But it's still rife with filthy charm. Other divey favorites include **Earl's (Map**

26), Eastlake Zoo (Map 20), Al's Tavern (Map 25), The Monkey Pub (Map 26), Nine Pound Hammer (Map 39), The Five Point (Map 1), the Nite Lite (Map 3), Canterbury Ale & Eats (Map 18), and **The Tug Tavern (Map 37)**.

Meat Is Always the Special

So you just bought a new sparkly halter top and you want to shake your tailfeather? The breeding grounds of Pioneer Square are the perfect neighborhood for you. **Trinity Night Club (Map 7)** and **The Last Supper Club (Map 7)** are popular destinations for plenty of sweaty radio hits. For those of you who prefer dancing on a bar or table top, check out **Cowgirls, Inc (Map 7)** or any number of bars in the Pioneer Square triangle.

When You Have to Dance

If the frat party annex isn't your scene, but you still have happy feet, you can get your hip-hop groove on at the **Baltic Room (Map 4)** or the **War Room (Map 4)**. The Baltic Room also boasts Bollywood mashups every other Saturday. For fun '80s, house, or funk beats, check out **Neighbours (Map 4)**, **ReBar (Map 2)**, or Belltown's **Bhudda (Map 1)** (which also has Brit Pop Wednesdays!). To relish the darkness in your soul, you can dance to the sounds of Joy Division and Skinny Puppy at the **Noc Noc (Map 3)**.

Want to hone your skills before hitting the town? You can take tango or swing lessons at the **Century Ballroom (Map 4)**.

The Kids Are Alright

All ages action, like in most cities, isn't easy to come by. The Moore Theatre and The Paramount are always all-ages, but their calendar isn't always geared toward a younger crowd. There are often indie rock shows at the **Showbox (Map 3)** and **Neumo's (Map 4)** and punk and metal at **El Corazon (Map 2)**. The **Vera Project** (www.theveraproject.org) is a non-profit that schedules all-ages shows around town in response to the oppressive Teen Dance Ordinance. Of course there's always a wealth of good cinema and allowance squandering at **Gameworks (Map 3)** to keep the kids out of trouble.

24-Hour Party People

Seattle can be tough on night owls. But if you're still raring to go at 3 am, there are a few options. **The Hurricane Café (Map 2)**, **The Five Point (Map 1)**, **The Mecca (Map 15)**, and **13 Coins (Map 2)** are all open 24 hours.

Map 1 • Belltown

	Address	Phone	
Amber	2214 1st Ave	206-728-8500	If Maxim Magazine owned a bar.
Belltown Billiards	90 Blanchard St	206-448-6779	Tries to be all things to all people and somehow pulls it off.
The Black Bottle	2600 1st Ave	206-441-1500	Damned if it ain't noisy, though the list is decent, and the flatbreads are the bomb.
Buddha	2222 2nd Ave	206-441-4449	Unassuming Thai restaurant by day, unmatched indie dance club by night.
The Crocodile Café	2200 2nd Ave	206-441-5611	Your one-stop shop for delectable diner food and rock.
Cyclops Café and Lounge	2421 1st Ave	206-441-1677	A tip of the fedora to old Belltown lounge days.
Del Rey	2332 1st Ave	206-770-3228	The bathroom is the most comfortable part of the bar.
Five Point Café	415 Cedar St	206-441-4777	Start and finish your Belltown adventure at this all-night joint.
Frontier Room	2202 1st Ave	206-956-7427	Cheap beer and BBQ happy hour. Addictive.
Hula Hula	106 1st Ave N	206-284-5003	Drink BOWLS full of rum in this ultra tiki lounge.
Lava Lounge	2226 2nd Ave	206-441-5660	Free shuffleboard and a great '80s jukebox offer a refuge from Belltown yuppies.
Marjorie	2331 2nd Ave	206-441-9842	Fresh cocktails in a Euro-style ambiance.
McLeod Residence Lounge	2209 2nd Ave	206-441-3314	Burning Man meets urban art gallery but with booze instead of peyote.
Palace Kitchen	2030 5th Ave	206-448-2001	Just getting started at midnight? Eat fine grub until 1 am, drink 'til 2 am.
Queen City Grill	2201 1st Ave	206-443-0975	Decent Northwest fare and loud Belltown crowd.
Rendezvous	2322 2nd Ave	206-441-5823	Dive bar with a touch of old Hollywood class.
Shorty's	2222 2nd Ave	206-374-0569	Pinball, hot dogs, and booze: the Holy Trinity of Awesome.
Spitfire Grill	2219 4th Ave	206-441-7966	"Urban sports bar" pleases all sorts with awesome happy hour.
Tia Lou's	2218 1st Ave	206-733-8226	Happy hour patio: Muy bonita. Night crowd: El Douche.
Tini Bigs Lounge	100 Denny Wy	206-284-0931	Be so very new millennium by heading back to the '50s at this martini lounge.
Twist Restaurant and Lounge	2313 1st Ave	206-448-9478	The twist is that you're the meat.
Umi Sake House	2230 1st Ave	206-374-8717	Late-night sushi happy hour in indoor zen garden!
Viceroy	2332 2nd Ave	206-956-8423	Linda's rather impressive attempt at swank. Two-fist Cristal with High Life.
Wasabi Bistro	2311 2nd Ave	206-441-6044	"Bistro" is Japanese for "Yuppie."
The Waterfront Seafood Grill	2801 Alaskan Wy	206-956-9171	The suits need somewhere to go.
Whisky Bar	2000 2nd Ave	206-443-4490	The walls are adorned with paintings of ladies with guns. Rad.

Map 2 • Downtown / Denny Triangle

13 Coins	125 Boren Ave N	206-243-9500	Sometimes you just gotta blow $50 on steak and lobster at 3 am.
Dimitriou's Jazz Alley	2033 6th Ave	206-441-9729	Seattle's longstanding jazz venue. Let them entertain you.
El Corazon	109 Eastlake Ave E	206-381-3094	If you like your punk and metal with a little teenager.
Feierabend	422 Yale Ave N	206-340-2528	Grab a bier and make new friends. Prost.
Hurricane Café	2230 7th Ave	206-682-5858	For the show after the show.
Lo Fi	429B Eastlake Ave E	206-254-2824	Dance to music that doesn't suck!
Rebar	1114 Howell St	206-233-9873	Fringe theater, live music, and decidedly drag-friendly. Experience the unexpected.

Map 3 • Downtown

Alibi Room	85 Pike St, Ste 410	206-623-3180	Dark, underground bar with a lounge feel.
Athenian Inn	1517 Pike Pl	206-624-7166	Drink with other Pike Place Market alcoholics.
Can Can	94 Pike St	206-652-0832	1940s cabaret is alive and well. Make reservations EARLY.
Contour	807 1st Ave	206-447-7704	Ongoing mix 'em up of live and DJ'd music.
Déjà Vu	1510 1st Ave	206-342-9160	It's no Lusty Lady.
Fado Irish Pub	801 1st Ave	206-264-2700	More like Frat-O.
Gameworks	1511 7th Ave	206-521-0952	Another dateless Friday night.
Kells Irish Restaurant and Pub	1916 Post Aly	206-728-1916	Where everybody gets a little Irish in them.
Le Pichet	1933 1st Ave	206-256-1449	Pretend you're in Paris.
The Lusty Lady	1315 1st Ave	206-622-2120	In case your Pioneer Square prowling proved fruitless.
Moore Theatre	1932 2nd Ave	206-467-5510	Architecturally stunning performance hall.
Nite Lite Restaurant & Bar	1926 2nd Ave	206-443-0899	Lethal drinks and Johnny Cash comfort lonely hearts and ironic hipsters.
Noc Noc	1516 2nd Ave	206-223-1333	Come for happy hour. Leave before nightfall to avoid goth swarm.
Oliver's Lounge	405 Olive Wy	206-382-6995	Feel wealthier and classier by buying overpriced martinis in a posh hotel scene.
The Owl & Thistle	808 Post Ave	206-621-7777	In true Irish fashion, you'll probably witness a fight.
Paramount Theatre	911 Pine St	206-467-5510	Opulent theater showcasing big-name musicals, concerts, and events.
The Pink Door	1919 Post Aly	206-443-3241	Wine, Italian food, and Cabaret!
Purple Café & Wine Bar	1225 4th Ave	206-829-2280	Dramatic in size, selection, and ambiance. Suits abound.
Shea's Lounge	94 Pike St #34	206-467-9990	Bore your friends with stories about when you lived in Paris.
The Showbox	1426 1st Ave	206-628-3151	Superb sight lines and crystalline sound on the city's biggest nightclub stage.
The Triple Door	216 Union St	206-838-4333	Live music venue with a Vegas nightclub slant.
Vino Vino Room	102 Cherry St	206-343-9517	Wine bar inside DeNunzio's. Italian music and good times.
The Virginia Inn	1937 1st Ave	206-728-1937	A one-drink destination.
W Bar	1112 4th Ave	206-264-6000	A bit of New York swank, if you're into that.
White Horse Trading Company	1908 Post Aly	206-441-7767	Top-secret English pub and bookstore. Enjoy a hearthside ale.
Zig Zag Café	1501 Western Ave	206-625-1146	Fitzgerald-esque cocktail lounge.

Map 4 • First Hill / Pike / Pine

611 Supreme	611 E Pine St	206-328-0292	Crepes for hipsters.
Bad JuJu Lounge	1425 10th Ave	206-709-9442	Dante would be proud.
Baltic Room	1207 Pine St	206-625-4444	Fashionable dance spot with the big velvet drapes.
Barca	1510 11th Ave	206-325-8263	Bitchy wait staff serve you drinks in the dark.
Capitol Club	414 E Pine St	206-325-2149	When you're date is more debonair than dive.
Century Ballroom	915 E Pine St	206-324-7263	Lindy, swing, salsa, tango anyone? Do it here in style, lessons available for klutzes.
Cha Cha Lounge	1013 E Pike St	206-322-0703	High-attitude tiki bar for hipsters.
Chapel	1600 Melrose Ave	206-447-4180	Former mortuary turned metrosexual martini party.
Chez Gaudy	1802 Bellevue Ave	206-329-4047	Like the Bleu Bistro with less places to sit.
Chop Suey	1325 E Madison St	206-324-8000	Alt-rock club with the ethnically insensitive moniker.
Clever Dunne's Irish House	1501 E Olive Wy	206-709-8079	Owned by real Irish people. Best pub quiz.

Map 4 · First Hill / Pike / Pine–continued

The Comet Tavern	922 E Pike St	206-323-9853	Order a Oly and get in a fight!
Crescent Lounge	1413 E Olive Wy	206-726-1774	Divey gay bar with karaoke seven nights a week.
The Cuff	1533 13th Ave	206-323-1525	Try (or try not) to get cuffed in the men's room.
The Eagle	314 E Pike St	206-621-7591	Quintessential leather bar.
Elysian Brewing Company	1221 E Pike St	206-860-1920	Super food and micros but lacks atmosphere. Bring interesting company.
The Garage	1130 Broadway	206-322-2296	Getting drunk and bowling is obviously a wise combination.
HaLo	500 E Pike St	n/a	New outpost of Century Ballroom. Salsa or swing on a huge dance floor.
Havana	1010 E Pike St	206-323-2822	Kick it like Castro.
The Hideout	1005 Boren Ave	206-903-8480	Drink tasty cocktails amidst paintings inspired by fever dreams. NFT pick.
Honey Hole	703 E Pike St	206-709-1399	Scrumptious cocktails and sandwiches that make you wish you had three hands.
King Cobra	916 E Pike St	n/a	A hard rockin' club risen from the ashes of Kincora.
Licorous	928 12th Ave	206-325-6947	High-brow drinks, small plates, gorgeous lighting, swanky setting.
Linda's Tavern	707 E Pine St	206-325-1220	Hipsters vie for seniority.
Madison Pub	1315 E Madison St	206-325-6537	Eat, drink, and be gay.
Neighbours Disco	1509 Broadway	206-324-5358	Straight-friendly all-night dance parties for the fabulous people.
Neumos	925 E Pike St	206-709-9467	Music club that welcomes Seattle's legions of hip-hoppers and punk rockers.
Poco Wine Room	1408 E Pine St	206-322-9463	Intimate and contemporary; Northwest emphasis with traveling international list.
Purr	1518 11th Ave	206-325-3112	Martini bar for classy cats.
R Place	619 E Pine St	206-322-8828	Karaoke, dancing, and all-male underwear contests.
The Redwood	514 E Howell St	206-329-1952	Hunting lodge chic. Vegetarians and Nuge fans come together!
Richard Hugo House	1634 11th Ave	206-322-7030	Pretend you like poetry, get laid.
Rosebud Restaurant	719 E Pike St	206-323-6636	$2 wells happy hour. Pre-func and get out before the snobbery peaks.
The Saint	1416 E Olive Wy	206-323-9922	Cleanse your soul with 80 different tequilas and super-fresh fare.
Satellite Lounge	1118 E Pike St	206-324-4019	Calm place for a nightcap on congested Cappie Hill, but order from the bar.
Six Arms	300 E Pike St	206-223-1698	Dude. They have tater tots.
Sugar	916 E Pike St	206-323-7128	Beautiful girls (and a few guys dressed as girls) who know how to party.
Tango	1100 Pike St	206-583-0382	Awesome if you're not paying.
Vito's Madison Grill	929 9th Ave	206-682-2695	$2 double vodka tonics will convince you that the food is edible.
The War Room	722 E Pike St	206-328-7666	Communist propaganda, capitalist drinks.
The Wild Rose	1021 E Pike St	206-324-9210	Friendly and fun lesbians. $1 Taco Tuesdays aren't a euphemism.

Map 5 · Central District (North)

Central Cinema	1411 21st Ave	206-686-6684	Drink beer and watch a cult or classic film. So simple yet so brilliant.
The Twilight Exit	2051 E Madison St	206-324-7462	Where hipsters go to avoid other hipsters.

Map 6 · Madrona

Madrona Ale House	1138 34th Ave	206-323-7807	Upscale bar food. Bring the whole family.

Map 7 • Pioneer Square / SoDo

Central Saloon	207 1st Ave S	206-622-0209	Frat boys have been drinking here since 1892.
Cowgirls Inc	421 1st Ave S	206-340-0777	Like Coyote Ugly, but sluttier.
Doc Maynard's	610 1st Ave	206-682-3705	Rock out to bands you've never heard of.
Double Header	407 2nd Ave	206-464-9918	Friendly old dudes who like dudes.
Elysian Fields	542 1st Ave S	206-382-4498	Stadium-size brewery a home-run shot from Safeco Field.
The Last Supper Club	124 S Washington St	206-748-9975	Three-tiered thumping nightclub attracting the skimpily-clad set.
New Orleans Creole restaurant	114 1st Ave S	206-622-2563	Blues and jazz in old hipster setting.
Pyramid Alehouse	1201 1st Ave S	206-464-0896	Get sh*t-faced like the Egyptians used to do.
Triangle Pub	553 1st Ave S	206-628-0474	Great spot for a Rainier before you watch the M's lose again.
Trinity Night Club	111 Yesler Wy	206-447-4140	Different action in three spacious rooms. Be twenty-something, wear less, enjoy more.

Map 8 • International District

Bush Gardens	614 Maynard Ave S	206-682-6830	Drunken late-night karaoke. Beware of bachelorettes.
Fort St George	601 S King St	206-382-0662	Japan meets the UK at this pub that also serves decent food.
Joe's	500 S King St	n/a	One of the last true dive bars in the city.

Map 9 • Central District (South)

Hidmo East African Cuisine	2000 S Jackson St	206-329-1534	Live African music on weekends.

Map 13 • Upper Queen Anne

Bricco Della Regina Anna	1525 Queen Anne Ave N	206-285-4900	Sexy Italian-style wine bar with an extensive list and simple, good food.
Hilltop Ale House	2129 Queen Anne Ave N	206-285-3877	Neighborhood pub.

Map 14 • Queen Anne (West)

Targy's	600 W Crockett St	206-285-9700	Time travel back to the old Queen Anne. Lovely.

Map 15 • Lower Queen Anne / Seattle Center

10 Mercer	10 Mercer St	206-691-3723	You'll think you've died and gone to a Bret Easton Ellis novel.
Chopstix Dueling Piano Bar	11 Roy St	206-270-4444	As lame as you'd imagined, if not more so.
Crow Restaurant and Bar	823 5th Ave N	206-283-8800	Good food and cocktails, but make a reservation or don't bother.
Fun House	206 5th Ave N	206-374-8400	Raw, blastin' punk bands, booze, and a basketball hoop outside.
Jabu's Pub	174 Roy St	206-284-9093	A friendly, comfortable place to get drizunk.
Mecca Café	526 Queen Anne Ave N	206-285-9728	Visit the Queen Anne of olden days.
Ozzie's Restaurant and Lounge	105 W Mercer St	206-284-4618	Where frat boys go to sing karaoke.
Peso's Kitchen and Lounge	605 Queen Anne Ave N	206-283-9353	If you like your meat market with a side of guac.
The Sitting Room	108 W Roy St	206-285-2830	Warm and orange. You'll see what I mean.
Solo Bar	200 Roy St	206-213-0080	Faith No More (remember them?) serves up some cocktails.
Sport	140 4th Ave N Ste 130	206-404-7767	If you really need to watch the Sonics one more time before they skip town.
Teatro Zinzanni Dinner and Dreams	222 Mercer St	206-802-0015	A fine night out. If someone else is paying.

Map 16 • Westlake / South Lake Union

| Mars Bar/Café Venus | 609 Eastlake Ave E | 206-624-4516 | Cool hangout next to the freeway. |

Map 17 • Capitol Hill (West)

Bleu Bistro	202 Broadway E	206-329-3087	Like chillin' in your own clubhouse.
Café Metropolitain	1701 E Olive Wy	206-324-0771	A portal to the most annoying parts of Belltown conveniently located on the Hill.
Dilettante	416 Broadway E	206-329-6463	Premium chocolate orgy.
Elite Tavern	1520 E Olive Wy	206-324-4470	Bitter queens still unite at the new location.
The Stumbling Monk	1635 E Olive Wy	206-860-0916	Discuss the waning political climate over Belgian beers. NFT fav.
Summit Public House	601 Summit Ave E Ste 102	206-324-7611	The quintessential neighborhood pub.
Sun Liquor	607 Summit Ave E	206-860-1130	What's better than freshly-juiced cocktails and warm nuts?

Map 18 • Capitol Hill (East) / Madison Valley

Bottleneck Lounge	2328 E Madison St	206-323-1098	Come meet your new neighbors at this cozy spot.
Canterbury Ales and Eats	534 15th Ave E	206-322-3130	Chaucer-approved dive bar. Not for the faint of heart.
Hopvine Pub	507 15th Ave E	206-328-3120	100% Pacific Northwest right down to the beer and fleece.
Liberty	517 15th Ave E	206-323-9898	Sushi and cocktails served by people who are more hip than you.
Smith	332 15th Ave E	206-322-9420	Linda's winning combination of animal heads and hipster pub fare.

Map 20 • Eastlake / Montlake / Portage Bay

Eastlake Zoo Tavern	2301 Eastlake Ave E	206-329-3277	Those grizzled old bartenders also own the joint.
Roanoke Park Place	2409 10th Ave E	206-324-5882	Drown another Husky football loss in their good beer selection.

Map 21 • Montlake

| Montlake Ale House | 2307 24th Ave E | 206-726-5968 | See Madrona Ale House blurb. |

Map 22 • Madison Park

| Impromptu Wine Bar Café | 4235 E Madison St | 206-860-1569 | Beach-side and cozy, featuring a traveling wine list and full bar. |

Map 23 • Ballard

DiVino	5310 Ballard Ave NW	206-297-0143	Wine is $10 a glass but condescending comments from the staff are free.
Hattie's Hat	5231 Ballard Ave NW	206-784-0175	Still gritty, but we're no longer afraid to eat there.
Hazelwood	2311 NW Market St	206-783-0478	Classy but not snooty, with two levels of dimly-lit ambiance.
Jolly Roger Taproom	1514 NW Leary Wy	206-782-6181	Nice and small with a subdued pirate theme. Fried pickles: Aarr!
King's Hardware	5225 Ballard Ave NW	206-782-0227	Über-hip bar with unhip crowd on weekends. Brought to you by Linda.
Matador	2221 NW Market St	206-297-2855	Lots of tequila. Lots.
Ocho	2325 NW Market St	206-784-0699	Like having an office party in your walk-in closet.
People's Pub	5429 Ballard Ave NW	206-783-6521	Like grandma's dining room, with late-night schnitzel and wurst.
The Sunset Tavern	5433 Ballard Ave NW	206-784-4880	Opium den-themed bar and concert venue for local bands.

The Tractor Tavern	5213 Ballard Ave NW	206-789-3599	Live alt twang.
Zayda Buddy's	5404 Leary Ave NW	206-783-7777	Fhaux-dive with Leinenkugel's!

Map 24 • Fremont

Brouwer's Café	400 N 35th St	206-267-2437	Could double as an S&M dungeon; amazing selection of beer but the food is torture.
The Buckaroo Tavern	4201 Fremont Ave N	206-634-3161	Cash- and beer-only biker bar for a quick one or a long, wild night.
El Camino	607 N 35th St	206-632-7303	Mexican frou-frou with covered outdoor seating.
George & Dragon Pub	206 N 36th St	206-545-6864	They call it football here.
High Dive	513 N 36th St	206-632-0212	BBQ and bands.
Nectar Lounge	412 N 36th St	206-632-2020	Good cheap happy hour pizza. Terrible piped-in music.
Norm's Eatery and Ale House	460 N 36th St	206-547-1417	Enjoy a beer with your dog after eating dinner elsewhere.
The Pacific Inn	3501 Stone Wy N	206-547-2967	When you need a break from the Fremont yuppies. NFT pick.
Smash	1401 N 45th St	206-547-3232	Accessible wine bar operated by former sommelier; international list.
Tost Lounge	513 N 36th St Space E	206-547-0240	Live music in a chilly blue room.
Triangle Lounge	3507 Fremont Pl N	206-632-0880	Endure the frat potential for the patio and bucket-o-beer.

Map 25 • Wallingford

Al's Tavern	2303 N 45th St	206-545-9959	Divey and lovable.
Blue Moon Tavern	712 NE 45th St	206-545-9775	Kerouac, Roethke, and other artists have fallen over drunk here.
Goldie's on 45th	2121 N 45th St	206-632-3453	Reliving frat-days-gone-by seven days a week.
Kate's Pub	309 NE 45th St	206-547-6832	Hidden gem. Specials and games galore. Easy on the Jaeger.
May Restaurant and Lounge	1612 N 45th St	206-675-0037	Pricey but delicious Thai bar food served late and sluggishly.
Moon Temple	2108 N 45th St	206-633-4280	Everyone loves stiff drinks.
Murphy's Pub	1928 N 45th St	206-634-2110	Drinks for Hibernians.
Sea Monster Lounge	2202 N 45th St	206-633-1824	Have a bagel dog with your jumpin' techno-rock.

Map 26 • U District

Big Time Brewery & Alehouse	4133 University Wy NE	206-545-4509	Laid back college pub for a brew and a slice of pizza.
College Inn Pub	4006 University Wy NE	206-634-2307	Best thing about the College Inn: You get older, they stay the same age.
Dante's	5300 Roosevelt Wy NE	206-525-1300	Seattle's only Satanic college-themed sports bar.
Earl's on the Ave	4333 University Wy NE	206-535-4493	Slightly less pungent since moving locations. Slightly.
Flowers Bar & Restaurant	4247 University Wy NE	206-633-1903	Vegetarian buffet by day, laid back bar by night.
Galway Arms	5257 University Wy NE	206-527-0404	If you're into Irish car bomb specials.
Monkey Pub	5305 Roosevelt Wy NE	206-523-6457	Frat-free oasis in U District.

Map 27 • Laurelhurst / Wedgwood / Sand Point

Wedgwood Ale House	8515 35th Ave NE	206-527-2676	Everyone who frequents this place went to high school together.

Map 28 • Ballard (West)

Sloop Tavern	2830 NW Market St	206-782-3330	Get drunk cheaply with enormous beers.

Map 29 • Ballard / Loyal Heights

Copper Gate	6301 24th Ave NW	206-706-3292	Pure Scandinavia, nude barbies and all.
The Dray	708 NW 65th St	206-453-4527	Beer on tap. Beer to go in growlers. Beer soaked raisins on the grilled cheese.
Tigertail	704 NW 65th St	206-781-8245	Decor reminiscent of an Asian massage parlor. Cocktail named the Pacific Rim Job.

Map 30 • Greenwood / Phinney Ridge

Barking Dog Alehouse	705 NW 70th St	206-782-2974	The dog barks for Belgian beer.
Duck Island Ale House	7317 Aurora Ave N	206-783-3360	The friendliest beer connoisseurs in Seattle.
El Chupacabra	6711 Greenwood Ave N	206-706-4889	Frighteningly delicious Mexican munchies and margaritas.
Kangaroo & Kiwi Pub	7305 Aurora Ave N	206-297-0507	Where homesick Australians get pissed with New Zealand ex-pats.
Molly Maguire's	610 NW 65th St	206-789-9643	Requisite neighborhood Irish pub, only with real Irish people!
Prost!	7311 Greenwood Ave N	206-706-5430	Small German-themed bar with a friendly attitude.
St Andrew's Bar & Grill	7406 Aurora Ave N	206-523-1193	The place for Scotch whiskey and kilt-fanciers.
Sully's Snow Goose Saloon	6119 Phinney Ave N	206-782-9231	Quaint country pub.
Tin Hat Bar & Grill	512 NW 65th St	206-782-2770	Even the jukebox has tattoos.
Uber Tavern	7517 Aurora Ave N	206-829-8922	Enjoy a cold brew at this small hangout.

Map 31 • Green Lake / Roosevelt

Die Bierstube	6106 Roosevelt Wy NE	206-527-7019	German beers the size of a German head.
Elysian Tangletown	2106 N 55th St	206-547-5929	Elysian micros in a cozy neighborhood pub.
La Casa Del Mojito	7545 Lake City Wy NE	206-525-3162	Mojitos are just the Tip of the Plantain.
Little Red Hen	7115 Woodlawn Ave NE	206-522-1168	Serious honky-tonk for urban cowboys. Slummers get bounced.
Luau Polynesian Lounge	2253 N 56 St	206-633-5828	Happy hour mai tais start flowing at noon. Perfect for your lunch break.
Pies and Pints	1215 NE 65th St	206-524-7028	Great concept. Poor execution.
Teddy's Tavern	1012 NE 65th St	206-526-9174	Easy going bar with a nice outside patio.

Map 32 • Ravenna

Knarr Tavern	5633 University Wy NE	206-525-3323	Play pool and shuffleboard with grizzled Seattleites.
The Pub at Third Place	6504 20th Ave NE	206-523-0217	Board games and wood decor make you feel comfortably snowed in.
Ravenna Alehouse	2258 NE 65th St	206-729-9083	An innofensive neighborhood pub.

Map 33 • Northwest Seattle

Rickshaw	322 N 105th St	206-789-0120	'70s karaoke paradise.

Map 34 • Northeast Seattle

Fiddler's Inn	9219 35th Ave NE	206-525-0752	When Wedgwoodies can find a babysitter.

Map 35 • Alki / West Seattle / North Admiral

Bamboo Bar & Grill	2806 Alki Ave SW	206-937-3023	The location and hours ('til 2 am) are the best thing they've got going.
Celtic Swell Irish Pub	2722 Alki Ave SW	206-932-7935	Children and fiddles welcome, just like Ye Olde Country.
Elliot Bay Brewpub	4720 California Ave SW,	206-932-8695	Top-notch beers and organic local beef.
The Matador	4546 California Ave SW	206-932-9988	Loud. Dark. Fifty kinds of tequila.
Poggie Tavern	4717 California Ave SW	206-937-2165	Not for the timid drinker.
West 5 Lounge & Restaurant	4539 California Ave SW	206-935-1966	Hip yet homey, but always crowded.
Yer Wor Village	2300 California Ave SW	206-932-1455	Known around the neighborhood as the Young Whore. Karaoke seven nights a week.

Map 36 • North Delridge

Skylark Café & Club	3803 Delridge Wy SW	206-935-2111	Real Seattle rock-n-roll happens here. No cover.

Map 37 • Fauntleroy / Arbor Heights

The Tug Tavern	2216 SW Orchard St	206-768-8852	Mini pitchers, shag carpeting, duct taped furniture—dive in.

Map 38 • White Center / South Park / Beverly Park

Loretta's	8617 14th Ave S	206-327-9649	Wood paneling and classic beer signs from the folks that brought you the Nine Pound Hammer.

Map 39 • SoDo / Beacon Hill / Georgetown

Beacon Pub	3057 Beacon Ave S	206-726-0238	Fantastic karaoke in a comfy dive setting.
Georgetown Liquor Company	5501 Airport Wy S	206-763-6764	Atari 2600 and beer. Can life get any better?
Hooverville Bar	1721 1st Ave S	206-264-2428	A bar for recovering corporate junkies.
Jules Maes Saloon	5919 Airport Wy S	206-957-7766	Century-old tavern where punk meets country.
Nine Pound Hammer	6009 Airport Wy S	206-762-3373	A Georgetown and NFT favorite. With shuffleboard!
Showbox SoDo	1700 1st Ave	206-628-3151	More Showbox for your buck.
Studio Seven	110 S Horton St	206-286-1312	Jam to live music with grandma and your teenager.
Uncle Moe's Watering Hole (a.k.a Planet Georgetown)	6266 13th Ave S	206-762-4009	Your alcoholic uncle's game room.

Map 40 • Columbia City / Mount Baker / Seward Park

Lottie's Lounge	4900 Ranier Ave S	206-725-0519	Comfortable neighborhood joint with live music and fun menu.

Map 45 • Bellevue (West) / Medina

Parlor	700 Bellevue Wy NE	425-289-7000	Upscale pool hall.

Map 46 • Bellevue (Central)

Skate King	2301 140th Ave NE	425-641-2047	Bounce. Roll. Skate.

Map 48 • Kirkland

The Shark Club	52 Lake Shore Plz	425-803-3003	Live music, crowded dance floor, and pool tables for the twenty somethings.
Tiki Joe's Wet Bar	106 Kirkland Ave	425-827-8300	$2 beer nights and rowdy karaoke for you and the frat boys.

Map 49 • Redmond

Celtic Bayou Brewpub	7281 W Lake Sammamish Pkwy NE	425-869-5933	Irish/Cajun hybrid in case you need to fill that void.

Seattle's spot among the country's culinary pantheon has ascended in recent years, and although we're not quite Zeus, we're definitely a Demeter. Or maybe, more like an Artemis. Casually upscale affairs are popping up on cozy little corners all over town—from the sexy roughhewn plates at gastropub **Quinn's (Map 4)** to the bright space and bright flavors of Belltown's **Txori Bar (Map 1)**. Seattle's restaurants have been able to fly mostly under the radar, resulting in a flourishing, inventive, and casual culinary scene that's been spared intense scrutiny—so get eating quick, because the ability to get a table without a wait is fast diminishing. We've now got a formidable contingent of award-winning chefs, it's true, but most of them have set up shop here to avoid the flashbulbs and fancy cars, and just cook some damn good food. The scene swells with top-notch restaurants (foie gras, foraged morels) that are decidedly unpretentious (fleece and Tevas usually permissible) and highly affordable (an entree under $30? Incredible!). It's just quality that's valued, rather than trendiness. The recent eco-friendly sustainably-free range organic fascination has always been a founding principle of Northwest cuisine, which relies on locally-sourced ingredients (chefs are downright obsessive about it). Flavor profiles range from Pan-Asian flair to rustic Italian or provincial French, but usually it's a little of this, a little of that (but don't you dare use the "f" word). Seafood is the crown jewel, of course, so do yourself a favor and eat as many Dungeness crabs and King salmon, when in season, as you can possibly afford. And while the variety in ethnic cuisines may not impress a New Yorker, Seattle's international selections are, for the more enterprising diner, worth seeking out. The point being that food here, above all, is accessible, and that's how we like it. It makes it a whole lot easier to get it into your mouth that way.

Seafood

Because of Seattle's proximity to the Pacific, it makes sense that seafood seems to wiggle its way onto every menu in town. Now, that's not to say that you're going to get the best stuff everywhere; selectivity is key. **Ray's Boathouse (Map 28)** is a venerable waterfront institution that's been doing it right for decades, with a prime waterfront location and a slightly older crowd (including, yes, lots of tourists). Downtown, our local chef-cum-restaurateur Tom Douglas serves up calamari and Copper River salmon for his adoring fans at **Etta's Seafood (Map 3)**. The luxuriously-minded might head over to the mahogany-sheathed den at Shuckers, or perhaps the old-school glitz of **The Oceanaire Room (Map 3)**, where piles of oysters and the sounds of Sinatra lure seafarers with a bit more swank (and cash) in their step. To get a true taste of Pike Place, go straight to **Matt's in the Market (Map 3)**, or the **Market Grill (Map 3)** for a blackened salmon sandwich. If you get a greasy jonesing for fish and chips, **Spud on Alki (Map 35)** and **Alki Crab and Fish Company (Map 36)** are classic, but newcomer **Pike Street Fish Fry (Map 4)** ups the ante with late-night hours, jars of homemade pickles, and fancy-schmancy sauces.

Seafood, Nippon-style

Sushi is huge in Seattle. Our easy access to fantastic things from the sea, coupled with a keen interest in Eastern cultures and a large Asian population, has resulted in a spread of sushi restaurants that would make any free-swimming fish shake in his fins. Purists requiring the very finest will seek a spot at **Nishino (Map 19)**, the eponymous establishment of Tatsu Nishino (a former disciple of famed Nobu Matuhisa). Put your dinner in his skilled hands omakase-style for a spectacular experience. A little more affordable is **Aoki (Map 17)** on Broadway, an unassuming little place serving good quality sushi and a selection of Japanese sakes. Or in West Seattle, make sure to try the chef specials at **Mashiko**

(Map 35). **Chiso (Map 24)** takes sushi for a spin in a hip, modern setting, inventing new rolls that are, more often than not, very oishii indeed. The ID offers more traditional sushi experiences, like at chef-favorite **Tsukushinbo (Map 8)** or **Maneki (Map 8)**—the oldest sushi bar in Seattle. And for the newly initiated, or those for whom California rolls are adventurous, **Blue C Sushi (Map 24, 26)** rolls out cheap and accessible dishes on a gimmicky (though admittedly fun) conveyor belt system.

Classy Joints

Most restaurants here don't have a dress code—Seattle is simultaneously famous and infamous for its constant state of casual dress. But there are those establishments that do request a bit more refinement from their diners, and sometimes, it's just dang refreshing to step out of the Birkenstocks and into leathered, crystalline luxury. The hands-down mother of them all is **Canlis (Map 13)**, a 55-year-old Seattle fixture with a view to die for, impeccable formal service, and spectacular food. Canlis is for when you not only want to eat fancy, but you want to feel fancy too. **Rover's (Map 19)**, helmed by the "chef in the hat" Thierry Rautureau, laces French-inspired Northwest with immaculate flair and boasts the best wait staff around. **Chez Shea (Map 3)** in Pike Place Market is tops for expensive dining of the romantic variety, and every C-note is worth the glory of its prix-fixe. Also in Pike Place, you can't go wrong at **Place Pigalle (Map 3)** for gourmet dining with a view. **Crush (Map 18)** is where the sexy people go, and where James-Beard nominated chef Jason Wilson's lusty dishes pop against the sleekest minimal interior. And if you never associated the word classy with a pizza joint, a trip to **Via Tribunali (Map 4)** will change your mind.

No Animals, Please

If your dietary preferences don't involve any fuzzy animals, or even their byproducts, you're not alone. Seattle's a haven for vegetarians and vegans, so much so that even the carnivorous can be found relishing tofu meat products. **Araya's Vegetarian Place (Map 26)** is popular with the college crowd, featuring tasty Thai and an excellent (and cheap) lunch buffet. **Flowers (Map 26)** is another great veggie buffet spot. They offer an amazing Mediterranean spread during the day. Vegans needn't be deprived of the late-night delight only greasy pizza can bring: **Pizza Pi (Map 32)** is an exclusively vegan pizzeria, and the dairy-free cheese is pretty decent. When die-hard meat lovers can't stop talking about how delicious the fake meat is at **Bamboo Garden (Map 15)**, it's worth taking note. The sweet and sour "pork," as well as anything deep-fried, is almost better than the real thing (well, maybe not). And if you imagine puny wheatgrass shots and flaccid faux patties when you think vegetarian, get thee to the gritty **Georgetown Liquor Company (Map 39)**, where you can dig into flavor-packed meatless sandwiches and Super Nintendo, quite literally, from the wrong side of the tracks.

Extra Meat, Please

But if you are into the eating of animals, Seattle will not disappoint. If you aren't lucky enough to work in Pioneer Square, it's worth taking a vacation day to grab a glorious sandwich and buy a few pounds of Armando Batali's amazing pork products at **Salumi (Map 7)**. To help you reach artery blockage bliss, order a double bacon deluxe at **Red Mill Burgers (Map 30)** or the criminally good "dork" (duck plus pork) burger at **Lunchbox Laboratory (Map 29)**. **Rancho Bravo (Map 25)** offers meat, Mexican-style, and primarily in the form of tacos. We guarantee you they'll be the most delicious brain, tripe, or tongue dishes you should probably ever get out of a truck. But the best way to get your meat fix in Seattle is to head straight to **Pecos Pit BBQ (Map 39)** and tell them to "spike it!" If you're a true meat aficionado, you'll probably end up crying puddles of protein-loving joy.

Eating Ethnic

Like most metropolitan cities in America, the cuisines of Mexico, Thailand, China, Vietnam, and Japan are well-served with numerous restaurants, of assorted quality, peppered throughout Seattle, but the adventurous foodie can find plenty other culinarily-minded cultures to sample from. **Tempero do Brasil (Map 32)** serves up Brazilian favorites with authentic atmosphere in the University District, while in West Seattle the **Salvadorian Bakery (Map 37)** specializes in fast food El Salvador-style. Fans of Malaysian fare need look no further than the **Malay Satay Hut (Map 8)** in the International District. Never had Cambodian? Head to **Phnom Penh (Map 8)** for some tasty noodles. The mysterious **Marrakesh Moroccan Restaurant (Map 1)** is housed in a dusty-pink, windowless building downtown, but inside all the romance and intrigue of Morocco comes alive. **Vios Café (Map 18)** brings homemade Greek fare in the friendliest family atmosphere (read: playground, toys, and crayons). Clustered around Seattle University you'll find a bunch of stellar Ethiopian spots, including the much loved **Mesob (Map 4)**, or head to **Enat Ethiopian (Map 34)** for the city's best. To venture further into African cooking, **Pan Africa (Map 3)** boasts a variety of earthily spiced dishes from around the continent. Freshly muddled mojitos and crispy empanadas have been packing the tiny dining room of **Isla Seattle (Map 23)**.

Cheap Eats

A high concentration of colleges and universities in the area means there are a lot of hungry, drunk, and otherwise intoxicated students prowling the streets for food they can buy with their Coinstar winnings and leftover laundry change. With most of a co-ed's budget going to beer and textbooks, cost efficiency is top priority; quality, irrelevant. Fortunately, there is an endless supply of local restaurants for the hard up, hungry, or hung over—with no unnecessary sacrifice in taste. Pho, the eminently filling and fragrant Vietnamese noodle soup, is one of the cheapest and most mouthwatering meals you can get for a scant $5 or so. **Pho Cyclo (Maps 17, 39)** ladles out a most intriguingly flavored version, but the ubiquitous local **Than Brothers' (Maps 17, 23, 26, 30, 35, 49)** chain does it a little more cheaply and a little more sweetly (you get a free cream puff with every bowl). For unique gourmet sandwiches on the relative cheap, stop by **Baguette Box (Map 4)** for their tasty tofu version, **Bakeman's (Map 3)** for an old-school hand-carved turkey on white bread, or queue up at the always popular **Paseo (Map 24)** for a hearty Cuban. Many a penny pincher have realigned their eating schedules to the happy hour at **McCormick and Schmick (Maps 3, 16)**, where the $1.95 half-pound burger and fries makes you wonder if you're dreaming—or, maybe for a moment, where they get their meat. The forward-thinking cheapskate heads to **Gorditos (Map 30)** for the infant-sized burritos that will feasibly supply at least two additional meals. And if a late-night craving for the lovably limp burgers you downed as a kid proves unshakable, local institution **Dick's (Map 25)** will sling you a paper sack full of 'em for not much more than your leftover change from that evening's bar-hopping.

Take Out

There is very little food delivery in Seattle. Agonized East Coasters are usually appalled; Seattleites, unfamiliar with

the wonders of doorstep-delivered Chinese, just sigh and order a pizza. Yup—those days when you're just too tired to cook, you'll still need to muster up enough energy to pick up your take out (unless, of course, you actually do want pizza). In the U District **Thai Tom (Map 26)** and **Thaiger Room (Map 26)** are always packed with pad thai devotees, but you can scant call ahead to pick it up. The effort and the calories are worth it at **Ezell's Fried Chicken (Map 2)**, an uncontested legend in the fried chicken arena. Seattle has a love/hate relationship with the Chinese from **Judy Fu's Snappy Dragon (Map 34)**; some can't stop yapping about it, others hate Judy's greasy guts. Judging by its always-packed dining room and brisk take-out business, it's worth a shot (hint: the dumplings are divine). Judy's also happens to deliver to the lucky few living close by. A newcomer to Capitol Hill, **In the Bowl (Map 17)**, will also deliver its tasty vegetarian noodle bowls—good thing, because it's usually impossible to find a seat.

Spots We Love

It's not just us; everyone's taking note. 2008 was a benchmark year for the Seattle food scene. Open later, looking sexier, sized smaller, and cooking better, these spots are the new pillars of Northwest cuisine. Places like Ethan Stowell's latest sensation, **How to Cook a Wolf (Map 13)**—everything shines golden, from the dramatic sloped roof to the perfect sea-sweet scallops. Seattle foodsters can't get enough. **Tilth (Map 24)**, **Lark (Map 4)**, **Pair (Map 32)**, and **Steelhead Diner (Map 3)** all exhibit the same golden touch in their quintessentially Northwest approaches.

Then there are the gastropubs like **Quinn's (Map 4)** and **Smith (Map 18)**, which prove a neighborhood watering hole's food needn't be watered down. They serve things like roasted marrow bones and wild boar sloppy joes, dishes that manage to both primal and elegant. For a Seattle take on the perfect French bar/cafe, **Café Presse (Map 4)** is your savior for a weekend brunch or late-night steak frites. The great Spanish bar food legacy, tapas, has effectively become official Seattle tradition as well. **Txori (Map 1)** is the place that nailed it on the head, with some truly magical San Sebastian-style pintxos.

The greatness goes one rung down further—the humble ice cream cone gets the royal Northwest treatment, an Airstream trailer grills up Kobe beef burgers, and a strip mall is a natural home for a quintessentially Seattle restaurant. Salted caramel, Thai iced tea—you may think you've dreamt up such wonderful flavors, but they're real, and they're but a few of the luscious options at **Molly Moon's (Map 25)**, a sustainably run ice creamery in the heart of Wallingford. Skillet (location varies, www.skilletstreetfood.com), a fancified meals-on-wheels, defies the idea of trailer trash—one taste of the bacon jam-topped burgers settles that score. And **Sitka & Spruce (Map 20)**, Matt Dillon's teensy 20-seat affair, has hit its exuberant stride, despite the dubious company it keeps (Subway and teriyaki are neighbors).

If the Seattle style of cooking was hard to pin down before, our new favorite spots indicate there's absolutely no confusion about what we do here now—our food is authentic, yet open to creative interpretation; it's accessible without sacrificing quality; it's conscious of its impact on our community and our environment. We love our Seattle, yes we do. And if you eat at these fantastic spots, you'll love it too.

Key: $: Under $10 / $$: $10–$20 / $$$: $20–$30 / $$$$: $30–40 / $$$$$: $40+
*: Does not accept credit cards. / † : Accepts only American Express. / †† : Accepts only Visa and Mastercard.
Time refers to weekend night closing time.

Map 1 • Belltown

		Phone	Price		
Anthony's Bell Street Diner	2201 Alaskan Wy	206-448-6688	$$$	10 pm	Casual (and affordable) offshoot of the popular Anthony's chain.
Anthony's Pier 66	2201 Alaskan Wy	206-448-6688	$$$$	10 pm	Pacific Northwest chain on Elliott Bay.
Assaggio Ristorante	2010 4th Ave	206-441-1399	$$$$	10 pm	If you don't mind the tourists, some of the food is pretty good.
Black Bottle	2600 1st Ave	206-441-1500	$$	1:30 am	Fill your jowls with flatbread and wine to drown out the noise.
Boat Street Café	3131 Western Ave	206-632-4602	$$	10 pm	Traditional French selections with an unabashed use of cream.
Brasa	2107 3rd Ave	206-728-4220	$$$$$	12 am	The roasted suckling pig: so primitive, and yet, so classy. And romantic.
Buenos Aires Grill	2000 2nd Ave	206-441-7076	$$$	11 pm	A Latin-flavored celebration of all things meaty.
Buffalo Deli	2123 1st Ave	206-728-8759	$*	5 pm	Pretty much determined to have the best French dip in town.
Cascadia	2328 1st Ave	206-448-8884	$$$$$	11:30 pm	Don't miss the classy happy hour.
Dahlia Bakery	2001 4th Ave	206-441-4540	$	6 pm	Take a hot steaming loaf of Tom Douglas home with you.
Dahlia Lounge	2001 4th Ave	206-682-4142	$$$$	11 pm	Another gem in Tom Douglas's juggernaut. Great for dates.
El Gaucho	2505 1st Ave	206-728-1337	$$$$	11 pm	Super-luxurious surf and turf, best for impressing the pants off someone.
Five Point Café	415 Cedar St	206-448-9993	$††	24 hrs	24-hour bar/diner with decent food. Just don't piss off the wait staff.
Flying Fish	2234 1st Ave	206-728-8595	$$$$	1 am	Fish for the fresh-faced younger set.
The Frontier Room	2202 1st Ave	206-956-7427	$$	12 am	A welcome dive in the midst of cosmo-laden Belltown.
Icon Grill	1933 5th Ave	206-441-6330	$$$	11 pm	Kitschy-crazy interior and familiar favorites bumped up a notch.
La Fontana Siciliana	120 Blanchard St	206-441-1045	$$	10 pm	Much-loved Sicilian spot.
La Vita E Bella	2407 2nd Ave	206-441-5322	$$	10 pm	Among the most delicious pizza crusts in town—crisp, chewy, perfect.
Lampreia	2400 1st Ave	206-443-3301	$$$$	9 pm	Minimalist, eclectic, and a little nouvelle from one of the country's best chefs.
Lola	2000 4th Ave	206-441-1430	$$	12 am	Always hoppin', so service can be spotty. Food's a little Greek and a little pricey.
Macrina Bakery & Café	2408 1st Ave	206-448-4032	$$	7 pm	Macrina's baked goods will make breakfast your most important meal.
Mama's Mexican Kitchen	2334 2nd Ave	206-728-6262	$$	10 pm	Kitschy Mexican cooking with a thing for Elvis (and cheese).
Marco's Supperclub	2510 1st Ave	206-441-7801	$$$	11 pm	Urban space, modern food, and fried sage leaves.
Marjorie	2331 2nd Ave	206-441-9842	$$$	1 am	Eclectic is an understatement. Nice patio.
Marrakesh Moroccan Restaurant	2334 2nd Ave	206-956-0500	$$	10 pm	Morrocan in all of its minty, buttery, fragrant theatricality.
Nara Grill	2027 5th Ave	206-727-2224	$$$$	10:30 pm	Pricey but excellently fresh sushi.
Noodle Ranch	2228 2nd Ave	206-728-0463	$	11 pm	Fusion-y Asian. Funky environment.
Ohana	2207 1st Ave	206-956-9329	$$	12:30 am	Pu-pus that are far from poo poo.
Palace Kitchen	2030 5th Ave	206-448-2001	$$$	1 am	Gourmet late-night dining in Seattle? This is your spot.
Queen City Grill	2201 1st Ave	206-443-0975	$$$$	12 am	Seafood's the focus, unless you count the horndogs hoping to score.
Restaurant Zoe	2137 2nd Ave	206-256-2060	$$$	11 pm	The brown butter-bathed ricotta gnudi is now officially Seattle legend.
Saito's Japanese Café & Bar	2122 2nd Ave	206-728-1333	$$$$	7 pm	Experienced sushi chef and impressive sake selection. Big lunch crowd.
Serious Pie	316 Virginia St	206-838-7388	$$$	11 pm	Truly amazing crust in tiny quarters, courtesy of Tom Douglas.
Shallots	2525 4th Ave	206-728-1888	$$$	10:30 pm	Great Asian fusion that's well-loved by the locals. The nine-flavor chicken rocks.
Shiro's Sushi	2401 2nd Ave	206-443-9844	$$$$	9:45 pm	Wait to sit at the bar, chat with Shiro, be utterly delighted.
Six Seven	Edgewater Hotel, Pier 67, 2411 Alaskan Wy	206-269-4575	$$$$	10 pm	Northwest seafood classics.
Tavolata	2323 2nd Ave	206-838-8008	$$	11 pm	Fantastically sexy space with handmade pastas to match.

Name	Address	Phone	Price	Close	Description
Two Bells Tavern	2313 4th Ave	206-441-3050	$$	12 am	A rare old soul in trendy Belltown. Tasty burgers.
Txori Bar	2207 2nd Ave	206-204-9771	$$	1 am	San Sebastian-style tapas. Translation: Awesome.
Wasabi Bistro	2311 2nd Ave	206-441-6044	$$$$	1 am	"Sushi" rolls usually involving avocado or cream cheese. Not for purists.
Waterfront Seafood Grill	2801 Alaskan Wy	206-956-9171	$$$$	11 pm	Puget Sound views. Upscale menu.
Zeek's Pizza	419 Denny Wy	206-448-6775	$$	10 pm	Pizzas with pizzazz, like the Thai one with peanut sauce.
Zoë	2137 2nd Ave	206-256-2060	$$$$	11 pm	A sophisticated place where execs, hipsters, and kids somehow all get along.

Map 2 • Downtown / Denny Triangle

Name	Address	Phone	Price	Close	Description
13 Coins	125 Boren Ave N	206-243-9500	$$$$$	24 hrs	Sometimes you just gotta blow $50 on steak and lobster at 3 am.
FareStart	700 Virginia St	206-443-1233	$$*	3 pm	Eat well, feel great: FareStart trains the disadvantaged to launch new lives as chefs.
The Hurricane Café	2230 7th Ave	206-682-5858	$	24 hrs	24-hour diner with full bar. Start or end your day with cheap, greasy eggs.
Shilla Restaurant	2300 8th Ave	206-623-9996	$$	12 am	Menu is a crash-course in Korean Food 101. Impressive panchan.
Venik Lounge	227 9th Ave N	206-233-3734	$	11 pm	The Russians know vodka and caviar. Swanky.

Map 3 • Downtown

Name	Address	Phone	Price	Close	Description
94 Stewart	94 Stewart St	206-441-5505	$$$$	10 pm	Funky feel, prime market location, and fried avocados!
Andaluca	407 Olive Wy	206-382-6999	$$$$	11 pm	Tasty upscale tapas will have you exclaiming "¡Qué sabroso!"
Bakeman's	122 Cherry St	206-622-3375	$*	3 pm	The plump turkey sandwiches are dirt-cheap, and damn tasty.
The Brooklyn	1212 2nd Ave	206-224-7000	$$$$	10:30 pm	Slurp down the oysters (the specialty here) in old-Seattle elegance.
Café Campagne	1600 Post Aly	206-728-2233	$$$	11 pm	Campagne's more laid-back sister. And the absolute best brunch downtown.
Café Zum Zum	823 3rd Ave	206-622-7391	$*	3 pm	Giant affordable lunch that is yum yum.
Campagne	86 Pine St	206-728-2800	$$$$	12 am	Frenchified Northwest loved for 20 years by tourists and locals alike.
Chez Shea	94 Pike St	206-467-9990	$$$$	10 pm	Seafood-centered menu, super-seductive, and an unbeatable view.
Crêpe de Paris	1333 5th Ave	206-623-4111	$$$	9 pm	Crepes, cabaret, and prix fixe = so French.
Crumpet Shop	1503 1st Ave	206-682-1598	$	5 pm	Fresh, buttery crumpets with sweet or savory toppings. Not just for Brits!
DeNunzio	102 Cherry St	206-343-9517	$$	11 pm	Expect Luigi to stop by for a chat; you'll feel a part of the famiglia in no time.
Dilettante Chocolates	400 Pine St	206-903-8595	$$	9 pm	Just skip dinner and indulge in a chocolate dessert orgy. You deserve it.
Dragonfish Asian Café	722 Pine St	206-467-7777	$$	1 am	Pop-culture Asian that takes a ride around the Pacific Rim.
Earth and Ocean	1112 4th Ave	206-264-6060	$$$$	10:30 pm	Find your culinary center piled high and gorgeous on the plate. Renowned.
El Puerco Lloron	1501 Western Ave	206-624-0541	$	8 pm	Cafeteria-style served carnitas and corn tortillas, which are fantastico.
Elliot's Oyster House	1201 Alaskan Wy	206-623-4340	$$$	11 pm	Get messy with the cioppino.
Emmett Watson's Oyster Bar	1916 Pike Pl	206-448-7721	$$	9 pm	Seattle's very first oyster bar, appropriately shabby—in a good way.
Entre Nous	216 Stewart St	206-905-1633	$$	1 am	Nuzzle over fondue and frites at this romantic, real-deal Provençal bistro.
Etta's Seafood	2020 Western Ave	206-443-6000	$$$	10 pm	Fresh seafood from Tommy D.
Gelatiamo	1400 3rd Ave	206-467-9563	$	8 pm	Some tasty pastries and heavenly gelato.
The Georgian	411 University St	206-621-7889	$$$$$	1:30 am	For impressing the spouse, the in-laws, or your boss.
Il Bistro	93A Pike St	206-682-3049	$$$$	1 am	Decent Italian off the market; nice scotch selection.
Il Fornaio	600 Pine St	206-264-0994	$$	10 pm	If you must eat in a mall, this place has decent Italian.
Jack's Fish Spot	1514 Pike Pl	206-467-0514	$	5 pm	No-nonsense counter that embodies the soul of the Market—for better or worse.
Kells Irish Pub	1916 Post Aly	206-728-1916	$$	12 am	Good Irish pub food: not an oxymoron.
La Creperie Voila	707 Pike St	206-447-2737	$$	9:30 pm	In the eating wasteland that is the Convention Center, Voila is your warm, buttery salvation.
Le Panier Very French Bakery	1902 Pike Pl	206-441-3669	$$	6 pm	Win instant popularity by doling out Panier's French macaroons--they will blow you away.

Arts & Entertainment • **Restaurants**

Map 3 • Downtown–*continued*

Le Pichet	1933 1st Ave	206-256-1499	$$	2 am	Eat roast chicken. Drink beaujolais. Pretend you're in Paris. Save airfare.
Library Bistro	92 Madison St	206-624-3646	$$	12 am	Swanky yet unfussy, and the food is equally lovely.
Mae Phim Thai Restaurant	94 Columbia St	206-624-2979	$	7 pm	Enormous portions of slightly authentic Thai for not much more than a fiver.
Market Grill	1509 Pike Pl #3	206-682-2654	$	5 pm	Homemade chowder and salmon sandwiches are worth the wait.
Matt's Famous Chili Dogs	801 Alaskan Wy	206-264-0446	$	6 pm	Midwestern folks affirm this is a true Chicago dog.
Matt's in the Market	94 Pike St	206-467-7909	$$$	9:30 pm	Market-fresh produce and fish tossed up to the second floor window? It's magic.
Maximilien in the Market	81A Pike St	206-682-7270	$$$	10 pm	Classic French in all its butter-sauced glory; classy and cheap happy hour.
McCormick & Schmick's	1103 1st Ave	206-623-5500	$$$	11 pm	Corporate club vibe and an unparalleled $1.95 happy hour burger.
McCormick's Fish House & Bar	722 4th Ave	206-682-3900	$$$	12 am	Corporate club vibe with weekly oyster specials.
Metropolitan Grill	820 2nd Ave	206-624-3287	$$$$$	11 pm	Martinis and meat.
Morton's, The Steakhouse	1511 6th Ave	206-223-0550	$$$$$	11 pm	Yet another dark wood, clubby, pricey steakhouse. Tableside service.
New Orleans Creole	114 1st Ave S	206-622-2563	$$	11 pm	Hush puppies, live jazz, and blues every night—and even vegetarian options!
Oceanaire Seafood Room	1700 7th Ave	206-267-2277	$$$	10 pm	Old-world glamor and top-notch fish.
Osaka Grill	128 Pike St	206-340-1793	$††	10 pm	Worth braving the grime for tasty teriyaki.
Pan Africa	1521 1st Ave	206-652-2461	$$	10 pm	Awesome African dishes in the Market.
Pellini	515 Madison St	206-267-2201	$$$$	11 pm	Italian made by an actual Italian, with a view and prices to impress any date.
The Pink Door	1919 Post Aly	206-443-3241	$$	10 pm	Acceptable Italian, cranky servers. And sometimes people swing from trapezes.
Place Pigalle	81 Pike St	206-624-1756	$$$$	11 pm	Great views highlight a nice seafood menu.
Porta by the Market	113 Virginia St	206-374-1301	$$$	1 am	Simple Greek straight from an Athenian taverna.
Purple Café & Wine Bar	1225 4th Ave	206-829-2280	$$$	12 am	Tome-like wine list can be intimidating; food is upscale café fare.
Qube Restaurant	1901 2nd Ave	206-770-5888	$$$$	12 am	Despite the atrocious name, the French/Asian fusion occasionally surprises.
Ruth's Chris Steak House	727 Pine St	206-624-8524	$$$$$	11 pm	Ubiquitous chain dishes out gargantuan portions of meat. Uninspired.
Sazerac	1101 4th Ave	206-624-7755	$$$$	11 pm	Fun and trendy twists on Southern classics.
Shuckers	411 University St	206-621-1984	$$$$	11 pm	Laced-up business-y types gulp oysters and make deals.
Steelhead Diner	95 Pine St	206-625-0129	$$	10 pm	Pitch-perfect dishes exude the essence of Seattle and the Northwest.
Tap House Grill	1506 6th Ave	206-467-1730	$$	12 am	160 beers on tap. We repeat: 160 beers. On tap.
Three Girls Bakery	1514 Pike Pl	206-622-1045	$	6 pm	The sandwiches are classic, no frills, and the hands-down favorite.
Tulio Ristorante	1100 5th Ave	206-624-5500	$$$$	11 pm	Fancified Italian dishes are loved by businesspeople. Great service.
Turkish Delight	1930 Pike Pl	206-443-1387	$*	5 pm	Brave the Market crowd for the 3 buck lentil soup.
Union	1400 1st Ave	206-838-8000	$$$$	11 pm	Daily changing menu; the ambience perfect for lingering over the ice cream.
Union Square Grill	621 Union St	206-224-4321	$$$$$	11 pm	A carnivore's dream: the fattest portherhouse, slathered in butter.
Vessel	1312 5th Ave	206-652-5222	$$$	12 pm	Pose in the window with a fine cocktail.
Von's Grand City Café	619 Pine St	206-621-8667	$$	10 pm	Red meat, Manhattans, and Martinis.
Wild Ginger	1401 3rd Ave	206-623-4450	$$$	10 pm	Wildly overrated, but still remains an eternal favorite.
World Class Chili Inc	93 Pike St	206-623-3678	$*	5 pm	Decent chili and cranky old man service.
Zaina Food, Drink & Friends	108 Cherry St	206-624-5687	$$	10 pm	Best falafel in Seattle.
Zaina Food, Drink & Friends	1619 3rd Ave	206-770-0813	$$	10 pm	Best falafel in Seattle.

Map 4 • First Hill / Pike / Pine

611 Supreme	611 E Pine St	206-328-0292	$$	11 pm	When the crepes are good, they're good; when they're bad, they're real bad.
Annapurna Café	1833 Broadway	206-320-7770	$$	10 pm	Warm, nourishing food from Nepal, Tibet, and India served in a cozy basement.
Ayutthaya Thai Cuisine	727 E Pike St	206-324-8833	$$	10 pm	Unbelievably fresh and satisfying Thai. Dubious musical accompaniment.
Baguette Box	1203 Pine St	206-332-0220	$	8 pm	Amazing tofu sandwich. And meat too.

Arts & Entertainment • **Restaurants**

Name	Address	Phone	$	Time	Description
Ballet Restaurant	914 E Pike St	206-328-7983	$	9 pm	Cheap Asian fusion with a vast selection.
Bill's Off Broadway	725 E Pine St	206-323-7200	$	2 am	Line your stomach with satisfying grease after a night of debauchery.
Bimbo's Bitchin' Burrito Kitchen	1013 E Pike St	206-322-9950	$††	2am	If Hunter S. Thompson opened a burrito joint.
Boom Noodle	1121 E Pike St	206-701-9130	$$	2 am	Japanese izakaya spot with flavors that explode in your mouth. Boom!
Café Presse	1117 12th Ave	206-709-7674	$$††	2 am	Authentic French bistro serving food until 2 am. Très magnifique!
Capitol Club	414 E Pine St	206-325-2149	$$	11 pm	Restaurant-cum-lounge with live flamenco and guest DJs.
Crave	1621 12th Ave	206-388-0526	$$	11 pm	A trendy formula that works: industrial space, noble ingredients, decent prices.
Dinette	1514 E Olive Wy	206-328-2282	$$$††	10 pm	Come for the lovely, fancy toast—it's more delicious and filling than it sounds.
Geneva	1106 8th Ave	206-624-2222	$$$$	11 pm	Haute spot.
The Green Papaya	600 E Pine St	206-323-1923	$$	11 pm	New and classic Vietnamese dishes.
Honeyhole Sandwiches	703 E Pike St	206-709-1399	$	2 am	22 sandwiches, hot and cold, meat and vegetarian, double-fisted and sloppy.
Hunt Club	900 Madison St	206-343-6156	$$$$	10 pm	Doesn't the name just ooze pretension? So does the setting and the prices.
In the Bowl Vegetarian Noodle Bistro	1554 E Olive Wy	206-568-2343	$	10 pm	Another example of fake meat made delicious. And they deliver.
Lark	926 12th Ave	206-323-5275	$$$$	10:30 pm	Little plates never had it so good. Casual elegance epitomized.
Machiavelli	1215 Pine St	206-621-7941	$$$	11 pm	Canoodle over some noodles in this hip, affordable Italian favorite.
Mediterranean Kitchen	1417 Broadway	206-860-3989	$$$	9:30 pm	Garlicky Greek goodness.
Mesob	1325 E Jefferson St	206-860-0403	$	10 pm	Ethiopian eats.
Osteria la Spiga	1429 12th St	206-323-8881	$$$	11 pm	Gorgeous pastas and sandwiches. Emilia-Romagna comes to Seattle.
Piecora's	1401 E Madison St	206-322-9411	$$	12 am	The best NY-style pizza, whole or by the slice.
Pike Street Fish Fry	925 E Pike St	n/a	$$	2 am	Unbelievably fresh fish and chips: a revelatory, late-night godsend on Cap Hill.
Poco Wine Room	1408 E Pine St	206-322-9463	$	1 am	Low-key, top-notch cheeses, meats, and, of course, great wine.
Quinn's	1001 E Pike St	206-325-7711	$$$	1 am	Grown up food for a grown up neighborhood.
Rosebud	719 E Pike St	206-323-6636	$$	10 pm	Elegant cuisine and great bartenders, plus an Orson Welles fetish.
Saley	1361 E Olive Wy	206-405-3444	$	8 pm	A sweet, small one-woman crepe shop.
Taco Gringos	1510 E Olive Wy		$*	3 am	Late-night tacos.
Tango	1100 Pike St	206-583-0382	$$$$	11 pm	Posh yet cozy; come for the half-price wine bottles on Mondays.
Taqueria Guaymas	1415 Broadway	206-860-3871	$$	10 pm	Cheap and filling.
Via Tribunali	913 E Pike St	206-322-9234	$$	1 am	One bite of the pizza will transport you back to Napoli.

Map 5 • Central District (North)

Name	Address	Phone	$	Time	Description
Assimba Ethiopian Cuisine	2722 E Cherry St	206-322-1019	$	n/a	Ethiopian utopia.
Café Salem	2715 E Cherry Sr	206-328-0404	$	8:30 pm	This hole-in-the-wall Ethiopian is a favorite with cabbies.
Catfish Corner	2726 E Cherry St	206-323-4330	$	10 pm	Like fried bottom feeders? This is the place.
Central Cinema	1411 21st Ave	206-328-3230	$††	12 am	Forget popcorn. Pair a movie with good beer and decent grub.
El Gallito	1700 20th Ave	206-329-8088	$	9:30 pm	Easy to overlook, but so perfect before a night of boozin'. Huge portions.
Ezell's Famous Chicken	501 23rd Ave	206-324-4141	$	10 pm	Oprah has Ezell's chicken FedExed straight from Seattle to her mouth. Really.
Meskel Ethiopian Restaurant	2605 E Cherry St	206-860-1724	$	11 pm	You'll need lots of napkins. And beer.
Thompson's Point of View	2308 E Union St	206-329-2512	$$$††	11:30 pm	A little creole, a little cajun, and all that jazz.

Map 6 • Madrona

Name	Address	Phone	$	Time	Description
Café Soleil	1400 34th Ave	206-325-1126	$$††	9 pm	Laid-back breakfast mornings and spicy Ethiopian nights.
Coupage	1404 34th Ave	206-322-1974	$$$$	11 pm	Only place in town for French-Korean fusion—sake infused kumquats, anyone?
Cremant	1423 34th Ave	206-322-4600	$$$	11 pm	Snuggle with your honeybun over a perfect bouillabaisse.

321

Map 6 • Madrona–*continued*

Dulce's Latin Bistro	1430 34th Ave	206-322-5453	$$$	10 pm	Hot and haute Mexican classics with class.
The Hi-Spot Café	1410 34th Ave	206-325-7905	$$††	2:30 pm	Locals love this place.
Lalibela	2800 E Cherry St	206-322-8565	$	11 pm	Standard Ethiopian; great combo platter.
Madrona Ale House	1138 34th Ave	206-323-7807	$$††	11 pm	Great bar food. Bring the whole family.
St Clouds	1131 34th Ave	206-726-1522	$$$	2 am	Upscale neighborhood joint with style and late-night dining.

Map 7 • Pioneer Square / SoDo

Al Boccalino	1 Yesler Wy	206-622-7688	$$$$	10:30 pm	Nice Southern Italian in a historic building.
Café Paloma	93 Yesler Wy	206-405-1920	$	5 pm	Lovingly made meze-style food and delicious pita.
Grand Central Bakery	214 1st Ave S	206-622-3644	$	5 pm	Great lunch spot with amazing pastries.
Green Leaf Vietnamese Restaurant	418 8th Ave S	206-340-1388	$	10 pm	Fresh, fantastic Vietnamese. One of the best and busiest in town.
Il Terrazzo Carmine	411 1st Ave S	206-467-7797	$$$	11 pm	Classic, well-executed Italian.
Marcela's Cookery	106 James St	206-223-0042	$$	n/a	Down-home grub, N'awlins style. Try the muffuletta.
Salumi	309 3rd Ave S	206-621-8772	$	2 pm	Mario Batali's dad makes damn good salami. NFT favorite lunch spot.
Slim's Last Chance Chili Shack & Watering Hole	663 1st Ave S	206-762-7900	$$	10 pm	Jalapeno mac n' cheese, brisket and bean chili—oh my.
Trattoria Mitchelli	84 Yesler Wy	206-623-3883	$	11 pm	Quality pasta, local art, and insanely good marinara.

Map 8 • International District

663 Bistro	663 S Weller St	206-667-8760	$	11 pm	Chinese with a rare, incomparably light touch. A shining highlight in the ID.
Blue & Pink	502 S King St	206-624-2611	$	10 pm	The must-order at this *very* good Korean spot: "Well-Being Stone Bowl BiBimbob".
China Gate Restaurant	516 7th Ave S	206-624-1730	$$††	1:30 am	Select your prey from its tank.
Hing Loon	628 S Weller St	206-682-2828	$$	2 am	The chicken dumpling soup is innocent, loving comfort. The smoked duck: primal, carnivorous pleasure.
House of Hong	409 8th Ave S	206-622-7997	$$	2 am	Great food, even better name.
Jade Garden	704 S King St	206-622-8181	$$	2:30 am	Some argue it's Seattle's best dim sum; honestly, it probably is.
Made In Kitchen	725 S Lane St	206-625-0909	$$$	9:30 pm	Vietnamese with an identity crisis and kinda fancy digs.
Malay Satay Hut	212 12th Ave S	206-324-4091	$$	10:30 pm	Three cuisines unite under one roof, with delicious results.
Maneki	304 6th Ave S	206-622-2631	$$	10 pm	Tasty traditional Japanese food. A Seattle institution.
Pho Bac	415 7th Ave S	206-621-0532	$	10 pm	A reliable pho filling station. Try the banh mi and spring rolls too.
Phnom Penh	660 S King St	206-748-9825	$	8:30 pm	Cambodian noodle joint.
Saigon Deli	1032 S Jackson St	206-329-4939	$$	10 pm	Some of the best banh mi you'll find. Cheap, fast, and so good.
Samurai Noodle	606 5th Ave S	206-624-9321	$	10 pm	If your experience has been more Top Ramen than top notch, prepare to get your mind blown.
Sea Garden	509 7th Ave S	206-623-2100	$$$	3 am	You can stay til 3 am and watch your food get snatched from the aquarium.
Shanghai Garden	524 6th Ave S	206-625-1689	$$	10:30 pm	Delicious hand-shaved barley noodles and at least 100 other options.
Szechuan Noodle Bowl	420 8th Ave S	206-623-4198	$††	10 pm	Perfect scallion pancakes. Perfect noodle soups. Perfect dumplings.
Tai Tung	655 S King St	206-622-7372	$$	1:30 am	Sit at the counter with the regulars and soothe yourself with one of many comforting soups.
Tamirind Tree	1036 S Jackson St	206-860-1404	$	11 pm	Exotically droolworthy Vietnamese cuisine. Gives portion of profits to Viet Nam Scholarship Foundation.
Tea Garden	708 Rainier Ave S	206-709-9038	$$*	10 pm	The dim sum flows freely, and it is fantastic. One of Seattle's best.
Tsukushinbo Japanese Restaurant	515 S Main St	206-467-4004	$*	10 pm	Hidden Japanese gem.
Uwajimaya Food Court	600 5th Ave S	206-624-6248	$	10 pm	Hawaiian, Filipino, Korean, and more. All food courts should be this tasty.
Vegetarian Bistro	668 S King St	206-624-8899	$	9:30 pm	Vegetarian dim sum enjoyed by hippies and carnivores alike.

Map 9 • Central District (South)

Hidmo East African Cuisine	2000 S Jackson St	206-329-1534	$$	12 am	Tasty Eritrean grub.
Island Soul	2608 S Judkins St	206-329-1202	$$	9 pm	Caribbean goodness like curried goat, sweet plaintains, and jerk chicken.
Magic Dragon Chinese Eatery	306 23rd Ave S	206-329-7011	$	9 pm	A la carte, no-frills Chinese.
Moonlight Café	1919 S Jackson St	206-322-3378	$	10 pm	Good vegan Vietnamese options in a shabby setting.
Taco del Mar	2309 S Jackson St	206-329-8383	$*	9 pm	Tacos del inauthentic.

Map 10 • Leschi

All Purpose Pizza	2901 S Jackson St	206-324-8646	$$	9 pm	Good beer selection. And they deliver!
Bluwater Bistro	102 Lakeside Ave	206-328-2233	$$	1 am	Pricy but perfect seafood and meat for appeasing the carnivore in your life.
Daniel's Broiler	200 Lake Washington Blvd	206-329-4191	$$$$	11 pm	Fancy folk (or those whose parents are paying) head here for decent steak.
Pert's, A Deli at Leschi	120 Lakeside Ave	206-325-0277	$	5 pm	Pick up a turkey and swiss before heading to the park.
Ruby Asian Dining	200 Lake Washington Blvd	206-322-7288	$	10 pm	Reliable Pan-Asian on the water.
That's Amore	1425 31st Ave	206-322-3677	$$	10 pm	A real gem in the restaurant doldrums of Mt. Baker, despite the cliched name.

Map 11 • Magnolia / Interbay

Bay Café	1900 W Nickerson St	206-282-3435	$$††	2:15 pm	Waterfront diner doin' it right: breakfast all day and malted milkshakes.
Chinook's at Salmon Bay	1900 W Nickerson St	206-283-4665	$$	11 pm	Perfect for getting out of the halibut/salmon rut.
Mondello Ristorante	2435 33rd Ave W	206-352-8700	$$	10 pm	Real Sicilian trattoria, run by merry Mamma Enza.
Palisade	2601 W Marina Pl	206-285-1000	$$$$$	10 pm	Fancy seafood dishes that range from so-so to spectacular.
Red Mill Burgers	1613 W Dravus St	206-284-6363	$	9 pm	The undisputed best burger in Seattle. And possibly, the best onion rings.
Szmania's	3321 W McGraw St	206-284-7305	$$$$	10 pm	Colorful, kind of crazy-looking food. Bring the platinum card.

Map 12 • Queen Anne (North)

La Palma	3456 15th Ave W	206-284-1001	$$	11 pm	Delicious and cheap Mexican of the lardy, salty, cheesy variety.
Macrina Bakery & Café	615 W McGraw St	206-283-5900	$$	7 pm	Macrina's baked goods will make breakfast your most important meal.
Yasuko's Teriyaki	3200 15th Ave W	206-283-9152	$††	10 pm	Seattleites love teriyaki. Go figure.

Map 13 • Upper Queen Anne

5 Spot	1502 Queen Anne Ave N	206-285-7768	$$	12 am	Rotating, regional experiments that are scrumptious more often than not.
Canlis	2576 Aurora Ave N	206-283-3313	$$$$	10:30 pm	The best view in town comes at a premium; food is fancy.
Chinoise Café	12 Boston St	206-284-6671	$$	10 pm	Modern sushi joint with a Pan-Asian flair and a heap of noodle dishes.
Hilltop Ale House	2129 Queen Anne Ave N	206-285-3877	$$	11 pm	Not your average pub grub. Baked goat cheese salad and curry cashews!
How to Cook a Wolf	2208 Queen Anne Ave N	206-838-8090	$$$	12 am	Ethan Stowell's newest iteration of clean, composed food is the talk of the town.
Kaosamai Thai	3 W Nickerson St	206-349-6533	$	10 pm	Get in line and get there early—the pad Thai practically flies from this teeny mobile kitchen.
Opal	2 Boston St	206-282-0142	$$$	11 pm	Rich dishes that border on ethereal. And no skimping on the foie gras, thank goodness.
Orrapin Thai Cuisine	10 Boston St	206-283-7118	$	10 pm	Mellow, candlelit Thai.
Ototo Sushi	7 Boston St	206-691-3838	$$$	11 pm	Super-fresh, nicely presented sushi that's a steal.
Pasta Bella	1530 Queen Anne Ave N	206-284-9827	$$$	9 pm	Your run-of-the-mill romantic Italian restaurant.
Pasta & Co	2109 Queen Anne Ave N	206-283-1182	$$	8 pm	One-stop gourmet chain has fresh bread, wine, and risotto cakes to go.
Ponti Seafood Grill	3014 3rd Ave N	206-284-3000	$$$$	11:30 pm	A very good seafood restaurant, and not overflowing with tourists.

Arts & Entertainment • **Restaurants**

Map 13 • Upper Queen Anne–*continued*

Queen Anne Café	2121 Queen Anne Ave N	206-285-2060	$††	8 pm	Absolutely superb breakfast dishes; dinner, however, is spotty.
Zeek's Pizza	41 Dravus St	206-285-8646	$$	10 pm	Pizzas with pizzazz, like the Thai one with peanut sauce.

Map 14 • Queen Anne (West)

Betty	1507 Queene Anne Ave N	206-352-3773	$$	10 pm	Comforting bistro dishes, not-so-cozy space. Still, locals are adoring.
Moxie	530 1st Ave N	206-283-6614	$$	11 pm	Plucky neighborhood spot for serious food taking serious chances.

Map 15 • Lower Queen Anne / Seattle Center

Bamboo Garden	364 Roy St	206-282-6616	$$	10 pm	A must. Chinese vegetarian spot that makes fake meat taste unnaturally good.
Blue Water Taco Grill	515 Queen Anne Ave N	206-352-2407	$	9 pm	Cheap, barely passable Ameri-Mexican.
Crow Restaurant and Bar	823 5th Ave N	206-283-8800	$$	11 pm	Scoff at the small plate trend and indulge in hearty, sausage-stuffed lasagna.
Dick's Drive-In	500 Queen Anne Ave N	206-285-5155	$	2 am	A local obsession, specializing in cheap burgers and shakes. Perfect at 1 am.
Gordito's	1507 Queen Anne Ave N	n/a	$	10:30 pm	Baby-sized burritos will be a delicious meal for days.
Kidd Valley	531 Queen Anne Ave N	206-284-0184	$	9 pm	Like a slightly fancier Burger King with not much more to offer.
Mecca Café	526 Queen Anne Ave N	206-285-9728	$	2 am	Your taste buds will thank you. Your heart and liver will disown you.
Mediterranean Kitchen	366 Roy St	206-285-6713	$$$	10:30 pm	Garlicky Greek goodness.
The Melting Pot	14 Mercer St	206-378-1208	$$$$	10:30 pm	Gimmicky and retro, perhaps, but dipping things in cheese can never be bad.
Pagliacci Pizza	550 Queen Anne Ave N	206-285-1232	$	12 am	Local pizza chain makes crispy-chewy delights with seasonal ingredients.
Peso's	605 Queen Anne Ave N	206-283-9353	$$$	1 am	Mexican with substance. Same can be said for the margaritas but not the patrons.
Racha	23 Mercer St	206-281-8883	$$$	12 am	Safe bet for pad thai, once you get past the yuppies.
Roti Cuisine of India	530 Queen Anne Ave N	206-216-7684	$$	10 pm	Tasty, reasonably priced lunch buffet. Guaranteed food coma.
Shiki Japanese	4 W Roy St	206-281-1352	$$	10:30 pm	One of the only places in the state to get fugu. Non life-threatening dishes, too.
SkyCity at the Space Needle	400 Broad St	206-905-2100	$$$	10 pm	Ridiculously overpriced, mediocre food—but what a view. For tourists.
Solo Bar	200 Roy St	206-213-0080	$$	12 am	ItalEthioSpaBulgarian cuisine. And tapas.
Sushi Land	803 5th Ave N	206-267-7621	$	9 pm	Fun, cheap sushi.
Ten Mercer	10 Mercer St	206-691-3723	$$	12 am	Hip bar and romantic upstairs area—heavy on the meat options.
Troiani	1001 3rd Ave N	206-624-4060	$$$$	11 pm	Leather, wood panels, dim lights: like eating in Grandpa's study.
Uptown China	200 Queen Anne Ave N	206-285-7710	$$	10:30 pm	Efficient, spice-a-licious Chinese, best complemented by a Tsingtao.
Veil	555 Aloha St	206-216-0600	$$$	10 pm	Slick, modern, and crazy-notorious for the peanut butter ice cream.

Map 16 • Westlake / South Lake Union

Chandler's Crabhouse	901 Fairview Ave N	206-223-2722	$$$$	11 pm	Not-bad crabs with an excellent view of Lake Union.
Daniel's Broiler	809 Fairview Ave N	206-621-8262	$$$$	2 am	Fancy folk (or those whose parents are paying) head here for decent steak.
I Love Sushi	1001 Fairview Ave N	206-625-9604	$$	10:30 pm	Sushi with a view.
McCormick & Schmick's Harborside	1200 Westlake Ave N	206-270-9052	$$$	11 pm	Corporate club vibe and an unparalleled $1.95 happy hour burger.

Map 17 • Capitol Hill (West)

Aoki Japanese Grill & Sushi Bar	621 Broadway E	206-324-3633	$$$	10 pm	Japanese owned, Japanese served.

Artemis	757 Bellevue Ave E	206-860-2752	$$	12 am	Up-and-coming hidden gem, with a most unexpected view.
Bleu Bistro	202 Broadway E	206-329-3087	$$	12 am	Best first date place in the city, with sexy dark corners and a milleu of cocktails.
Broadway Grill	314 Broadway E	206-328-7000	$$	3 am	The eggs benedict is to die for. So are the cocktails. Shoot, it's all good.
Café Septieme	214 Broadway E	206-860-8858	$	12 am	Lovely ambience, pastas, and schnitzel right on Broadway.
Charlie's on Broadway	217 Broadway E	206-323-2535	$$	2:30 am	Bar food that tastes like home cookin'...almost.
Deluxe Bar & Grill	625 Broadway E	206-324-9697	$$	2 am	Kitchen stays open late, and the fries will leave you begging for mercy.
Dick's Drive-In	115 Broadway E	206-323-1300	$	2 am	A local obsession, specializing in cheap burgers and shakes. Perfect at 1 am.
Dilettante Chocolates	416 Broadway E	206-329-6463	$$	1 am	Just skip dinner and indulge in a chocolate dessert orgy. You deserve it.
Galerias	611 Broadway E	206-322-5757	$$	11:30 pm	Funky twists on Mexican fare and an impressive tequila display.
Glo's	1621 E Olive Wy	206-324-2577	$††	4 pm	Almost puts grandma's biscuits and gravy to shame. Great on a rainy morning.
Jai Thai	235 Broadway E	206-322-5781	$	10 pm	The curries are always kickin', and the happy hour menu is tops.
Noah's Bagels	220 Broadway E	206-720-2925	$††	5 pm	Better to wait for your next trip to New York.
Pagliacci Pizza	426 Broadway E	206-324-0730	$$	11 pm	Local pizza chain makes crispy-chewy delights with seasonal ingredients.
Pho Cyclo	406 Broadway E	206-329-9256	$	9:30 pm	Hella-tasty bowls of pho. Not the cheapest, but one of the yummiest.
Pho Thàn Brothers'	516 Broadway E	206-568-7218	$*	9 pm	Three words: free cream puff.
Piroshki on Broadway	128 Broadway E	206-322-2820	$	10 pm	Fresh piroshkis are cheap. Dirty looks from Russian ladies are free.
Queen Sheba	916 E John St	206-322-0852	$††	11 pm	Finger-lickin' spicy goodness to mop up with injera bread. Bring friends.
Rom Mai Thai	613 Broadway E	206-726-9058	$	11 pm	Friendly people and top-notch Thai; one of the best on Broadway.
Siam on Broadway	616 Broadway E	206-324-0892	$	11 pm	In a town with tons of Thai, the Tum Kha Gai here reigns supreme.
Table 219	219 Braodway E	206-328-4604	$$	9 pm	Same brunch classics from the El Greco days; dinner's got new creative touches.
Taqueria Guaymas	213 Broadway E	206-860-7345	$$	10 pm	Cheap and filling.

Map 18 • Capitol Hill (East) / Madison Valley

22 Doors	405 15th Ave E	206-324-6406	$$$	10:30 pm	Friendly neighborhood gastropub dishing out decidedly non-bar food.
Coastal Kitchen	429 15th Ave E	206-322-1145	$$$	11 pm	A quarterly rotating menu focusing on a different global cuisine. And blunch!
Crush	2319 E Madison St	206-302-7874	$$	10:30 pm	Foodie food.
Essential Baking Company	2719 E Madison St	206-328-0078	$	8 pm	You'll think you're in a European bakery.
The Harvest Vine	2701 E Madison St	206-320-9771	$$	10 pm	Gorgeous, perfect tapas.
Karam's Lebanese Cuisine	340 15th Ave E	206-324-2370	$	9 pm	Acquaint yourself with the kibbah.
Kingfish Café	602 19th Ave E	206-320-8757	$$	10:30 pm	The place for comforting soul food. Eat up, get fat, be grateful.
Monsoon	615 19th Ave E	206-325-2111	$$$	10 pm	Sublimely elegant Vietnamese, and oh-so-affordable. Great dim sum brunch.
Remedy Teas	345 15th Ave E	206-323-4832	$$	10 pm	150 incredible loose teas, the friendliest staff, lovely treats, and a clean, modern interior.
Samui Thai Cuisine	524 15th Ave E	206-328-2406	$††	10 pm	Mouth-watering Thai served with Soup Nazi attitude.
Smith	332 15th Ave E	206-322-9420	$$	11 pm	Perfect sweet potato fries, "devils on horseback", and brunch make for elegantly eclectic pub fare.
Vios Café & Marketplace	903 19th Ave E	206-329-3236	$	8:30 pm	Beautiful Greek dishes. Wines for the adults, play area for the kiddies.

Map 19 • Madison Valley / Denny Blaine

Café Flora	2901 E Madison St	206-325-9100	$$	10 pm	Eat fancy vegetarian food (considered one of the country's best) in a Zen garden.
Chinoise Café	2801 E Madison St	206-323-0171	$$	9:15 pm	Modern sushi joint with a Pan-Asian flair and a heap of noodle dishes.
Nishino	3130 E Madison St	206-322-5800	$$$	10:30 pm	One of the premier sushi places in town. Reservations requisite.

Map 19 • Madison Valley / Denny Blaine–*continued*

Rover's	2808 E Madison St	206-325-7442	$$$$$	10 pm	One of Seattle's favorite haute spots; say hello to the Chef-in-the-Hat.
Voilà! Bistrot	2805 E Madison St	206-322-5460	$$$	10:30 pm	Classic French in a classy setting. Stupid name.

Map 20 • Eastlake / Montlake / Portage Bay

14 Carrot Café	2305 Eastlake Ave E	206-324-1442	$$	4 pm	Typical breakfast fare that's, well, typical. Popular anyway.
Louisa's Café & Bakery	2379 Eastlake Ave E	206-325-0081	$	8 pm	Baked goods, espresso, counter service.
Red Robin Gourmet Burgers	3272 Fuhrman Ave E	206-323-0918	$$	11 pm	It all started here—for better or worse.
Serafina	2043 Eastlake Ave E	206-323-0807	$$	1 am	Rustic and charming Italian. A very loyal Eastlake following.
Sitka & Spruce	2238 Eastlake Ave E	206-324-0662	$$	10:30 pm	Daily menu based on the freshest local ingredients. Tiny, busy, worth it.

Map 21 • Montlake

Café Lago	2305 24th Ave	206-329-8005	$$$	10 pm	Heartbreakingly wonderful neighborhood Italian.
Volunteer Park Café and Marketplace	1501 17th Ave E	206-328-3155	$	9 pm	Stop by after a stroll through Volunteer Park to grab a light-as-air scone.

Map 22 • Madison Park

Cactus	4220 E Madison St	206-324-4140	$$$	11 pm	Outstanding mojitos and Mexican.
Madison Park Café	1807 42nd Ave E	206-324-2626	$$$	10 pm	Superb French-inspired menu, superb owner, superb location.
Scoop du Jour	4029 E Madison St	206-325-9562	$	9 pm	32 flavors of ice cream and a deli.
Sostanza Trattoria	1927 43rd Ave E	206-324-9701	$$$$	10:30 pm	Good go-to if you need to seduce a special friend.

Map 23 • Ballard

Anne's Teriyaki	2246 NW Market St	206-789-5838	$	10 pm	Huge menu, gigantic portions, quick. And cheap!
Ballard Mandarin Chinese Restaurant	5500 8th Ave NW	206-782-5531	$$	10 pm	I wouldn't do it...unless it were on a bet.
Café Besalu	5909 24th Ave NW	206-789-1463	$	3 pm	Beautifully-made pastries, quiches, cookies, brioches…
Dandelion	5809 24th Ave NW	206-706-8088	$$$	10 pm	Incredibly tiny and crowded, but you'll forgive 'em after a bite or two.
The Dish	4358 Leary Wy NW	206-782-9985	$$*	1:45 pm	Probably one of the best tofu scrambles of all the local hippie-dippies.
Hale's Ales Pub	4301 Leery Wy NW	206-706-1544	$$	11 pm	Seattle's oldest microbrewery with unfortunate corporate-like atmosphere; try the beer sampler.
The Hi-Life	5425 Russell Ave NW	206-784-7272	$$	11 pm	Breakfast, lunch, dinner, and quart-sized Bloody Marys in a 1911 firehouse.
India Bistro	2301 NW Market St	206-783-5080	$$	9:30 pm	Perfectly spiced entrees with excellent seafood.
Isla Seattle	2320 NW Market St	206-789-0516	$$	11 pm	A half-dozen Puerto Rican platos that are addictive and satisfying.
Jolly Roger Taproom	1514 NW Leary Wy	206-782-6181	$$††	12 am	Yes, it's a brewery, but to call it pub food would be sacrilegious.
La Carta de Oaxaca	5431 Ballard Ave NW	206-782-8722	$$	12 am	Authentic Oaxacan—think deep, dark sweet mole—at bargain prices. NFT fave.
Louie's Cuisine of China	5100 15th Ave NW	206-782-8855	$$	1 am	Chinese comfort food since 1930-something.
Madam K's Pizza Bistro	5327 Ballard Ave NW	206-783-9710	$$††	11 pm	Bordello-themed gourmet pizza house with perversely thick pizzas.
Market Street Grill	1744 NW Market St	206-789-6766	$$$	11 pm	The food is as busy as the restaurant, which is not necessarily a bad thing.
Matador	2221 NW Market St	206-297-2855	$$	11 pm	If you can't get a table at Oaxaca.
Matt's Famous Chili Dogs	2325 NW Market St	206-789-1144	$	10 pm	Midwestern folks affirm this is a true Chicago dog.
The Other Coast Café	5315 Ballard Ave NW	206-789-0936	$*	7 pm	Sloppy sammies and super subs like they slather up way out east.
Pasta Bella	5909 15th Ave NW	206-789-4933	$$$	10:30 pm	Your run-of-the-mill romantic Italian restaurant.
Pho Thàn Brothers'	2021 NW Market St	206-782-5715	$*	9 pm	Cheap, fast, and filling, with a free cream puff to boot.
Senor Moose	5242 Leary Ave NW	206-784-5568	$	9 pm	New, soon-to-be Ballard breakfast institution.
Tall Grass Bakery	5907 24th Ave NW	206-706-0991	$	8 pm	Bring extra bread to pay for these award-winning loaves.
Thaiku	5410 Ballard Ave NW	206-706-7807	$$	10: 30 pm	Fun Thai, yes. But the main draw is the aphrodisiac drinks—limit one per person.

Vera's	5417 22nd Ave NW	206 782 9966	$	2 pm	Good old breakfast with crusty regulars.
Volterra	5411 Ballard Ave NW	206-789-5100	$$$	1 am	Lovely Italian specialties with contemporary flair.
Zayda Buddy's	5404 Leary Ave NW	206-783-7777	$$	11 pm	Midwestern comfort food and Schlitz. Burn in hell, Wisconsin, for sending us more hipsters.

Map 24 • Fremont

35th Street Bistro	709 N 35th St	206-547-9850	$$$	11pm	Sidewalk seating; good wine list.
Art of the Table	1054 N 39th St	206-282-0942	$$$$	7:30	A weekend dinner club with harmonic pairings and intimate company. You won't forget it.
Asteroid Café	3601 Fremont Ave N	206-547-2514	$$$	2 am	Surprisingly good Italian.
Bizzarro Italian Café	1307 N 46th St	206-632-7277	$$	11 pm	Tasty pasta dishes in a funky, yet intimate, setting. Bizzarre name.
Blue C Sushi	3411 Fremont Ave N	206-633-3411	$	11 pm	What's cooler than an extensive selection of sushi on a conveyer belt?
Brad's Swingside Café	4212 Fremont Ave N	206-633-4057	$$	10 pm	Homey and intimate neighborhood favorite.
Brouwer's Café	400 N 35th St	206-267-2437	$$	2 am	Belgian cuisine and a staggering beer menu.
Chillies Paste	119 N 36th St	206-633-1433	$	10 pm	Delicious curries, wide noodle dishes, and a fantastic seafood soufflé.
Chiso	3520 Fremont Ave N	206-632-3430	$$$	10 pm	Sushi served up chic.
Costa's Opa Greek Restaurant	3400 Fremont Ave N	206-633-4141	$$	12 am	You'll have dreams about the avgolemono soup.
Dad Watson's	3601 Fremont Ave N	206-632-6505	$$	11 pm	Great pub food—try the reuben.
Eggs Cetera's Blue Star Café	4512 Stone Wy N	206-548-0345	$$	10 pm	Stellar breakfast menu.
El Camino	607 N 35th St	206-632-7303	$$	11 pm	Flavorful Mexican food with patio dining. Few veg options.
Jai Thai	3423 Fremont Ave N	206-632-7060	$	10:30 pm	The curries are always kickin', and the happy hour menu is tops.
Kid Valley	4910 Green Lake Wy N	206-547-0121	$	9 pm	Hey, at least they have veggie burgers.
Kwanjai Thai	469 N 36th St	206-632-3656	$††	10:30 pm	Cheap, reliable, lightning-fast.
Le Gourmand	425 NW Market St	206-784-3463	$$$	10 pm	A cozy-tiny affair, ethereal French food, and chicks totally dig it.
Musashi's	1400 N 45th St	206-633-0212	$$*	10 pm	Cozy up to the Japanese regulars and chow down on a bento box.
Paseo	4225 Fremont Ave N	206-545-7440	$*	9 pm	Restaurant the size of a garage, and so is the pork sandwich. So damn good.
Perche No Pasta & Vino	1319 N 49th St	206-547-0222	$	11 pm	Housemade pasta (!); high on faux brick and friendliness.
Persimmon	4256 Fremont Ave N	206-632-0760	$$	9:30 pm	Comfy brunch bistro serving locally-grown ingredients.
Pontevecchio	710 N 34th St	206-633-3989	$$	10 pm	Take your amore for noodles and canoodling.
Postmark Gelato	3526 Fremont Pl N	206-545-7560	$††	11 pm	Very respectable gelato, plus sandwiches and postcards.
The Red Door	3401 Evanston Ave N	206-547-7521	$	12 am	A better class of pub grub.
Rocking Wok	4301 Interlake Ave N	206-545-4878	$††	10 pm	Not the prettiest place to look at, but the bargain-priced dim sum is true Taiwanese.
Roxy's Deli	462 N 36th St	206-632-3963	$	8 pm	As close to Katz's as Seattle's going to get. The best is the pastrami on rye.
Silence-Heart-Nest	3508 Fremont Pl N	206-633-5169	$	3 pm	Delectable vegetarian dishes made with love by Sri Chinmoy devotees.
Simply Desserts	3421 Fremont Ave N	206-633-2671	$	11:30 pm	Simply the best chocolate cake. Anywhere.
Tawon Thai	3410 Fremont Ave N	206-633-4545	$††	10:30 pm	Pad Thai here is a beacon in the sea of Fremont's Thai restaurants.
Theo Chocolate	3400 Phinney Ave N	206-632-5100	$$	10 pm	Portobello chocolate soup? Coconut curry chocolate bars? It's Willy Wonka meets Marco Polo.
Tilth	1411 N 45th St	206-633-0801	$$$	10:30 pm	The definition of seasonal, organic, local cooking. And it's delicious to boot.
Tutta Bella Neopolitan Pizzeria	4411 Stone Wy N	206-633-3800	$$	10 pm	Their pizza has been certified by the Italian government. 'Nuff said.
Veraci Pizza	500 NW Market St	206-525-1813	$	10 pm	A traveling wood-fired oven turns out delightful Neopolitan-style slices. Queue up at their new permanent location.

Map 25 • Wallingford

Boulangerie	2200 N 45th St	206-634-2211	$*	8:30 pm	Even a Frenchman would admit les croissants sont authentiques.
Chinoise Café	1618 N 45th St	206-633-1160	$$	9:15 pm	Modern sushi joint with a Pan-Asian flair and a heap of noodle dishes.

Arts & Entertainment • **Restaurants**

Map 25 • Wallingford–*continued*

Name	Address	Phone	Price	Hours	Description
Chutney's Bistro	1815 N 45th St	206-634-1000	$$	10 pm	Curry cuts across the socioeconimc divide.
Dick's Drive-In	111 NE 45th St	206-632-5125	$	2 am	A local obsession, specializing in cheap burgers and shakes. Perfect at 1 am.
Elemental@Gasworks	3309 Wallingford Ave N	206-547-2317	$$	12 am	Highly experimental dishes can be a hit (shortribs on waffles!) or a miss (bacon truffles?).
Essential Baking Company	1604 N 34th St	206-545-0444	$	8 pm	You'll think you're in a European bakery.
Joule	1913 N 45th St	206-632-1913	$$$	11 pm	Inspired small plates pack a punch, fusing Korean spice with French precision.
Julia's	4401 Wallingford Ave N	206-633-1175	$$††	9 pm	Quirky space, awesome breakfast. And your mom will like it, too.
Kabul Afghan Cuisine	2301 N 45th St	206-545-9000	$$	10 pm	Warm family setting with a traditional Afghan menu.
May Restaurant and Lounge	1612 N 45th St	206-675-0037	$$	1 am	Refreshing, subtly balanced Thai dishes that are utterly devoid of ketchup.
Molly Moon's	1622 N 45th St	206-618-4934	$	10 pm	Fresh, local, sustainably organic ice cream—down to the dairy and the compostable dishes.
Rancho Bravo Tacos	211 NE 45th St	n/a	$*	2:30 am	Mexican served out of a silver trailer. Locals are fanatical for the tacos.

Map 26 • U District

Name	Address	Phone	Price	Hours	Description
Agua Verde	1303 NE Boat St	206-545-8570	$$	10 pm	Eat authentic Baja-style Mexican cuisine then rent a kayak.
Aladdin Gyrocery	4541 University Wy NE	206-548-9539	$*	1 pm	Best falafel on the Ave. Standing room only.
Araya's Vegetarian Place	1121 NE 45th St	206-524-4332	$$*	9:30 pm	We can't believe it's not meat.
Atlas Foods	2675 NE Village Ln	206-522-6025	$$	10 pm	Fresh fish dishes, great Cobb salad, and mouthwatering blackberry cobbler.
Blue C Sushi	4601 26th Ave NE	206-525-4601	$	11 pm	Enjoy the same delicious sushi as the Fremont location but with yuppies.
Burger & Kabob Hut	4142 University Wy NE	206-632-0324	$††	2 am	A good place to stumble into for onion rings after the bars kick you out.
Cedars	4759 Brooklyn Ave NE	206-527-5247	$$	10 pm	Indian food that's naan stop delicious. Plus, a nice view of the Safeway parking lot.
Chaco Canyon Café	4757 12th Ave NE	206-522-6966	$	8 pm	An amazing voyage into the raw-food universe; the mocha shakes rock!
Delfino's Chicago Style Pizzeria	2631 NE University Vlg	206-522-3466	$$	10 pm	You may have to wait, but the thickly gooey Chicago-style 'zas are worth it.
Flowers Bar & Restaurant	4247 University Wy NE	206-633-1903	$$	2 am	Mediterranean veggie buffet may be the best lunch deal in Seattle.
Hillside Quickie's	4106 Brooklyn Ave NE	206-632-3037	$*	9 pm	Seattle's best all-vegan hip hop sandwich shop and deli.
Jimmy John's	4141 University Wy NE	206-548-9500	$	4 am	Fast sandwiches that can be delivered within the U District.
Kai's Bistro & Lounge	1312 NE 43rd St	206-547-2784	$	9 pm	Side-street bistro with quality cocktails and great happy hour.
Le Casa Del Mojito	5253 University Wy NE	206-524-4615	$$	11:30 pm	Rice, beans and smashed plantains. Go.
Mamma Melina	4759 Roosevelt Wy NE	206-632-4333	$$	10:30 pm	An Italian experience that will get you laid.
Matt's Famous Chili Dogs	1301 NE 45th St	206-545-4490	$	12 am	Midwestern folks affirm this is a true Chicago dog.
Memo's Mexican Food	4743 University Wy NE	206-729-5071	$*	24 hrs	If a 24-hour Taco Bell had real Mexican names for food.
New China Express	4232 University Wy NE	206-632-5833	$	10 pm	Generically named restaurant delivers miracle hangover cure.
Orange King	1411 NE 42nd St	206-632-1331	$*	9 pm	A UW student's wet dream. Burgers and teriyaki under one roof.
Pagliacci Pizza	4529 University Wy NE	206-632-0421	$$	12 am	Local pizza chain makes crispy-chewy delights with seasonal ingredients.
Pam's Kitchen	5000 University Wy NE	206-696-7010	$††	10 pm	A taste of the Carribean arrives on the ave.
Paoli's Pizza and Pasta	4510 University Wy NE	206-632-3657	$††	11 pm	Cheap eats, open late.
Pasta & Co	4622 26th Ave NE	206-523-8594	$$	9 pm	One-stop gourmet chain has fresh bread, wine, and risotto cakes to go.
Pho Thàn Brothers'	4207 University Wy NE	206-633-1735	$*	9 pm	Cheap, fast, and filling, with a free cream puff to boot.
Pho Vietnam 2	4235 University Wy NE	206-547-1709	$††	10 pm	Lots of love for the noodle soup here, pho good reason.
Pizza Ragazzi	5201 University Wy NE	206-525-1700	$	4 am	At 4 am, who cares what the pizza tastes like?
Portage Bay Café	4130 Roosevelt Wy NE	206-547-8230	$$	3 pm	Local organic breakfasts and lunches.

Ruby	4241 University Wy NE	206-675-1770	$††	10 pm	Just like Flowers, except they serve soup and lack the cool evening ambiance.
Shultzy's Sausage	4114 University Wy NE	206-548-9461	$	10 pm	Purveyors of fine encased meats, plus a great beer menu.
Sunney's Café Restaurant	4736 University Wy NE	206-522-3500	$	9 pm	Affordable, authentic Korean—just wish you got a bit more *banchan* for your buck.
Tandoor Indian Restaurant	5024 University Wy NE	206-523-7477	$	10 pm	Consistently excellent, and the best pakora $2.50 can buy.
Thai 65	4214 University Wy NE	206-632-1371	$	10 pm	Another of the U District Thai favorites. Lots of seating.
Thai Tom	4543 University Wy NE	206-548-9548	$*	9 pm	Come for the best open kitchen show (and best Thai) in Seattle. Always busy.
Thaiger Room	4228 University Wy NE	206-632-9299	$	9:30 pm	Thai's a dime a dozen on the Ave, but Thaiger's one of the standouts.

Map 27 · Laurelhurst / Wedgwood / Sand Point

Black Pearl	7347 35th Ave NE	206-526-5115	$$	10 pm	Great housemade noodles and noticeably ungreasy food.
Ciao Bella	3626 NE 46th St	206-524-6989	$$	10 pm	Simple homecooked Italian from a native Umbrian. Buonissimo!
Jak's Grill	3701 NE 45th St	206-985-8545	$$$$	11 pm	Best place for a classy, meaty, potatoey night out.

Map 28 · Ballard (West)

| Anthony's HomePort | 6135 Seaview Ave NW | 206-783-0780 | $$$ | 11:30 pm | Pacific Northwest chain with an impressive view. |
| Ray's Boathouse Café | 6049 Seaview Ave NW | 206-782-0094 | $$$ | 10 pm | Venerable institution that's been doing seafood right for decades. Watch out for tourists. |

Map 29 · Ballard / Loyal Heights

Kasbah Authentic Moroccan	1471 NW 85th St	206-788-0777	$$	10 pm	Your heart will be still for the b'stilla. And belly dancers are always fun.
Lunchbox Laboratory	7302 15th Ave NW	206-722-3229	$	10 pm	Stunning burger specimens among Seattle's very best—the "dork" is a thing of beauty.
The Original Pancake House	8037 15th Ave NW	206-781-3344	$$	10 pm	Homemade batter! A dozen types of flapjacks! It's breakfast heaven.
Smokin' Pete's BBQ	1918 NW 65th St	206-783-0454	$$	9 pm	All meat, all the time. Stacks of napkins requisite.
Thai Siam	8305 15th Ave NW	206-784-5465	$	10 pm	Skip the phad thai; go for the huge, drool worthy steak salad.
Wild Mountain Café	1408 NW 85th St	206-297-WILD	$$$	10 pm	Tasty, funky, spirited home-grown food.
Zagi's Pizza	2408 NW 80th St	206-706-0750	$*	12 am	New Yorkers may dispute the authenticity, but this NY-style pizza is just good.

Map 30 · Greenwood / Phinney Ridge

74th St Ale House	7401 Greenwood Ave N	206-784-2955	$$	11 pm	Serious about food and beer.
Barking Dog Alehouse	705 NW 70th St	206-782-2974	$$	11 pm	Cozy dinners, weekend brunch, and generous beer selection.
Beth's Café	7311 Aurora Ave N	206-782-5588	$††	24 hrs	12-egg omelets, unlimited hashbrowns. You'll either die and go to heaven, or just…die.
Carmelita	7314 Greenwood Ave N	206-706-7703	$$$	10 pm	Seattle's second best vegetarian restaurant.
El Chupacabra	6711 Greenwood Ave N	206-706-4889	$††	2 am	Hearty Mexican, loud music, wacky interior.
Gorditos	213 N 85th St	206-706-9352	$	9:30 pm	Burritos bigger than a newborn baby.
Mae's Phinney Ridge Café	6412 Phinney Ave N	206-782-1222	$	3 pm	Fun, funkily creative breakfast.
Olive You	8516 Greenwood Ave N	206-706-4121	$	12 am	Casual, dang-good homemade Mediterranean.
Pho Thân Brothers'	7714 Aurora Ave N	206-527-5973	$*	9 pm	Cheap, fast, and filling, with a free cream puff to boot.
Red Mill Burgers	312 N 67th St	206-783-6362	$*	9 pm	The undisputed best burger in Seattle. And possibly, the best onion rings.
Santa Fe Café	5910 Phinney Ave N	206-783-9755	$$$	10 pm	Nuevo Mexican/Southwestern improvisations like blue-corn crepes. ¡Delicioso!
Stacia's	305 NW 85th St	206-781-0292	$$	11 pm	Free cookies with your pizza!
Stumbling Goat Bistro	6722 Greenwood Ave N	206-784-3535	$$$	10 pm	As a bistro should be: Simple, uncomplicated, romantic.
Yanni's	7419 Greenwood Ave N	206-783-6945	$$$	10 pm	Great place to convert Greek food naysayers. Exceptional dolmathes.
Zeek's Pizza	6000 Phinney Ave N	206-789-0087	$$	10 pm	Pizzas with *pizzazz*, like the Thai one with peanut sauce.

Map 31 • Green Lake / Roosevelt

Blue Onion Bistro	5801 Roosevelt Wy NE	206-729-0579	$$	10 pm	Down-home artery-overwhelming cooking.
Duke's Chowder House	7850 Green Lake Dr N	206-522-4908	$$	2 am	For all you chowda' heads.
Eva	2227 N 56th St	206-633-3538	$$$	10 pm	An elegant meal (ties, high heels, expense accounts not necessary).
Krittika Noodles & Thai Cuisine	6411 Latona Ave NE	206-985-1182	$$	10 pm	Touch-and-go Thai—some people scarf it up, others barf it up. You decide.
Latona Pub	6423 Latona Ave NE	206-525-2238	$$	12 am	Refuel after a loop around Greenlake with a superb beef pot pie.
Mighty-O Donuts	2110 N 55th St	206-547-0335	$*	5 pm	Those vegans really know how to make a damn fine donut.
Mona's Bistro & Lounge	6421 Latona Ave NE	206-526-1188	$$	11 pm	Swank neighborhood date spot featuring inventive cocktails, classic food.
Nell's	6804 E Green Lake Wy N	206-524-4044	$$$$$	10 pm	Subtle, lovely dishes showcasing tip-top local ingredients.
Pies and Pints	1215 NE 65th St	206-524-7082	$	12 am	Butterly, flaky, savory pies and, um... pints.
Primo Burgers	6501 Roosevelt Wy NE	206-525-3542	$	9 pm	A reliable burger place, complete with special sauce and Hawaiian kitsch.
Salvatore Ristorante	6100 Roosevelt Wy NE	206-527-9301	$$$	10:30 pm	Straightforward and spensy Italian.
Spud Fish & Chips	6860 E Green Lake Wy N	206-524-0565	$*	9 pm	This place has been around for 75 years for a good reason.
Sunlight Café	6403 Roosevelt Wy NE	206-522-9060	$††	9 pm	Super-crunchy vegetarian place—aptly named, too.
Sushi Tokyo	6311 Roosevelt Wy NE	206-526-2935	$$	9:30 pm	Sushi + teriyaki = yum.
Taqueria Guaymas	6808 E Green Lake Wy N	206-729-6563	$$	10 pm	Cheap and filling.
Taste of India	5517 Roosevelt Wy NE	206-528-1575	$$††	10 pm	A decidedly better buffet, with above-average Indian standards.
Wayward Café	901 NE 55th St	206-524-0204	$$††	9 pm	Vegan comfort food with punk vibe.
Zeek's Pizza	7900 E Green Lake Dr N	206-285-8646	$$	10 pm	Pizzas with pizzazz, like the Thai one with peanut sauce.

Map 32 • Ravenna

Bagel Oasis	2112 NE 65th St	206-526-0525	$	4 pm	Tasty bagels with a wide array of toppings.
Blue Dog Kitchen	5509 University Wy NE	206-523-1933	$	n/a	Students love the pumpkin bread, blueberry pancakes and free WiFi.
Guadi	3410 NE 55th St	206-527-3400	$$$	10 pm	Just like Spain (except the early closing time).
Hot Dish	2255 NE 65th St	206-524-5555	$$	9 pm	Family-friendly comfort food favorites with a twist.
Kidd Valley	5502 25th Ave NE	206-522-0890	$	9 pm	Hey, at least they have veggie burgers.
Mr Villa	8064 Lake City Wy NE	206-517-5660	$	9 pm	Solid Mexican.
Nana's Soup House	3418 NE 55th St	206-523-9053	$	9 pm	Unpretentious soups, sandwiches, and beer.
Pair	5501 30th Ave NE	206-526-7655	$$$	10 pm	Small, seasonal plates—you guessed it—"paired" with wine. NFT approved.
Pizza Pi Vegan Pizzaria	5500 University Wy NE	206-343-1415	$*	10 pm	Who says vegans have to compromise? All vegan, all the time.
Queen Mary Tea Room	2912 NE 55th St	206-527-2770	$$$	5 pm	Snack on proper British crumpets and tea. Don't forget to raise your pinky.
Tempero do Brasil	5628 University Wy NE	206-523-6229	$$$††	10 pm	A thrilling mix of cuisines is the remedy for "what-to-try-next" syndrome.
Zeek's Pizza	2108 NE 65th St	206-525-0250	$$	10 pm	Pizzas with pizzazz, like the Thai one with peanut sauce.

Map 33 • Northwest Seattle

Acorn Eatery & Bar	9041 Holman Rd NW	206-297-0700	$$$	12 am	It's looks like a tavern, so it's easy to miss. Don't—fantastic Italian fare.
Baranof	8549 Greenwood Ave N	206-782-9260	$	2 am	A clasic dive bar with low level hipster encroachment andd sloppy burgers galore.
Bick's Broadview Grill	10555 Greenwood Ave N	206-367 8481	$$$	10 pm	Fusion that's in your face.
Burgermaster	9820 Aurora Ave N	206-522-2044	$	1 am	Drive up, park, and let the old-school car-side service do all the work.
Burrito Loco	9211 Holman Rd NW	206-783-0719	$$	10 pm	The burritos here are loco good.
Cyndy's House of Pancakes	10507 Aurora Ave N	206-522-5100	$$	1:30 pm	Dutch baby pancakes in a 1970s flashback.
Dick's Drive-In	9208 Holman Rd NW	206-783-5233	$	2 am	A local obsession, specializing in cheap burgers and shakes. Perfect at 1 am.
Kidd Valley	14303 Aurora Ave N	206-364-8493	$	9 pm	Hey, at least they have veggie burgers.
Patty's Eggnest	9749 Holman Rd NW	206-297-1545	$††	3 pm	Fat omelets and fresh-squeezed OJ make this the best breakfast in town.
Taqueria la Pasadita #2	2143 N Northgate Wy	n/a	$*	11 pm	Calling these tacos some of Seattle's best is a serious claim. We're serious.

Map 34 • Northeast Seattle

Café Long	12517 Lake City Wy NE	206-362-6259	$	8 pm	Hidden family-run Vietnamese restaurant heavy on the veggie fare.
Café Weini	1510 NE 117th St	206-365-0757	$	9 pm	The hidden gem that makes buying this book worthwhile.
Dick's Drive-In	12325 30th Ave NE	206-363-7777	$	2 am	A local obsession, specializing in cheap burgers and shakes. Perfect at 1 am.
Enat Ethiopian	11546 15th Ave NE	206-362-4901	$	11 pm	Best Ethiopian restaurant in Seattle.
Judy Fu's Snappy Dragon	8917 Roosevelt Wy NE	206-528-5575	$	9:30 pm	Sopping-greasy Chinese—and still, mysteriously, a Seattle favorite.
Toyoda Sushi	12543 Lake City Wy NE	206-367-7972	$$$	9:30 pm	Trend seekers go elsewhere: the sushi here is simple, fast, affordable.

Map 35 • Alki / West Seattle / North Admiral

Alki Bakery	2738 Alki Ave SW	206-935-1352	$	9 pm	Repeatedly voted best apple pie in Seattle. We agree.
Alki Café	2726 Alki Ave SW	206-935-0616	$$	9 pm	A hefty helping of the basics plus a view.
Alki Homestead	2717 61st Ave SW	206-935-5678	$$††	10 pm	This historic landmark is famous for its all-you-can-eat fried chicken.
Ama Ama Oyster Bar	4752 California Ave SW	206-937-1514	$$$††	12 am	Fifty-cent oysters during happy hour!
Angelina's Trattoria	2311 California Ave SW	206-932-7311	$$	11 pm	Affordable, cozy, and consistently delicious Italian.
Bakery Nouveau	4737 California Ave SW	206-923-0534	$	10 pm	World Cup-winning baker crafts inexplicably perfect croissants. The twice-baked almond one is a must.
Blackbird Bistro	2329 California Ave SW	206-937-2875	$$$	10 pm	Eat seasonal, socially-conscious dishes in a lovely setting.
Cactus	2820 Alki Ave SW	206-933-6000	$$	11 pm	Pretend you're in SoCal, straight chillin' with a margarita by the beach.
Christo's on Alki	2508 Alki Ave SW	206-923-2200	$$	11 pm	Family friendly with Greek gusto.
Circa Neighborhood Grill and Alehouse	2605 California Ave SW	206-937-1102	$$	10 pm	Exquisite food makes you forget about the uncomfortable booths.
Duke's Chowder House	2516 Alki Ave SW	206-937-6100	$$	11 pm	The chowder truly is what it's cracked up to be.
Easy Street Records	4559 California Ave SW	206-938-3279	n/a	n/a	You can't go to West Seattle without stopping here for coffee, food, or music.
Elliott Bay Brewery & Pub	4720 California Ave SW	206-932-8695	$$	12 am	Ice cream floats made with stout. C'mon, you know you wanna try it.
Jak's Grill	4548 California Ave SW	206-937-7809	$$$$	11 pm	Both the food and atmosphere are upbeat.
La Rustica	4100 Beach Dr SW	206-932-3020	$$$$$	10 pm	Escape the beach buzz. Meat, seafood, and pasta in a seemingly remote setting.
Lee's Asian Restaurant	4510 California Ave	206-932-8209	$$††	10 pm	The Seven-Flavor Beef will haunt your dreams.
Mashiko	4725 California Ave SW	206-935-4339	$$	11 pm	Sit back and let the chef choose for you. Good luck.
The Mission Tapas and Bar	2325 California Ave SW	206-937-8220	$$$	12 am	Expensive and inviting atmosphere. Appetizers outdo the entrees.
Pagliacci Pizza	4449 California Ave SW	206-726-1717	$$	11 pm	Local pizza chain makes crispy-chewy delights with seasonal ingredients.
Pailin Thai	2223 California Ave SW	206-937-8807	$$††	10 pm	Gigantic fish tank and fresh food makes for peaceful dining.
Pegasus Pizza	2758 Alki Ave SW	206-932-4849	$$	11:30 pm	Starved? Generous salads and loaded pizzas will do the trick.
Pepperdock's Restaurant	2618 Alki Ave SW	206-935-1000	$	8 pm	Tasty, cheap, beach food.
Pho Thân Brothers'	4822 California Ave SW	206-937-6264	$*	9 pm	Cheap, fast, and filling, with a free cream puff to boot.
Shadowland	4458 California Ave SW	206-420-3817	$$	10 pm	Hearty.
Spud Fish & Chips	2666 Alki Ave SW	206-938-0606	$*	9 pm	This place has been around for 75 years for a good reason.
Sunfish Seafood	2800 Alki Ave SW	206-938-4112	$$*	9 pm	The best grilled halibut kabobs—batter not included.
Talarico's	4718 California Ave SW	206-937-3463	$	2 am	Huge slices of pizza, but we miss the old New Luck Toy.
Taqueria Guaymas	4719 California Ave SW	206-935-8970	$	10 pm	Cheap and filling.
Zatz A Better Bagel	2348 California Ave SW	206-933-8244	$*	5:30 pm	Super fresh.

Map 36 • North Delridge

Alki Crab & Fish Company	1660 Harbor Ave SW	206-938-0975	$*	9 pm	Greasier than most, and—mmm!—live bait for sale in adjacent room.
Buddha Ruksa	3520 SW Genesee St	206-937-7676	$$	10 pm	Enlightenment attained.
Luna Park Café	2918 SW Avalon Wy	$	10 pm	Plenty of fun for the kids; mimosas and piles of eggs for the adults.
Salty's on Alki Beach	1936 Harbor Ave SW	206-937-1600	$$$$	10 pm	The brunch is a must at least once in your lifetime.

Note: Luna Park Café phone is 206-935-7250.

Map 37 • Fauntleroy / Arbor Heights

88 Restaurant	9418 Delridge Wy SW	206-768-9767	$	8 pm	Your standard, ol' reliable pho/banh mi purveyor.
Eats Market Café	2600 SW Barton St	206-933-1200	$$	9 pm	A dual-purpose after-work pub and post-hangover breakfast spot.
Endolyne Joe's	9261 45th Ave SW	206-937-5637	$$	11 pm	American classics that are updated every season.
Salvadorean Bakery	1719 SW Roxbury St	206-762-4064	$*	9 pm	Specialties from El Salvador: Stay for the sopa de pollo and the pupusas.
Taqueria Guaymas	1622 SW Roxbury St	206-767-4026	$$	10 pm	Cheap and filling.
Zippy's Burgers	1513 SW Holden St	206-763-1347	$	11 pm	How a quarter-pounder should be—chargrilled and served with a smile.

Map 38 • White Center / South Park / Beverly Park

Muy Macho	8515 14th Ave S	206-763-3484	$	9:30 pm	Good and cheap. Brain and tripe.

Map 39 • SoDo / Beacon Hill / Georgetown

By's Drive-In	2901 4th Ave S	206-622-9901	$	8 am	It's no Dick's, but better than the chains.
Calamity Jane's	5701 Airport Wy S	206-763-3040	$$	10 pm	The vegetarian shepherd's pie will make you a believer of both vegetarian food and shepherd's pie.
Dahlak Eritrean Cuisine	2007 S State St	206-860-0400	$$	12 am	Complex and layered dishes that outshine most. Superfun with friends.
Georgetown Liquor Company	5501 Airport Wy S	206-763-6764	$	10 pm	Veggie sandwiches that Yoda would approve of.
Jones Barbeque	2454 Occidental Ave S	206-625-1339	$††	7 pm	The tenderest, juiciest dead cows one could imagine.
La Cabana Café	2532 Beacon Ave S	206-322-9643	$$	9:30 pm	The free cinnamony sugar sopapillas are so very yummy.
Matt's Famous Chili Dogs	6615 E Marginal Wy S	206-768-0418	$	5:30 pm	Midwestern folks affirm this is a true Chicago dog.
Pecos Pit BBQ	2260 1st Ave S	206-623-0629	$*	3 pm	Spicy sandwiches for hardworkin' tongues.
Pho Cyclo	2414 1st Ave S	206-382-9256	$	9:30 pm	The fragrant pho ga really is chicken soup for the soul.
Pig Iron Bar-B-Q	5602 1st Ave S	206-768-1009	$$	8:30 pm	Southern-style eats and a tattooed ambiance.
Smarty Pants	6017 Airport Wy S	206-762-4777	$$††	12 am	Vegetarian sandwiches, vegetarian frito pie… mmm.
SODO Deli	3228 1st Ave S	206-467-0306	$	4 pm	The food is Sodo-licious.
Squid & Ink	1128 S Albro Pl	206-763-2696	$	12 am	Tempeh subs that die-hard carnivores can get down with. Cocktails sweeten the deal.
Stellar Pizza, Ale & Cocktails	5513 Airport Wy S	206-763-1660	$††	12 am	Stellar. Really.
Viengthong	2820 Martin Luther King Jr Wy S	206-725-3884	$	10 pm	Quality Thai-Laotian dishes that tend toward fire-engine spiciness.
Willie's Taste of Soul BBQ	3427 Rainier Ave S	206-722-3229	$	10 pm	Soul-satisfying baby backs and some insanely buttery yams.

Map 40 • Columbia City / Mount Baker / Seward Park

Café Ibex	3218 Martin Luther King Jr Wy S	206-721-7537	$	2 am	Decent Ethiopian open late.
Columbia City Ale House	4914 Rainier Ave S	206-723-5123	$$	12 am	Not a chicken wing in sight: just catfish sandwiches, gumbo, fish tacos. Poor you.
Columbia City Bakery	4865 Rainier Ave S	206-722-9138	$	4 pm	Bread to make your grandmamma proud. Fabulous baguettes.
Da Pino's	4225 Rainier Ave S	206-725-1772	$$	9 pm	Unreal cured meats (mmm, spicy capicola), plus pastas and wine dinners.
El Asadero Taco Truck	3517 Rainier Ave S	n/a	$*	10 pm	Mexi cola and carne asada for less than a latte.
Mioposto	3601 S McClellan St	206-760-3400	$$	10 pm	A splendid park view and light, family-friendly fare from the Chow Foods crew.
Geraldine's Counter	4872 Rainier Ave S	206-723-2080	$$*	10 pm	Diner fare that's far better than it needs to be.

Jones Barbeque	3216 S Hudson St	206-725-2728	$††	10 pm	The tenderest, juiciest dead cows one could imagine.
Jones Barbeque	3810 S Ferdinand St	206-722-4414	$††	10 pm	The tenderest, juiciest dead cows one could imagine.
La Medusa	4857 Rainier Ave S	206-723-2192	$$$	10 pm	Sicilian food for the soul meets the neighborhood farmer's market.
Roy's BBQ	4903 Rainier Ave S	206-723-7697	$††	7 pm	How does Roy gets that brisket so tender? Don't question, just eat.
Silver Fork	3800 Rainier Ave S	206-721-5171	$	4 pm	Classic greasy spoon, complemented by lots of butter.
Tutta Bella Neopolitan Pizzeria	4918 Rainier Ave S	206-721-3501	$	10 pm	Their pizza has been certified by the Italian government. 'Nuff said.
Verve Wine Bar and Cellar	3820 S Ferdinand St	206-760-0977	$	10 pm	Wines, and especially great cheese, to enjoy AND take home with you.
Wellington Tea Room	4869 Rainier Ave S	206-722-8571	$$$	10 pm	Southern country menu with live weekend jazz.

Map 41 • Rainier Beach / Rainier View / Skyway

Hong Kong Seafood Restaurant	9400 Rainier Ave S	206-723-1718	$$	10 pm	Great Cantonese dim sum and noodles.
King Donut	9170 Rainier Ave S	206-721-3103	$	7:30 pm	Terrific trifecta of donuts, teriyaki, and laundromat. We kid you not.
Maya's Mexican Restaurant	9447 Rainier Ave S	206-725-5510	$	11 pm	Seafood is the speciality; wash it down with a fresh-queezed 'rita.

Map 42 • Mercer Island

Bennett's Pure Food Bistro	7650 SE 27th St	206-232-2759	$$	10 pm	Deli by day, fine dining by night.
Pon Proem	3039 78th Ave SE	206-236-8424	$$	10 pm	They don't mess around with the chiles here.
Roanoke Inn	1825 72nd Ave SE	206-232-0800	$$	11 pm	Nuzzle up to the cozy fire in the company of millionaires.
Roberto's	7605 SE 27th St	206-232-7383	$*	10 pm	A pizza place with salads that are actually tasty.
Seven Star	2775 78th Ave SE	206-230-8665	$††	10 pm	More like two stars.
Thai on Mercer	7691 27th St	206-236-9990	$$$	10 pm	Ugh.

Map 43 • Bellevue (Southwest)

Grazie Ristorante	3820 124th Ave SE	425-644-1200	$$	10 pm	Grazie for yet another Olive Garden.
Shanghai Café	12708 SE 38th St	425-603-1689	$$	10:30 pm	Homemade noodles keep 'em coming back.
Top Gun Seafood	12450 SE 38th St	425-641-3386	$$	12 am	Take a ride into the dim-sum zone.

Map 45 • Bellevue (West) / Medina

Bamboo Garden Restaurant	202 106th Ave NE	425-688-7991	$	10 pm	Cheap, spicy Sichuan in a strip mall (adjacent to an adult entertainment store).
Bis on Main	10213 Main St	425-455-2033	$$$$	10 pm	Perfect for wining and dining—as long as you got the dough.
Cheesecake Factory	401 Bellevue Sq	425-450-6000	$$$	12:30 am	Overpriced food straight from the assembly line.
Daniel's Broiler	10500 NE 8th St	425-462-4662	$$$$$	10 pm	Fancy folk (or those whose parents are paying) head here for decent steak.
Facing East Taiwanese Restaurant	1075 Bellevue Wy NE	425-688-2986	$	9 pm	Bet you never thought you'd the words oysters and pancakes together.
Mediterranean Kitchen	103 Bellevue Wy NE	425-462-9422	$$$	9:30 pm	Garlicky Greek goodness.
The Melting Pot	302 108th Ave NE	425-646-2744	$$$$	10 pm	Gimmicky and retro, perhaps, but dipping things in cheese can never be bad.
Moghul Palace	10303 NE 10th St	425-451-1909	$$	10 pm	Deemed one of the finest Indian joints, though service is another story.
Pagliacci Pizza	563 Bellevue Sq	425-453-1717	$$	11 pm	Local pizza chain makes crispy-chewy delights with seasonal ingredients.
Pasta & Co	10218 NE 8th St	425-453-8760	$$	8 pm	One-stop gourmet chain has fresh bread, wine, and risotto cakes to go.
PF Chang's China Bistro	525 Bellevue Wy SE	425-637-3582	$$$	12 am	Shamelessly Americanized Chinese food.
Ruth's Chris Steak House	565 Bellevue Sq	425-451-1550	$$$$$	11 pm	Ubiquitous chain dishes out gargantuan portions of meat. Uninspired.
Seastar Restaurant and Raw Bar	205 108th Ave NE	425-456-0010	$$$	10 pm	Known for the seafood and oysters.
Tap House Grill	550 106th Ave NE	425-467-1728	$$$	2 am	160 beers on tap. We repeat: 160 beers. On tap.

Map 46 • Bellevue (Central)

Name	Address	Phone	Price	Close	Description
Andre's Eurasian Bistro	14125 NE 20th St	425-747-6551	$$$	9 pm	Mismash of European/Asian cuisines for the indecisive.
Blue Ginger Korean Grill and Sushi	14045 NE 20th St	425-746-1222	$$	10 pm	BBQ up some Korean beef at your table.
Dixie's BBQ	11522 Northup Wy	425-828-2460	$$*	5:30 pm	Louisiana-style brisket slopped into styrofoam—it's so right.
I Love Sushi	11818 NE 8th St	425-454-5706	$$$	10:30 pm	We love I Love Sushi.
Jeem Asian Restaurant	14850 NE 24th St	425-883-8858	$	10 pm	Fluctuating-in-quality dim sum.
Malay Satay Hut	15230 NE 24th St	425-564-0888	$$	10:30 pm	Three cuisines unite under one roof, with delicious results.
Noble Court	1644 140th Ave NE	425-641-6011	$$	3 am	Freakin' huge Hong Kong-style treats and dim sum. Gets packed.
Pho Hoa	15169 NE 24th St	425-641-7898	$	11:45 pm	Pho for an MSG fix.
Regent Bakery & Café	15159 NE 24th St	425-378-1498	$*	9 pm	Family run Chinese bakery well known for their massive selection of cakes.
Saigon City	15045 Bel Red Rd	425-401-0823	$	11 pm	Mediocre pho, but cute menu adorned with family photos.
Sichuanese Cuisine	15005 NE 24th St	425-562-1552	$	11 pm	Greasy and spicy.
Szechuan Chef	15015 Main St	425-746-9008	$$	10 pm	Spicy red Szechuan hotpots with floating peppercorns are the trend.
Thai Kitchen	14115 NE 20th St	425-641-9166	$	11 pm	Curries and peppers will have you oohing and aahing in satisfaction.
Tosoni's	14320 NE 20th St	425-644-1668	$$$$$	10:30 pm	Loyal regulars hope the secret doesn't get out. Oops.

Map 47 • Bellevue (East) / Redmond

Name	Address	Phone	Price	Close	Description
Firenze Ristorante Italiano	15600 NE 8th St	425-957-1077	$$$	10:30 pm	A go-to date place; the simplest dishes are the bestest.

Map 48 • Kirkland

Name	Address	Phone	Price	Close	Description
21 Central Steakhouse	21 Central Wy	425-822-1515	$$$$$	10 pm	Well-dressed older men and their younger wives gobble up fat steaks.
Anthony's	135 Lake St S	425-822-0225	$$$$	10:30 pm	Pacific Northwest fare with expansive view of Lake Washington.
Blue Fish Sushi Bar & Grill	166 Lake St S	425-822-8245	$$	10:30 pm	A lousy Korean attempt at Japanese food.
Boston Wood Fired Pizza	13200 Old Redmond Rd	425-883-9700	$$	10 pm	Too bad it's take out and limited delivery only; 16" specialty pizzas get cold fast.
Cactus	121 Park Ln	425-893-9799	$$	11 pm	Outstanding mojitos and Mexican.
Café Juanita	9702 NE 120th Pl	425-823-1505	$$$$$	10 pm	Serenity exemplified, and stellar Italian. A must.
Calabria Ristorante Italiano	132 Lake St S	425-822-7350	$$$	12 am	Pastas are the specialty, and a good range of Italian cuisines are represented.
Hanuman Thai Café	115 Central Wy	425-605-2182	$	10 pm	Too satisfying for words. You'll actually think you're in Thailand.
Izumi	12539 116th Ave NE	425-821-1959	$$$	9:30 pm	An affordable Eastside alternative to Seattle's uberspendy sushi spots.
Lynn's Bistro	214 Central Wy	425-889-2808	$$$$	10 pm	Bistro fare with an Asian flair.
The Original Pancake House	130 Parkplace Ctr	425-827-7575	$$	2:30 pm	Homemade batter! A dozen types of flapjacks! It's breakfast heaven.
Pegasus Pizza	12669 NE 85th St	425-822-7400	$$	11 pm	Starved? Generous salads and loaded pizzas will do the trick.
Purple Café & Wine Bar	323 Park Pl Ctr	425-828-3772	$$	11 pm	Tome-like wine list can be intimidating; food is upscale café fare.
Ristorante Paradiso	120A Park Ln	425-889-8601	$$$	10:30 pm	A little bit of Sardinia on the Eastside.
Shamiana	10724 NE 68th St	425-827-4902	$$$	10 pm	Generous buffet.
The Slip	80 Kirkland Ave	425-739-0033	$$	10:30 pm	Burgers so juicy they... slip.
Thai Kitchen	11701 124th Ave NE	425-8205630	$	11 pm	Curries and peppers will have you oohing and aahing in spicy satisfaction.
Thin Pan Siam Bistro	170 Lake St S	425-827-4000	$$$	10 pm	Contemporary Thai cuisine right on the sidewalk.
Third Floor Fish Café	205 Lake St S	425-822-3553	$$$$	9:30 pm	Fine Northwest seafood with live music.
Wing Dome	232 Central Wy	425-822-9464	$	10 pm	Flamin' baskets of flavored chicken wings.

Map 49 · Redmond

Desert Fire Southwestern Grill	7211 166th Ave NE	425-895-1500	$$	10 pm	Mexican + American ingredients = Southwestern cuisine.
Family Pancake House	17621 Redmond Wy	425-883-0922	$††	10 pm	Chocolate chip pancakes that melt in your mouth.
Frankie's Pizza and Pasta	16630 Redmond Wy	425-883-8407	$$	10 pm	Local favorite serving gourmet pizza and the usual Italian fare.
Kikuya	8105 161st Ave NE	425-881-8771	$$$	8:45 pm	A formerly great sushi joint suffering under new owenrship.
Matt's Rotisserie & Oyster Lounge	16651 NE 74th St	425-376-0909	$$	12 am	Almost upscale, but tempered by kids and baseball caps.
Nara Japanese Restaurant	16564 Cleveland St, #M	425-885-0703	$$††	9:30 pm	Head for the sushi bar.
Ooba's Mexican Grill	15802 NE 83rd St	425-702-9614	$	8 pm	Flavorful, fresh Mexican.
Pasta & Co	7625 170th Ave NE	425-881-1992	$$	7:30 pm	One-stop gourmet chain has fresh bread, wine, and risotto cakes to go.
Pho Thân Brothers'	7844 Leary Wy NE	425-881-3299	$*	9 pm	Cheap, fast, and filling, with a free cream puff to boot.
Pizza Schmizza	16552 NE 74th St	425-885-2720	$	10 pm	Hope you like cold pizza.
Pomegranate Bistro	18005 NE 68th St	425-556-5872	$$	10 pm	Cute and tasty.
Sages Restaurant	15916 NE 83rd St	425-881-5004	$$$	5 pm	ntimate, rustic, mouthwatering Italian with candles and white tablecloths.
Sushi Land Marinepolis	8910 161st Ave NE	425-284-2587	$$	9 pm	Fun, cheap sushi.
Taste the Moment	8110 164th Ave NE	425-556-9838	$$$	9 pm	Feel the passion! Drink from the tea cups!
Thai Ginger	16480 NE 74th St	425-558-4044	$$$††	10 pm	Try their trout salad.
Todai Redmond	7548 164th Ave NE	425-376-1922	$$$††	10 pm	Feel the marine ecosystem collapse. Free on your birthday.
Typhoon!	8936 161st Ave NE	425 558-7666	$$$	10 pm	Upscale Thai, popular with businessmen during lunch hour.
Yummy Teriyaki	17218 Redmond Wy	425-861-1010	$	8:30 pm	Big portions of just that.

Seattle is nothing if not eclectic, and that's good news for all you shopaholics. Whether your last name is Gates or you're scrounging for dollars, Seattle provides plenty of opportunities for retail therapy.

Clothes

Some people think Seattle dresses too casually. Well, we've got news for them. What we lack in formality, we make up for in style. There is no shortage of clothes shopping in Seattle, and no matter where you are in this city; you will never be far from a cute boutique or funky thrift shop. If you like to go a little easy on your wallet, try **Buffalo Exchange (Map 26)**, where you can buy and sell used, fashionable clothes from name brand designers. Going for a more vintage look? Head to **Atlas Clothing Co (Map 4)** or **Red Light (Maps 17, 26)**. If you have a guilty conscience about your clothes (and a killer bod), try **American Apparel (Maps 17, 26)** to sport some sweatshop-free duds. For those of you with money to burn, it's all about the original **Nordstrom (Map 3)**, For those who don't, you can sometimes find the same stuff for less at cheap sister store the **Nordstrom Rack (Map 3)**.

Music

Some cities have let the internet eat up all their music stores. But in Seattle, independent record shops are thriving. Maybe that whole grunge thing wasn't so bad after all. **Sonic Boom (Maps 23, 24)** is a great place to see a live band and buy their music simultaneously. Find that ultra-rare album at **Bud's Jazz Records (Map 7)**. If you prefer to make your own music, you can get your gear cheap at **Trading Musician (Map 31)**. For new and used tunes, any of these places will do you just fine: **Easy Street Records (Map 25, 35)**, **Jive Time Records (Map 24)**, **Everyday Music (Map 17)**, and **Bop Street Records (Map 23)**.

Don't Toy With Me

Quality baubles and gadgets for the pre-pubescent crowd are easy to score in Seattle, thanks to progressively-minded toy stores like **Curious Kidstuff (Map 35)** and **Magic Mouse (Map 7)**, but this is a city full of adults in various stages of arrested development and they demand to be catered to. Enter **Schmancy (Map 3)**, a cozy boutique for vinyl and plush toys made for whimsical folk of voting age who need a cuddly T-bone steak doll or a sock monkey to get them through the night. Head out to Ballard to **Archie McPhee's (Map 23)**, a veritable supermarket of kitschy gag gifts and other wacky wares for adults who miss the thrill that only whoopee cushions and potato guns can provide. Speaking of adults and toys, **Babeland (Map 4)** up on Capitol Hill offers an utterly shame-free zone to casually shop for all manner of stimulating marital (or otherwise) aids—dildos, vibrators, leather whips,

silicone sleeves, and how-to books are available in a clean, well-lit atmosphere with helpful sex-positive salespeople. Oh, didn't think we'd go there, did you? If it bugs you, check out **Goodwind's Kites (Map 24)** over by Gas Works Park. You just can't get any more wholesome than a kite.

Eat, Drink, and Spend Money

Try the wieners at **Uli's Famous Sausage (Map 3)** and grab some beer to go with it at **Bottleworks (Map 25)**, where you'll get drunk just looking at the selection. **Pike Place Market (Map 3)** is unbeatable when it comes to fresh seafood; just don't go to the guys throwing fish around. That's for tourists, which you are not. Go to Harry at **Pure Food Fish (Map 3)**. While you're down in the market load up on cheese at **Beecher's (Map 3)**, fresh dairy products at **Pike Place Creamery (Map 3)**, and gelato at **Bottega Italiana (Map 3)**. Ballard clings to its Scandinavian culinary heritage at **Olsen's (Map 23)**. **Uwajimaya (Map 8, 46)** is a wonderland of Asian food and gifts that can't be missed. For all you wine snobs, **Madison Park Cellars (Map 22)** has got you covered. Fresh produce on your mind? **Lenny's Fruits and Vegetables (Map 33)** is the place to be.

Mallrats

If you must patronize a mall, it's good to know which to hit and which to avoid. Let's start with the malls to avoid. **Westlake Center (Map 3)** is well-known as the most useless mall in Seattle. It is one of the two stops on the monorail which makes it a bona fide tourist trap. The other mall downtown, Pacific Place, is really nice, but with Tiffany's, Cartier, and Coach only Amazon and Microsoft executives can afford to shop there. The mall for the masses is **Northgate (Map 34)**. It appeals to the simple folk who enjoy the mindless pleasures of The Gap, Macy's, JC Penney, and Express. Somewhere in between Northgate and Pacific Place is **University Village (Map 26)** with shops like Apple and Eileen Fisher. It is outdoors, but they provide shoppers with free yellow umbrellas while they stroll around. Other malls worth some consideration are **Crossroads (Map 47)** in Bellevue and Westfield Southcenter in south Seattle.

Cool Commercial Strips

If you're looking to do some one-stop shopping, but can't stand the soul-killing atmosphere of a mall, there are a number of funky and/or chic commercial strips in Seattle. Get yourself to the: **Pike/Pine Corridor (Map 4)**, **Broadway on Capitol Hill (Map 17)**, **Ballard Avenue (Map 23)**, **36th Street & Fremont Avenue (Map 24)**, **University Way ("The Ave") in the U District (Map 26)**, and pretty much anywhere in **Belltown (Map 1)**.

Map 1 • Belltown

	Address	Phone	
Dahlia Bakery	2001 4th Ave	206-441-4540	Take a hot steaming loaf of Tom Douglas home with you. The coconut cream pie is dreamworthy.
I Heart Rummage at Crocodile Café	2201 3rd Ave	n/a	Craft collective of local artists selling their unique wares.
Rudy's Barbershop	89 Wall St	206-448-8900	Absolute best cheap haircut.
Singles Going Steady	2219 2nd Ave	206-441-7396	Terrific range of new/used punk and indie music sold by friendly crusties.

Map 2 • Downtown / Denny Triangle

Play it Again Sports	1304 Stewart St	206-264-9255	Used sports equipment, check here before walking the block to REI.
REI	222 Yale Ave N	206-223-1944	The granola flagship store with an impressive rock wall.

Map 3 • Downtown

American Apparel	1504 6th Ave	206-381-3400	Soft t-shirts and free porn!
Baby and Company	1936 1st Ave	206-448-4077	Want to pay to dress like you live in Manhattan? Try here.
Beecher's Cheese	1600 Pike Pl	206-956-1964	Stop in everyday for a free sample.
Bottega Italiana	1425 1st Ave	206-343-0200	Seattle's best gelato.
Chocolate Box	108 Pine St	206-443-3900	Think Willy Wonka's Chocolate Factory.
Decaro Sartoria Custom Tailors	2025 1st Ave	206-448-2812	Gian transforms your Polartek boy into a suave Italian lover for a tailor made sum.
Don & Joe's Meats	85 Pike St	206-682-7670	Old-school butcher shop.
First and Pike News	93 Pike St	206-624-0140	Classic Pike Place Market newstand.
Golden Age Collectibles	1501 Pike Pl	206-622-9799	Essential geek merchandise.
Hair Fair Wig Shop	124 Pike St	206-623-9430	The Blade's best and only wig shop. RIP Wigland.
Isadoras	1915 1st Ave	206-447-7711	The queen of vintage. Prices to match.
Left Bank Books Collective	92 Pike St	206-622-0195	Anarchist, revolution, Chomsky—everything that made the '60s great.
Leroy's Menswear	204 Pike St	206-682-1033	Classy duds for classy dudes.
Market Magic	1501 Pike Pl	206-624-4271	Make your social life magically disappear.
Market Optical	1906 Pike Pl	206-448-7739	Contact lenses are so yesterday. Whack out with really expensive frames.
Metsker Maps	1511 1st Ave	206-623-8747	A geographer's paradise.
Nordstrom	500 Pine St	206-628-2111	It all began here: The legendary customer service, the fine designer goods.
The Nordstrom Rack	1601 2nd Ave	206-448-8522	Nordstrom stuff, a half season later and much cheaper.
Peter Miller Books	1930 1st Ave	206-441-4114	Top-notch selection of architecture and design books.
Pike Place Creamery	1514 Pike Pl	206-622-5029	Who can resist Nancy Nipples' dairy products?
Pike Place Market	Pike St & 1st Ave	206-682-7453	Still going strong after 100 years. Locals get up early to shop.
Pure Food Fish	1515 Pike Pl	206-62-5765	No flying fish, just great seafood and service.
Riveted	1113 1st Ave	206-624-5326	Denim junkie heaven (and cheapskate hell).
Schmancy	1932 2nd Ave	206-728-8008	Coolest stuffed animals ever.
Seattle Art Museum Gallery	1220 3rd Ave	206-343-1101	Rent art for your new condo.
Seattle Mystery Bookshop	117 Cherry St	206-587-5737	It's all here. Detective fiction, suspense, thrillers, true crime.
Sephora	415 Pine St	206-624-7003	All the make-up you can dream up in one store.
Sneaker City	110 Pike St	206-621-7923	Fill your proverbial wazoo full of sneakers.
Spanish Table	1427 Western Ave	206-682-2827	We're in love with Catherine. She sends us home with fine sherries and fixings for tapas.
Sway & Cake	1631 6th Ave	206-624-2699	Fun, flirty LA labels for the ladies. Cake not included.
Tenzing Momo	93 Pike St	206-623-9837	Herbs, teas, incense, tarot readings. Get your hippie supplies here.
Twist	600 Pine St	206-315-8080	Gorgeous jewelry, eclectic ceramics, and other fine, expensive breakables.
Uli's Famous Sausage	1511 Pike Pl	206-839-1000	Tasty sausagefest.
Vain	2018 1st Ave	206-441-3441	Hair. Shop. Art.
Watson Kennedy Fine Living	1022 1st Ave	206-652-8350	Swanky Frenchy things your lady friends will like.
Westlake Center	1601 5th Ave	206-467-3044	Maybe, if every other store in Seattle goes out of business. Maybe.
Zanadu Comics	1923 3rd Ave	206-443-1316	The best place to satisfy the new comics Wednesday jones.

Map 4 • First Hill / Pike / Pine

The Anne Bonny	1355 E Olive Wy	206-382-7845	Art, home accoutrements, and dead people's furniture.
Atlas Clothing Co	1515 Broadway	206-323-0960	Retro treasures, new and used.
Babeland	707 E Pike St	206-328-2914	A sex shop you can be proud to visit, staffed by enlightened women.
Bootyland	1317 E Pine St	206-328-0636	Because your baby really needs a Ramones t-shirt.
I Heart Rummage at Chop Suey	1325 E Madison St	206-324-8000	Indie arts and farts and crafts by local folk.
Le Frock	317 E Pine St	206-623-5339	Swanky vintage clothing for dudes and dolls.
Life Long Thrift	1017 E Union St	206-957-1655	Proceeds help people affected by AIDS.
Lucky Devil Tattoo	1720 12th Ave	206-323-1637	Personable, versatile artists help you piss off your parents for a reasonable price!
RE Load Baggage/Tandem	1205 E Pike St, Ste 1D	206-329-2546	Handsome handmade messenger bags and other cool stuff.
Revolution Books	1833 Nagle Pl	206-325-7415	Still waiting for Seattle to secede.
Rudy's Barbershop	614 E Pine St	206-329-3008	Absolute best cheap haircut!
That's Atomic	1502 E Olive Wy	206-325-3794	Weird hours. Even weirder antiques and knick-knacks.
Whimsy Home Décor	1535 14th Ave	206-324-4679	Unique gifts for your new Brix condo.
Zero Zero	1525 Summit Ave	206-568-3996	The best hipster hairstyling bang for your buck.

Map 6 • Madrona

Décor on 34th	1421 34th Ave	206-219-1500	Stylish home décor shop.
Jaywalk	1105 34th Ave	206-328-7776	Whimsical, tiny gift store—vintage, local artists, jewelry, odd delights
King's Palace	1411 34th Ave	206-720-1961	Doggie daycare.
Madrona Moose	1421 34th Ave	206-320-7900	If Park Plaza's Eloise shopped in Seattle, she'd stop by the Moose.

Map 7 • Pioneer Square / SoDo

Bud's Jazz Records	102 S Jackson St	206-628-0445	One of the West Coast's greatest collections of jazz CDs and rare vinyl.
Ebbets Field Flannels	408 Occidental Ave S	888-896-2936	Only store for the finest maker of historic and authentic baseball uniforms.
Elliot Bay Book Company	101 S Main St	206-624-6600	Do not pass out of this lifetime without going to Elliott Bay Books.
Magic Mouse Toys	603 1st Ave	206-682-8097	We think it's run by elves.
Pioneer Square Antique Mall	602 1st Ave	206-624-1164	A mall that even grandma can enjoy.
Rialto Movie Art	81 1/2 S Washington St	206-622-5099	Buy your H.R. Pufnstuf bobblehead or Bettie Page address book here.
Salumi	309 3rd Ave S	206-621-8772	Take home some gnocchi on Tuesdays.
Synapse 206	206 1st Ave S	206-447-7731	Clothing boutique featuring emerging designers.

Map 8 • International District

Kinokuniya Bookstore	525 S Weller St	206-587-2477	If NFT was available in Japanese, it would be sold here.
Re-Pc Recycled computers	1565 6th Ave S	206-623-9151	Bins and bins of computer stuff.
Uwajimaya	600 5th Ave S	206-624-6248	Asian superstore with groceries, gifts, restaurants, even apartments.

Map 9 • Central District (South)

Africa Braids and Jewelry	2506 S Jackson St	206-860-7235	Your hair will thank you.
Flowers Just For You	2216 S Jackson St	206-324-1440	Family owned, friendly, and helpful staff.
Jackson St Books	2301 S Jackson St	206-324-7000	A decent cove that smells like books.
Two Big Blondes Plus Consignment Shop	2501 S Jackson St	206-762-8620	Phat shirts, phat pants, phat skirts, etc for those livin' large.
Western Beauty	2301 S Jackson St	206-329-2582	Disney World for beauticians.

Map 10 • Leschi

Il Vecchio Bicycles	140 Lakeside Ave	206-324-8148	The Leschi bicycling scene gathers here for gear and gossip
Leschi Food Mart	103 Lakeside Ave	206-322-0700	Amazing wine selection.
Sweet and Savory's Parisian Bakery	1418 31st Ave S	206-325-2900	Pastry paradise.

Map 11 • Magnolia / Interbay

Wild Salmon Seafood Market	1900 W Nickerson St	206-283-3366	How fresh is this? Dockside store gets fish right off the boats.

Map 13 • Upper Queen Anne

A & J Meats & Seafood	2401 Queen Anne Ave N	206-284-3885	Great neighborhood butcher and fish monger.
Oslo's A Men's Store	1519 Queen Anne Ave N	206-282-6756	East coast chic (AG, Theory) meets West coast casual (resident golden retriever, Oslo).

Map 15 • Lower Queen Anne / Seattle Center

Easy Street Records	20 Mercer St	206-691-3279	Leading the revival of independent music stores, regular in-store performances.
Twice Sold Tales	7 Mercer St	206-282-7687	Large collection of books not for folks with cat allergies.

Map 17 • Capitol Hill (West)

American Apparel	200 Broadway E	206-709-8100	Soft t-shirts and free porn!
Bailey-Coy Books	414 Broadway E	206-323-8842	Meet the same-sex love of your life, or console yourself with a really good book.
Broadway News	605 Broadway E	206-324-7323	Periodical paradise.
Castle Superstore	206 Broadway E	206-621-7236	An adult mega-store.
Crossroads Trading Co	325 Broadway E	206-328-5867	Buys and sells only fashionable designer clothing.
Everyday Music	112 Broadway E	206-568-3321	Two floors of used CDs, DVDs, and LPs. Your wallet is screwed.
Metro Clothing	231 Broadway E	206-726-7978	Goth Wear. Costumes for some. Business Casual for others.
Pretty Parlor	119 Summit Ave E	206-405-2883	Vintage and locally designed couture that make you feel pretty.
Red Light Vintage Clothing	312 Broadway E	206-329-2200	Vintage clothing for people with 10 inch waists.
Twice Sold Tales	905 E John St	206-324-2421	Buy and sell used books whilst petting kitties.
Urban Outfitters	401 Broadway E	206-322-1800	Fashionable and affordable clothes for faux-city dwellers.

Map 18 • Capitol Hill (East) / Madison Valley

Rainbow Natural Remedies	409 15th Ave E	206-329-8979	Score some herbs.
Shoprite	432 15th Ave E	206-328-5138	Sort of like a dollar store, but better—and more random.
Sonic Boom Records	514 15th Ave E	206-568-2666	See indie bands play live and then buy their records.

Map 19 • Madison Valley / Denny Blaine

City People's Garden Store	2939 E Madison St	206-324-0737	Yes, you too can have flowers blooming and veggies growing year round in Seattle.
Fury Extraordinary Consignment	2810 E Madison St	206-329-6829	Seattle's got-bucks women consign clothing off their backs onto the racks of Fury.
Gentlemen's Consignment	2809 E Madison St	206-328-8137	Used business wear.
The Lavender Heart	2812 E Madison St	206-568-4441	Walk into the store, breathe in the creative mind of owner Holly Henderson, exhale.

Map 20 • Eastlake / Montlake / Portage Bay

The Flower Lady	3230 Eastlake Ave E	877-325-5751	Finally out of the parking lot and into her own shop—delightful flowers within budget.

Map 21 • Montlake

Mont's Market	2350 24th Ave E	206-325-5537	Gourmet goods for the 'hood.
Montlake Bicycle Shop	2223 24th Ave E	206-329-7333	Used bikes rentals, and sales. Knowledgeable staff.
Mr Johnson's Antiques	2315 24th Ave E	206-322-6033	Fair prices, some negotiable.

Map 22 • Madison Park

Madison Park Cellars	4227 E Madison St	206-323-9333	Artistic postcard of a wine store—the tiny cellar boasts an eclectic selection.
Scoop du Jour	4029 E Madison St	206-325-9562	32 flavors of ice-cream and a deli!

Map 23 • Ballard

Anchor Tattoo	2313 NW Market St	206-784-4051	You'll be in good, (and clean) hands here.
Archie McPhee	2428 NW Market St	206-297-0240	For all your rubber chicken/invisible ink needs.
Ballard Farmers Market	5330 Ballard Ave NW	206-781-6776	Organic farmers, restauranteurs, and sidewalk buskers.
Bop Street Records	5219 Ballard Ave NW	206-297-2232	Huge basement full of vinyl. Certain piles off limits.
Damsalfly	5346 Ballard Ave NW	206-297-8146	Small boutique featuring affordable fashions, accessories, and décor.
Electric Vehicles Northwest	4810 17th Ave NW	206-547-4621	Electric bicycle sales and repairs.
Epilogue Books	2001 NW Market St	206-297-2665	General used books.
Fred Meyer	915 NW 45th St	206-297-4300	Just like Target but with groceries too!
Greener Lifestyles	5317 Ballard Ave NW	206-545-4405	Interesting, environmentally-friendly, sustainable (re: expensive) goods.
JoAnn Fabrics	2217 NW 57th St	206-782-6242	Fabrics supplies and fun decorations at excellent prices.
La Tienda Folk Art Gallery	2050 NW Market St	206-297-3605	The difference between "folk art" and "tourist trap" is location.
Ok Ok	5107 Ballard Ave NW	206-789-6242	Seattle's coolest store/art gallery.
Olsen's Scandinavian Foods	2248 NW Market St	206-783-8288	Smorgasboard of herring and head cheese.
Re-Soul	5319 Ballard Ave NW	206-789-7312	Where one goes to blow a paycheck on a pair of shoes.
The ReStore	1440 NW 52nd St	206-297-9119	Funky reused building material and all the cheap knick-knacks you could possibly want.
Second Ascent	5209 Ballard Ave NW	206-545-8810	New and used sporting equipment.
Sonic Boom Records	2209 NW Market St	206-297-2666	National and international acts perform free live sets at the Ballard location.
Sugartown Vintage	2421 NW Market St	206-789-1400	80s vintage. Sweet.
Velouria	2205 NW Market St	206-788-0330	Friendly boutique featuring indie designers.

Map 24 • Fremont

Bliss	3501 Fremont Ave N	206-632-6695	Small clothing boutique with designer duds mixed in.
Blue Video	4100 Aurora Ave N	206-632-9886	No one is surprised that this adult video rental store is on Aurora.
Deluxe Junk	3518 Fremont Pl N	206-634-2733	Well organized shop of vintage clothing and accessories.
Destee Nation	3412 Evanston Ave N	888-332-6437	T-shirts emblazoned with logos of local bars and record shops.
Electric Vehicles Northwest	110 N 36th St	206-547-4621	Electric bicycle sales and repairs.
Fremont Antique Mall	3419 Fremont Pl N	206-548-9140	Huge antique store full of one-of-a-kind finds.
Fremont News	3416 Fremont Ave N	206-633-0731	If you want to read it, they have it.
Fremont Sunday Market	N 34th St & Phinney Ave	206-781-6776	The world's most fabulously bizarre bazaar.
Fusion Beads	3830 Stone Wy N	206-782-4595	A well-organized bead store that also offers classes.
Goodwind's Kites	3420 Stone Wy N	206-633-4780	You can't go to Gasworks without a kite! Good thing they're so close.
The Indoor Sun Shoppe	160 N Canal St	206-634-3727	When you don't have a garden, they'll help you create one, inside.
The Industry	3516 Fremont Pl N	206-547-9961	Unisex boutique offering hip, sexy, urban things of a higher cailber.
Jive Time Records	3506 Fremont Ave N	206-632-5483	Rare vinyl, used CDs, 99¢ bins.
Marketime Foods	4416 Fremont Ave N	206-632-8958	The TARDIS of convenience stores. It's bigger on the inside!
PCC Natural Markets	600 N 34th St	206-632-6811	One-stop shopping for overpriced organic groceries.
Portage Bay Goods	706 N 34th St	206-547-5221	Eclectic gifts for babies, children, and adults in a range of prices.
Private Screening	3504 Fremont Pl N	206-548-0751	When you want to look like Jackie O. or Frank Sinatra.
Rudy's Barbershop	475 N 36th St	206-547-0818	Absolute best cheap haircut!
Sonic Boom Records	3414 Fremont Ave N	206-547-2666	Top-rated local indie record store; great for imports.
Twice Sold Tales	3504 Fremont Ave N	206-632-3759	Large collection of books not for folks with cat allergies.

Map 25 • Wallingford

Bottleworks	1710 N 45th St	206-633-2437	The world's finest beers ripe for the six-packing.
Comics Dungeon	250 NE 45th St	206-545-8373	Preventing geeks from getting girlfriends since the early '90s!
The Erotic Bakery	2323 N 45th St	206-545-6969	What a lovely flower cake...er...oh MY!
I Do Bridal	2206 N 45th St	206-633-7926	Small bridal shop with a broad range of dress sizes and prices.
Open Books: A Poem Emporium	2414 N 45th St	206-633-0811	One of the few poetry-only bookstores in the nation.
Trophy Cupcakes	1815 N 45th St	206-632-7020	The perfect combo: cute & tasty.
Wide World Books & Maps	4411 Wallingford Ave N	206-634-3453	The nation's first travel-only bookstore is now 30 years old.

Arts & Entertainment • **Shopping**

Map 26 • U District

American Apparel	4345 University Wy NE	206-547-0399	Non-sweatshop basics.
Anthropologie	2520 NE University Village	206-985-2101	Higher end clothing and home accessories.
Borseno's Barber Shop	1406 NE 50th St	206-523-3119	Female stylists with tattoos. Cool.
Buffalo Exchange	4530 University Wy NE	206-545-0175	Second-hand clothes for girls who drink Zima.
Bulldog News	4208 University Wy NE	206-632-6397	Pick up a copy of *Obscure French Cinema Monthly* and *People* simultaneously.
Cellophane Square	4538 University Wy NE	206-634-2280	New and used CDs and DVDs.
Cinema Books	4753 Roosevelt Wy NE	206-547-7667	Reel literature.
Fireworks	2617 NE Village Ln	206-527-2858	Eclectic gift shop.
Gargoyles Sanctuary	4550 University Wy NE	206-632-4940	For all your gothic, home decorating needs.
Half Price Books	4709 Roosevelt Wy NE	206-547-7859	Books, music, video, magazines.
Hardwick's	4214 Roosevelt Wy NE	206-632-1203	An adventure in hardware.
Lucky Vintage	4742 University Wy NE	206-523-6621	Come in looking like Hilary Clinton, leave like Bettie Page.
Magus Bookstore	1408 NE 42nd St	206-633-1800	Used bookstore with a friendly, helpful, and knowledgeable staff.
Recycled Cycle	1007 NE Boat St	206-547-4491	Comprehensive bike store specializing in used and DIY bikes.
Red Light Vintage Clothing	4560 University Wy NE	206-545-4044	Vintage clothing for people with 10 inch waists.
Rudy's Barbershop	4738 University Wy NE	206-527-5267	Absolute best cheap haircut!
Scarecrow Video	5030 Roosevelt Wy NE	206-524-8554	Best video store in Seattle? No, best in the world.
Sephora	2618 NE University Village	206-526-9110	All the make-up you can dream-up in one store.
Shiga's Imports	4306 University Wy NE	206-634-1327	Decorate your dorm room like an opium den.
Something Silver	4628 Village Ct NE	206-523-7545	Unique silver jewelry.
Tiger Tiger	4321 University Wy NE	206-547-8888	Used clothing for men and women, erratically priced.
Trader Joe's	4555 Roosevelt Wy NE	206-547-6299	Don't let the yuppies walking in fool you, this place is really inexpensive.
Twice Sold Tales	4501 University Wy NE	206-545-4226	General used books and a cat.
University Bookstore	4326 University Wy NE	206-634-3400	Huge bookstore and gift shop. Don't go there the first week of any quarter.
University Village	2624 NE University Village	206-523-0623	Upscale outdoor shopping mall.
Weaving Works, Inc	4717 Brooklyn Ave NE	206-524-1221	Complete explosion of colors and textures, skilled advice for Seattle's needleworkers.
Wooly Mammoth	4303 University Wy NE	206-632-3254	Sensible shoes for the masses.
Zanadu Comics	1307 NE 45th St	206-632-0989	The best place to satisfy the new comics Wednesday jones.

Map 27 • Laurelhurst / Wedgwood / Sand Point

Metropolitan Market	5250 40th Ave NE	206-938-6600	High end groceries, high end prices.
PCC Natural Markets	6514 40th Ave NE	206-526-7661	A great natural market that will leave your wallet unnaturally empty.

Map 29 • Ballard / Loyal Heights

Goodwill	6400 8th Ave NW	206-957-5544	Make sure to check for stains.

Map 30 • Greenwood / Phinney Ridge

Couth Buzzard Used Books	7221 Greenwood Ave N	206-789-8965	General used books.
Fred Meyer	100 NW 85th St	206-784-9600	Just like Target but with groceries too!
Greenwood Hardware	7201 Greenwood Ave N	206-783-2900	Makes you really, really, really hate Home Depot.
Ken's Market	7231 Greenwood Ave N	206-784-3470	Last of the old-fashioned neighborhood markets.
PCC Natural Markets	7504 Aurora Ave N	206-525-3586	One-stop shopping for overpriced organic groceries.
Rudy's Barbershop	6415 Phinney Ave N	206-782-9861	Absolute best cheap haircut!
The Sneakery	612 NW 65th St	206-297-1786	Hipsters will notice your feet for the cool shoes rather than your jacked up ingrown toenail.

Map 31 • Green Lake / Roosevelt

Arnie's Vintage Costumers	7011 Roosevelt Wy NE	206-522-5234	Specializing in vintage costumes, many of which are created on-site.
East West Bookshop	6500 Roosevelt Wy NE	206-523-3726	When you feel like some new-age reading or learning how to meditate.
Fish Store	6109 Roosevelt Wy NE	206-522-5259	Specialized equipment for the aquarium enthusiast.
Gregg's Greenlake Cycle	7007 Woodlawn Ave NE	206-523-1822	Voted best bike shop in Seattle.
J n S Phonograph Needles	1028 NE 65th St	206-524-2933	No idea what they sell.
The Last White Elephant	902 NE 65th St	206-525-0170	Animal compassion through fashion.
Mamo Jewelry Design	6317 Roosevelt Way NE	206-525-4653	Custom jewelry and services.

Map 31 · Green Lake / Roosevelt–continued

Pop Tots	6405 Roosevelt Wy NE	206-522-4322	Child-size CBGB t-shirts for ex-punk parents who miss being hip.
Science, Art and More	6417 Roosevelt Wy NE	206-524-3795	Brainy toys for girls and boys.
Trading Musician	5908 Roosevelt Wy NE	206-522-6707	Good prices on great gear for musicians of all kinds.

Map 32 · Ravenna

3rd Place Ravenna	6504 20th Ave NE	206-525-2790	Revitalized neighborhood bookstore, coffee shop, deli, performance place; bar downstairs.
Sidecar for Pigs Peace	5270 University Wy NE	206-523-9060	Ethically-minded consumers shop at the only 100% vegan store in WA.

Map 33 · Northwest Seattle

Lenny's Fruits & Vegetables	10410 Greenwood Ave N	206-781-0619	Cheaper cilantro, you'll never find.
The Maltese Falcon	9921 Aurora Ave N	206-524-1940	Video rental run by film devotees.
Value Village	8700 15th Ave NW	206-783-4648	Enormous second-hand store that sells everything from furniture to clothes.

Map 34 · Northeast Seattle

Display & Costume	11201 Roosevelt Wy NE	206-362-4810	Go here if you are throwing a party or need a costume. Amazing Christmas displays.
Fred Meyer	13000 Lake City Wy NE	206-440-2400	Just like Target but with groceries too!
The Northgate Mall	401 NE Northgate Wy	206-362-4777	Large indoor shopping mall. Ugh.

Map 35 · Alki / West Seattle / North Admiral

Capers	4521 California Ave SW	206-932-0371	Classy, overpriced house wares that you really can't live without.
Click! Design that Fits	2210 California Ave SW	206-328-9252	Drool over cement-in-silver jewelry.
Coastal Surf Boutique	2532 Alki Ave SW	206-933-5605	Costly surf brand names. Offers bike rental in summer.
Curious Kidstuff	4740 California Ave SW	206-937-8788	Let your kids run wild while you buy them super-cool toys.
Easy Street Records	4559 California Ave SW	206-938-3279	You can't go to West Seattle without stopping here for coffee, food, or music.
Husky Deli	4721 California Ave SW	206-937-2810	Old-fashioned deli counter and homemade ice cream.
Metropolitan Market	2320 42nd Ave SW	206-937-0551	Fine grocery shopping.
Northwest Art & Frame	4733 California Ave SW	206-937-5507	Find an equal amount of useless gifts and art necessities.
PCC Natural Markets	2749 California Ave SW	206-937-8481	Organic to the core.
Seattle Fish Company	4435 California Ave SW	206-938-7576	Support the independents who don't sell farm-raised fish.
Small Clothes	3236 California Ave SW	206-932-2222	Upscale second-hand for the toddler set.
Square One Books	4724 42nd Ave SW	206-935-5764	West Seattle's one and only independent bookstore for new books.
West Seattle Farmer's Market	SW Alaska St & California Ave SW		May thru December.
Zamboanga	4531 California Ave SW	206-933-6399	Eclectic trinkets and flowy clothes.

Map 39 · SoDo / Beacon Hill / Georgetown

Daniel Smith	4150 1st Ave S	206-223-9599	Mega mart art supplies. Make an artist happy.
Esquin Wine Merchants	2700 4th Ave S	206-682-7374	Guess what they sell?
George	5633 Airport Wy S	206-763-8100	Up and coming boutique and gallery.
Georgetown Records / Fantagraphics	1201 S Vale St	206-762-5638	Cool record store that now shares a space with the Fantagraphics flagship store.
Goodwill Outlet	1765 6th Ave S	206-957-5516	Wear a bio-hazard suit and paw thru bins of cast offs from the unwashed masses.
JC Marble & Granite	2735 1st Ave S	206-388-0909	Stone good enough for Jesus Christ's tomb.
Maruta	1024 S Bailey St	206-767-5002	Ultra-authentic Japanese grocery; like a tiny Uwajimaya without the foreign influence.
Moe's Home Collection	1926 6th Ave S	206-405-4411	Furniture for Modern snobs.
Northwest Shower Door	3223 1st Ave S	206-264-1010	Elegant doors for clean people.
Pacific Industrial Supply	2960 4th Ave S	206-682-2100	Industrial hardware junkie? Get your fix here.
Remo Borracchini's	2307 Rainier Ave S	206-325-1550	An adored local bakery with an emphasis on affordable.
Seattle Pottery Supply	35 S Hanford St	206-587-0570	When you want to recreate *Ghost*.
Visions Espresso Service	2737 1st Ave S	206-623-6709	The Wizard of Oz would be jealous of their coffee machine collection.

Map 40 • Columbia City / Mount Baker / Seward Park

Bike Works!	3709 S Ferdinand St	206-725-9408	Non-profit bike shop that teaches maintainance to kids.
Grocery Outlet	2929 27th Ave S	206-723-2767	Why is the food so cheap? Don't ask just buy.
PCC Natural Market	5041 Wilson Ave S	206-723-2720	Organic to the core.

Map 41 • Rainier Beach / Rainier View / Skyway

Van Asselt Beauty Salon	7136 Beacon Ave S	206-725-2058	They are committed to you looking fabulous.

Map 45 • Bellevue (West) / Medina

Bellevue Square	Bellevue Wy NE & NE 8th St	n/a	Bellevue behemoth.
Fireworks	196 Bellevue Sq	425-688-0933	Colorful gifts and home décor handmade by local artists.
Lincoln Square	Bellevue Wy NE & NE 8th St	n/a	Just what Bellevue needed—an expansion of Bellevue Square.
Made In Washington	190 Bellevue Sq	425-454-6907	If you must give Northwest smoked salmon as a gift.
Rudy's Barbershop	5 Bellevue Wy NE	206-467-1462	Absolute best cheap haircut!
Sephora	141 Bellevue Sq	425-467-1337	All the make-up you can dream-up in one store.

Map 46 • Bellevue (Central)

Paldo World	549 156th Ave SE	425-641-1970	Korean foodie paradise.
Uwajimaya	15555 NE 24th St	425-747-9012	Awesome Asian superstore.

Map 47 • Bellevue (East) / Redmond

Crossroads Bellevue	NE 8th St & 156th Ave NE	n/a	Less than glitzy shopping mall.

Map 48 • Kirkland

Champagne Taste	147 Park Ln	425-828-4502	Designer gown consignment store.
PCC Natural Market	10718 NE 68th St	425-828-4622	Organic to the core.
Reasons to Believe	92 Kirkland Ave	425-893-8159	Handcrafted Santa Clauses. Ho ho ho.
Rebekah's	117 Lake St S	425-827-5455	Nicer end of consignment selections.
Simplicity Décor	126 Park Ln	425-803-0386	Classy, simple Thai-style furniture.
Tim's Seafood	224 Park Ln	425-827-0195	Fresh, seasonal seafood for sale. They pack and ship for you.

Map 49 • Redmond

Bergman Travel Shop	16516 NE 74th St	425-883-8400	Serious stuff for serious travelers.
Half Price Books	7805 Leary Wy NE	425-702-2499	New and used books at discounted prices.
PCC Natural Market	11435 Avondale Rd NE	425-285-1400	Organic to the core.
Redmond Saturday Market	7730 Leary Wy NE	425-556-0636	Eastside's oldest market—go early for the best pick in local fruits and vegetables.
Redmond Town Center	16495 NE 74th St	425-867-0808	A mall. At least it's Outdoors.
REI	7500 166th Ave NE	425-882-1158	Heaven for wealthy weekend warriors.
Tree Top Toys	15752 Redmond Wy	425-869-9713	Toys galore.

A Contemporary Theatre (ACT) (Map 3) provides some of Seattle's best drama, with two stages to host new plays from nationally-recognized playwrights as well as the occasional revival. **The Intiman Theatre (Map 15)** won a Regional Theatre Tony Award in 2006, and currently is in the midst of a five-year project called *American Cycle*, exploring what it means to be an American citizen via classic plays and community forums. Another big player in Seattle performance arts is **On the Boards (Map 15)**, a risk-taking organization that specializes in artist development, particularly through their *12 Minute Max* series, which offers brief glimpses of new and in-progress works from up-and-coming performers and writers.

Seattle's live theater scene is also robust enough to support a slew of small stages where aficionados can catch the latest experimental performances, new works from local playwrights, or revivals of much-loved classics. **Theater Schmeater (Map 4)**, **Bathhouse Theatre (Map 31)**, **Odd Duck Studios (Map 3)**, and others toil tirelessly in often-cramped conditions and stumble as often as they soar, but that's how great theater is made. Check out seattleperforms.com for the latest theatrical happenings in the Emerald City. A few years ago, indie weekly paper *The Stranger*, moved their annual amateur porn film festival to On the Boards to better accommodate supply and demand, thus proving that porn IS art.

Theaters	Address	Phone	Map
5th Avenue Theatre	1308 5th Ave	206-625-1900	3
ACT Theatre	700 Union St	206-292-7676	3
ArtsWest Theatre	4711 California Ave SW	206-938-0339	35
Bathhouse Theater	7312 W Green Lake Dr N	206-524-1300	30
Benaroya Hall	200 University St	206-215-4800	3
Capitol Hill Arts	1621 12th Ave	206-388-0569	4
Center House Theatre	305 Harrison St	206-216-0833	15
Historic University Theater	5510 University Wy NE	206-781-3879	32
Intiman Theatre	201 Mercer St	206-269-1900	15
Kirkland Performance Center	350 Kirkland Ave	425-893-9900	48
Langston Hughes Permorning Arts Center	104 17th Ave S	206-684-4657	9
The Little Theatre	608 19th Ave E	206-675-2055	18
Magnuson Community Center Auditorium	7400 Sand Point Wy NE, Bldg 47	n/a	27
Market Theater	1428 Post Aly	206-587-2414	3
McCaw Hall	321 Mercer St	206-733-9725	15
Meany Hall for the Performing Arts	4001 University Wy NE	206-543-4880	26
Meydenbauer Center	11100 NE 6th St	425-637-1020	45
Moore Theatre	1932 2nd Ave	206-467-5510	3
Northwest Puppet Center	9123 15th Ave NE	206-523-2579	34
Odd Duck Studio	1214 10th Ave	206-375-8945	4
On The Boards	100 W Roy ST	206-217-9886	15
Open Circle Theater	429 Boren Ave N	206-382-4250	2
Paramount Theatre	911 Pine St	206—682-1414	3
R.E.D. Performance Loft	89 Yesler Wy	206-331-6673	7
Richard Hugo House	1634 11th Ave	n/a	4
Seattle Children's Theatre at Seattle Center	201 Thomas St	206-441-3322	15
Seattle Repertory Theatre - Bagley Wright Theatre	155 Mercer St	206-443-2222	15
Second Story Repertory	16587 NE 74th St	425-881-6777	49
Spectrum Dance Theater	800 Lake Washington Blvd	206-325-4161	6
Taproot Theatre	204 N 85 St	206-781-9707	30
Teatro Zinzanni	222 Mercer St	206-802-0015	15
Theater Schmeater	1500 Summit Ave	206-324-5801	4

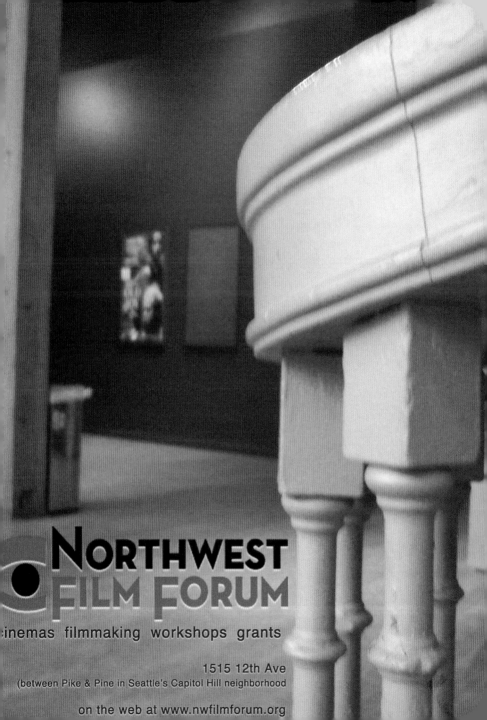

NORTHWEST FILM FORUM

cinemas filmmaking workshops grants

1515 12th Ave
(between Pike & Pine in Seattle's Capitol Hill neighborhood

on the web at www.nwfilmforum.org

Think local. Act global.

When Volunteers return home from
making a difference in another country,
they bring back real-world skills and
experience for their own community.

800.424.8580
www.peacecorps.gov

Life is calling. How far will you go?

LIFE,
LIBERTY
AND THE
PURSUIT OF
HAPPY HOUR
>JOIN THE PARTY
SVEDKA
Imported Swedish
VODKA
Product of Sweden

Note: Most of Seattle uses a strict Cartesian grid for street numbering, meaning that streets that are diagonal or change direction may change number sequences unexpectedly. Where possible, we've indicated these shifts with a *. Also, central Kirkland uses some street names which can be found elsewhere in Seattle, these streets bear no relation to each other, and are indicated with "(Kirkland)".

Street Index

Street Index

Street Index

Street / Range	Page	Grid
NE 46th St		
(100-199)	25	A2
(2200-2299)	26	A2
(4000-4099)	27	C1
(10500-10699)	45	A2
(16200-16699)	47	A1
NW 46th St		
(100-599)	24	A1
(600-1599)	23	C1/C2
SE 46th St		
(8300-9499)	42	B1/B2
(11600-13399)	43	B2/C1/C2
(13900-17699)	44	—
SE 46th Way	44	C1/C2
47th Ave NE	27	A1/B1/C1
47th Ave S		
(3900-6499)	40	B1/C1
(7946-11099)	41	A2/B2/C2
47th Ave SW		
(1700-5999)	35	A2/B2/C2
(6000-9799)	37	A1/B1
47th Ave W	11	A1
NE 47th Ct	47	A1
SE 47th Ct	44	C1/C2
SE 47th Ln	44	C2
47th Pl NE	27	C1
47th Pl SW	37	A1
NE 47th Pl	45	A2
SE 47th Pl		
(8400-8599)	42	B2
(11614-13099)	43	C1/C2
(14469-17299)	44	C1/C2
N 47th St		
(100-1599)	24	A1/A2
(1600-2099)	25	A1
NE 47th St		
(200-899)	25	A2
(900-2499)	26	A1/A2
(3500-4899)	27	B1
(9000-10999)	45	A2
(13200-13499)	46	A1/A2
NW 47th St		
(100-599)	24	A1
(600-899)	23	B2/C2
SE 47th St		
(8400-9499)	42	B2
(11600-13156)	43	C1/C2
(13900-17699)	44	C1/C2
SE 47th Way	44	C2
48th Ave NE		
(3700-7499)	27	A1/B1/C1
(9400-10499)	34	B2/C2
48th Ave S		
(3900-7099)	40	B2/C2
(7100-10899)	41	A2/B2/C2
48th Ave SW		
(1900-5999)	35	A2/B2/C2
(6000-9799)	37	A1/B1
NE 48th Ct	47	A1
SE 48th Ct	44	C2
SE 48th Dr	44	C1/C2
48th Pl NE	27	C1
NE 48th Pl		
(10400-11199)	45	A2
(11700-13899)	46	A1/A2

Street / Range	Page	Grid
SE 48th Pl		
(12500-12999)	43	C2
(16400-16799)	44	C2
N 48th St		
(100-1599)	24	A1/A2
(1600-2099)	25	A1
NE 48th St		
(800-899)	25	A2
(2300-2399)	26	A2
(3600-3899)	27	B1
(10800-11098)	45	A2
(16400-19199)	47	A1/A2
NW 48th St		
(2-599)	24	A1
(600-1699)	23	B1/B2
SE 48th St		
(8100-9099)	42	B1/B2
(11600-12299)	43	C1/C2
(16100-16399)	44	C2
49th Ave NE		
(3624-7399)	27	A1/B1/C1
(9000-10299)	34	C2
49th Ave S		
(4000-6699)	40	B2/C2
(7900-11399)	41	A2/B2/C2
49th Ave SW		
(2100-5999)	35	A2/B2/C2
(6000-9999)	37	A1/B1
NE 49th Ct	47	A1
NE 49th Pl	47	A1/A2
SE 49th Pl		
(11800-11899)	43	C2
(14000-17299)	44	C1/C2
N 49th St		
(100-1599)	24	A1/A2
(1600-2099)	25	A1
NE 49th St		
(2500-2899)	26	A2
(10900-11099)	45	A2
(15800-15899)	47	A1
NW 49th St		
(100-599)	24	A1
(600-1599)	23	B1/B2
SE 49th St		
(11600-13299)	43	C1/C2
(14300-16799)	44	C1/C2
50th Ave NE	27	A1/B1/C1
50th Ave S		
(4000-5399)	40	B2/C2
(7900-11199)	41	A2/B2/C2
50th Ave SW		
(2100-5199)	35	A2/B2/C2
(6000-9999)	37	A1/B1
NE 50th Ct	47	A1
NE 50th Pl	46	A1/A2
SE 50th Pl		
(8100-8399)	42	B1
(1100-1199)*	43	C1
(11600-13609)	43	C1/C2
(16500-16699)	44	C2
N 50th St		
(100-1499)	24	A1/A2
(1500-2599)	25	A1/A2

Street / Range	Page	Grid
NE 50th St		
(100-899)	25	A2
(900-3450)	26	A1/A2
(3451-5399)	27	B1
(13200-13599)	46	A1/A2
(16201-19831)	47	A1/A2
NW 50th St		
(100-620)	24	A1
(621-1699)	23	B1/B2
SE 50th St		
(4845-9099)	42	B2
(12000-12199)	43	C2
(14000-15899)	44	C1/C2
NE 50th Way	47	A1
51st Ave NE		
(3800-7599)	27	A1/B1/C1
(9000-9299)	34	C2
51st Ave S		
(4000-6999)	40	B2/C2
(9200-11399)	41	B2/C2
51st Ave SW		
(2300-5211)	35	—
(9623)	37	B1
NE 51st Ct	47	A2
51st Pl S	40	C2
51st Pl SW	35	C1
NE 51st Pl	46	A1/A2
SE 51st Pl		
(9000-9049)	42	B2
(12600-13299)	43	C2
(13600-14199)	44	C1
N 51st St		
(100-1599)	24	A1/A2
(1600-2399)	25	A1
NE 51st St		
(100-499)	25	A2
(2200-2399)	26	A2
(3900-3999)	27	B1
(14800-15543)	46	A2
(15600-19199)	47	A1/A2
NW 51st St		
(100-599)	24	A1
(600-1699)	23	B1/B2
SE 51st St		
(12000-13399)	43	C2
(14100-15099)	44	C1
52 Ave SW	35	C1
52nd Ave NE	27	A1/B1/C1
52nd Ave S		
(4500-6999)	40	B2/C2
(7700-9699)	41	A2/B2
52nd Ave SW	35	—
52nd Pl SW	35	B1
NE 52nd Pl	27	B1
SE 52nd Pl		
(8700-8799)	42	B2
(13200-13399)	43	C2
(13800-14399)	44	C1
N 52nd St		
(100-1599)	24	A1/A2
(1600-2399)	25	A1
NE 52nd St		
(100-499)	25	A2
(1000-2999)	26	A1/A2
(3500-5399)	27	B1
(10201-10799)	45	A2
(15400-15599)	46	A2

Street / Range	Page	Grid
NW 52nd St		
(100-599)	24	A1
(600-1699)	23	B1/B2
SE 52nd St		
(9400-9599)	42	B2
(11600-13599)	43	C1/C2
52nd Ter S	40	C2
53rd Ave NE		
(4200-7399)	27	A1/B1/C1
(8500-8599)	34	C2
53rd Ave S		
(4600-4999)	40	B2
(8600-11788)	41	B2/C2
53rd Ave SW	35	A1/B1
53rd Ct NE	34	C2
NE 53rd Pl	46	A2
SE 53rd Pl		
(8391-9399)	42	B2
(13600-15356)	44	C1
53rd St SE	42	B2
N 53rd St		
(300-1599)	24	A1/A2
(1600-2299)	25	A1
(2300-2399)	31	C1
NE 53rd St		
(100-899)	25	A2
(900-2924)	26	A1/A2
(10400-11219)	45	A2
(11220-11451)	46	A1
(15600-18699)	47	A1/A2
NW 53rd St		
(100-599)	24	A1
(600-1699)	23	B1/B2
SE 53rd St		
(8800-8999)	42	B2
(12500-13499)	43	C2
(15300-15510)	44	C1
54th Ave NE		
(4300-7399)	27	A1/B1/C1
(8500-8599)	34	C2
54th Ave S		
(4700-6599)	40	B2/C2
(7200-11851)	41	A2/B2/C2
54th Ave SW	35	B1/C1
SE 54th Ct	44	C1
54th Pl SW	35	A1
NE 54th Pl		
(13200-15525)	46	A2
(18700-18799)	47	A2
SE 54th Pl		
(9160-9170)	42	B2
(11700-13399)	43	C2
(13600-17399)	44	C1/C2
N 54th St		
(100-1599)	24	A1/A2
(1600-2399)	31	C1
NE 54th St		
(100-499)	31	C1/C2
(2000-2999)	32	C1/C2
(4500-5499)	27	B1
(15400-15436)	46	A2
NW 54th St		
(100-599)	24	A1
(600-2599)	23	B1/B2
(2600-3499)	28	C1/C2

Street Index

Street Index